HOW INDIA WROUGHT FOR FREEDOM

HOW INDIA WROUGHT FOR FREEDOM

THE STORY OF THE NATIONAL CONGRESS
TOLD FROM OFFICIAL RECORDS

ANNIE BESANT

GYAN

Published by

GYAN

Gyan Publishing House
5, Ansari Road
Daryaganj, New Delhi-110002
Phone: 011-47034999, 9811692060
E-mail: books@gyanbooks.com

Distribution Network
gyanbooks.com
India, USA, Canada, UK, Australia, France

ISBN: 978-81-212-8876-7 (PB)
First Published, 1915

2nd Impression 2023

Printed at: Gyan Press, Delhi.

HOW INDIA WROUGHT FOR FREEDOM
AUTHOR: ANNIE BESANT

HOW INDIA WROUGHT FOR FREEDOM

HOW INDIA WROUGHT FOR FREEDOM

THE STORY OF THE NATIONAL CONGRESS
TOLD FROM OFFICIAL RECORDS

BY ANNIE BESANT

THEOSOPHICAL PUBLISHING HOUSE
ADYAR, MADRAS, INDIA
T. P. S., LONDON; T. P. H., BENARES
THE INDIAN BOOK DEPOT, BOMBAY
1915

DEDICATED

WITH PROFOUND DEVOTION TO THE

MOTHERLAND

AND WITH RESPECTFUL ADMIRATION TO HER NOBLE SON

DADABHAI NAOROJI

BY HER SERVANT

ANNIE BESANT

NOTE

I offer most grateful thanks to a Fellow of the Theosophical Society who has made the splendid Index which adds quite indefinitely to the value of the book.

ANNIE BESANT

FOREWORD

LITTLE is needed to explain the purpose of this book. It is a plain story of India's constitutional struggle for Freedom, a story so pathetic in its patience, so strong in its endurance, so far-seeing in its wisdom, that it is India's justification—if any justification can be needed for asserting the right to Freedom—for her demand for Home Rule.

The younger generation are impatient under the repetition of disregarded demands, and they are right. The time has come for the definite agitation for Home Rule, to continue till it is granted. But they are wrong if they fail to recognise that these thirty years of work alone make it possible that the full demand for Freedom can now be effectively made. And they are doubly wrong if they are not grateful to these builders of the Indian Nation, who, when all was dark around them, believed in the dawning of the Day. They have laid the foundation on which their youngers can build. Homage then to the veterans, living still with us here, and living in the world beyond. That the younger generation may know how splendidly they wrought, this book is written.

I fearlessly place this volume before the public, as a proof of India's fitness for Home Rule. The grasp of the questions dealt with, the sagacity of the remedies proposed for poverty and misrule, the sobriety of the claims urged, the knowledge of, and the sympathy with, the sorrows of the people, prove how much better off India would be under Self-Rule than under Other-Rule. Let any unprejudiced student turn over the Resolutions passed by the Congress during thirty years, and see how it laid bare the popular suffering, and how it pointed with unerring finger to the causes of that suffering—the drain of Indian wealth to England, the exorbitant cost of the alien rule, the ever-increasing military expenditure, the sacrifice of Indian industries, the land-tax ever rising and condemning the peasantry to perpetual indebtedness, and to a hopeless poverty and semi-starvation that have no parallel in any other civilised Nation. It is these facts, covered up by officials, but laid bare by the Congress, which make Home Rule necessary, if a catastrophe is to be avoided.

The daily insult of the Arms Act, the constant oppression of the Press and Seditious Meetings Acts, the exclusion of Indians from the higher grades of the Army, the Police, the Educational Service, and a score of other wrongs, while bitterly felt by a high-spirited people, have not in them the immediate menace that lies in the grinding poverty of the masses of the population. People become more or less accustomed to the "atmosphere of inferiority," and oppression, long submitted to, at last dulls pride and weakens self-respect. But people never become accustomed to Hunger, and they become desperate when they see no hope of relief for themselves, nor for their children after them. The danger to British Rule lies far more in the misery of the masses than in the discontent of the educated. To call attention to that danger before it is too late, this book is issued.

The Historical Introduction is the background of the story. It is the testimony of 5,000 years to India's success in ruling herself. Let Indian history be set side by side with European history—with what there is of the latter—century by century, and let us see whether India need blush at the comparison. Take but the sixteenth, seventeenth, eighteenth centuries, to go back no further. Compare Akbar's tolerance with the persecution of Protestants by Mary, of Roman Catholics by Elizabeth, and of Puritans by James and Charles. Read the Penal Laws against Roman Catholics in Ireland, and ask if the English, who enacted and enforced them, were fit for Self-Government. See the misery and starvation of France in the eighteenth century ending in the Revolution, review the Peasants' War in Germany, the constant Wars in Italy, the turbulence of Hungary and Poland, the royal murders and revolutions in England, and say if all these countries were more fit for Self-Government than India. Yet they, unworthy, took it, and have purified themselves by it, becoming more fit in the using of it. India, more worthy than they to take it, is deemed unfit. The only argument against India's fitness is her submission.

May this book help Britain to understand the shame of her autocratic rule in India, her broken pledges, her selfishness, her preference of her own to India's interests. May it help India to realise her duty to Herself.

ANNIE BESANT

CONTENTS

HISTORICAL INTRODUCTION

AND SOME

DEDUCTIONS AND ANTICIPATIONS

THE DAWNING

THE great Nations of the far Past spring suddenly on to the stage of history, as Bunsen said of Egypt, full-grown. Truer perhaps would be the simile, if we said that a curtain rises, and we see the Nation on the stage, full-panoplied, complete, as no Nation could be without centuries, perhaps millennia, of civilisation behind it. This is true of India, as of Assyria, Persia, Egypt, but in one thing India differs from those whose contemporary she was. They are dead. She still lives; and in these modern days she is showing a vigour and a strength which bid fair to place her again in the forefront of the world's history. They are known by unburied cities, by ruins, by fragments, by papyri, by tiles, by coins, found by burrowing in their sepulchres. India is continuous, with a history running backwards to most archaic times—how ancient, who may say?—and she has a literature which also runs backward, claiming an antiquity not yet acknowledged in the West: Vedas, Institutes, Purāṇas, Epic Poems, which, as regards the historical books—the Purāṇas, and the Epics—can be checked in their later records as regards dynasties, by Greek history, and yet more by the fragments of the past dug up from time to time. Says Vincent A. Smith:

> Modern writers have been inclined to disparage unduly the authority of the paurāṇic lists, but closer study finds in them much genuine and valuable historical tradition. For instance the *Vishṇu Purāṇa* gives the outline of the history of the Maurya dynasty with a near approach to accuracy, and the Redcliffe manuscript of the *Maṭsya* is equally trustworthy for Āndhra history. Proof of the surprising extent to which coins and inscriptions confirm the *Maṭsya* list of the Āndhra Kings has recently been published.[1]

Entrancing as are the records of the far-off times, the stories of Sages and Warriors, of Rāmachandra, the Hero-King of the *Rāmāyaṇa*, of the doings in peace and war of the Kauravas and Pāṇḍavas and Shrī Kṛshṇa, that make the story of the *Mahabharata*, of these who live by scores and hundreds enshrined in legend, tradition, drama, song, and—the greatest of them—live still more vitally in Indian hearts and prayers and ceremonies to-day, showing the historical continuity —from all of these we must turn aside for want of space with only this one fact writ large: *It is on this literature and on the past embodied in it that the foundation of Indian Nationality is indestructibly laid.* The National Self-consciousness strikes its roots deeply into

[1] *Early History of India*, p. 10, Ed. 1908. In so brief a sketch, it is better not to overburden the pages with continuous references, but a bibliography of the books consulted on the history here condensed, which will guide the serious student in his research, will be found at the end of this Introduction.

this rich soil, and whatever may contribute to its later growth—and the contributions are enormous—the Nation's Life and Unity are rooted here. He who knows nothing of the infinite wealth of this "unhistorical" past will never understand the Indian heart and mind, and Sir Valentine Chirol, in his malicious and unscrupulous book on *Indian Unrest*, saw accurately the truth that from the "Hindu Revival" was born the National Movement of Modern India, as from a similar Revival was born the Maratha Confederacy. Moreover, very many of the institutions and customs of "historical" times are continuous with those of the "legendary" past, and are incomprehensible and without significance save for that past. The horse-sacrifices of Pushyamitra in the second century B.C., of Adityasena in the seventh century A.D., link with the tradition of that of Sagara, uncounted millennia backward, and with that of Yudhishthira in 3000 B.C. odd—in each equally the sign of the acknowledged Lord Paramount of India as a whole. So again with the Pañchayat, "the Five," whether the Council of Village Elders of time immemorial, or Chandragupta's Boards in the fourth century B.C. India is a continuum, and her Âryan civilisation an unbroken whole. There are invasions and conquests, periods of strength and weakness, of unity and division, in her æonian story. But she is always India; always Aryan, the MOTHER Imperishable, who has borne uncounted millions from her womb, but whose own birth no historian can guess at, whose death no prophet can foretell. And this it is well to remember, in our judgments of to-day. With an admitted history of nearly 5,000 years, from the commerce between India and Babylon, according to Dr. Sayce, in 3000 B.C.,[1] and the proofs of high civilisation and wealth then existing; with an admitted literature of at least 7,000 years; the period of English rule in India, barely a century and a half, is microscopically small, a tiny ripple on her ocean. Invasions flow and ebb; conquerors come and go; India assimilates what is left of them, is the richer for them, and remains herself. She did without England for millennia, and flourished amazingly; she could do without England for millennia to come; but the two need each other, and will be the better for each other in the near future, and India desires to be linked with England in that future, but on a footing of perfect equality, and *on none other.*

INDIA'S MIDDLE HISTORY

THE COMING OF THE ARYANS

They were no wild tribes that crossed the Himālayan passes and flooded India in successive waves of invasion from 18000 B.C. onwards.[2] They came from an archaic Middle Asian civilisation, the cradle of the Āryas, whence came successively the immigrants who made the Mediterranean civilisation, colonised Persia and Mesopotamia, and sent the forefathers of the Latin, Slav and Teuton Nations to people Europe. Later, they came down into India, penetrated first to

[1] *Hibbert Lectures*, 1887, quoted in *Indian Shipping*, p. 85, Ed. 1912.

[2] This first paragraph is not "historic".

the south—the Āryan Dravidians—and later settled in the north. But this is still the region of dreams, and no sober western historian will yet accept it. And yet perhaps this is hardly so, for Sir William Hunter, though he gives no dates, speaks of the Āryan home as in Central Asia, of settlements round the shores of the Mediterranean, of a western offshoot founding Persia, of another becoming the Greek Nation, Italy and Rome, Spain and Britain, and of others descending through the passes of the Himālayas into India.

It is not without significance, as Professor Radhakumud Mukerji points out in his *Fundamental Unity of India*, that India is one country in her religious literature. She is Jambūdvīpa—Ashoka is called "King of Jambūdvīpa," and Bharatavarsha, Āryāvarta; "India" is a name given by foreigners. In Hindu prayers, the names of the great rivers are recited, the northern only in the earlier, later the southern as well, as the Āryans spread southward. The sacred places range from Hardwar to Kanchi, and later, Badarikedarnath to Rameshvara, from Dvaraka to Jagannath. And the people, ever reciting these, knew them all as in their Motherland. Pilgrimages took the devout to all of these as Hindu. The student will find in that useful little book many more proofs that India was a unity, had, even then, a National Self-consciousness in her religion. Patriotism was inspired and hallowed by these loving recitations.

Despite the fact that "India's history only begins with Alexander," as western writers say, we submit in passing that, as above noted, Babylon was trading with her in 3000 B.C.; that Semiramis of Nineveh invaded India in 2034 B.C. and penetrated as far as Jammu, as stated on a column erected by her, and was finally put to flight by an Indian Prince, named Strabrobates by Diodorus Siculus; that mummies in Egyptian tombs, dating from 2000 B.C. have been found wrapped in Indian muslin of the finest quality, and that their indigo dye is said to have come from India; that Diodorus Siculus tells of an invasion of India, 981 B.C., by Rameses II; that Hiram of Tyre, 980 B.C. traded with India from harbours in the Arabian Gulf, and Tamil names for Indian products are found in the Hebrew Bible.[1] There is plenty of evidence by such contacts, apart from Indian literature, of a civilisation rivalling at least those of Egypt and Assyria.

In A.D. 883, the first Englishman whose visit to India is recorded, was Sighelmas, Bishop of Sherborne, sent by King Alfred (A.D. 849-901) to visit the Christian Church, named after S. Thomas. He travelled comfortably, and brought back to England "many splendid exotic gems and spices, such as that country plentifully yielded".[2]

"History" Begins

For our purposes we can arbitrarily begin at the period recognised as "historical" by the wider western

[1] *Indian Shipping*, p. 89.

[2] These facts and many others of undoubted historicity, may be found summarised in the *Manual of Administration of the Madras Presidency*—a book containing a vast amount of information, with some astounding lapses of knowledge.

historians, the middle of the 7th century B. C., when we find, as said above, highly civilised communities—having existed there " for untold centuries," admits Vincent Smith—commerce with foreign countries going on, making India " historical," the knowledge of writing widely spread, and the country between the Himālayas and the Nerbudda river divided into sixteen States—some monarchical, some aristocratic-republican—with great stretches of forests, jungles, and unsettled lands interspersed among them. The beginning of the seventh century, A.D. 600, sees the first "historical" dynasty ruling over Magadha (Bihar). In the time of the Lord Buddha—a time of obviously high civilisation and much philosophical discussion (623 B.C. to 543 B.C. according to Sinhalese traditions, died 487 B.C. according to Vincent Smith)—Kosala (Oudh) and Magadha stand out prominently, Kosala being the premier State and having swallowed up Kashi (Benares). Very soon afterwards Magadha took the lead, including the territory from the Himālayas to the Ganga, with Pataliputra (where Patna and Bankipur are now) as capital—the first capital of India in "historical" times, as we shall see later.

Ajatashatru, its founder and the King of Magadha, was contemporary with Darius of Persia (521-485 B.C.), who annexed Sindh and part of the Panjab, and formed them into a Persian satrapy, interesting to us merely from the proof of the enormous wealth at that time of that part of India—implying thereby high civilisation—for it paid an annual tribute in gold-dust equal to one million pounds sterling.

We can pass on to the first "historical" Emperor of India, Chandra Mori, or Chandragupta; he came, according to the paurāṇic lists, from a branch of the Pramaras, one of the thirty-six royal races, of the "line of the Sun," descended from King Rāmachandra or one of his brothers; the Pramaras were one of the four Agnikulas, "Fire Families," descended from his brother Bharata. Chandragupta was the founder of the Maurya dynasty, and seized the throne of Magadha in 321 B.C. Six years before that date Alexander the Great had invaded what is now Afghanistan; crossing the Hindu Khush, fighting his way to the Indus, and, crossing it about March, 326 B.C., he entered on Indian soil, "which no European traveller or invader," says Vincent Smith, "had ever before trodden"—a rash and mistaken statement. Alexander did not remain long; he advanced to and crossed the Jhelum, defeated Poros, penetrated beyond Sialkot into Jammu, and then, much against his will, forced by a mutiny in his army, began his retreat in September of the same year, and quitted India finally about September, 325, and marched to Persia, reaching Susa in April-May, 324. His death in 323 put an end to his hopes, and young Chandragupta—belonging to the Magadha royal family, but unfriendly to its head and in exile—gathered an army, attacked the Greeks left in the Panjab and Sindh, drove them out and subdued the country. He then attacked the King of Magadha, and seated himself on his throne, added to his troops till he gathered an army of 690,000 men—infantry, cavalry, chariots and elephants—swept everything before him with amazing celerity, and finally established himself as Emperor of India, ruling from the Hindu Khush to the Nerbudda, from the Arabian Sea to the Bay of Bengal.

THE EMPERORS OF INDIA

The organisation of his Empire by this extraordinary man was as marvellous as his military capacity. Megasthenes, the Greek, lived for some time in Pataliputra, Chandragupta's capital, observed closely his administration in all its details, and left his observations on record; so we are on ground that cannot be challenged. Hunter sums up the views of Megasthenes as follows:

> The Greek ambassador observed with admiration the absence of slavery in India, the chastity of the women, and the courage of the men. In valour they excelled all other Asiatics; they required no locks to their doors; above all, no Indian was ever known to tell a lie. Sober and industrious, good farmers, and skilful artisans, they scarcely ever had recourse to a lawsuit, and lived peaceably under their native Chiefs. The kingly government is portrayed almost as described in the Code of Manu. Megasthenes mentions that India was divided into 118 kingdoms; some of which, as the Prasii under Chandragupta, exercised suzerain powers. The village system is well described, each little rural unit seeming to the Greek an independent republic. Megasthenes remarked the exemption of the husbandmen (Vaishyas) from war and public services; and enumerates the dyes, fibres, fabrics, and products (animal, vegetable, and mineral) of India.[1]

Megasthenes tells how Chandragupta had established a War Office of 30 members, divided into six Boards each of five members—Pañchayats: I. Admiralty, in

[1] Hunter's *Brief History of the Indian People*, pp. 77, 78 (printed for the Madras Schools) 1881. Perhaps because intended to teach Indian boys, it is often unfair and prejudiced, *e.g.*, in its account of the great Shivaji.

touch with Admiral; II. Transport, Commissariat, Army Service; III. Infantry; IV. Cavalry; V. War-chariots; VI. Elephants. The civil administration was similar, and Megasthenes describes specially the Municipality of Pataliputra, consisting again of 30 members, divided into six Pañchayats: I. is specially interesting as showing the care—noticeable in the books describing "pre-historic" times—exercised by the State over Arts and Crafts; it supervised all industrial matters, materials, wages, etc. II. looked after foreigners, acting as Consuls, Vincent Smith remarks, and giving proof that the Empire "was in constant intercourse with foreign States". III. was in charge of the registration of births and deaths, rigidly kept as a basis for taxation. IV. looked after trade, and kept the official weights and measures to which all must conform. V. supervised manufactures, and VI. collected the tax of a tithe of the value of all goods sold. The Municipality as a whole was responsible for markets, harbours, temples, etc. The Empire was divided into Provinces ruled by Viceroys, and officers travelled over the land, inspecting. It is noticed, as so often in later times, that the Indians bore the highest reputation for truth and honesty. Irrigation had its own Department, which regulated "the sluices by which water is distributed into the branch canals, so that every one may enjoy his fair share of the benefit," says Megasthenes. A mass of details has been accumulated, and may be found in the *Art of Government*, ascribed to Chanakya, Chandragupta's Brāhmaṇa minister, that has been translated. The Emperor died 297 B.C., and was succeeded by Bindusara, his son, and either the father or son extended the Empire almost as far south as what is now Madras. He was followed by Ashoka, who added to the Empire the Kingdom of Kalinga on the Bay of Bengal, and he ruled for 40 years—273 or 2 B.C. to 232 or 1—from the Hindu Khush to Madras. The Āndhra State (Āndhradesha), between the Godaveri and the Kistna, had its own Rāja, acknowledging Ashoka's overlordship, but the Pandya, Chola, Keralaputra and Satyaputra States, occupying the extreme south, were independent. Four Viceroys administered the north-western, eastern, western and southern Provinces, Ashoka himself administering the central. His wisdom, his power, his piety, his splendour, are they not written in his edicts, engraved on Rock and Pillar, and by these his Empire was ruled. Rock Edict II and Pillar Edict VII declare :

> On the roads I have had banyan trees planted to give shade to man and beast; I have had groves of mango-trees planted: and at every half kos I have had wells dug: rest-houses have been erected; and numerous watering-places have been prepared here and there for the enjoyment of man and beast.

Care of the sick, distribution of drugs and herbs, hospitals for animals, were among his institutions.

After his death, many Provinces broke away, until the sixth of his descendants, Brehidrita, or Brihadratha, was expelled from Magadha, 184 B.C., and seized Dhar and Chittoor in Mewar, Rajputana, where his descendants ruled till A.D. 730. But Vincent Smith says he was assassinated by Pushyamitra, the commander of his army. The Mori Chiefs certainly reigned in Mewar, and the transfer as stated is probable. In any case, the Maurya dynasty in Magadha ended, and Pushyamitra founded a new dynasty, the Sunga. Moreover he finally celebrated the horse-sacrifice a few years before his death, in 148 B.C., being acknowledged as Lord Paramount. His dynasty came to an end in 74 B.C., and was succeeded by the Kanva dynasty of four short-lived Kings, the last of whom perished in 27 B.C. at the hands of the ruler of the great Āndhra Kingdom.

The Kingdoms of India

The unity of India for the time had gone, as embodied in an Empire, and great Kingdoms arose and flourished. In the south the Āndhra Nation (later the Telugu-speaking population), occupying the Deccan, which had acknowledged the overlordship of Ashoka, after his death became independent, in 220 B.C., extended its sway as far as Nasik, thus stretching across India, and coming into touch with, and striving to hold, Gujerat and Kathiawar. From A.D. 85—138, the Āndhras were constantly struggling on their western borders with invading foreigners, and ultimately Kathiawar, Sindh and Cutch passed from Āndhra hands into those of the invaders. The Āndhra kingdom lasted another hundred years, ending in A.D. 236.

South of the Kistna was the Tamil country, divided into four kingdoms : Pandya, in the south, with Madura as capital ; Chola, with the river Pennar to the north and Pandya to the south ; while Keralaputra lay between it and the western sea, the later Malabar ; and

Satyaputra was a small State round the present Mangalore. The Tamil land was wealthy and civilised and inhabited by a great trading people. They exported pepper, pearls and beryls chiefly, and did an immense trade, especially with Egypt and Rome. We read of an embassy to congratulate Augustus Cæsar in 20 B.C., mentioned by Strabo. The routes chiefly followed were those by the Persian Gulf and the Red Sea, the monsoon weather, May to August, being avoided by the merchants. In the 14th century, Marino Sanuta, a Venetian noble, said that goods of small bulk and high value—spices, pearls, gems—went to a Persian Gulf port, then up the Tigris to Bassorah, thence to Baghdad. More bulky goods went by the Red Sea, crossed the desert, and down the Nile to Alexandria. Dacca fabrics were favourite wear in Rome in the imperial Court. This Roman trade led to the establishment of Roman Colonies among the Tamils during the first and second centuries A.D. Roman coins circulated, and some bronze vessels from the West have been dug up in the Nilgiris. Tamil literature grew abundantly during the first three centuries, and music, painting and sculpture flourished.

The Manual of the Administration of the Madras Presidency, putting the events of the *Rāmāyaṇa* at 2000 B.C. (an absurdly late date from the Hindu standpoint), notes that Rāma met Agastya, the great Sage of South India ; and that Agastya had much influence over an early Pandyan King, Kulashekara. For our purposes we may take the kingdom as it existed in 543 B.C., when Vijaya, from the Gangetic region, invaded Ceylon, and married a daughter of the reigning Pandyan King. Madura, the capital, was famous for its learning, and had a famous Sangha, or Collegium, an assembly of learned men, and among them Tiruvalluvar, the author of the famous poem, Kural.[1] The story of the Pandyan Kingdom's struggles with Chola, and of its invasions of Ceylon, shows a powerful State; and it continued, passing through many vicissitudes, down to 1731, when its last Hindu Monarch died, leaving a widow, Minakshi Ammal, who adopted a son, but was attacked and betrayed, and poisoned herself in Trichinopoly Fort—a Kingdom of more than 2,000 years within "historical" limits, ending in a tragedy in the frightful 18th century.

The Chola Kingdom was, as we have seen, an independent State in the time of Ashoka, and like Pandya was actively commercial, sending its ships across the Bay of Bengal and the Indian Ocean eastwards, and internal commerce being also carried on, goods from the east going to Kerala and Kerala sending Egyptian merchandise to Chola. Both the Chola and the Pandya kingdoms suffered much from the depredations of the Pallavas, thought by some to be an immigrating offshoot from the Parthian Pahlavas, who invaded north-west India. When Hiuen Tsang in A.D. 640 visited Kanchi, where the Pallavas had established

[1] The date of the Kural is a matter of dispute. Mr. V. Kanakasabhai, in *The Tamils 1,800 years ago*, puts it between A. D. 100 and 130. Dr. K. Graul, who translated it into German, says between A. D. 200 and 800. The Rev. Mr. Pope, who translated it into English, says A.D. 800 to 1000. The *Encyclopædia Britannica* offers from the 9th or 10th century to the 13th.

themselves, he mentions the Chola people, just then in a depressed condition. The Pallavas had no fixed borders, but are said to have lived as a predatory tribe; this seems scarcely likely, as they were powerful from the 4th to the 8th century A.D., but they were crushed, to the satisfaction of all, by a Chola Rāja Aditya, between about 880 and 907. Then the Chola Kingdom grew and flourished exceedingly, until the beginning of the fourteenth century; its capitals at different periods were Warriore, a suburb of Trichinopoly, Kumbhakonam and Tanjore. It was crippled by the Muhammadan invasion of South India in 1310, and though the invaders were driven out again in 1347, Chola soon after disappears.

Kerala occupied the western coast, comprising the present Travancore, Cochin and Malabar, trading chiefly with Egypt and Arabia. Its history has been largely recovered of late years, and teems with interest, most of it living unbrokenly from its ancient past right down to the present day, under its own Princes. Owing to the constant communication with the West, Christianity was early introduced into Kerala, some say in the first century A.D. by S. Thomas; others, including Vincent Smith, in the sixth century from the Syrian Church. The matter is not important for us, as Christianity made no way outside Kerala, and is not a factor in India during her long and prosperous life. It came to her with European trading companies, and her loss of power and prosperity.

In Northern India, owing to the powerful Kingdoms beyond the north-west frontier and also to raids and immigrations from China and Central Asia, the break up of the Mauryan Empire brought about disturbed conditions for many centuries; Bactria and Parthia, ruled by Princes of Greek descent, became independent States, breaking the yoke of the Seleukidæ in the middle of the third century B.C.; they invaded the north-western districts from time to time, and much of the Panjab and the Indus valley was definitely under Greco-Parthian rule (Indo-Parthian or Indo-Greek), from about 190 B.C. to A.D. 50, and these were finally crushed by the Kustans about A.D. 90. These invasions produced but little effect and wrought little destruction. It was other with hordes of nomad tribes, which swept down from the Central Asian steppes and China, destroying as they passed, from 170 B.C. onwards, some even reaching Kathiawar, where they settled, founding a Saka dynasty, destroyed A.D. 390. Among these the Yuch-chi from China definitely established themselves, crushing out the Indo-Parthian kingdom, and establishing their own—the Kushan dynasty—under Kadphises I and II, the latter sending an embassy to Rome to Trajan, about A.D. 99, to announce his conquests. He ruled the whole north-west of India, from Benares as easternmost point, as well as Afghanistan to the Hindu Khush, and his successor added Kashmir. This successor, Kanishka (about A. D. 120—150) is interesting for his famous Buddhist tower—13 storeys high—his splendid monastery for Buddhist education still existing in the ninth century, the Buddhist council called by him, at which Ashvaghosha was vice-president, held in Kashmir. The dynasty perished in the third century, about the same time as the Āndhra Kingdom in the Deccan, so far as India was concerned, but Kushan Kings were reigning in Kabul in the fifth century, when they were conquered by the Huns.

ANOTHER EMPIRE

Another vast Empire rises out of the darkness of seventy years which covers northern India from historical eyes, from the disappearance of the Kushan Kingdom, about A. D. 240, until A.D. 308, when Chandragupta, a Prince reigning in Pataliputra, weds a Lichchavi Princess, Kumari Devi, and the royal pair, between them, come to rule a Kingdom comprising Bihar, Oudh, Tirhut, and some adjacent lands. Chandragupta I became "Mahārāja of Mahārājas," and started an era, the Gupta era, from February 26, A. D. 320. To him was born a son, Samudragupta, who ruled from 326 to about 375, and built a new Empire.

He subdued all the Chiefs of the Gangetic plain and then those of the centre, then invaded the south, going by the east coast and returning by the west, but invading and gathering huge spoils, not holding, the southern States; he incorporated in his Empire half Bengal—from the Hooghly westwards, and all the country right across India including Gujerat, with the Nerbudda for southern boundary, the Central and United Provinces, much of Panjab, with almost all the rest of it and north Rajputana as a Protectorate, and many outlying States and the South acknowledged him as Overlord; he finally performed the horse-sacrifice as Lord Paramount of India, probably about A. D. 340. He died about 375. His son and successor was Chandragupta II, sometimes called Chandragupta-Vikramaditya. He must not be confused with the ruler of the same name, whose era, called also Samvat, began 56 B. C., the Vikramaditya at whose Court was the famous poet-minister, Bhattumurti.

He added to the Empire Malwa and Surashtra, abolished the Saka dynasty in the latter, and died in A. D. 413. Fa-Hien, the Chinese traveller who visited India at the beginning of the 5th century, spent six years in the Empire, during three of which he studied Samskrit in one of the large Buddhist monasteries at Pataliputra. He speaks with intense admiration of the wealth, prosperity, virtue, and happiness of the people, and the great liberty they enjoyed. "Those who want to go away may go; those who want to stop may stop." Most offences were punished by fines, and there was no capital punishment, and no judicial torture. Repeated rebellion, however, was punished by cutting off the right hand, "but such a penalty was exceptional". The roads were safe, for in all his travels Fa-Hien was not once attacked by robbers. "They do not keep pigs or fowls, there are no dealings in cattle, no butchers' shops, or distilleries." "No one kills any living thing, or drinks wine, or eats onions or garlic." Charitable institutions were numerous, rest-houses were kept on the roads. In the capital was a free hospital, supported by the voluntary contributions of the rich. Fa-Hien says:

> Hither come all poor or helpless patients suffering from all kinds of infirmities. They are well taken care of, and a doctor attends them; food and medicine being supplied according to their wants. Thus they are made quite comfortable, and when they are well they may go away.

(The first hospital in Europe was the Maison Dieu in Paris, in the seventh century.) It is worthy of notice that the King was a Hindu, and Fa-Hien a Buddhist, so he was the less likely to praise overmuch.

Some think that the last recension of the great Purāṇas and of the legal Institutes was made at this time. Sure it is that Saṃskrit was sedulously honoured, while art prospered, and architecture became ornate and splendid.

Chandragupta's son, Kumaragupta I, succeeded in A.D. 413 and Vincent Smith thinks he must have added to the Empire, as he celebrated the horse-sacrifice; he died in 455, leaving his son and successor Skandagupta to bear the burden of Empire, and to face the oncoming Huns. He defeated them at the beginning of his reign, if not as Yuvarāja (Crown Prince), but they returned about 470 and pressed him hardly, and when he died ten years later, the Empire died with him, though his half-brother succeeded to the throne and reigned in Magadha, its centre, the family continuing there till A.D. 720; while other members of the Gupta family ruled other portions, and a descendant of it was the grandmother of Harsha of Thanesar, in the Panjab, who became famous.

The fall of the Empire was due to the appearance of the Huns, who invaded India and Europe in two mighty streams, crushing Persia, and over-running the civilised world. Their power was broken by the Turks, in the middle of the sixth century, after they had devastated both Europe and Northern India.

Harsha, who came to the throne in A.D. 606 restored and somewhat enlarged on the east the Gupta Empire, but it was less in Rajputana. His rule was much approved by Hiuen Tsang, who visited India 630 and 644, but it did not reach the level of the Gupta administration. After many years of War, Harsha was more or less attracted to Buddhism by Hiuen Tsang, and was fond of religious debates, a fondness shared by his widowed sister, who attended them with him and was a most learned lady. He died in A.D. 648. After his death, Adityasena of the Gupta dynasty performed the horse-sacrifice, for no very definite reason known to history; there is no record of any later performance thereof. Sixty-four years after Harsha's death, in A.D. 710-11, the Arabs from Bassorah—who had conquered Mukuram (Baluchistan) and were settled there by A.D. 644—under Muhammad Ben Kasim, crossed the Indus, overran Sindh, which was held by Musalmans thereafter, and advanced into Rajputana. Young Bappa, a lad of 15, a Mori of Chittoor, led an army against them and defeated them, but the Crescent of Islam had risen over India's horizon, a New Era had begun.

Before passing on into the Muhammadan invasions, it is well to pause at this point for a moment, for western historians have failed to note the general prosperity and happiness of the Indian populations, save where such incursions as the nomads and Huns temporarily ravaged a part of the country. They have glanced lightly over the wealth, the trade, the happiness of the masses of the people, during an acknowledged period, from Semiramis to Muhammad Ghori, of 3,000 years—to say nothing of the "untold centuries" beyond—and have fixed their gaze on the local wars, ignoring the vast accumulation of wealth, which proved that the industrial life and prosperity of the people went steadily on, unaffected by temporary and local disturbances, in a huge stream of content and progress. If this be compared with the state of Germany before the Peasants' War, with the state of France before the great Revolution, western nations may begin to realise that eastern nations may have something to say for themselves, and that the "blessings" of foreign occupation are not fully recognised in India.

A very striking illustration of this was the seventy-five days' festival of Harsha, in A.D. 644, held at the confluence of the Ganga and Jumna at Prayag (Allahabad), at which Hiuen Tsang was present. Harsha had held such a festival every five years for thirty years, "in accordance with the custom of his ancestors," to distribute among ascetics, religious orders and the poor, *the accumulations of wealth of the preceding five years.* About half a million of people assembled, gifts were distributed on the first three days in the name of the Buddha, the Sun, and Shiva; on the fourth day, to 10,000 Buddhist monks, who each received 100 gold coins, a pearl and a cotton garment; then, for twenty days, gifts to Brāhmaṇas, for ten days to "heretics"; for a month to the poor, destitute and orphans. Harsha gave everything, except horses, elephants and army equipments, down to his personal jewels. And this was done every five years. The great festival is still held every twelfth year, but there is no King Harsha, and no distribution of gifts. Nor, if there were such a Monarch, could the country support such quinquennial accumulations. Only a huge and well-to-do manual labour class could have rendered possible the great trading, manufacturing and commercial classes, who existed at the coming of the East India Company; history confirms these facts. The Emperors, Kings and Chiefs were enormously wealthy because they ruled a wealthy people, and nurtured their prosperity. When Sir William Hunter wrote, "40,000,000 of the people never had a full meal," and a larger number are in that condition to-day.

So long as the wars were internecine, between Hindu Kingdoms, the caste system confined the fighting to the Kshattriya (military) order; the universal Pañchayats of the village organisation carried on smoothly the all-important village life, and Hiuen Tsang notes that villagers quietly went on with their agricultural work while a battle was proceeding close by; it was the policy of the contending Chiefs to safeguard the peasantry, on whose labour depended the prosperity of the land they hoped to rule. Only raiders like the Huns devastated, and their devastations were local.

How much the ordinary life runs on with little change may be judged by comparing life in Malabar to-day with Marco Polo's description of what he observed in the same district, then Kerala, in A.D. 1292. He said that the people wear but one cloth.

Women burn themselves with their dead husbands. Many worship the cow. They rub their houses with cow-dung and sit on the ground. They chew "tembal" (Persian for "betel"). Cail (Canyal in Tinnevelly) is a great and noble city where touch all ships from the west. Coilum (Quilon) produces ginger, pepper and fine indigo. No corn is grown, only rice. Gozurat (Gujarat) produces pepper, ginger, indigo and cotton, and manufactures beautiful mats. Tannah (near Bombay) exports leather, buckram and cotton, and imports gold, silver, copper and other articles. Fine buckrams seem to have been very largely exported. Other travellers in the 14th, 15th and 16th centuries give similar testimony. India's trade for thousands of years was enormous, and Pliny the Elder in his *Natural History* (about A.D. 77) [1] complains that the annual drain of gold from the Roman Empire to India, Arabia, and China, was never less than 100,000,000 sestercia, "giving back her own wares in exchange, which are sold at fully one hundred times their prime cost". "That is what our luxuries and women cost us," says he sardonically. [2]

Islam in India

A new element now enters into Indian history, an element which is still only in process of assimilation,

[1] Edition Mayhoff, Leipzig, 1906, Bk. VI, p. 101. The readings vary, some giving 500 × 100,000 = 50,000,000, others 55,000,000, as adopted in the *Imperial Gazetteer*.

[2] The *Imperial Gazetteer of the Indian Empire* allots 55,000,000 of this 100,000,000 to India, from another reading, and reckons this at £458,000. This calculation again is vitiated by the fact that the value of the sestercium varied from 2·1 to 2·4 pence.

which caused inevitably disturbance and much evil feeling on both sides, but brought to the building of the Indian Nation most precious materials, enriching the Nationality and adding new aspects to its many-faced splendour. As "Saxon and Norman and Dane," to say nothing of other elements, are the English, and as English and Scotch and Irish are forming one Kingdom, the Irish, after eight hundred years, yet unassimilated, so in India, Indians, Persians (Parsīs) and Musalmāns are not yet wholly one Nation, though becoming one with great rapidity. We must now, as roughly as before, trace the outline of this Muhammadan entrance into and fixation in India, up to this time a Hindu Nation.

We have seen that the Arabs invaded and conquered Sindh early in the eighth century, and were thrown back from Rajputana by Bappa. Rajputana was a congeries of States, each with its own Chief, war-loving, chivalrous, and quarrelling constantly with each other—a poor barrier, therefore, against warriors of a faith resting on one Prophet, one book and a sword consecrated to both. The whole story is one of heroic, incredible valour, rendered futile by ceaseless dissensions, which led to angry alliances with the common foe against the estranged brother.

A Kingdom comprising the greater part of the Panjab and the upper Indus was the first, after the Rajput repulse, to face the Muslims, when Sabuktinin, Sultān of Ghazni, Afghanistan, invaded India in A.D. 986, and after some battles established himself in

Peshawar. His son, Muhammad, raided Indian territory seventeen times between A.D. 1001 and 1024, starting in October on a three months' march into the interior, and returning when he had satisfied himself with plunder, but holding Lahore strongly from 1021. He died A.D. 1030. Five centuries followed of incessant struggle. In the Empire, broken into pieces, each fragment had its Chief, fighting his neighbour. The rule of the Huns seemed to have bred divisions. As the robber Barons fought in Europe, after the breaking up of the Constantinople Empire, so the clans and their Chiefs fought in India. The invaders naturally took advantage of it, siding with either party, the weaker for preference, to destroy that weaker when the stronger was crushed. Rajput Chiefs, both in Rajputana and Panjab, battled unceasingly against each other, and alas, with Muslims against Rajputs, with varied fortunes; Prithvirāj succeeded to the gadi of Delhi in A.D. 1164, rolled back the Musalmāns, broken, on Lahore, but fought his last battle in 1193, the flower of Rajput chivalry around him but some Rajputs against him, fought until the dead lay in swathes on the field, 13,000 of them "asleep, on the banks of the Ghuggur"; and he, the darling of the bards, seeking death, alas, in vain, was caught under his fallen horse, was taken prisoner, answered a taunt from his capturers with a bitter jest, and was stabbed; the Hindu throne of Delhi was empty. The Pathan seated himself thereon, ruled, and set up other kingdoms in India, and fought, conquered and was conquered; and so fierce battles raged up and down the northern lands, with inroads from Afghanistan, and rival Muhammadan Chiefs and changes, Pathans, Tartars, Mughals, until Babar and his Turks and Mughals came in 1519, and 1520, and 1524, and finally fought the battle of Panipat against Sultan Ibrahim Lodi, the Pathan, in 1526, and was proclaimed Emperor of India at Delhi, the first of the "great Moguls".

But we must turn aside for a moment, and run backwards to take a bird's eye-view of the south, where later, Musalmān and Hindu fought for rule, until the Maratha Power rose to dominance. The Āndhra Kingdom had disappeared, we know, about A.D. 230, and the great table-land of the Deccan, south of the Nerbudda, becomes again the scene of pregnant history, when the Chief of the Chalukyas, or Solankis, a Rajput Agnikula clan, conquered the Deccan and built a Kingdom about A.D. 550, and reigned in Vatapi, in the Bijapur District, gloriously and well. In a century the dynasty had grown strong and famous, and exchanged embassies with Khusru II of Persia—as shown in a fresco in an Ajanta cave. Many fights with Pallavas and others need not detain us; enough that the Chalukya kingdom in the Deccan and Maharashtra continued to A.D. 1190; just before the Pathan, Muhammad Ghori, seated himself on Delhi throne. A hundred years later, in 1294, the Sultan Ala-ud-din, after the sack of Chittoor, invaded the Deccan, and crushed the Gadavas who had succeeded the Chalukyas, and took as ransom six maunds of pearls, two maunds of diamonds and other gems. (A maund=82 lb. avoirdupois.) In 1309 came the invasion of his lieutenant Malik Kafur, who overran the south, right down to Rameshvara, where he built a Mosque, and then returned whence he came; and in 1336, south of the Krishna and west of the Tungabhadra river, dividing it from the Chola Kingdom, rose the great Hindu Kingdom of Vijayanagar, that held its own for two centuries of pride, despite the growing power of the Muslims.

Babar, we resume, of Turki race, descendant of Tamerlane, sat enthroned in Delhi, the founder of the splendid Mughal dynasty. Two years after Panipat, a great battle was fought at Fatehpur Sikri between the new Emperor and the Rajputs, and he conquered, only to die four years later, in 1530. Then Humayun, his son, became Emperor, but was driven out by a Pathan Chief, and fled to Kandahar in 1543, coming back in 1555; for his twelve-year old son, Akbar, conquered the Pathan, and re-opened to his father the gates of Delhi. Akbar succeeded to the throne in 1556, to be India's greatest Muḥammadan Emperor; perhaps the only serious stain upon his name—and he was then only fourteen years old—is the sack of Chittoor in 1557. So great was he, so tolerant, that he welded together Hindu and Musalmān; Hindu Princesses were the mothers of the Emperors Jehangir (Salim) and Shah Jahan; Rajputs were generals in his army, and ministers in his State; the Rajput Man Sinha was his greatest general, Rāja Toda Mall his greatest minister. Akbar's dream was a United India, and he renewed the Empire of Chandragupta Maurya, though some Rajput States defied him to the end. He "laid down the principle that men of all faiths were to be treated alike by the law; he had opened all posts of authority to men of ability, without restriction of creed; he had abolished the slavery of captives, the capitation tax on non-Musalmāns, and the tax on Hindu pilgrims. He forbade the forcing of a widow to burn herself on her husband's funeral pyre, sanctioned widow re-marriage, forbade child-marriage, and the killing of animals for sacrifice." He also laid down a land-system which caused great content. Three classes of land were made, according to fertility. The value of the produce was decided by an average of nineteen years. The Government took one-third, for land revenue and support of militia, amounting to 22 millions sterling a year, the land-tax bringing in from 16½ to 17½ millions; all other taxes were abolished. A settlement was made every ten years.

The Emperor Jehangir, succeeding to the throne in 1605, did naught to strengthen his father's work, but he did one thing pregnant with ruin for his house. In 1613, he gave permission to the English to trade in his dominions, and factories were established in Surat, Cambay, Gogo and Ahmedabad. Two years later Sir Thomas Roe came to him as ambassador from James I. His land-tax amounted to 17½ millions. Shah Jahan, 1627-1658, under whom, by new conquests, the land-tax came to 22 millions, continued his grandfather's policy; and had others followed in the steps of these twain, there had been no Hindu-Musalmān question in modern India. But Aurungzeb, the destroyer, succeeded, and his persecutions and his cruelties drove his subjects into rebellion. "At last revolts broke out on every side, his sons rebelled, debts accumulated, disorders of every kind arose, and in 1706 he died, alone and miserable, amid the ruins of the Empire he had shattered. With his accession the hope of a United India vanished, and at his death the work of Akbar was destroyed." Materially his wealth was immense; his conquests added again to the land revenue, and raised it to 38 millions sterling. A hundred years later it was still £34,506,640.

In the year of Shah Jahan's accession to the Imperial throne was born a child destined to lead in the shaking of the Mughal Power; it was Shivaji, "crowned in Raigad in 1674, as the Hindu Emperor, and the Maratha Kingdom of the South faced the Mughal Kingdom of the North".[1]

The State of the People

During these centuries of war, raids and forays, what was the condition of the people of northern India? The answer comes from the travellers who observed it, from the merchants who struggled and intrigued for the right to exploit it. They were bitterly prejudiced and speak of "heathen" and "heathen customs," but they drove good bargains and bought, bought largely, to sell again at huge profits, and die in Europe, wealthy from their trading.

Bernier, in his letter to Colbert, complains, even more vigorously than Pliny, seventeen centuries before, that " this Hindustan is an abyss into which a great

[1] The extracts are from *Children of the Motherland*, pp. 143, 145, 165.

part of the gold and silver of the world finds plenty of ways of going in from all sides, and hardly one way out". After a vivid description of the military strength of the great Mughal, he speaks of his immense treasures, gold and silver and jewellery, "a prodigious quantity of pearls and precious stones of all sorts . . . one throne is all covered with them". Woman wear rings and anklets, chains, ear-rings and nose-rings; most of all he marvels over the incredible quantity of manufactured goods, "embroideries, streaked silks, tufts of gold for turbans, silver and gold cloth, brocades, network of gold"—he is evidently dazed. He can hardly find words to describe the Emperor, with his golden turban, and his spray of diamonds, and a matchless topaz that shone like a little sun, and his huge collar of rows of pearls down to his waist, and so on and on for pages. Tavernier describes him on similar lines, with his seven thrones, and the marvellous peacock throne, with the natural colours of the peacock's tail worked out in jewels, valued by him at 6½ millions sterling; he gives very full descriptions of the manufactured goods. Kasembasar, "a village in the kingdom of Bengal," exported yearly 22,000 bales of silk, weighing "2,200,000 pounds, at 16 oz. to the pound". Carpets of silk and gold, satins with streaks of gold and silver, endless lists of exquisite works, of minute carvings, and other choice objets d'art. The facts speak for themselves. It was this enormous wealth that drew Europeans to come hither to "shake the pagoda tree"; the stories carried back by successful shakers, drew others to the golden land. This was the country of which Phillimore wrote in the middle of the 18th century, that "the droppings of her soil fed distant Nations". To share in this incredible wealth, the first English factories were established on the western coast.

The proof of India's prosperity under Indian rule, Musalmān as well as Hindu, lies in India's wealth. The wars scratched the country here and there, now and then; the peasants, artisans, traders, wrought industriously everywhere, always. The invading raiders laid all waste, and travellers come across such scenes and describe them, as though they pictured the normal state of the country. They carried away enormous wealth, but the producers remained and piled it up again. But when the Musalmāns settled down as rulers, their own prosperity depended on that of the people and they took with discrimination. Firoze of the Toghlak dynasty (A.D. 1351—1388), like Hindu Rulers before him, constructed great irrigation works, canals, etc. It was this care for irrigation, characteristic of Indian Rulers, which gave such marvellous fertility to the soil through the centuries. Ever the immense foreign trade went on, enriching the land, and they exported luxuries and surplus, never the food wanted to feed the people; that remained from the fat years against the lean. A disadvantage of the swift communication between Britain and India now is that the rulers no longer come to stay; but, under the decencies of modern ways, gather wealth like the old raiders, and like them carry it abroad for enjoyment.

THE MARATHA CONFEDERACY

The Hon. Mr. Justice Ranade, in his small volume on the *Rise of the Maratha Power*, has done more than any other writer to point out the significance of the Maratha story in the long history of India, and to make the reader feel its inspiration and its teaching.

While Delhi was the seat of Mughal Power, the Musalmāns in the Deccan had made themselves independent of it in A.D. 1347, and had chosen Ala-ud-din Hasan as King, who founded the Bahāmani kingdom, which broke up from 1484 to 1572 into the five kingdoms of Berar, Ahmednagar, Bijapur, Bidar and Golconda, whose quarrels with the Delhi Empire facilitated the breaking up of the Musalmān domination. The rise of the Maratha Power was preceded by a great Hindu Revival, Tukaram, Veman Pandit, Eknath and Ramdas, the Guru of Shivaji, were its inspiration. Shivaji himself was a Mystic, materialised into a man of action. His aim was the building of a Nation; his means patriotism and union. His spirit, his aim, his means, are the spirit, the aim, the means of the National party in India to-day; a Hindu Revival preceded the modern National movement; its one aim is India, a Nation; its fervent patriotism and its striving after union are its means to success. Where it differs from its forerunner is that instead of fighting against the Musalmāns it welcomes them as a part of the Nation, instead of using the sword, it uses as weapons, education, the platform and the pen.

Shivaji's careful organisation of the Government recalls the work of Chandragupta-Maurya. First came the Peshwā, or Prime Minister; then the Minister of War (Senapati—Army Lord); the Minister of Finance (Amātya); the Accountant-General (Pant Sachiv); the Private Secretary (Mantri); the Foreign Secretary (Sumant); the Minister of Religion (Panditrao); the Chief Justice. But it was Shivaji himself who created the new Maharashtra, and made the men, who, after his death, broke the Mughal power. The building up of his great Kingdom from Surat in the north to Hubli in the South, from the sea on the west to Berar, Golconda and Bijapur on the east, his coronation at Raipur in 1674 as Pādshāha, his recognition by the rulers of Golconda and Bijapur as Suzerain by the paying of tribute, his death in 1680—all this may be read at leisure. He died, but he had "created a Nation," and when Aurungzeb came in 1682 to crush the Marathas and the Musalmān Kingdoms, although he with his huge army carried everything before him, Shivaji's younger son, Rajaram, rallied the Maratha leaders round him, and began the great twenty-years' War of Independence; at his death his nephew Shaku succeeded him and the War went on, till in 1705 a treaty was made, though not kept; Aurungzeb died two years later, broken-hearted, after a war of 25 years, which ended in failure. Shaku was crowned, regaining his grandfather's realm. Thus Svarāj, "own-rule," was gained, and, after a period of quarrelling and unrest, Balaji Vishvanath became the Peshwā of the Maratha Kingdom, and is called in Hunter's history and even in Ranade's, the First

Peshwā. He it was who bound together the great Maratha Chiefs, built up the Confederacy that lasted for a hundred years, that broke the Mughal Empire, and practically ruled India. Balaji marched to Delhi in 1718, and in the next year compelled the Emperor to recognise the right of Shaku to a quarter and a tenth of the land revenue of the Deccan (the chouth and sardeshmukti), and when he was succeeded in 1720 by his son, Baji Rao, he left the Confederacy so strong that it was able to extend its power gradually under the second and third Peshwās from Gujerat and Kathiawar to Bengal and Orissa, from Delhi to Maharashtra.

The Peshwā at Poona represented the centre of the great Confederacy; the Bhonsla General was at Nagpur; Holkar was at Indore; Scindia at Gwalior; the Gaekwar at Baroda. These five represented the five Maratha Branches, each with its Chief. The great defeat of the Marathas at Panipat, fighting against the Afghans, threw them back from the extreme north, but they regained their power there, and held the Delhi Emperor as their puppet in 1803. In fact the Marathas ruled India, save where a new Power was making its way, a Power against which they broke, as the power of the Musalmāns had broken against them. It was that of Great Britain.

The British in India

Long and strange was the struggle for European Empire in India from the days when the Mughal Empire was in the heights of its splendour, through the

Maratha Empire, until the final triumph of the British. Portuguese, Dutch, French, British—such the succession of the foreign ventures, with a gleam of Denmark in 1620; of the German Empire headed by Austria, the "Ostend Company" in 1722; of Prussia, the Emden Company in 1744—ghosts flitting across the Indian stage. They were all seeking for trade. It was a traders' war when they fought; the soldiers were mostly adventurers; European Governments looked on complacently and helped with a few soldiers now and then. But the flag followed trade, not trade the flag. And the fighting was traders' fighting rather than that of soldiers, not careful of honour, nor treaty, but only of gain. Bold unscrupulous adventurers, they were for the most part, the "bad boys" of the family, like Clive. *Punch* wrote a fearful epitaph on "John Company" and his crimes, after the Sepoy War, and when the Crown took over the Empire the Company had made, it marked the New Era with the noble proclamation of Queen Victoria, the Magna Carta of India. But the making of that Empire by the adventurers is a wonderful story of courage, craft, unscrupulousness—were they not dealing with "heathen"?—ability rising to genius, as in Clive, and great administrators after great soldiers. At the beginning conquest was not thought of, no one made any pretence that he was here for "the good of India". Quite frankly, it was the immense wealth of India that lured them, wealth to be carried "home" for enjoyment; the "white man's burden" was golden. The breaking up of the Mughal Empire and the quarrels of Viceroys who became

Kings, of Generals who became Chiefs, these gave the opportunity. Britain succeeded, because she was the Power that held in her the most fertile seed of free institutions, because she was on the eve of establishing democratic Government on her own soil on the surest basis, so that while she might enthrall for a time, ultimate freedom under her rule was inevitable. France had behind her then only the traditions of tyranny; the Bourbons ruled and rioted. India needed for her future a steady pressure, that would weld her into one Nation on a modern basis, that she might become a Free Nation among the Free. The High Powers that guide the destinies of Nations saw Britain as fittest for this intermediate and disciplinary stage.

Early in the sixteenth century the Portuguese formed trading settlements on the western coast in Calicut and Goa. Early in the seventeenth century, the Dutch traded on the eastern coasts, established very many factories, but finally settled down, after many vicissitudes, struggles and battles, in Java, etc., "the Dutch Indies". France began to nibble in 1537, and established her first factories in Surat and Golconda in 1668, and in 1672 bought the site of Pondicherry; she made a great bid for an Indian Empire in the eighteenth century through the genius of Dupleix chiefly, and failed.

Denmark was stirred to rivalry in 1612, and made an East India Company, but never was strong enough for the Empire game. She began by a shipwreck on the Tanjore coast in 1620, the survivors from the shipwreck, except the Captain, Roelant Crape, being murdered. The Raja of Tanjore gave him permission to settle at Tranquebar. The settlement was never important, but it started the Protestant missionaries in India in 1706, and Schwarz (1750-1798) founded the missions in Trichinopoly, Tanjore, and Tinnevelly, still the strongest missionary centres in India. England bought the settlement finally in 1845, with Balasore, and with another missionary settlement in Serampur, Bengal. In 1847, the Tranquebar mission was handed over to the Lutherans. From the 18th century onwards all the missionary Nations—German, American, French, Italian, Swiss—have freely established their missions in India, *imperia in imperio*, a dangerous policy, a menace to British rule, and a running annoyance and irritation to Indians.

Britain began humbly. On December 31, 1600, Elisabeth chartered "The Governor and Company of Merchants of London trading in the East Indies" for exclusive trading there—at that time no trading having been done—and they fitted out some ships, one, under Captain Hawkins, reaching Surat, on the West Coast, in 1606. In 1611, a Captain Hippon, on his own account, set up a little trading establishment on the East Coast at Pettapoli, and another at Masulipatam. In 1613, the Emperor Shah Jahan gave duly written permission for setting up factories at Surat and Cambay, Gogo and Ahmedabad, and in 1616 the Zamorin of Calicut allowed a factory to be set up in his capital city. Thus was a footing made on the West Coast, and Surat became a Presidency Town in the time of Cromwell (1653), and moved its

Government in 1661 to the island of Bombay, given by Portugal as a kind of wedding gift, when Charles II married Catherine of Braganza.

Meanwhile the East Coast was factorised, and in 1626, a factory was established at Argeman, 70 miles north of Madras, with a fort to protect it. Factory, fort, town, "necessary" extensions—so it went thenceforth, all natural and inevitable. In 1634, Shah Jahan allowed another trading centre, at Pipli, in Bengal, and in the next year, Charles I issued another charter. But Argeman was not convenient, and the kind Rāja of Chandragiri, descendant of the royal house of Vijayanagar, in 1639, gives Mr. Day permission to have a factory at Chennaputnam, with land one mile broad and six miles along the shore, and he generously builds them a fort to protect it, Fort S. George. And Day builds a wall round the fort, on the island made by the two branches of the Coum River, 400 yards long and 100 wide, and allows only white people to live inside his wall, any Nation, if only white—White Town; and outside it an Indian town grows up—Black Town. And these twain are Madraspatam—Madras. In 1564, it had a garrison of 26 men. Its official records begin from 1670. Cromwell lets the two companies of Elisabeth and Charles I amalgamate, and makes Fort S. George a Presidency, in 1653, with authority over the Bengal factories.

In 1690, Job Charnock sets up a factory in Calcutta, though trading privileges were not granted to the English in Bengal until between 1713 and 1719 by the Mughal Emperor Firokshere, and builds a fort; so we have three big forts ere the end of the first quarter of the 18th century—Bombay, Madras, Calcutta, a Fort S. David also, a mile from Cuddalore; in 1686, Sir John Child, at Bombay, makes the ominous announcement, that thenceforth if the "natives"—the owners of the country—attack, he will retaliate. Until then, they had been yielding and submissive, as became foreign traders. In 1702, various Companies having arisen in England, who all quarrelled bitterly, it was thought well to amalgamate them, and so present a solid front; and amalgamated they were, as the United East India Company, in 1702. The position was a most peculiar one. Here was a Company, to all intents and purposes independent; it was ruled by a Board of Directors in London; it chose its own agents, it made its own armies; after a time it appointed a Governor, then a Governor-General; it applied for Charters, for Courts of Justice, and got them—with subsequent horrors related by Macaulay. There was no effective control over its proceedings, although Parliament interfered for the first time in 1773, and a Board of Control was established in 1784, and the Court of Directors placed under it—a clumsy dual arrangement, making no real difference. The one useful thing was the renewal of the Charter, preceded by an enquiry, which at least revealed the state of things—and terrible are the records. When things became too outrageous, Parliament interfered, as in the impeachment of Warren Hastings; but, for the most part, Britain was far too busy with her own troubles, her loss of her American Colonies, her

Napoleonic Wars, the struggles of her rising Democracy, the miserable condition of her people, her Chartists, her agricultural riots, and the rest, to trouble much about what a trading Company was doing in far-away heathen India; the Company made treaties and broke them, or forged them, if more convenient; it cheated, robbed, murdered, oppressed, and —built an Empire in about a century. Clive was the first Governor under the East India Company in 1758; Earl Canning the last in 1856. The Company ended in the Sepoy War of 1857, and the Crown assumed the sovereignty in 1858.

The policy of the Company was shrewd and effective. The Indian rulers borrowed European officers to drill their soldiers, borrowed European soldiers too. Presently, if French officers and men were with one Chief, English officers and men were with the rival. Dupleix had allied himself with one claimant to the throne of the dead Nizām of the Deccan; the English therefore were with the Nawāb of the Carnatic, who had an eye to a possible chance. Princes, English and French all tried to use each other—the Princes to play off English against French, the English and French severally to use opposing Princes against each other. It is a sorry story of intrigue, of utter disregard of honour and good faith on all sides. Dupleix, that French genius, master of the military art and of unscrupulous statecraft, was carrying all before him and carving out a French Empire in Southern India, when Robert Clive, a writer in the service of the Company, who was also a captain for the nonce, offered a bold plan of attack, and was bidden carry it out; marched rapidly to Arcot (1751) with 200 English and 300 sepoys, seized it, held it against all comers, struck here, struck there, won everywhere, and laid the first stone of the British Empire in India. The French hopes in the South were finally destroyed by the victory of Colonel Coote at Wandiwash in 1760.

After a visit to England, the Directors made Clive Governor of Fort S. David, and he returned to India in 1755 for five marvellous years of glory and shame. Trouble in Bengal, where Siraj-ud-daula was Viceroy for Delhi, and had attacked and captured Fort William; he thrust his 146 captives, for the night into the Fort military gaol, the "Black Hole," a room 18 feet square with two small windows, and, says the *Imperial Gazetteer*, "although the Nawāb does not seem to have been aware of the consequences, it meant death to a huddled mass of English prisoners in the stifling heat of June" (ii, 474). Only 23 survived that night of agony. Clive started for Calcutta, managed, despite the Black Hole, to persuade the Nawāb that he was a friend—"I will . . . stand by him as long as I have a man left," wrote he—seduced by bribery some of the Nawāb's officers, forged a treaty, and Admiral Watson's signature thereto, to deceive Omichand, himself a traitor, defeated his dear friend the Nawāb at Plassey (June 23, 1757), and sold his throne—our Bengal, Bihar and Orissa—to Mir Jafar for a sum that amounted to £2,340,000 sterling, of which Clive received £200,000. Omichand, when he found the treaty was forged, swooned, and never recovered the shock; Clive advised him to go on a pilgrimage, but the wretched man sank into idiocy, "languished a few months and then died". Macaulay, though he makes excuses for his hero of meeting craft with craft, says of his general policy, that "he descended, without scruple, to falsehood, to hypocritical caresses, to the substitution of documents and to the counterfeiting of hands" (*Essays*, ii. 101, 102. Ed. 1864). By these means, joined to marvellous courage and military genius, he founded the British Empire in India, which historians date from Plassey.

Clive obtained in addition from Mir Jafar a tract of 882 square miles—the 24 Perganas—to go to the Company after his death, he having meanwhile the rental; this rental was paid to him by the Company from 1765—when they took over the land—till he died in 1774; the quit-rent was about £30,000 sterling a year. At the age of 34, starting with nothing, he had accumulated, between 1755 and 1760, admittedly, £220,000 remitted to business houses in England; £25,000 in diamonds; "considerable" sums and a "great mass of ready money," as well as the huge estate, which he valued at £27,000 a year. All this was challenged in the House of Commons, in 1773, after his last return to England (1767), and a vote of censure was shelved by the previous question, and the words that "he did, at the same time, render great and meritorious services to his country". He committed suicide in 1774. Macaulay says of the enquiry: "It was clear that Clive had been guilty of some acts which it was impossible to vindicate without attacking the authority of all the most sacred laws which regulate the intercourse of individuals and of States. But it was equally clear that he had displayed great talents, and even great virtues"—talents, undoubtedly. Macaulay thinks that the enmity he roused was due to his efforts to stop corruption; for, in 1765, he had returned to India for a year and a half as Governor, and had devoted himself to the purifying of the administration, perhaps repenting of his own rapacity. That, at least remains to his credit, but he kept hold of his own ill-gotten wealth. His new ardour for purity had been more admirable, had he disgorged his own spoils, and it may well be that the attack on him was largely due to the fact that he had enriched himself by methods which he forbade to others.

Macaulay gives a terrible account of the oppressions of the Company at this time: "thirty millions of human beings were reduced to the extremity of wretchedness. They had been accustomed to live under tyranny, but never under tyranny like this ... That Government, oppressive as the most oppressive form of barbarian despotism, was strong with all the strength of civilisation." He quotes a Musalmān historian, who praises the extraordinary courage and military skill of the English: "but the people under their dominion groan everywhere, and are reduced to poverty and distress. O God! come to the assistance of thy afflicted servants, and deliver them from the oppressions which they suffer." In 1770 there was an awful famine; "the Hooghly every day rolled down thousands of corpses close to the porticoes and gardens of the English conquerors. The very streets of Calcutta were blocked up by the dying and the dead." It was "officially reported to have swept away two-thirds of the inhabitants" (*Imperial Gazetteer*, ii, 480), or 10,000,000 persons.

The terrible years roll on; Macaulay again lays stress on them in his Essay on Warren Hastings; of his ability, again, there is as little doubt as of his crimes. He was Governor from 1772 to 1785, taking in 1774 the title of Governor-General. He laboured at administration, and filled the Company's coffers with gold. The gathering of this seems to have been his chief object, and was the cause of his greatest crimes. The Nawāb of Bengal had had an income of 53 lakhs promised him by Clive, when deprived of his power; Clive cut the allowance down to 41 lakhs on the accession of a new Nawāb, and the third was reduced to 32 lakhs. Hastings found a child as the fourth, and, the child being helpless, cut him down to 16 lakhs. He sold Allahabad and Kora to Oudh for 50 lakhs (then worth half a million pounds sterling), and stopped the tribute of 26 lakhs guaranteed to the Emperor of Delhi in return for Bengal. To these "conquerors" every treaty was a mere "scrap of paper," to be repudiated at pleasure. These "economies" were highly appreciated by the Company; they left the Company wealthy in gold, but bankrupt in honour. Had they only stained their own honour, it would have been their own business. But they stained the honour of England in India's eyes. These were the first "English" whom she knew; England made some amends by giving English education with its liberty-inspiring ideals. She will make her final amends by co-operating with India, as she has co-operated with Ireland, to shape Home Rule.

But worse crimes followed this auspicious beginning; the sale of the Rohillas to pillage and slaughter: the hanging of Nanda-kumara; the coercion of the Princesses of Oudh. The Rohillas were a long-Indianised Afghan people, whose "little territory" says Macaulay (*Essays*, ii. 193), "enjoyed the blessings of repose under the guardianship of valour. Agriculture and commerce flourished among them; nor were they negligent of rhetoric and poetry." Sujah Daula, Nawāb of Oudh, coveted this rich territory, but feared the valour of the Rohillas, numbering some 80,000 warriors. Hastings sold him the use of the British army for £400,000 sterling, and they, with the Nawab's troops, were let loose on this noble people. Fire and sword devastated the land and slew the people, and "the rich province which had tempted the cupidity of Sujah Daula became the most miserable part even of his miserable dominions". In two years, by such transactions, Hastings gave the Company about a million sterling and £450,000 increase of annual income. He also had saved Bengal from an annual military expenditure of £250,000.

Nanda-kumara was a wealthy Brāhmaṇa who accused Hastings of some of his crimes; before this, there was a long story of antagonism; he was a man of high rank, talent and wealth. His accusation was met by his arrest for an alleged forgery six years before. The infamous Sir Elijah Impey was the judge, the jury English. The verdict was a foregone conclusion, and Impey pronounced a sentence of death. He died with peaceful dignity, hanged on the public gallows before an enormous crowd, amid shrieks and shouts of horror and despair.

The Princesses of Oudh, the mother and widow of Suraj Daula were enormously wealthy, reputed to possess a treasure of £3,000,000 sterling, and great revenues from land. The safety of their wealth was guaranteed to them by the Government of Bengal. But what of that? They were accused of complicity in some rioting, but as there was no evidence they were not brought to trial; Hastings and the new Nawāb, grandson and son of the Princesses, agreed to an act of confiscation, stripping them of everything. The son repented, but not so Hastings. He imprisoned the Princesses. He then seized the two eunuchs who were at the head of their household, imprisoned, ironed, starved them, and at last gave them up to torture, the Nawāb's officers being empowered in writing to "have free access to the prisoners and be permitted to do with them as they shall see proper," as the Nawāb had "determined to inflict corporal punishment" on them. Their only crime was their refusal to surrender the charge given to them by their dead lord. The Princesses were kept in prison half-starved, till they had paid £1,200,000.

Warren Hastings was a man of magnificent abilities, and made a strong administration, but the record of his crimes is long and terrible. He left India in 1785, and was impeached by the House of Commons, which had before censured him, after long debate, for his crimes, while the King favoured him, the Company adored him, Lord Chancellor Thurlow protected him; the result was sure, despite the marvellous eloquence of Burke. In vain his passionate peroration rang out:

> I impeach him in the name of the Commons' House of Parliament, whose trust he has betrayed. I impeach him in the name of the English Nation, whose ancient honour he has sullied. I impeach him in the name of the people of India, whose rights he has trodden under foot, and whose country he has turned into a desert. Lastly, in the name of human nature itself, in the name of both sexes, in the name of every age, in the name of every rank, I impeach the common enemy and oppressor of all!

The trial began in 1788 and the decision was pronounced in 1795. 160 nobles began the trial; 29 voted at the close, a majority in his favour. Meanwhile Hastings, secure in the King's favour, had spent £40,000 in building a house and in laying out its grounds.

Within our limits we cannot trace fully the growth of the Indian Empire: Lord Cornwallis followed Hastings in 1786 and left his mark in the Permanent Settlement of Bengal. Fighting as usual went on in the South, and in the Third Mysore War (1790-92), Lord Cornwallis, Governor-General, allied with the Nizam of the Deccan and the Maratha Confederacy, conquered Tipu Sultan of Mysore, robbed him of half his territories—which they divided between them—and exacted from him three million pounds sterling, thus ensuring another war.

Marquess Wellesley and the Nizam, in the fourth Mysore War (1799), finished him, and he died, fighting gallantly to the end, in the breach at the storming of Seringapatam. This added the Carnatic to the Madras Presidency. The quarrels of the Maratha Chiefs enabled Marquess Wellesley to detach the Peshwā from them, and he became a vassal of the Company; the third Maratha War followed (1802-04), and in 1817-18, the last, the Maratha Empire perished, and left its Princes as feudatories of the English.

Ranjit Singh, the "Lion of the Panjab," who created the Sikh kingdom, and seized Lahore as his capital in 1799, when only 19 years of age, was the creator of the last Power the British had to meet. His army was united by religion not by territory; they were the Sikhs, the disciples of the ten Gurus who had built up the Khalsa (Society), from Nanak the Saint to Govinda Singh, the Warrior (1675-1708). He made his Kingdom in the Panjab as far south as Multan; in 1809, Metcalfe visited Ranjit Singh as envoy from the British, and concluded a treaty with him, making the Sutlej River the boundary between his Kingdom and the British territory. With him there was peace till his death in 1839, but in 1845 the Sikh army crossed the Sutlej, and after four battles was driven back. In 1848 the second Sikh War broke out; the British were defeated at Chilianwala (1849), but soon after Multan was stormed, the victory of Gujrat won, and the Panjab was annexed two months later.

Lord Dalhousie (1848-56) started the convenient theory that "Native States" were less well governed than British Provinces, and should be annexed wherever possible, *e.g.*, as when a ruler died without a son. Under these conditions he annexed Satara in 1849, Jhansi in 1853, Nagpur in 1853. Oudh he annexed in 1856, on high moral grounds, because its administration was "fraught with suffering to millions"—a dangerous argument from an official of the East India Company. It was looked on with alarm by the "Natives," and contributed to the Sepoy Revolt of 1857, when Lord Canning was Viceroy. This broke out in May 10, 1857, in Meerut, and ended in January, 1859.

From that time we may date the famous "Pax Britannica," for until that time there were continual wars and annexations, while since then there have been none further within India itself. There have been frontier wars, the iniquitous Afghan wars, the annexation of Burma, but internal order has been maintained.

On November 1, 1858, was held the Darbar of Allahabad, in which was published the Queen's Proclamation, assuming the Government of India, and making the Governor-General a Viceroy. The Company perished in the Sepoy Rebellion, in which poured out the hatreds accumulating since Plassey, in 1757. The Queen's Proclamation contained the memorable words:

> It is our further will that, so far as may be, our subjects, of whatever race and creed, be freely and impartially admitted to office in our service, the duties of which they may be qualified by their education, ability and credit duly to discharge. In their prosperity will be our strength; in their contentment our security; and in their gratitude our best reward.

Fifty-seven years have rolled away since those noble words were spoken; they remain unfulfilled, and, as the inevitable consequence, the security of contentment is not yet ours.

The existing conditions in India, bearing on the religious, economic, educational and political problems of the present, are dealt with in the Congress story. They will be better understood against the historical background, which shows that Indian Nationality is not a plant of mushroom growth, but a giant of the forest, with millennia behind it.

India is now full of unrest, righteous unrest; she is consequently held down by a series of enactments unparalleled in any modern civilised country; Lord Morley has had the audacity to state, according to Sir Valentine Chirol (*Indian Unrest*, 154, ed. 1910) that the Government of India "must be an autocracy," and India loathes autocracy. She has enjoyed all the benefits which flow from it during her childhood and youth as a Nation, and she has felt its weight in British hands; she is now mature; she demands freedom, and she is resolute to take her destiny into her own hands, as one of the Free Nations in a Crowned Commonwealth, if Britain will work with her, in making the transit. Vincent A. Smith (*Early History of India*, p. 331), in tracing the annals of some "Indian petty States," says that they show "what India always has been when released from the control of a supreme authority, and what she would be again, if the hand of the benevolent despotism which now holds her in its iron grasp, should be withdrawn". If a central authority is wanted, and all Free Nations need it, to prevent centrifugal forces from causing disintegration, India demands that it shall be her own Parliament. Why should she, alone among civilised modern Nations, require a foreign supreme authority ?

But there is one danger to India's future which it is well to recognise—the effect of the concomitants of the famous Pax Britannica of fifty-seven years. India has never before been under foreign domination *as a whole.* If one part of her was invaded, other parts were tranquil : if there was a foreign conquest, the new rulers settled down on the old lines ; there were no barriers put up round State offices, differentiating between the new-comers and the earlier inhabitants ; in fact the aim of the new was assimilation with the older elements in a common civic life, and when the Musalmans made their Kingdoms and Empire, everything was done to induce the people to accept the new rulers and live in peace. Aurangzeb, the sixth Mughal Emperor, was the first persecutor, and his brutalities broke the Mughal power. The British policy has been different ; the whole administration of British India has been in its own hands, and all the chief positions of responsibility and power have been rigidly confined to the foreigners ; it is thought a wonderful concession that the Minto-Morley reforms allowed *one* Indian to enter the Imperial Council ! All initiative, all originality have been rigorously repressed, while manly independence has been resented, and even punished. It has seemed as though it were the British aim to turn the whole Indian Nation into a race of clerks.

This steady crushing pressure over the whole population has produced a serious result, and has emasculated the Nation. Indians hesitate, where they should act; they ask, where they should take; they submit, where they should resist; they lack self-confidence and the audacity that commands success. Prompt, resolute, effective action is but too rare; they lack fire and decision. Mr. Gokhale, in his answer before, the Royal Commission on Indian Expenditure (Ans. 18,331), voiced the same idea, after pointing to the 2,388 officials drawing annual salaries of Rs. 10,000 and upwards, of whom only 60 were Indians. "The excessive costliness of the foreign agency is not, however, its only evil. There is a moral evil, which, if anything, is even greater. A kind of dwarfing or stunting of the Indian race is going on under the present system. We must live all the days of our life in an atmosphere of inferiority, and the tallest of us must bend in order that the exigencies of the existing system may be satisfied." This is the deepest, gravest, wrong that Great Britain has inflicted on a once mighty and imperial race. Unless Indians can again develop the old vigour, courage and initiative, India can have no future. But the old spirit is awaking on every side, and therein lies our hope.

We doubt if those, who read and *verify* the above, will think that she has got on so badly in the past, left to her own resources.

Some Deductions and Anticipations

We submit from a review of this rough sketch:

That India, despite foreign invasions and local disturbances, which all nations have suffered in their time—what peace had England from the Conquest up to the final defeat of Charles Edward in 1745 ?—was a prosperous and wealthy Nation before the coming of the East India Company, and that her huge wealth, down to the end of the 18th century, is a proof of general industry and security and immense industrial output among the masses, while the wealth of the merchants, and of the banking and trading communities shows a settled condition, where credit was good; that commercial integrity was so great that receipts and bonds were not demanded in financial transactions.

That the English connection, under the Company, reduced India to poverty, and dislocated her industries, and that, under the Crown, the Government still hamper her industries, make a cruelly severe drain upon the country, and by their fiscal arrangements prevent the return of prosperity. That between 1770 and 1900—130 years—there have been twenty-two famines, eighteen according to the Report of the Famine Commission of 1880 and four after 1880. In 1770, as we have seen, there was a famine in Bengal with 10,000,000 deaths; in 1783 in Madras; in 1784, in Upper India, which left Oudh in a pitiable condition; in 1792 in Bombay and Madras; in 1803 in Bombay; in 1804 in northern India; in 1807 in Madras; in 1813 in Bombay; in 1823 in Madras; in 1833 in Madras, where in one district, Guntur, 200,000 died out of 500,000 population, and the dead lay unburied about Madras,

Masulipatam and Nellore; in 1837 in north India, in which a calculation of 800,000 deaths is thought too low by the Famine Commission; in 1854 in Madras; in 1860 in northern India, about 200,000 deaths; in 1866 in Orissa and Madras, in Orissa a third of the people died, about 1,000,000, in Madras about 450,000; in 1869 in north India, about 1,200,000 deaths; in 1874 in Bengal, over 1,000,000 were relieved and life was saved; in 1877 in Madras, 5,250,000 deaths; in 1868 in north India, 1,250,000 deaths; in 1889 in Madras and Orissa; in 1892 in Madras, Bengal and Rajputana; in 1896-7 in North India, Bengal, Madras and Bombay—the number of deaths is not given, but 4,000,000 persons received relief; and in 1899-0, in north India, Central Provinces and Bombay, 6,500,000 persons were in receipt of relief—the worst famine on record. In 1892 and 1897, Burma also suffered from famine. In 1896, bubonic plague broke out in Bombay, and has slain its millions.

That even if Self-Government should cause—as we do not think it would—any recrudescence of local jealousies and divisions, they would be local and temporary troubles, out of which India would emerge prosperously, as she has done before.

That after an admitted prosperous and wealthy existence for 5,000 years under eastern rulers, she could not fall into barbarism even by the total and sudden withdrawal of a rule that has only been here in any kind of power for a poor 158 years, of which the first fifty were spent entirely in plundering, and which only stopped constant wars and annexations in

1856. Has the history of British rule in India proved to be more peaceful than the worst of its predecessors up to the Sepoy Rebellion? And it must not be forgotten that nearly all the current history is the special pleading of an advocate, who is representing his own side and blackening his antagonists, minimising every wrong committed by his own side, exaggerating every wrong done upon the other.

That in the very limited educational work she has done, Britain has been immensely useful, for the study of her own history has strengthened and given point to the National feeling that was powerfully aroused in the rise of the Marathas; from 1835 she took up education, and though it has spread very slowly, and is doing badly now in consequence of the strangling policy initiated by the Universities Act of 1904, India's debt here to Britain is great and is fully recognised.

That Britain has done much in railways—of mixed benefit, being chiefly strategic instead of economic, but on the whole desirable; much less well than the old rulers in irrigation works, in forestry, in village government, and in sanitation.

That India welcomes English co-operation, but is getting very tired of English domination; that she is determined to get rid of coercive legislation, and to enjoy Self-Government. That she earnestly desires to have it with English help, but is resolved to have it.

That she is perfectly well aware that England did not "conquer her by the sword," but by the help of her own swords, by bribery, intrigue, and most acute diplomacy, fomenting of divisions, and playing of one party against another. But she is willing to let bye-gones be bye-gones, if Britain will now treat with her on equal terms, and welcome her as a partner, not a dependent.

INDIA WANTS SELF-GOVERNMENT BECAUSE:

1. British rule has destroyed her Village and Council Government, and has put in its place a hybrid system of Boards and Councils which are impotent for good, because well-informed Indian opinion is over-ruled by officials who come, knowing nothing of India, and seek to impose English methods on an ancient land which has its own traditions. They then complain that their hybrid is sterile. It is the way with hybrids. India wants to rebuild and improve her own system, beginning with Panchayats, and working upwards, untrammelled by foreign experts.

2. British rule after eighty years of its education is educating 2·6 of the population, and bases her denial of liberty on the "microscopical minority" of the educated, due to her own policy. Japan, under eastern rule, has educated her whole population in 40 years. British education is not only microscopic, but it is ill-directed; it was arranged with a view of supplying clerks and some professional men in order to enable the British Government to be carried on. India wants a system which will develop her resources by supplying scientific experts in every branch wherein applied science is needed, by supplying practical experts in all industries and crafts; a system which

will educate her whole population for useful ends, as the United States and Germany have done for their populations and Britain is now doing for hers. India also desires to check the lavish expenditure of her money on the schools and colleges of foreign missions —British, Scotch, American, German, Danish, French, Swiss, Italian—while those under her own control are discouraged and crippled in their natural development on lines shaped by Indians.

3. British rule has destroyed India's finest arts and industries in order to favour the importation of cheap foreign goods, and even in machine industry, such as cotton, taxes the home-produce in order to balance the customs duty on imported goods. It encourages the export of raw materials, which come back as manufactured articles, thus paralysing Indian industrial efforts for the benefit of foreigners. The export industry being in full swing, when England goes to War, India's materials are suddenly thrown on her hands, and as she has neither plant, nor knowledge how to use it, they rot on the ground and their producers starve. India would train her own sons to utilise her vast stores of raw material, for her own profit, and would only send abroad her surplusage.

4. British rule has neglected irrigation —only lately taken up because of the awful famines, and even now starved for want of funds—and while recklessly cutting forests down has, also until lately, neglected replanting. Huge tracts of land, especially in the north-west, have consequently become deserts, which were formerly rich

and fertile. India would place irrigation and forestry among the first duties of Government.

5. British rule has neglected sanitation, while the tendency to centralise in towns and neglect villages has necessitated changes from the old methods. Alarmed by the plague—a disease of dirt, which decimated Europe dirty and vanished before Europe semi-clean—it took some hasty and injudicious methods, which alienated Indian sympathy, and is now more busy with injecting serums into Indian bodies, thus really perpetuating disease, than with sanitation. The trouble is increased by the arrogant contempt for indigenous systems, and the ousting of them by Government, while it is impossible to replace them adequately everywhere with the costly modern appliances. India would insist on sanitation as among the first duties of Government, would encourage all that is good in the old systems, and utilise what is good in western methods.

6. British rule is extremely costly; it employs Europeans in the highest posts at the highest salaries, and introduces them everywhere as "experts"—experts ignorant of the conditions in which they are working; it keeps special preserves wholly for Europeans; others into which Indians may enter at the heavy cost of going to England to obtain "English degrees"; it pensions its servants, so that the English ones live on Indian money when they retire to England, making a huge annual drain; it encourages exploitation of the country by English companies and English capital, making another

drain; it makes India pay for an Indian army, maintained to keep India in subjection; it makes India pay for a costly English establishment, the central autocracy, irresponsible to Parliament. India would do away with all this; would open everything to Indians —as indeed the Proclamation of 1858 promised—and require no foreign degrees as credentials; would abolish the India Office; would acknowledge, outside India, the authority only the Crown and the Imperial Parliament, in which she enjoyed adequate representation. She would have her own Army and Navy, for protection and Imperial needs, not to hold her people down.

7. British rule has substituted coercion for improvements in Government, like any other autocracy. India would sweep all this coercive legislation away; she would not be afraid of her people possessing arms; she would not be afraid of the criticism of free speech and a free Press; she would reform abuses instead of strangling the expression of the discontent which abuses produce; she would emulate British rule in Britain, not British rule in India.

In a phrase:

India is enthralled, and she is determined to be free.

HOW INDIA WROUGHT FOR FREEDOM

CHAPTER I

In late December in 1884, seventeen men met in Madras, in the house of that stalwart advocate of religion and reform, Dewan Bahadur Raghunath Rao. Nearly all of them had been delegates to the just-ended Annual Convention of the Theosophical Society at Adyar, and the others had been there as friends and sympathisers. But surely this new pride in India's mighty faiths throbbing in their hearts, this dawning hope of India's greatness in the future to correspond with the greatness of her past, this feeling that the discrowned East is not always to remain a thrall to the younger western Nations, and that Asia, once the cradle of mighty Empires, shall again stretch out her hands to grasp the sceptre and the imperial ball—these dreams sent out the dreamers to take counsel together, and they resolved, greatly daring, to form themselves into a group of provisional Committees, men from different towns to win others, each in his place, and to meet later for further consultation. Let us place on record their names, for they were the seed of a mighty tree. Norendranath Sen of Calcutta, that sturdiest of fighters, was one of the little group, and he gave their names later in his paper, *The Indian Mirror*; he remarks that "the delegates who attended the Convention were most of them men who, socially and intellectually, are the leaders of the Society in which they move in different parts of the country". They were:

Madras: The Hon. Mr. S. Subramania Iyer (subsequently Judge of the High Court, Acting Chief Justice, K.C.I.E., and LL.D.), and Messrs. P. Rangiah Naidu and P. Ananda Charlu.

Calcutta: Messrs. Norendranath Sen, Surendranath Bannerji (the "uncrowned King of Bengal," the great orator, and National leader), and M. Ghosh.

Bombay: The Hon. Messrs. V. N. Mandlik and K. T. Telang (later, Judge of the High Court) and Mr. Dadabhai Naoroji (the G.O.M. of India).

Poona: Messrs. C. Vijiaranga Mudaliar, and Pandurang Gopal.

Benares: Sardar Dyal Singh.

Allahabad: Mr. Harishchandra.

N. W. P.: Mr. Kashi Prasad and Pandit Lakshminarayan.

Bengal: Mr. Charuchandra Mitter.

Oudh: Mr. Shri Ram.

Seventeen good men and true, who out of their love and their hope conceived the idea of a political National Movement for the saving of the Motherland.

There seems to be no record of the work done in their own towns and provinces on their return home, but the *Proceedings of the First Indian National Congress* tells us that "in March, 1885, it was decided to hold a meeting of Representatives from all parts of India at the then coming Christmas. Poona was considered the most central and therefore suitable place." From this onwards we have the official Reports to guide our steps.

From this meeting the following circular was issued, profoundly interesting now, in 1915, as showing the minds of the Fathers of the Congress in these days of origin, in 1885, just thirty years ago. It shows the first ideas of those who were to be the leaders of the Indian Nation in her struggles to regain her lost liberty, and to become a Self-governing Nation, free amid the Free Communities which form the mighty Empire "on which the Sun never sets".

Here is the circular:

A Conference of the Indian National Union will be held at Poona from the 25th to the 31st December 1885.

The Conference will be composed of Delegates—leading politicians well acquainted with the English language—from all parts of the Bengal, Bombay and Madras Presidencies.

The direct objects of the Conference will be: (1) to enable all the most earnest labourers in the cause of national progress to become personally known to each other; (2) to discuss and decide upon the political operations to be undertaken during the ensuing year.

Indirectly this Conference will form the germ of a Native Parliament and, if properly conducted, will constitute in a few years an unanswerable reply to the assertion that India is still wholly unfit for any form of representative institutions. The first Conference will decide whether the next shall be again held at Poona, or whether, following the precedent of the British Association, the Conferences shall be held year by year at different important centres.

This year the Conference being in Poona, Mr. Chiplonkar and others of the Sarvajanik Sabha, have consented to form a Reception Committee in whose hands will rest the whole of the local arrangements. The Peshwah's Garden near the Parbati Hill will be utilised both as a place of meeting (it contains a fine Hall, like the garden, the property of the Sabha) and as a residence for the delegates, each of whom will be there provided with suitable quarters. Much importance is attached to this, since, when all thus reside *together* for a week, far greater opportunities for friendly intercourse will be afforded than if the delegates were (as at the time of the late Bombay demonstrations) scattered about in dozens of private lodging houses all over the town.

Delegates are expected to find their own way to and from Poona—but from the time they reach the Poona Railway Station until they leave it again, everything that they can need, carriage, accommodation, food, etc., will be provided for them gratuitously.

The cost thus involved will be defrayed from the Reception Fund, which the Poona Association most liberally offers to provide in the first instance, but to which all delegates, whose means warrant their incurring this further expense, will be at liberty to contribute any sum they please. Any unutilised balance of such donations will be carried forward as a nucleus for next year's Reception Fund.

It is believed that exclusive of our Poona friends, the Bombay Presidency, including Sindh and the Berars, will furnish about 20 delegates, Madras and Lower Bengal each about the same number, and the N. W. Provinces, Oudh, and the Panjab together about half this number.

Very modest were they, and very accurate withal in their estimate of seventy delegates, for seventy-two actually recorded their names as Representatives, while another thirty attended as friends, being, as Government servants, precluded from acting as Representatives in a political gathering. The first meeting did not, however, take place at Poona, for, only a few days before Christmas, some sporadic cases of cholera occurred, possibly presaging an outbreak, and it was thought wiser to move the Conference, now called the Congress, to Bombay. The Managers of the Gokuldas Tejpal Samskrit College and Boarding House placed the whole of their fine buildings at the disposal of the Congress, and all was ready by the morning of the 27th December for the reception of the Representatives of the Indian Nation. As we glance over the lists of those who were present, how many we see who became famous in the annals of India's struggle for Freedom. Among those who could not act as Representatives—for the reason given above—we note the Reformer, Dewan Bahadur R. Raghunath Rao, Deputy Collector of Madras, the Hon. Mr. Mahadev G. Ranade, then member of the Legislative Council and Small Cause Court Judge of Poona, later to be a Judge of the High Court of Bombay, and leader honoured and trusted; Lala Baijnath of Agra was there, to be known as scholar and writer later on; and Professors K. Sundararaman and R. G. Bhandarkar. Among the Representatives may be noted editors of well-known Indian papers, of *The Dnyan Prakash*, *The Quarterly Journal* of the Poona Sarvajanik Sabha, *The Maratha*,

The Kesari, *The Nababibhakar*, *The Indian Mirror*, *The Nassin*, *The Hindusthani*, *The Tribune*, *The Indian Union*, *The Indian Spectator*, *The Indu Prakash*, *The Hindu*, *The Crescent*. How many names shine out, familiar and honoured : Mr. A. O. Hume is there from Simla; W.C. Bannerji and Norendranath Sen from Calcutta; W. S. Apte and G. G. Agarkar from Poona; Gangaprasad Varma from Lucknow; Dadabhai Naoroji, K. T. Telang, Pherozeshah M. Mehta—then, as now, leader of the Bombay Corporation—D. E. Wacha, B. M. Malabari, N. G. Chandavarkar from Bombay; P. Rangiah Naidu, President of the Mahajana Sabha, S. Subramania Iyer, P. Ananda Charlu, G. Subramania Aiyar, M. Viraraghavachariar from Madras; P. Kesava Pillai from Anantapur. These were among the earliest who wrought for India's Freedom, and those yet on earth are working for her still.

At 12 noon, on December 28th, 1885, in the Hall of the Gokuldas Tejpal Samskrit College, the First National Congress met. The first voices heard were those of Mr. A. O. Hume, the Hon. Mr. S. Subramania Iyer and the Hon. Mr. K. T. Telang, who proposed, seconded and supported the election of the first President, Mr. W. C. Bannerji. A solemn and historic moment was that in which the first of the long line of men thus honoured by the Motherland took his seat, to preside over her first National Assembly.

After alluding to the representative and weighty character of the Congress, he laid down under four heads the objects of the Congress :

(*a*) The promotion of personal intimacy and friendship amongst all the more earnest workers in our country's cause in the various parts of the Empire.

(*b*) The eradication by direct friendly personal intercourse of all possible race, creed, or provincial prejudices amongst all lovers of our country, and the fuller development and consolidation of those sentiments of national unity that had their origin in their beloved Lord Ripon's ever memorable reign.

(*c*) The authoritative record, after this has been carefully elicited by the fullest discussion, of the matured opinions of the educated classes in India on some of the more important and pressing of the social questions of the day.

(*d*) The determination of the lines upon and methods by which during the next twelve months it is desirable for native politicians to labour in the public interests.

Of these the first three have been well worked out, but the fourth has been less regarded, and needs urging to-day. Such guidance is supremely necessary, and the Nation has the right to demand it from its best men. In all organised movements some direction from the centre is necessary. The Congress has admirably focussed educated opinion, passing valuable judgments on events and policy, and demanding necessary reforms from Government, but it has not adequately outlined the work to be done during each coming year; hence political work has lacked point and vigour; it is impossible to agitate for all the matters touched on by resolutions, and hence political work in the whole country has been spasmodic and sporadic, and therefore largely ineffective; there is no concerted work. Yet what

India can do in the way of agitation when she has an objective is clearly shown by the agitation on South African grievances.

The nine resolutions of the first National Congress mark the beginning of the formulation of India's demands.

The first asked for a Royal Commission to enquire into the working of Indian administration.

The second for the abolition of the India Council.

The third dealt with the defects of the Legislative Councils in which then all the members were nominated, and asked for the admission of elected members, for the right of interpellation, for the submission of budgets to the Councils, for the creation of Councils in the N. W. P. and Oudh, and in the Panjab, and for a Standing Committee in the House of Commons to consider formal protests from majorities in the Councils.

The fourth prayed for simultaneous examinations for the I. C. S. and the raising of the age of candidates.

The fifth and sixth dealt with military expenditure.

The seventh protested against the annexation of Upper Burma and the proposed incorporation of it with India.

The eighth ordered the sending of the resolutions to Political Associations, and they were discussed and passed all over the country by political bodies and public meetings, an admirable plan which has fallen into desuetude; they were carried with much enthusiasm, and here and there amended on minor points, while Bapatla objected to the abolition of the India Council, which it regarded as a check on the Secretary of State, and wanted its power over him made effective.

The final resolution fixed the next Congress at Calcutta, on December 28th, 1886.

Of these resolutions, the first has been partially granted by the Decentralisation and Public Services Commissions; the second is still being demanded; much of the third was given in the Minto-Morley reforms; the prayer of the fourth is still ungranted as regards simultaneous examinations, but the age of candidates has been raised; the fifth, sixth and seventh had no effect. The eighth and ninth were, of course, carried out.

Mr. G. Subramania Iyer of Madras, the Editor of *The Hindu* and one of the boldest and farthest-sighted of the Madras leaders, moved the first resolution in an admirable speech, much of which is valid for to-day. It ran: "That this Congress earnestly approves of the promised Committee to enquire into the working of the Indian administration." He pointed out that in the days of the East India Company, the renewal of its Charter at twenty years' intervals brought about a most valuable enquiry into the condition of the country, but that since the Crown had taken it over in 1858, these had ceased, and the distressing deterioration of the condition of the people was going on unnoticed. Parliament took control in theory, but abandoned it in fact—except where English party-interests were concerned—and the India Council took up the place of the defunct Company, but ruled without enquiry; he appealed to "the justice and fairness of the English people," and asked for an enquiry into facts. Mr. Pherozeshah Mehta seconded, and remarked that there must not be an enquiry by "Anglo-Indians, sitting in judgment on themselves". Mr. Norendranath Sen supported, pointing out that the enquiry would be a sort of stock-taking as to the results, after twenty-seven years, of direct Government by the Crown. A lively debate ensued, an amendment being proposed, and the resolution was finally carried in the amended form. (The resolutions are printed at the end of the Chapter.)

The second resolution was moved on December 29th by Mr. Chiplonkar, and asked for the abolition of India's Old Man of the Sea, the India Council. He pointed out that India was not governed by the Crown, but by retired Anglo-Indian officials, looked on doubtfully by Lord Beaconsfield in 1858. (Those who care to read the debate over the Government of India Bill will find what now sound astonishingly democratic statements, and regrets that the Rebellion barely ended made proper representation of India impossible just then.)

Mr. Ananda Charlu was very caustic in seconding the resolution, and commented on the oddity of the "oligarchy of fossilised Indian administrators," who were "superannuated for service in India," being competent to deal with increased complexity of problems in England, where the improved climate could only diminish the rate of decline. The abolition of the Council was a primary condition of all other reforms. Mr. Pherozeshah Mehta also thought that effete Anglo-Indians, who would be partial to their brethren in India, were a very unsatisfactory appellate tribunal.

The resolution was carried unanimously and has been carried at intervals ever since, but in vain.

The third resolution was moved in a very full and careful speech by the Hon. Mr. K. T. Telang, who usefully indicated possible electorates for members of the Legislative Councils, and the Hon. Mr. S. Subramania Iyer seconded, both by personal experience as members knowing how "little influence they possessed in the Councils either for good or for evil". They could not be "of any great use to the country". Mr. Dadabhai Naoroji cogently said that they had learnt from "the English people how necessary representation is for good Government"; without it "what good is it to India to be under the British sway? It will be simply another Asiatic despotism. . . . We are only British drudges or slaves." There was a long debate, and the resolution was carried unanimously on the following day. It was partly granted in the Minto-Morley reforms 24 years later.

The fourth resolution was moved by Mr. Dadabhai Naoroji, and the discussion was remarkable for the speech of Mr. D. S. White, who wished to stop the importation of boys from England at great expense, and to abolish the Civil Service, utilising, both from England and India, men of experience and reputation.

The resolution was carried, and the age limit has been raised, but the main prayer is not yet granted. It is pathetic to read the reiterated confidence of the speakers " in the justice of the English people," and to see that that confidence is still unjustified.

Mr. P. Rangiah Naidu, in the next resolution, after pointing out that military expenditure had increased from £11,463,000 in 1857 to £16,975,750 in 1884, pleaded with the Government to " change their present policy of suspicion and distrust for a generous and confiding one," to improve the " Native Army," to accept the offers of the people to enrol as Volunteers; then no more European soldiers would be needed. Mr. D. E. Wacha, in seconding, made the first of many great Congress speeches, an able and exhaustive review of the military position, cruelly unfair to India and placing on her most unjust burdens. The resolution was carried, as was the next, urging that if military expenditure was not diminished, it should be met by re-imposition of the import duties, the abolition of which had robbed poverty-stricken India to enrich wealthy Lancashire. The debate showed the thorough knowledge and rare ability of the men taking part in it, and we hear also their repudiation of opinions now long familiar through thirty years of repetition, that educated Indians were disloyal, and that English education had awakened dangerous aspirations.

The resolution on Burma, and the remaining two were quickly passed, and the first National Congress dissolved, leaving a happy and inspiring memory of fine work done, and unity demonstrated. India had found her Voice. India was realising herself as a Nation. Strange and menacing was the portent in the eyes of some. Splendid and full of hope in the eyes of others. The rosy fingers of the Dawn-Maidens had touched the Indian skies. When would her Sun of Freedom rise to irradiate the Motherland ?

RESOLUTIONS

1. That this Congress earnestly recommends that the promised enquiry into the working of Indian Administration, here and in England, should be entrusted to a Royal Commission, the people of India being adequately represented thereon, and evidence taken both in India and in England.

2. That this Congress considers the abolition of the Council of the Secretary of State for India, as at present constituted, the necessary preliminary to all other reforms.

3. That this Congress considers the reform and expansion of the Supreme and existing Local Legislative Councils by the admission of a considerable proportion of elected members (and the creation of similar Councils for the N.W. Provinces and Oudh, and also for Panjab) essential; and holds that all Budgets should be referred to these Councils for consideration, their members being moreover empowered to interpellate the Executive in regard to all branches of the administration; and that a Standing Committee of the House of Commons should be constituted to receive and consider any formal protests that may be recorded by majorities of such Councils against the exercise by the Executive of the power, which would be vested in it, of overruling the decision of such majorities.

4. That in the opinion of this Congress the competitive examinations now held in England, for first appointments in various civil departments of the public service, should, henceforth, in accordance with the views of the India Office Committee of 1860, be held simultaneously one in England and one in India, both being as far as practicable identical in their nature, and those who compete in both countries being finally classified in one list according to merit, and that the successful candidates in India should be sent to England for further study, and subjected there to such further examinations as may seem needful. Further, that all other first appointments (excluding peonships, and the like) should be filled by competitive examinations held in India, under conditions calculated to secure such

intellectual, moral, and physical qualifications as may be decided by Government to be necessary. Lastly, that the maximum age of candidates for entrance into the Covenanted Civil Service be raised to not less than 23 years.

5. That in the opinion of this Congress the proposed increase in the military expenditure of the empire is unnecessary, and regard being had to the revenues of the empire and the existing circumstances of the country, excessive.

6. That in the opinion of this Congress, if the increased demands for military expenditure are not to be, as they ought to be, met by retrenchment, they ought to be met, firstly, by the re-imposition of the Customs duties; and, secondly by the extension of the licence-tax to those classes of the community, official and non-official, at present exempted from it, care being taken that in the case of all classes a sufficiently high taxable minimum be maintained. And further, that this Congress is of opinion that Great Britain should extend an imperial guarantee to the Indian debt.

7. That this Congress deprecates the annexation of Upper-Burma and considers that if the Government unfortunately decide on annexation, the entire country of Burma should be separated from the Indian Viceroyalty and constituted a Crown Colony, as distinct in all matters from the Government of this country as is Ceylon.

8. That the resolutions passed by this Congress be communicated to the Political Associations in each province, and that these Associations be requested with the help of similar bodies and other agencies within their respective provinces to adopt such measures as they may consider calculated to advance the settlement of the various questions dealt with in these resolutions.

9. That the Indian National Congress re-assemble next year in Calcutta, and sit on Tuesday, the 28th of December, 1886, and the next succeeding days.

CHAPTER II

The different character of the second Congress as compared with the first has rightly been emphasised in the official record. As it points out, the first Congress was composed of Volunteers, the second of Delegates, and in those two words lies the essential difference, and they mark the immense progress in the country which lay between the two. The Congress had captured the heart as well as the brain of India. It is interesting to turn over the pages containing extracts from papers published in all parts of India, and to glance at the reports of the meetings held for the election of delegates; in these early days any association of any kind, or any public meeting, might elect; there was no organisation to speak of; only an effort to find out that which the Nation wished. In this way 500 delegates were elected, of whom 434 actually registered their names and credentials as present, and it is thought that 4 or 5 left without doing so. Various circulars were issued suggesting subjects for discussion and outlining proposals, so that delegates might not come unprepared—a plan that, unfortunately, fell into desuetude. The representation of the Provinces is noteworthy, as showing the amount of interest taken in each. The N. W. P. and Oudh head the list—outside Bengal—with 74 delegates, marking the enlightenment of the great Province which contains Lucknow, Cawnpur, Agra, Allahabad, Benares, Bareilly, Meerut, active centres of thought; Bombay and Madras each sent 47. Panjab only 17; Central Provinces and Assam 8 each. Bengal naturally sent a very large number, 230, but she had 70 millions of people, while the next, the N. W. P. and Oudh, had only 44. Reckoned by percentages Bengal had 3·3 per million, and Bombay 2·7.

The delegates began to stream into Calcutta on the 25th, and the first meeting of the Congress was held on December 28th, in the Town Hall, packed to its limit of holding; the famous scholar, Dr. Rajendralala Mittra, welcomed the delegates and the visitors; he demanded with no uncertain voice that representatives of the people should be elected to the Legislative Councils:

> We live, not under a National Government, but under a foreign bureaucracy; our foreign rulers are foreigners by birth, religion, language, habits, by everything that divides humanity into different sections. They cannot possibly dive into our hearts; they cannot ascertain our wants, our feelings, our aspirations. They may try their best, and I have no reason to doubt that many of our Governors have tried hard to ascertain our feelings and our wants; but owing to their peculiar position, they have failed to ascertain them.

Then came a striking episode. A very old man, a great landed proprietor, "blind and trembling with age," Jaikishan Mukerji, proposed the Hon. Mr. Dadabhai Naoroji as President. In a few words he explained their wish for such improvements in administration as should keep pace with the spread of education and enlightenment, saying that it was no wonder that their object had drawn distinguished men "from all parts of the country, when you find a blind old man like myself of 79 years of age, bending under the infirmities of age, taking a part in the deliberations". Most surely these three men above—to say nothing of the support of the venerable Debendranath Tagore—disproved the slander that the Congress was the work of turbulent youths and disappointed place-hunters.

Mr. Dadabhai Naoroji, in some preliminary observations drew attention to the refusal of the Government to grant the prayer of the first Congress for a Royal Commission of enquiry, but noted that they had agreed to giving a Council to the N. W. P. He laid stress on the bitter poverty of India, and urged that it was "the right as well as the duty of this Congress to set forth its convictions, both as to this widespread destitution and the primary steps needed for its alleviation". The first meeting was closed by Babu Jaikishan, who said that the India of 1886 was very different from that of 1835, yet a Free Press had then been granted to India by Sir Charles Metcalfe: "Standing as I do, one of the few remaining links between the Old India of the past and the New India of to-day, I can scarcely hope to see or enjoy the fruit of those labours on which this Congress and the Nation it represents are entering; but I am glad to have lived to see this new departure, and if an old man's sympathy and good wishes can aid or encourage you in the noble work you are undertaking, I can say from the bottom of my heart that that sympathy and those good wishes are already yours." Thus blessed by the aged, the Congress took up its work.

The President, in his opening address, made one often-disputed point admirably clear, and defined the scope of the Congress. He pointed out that the Congress was a purely political body, and while he was himself profoundly alive to the necessity of social reforms, he held that the Congress should deal only with political matters, on which Indians were united, and not with other questions on which they were necessarily divided, and on which no common action was therefore possible. Each community had its own social needs, and those of one were not those of another. But they had common political needs, and could unite on a common political platform. "A National Congress must confine itself to questions in which the entire Nation has a direct participation, and it must leave the adjustment of social reforms and other class questions to class Congresses." The National Movement, the National Party, as a whole, has its aspects, religious, educational, social, political, and the Congress is the organ of that Movement, that National Party, for political action, and for political action only. The Congress has steadily continued on the line thus early laid down.

As it was impossible to carry on business in the huge Town Hall, the Congress met on the second day in the rooms of the British Indian Association. The first Resolution on the Queen-Empress' Jubilee was carried with enthusiasm, and then Mr. D. E. Wacha moved the second, drawing attention to the "increasing poverty of vast numbers of the population of India". He pointed out that the condition of the ryots had steadily deteriorated since 1848, and that 40 millions of people had only one meal a day, and not always that. He pointed to the main cause "in the tribute to Great Britain, exported to fructify there, and swell still further the unparalleled wealth of those distant isles, never in any shape to return here to bless the country from whose soil it was wrung, or the people, the sweat of whose brows it represents". The foreign agency must be minimised, otherwise poverty could not be relieved. They must have representative institutions to ensure the reforms essential to National prosperity. The Hon. Mr. S. Subramania Iyer added his testimony from Madras, saying it was impossible to control "the extortions of the revenue authorities". Several amendments were proposed—permanent settlement, wider employment of Indians, encouragement of indigenous trade, as palliatives—but all were rejected and the original resolution carried.

The most remarkable speech on the third resolution was that of Malik Bhagavan Das, from Dehra Ismail Khan, who, speaking in Urdu, said he came "from a land where men handle the sword more readily than the pen"; some said that the only people who wanted changes were Bengali Babus;

"Do I look like a Bengali Babu?" he asked, drawing up his great frame in his frontier dress. All the more intelligent persons wanted them, he said. After recounting some special cases of able men in his own district, he concluded :

> There is not a district, not a town, that does not contain many such or better men; and do you suppose that any of them are greatly pleased with a form of administration which denies, to ninety-nine out of every hundred of them, any career? or that any of them fail to see that representative institutions, and a much larger employment of Indians in the higher offices of State, would be important steps towards the opening they want? I will not detain you longer. I will only repeat that this Congress and the objects it aims at have the sympathy of every thinking man in India, be he educated or uneducated; and though the newspapers may misunderstand the subject, I think the Government knows better, and as, despite mistakes that it makes, the Government is a generous Government, I hope, and *think* too, that, coming to realise how universal is the feeling, it will yield to our desire, and concede, if not at once, yet piece by piece, all we ask for. If I speak plainly it is not that I am opposed to British rule—far from it; that rule has no more earnest supporter than myself. But good as it is, there are many things yet that should be improved, and amongst them the matters dealt with by this Congress. And while I say: May God prosper British rule in India for ever, I also say: May He give our rulers wisdom to understand the reasonableness of our demands for reform, and the magnanimity to concede what we ask for.

The resolution was unanimously carried. The rest of the time was spent in discussing the draft of the fourth resolution, making many amendments, and finally, by Resolution VI, appointing a Committee to consider and report on the Public Service question. (All the Resolutions will be found on page 29, *et seq.*)

On the third day, December 29th, the Congress—meeting again in the Town Hall—Resolution VIII, asking for the extension of the jury system was, after some discussion, carried unanimously; in the course of it, one delegate, Lala Murlidhar, from the Panjab, said that he came to the Congress from gaol, released on bail, convicted without evidence "because I am considered a political agitator, because I have my own opinions and speak what I think without fear," and the protection of the jury was necessary against such abuses.

Government is always angry, as we know, when defects in the "administration of justice" are pointed out; but far more harm is done to it by the loud and prolonged cheers with which this eminently respectable assemblage of 1886 greeted this "convicted" prisoner out on bail, than by the criticisms which should lead the Government to amend the matters complained of.

This Resolution was completed by No. IX, carried a little later, urging that the "innovation made in 1872," which deprived the verdicts of juries of finality, and "for the first time" gave power to set aside verdicts of acquittal, "should be at once withdrawn". Some opposed it, on the ground that Englishmen were sometimes wrongfully acquitted by juries of their countrymen, but a large majority, despite this temporary inconvenience, carried the right principle. The abuse, however, still continues and has been terribly used, as in the hands of Sir John Hewett.

Resolution X, carried while the preceding one was being drafted, sought to give accused persons the right of demanding a committal to Sessions instead of being tried by Magistrates. It was pointed out that first-class Magistrates, "often quite young and inexperienced," could give a sentence of two years' imprisonment and a fine of Rs. 1,000, and that if the Government desired "to maintain the character of their Courts for justice," they must give the option of a trial at Sessions. Complaint was made that some of the Magistrates were "devoid of that conscientiousness that in former days was the characteristic of British officers". The truth is that the Courts do justice in ordinary cases as between Indian and Indian, but, since political agitation has arisen, British officials, like those of every autocracy, have a bias against every one who advocates political changes, and such men—as in the case of Lala Murlidhar—are discriminated against, consciously or unconsciously; hence, as Mr. T. Chidambara Rao pointed out, and as all of us know, our liberties remain at the mercy of magistrates "often far from competent, from a legal point of view, to exercise such great powers". The next Resolution, still legal, demanded the separation of judicial and executive functions.

Then came a Resolution (XII) of vital importance, where Indian foresight far outstripped British—a Resolution appealing to Government to sanction volunteering, so that Indians might be able to support them in any crisis. It was moved by Raja Rampal Singh in a most remarkable speech, a speech which showed that in him, at least, the old martial spirit was not dead. He began by saying that the loyal and conciliatory spirit of the Congress should protect them from blame when they spoke on a matter on which they were "distinctly at variance with Government". The whole country had petitioned Government on the matter and had been refused, "not over-graciously"; none the less must they press it, as "the highest interests of Great Britain as well as India" were concerned:

> We are deeply grateful to Government for all the good that it has done us, but we cannot be grateful to it when it is, no matter with what best of intentions, doing us a terrible and irreparable injury. . . . . . We cannot be grateful to it for degrading our natures, for systematically crushing out of us all martial spirit, for converting a race of soldiers and heroes into a timid flock of quill-driving sheep. Thank God, things have not yet gone quite so far as this. There are some of us yet, everywhere, who would be willing to draw sword, and if needful lay down our lives, for hearth and homes, aye and for the support and maintenance of that Government to which we owe so much. But this is what we are coming to . . . . and when we once come to that, then I think that, despite the glories of the Pax Britannica, despite the noble intentions of Great Britain, despite all the good she may have done or tried to do us, the balance will be against her, and India will have to regret rather than rejoice that she has ever had anything to do with England.
>
> This may be strong language, but it is the truth; nothing can ever make amends to a Nation for the destruction of its National spirit, and of the capacity to defend itself and the soil from which it springs.
>
> Nor is it only we who shall have to regret and suffer for the mistaken policy that our Government is unhappily

pursuing in this matter. Look where you will around you in the world, and you will see gigantic armies and armaments. There is trouble in store for the whole civilised world, and sooner or later a tremendous military struggle will commence, in which, assuredly, before it terminates, Great Britain will be involved. Great Britain with all her wealth cannot put one hundred men into the field for every thousand that several Continental Powers can. England herself is isolated, and by her insular position to a certain extent protected, but no friendly sea rolls between Europe and Asia, the landward path to India is known and open; India is not isolated, and it will be India, on whose possession half Great Britain's wealth and status depends, that will be the scene of any serious attack by any Continental Powers on Great Britain.

Then will England regret that, instead of having millions of brave Indians trained to arms to fling back invaders, she has only her scanty legions to oppose to them, and from her timid subjects can only look at most for good wishes—good wishes, truly good things in their way, but poor bulwarks against Berdan rifles and steel ordnance.

But on our own account we deprecate the existing policy. High and low we are losing all knowledge of the use of arms, and with this that spirit of self-reliance which enables a man to dare, which makes men brave, which makes them worthy of the name of men. When I was only five years of age my grandfather made me begin to learn all physical exercises in vogue amongst us, and I was trained to the use of all arms and in all martial exercises. But what man now sends his son for such training? What young man nowadays knows anything of these things? Fifty years ago, without desiring warfare, every young man's heart glowed within him at the thought of some day showing his prowess in a fair field. Now most young men would, I fear, contemplate any such possible contingency with very, let me say, mixed feelings. If men are to be fit for soldiers, fit to fight to any purpose when the time of trial comes, and come it must for every country, then they must be trained in the use of arms, they must from their childhood see their parents, their elders, using arms and participating in those martial exercises which only 35 years ago, in Oudh at least, were part of every gentleman's occupation.

And there is another very important point—India is practically being impoverished, to a great extent, by the enormous expense of her standing army. Sooner or later the crushing weight of this (for her resources) enormous expenditure will break down either the country or the Government. Now by a judicious encouragement of Indian Volunteers, it would be possible to reduce very greatly this military expenditure, and yet leave the country far stronger for defensive purposes than it now is.

But I might go on for hours. I might dwell on the fact that in the way the Arms Act is now worked in many localities, the people, their herds, their crops, are wholly at the mercy of wild beasts. I might dwell on the insult, the injustice, the violation of the most sacred and solemn pledges by England to India, that are involved in the rules that permit Indian Christians, but do not permit Indian Hindus or Muhammadans, to volunteer. But I have said enough, and indeed being, as we are, all of one mind, too much already I fear on this subject, in which I am deeply interested. I will only now add that we do not ask Government to put arms blindly into all men's hands, but only to permit under such rules and restrictions as it sees fit, the better and more educated classes of its loyal Indian subjects to qualify themselves to defend, when occasion may require, their homes, their country and their Government.

Needless to say that the resolution was carried, and yet, 29 years later, the Arms Act is still on the Statute Book, and only Indian Christians are permitted to volunteer. None the less, the feelings expressed so passionately by Raja Rampal Singh throb as passionately in the hearts of all Indian gentlemen to-day.

The fourth and last day of the Congress dealt with the all-important subject of representative institutions. Mr. Surendranath Bannerji brought up the Report of the Committee appointed to consider the Public Service Question, and it was unanimously approved by Resolution VII. He then moved Resolution IV, and the tentative suggestions embodied in it, urging :

> Self-Government is the ordering of nature, the will of Divine Providence. Every Nation must be the arbiter of its own destinies—such is the omnipotent fiat inscribed by Nature with her own hands and in her own eternal book. But do we govern ourselves ? The answer is no. Are we then living in an unnatural state ? Yes, in the same state in which the patient lives under the ministrations of the physician. We are passing through a period of probation and a period of trial under the auspices of one of the most freedom-loving Nations in the world. And we claim that the period of probation may now fairly terminate, that the leading-strings may be taken off, and the child, having emerged into the dawn of mature manhood, may at any rate be partially entrusted with the management of his own affairs. If it were otherwise, the circumstance would imply the gravest slur upon the character of British rule in India ; for it would mean that after more than a century of British rule and of English education, we are still unfit to appreciate the principles and to practise the art of Self-Government. But I have no fears on this score. In our own Province, local self-government has been remarkably successful. We have it on the highest authority ; for no less a personage than His Honour the Lieutenant-Governor has declared that in Bengal local self-government has on the whole been a success ; and I am quite sure similar testimony would be forthcoming in reference to the other Provinces of India. It would indeed be a marvel if it were otherwise. Our Panchayat system is as old as the hills and is graven on

the hearts and the instincts of the people. Self-Government is therefore nothing new to the habits or the ways of thought of the people of India.

The motion was seconded by Mr. N. G. Chandavarkar in a powerful speech, in which he showed, by quotations, that the great Englishmen who had ruled in India had contemplated Self-Government. Other speeches followed—they all deserve reading, so good were they—and then came Pandit Madan Mohan Malaviya, making his maiden speech in the Congress, and fairly carrying his audience away with the eloquence which has ever since been at India's service. One quotation we must have:

> It is not to the great British Government that we need demonstrate the utility, the expediency, the necessity of this great reform. It might have been necessary to support our petition for this boon with such a demonstration, were we governed by some despotic monarch, jealous of the duties, but ignorant and careless of the rights of subjects; but it is surely unnecessary to say one word in support of such a cause to the British Government or the British Nation—to the descendants of those brave and great men who fought and died to obtain for themselves and preserve intact for their children those very institutions which, taught by their example, we now crave, who spent their whole lives and shed their hearts' blood so freely in maintaining and developing this cherished principle.
>
> What is an Englishman without representative institutions? Why, not an Englishman at all, a mere sham, a base imitation, and I often wonder as I look round at our nominally English magnates, how they have the face to call themselves Englishmen and yet deny us representative institutions, and struggle to maintain despotic ones. Representative institutions are as much a part of the true Briton as his language and his literature.

> Will any one tell me that Great Britain will, in cold blood, deny us, her free-born subjects, the first of these, when, by the gift of the latter, she has qualified us to appreciate and incited us to desire it?
>
> No taxation without representation. That is the first commandment in the Englishman's Political Bible; how can he palter with his conscience and tax us here, his free and educated fellow-subjects, as if we were dumb sheep or cattle? But we are not dumb any longer. India has found a voice at last in this great Congress, and in it, and through it, we call on England to be true to her traditions, her instincts, and herself, and grant us our rights as free-born British citizens.

The resolution was, of course, carried unanimously.

Resolution V was next brought on, as helping to give effect to the all-important Resolution IV, and was quickly carried.

Resolutions XV, XIII, XIV were then passed in the order given, to send the resolutions to the Viceroy, to be forwarded by him to the Queen-Empress and the Secretary of State; to establish Standing Congress-Committees; and to hold the next Congress in Madras. This memorable sitting then closed with a vote of thanks to the President.

The Statesman (Calcutta) had a remarkable article on the Congress, saying that the Congress was composed of "men to whom we can point with pride, as the outcome of a century of our rule". The London *Times*, on the other hand, burst into violent invective, declaring that the Congress—our readers can judge of the truth of the statement—was "merely an affair of discontented place-seekers—men of straw, with little or no stake in the country. . . .

persons of considerable imitative powers . . . of total ignorance of the real problems of Government . . . delegates from all these talking clubs . . . might become a serious danger to public tranquillity ". Virulent rubbish, which did its mischievous work in Great Britain.

The Viceroy, Lord Dufferin, received some of the members, not as delegates but as " distinguished visitors to the capital "! He also invited them to a garden party, carefully explaining that he did not ask them as representatives. Unconsciously humorous was His Excellency. But he doubtless meant well. In any case, the representative character of the Congress was recognised by India, if not by this amiable gentleman.

RESOLUTIONS

I. That this Congress of Delegates from all parts of India do humbly offer its dutiful and loyal congratulations to Her Most Gracious Majesty, the Queen Empress, on the approaching completion of the first half century of her memorable, beneficent and glorious reign, and heartily wish her many, many more, and happy, years of rule over the great British Empire.

Representation

II. That this Congress regards with the deepest sympathy, and views with grave apprehension, the increasing poverty of vast numbers of the population of India, and (although aware that the Government is not overlooking this matter and is contemplating certain palliatives) desires to record its fixed conviction that the introduction of Representative Institutions will prove one of the most important practical steps towards the amelioration of the condition of the people.

III. That this Congress do, emphatically, reaffirm the 3rd Resolution of the Congress of 1885, and distinctly declare its belief that the reform and expansion of the Council of the Governor-General for making Laws and of the Provincial Legislative Councils therein suggested, have now become essential alike in the interest, of India and England.

IV. That this Congress is of opinion that in giving practical effect to this essential reform, regard should be had (subject to such modifications as, on a more detailed examination of the question, may commend themselves to the Government) to the principles embodied in the following tentative suggestions:

(1) The number of persons composing the Legislative Councils, both Provincial and of the Governor-General, to be materially increased. Not less than one-half the Members of such enlarged Councils to be elected. Not more than one-fourth to be officials having seats *ex-officio* in such Councils, and not more than one-fourth to be Members, official or non-official, nominated by Government.

(2) The right to elect members to the Provincial Councils to be conferred only on those classes and members of the community, *prima facie*, capable of exercising it wisely and independently. In Bengal and Bombay the Councillors may be elected by the members of Municipalities, District Boards, Chambers of Commerce and the Universities, or an electorate may be constituted of all persons possessing such qualifications, educational and pecuniary, as may be deemed necessary. In Madras, the Councillors may be elected either by District Boards, Municipalities, Chambers of Commerce and the University, or by Electoral colleges composed of members partly elected by these bodies and partly nominated by Government. In the North-West Provinces and Oudh and in the Panjab, Councillors may be elected by an Electoral College composed of members elected by Municipal and District Boards and nominated, to an extent not exceeding one-sixth of the total number, by Government, it being understood that the same elective system now in force where Municipal Boards are concerned will be applied to District Boards, and the right of electing members to these latter extended to the cultivating class. But whatever system be adopted (and the details must be worked out separately for each province) care must be taken that all sections of the community, and all great interests, are adequately represented.

(3) The elected Members of the Council of the Governor-General for making Laws, to be elected by the elected Members of the several Provincial Councils.

(4) No elected or nominated Member of any Council, to receive any salary or remuneration in virtue of such membership but any such Member, already in receipt of any Government salary or allowance, to continue to draw the same unchanged during membership, and all Members to be entitled to be reimbursed any expenses incurred in travelling in connection with their membership.

(5) All persons, resident in India, to be eligible for seats in Council, whether as electees or nominees, without distinction of race, creed, caste or colour.

(6) All legislative measures and all financial questions, including all budgets, whether these involve new or enhanced taxation or not, to be necessarily submitted to and dealt with by these Councils. In the case of all other branches of the administration, any Member to be at liberty, after due notice, to put any question he sees fit to the *ex-officio* Members (or such one of these as may be specially charged with the supervision of the particular branch concerned) and to be entitled (except as hereinafter provided) to receive a reply to his question, together with copies of any papers requisite for the thorough comprehension of the subject, and on this reply the Council to be at liberty to consider and discuss the question and record thereon such resolution as may appear fitting to the majority. Provided that, if the subject in regard to which the enquiry is made involves matters of Foreign policy, Military dispositions or strategy, or is otherwise of such a nature that, in the opinion of the Executive, the public interests would be materially imperilled by the communication of the information asked for, it shall be competent for them to instruct the *ex-officio* Members, or one of them, to reply accordingly, and decline to furnish the information asked for.

(7) The Executive Government shall possess the power of overruling the decision arrived at by the majority of the Council, in every case in which, in its opinion, the public interests would suffer by the acceptance of such decision; but whenever this power is exercised, a full exposition of the grounds on which this has been considered necessary, shall be published within one month, and in the case of local Governments they shall report the circumstances and explain their action to the Government of India, and in the case of this latter, it shall report and explain to the Secretary of State; and in any such case on a representation made through the Government of India and the Secretary of State by the overruled majority, it shall be competent to the Standing Committee of the House of Commons (recommended in the 3rd Resolution of last year's Congress which this present Congress has affirmed) to consider the matter, and call for any and all papers or information, and hear any persons on behalf of such majority or otherwise, and thereafter, if needful, report thereon to the full House.

V. That this Congress do invite all Public Bodies and all Associations throughout the Country, humbly and earnestly, to entreat His Excellency the Viceroy to obtain the sanction of Her Majesty's Secretary of State for India to the appointment of a Commission, to enquire exhaustively into the best method of introducing such a tentative form of Representative Institutions into India, as has been indicated in Resolutions III of the past, and IV of the present year's Congress.

Public Service

VI. That a Committee composed of the gentlemen named in the margin be appointed to consider the Public Service Question and report thereon to this Congress.

Hon. Dadabhai Naoroji (Bombay).
 „ S. Subramania Iyer (Madras).
 „ Peary Mohan Mukerji (Calcutta).
Mr. G. Subramania Iyer (Madras).
Babu Motilal Ghose (Calcutta).
 „ Surendra Nath Bannerji (Calcutta).
 „ Gangaprasad Varma (Lucknow).
 „ Ramkali Chaudhuri (Benares).
 „ Guru Prasad Sen (Patna).
Pandit Prannath (Lucknow).
Munshi Kashiprasad (Allahabad).
Nawab Reza Ali Khan (Lucknow).
Mr. Hamid Ali (Lucknow).
Lala Kanyalal (Amritsar).
Rao Sahab Gangadhar Rao Madhaw Chitnavis (Nagpur).
Mr. Rahimtulla M. Sayani (Bombay).

VII. That this Congress approves and adopts the report submitted by the Committee appointed by Resolution VI.

REPORT

We, the Members of the Committee appointed by the Congress to submit a statement in connection with the Public Service question, have the honour to report that the following resolutions were unanimously adopted by us at a meeting held yesterday:

1. That the open Competitive Examination be held simultaneously both in India and in England.

2. That the simultaneous examinations thus held be equally open to all classes of Her Majesty's subjects.

3. That the classified list be prepared according to merit.

4. That the Congress express the hope that the Civil Service Commissioners will give fair consideration to Samskrit and Arabic among the subjects of examination.

5. That the age of candidates eligible for admission to the open Competitive Examination be not less than 19, or, as recommended by Sir C. Aitchison, more than 23 years.

6. That simultaneous examinations being granted, the Statutory Civil Service be closed for first appointments.

7. That the appointments in the Statutory Civil Service, under the existing rules, be still left open to the Members of the Uncovenanted Service and to professional men of proved merit and ability.

8. That all appointments requiring educational qualifications, other than covenanted first appointments, be filled by Competitive Examinations held in the different Provinces, and open in each Province to such natural-born subjects of H.M. only as are residents thereof.

These Resolutions it is hoped, cover the main principles which underlie the questions set by the Public Service Commission. For a more detailed consideration there was no time.

(Sd). DADABHAI NAOROJI,

30th December, 1886 *President of the Committee*

Legal

VIII. That, in the opinion of this Congress, the time has now arrived when the system of trial by jury may be safely extended into many parts of the Country where it is not at present in force.

IX. That, in the opinion of this Congress, the innovation made in 1872 in the system of trial by jury, depriving the verdicts of juries of all finality, has proved injurious to the Country, and that the powers then, for the first time, vested in Sessions Judges and High Courts, of setting aside verdicts of acquittal, should be at once withdrawn.

X. That, in the opinion of this Congress, a provision, similar to that contained in the Summary Jurisdiction Act of England (under which accused persons in serious cases have the option of demanding a committal to the Sessions Court), should be introduced into the Indian Code of Criminal Procedure, enabling accused persons, in warrant cases, to demand that, instead of being tried by the Magistrate, they be committed to the Court of Sessions.

XI. That this Congress do place on record an expression of the universal conviction, that a complete separation of executive and judicial functions (such that in no case the two functions shall be combined in the same officer) has become an urgent necessity, and that, in its opinion, it behoves the Government to effect this separation without further delay, even though this should, in some Provinces, involve some extra expenditure.

Volunteering

XII. That in view of the unsettled state of public affairs in Europe, and the immense assistance that the people of this country, if duly prepared therefor, is capable of rendering to Great Britain in the event of any serious complications arising, this Congress do earnestly appeal to the Government to authorise (under such rules and restrictions as may to it seem fitting) a system of Volunteering for the Indian inhabitants of the country, such as may qualify them to support the Government, effectively, in any crisis.

Organisation

XIII. That Standing Congress-Committees be constituted at all important centres.

XIV. That the Third Indian National Congress assemble at Madras on the 27th of December 1887.

XV. That copies of these Resolutions be forwarded to His Excellency the Viceroy in Council, with the humble requests, that he will cause the 1st Resolution to be submitted in due course to Her Majesty the Queen Empress, that he will cause all the Resolutions to be laid before Her Majesty's Secretary of State for India, and that he himself will be graciously pleased, in consultation with his colleagues, to accord them his best consideration.

(Sd.) DADABHAI NAOROJI,

President of the Second Indian National Congress

CHAPTER III

The spirit of the third National Congress is shown by the heading of the official Report, taken from the speech of Raja Sir T. Madhava Rao, K. C. S. I., the Chairman of the Reception Committee, who, speaking of the Congress, declared that it was "the soundest triumph of British Administration, and a Crown of Glory to the British Nation". The words recall those of Macaulay, when he said that the noblest monument of British Rule in India would be the establishment of Britain's free institutions in the land.

The third Congress met at Madras in December, 1887. As early as May 1st, 1887, a strong Reception Committee of some 120 members was formed, with Raja Sir T. Madhava Rao as Chairman, and embracing Hindus of all castes, Muhammadans, Indian Christians and Eurasians, a thoroughly representative body. Every town of over 10,000 inhabitants was asked to form a sub-committee, and a vigorous political propaganda was carried on, 30,000 copies of a Tamil *Congress Catechism*, by Mr. Viraraghavachariar, being distributed. A striking proof of the result of this was the fact that Rs. 5,500 were contributed by 8,000 subscriptions varying from anna one to Rs. 1-8, and another Rs. 8,000 varying from Rs. 1-8 to Rs. 30. Poor people even sent collections from Mandalay, Rangoon, Singapore and the eastern islands. It is pleasant to see the names of the Ruling Princes of Mysore, Travancore and Cochin, and Their Highnesses the Maharaja of Vizianagaram and the Raja of Venkatagiri at one end of the subscribers, with one-anna coolies at the other—a truly National work. The Standing Congress Committees were asked to send up subjects for discussion, and the energetic Committee, greatly daring, set up a huge Pandal, capable of holding 3,000 persons.

760 delegates had been elected, and 607 were actually present. The table was as follows :

Madras	362
Bombay and Sindh	99
Bengal, Orissa and Assam	79
N. W. P. and Oudh	45
Central Provinces	13
Panjab	9
	607

The Panjab had elected 42 delegates, though only 9 appeared. From the Panjab to Madras is a far cry. A good feature was the presence of 45 ryots and 19 artisans. A noteworthy delegate was Mr. John Adam, "the Principal of the great Pachaiyappa's Collegiate establishment". The Report also notes the friendliness of *The Madras Mail, The Bombay Gazette,* the Calcutta *Daily News* and *Statesman.* Among the many who sent letters of sympathy were the Shri Mahant of Tirupati, and the Maharaja of

Darbhanga, and of course the Hon. Mr. K. T. Telang, while the Hon. Mr. G. M. Ranade was present in person, though, as before, unable to serve as a delegate.

The Congress met on December 27th, in the Pandal, erected in Mackay's Gardens, some 3,000 spectators assembling in and around the great tent. Sir T. Madhava Rao in a few words welcomed the delegates, and, being in very weak health, gave his brief speech to Mr. C. V. Sundaram Shastri to read; he justified the Congress, expressed his belief that the Government was willing to help India to advance, and urged caution on "all parties concerned". Mr. W. C. Bannerji proposed and the Hon. Mr. S. Subramania Aiyar seconded, the election as President of Mr. Budrudin Tyabji, who took the chair amid great applause; it is interesting to note that the first Congress was presided over by a Hindu, the second by a Parsi, the third by a Musalman.

Mr. Tyabji laid stress on the representative character of the Congress, asserted its loyalty, and finally advised that a Committee—the names of which he read out—should be appointed to consider the many suggestions sent in for discussion and to draw up a programme for the work of the Congress. The proposal was warmly approved and the following Committee was accepted:

Bengal, Assam and Orissa.—Mr. W. C. Bannerji, Dr. Trailokyanath Mitra, Messrs. Surendranath Bannerji and Norendranath Sen. *Behar.*—Messrs. Saligram Singh, and Guru Prasad Sen. *Bombay and Sindh.*—Messrs. Chandavarkar, Khare, Dhruva, Nam Joshi, and Gobind Buksh.

North-West Provinces and Oudh.—Mr. Moulvi Hamid Ali, Raja Rampal Singh, Mr. Ram Kali Chaudhuri and Pandit Madan Mohan Malaviya. *Panjab.*—Pandit Satyanand Agnihotri and Lala Murlidhar. *Madras.*—Messrs. Hume, Sabapathy Mudaliar, Sankara Nair and W. S. Gantz.

The appointment of this Committee is interesting, as it was really the first "Subjects Committee," the body to which all real debate has gradually been transferred. It is a question whether the plan is a good one, since the Committee sits in private, and hence both the members and the public lose the healthy influence of open debate, which added so much to the vitality and interest of the Congress; the public sittings become a mere formal passing of resolutions debated in Committee. Besides, the younger delegates lose the training in debate which they enjoyed in earlier days, and become the more critical when they have no fair opportunity of expressing dissent and moving amendments. In the days we are now studying, amendments were frequently brought forward and thoroughly debated.

On the second day, December 28th, the first Resolution appointed a Committee to consider what, if any, rules should be framed for the constitution and working of the Congress, to report on the 30th (the list of names will be found in the Resolution, two names, that of the mover and of Mr. R. P. Karandikar, being added to the original list). The Resolution was moved by Dr. Trailokyanath Mitra, who remarked that some opponents said that the delegates represented no one but themselves; while they must not check the growth and development of the Congress by hard and fast rules, too early imposed, the world should know who elected the Congress, and that the Congress was really representative. Mr. Hamid Ali Khan seconded, and Mr. W. S. Gantz supported, pointing out that little work was done between Congresses, whereas work should continue throughout the year. At this point Dr. Trailokyanath Mitra's name was added. Mr. R. P. Karandikar moved an amendment, narrowing the scope of the Committee to framing rules, and proposing to defer the question of a Constitution till the Congress had gained more experience and had visited other Provinces. Others supported the amendment, regarding the proposal to frame a Constitution as premature, but on the appeal of the President the amendment was withdrawn, as the whole matter could be considered on the report of the Committee ; this was done, Mr. Karandikar's name was added to the Committee, and the Resolution was carried unanimously.

The second Resolution re-affirmed the necessity of the admission of representatives to the Legislative Councils, and Mr. Surendranath Bannerji said in proposing it : "We unfurl the banner of the Congress, and upon it are written, in characters of glittering gold, which none may efface, the great words of this Resolution : 'Representative Institutions for India.'" He declined to enter into details, affirming only the principle, pointing out that they were not legislators, and saying : "The Government has highly paid officials, drawing thousands of rupees a month, and it is for them to elaborate the Bill and settle the details, upon principles which may find acceptance with the Government." It is significant that Raja Sir T. Madhava Rao seconded the proposal, remarking that, prudent and conservative as he was, he regarded as necessary for India representative institutions; he said the principle was "one which the British Government, I am sure, will not, and cannot, refuse to recognise". He was optimistic enough to believe, this cautious old statesman, that in "a year or two" they would "receive a satisfactory response to our very reasonable recommendations"! Only 28 years have passed since then.

A long discussion followed, in which Mr. Eardley Norton made a remarkable speech, in which he urged resolution, courage and endurance, until the right demanded was obtained. "I was told yesterday by one, for whose character and educated qualities I cherish a great esteem, that in joining myself with the labourers in this Congress, I have earned for myself the new title of 'a veiled seditionist'. If it be sedition, gentlemen, to rebel against all wrong; if it be sedition to insist that the people should have a fair share in the administration of their own country and affairs; if it be sedition to resist tyranny, to raise my voice against oppression, to mutiny against injustice, to insist upon a hearing before sentence, to uphold the liberties of the individual, to vindicate our common right to gradual but ever advancing reform—if this be sedition I am right glad to be called a 'seditionist,' and doubly, aye, trebly glad, when I look around me to-day, to know and feel I am ranked as one among such a magnificent array of 'seditionists'." He spoke in 1887. These things, and indeed much less important things, are still "sedition" in 1915.

Pandit Bishen Narayan Dhar was another fine speaker, and he pointed out the value of free institutions as "the best practical school for mental and moral discipline". "To be called on from time to time to take part in the affairs of your country, to discuss, with the sense of responsibility that power gives, public questions; to have to employ your highest faculties in the management of affairs that have a direct bearing on your country's glory, and on the happiness of her people, these things, I say, are all steps in the education necessary for the unfolding of all the speculative and practical faculties of a Nation." Without this, "it will lack that instinctive sense of liberty, that robustness of character which are essential to all healthy and, therefore, progressive, National life". He appealed to the views taken by eminent Englishmen on this matter, giving the following striking opinions. Sir Richard Temple, who was hardly regarded as a friend of India, said:

> For all that it must be remembered that the elective principle is essential to that political training which every stable government (like that of the British in India) must desire to see possessed by its subjects . . . . Public spirit cannot be created without entrusting the people with a part of their own public business, a part limited at first, but increasing as their fitness shall grow. Even if political risks should accrue, they must be borne in

performing the duty which the British Government owes to the people of India. In that country, a trustful policy will be found a wise one, and that which is sound morally will prove to be the safest politically.

Sir John Lawrence, as long ago as 1864, said:

> The people of India are quite capable of administering their own affairs, and the municipal feeling is deeply rooted in them. The village communities, each of which is a little republic, are the most abiding of Indian institutions. Holding the position we do in India, every view of duty and policy should induce us to leave as much as possible of the business of the country to be done by the people.

And Mr. Gladstone, who loved Liberty in his old age even more fully than he loved her in his youth, declared:

> I hold that the capital agent in determining finally the question whether our power in India is or is not to continue, will be the will of the two hundred and forty millions of people who inhabit India. The question who shall have Supreme Rule in India is, by the laws of right, an Indian question; and those laws of right are from day to day growing into laws of fact. Our title to be there depends on a first condition, that our being there is profitable to the Indian nations; and on a second condition, that we can make them see and understand it to be profitable.

It was England, said the eloquent Pandit, who had created the desire which the Congress was voicing:

> England has moved us from our ancient anchorage. She has cast us adrift, against our will, upon the wide waters of a seething proletariat; and we turn back to England, and ask her to grant us that compass of representative institutions by which, amid a thousand storms, she has steered her prosperous course to the safe haven of regulated political freedom.

It was a noble appeal; but, like many others, it fell upon deaf ears. England sowed the seed of Freedom, but when its fair harvest showed itself in the Congress, she feared the result of her work, she hesitated, and finally sent Lord Curzon to destroy her own success; then there came, as there ever come, from dammed-up aspirations, unrest and trouble, and then coercion and half-hearted reforms, and growing trouble, until the War broke out and saved the Empire, and gives now the possibility of a blessed change, which shall bind together the hearts of India and Great Britain—if Britain will be as wise as Russia.

Another Pandit, Madan Mohan Malaviya, came next, and spoke with the passionate earnestness natural to him; we give a long extract, to show how reasonable was the plea. It is as valid now as then, for though the Minto-Morley reforms of 1910 gave some representation, the details were so juggled with as to leave the representatives in a hopeless minority, and to give them absolutely no control over the Budget.

Allow me to say this much, that, placed as we are in this country under a foreign Government, however benevolent and generous its motives—the motives of those who take part in the administration—we stand in the greatest need of our own representatives in the Legislative Councils. Gentlemen, the whole of Europe, with the exception of Russia, has declared that the most efficient and best form of Government for any country, which has made any advance in civilisation, is a Government, conducted not solely by the few for the many, but to a greater or less extent by the many for themselves—

a Government, in fact, in which the representatives of the people have some potential share—and if this be expedient for European countries, where the rulers and the ruled are of the same Nationality, and where they are of the same religion, I think it must be conceded that it is even more essential for India, which is inhabited by people whose habits, manners, customs, language, race and creed differ from those of their rulers. If we demand for India that there should be representatives of her people in the State Councils, we only ask for what, not simply Europe, but America, Australia, and almost the whole civilised world have declared with one unanimous voice to be essential for any Government that is to be suitable to any country, as it is only where the representatives of the people are allowed to take part in that administration, that the wants and wishes, the aspirations and grievances of the people can be adequately set forth, properly understood, or duly provided for. That being so, gentlemen, I think there cannot possibly be two opinions on the point, that the reform which we crave for from Government is one so essential for the well-being of this country, that it should be conceded to us without the least avoidable delay. This is now the third time that we have thus been meeting at yearly intervals, we have come from every district, from the most distant portions of this Empire, and in many cases, at the cost of great personal sacrifice. We have nothing personally to gain, no selfish aim to serve. We come together, chosen by our fellow-countrymen, primarily to press upon Government the fact that the country stands badly in need of this reform, and that the entire Nation prays for it. But, unhappily, Government has not as yet listened to our people's prayer!

What is it that we see year after year? People assembling from all parts of India—from the Panjab, Sindh, Assam, Madras, Bengal, Bombay, the N. W. Provinces, Oudh, the Central Provinces, from every Province, from every town—coming together to implore Government humbly to grant this reform, which is, after all, their birthright as free-born British subjects. It is no desire or motive of self-ambition that brings these people together at such heavy cost, and at such great personal inconvenience. There is no taint of self-interest in the matter. No. Their sole idea is that India, their country, of all things stands badly in need of this fundamental reform and they hope, and God grant that they may not hope in vain, that their unselfish persistence in asking may secure for their native land this great boon! I cannot possibly believe that there is one single educated Indian, who after studying this question can rest happy in his mind, without trying his very best to secure this reform. I cannot possibly believe that any good man who once really understands what this reform truly means for his country and his countrymen, for his kinsmen, his children and himself, can remain indifferent to it. And, gentlemen, neither we nor any other intelligent Indians are indifferent to it—and though thus far success has not crowned our efforts, we must only go up to Government again and ask their earliest consideration of our demands, or of our prayers (call them which you will), and entreat them, again and again, to concede to us this reform. Gentlemen, it is nothing very great we are asking them to do. The British Government has already made this concession to so many countries. So many Colonies, so many British Colonies enjoy it. Canada, the Cape, the Australian Colonies, innumerable smaller places, even the so-called Crown Colonies, except perhaps the Fiji Islands and some purely military posts, all enjoy some measure, and most of them the fullest measure, of Representative Government. Britain has granted or conceded this concession to all these places. Why should she withhold it from the people of India? Does she think that we are less loyal than her subjects in other lands? Australia would break with her to-morrow if she ventured to prevent Australia from taxing British goods, while we, in all good temper, accept an odious income-tax, vilely administered, and imposed not to meet the expenses of our own Government, but to provide funds to enable Great Britain to annex Burma or menace Russia. Does she think we are not prepared for the privilege? I think this very Congress is proof positive of our ripeness for the task, and of the intelligence and knowledge which would be brought to bear upon the affairs of the nation if only the Government were kind enough to accede to our wishes.

Pandit Madan Mohan Malaviya laid great stress on the neglect of Indian affairs in Parliament, as a cogent reason why India herself should be allowed to look after them. He quoted Mr. Bradlaugh, M.P., who spoke strongly in the House on this neglect:

> Last year the Budget was considered on June 21st and the year before on August 6th. It was not right to leave to the last moment of the Session the only opportunity that was afforded to Parliament of considering the wishes and the grievances of the 200,000,000 of people whom we rule. That any Parliamentary control should be exercised over the affairs of India was impossible, when the Indian Budget figured upon paper as the 8th order upon one of the last days of an expiring Session.

Was it any wonder that India felt indignant? At this very Budget debate, said the Pandit, 29 members had been present in the House of Commons out of 675: "How would they like their own affairs to be treated in that way? Would they, I repeat, stand it for one week?" "They will not do their duty by the country themselves, and they will not allow us to do it."

Many other members spoke, and one of them, Mr. A. Kumar Dutt, who brought a petition from over 45,000 persons asking for reform, told of the interest of the people of his Province in the question, and how a Chandala (the lowest class of outcaste) had come forward after his lecture, forgetting all his surroundings and saying: "We are going to have our own men to be our Legislators; that is very good, that is very good." At another, a very poor Musalman came forward with a four-anna bit "to help on your cause". Another Musalman explained to an enquirer: "Look here, as we elect our arbitrators and as we hold ourselves bound by the decisions of such people, so let us elect our own men to be our Legislators, and they will pass laws by which we will gladly be bound." As the speaker said, the common people have common sense. The Resolution was put and carried unanimously.

On the third day, December 29th, the third resolution, demanding the separation of executive and judicial functions was put and carried unanimously, but the feeling in favour of it was so strong that two hours were occupied in speeches in support of it. It is interesting to note that it was moved by Mr. N. Subramaniam, an Indian Christian Barrister, and seconded and supported by men of the most diverse opinions on non-political questions.

Resolution IV was moved by Mr. Norendranath Sen, who pithily remarked that India needed to be "equally qualified for Self-Government in times of peace, and Self-Defence in times of war". Mr. Saligram Singh seconded. As the original form only asked admission for the "sons of noblemen and gentlemen of all classes resident in India," amendments were proposed, widening its scope, and it was finally passed in the all-embracing form found in the list of Resolutions.

Resolution V was the same as Resolution XII of the Congress of 1886, but is noteworthy for the speech of Mr. (now Sir) Sankaran Nair, who pointing to the troubled state of affairs, and the likelihood of England being involved in war, asked if Indian civilisation was "to be broken into and destroyed by Northern invaders." He went on :

> Of course, we have this much freedom, that we have full liberty to offer our prayers for the success of the British Government. But prayers, I fear, are not likely to be of much use to us or to them. Is the peace and tranquillity, I say, which we now enjoy, to be ravished from us, without our voices being heard, our arms being raised in the settlement of the dispute? It appears to me absurd to entertain such an idea. It appears to me intolerable, the more especially as even the English themselves cannot assert what the result of the struggle here is likely to be, if India continues debarred from helping herself and them. It is impossible to foresee what will happen, if this policy of Government, of refusing our co-operation, is persisted in. It appears to be absolutely suicidal and we only hope, equally for our own and their sakes, that the English may not some day regret that she has refused, while there was yet time, and we could have been trained into serviceable allies, those prayers which we have so repeatedly put up in regard to this matter. The Russians have armed their foes of yesterday to fight on their own behalf to-day, and the result shows that they have been justified in their action. Have we been less loyal to the British than the Turkomans to the Russians, whom they fought with only yesterday? They lie who say that our loyalty cannot be depended upon in the hour of danger.

Some very earnest and warm speeches were delivered, the feeling as to the Russian menace being very strong. The Resolution was carried unanimously, and the Congress then turned to the less exciting question of the income-tax, which was discussed in a very business-like way, and the

Resolution thereon was carried unanimously; therewith the business of the day ended.

On the following day, Resolution VII was very earnestly and competently discussed; a working carpenter—sent with two other artisans from Tanjore—made a very sensible speech, saying, among other things:

> These factories and workshops, gentlemen, when they spring up, will be a source of gaining an honest livelihood to thousands of our countrymen who now, destitute of any means, are driven to despair how to keep body and soul together. And, gentlemen, how welcome will be the day for India, when, by the immense and growing development of her arts and industries, she will be able to find at least a wholesome morsel of food for her 45 millions of completely destitute children, who are now, by official admission, going without even one single full meal a day.

How these words recall Shelley's apostrophe to Liberty:

> To the labourer thou art bread,
> And a comely table spread. . . .
> No, in countries that are free
> Such starvation cannot be
> As in England now we see.

Change "England" into India.

The official Report of the Congress remarks on this:

> Referring to Mr. Mookkanasari's concluding words, it may not be amiss to explain that it is due to no want of sympathy for the miserable half-starving millions of their fellow-countrymen that so little has been said during this last Congress of that cruel poverty which is year by year decimating the lowest classes and

as many, perhaps a majority, believe is surely, if slowly, creeping higher up the social scale. The fact simply is that since the resumption of the aggressive annexive policy and the enormous increases of taxation, that have, thus far, been the chief features of Lord Dufferin's administration, the Indian community despair of obtaining any material alleviation of the misery they see around them, until they can secure a potential voice in the administration, and it is this conviction, more than anything else, that is giving such an intense earnestness to their efforts in the direction of representation.

After this a Resolution to repeal the Arms Act came up, and gave rise to what the official record calls "an animated, almost fiery, discussion which lasted some hours". It was a question then, as now, which cuts Indians to the quick; as the record says: "No native of India may possess or carry arms without special licence, whereas Europeans, Eurasians, Negroes, Hottentots or Fiji Islanders, any scum of the earth, even, that the ocean casts on India's shores, may wear arms unquestioned." That is the sting; any foreigner may bear arms; the native of the country may not. And it is very curious that Indians carried arms after the Sepoy Rebellion, and were not forbidden them until 1878. The mover of the Resolution, Rao Bahadur Sabapati Mudaliar spoke of the degradation and the slur imposed by the Act, and the practical hardship to the farmers and ryots, unable to protect themselves from wild beasts and robbers. It was seconded by Mr. Bepin Chandra Pal who—though wanting no weapon himself but his steel pen and his sharp tongue—demanded the repeal of the Act to save thousands of men and women from being killed by tigers and leopards, and also because the Act "is wrong in principle, injurious in its effect, and is simply suicidal to the Government". An amendment in favour of modification instead of repeal was proposed, and after much discussion, Resolution VIII was carried as printed below, the first of many appeals, as righteous as they were, and are, useless.

Mr. A. O. Hume then brought up the report of the Committee appointed by Resolution I, giving a long series of tentative rules, and proposed that they should be circulated to all Standing Committees, and reported with suggestions next year. The Resolution —No. IX—was seconded by Dr. Trailokyanath Mitra and agreed to. Allahabad was chosen for the next Congress, and the formal last Resolution passed. The Congress then closed with the usual vote of thanks.

Lord Connemara, the Governor of Madras, Sir Savalai Ramasami Mudaliar, C. I. E., the Sheriff, and Mr. Eardley Norton, an English barrister, practising in Madras, gave entertainments to welcome the members, and the whole atmosphere of Madras seems to have been friendly.

RESOLUTIONS

Constitution

I. That a Committee is appointed, consisting of the gentlemen (marginally enumerated*) to consider what rules, if any, may now be usefully framed in regard to the constitution and working of the Congress, with instructions to report thereon to the Congress, on the 30th instant.

* Messrs. Nam Joshi, Chandavarkar, Mir Humayun Jah Bahadur, Hajee Mahomed Abdul Shakoor Badshaw Sahib, S. Subramania Iyer, W. S. Gantz, Rangiah Naidu, Surendranath Bannerji,

Trailokyanath Mitra, Kali Charan Bannerji, Guru Prasad Sen, Saligram Singh, Ramkali Chaudhuri, Hafiz Abdul Rahim, Rampal Singh, Pandit Madan Mohun, Ganga Prasad Varma, Bishen Narayen Dar, Hamid Ali, Murlidhar, Satyanand Agnihotri, H. H. Dhruva, W. C. Bannerji, Norendranath Sen, Eardley Norton, Joy Govind Shome, Iswari Lal Sircar, G. Subramania Iyer, D. A. Khare, S. A. Saminada Iyer, Sabapathy Mudaliar, A O. Hume, C. Vijiya Raghava Chariar, Govind Buksh, Karandikar.

IX. That the rules drafted by the Committee appointed under Resolution I, stand over for consideration till next Congress, but that, in the meantime, copies be circulated to all Standing Congress Committees, with the request that they will, during the coming year, act in accordance with these rules, so far as this may seem to them possible and desirable, and report thereon to the next Congress, with such further suggestions as to them may seem meet.

Representative

II. That this Congress re-affirms the necessity for the expansion and reform of the Council of the Governor-General for making Laws, and the Provincial Legislative Councils, already set forth in Resolutions III of the Congresses of 1885 and 1886, and expresses the earnest hope that the Government will no longer delay action in the direction of this essential reform.

Legal

III. That this Congress once again places on record an expression of the universal conviction that a complete separation of the Executive and Judicial functions (such that in no case the two functions shall be combined in the same officer) has become an urgent necessity, and declares that, in its opinion, it behoves the Government to effect this separation, without further delay, even though this should, in some provinces, involve some extra expenditure.

Military

IV. That in view of the loyalty of Her Majesty's Indian subjects, this Congress considers it desirable that the Queen's Proclamation should be given effect to; that the Military Service in its higher grades should be practically opened to the natives of this country, and that the Government of India should establish Military Colleges in this country, whereat the natives of India, as defined by Statute, may be educated and trained for a military career as officers of the Indian Army.

V. That in view of the unsettled state of public affairs in Europe, and the immense assistance that the people of this country, if duly prepared therefor, are capable of rendering to Great Britain in the event of any serious complications arising, this Congress once again earnestly appeals to the Government to authorise (under such rules and restrictions, as may to it seem fitting,) a system of volunteering for the Indian inhabitants of the country, such as may qualify them to support the Government, effectively, in any crisis.

VIII. That in view of the loyalty of the people, the hardships which the present Arms' Act (XI of 1878) causes, and the unmerited slur which it casts upon the people of this country, the Government be moved so to modify the provisions of Chapter IV and, if necessary, other portions of the said Act, as shall enable all persons to possess and wear arms, unless debarred therefrom, either as individuals or members of particular communities or classes, by the orders of the Government of India (or any local authority empowered by the Government of India on that behalf) for reasons to be recorded in writing and duly published.

Taxation

VI. That as the administration of the Income-Tax, especially, as regards incomes below Rs. 1,000, has proved extremely unsatisfactory, it is essential, in the opinion of the Congress, that the taxable minimum be raised to Rs. 1,000, the loss of revenue thus involved, being made good, and further financial difficulties, if any, met, by reductions in the existing public expenditure, or, should this prove impossible, by the re-imposition of an import duty on the finer classes of cotton goods.

Educational

VII. That having regard to the poverty of the people, it is desirable that the Government be moved to elaborate a system of Technical Education, suitable to the condition of the country, to encourage indigenous manufactures by a more strict observance of the orders, already existing, in regard to utilising such manufactures for State purposes, and to employ more extensively, than at present, the skill and talents of the people of the country.

Formal Business

X. That the Fourth Indian National Congress assemble at Allahabad, on the 26th December, 1888.

XI. That copies of these Resolutions be forwarded to His Excellency the Viceroy-in-Council with the humble request, that he will cause all the Resolutions to be laid before Her Majesty's Secretary of State for India, and that he himself will be graciously pleased, in consultation with his colleagues, to accord them his best consideration.

CHAPTER IV

"The Fourth Indian National Congress was heralded by a tumultuous outbreak of opposition." Thus remarks the official Record, on beginning its summary of the Fourth Congress, that of 1888. It met in Allahabad, and Sir Auckland Colvin signalised himself by his opposition, while Lord Dufferin, the Viceroy, had the bad taste to attack it and brand it as seditious in a banquet given him on his leaving office. The most outrageous efforts were made to prevent its being held in Allahabad. The Chairman of the Reception Committee recounted, in his speech of welcome, the obstacles which the Committee had had to surmount, for all the re-actionary and tyrannical elements in India had risen against the Congress, terrified at its growing strength. They were first informed that they could use the Khusro Bagh, but the permission was, a little later, withdrawn. Then, in April, they were given permission to rent a large piece of waste land near the fort; *four months later* the rent was returned, with the information that it was refused on sanitary grounds. Thirdly, they secured a group of houses belonging to friends, but these were near *The Pioneer* office, and as this was intolerable to the stately journal, and some of the houses were within Cantonment limits, the military authorities refused to allow these to be used, and so all were rendered impossible. Finally, just seven weeks before the meeting—while the authorities were chuckling over their success—a representative of the Reception Committee slipped quietly over to Lucknow, with a carefully drawn lease and the rent in his pocket, went to a Nawab whose splendid house in Allahabad, standing in large grounds, happened to be vacant, and persuaded him to accept the rent and sign the lease. On the very next day, the Reception Committee walked in and took possession, and Lowther Castle, in the very middle of the civilian quarter, nodded to its next-door neighbour, Government House, where Sir Auckland Colvin fumed in helpless wrath. It was outside the Cantonments, so the military authorities could not again interfere, and the lease foiled the civilians. So there the Congress met, and a huge pandal was raised, seating 5,000 persons, while a splendid shamiana (tent) lent by the Maharaja of Darbhanga, served as a general reception room, and another was lent by a Muhammadan nobleman to serve as a reading-room, almost every paper in India—except the Anglo-Indian—being sent gratuitously; round these arose blocks of tents, divided by wide roads, each block having its own dining and meeting halls, the whole forming a finely decorative city, while Lowther Castle itself was used for the President, Secretaries and leading delegates, with all the business offices. A quarter was set aside for shops, where salesmen offered the beautiful Indian manufactures of the U. P., but, the Report says, spirituous liquors and intoxicants of all kinds were rigidly excluded.

An attempt at counter-opposition to the Congress movement was made, and some Anti-Congress Associations were formed, attended by the officials, adding much warmth and enthusiasm to the Congress; and many secret gifts reached it at Lowther Castle, the Nicodemuses coming by night and the anxiety that the names of the givers should not be known being pathetic. Nor was it unreasonable, for one means of oppression often resorted to then, as now, was demanding heavy security for good behaviour, without any charge being made. A gentleman who had attended the Madras Congress, "in defiance of his district officer, a most rabid anti-Congressman," was called on to give security of Rs. 20,000 to keep the peace. He gave it and went away, feeling that if he appealed and won his case, there would be some serious charge made up against him by the police. "In one district of the Panjab, in one year, security for good behaviour, etc., was demanded from between 5,000 and 6,000 people. Free English people should realise something of all this, before they condemn our poor people too strongly for not having the courage of their convictions." This was written in 1889, long before there was any "unrest".

The Report says:

> Whether there is any wisdom in a system of persecution, that, while it stimulates to greater activity in secret, keeps nearly three-fourths of a movement like the

Congress out of sight, we must leave it to others to decide. But this much is certain: The Congress idea has now obtained such a hold upon the mind of the country that no earthly power can extinguish it. If ten thousand of the most prominent Congressmen were deported to-morrow, the idea would still creep on, spreading from mind to mind, till it had seized every man, woman and child amongst the Indian population, ever growing stronger and stronger in every mind which had received the seed. It is essentially beneficent in its character and, in its open growth, instinct with peace and goodwill to men. Official opposition and persecution will not only add to its growth, but will operate to convert an open, above-board, constitutional movement, into a secret, underground, and, therefore, unconstitutional one. There was towards the close of Lord Lytton's administration a great deal of secret organisation for unavowed, and, probably, even to its originators scarcely understood, purposes: though none who have studied history can doubt in what this would have eventuated. It has been the chief glory of the Congress movement that, aided by the enthusiasm elicited by good Lord Ripon's sympathetic rule, it has swept away all this fungoid undergrowth, and sweetened all political agitation by working it out into the wholesome light of the open day. It will be the fault of the Bureaucracy—and the Bureaucracy alone—if, by the unconstitutional abuse of their authority and powers, they drive a portion of the national energy back into the old, disused and illegitimate channels.

Alike for England and India, whose fortunes are now inextricably interwoven, no more gravely significant question exists at the present day for consideration. If England only invites and welcomes the confidence of India, and receives, with kindly consideration, the loyal suggestions (not necessarily adopting all, but treating them with the respect to which they are entitled) of the Congress which, year by year, more and more thoroughly represent the views of the whole thinking portion of the nation, all will be well for both countries. As a great Indian Prince recently said, after hearing the resolutions passed at the several Congresses: "If only these things be conceded, the rule of the British in India will last for ever." But if Viceroys and other high functionaries are to be permitted to sneer at and misrepresent the aspirations of a great nation, if subordinate officials are to be allowed unconstitutionally to oppose loyal political movements and persecute honest and earnest men for temperately and candidly setting forth what they hold to be their grievances and the best methods of redressing these—if England fancies, in a word, that she can maintain by fear a rule that only love can immortalise, then serious troubles only too probably await both countries.

The development of the Congress movement during 1888 was very great; hundreds of thousands of pamphlets and leaflets were distributed, hundreds of men travelled and gave lectures, and, as a result, three millions of men "took a direct part in the elections for the delegates". In Calcutta the women of some of the highest Hindu families discussed the "Kangress," and in Allahabad some even quarrelled with old friends because they were "anti"; some even did puja (offered worship) for it. The result of all this was that the number of delegates attending doubled that of Madras in 1887; 1,500 were elected and 1,248 attended. They were thus made up:

Madras	95
Bombay and Sindh	163
Panjab	80
N. W. P. & Oudh	583
C. P. & Berar	73
Bengal, Behar, Orissa & Assam	254
	1,248

Moulvi Muhammad Hidayut Rasul explained the large band of delegates from Oudh as "due to the kindness of our brethren in the Aligarh camp—the opponents of the Congress". This doubling of delegates was the more remarkable, as each delegate was, for the first time, required to pay a fixed fee before taking his seat.

The Congress opened on December 26th, 1888, at 2 p.m., the Hon. Pandit Ayudhianath, the Chairman of the Reception Committee, in the chair. He gave the details above mentioned as to their tribulations in house-hunting, and protested warmly against the unwarrantable accusations made by Sir Auckland Colvin and Lord Dufferin, resenting especially the letter of the former to "our most esteemed but much abused friend, Mr. Hume".

The Hon. Mr. Pherozeshah Mehta proposed and Sardar Dayal Singh seconded the election of Mr. Yule as President. Sheikh Raza Hassein Khan, in supporting the election, produced a Fatwa, supporting the Congress, from the Shamsululma, the leader of the Sunni community of Lucknow, and declared that "it is not the Muhammadans, but their official masters, who are opposed to the Congress".

Mr. Yule, in his presidential speech, argued for the right of representation, pointing out that in 1858, the objection raised to the Bill for the Government of India brought in by Lord Palmerston was that it gave no representation. Mr. Disraeli, succeeding almost immediately, brought in another Bill, in which he regretted that the unsettled state of the country made representation impossible at that time, and suggested a queer hybrid scheme which was withdrawn, and a third scheme was brought in, a provisional one, to continue while education spread so as to enable the political powers of Indians to be enlarged. The House of Commons, meanwhile, was to regard India as "a great and solemn trust committed to it by an all-wise and inscrutable Providence". "The 650 odd members," said Mr. Yule caustically, had thrown the trust "back upon the hands of Providence, to be looked after as Providence itself thinks best". The Congress was only asking for that which, thirty years before, the Government declared to be desirable. India had an immense trade, but no member of the mercantile class had power to influence the laws controlling it. India paid £77,000,000 in taxes, and not a man of the country had a voice in its disposal. It had 3,300,000 students, a number only lately reached in England, and they should supply material for some representatives. "In England, we should be trusted citizens. In India, well, the charitably minded among our opponents say that we are incipient traitors."

A Subjects' Committee was then elected, the country being divided into Circles, and a number of members being appointed to each, 106 in all, each circle electing its own members.

The first thing next day was the presentation of a silver casket containing rupees to the President, the rupees for Congress expenses, the casket for himself. Resolution I up to the words "Resolution IV of the Congress of 1886," was then proposed by the Hon. Mr. K. T. Telang, who, in moving it, effectively answered Sir Auckland Colvin's and Lord Dufferin's attacks. Mr. Surendranath Bannerji seconded, remarking that he was thankful for the opposition to the Congress. "Causes the noblest, the most beneficent, the most far reaching in their consequences for good, have never prospered or triumphed except under the stress of adverse criticism." Moreover Lord Dufferin's attack had reached the English Nation, and Mr. Gladstone, who three months before had not known the programme of the Congress, had said, speaking at a great meeting: "It will not do for us to treat with contempt, or even with indifference, the rising aspirations of this great people." Mr. Bannerji remarked on the extreme moderation of their proposals—and in truth they were absurdly moderate. They asked to substitute for the one-third non-official members who were nominated, one half non-official members, who should be elected; they asked that the Budgets for which they supplied the money should be submitted to them, and that they should have the right of interpellation and calling for papers. 27 years have passed, and these demands are but very partially granted. Pandit Bishan Narayan Dhar assured his hearers that "if you go on making your appeal with fairness, courage and moderation to the great English Nation, they will assuredly respond to your prayers, for as the harp responds to the harper's touch, so does the great deep heart of England respond to every reasonable prayer for justice and freedom". A very beautiful simile, and it is true, except in the case of India, where the harp has been touched for thirty years, and has not yet moved that heart to respond.

Lala Lajpat Rai—whose name, so loved and honoured now, appears for the first time among the Congress speakers—very usefully quoted the opinions of Sir Syed Ahmed, who was a strong opponent of the Congress, but who, in his book, *Causes of the Indian Revolt,* written in 1858, had stated "that the people should have a voice in its Councils" was necessary to the stability of the Government, so as to "warn us of dangers before they burst upon and destroy us". "The evils which came to India," wrote Sir Syed, "from the non-admission of natives into the Legislative Councils of India were various." At the time Sir Syed wrote, even nominees of Government to the Council were not allowed.

Mr. S. Ramaswami Mudaliar placed a simple fact before the Congress, showing that the Resolution did not advocate a leap in the dark :

> Gentlemen, while we are humbly praying our Government to grant us some small representative element in the Government, we have actually got full-blown representative institutions flourishing in this country under our very noses. I do not know whether you are aware how they are flourishing in Pondicherry and other places which are subject to the French Government. England will not as yet allow us the smallest modicum of representative institutions, but in Pondicherry every man has a right to elect his representative. He enjoys manhood suffrage! Not only that, but the people of Pondicherry

have got a member of their own in the Chamber of Deputies and another in the Senate. Then in Pondicherry itself they have got a Council which is called the Council-General, and which meets every year, and this is an elective body elected by the whole people. Before this Council is placed the Annual Budget, and the Budget is fully discussed by the members. The Budget is there threshed out by that body, and it is not until, after this discussion, it has been approved that it comes into operation. Gentlemen, it is said that we are not fit for representative institutions, but it is our fellow countrymen, our relatives in many cases, no better educated than, and in no wise different from ourselves, whom the French Government has found to be fitted, not only for the small instalment of representative institutions that we ask for, but for fully-developed representative institutions, including manhood suffrage, which none of us ever even dream of demanding. I commend this fact to the careful consideration of our opponents, who deny our fitness for even those small reforms we crave.

It would hardly be possible to imagine an argument more cogent, a contrast more poignant.

A most extraordinary incident then occurred. Raja Shiva Prasad, who had become notorious as a leader of the anti-Congress movement, had by some curious accident obtained election at a public meeting at Benares, and claimed his seat as a delegate. He rose to move an amendment, and used his time in attacking the Congress and presented as an amendment a draft of a petition to the Lieut.-Governor, quoting without references supposed statements made in unnamed pamphlets and articles, till the President stopped him, as the petition was in no sense an amendment; whereupon the egregious Raja sat down, and the Congress became serious again. A proposal was made, seconded and accepted, to add to the Resolution the concluding words as printed, and it was then carried unanimously.

Mr. Eardley Norton made a vigorous speech in moving Resolution II; he quoted the views of Sir Robert Peel and Mr. Charles Grant. Sir Robert Peel had declared that the duty of England was "to endeavour while we still keep them under British rule, to atone to them for the sufferings they endured, and the wrongs to which they were exposed in being reduced to that rule, and to afford them such advantages and confer on them such benefits as may in some degree console them for the loss of their independence. These, Sir, are considerations which, whatever may be the anxiety to extend British conquest, and to maintain the rights of British subjects, must indisputably be entertained in a British Parliament." The fact is that during the rule of the East India Company, Parliament interfered at 20 years' intervals to check the oppression of the Indian people. After 1858, Parliament grew indifferent, and a Bureaucracy developed. Mr. Norton said that, as an Englishman, he was ashamed of England's broken promises to India. He quoted the Duke of Argyll, who said that they had not fulfilled "the promises and engagements which we have made," and Lord Lytton who said that the Indians had been "cheated" of their hopes. The Hon. Mr. Pherozeshah Mehta briefly seconded, but the Resolution was not in the form finally passed, but approved and recited the report of the Congress of 1886.

Mr. John Adam moved and Mr. Sankara Menon seconded an amendment, acknowledging that the proposals of the Public Services Commission were an improvement, and reaffirming Resolution IV of the Congress of 1885. On this the Congress adjourned.

The third day began by sending a telegram of thanks and good wishes to Mr. John Bright, then lying ill, and after this Mr. Ramaswami Mudaliar moved another amendment, suggesting that the consideration of the questions dealt with by the Public Service Commission be postponed to the next Congress, and the Hon. Mr. K. T. Telang seconded. Then Mr. Monomohan Ghose proposed Resolution II as it stands below, and Mr. N. D. Chandavarkar seconded. The original resolution and the various amendments were withdrawn, and the Resolution unanimously carried.

Resolution III, re-affirming Resolution XI of the Congress of 1886 was carried unanimously, and then Resolution IV, embodying three former ones, was carried, the only noticeable point being the first appearance of Mr. N. Subba Rao as a speaker. I like to note the coming on to the stage of one after another of our present workers.

Perhaps one of the most sarcastic and effective speeches ever delivered on the Police introduced Resolution V on Police Administration; the mover was Munshi Sajjad Husain, the editor of the Lucknow *Punch*. He spoke in Urdu, but even the translation is delightful. The British Government had bestowed on them many blessings, and had also given them the Police. No Lieut.-Governor, no Viceroy, had such power over his comfort as a simple chowkidar or his honour the constable.

> The humblest labourer in the village, the most exalted noble in the city, are equally under the control of these distinguished officials. There is no place, no spot, where Their Highnesses the Police, like the Angel of Death, are not present. Let a man displease them in the slightest, and see the beneficence of our kind Police. He may know nothing about it, but there will be a criminal case filed against him, and arrangements made for requiring him to give security for good behaviour, before he can reach his home.

On the whole, the editor of *Punch* thought that the Police were more troublesome to the honest people than to the thieves and badmashes, and the investigation into a theft was more annoying than the robbery. So let other people advocate reforms of Legislative Councils and other such questions. He wanted the reform of the Police.

Mr. R. N. Mudholkar seconded the Resolution in an admirable speech, pointing out that the policeman, who ought to be loved, was detested, because, being shamefully underpaid and quite illiterate, he was invested with enormous powers, so that he could annoy and insult all around him with impunity. Mr. Pringle noted the importance of the Resolution, because the police, like the poor, were always with us, and he gave instances of their ill behaviour, declaring that "to the character and conduct of the police in my own part of the country I can speak with confidence, and can boldly assert that it leaves almost everything to be desired". One after another rose, all speaking in the same strain, and the Resolution, asking for a Commission of Enquiry, was carried unanimously.

Then came the reaffirmation of three military resolutions passed at previous Congresses, and much stress was laid on the enormous cost of English soldiers, and the remark of Lord Randolph Churchill was quoted that the new taxation, which was wholly "a consequence of the foreign rule imposed on the country" was "a serious political danger . . . . of the most serious order". Mr. Ali Muhammad Bhimji remarked that he might have a West Indian servant who might carry arms, while his Indian master might not. Amendments were proposed, modifying or omitting one part of the Resolution or another; especially as regarded the Arms Act, but the Hon. Mr. P. M. Mehta urged that "you cannot and ought not to emasculate a whole nation. . . . Remember, that when once the Indian people become emasculated, it will be a very long time indeed before you can get them to recover their manliness and their vigour," and the Resolution was finally carried by a large majority.

Mr. D. E. Wacha moved a less vigorous form of Resolution VII, asking that the Government would look into the question of Abkari and Excise, and rejoiced that the Congress had taken up the question. But an amendment was agreed to, which was shorter and more pointed, and was carried unanimously.

Pandit Madan Mohan Malaviya proposed Resolution VIII, and at the close of his speech warmly protested against the assertion by a high official that the promises in the Queen's Proclamation of 1858 "were made more as a matter of policy than in honest good faith," and read an extract from a letter from the Queen, showing Her Majesty's wish that the Indians should be "placed on an equality with the subjects of the British Crown," and saying that she was "giving them pledges which her future reign is to redeem". The learned Pandit remarked that "we hope and trust they will be soon redeemed". He is still hoping and trusting.

After other speeches, the Resolution was carried and the Congress adjourned.

The fourth day of the Congress opened with the gift of a hall for the Divisional Congress in the Southern Maratha country by Mr. Ramachandra Bahdeva Apte, and the mention of innumerable letters and telegrams of congratulation. Mr. Adam, the Principal of Pachaiyappa's College, then moved Resolution IX on Education, saying that they desired "to extend primary education, to broaden secondary education, and to maintain at the highest now possible, and an ever rising level, higher education". He complained that Government policy in education was retrograde, and that Schools and Colleges were being closed for want of support from the Imperial Government. The Hon. Mr. K. T. Telang seconded, complaining that while Government had always money for its very varied activities, it gave only 1 per cent of its revenues to education. Mr. G. Subramania Iyer supported, urging that only by the spread of education could the country adapt itself to the abandonment of old ways and the acceptance of new, brought about by the English connexion, and that there was a growing idea, which he himself did not share, that the check to higher education was an answer to the Congress demands for political power. Other speakers followed and the Resolution was unanimously passed.

As it was Mr. Gladstone's birthday a telegram of good wishes was then sent amid loud applause.

Rai Tej Narayan Singh Bahadur next moved Resolution X, asking for a Commission to enquire into the industrial condition of the country, and it was seconded by Mr. Ananda Charlu. Some of the delegates wished to add riders on emigration and on technical schools, but the Resolution as it stood was eventually carried. Then Mr. W. C. Bannerji—after a proposal on Land Settlement had been made and withdrawn—moved Resolution XI, submitting the Resolutions to the Viceroy and Her Majesty's Government, and asking for a Parliamentary Committee to look into the grievances complained of. In 1885 the Congress had asked for a Royal Commission, but they asked now only for a Parliamentary Committee as swifter in its action, and appealed to Mr. Bradlaugh, M. P., to support their prayer. He again declared that the British public, "a truth-loving and a justice-loving public," would give them what they wanted. Pandit Bishambhar Nath, in seconding, remarked that if Sir Auckland Colvin had been in that assembly, he would have seen that "the creation of a healthy tone of independence in India," which he declared was impossible, was developing hand-in-hand with enthusiastic loyalty to Her Majesty's Throne. After four other speakers had supported it, the Resolution was carried unanimously.

Resolution XII was moved by Captain Banon in a strong speech, and seconded by Captain Hearsay, who pointed out that over 2,000 Indian women were procured by Government "for the hideous purpose alluded to," that the provision encouraged the boy-soldiers to loose living, and that it would be better to encourage the soldiers to marry. The resolution was supported by Mr. Howard and Moulvi Muhammed Hafiz, and carried unanimously. Resolution XIII was then warmly supported and passed, so as to avoid the acceptance of any resolution dealing with a purely Hindu or Muhammadan question against the will of those who would be affected by it—a resolution bearing witness to the sagacity and impartiality of the Congress.

The question of Permanent Settlement, which had been withdrawn, was again brought up by a show of hands in favour of it, and a resolution on it was proposed, seconded and supported. The question was felt to be of such magnitude, that an amendment, Resolution XIV, proposed by the Hon. Mr. K. T. Telang, was unanimously passed, the original resolution being withdrawn. Resolution XV had been rejected by the Standing Committee as useless, but was insisted on by the Congress and unanimously carried. Bombay or Poona was then chosen for the next Congress, and Mr. A. O. Hume was, amid great applause, "re-elected" General Secretary. It is curious that this is the first resolution on the record with regard to a General Secretary, an office filled practically by Mr. Hume from the first Congress. His courage, the attacks made on him, and his devotion, marked him out for the post.

A vote of thanks to the President followed, and the Fourth Congress was dissolved.

RESOLUTIONS

Representation

I. Resolved—That this Congress affirms the necessity for the expansion and reform of the Council of the Governor-General for making laws and regulations, and of the existing Provincial Legislative Councils, already set forth in Resolutions III of the Congress of 1885 and 1886, and Resolution II of the Congress of 1887 (a tentative scheme for which expansion and reform was suggested in Resolution IV of the Congress of 1886); and further urges that a Legislative Council (of the same character as those which have been suggested for Provinces where Legislative Councils already exist) be established for the Panjab.

Public Service

II. Resolved—That this Congress, while appreciating the concessions proposed in the Report of the Public Service Commission, yet feels it necessary to put distinctly on record its opinion that full justice will never be done to the people of this country until the open competitive examination for the Civil Service of India is held simultaneously in England and in India.

Legal

III. Resolved—That this Congress, having read and considered Resolution XI of the Congress of 1886, to wit—

(See Resolution XI, 1886)

and Resolution III of the Congress of 1887, to the same effect, does now, hereby, affirm the same respectively.

IV. Resolved—That this Congress, having read and considered Resolution VIII of the Congress of 1886, to wit—

(See Resolution VIII, 1886)

Resolution IX of the Congress of 1886, to wit—

(See Resolution IX, 1886)

and Resolution X of the Congress of 1886, to wit—

(See Resolution X, 1886)

does now, hereby, affirm the same respectively.

Police

V. Resolved—That, as it is the general belief of the people of this country that the existing system of police administration in India is highly unsatisfactory in itself and oppressive to them, the Government be respectfully urged to appoint a Commission, consisting of official and non-official members, to investigate the entire question as speedily as possible.

Military

VI. Resolved—That this Congress having read and considered Resolution IV of the Congress of 1887, to wit—

(See Resolution IV, 1887)

Resolution XII of the Congress of 1886, and Resolution V of the Congress of 1887, to wit—

(See Resolution XII, 1886, and Resolution V, 1887)

and Resolution VIII of the Congress of 1887, to wit--

(See Resolution VIII, 1887)

does now, hereby, affirm the same respectively.

Temperance

VII. Resolved—That, having regard to the fact that a serious increase in the consumption of intoxicants has taken place under the systems of Abkari and Excise now prevailing in India, the Government be respectfully urged to adopt some such improved system as shall tend to discourage insobriety.

Taxation

VIII. Resolved—That as the administration of the Income Tax, especially as regards incomes below Rs. 1,000, has proved extremely unsatisfactory, it is essential, in the opinion of the Congress, that the taxable minimum be raised to Rs. 1,000.

Education

IX. Resolved—That this Congress being of opinion that it is the first duty of the British Government in India to foster and encourage education, as well general as technical, in all its branches, and that the declaration made in the recent resolution of the Government of India on the subject of education is calculated to encourage the tendency to reduce imperial expenditure on education, and to withdraw from the control of it, respectfully urges upon Government the extreme importance of increasing, or at any rate of not decreasing, the present expenditure on education, and of the Government continuing to control the Educational Institutions of all kinds now existing.

X. Resolved—That having regard to the poverty of the people, the importance of encouraging indigenous manufactures, and the difficulty of practically introducing any general system of technical education with the present imperfect information, Government be moved to delay no longer the appointment of a mixed Commission, to enquire into the present industrial condition of the country.

Request for a Parliamentary Committee

XI. Resolved—That the foregoing Resolutions be submitted for the favourable consideration of His Excellency the Viceroy, and for transmission by him to Her Majesty's Government, with the humble request of this Congress that the reforms suggested in the said Resolutions (based as most of these are on Her Gracious Majesty's Proclamation of 1858, may now be effected; and that should it be deemed necessary first to institute any enquiry into any of the matters forming the subjects of these Resolutions, such enquiry may be made, as speedily as possible, by a Parliamentary Committee.

Prostitution

XII. Resolved—That this Congress, having watched with interest and sympathy the exertions that are being made in England for the total abrogation of laws and rules relating to the regulation of prostitution by the State in India, places on record its appreciation of the services thus rendered to this country, and its desire to co-operate by all means in its power in the attainment of this laudable object.

Congress Constitution

XIII. Resolved—That no subject shall be passed for discussion by the Subjects Committee, or allowed to be discussed at any Congress by the President thereof, to the introduction of which the Hindu or Muhammadan Delegates as a body object, unanimously or nearly unanimously; and that if, after the discussion of any subject which has been admitted for discussion, it shall appear that all the Hindu or all the Muhammadan Delegates as a body are unanimously or nearly unanimously opposed to the Resolution which it is proposed to pass thereon, such Resolution shall be dropped; provided that this rule shall refer only to subjects in regard to which the Congress has not already definitely pronounced an opinion.

Permanent Settlement

XIV. Resolved—That the question of the introduction of a Permanent Settlement of the Land Revenue Demand into the Madras and Bombay Presidencies and other Provinces be referred to the several standing Congress Committees, with instructions to report upon the same, in so far as it affects their respective circles, to the Congress of 1889.

Salt Tax

XV. Resolved—That this Congress puts on record its disapproval of the recent enhancement of the Salt Tax, as involving a perceptible increase to the burthens of the poorer classes, as also the partial absorption, in a time of peace and plenty, of the only Financial Reserve of the Empire.

Formal

XVI. Resolved—That the Fifth Indian National Congress do assemble in the Bombay Presidency (either at Bombay itself or at Poona, as may be settled hereafter) on the 26th of December, 1889.

XVII. Resolved—That Mr. A. O. Hume be re-appointed General Secretary for the ensuing year.

CHAPTER V

The Congress of 1889 was signalised by the extraordinary welcome given by it, and by India, to Mr. Charles Bradlaugh, M. P., that noble English Democrat, who might say with Thomas Paine: "The world is my country, and to do good my religion"; for wherever there was a country striving to free itself from oppression, there his trumpet-voice rang out for Liberty, there he stood in the breach to defend and to strengthen. "Member for India," he was rightly called, for he spoke for her in the Council Chamber of the Empire.

The Fifth Congress met in Bombay on December 26th, 1889, and found there warm welcome, the clouds which lowered over Allahabad having wholly dissolved away. Sir Albert Sassoon lent the site for the great temporary Hall, into which 6,000 people packed themselves, 1,913 of whom were delegates. 2,500 delegates had been elected, 1,889 registered their names, and another 24 paid for their tickets, but unfortunately did not register. Glancing over the register, we find people of all professions and trades from all parts of the country—princes, landlords, peasants, merchants, contractors, barristers, vakils, pleaders, solicitors, attorneys, principals, headmasters, professors, teachers, editors, money-lenders, bankers, brokers, manufacturers, traders, shopkeepers, artisans, doctors, sardars, printers, authors, reises, taluqdars, a judge, a munsiff, nine clergymen and missionaries, and ten ladies, seven of whom were Indians. A striking fact is the large number of merchants and zemindars, and also of secretaries of public bodies, municipal commissioners and members of boards. The delegates divided by Provinces were :

Madras	366
Bombay and Sindh	821
Panjab	62
N.W.P and Oudh	261
C.P. and Berar	214
Bengal, Behar, Orissa, Assam	165
	1,889

Bombay sent 38 delegates to the Bombay Congress of 1885, and to this Bombay Congress in 1889 it sent 821. There were 2 Muhammadans at the first Congress, 254 at the fifth. Comment is needless.

Mr. Pherozeshah M. Mehta was the Chairman of the Reception Committee, and to him fell, therefore, the pleasant duty of welcoming the Congress, and of asking it to elect formally its President. He spoke of "the nationalising tendency which is now so powerfully leavening New India," and after alluding to the way in which the Congress had surmounted all difficulties, he welcomed him "whom we have learned to hail as the Member for India in the British House of

Commons," on whom had descended the mantle of John Bright and Professor Fawcett.

Mr. W. C. Bannerji then proposed, the Hon. Pandit Ayodhyanath seconded, and Raja T. Rama Rao supported, the election of Sir William Wedderburn as President, and he took the Chair amid enthusiastic cheers.

Sir William Wedderburn laid stress on the destruction of the safeguards—which existed in the time of the East India Company in Parliamentary control and periodical enquiry—by the Crown taking over the Government of India in 1858, from which he dated India's principal misfortunes. He showed how the India Office had strangled the scheme for Agricultural Banks, sent up by Lord Ripon, saying that it was not "practicable". "I wonder," said Sir William, "whether Sir J. Gorst is aware that in Germany alone there are 2,000 such Agricultural Banks in active working, and that throughout the Continent of Europe it is admitted that without such financial institutions the peasant proprietor is absolutely unable to maintain himself without falling into the clutches of the village usurer." He praised the work of the Congress, and of the Congress Agency in England, with "its indefatigable Secretary Mr. William Digby," and rejoiced over the going to England of a deputation to appeal to the people of England "to perform their trust and duty towards the unrepresented millions of India: appeals to unselfishness, to justice and to humanity will ever find a sure response from the great heart of the British people". The response has not yet reached India; it has a long way to come.

Two presentations were made to the President, at the close of his address, towards the expenses of the Congress, with a book and a silver salver as mementoes for himself. The names of the delegates elected from each circle to the Subjects Committee—among which we note that of Mr. B. G. Tilak—were then read out, 107 in number, and ratified by Congress, the President and Secretary making 109, sitting on it *ex officio*, and the Congress adjourned to the following day, leaving the Committee to its labours.

The second day's sitting began with the presentation of the report from the Standing Committee of Madras, but none other was forthcoming. Mr. Pherozeshah M. Mehta then proposed Resolution I; he said it was impossible to present all the addresses and telegrams which had come pouring in from all parts of the country, so it was better to frame an address to Mr. Bradlaugh from the Congress and take the rest as read. The Hon. Pandit Ayodhyanath and Mr. John Adam seconded and supported, and the resolution was carried by acclamation.

The President then opened the important business of the day, the reform of the Legislative Councils, saying that a draft Bill had been prepared by Mr. Bradlaugh and circulated, embodying the view of the Congress as so far expressed. Mr. Bradlaugh wished to obtain the mature opinion of the Indian people on certain matters, so that they might be embodied in the Bill. Certain proposals had therefore been drafted, and must be considered.

Mr. Eardley Norton moved Resolution II with the Scheme, giving an outline of principles to be embodied in a Bill. The existing Councils were shams, and they demanded to be given half of each Council, "to do with as we choose". Given this principle of election: "We shall have the right to control ourselves; we shall have the right, to a certain extent, to control our taxation; we shall have the right to criticise the Budget; and last, but not least, we shall have the glorious privilege of interpellation, a right which, if properly applied, will inure to the enormous benefit both of the rulers and of the ruled." The indirect method of election was proposed, because there was no chance of obtaining direct, and because the various bodies already existing, Municipalities, Boards, Universities, etc., would really give to Government the power of manipulating the electorates. The Hon. Pandit Ayodhyanath, in seconding, said that the existing Councils were a farce, and Pandit Bishen Narayan Dhar remarked that if the Government really wished to know the opinion of the people, the principle of election must be accepted:

> The chief plank of the Congress platform is the *elective* principle, and we are not going to be satisfied with a thing that will be a snare, a mockery, and a delusion, leading men to believe that they have something which they do not really possess. What we want is not sham, but reality; not shadow, but substance; not nomination, which is another name for deception, but representation, which is the essence of political reform.

Among the speakers who supported the resolution were Mr. G. Subramania Iyer, Mr. Bepin Chandra Pal, Lala Lajpat Rai, Pandit Madan Mohan Malaviya —who showed, by the increase of the Salt Tax and the compelling of the ryot to pay the Patwari Cess twice over, how much out of touch with the poor were the nominated members—and Mr. Surendranath Bannerji, who once more expressed his certainty that there could " come but one response, which, I am confident, will be in accord with the great traditions of the English people, and will serve to consolidate the foundations of British rule in India, and to broad-base it upon the affections of a happy, prosperous and contented people ". Congress speakers show a remarkable readiness to prophesy, with an equally remarkable failure to prophesy correctly.

The Scheme was put clause by clause, and 1 and 2 passed unchallenged. On clause 3 it was moved, unsuccessfully, to strike out the word " male," so that qualified women might vote.

On clause 5 an amendment was moved by Mr. Tilak and seconded by Mr. Gokhale, that the Imperial Council should be elected by the Provincial Councils, instead of by the Electoral College. The amendment is noteworthy as coming from two strong men, speaking in the Congress for the first time, men who were to leave on Indian history an ineffaceable mark. The amendment was lost, as was another leaving the representatives of minorities to be nominated by Government. A lively little incident then occurred, one of the Musalman delegates making a violent speech, in which he claimed that his co-religionists should be elected in equal numbers with Hindus although the population was smaller; the proposition was seconded, but was also opposed by Musalmans, who regarded it as unjust; finally the original clause was carried by an overwhelming majority of both communities, and the Congress was adjourned.

The third day, December 28th, was overloaded with business, and the Congress, this year, met for three days only; a meeting was fixed at 6 p. m. for the presentation of an address to Mr. Bradlaugh, so the sitting had to close at 5. The first business was the passing of Resolution III, an "Omnibus Resolution," in which were re-affirmed, in ten clauses, important decisions arrived at in previous Congresses. It was moved by Mr. Kalicharan Bannerji, seconded by Mr. N. G. Chandavarkar, and supported by Mr. S. B. Senkaram, who stated that he was a Brahmana and a Volunteer, having been admitted to the Vizagapatam Rifle Volunteer Corps. The Resolution was then carried.

Resolution IV was proposed by the Rev. G. M. Cobban, and seconded by Mr. D. E. Wacha, who pointed out that the House of Commons had directed the Government of India to modify their excise policy so as to meet the wishes of the people; after nine months, however, the Government had done nothing. The Rev. Messrs. R. A. Hume and Evans supported it, and the Resolution was carried unanimously.

Mr. S. Ramaswami Mudaliar then moved Resolution V, and criticised very adversely the despatch of the Secretary of State on the Report of the Public Service Commission, making the position of Indians, except as to age, worse than it was before the Commission, for the Indian officials were compelled either to remain in the positions they then held in the Statutory Service, or to enter the Provincial Service, the members of which were barred from all the higher executive offices. Indians, he said, only asked for "a fair field and no favour"; "we want the best men we can get, and if the Europeans can beat the Indians in a fair competition, let them do so". Mr. G. K. Gokhale seconded the Resolution, and spoke plainly and sternly, with the ring of steady purpose for which he afterwards became famous:

Fifty-six years have come and gone since the promise was first made that no distinction of race or creed or colour should be allowed to stand in the way of the prospects of preferment of any native of India. That noble promise then made—a promise worthy of the highest and most generous attitude of England towards any of the countries with which she has ever come into contact—was reiterated in yet stronger terms in the proclamation of 1858. The terms of the enactment of 1833 and of the proclamation of 1858 are so explicit that those who now try to withhold from us the privileges then assured to us must be prepared to face the painful dilemma of hypocrisy or treachery—must be prepared to admit that England was insincere when she made those promises, or that she is prepared to break faith with us now.

Gentlemen, you may be aware that an English Judge famous (or infamous) in a way, did not scruple to accept this latter position, and propound the preposterous doctrine that the proclamation of 1858 was never meant to be seriously taken. I hope however that there are not many Englishmen of that kind. With these noble promises of 1833 and 1858 before us, I ask you, are we not entitled to say that the least we expect from our English rulers is that they should always show a steadily progressive tendency towards the fulfilment of these promises?

Mr. Gokhale urged that there were three points, before the Commission sat, of importance to Indians: first, competitive examinations; secondly, in the Statutory Covenanted Service, one-sixth of the posts, by the enactment of 1861, were reserved for Indians; thirdly, the Uncovenanted Service was wholly Indian. The Commission refused simultaneous examinations, though "for posts in our own country, if we are not to be examined in our own country, I do not know what justice and equity are". Secondly, only 108 posts, out of 941 reserved for the Covenanted Service, instead of 158, the one-sixth belonging to Indians, might be reserved for Indians in the higher branch of the Uncovenanted Service, re-named the Provincial Service. The Commissioners recommended that 108 *should* be given; The Secretary of State said *may*. "We may be given 108 places, leaving it to the discretion of the Government, and we know what that means. For every one of these 108 places that we shall have, half a dozen will go to the European official class." The status of Indians was distinctly changed for the worse by the Commission, and this is one of the many cases in which the Crown—which is not Crown but Bureaucratic—Government has proved worse for

India than the old East India Company rule. The Resolution, supported by Mr. John Adam and Mr. Ali Muhammad Bhimji was unanimously passed.

The official Report says that a suspicion is "beginning to gain ground in India, that England's policy towards us is changing, and is no longer actuated by quite those same noble and lofty motives that, in bye-gone days, threw a halo round the British name". That suspicion has grown during the 26 years since those words were written. Mr. Ali Muhammad Bhimji pointed to the Commission of 1860, recommending simultaneous examinations; Lord Stanley had said with regard to this, that

> he could not "refrain from expressing his conviction that in refusing to carry on examinations in India as well as in England, a thing that was easily practicable, the Government were in fact negativing that which they had declared to be one of the principal objects of their Bill, and confining the Civil Service as heretofore to Englishmen. The result was unjust and he believed it would be most pernicious." Then again Lord Stanley further said: "Let them suppose for instance, that instead of holding these examinations here in London, they were to be held in Calcutta; well, how many Englishmen would go there, or how many would send their sons perhaps to spend two or three years in the country, on the chance of obtaining an appointment? Nevertheless that was exactly the course proposed to be adopted towards the natives of India." These are the opinions that were expressed at the time, when the Commissioners came to the conclusion that simultaneous examinations should be held in India, and we are asking nothing more nor less than what they decided in 1860; and now 29 years have gone by, and the prospects then held out to us by one of England's wisest statesmen and endorsed by a Parliamentary Commission, prospects

based upon our Gracioùs Queen-Empress' solemn promises, have not yet been realised. I know that men have been found base enough—men traitors alike to their Queen and country—to assert that our beloved Empress' words were no promises, merely emotional utterances never intended to be acted upon. But how did an honest English statesman treat this dastardly stuff? What did Lord Ripon say? "The document (Her Majesty's Proclamation) is not a Treaty, it is not a diplomatic instrument; it is a declaration of principles of Government; if it is obligatory at all, it is obligatory in respect to all to whom it is addressed. The doctrine, therefore, to which Sir James Stephen has given the sanction of his authority, I feel bound to repudiate to the utmost of my power. It seems to me to be inconsistent with the character of my Sovereign and with the honour of my country, and if it were once to be received and acted upon by the Government of England, it would do more than anything else could possibly do to strike at the root of our power and to destroy our just influence."

Sir James Fitzjames Stephen was the man of whom Mr. Gokhale spoke as "an English Judge famous or infamous". But after all, Sir James has proved right.

Next came our old friend the Arms Act in Resolution VI, very carefully worded this year: proposed by Mr. John Adam, seconded by Lala Harbhagavan Das, and supported by three others, it was unanimously carried.

Resolution VII was moved by Mr. Baikunthnath Sen in an able and thoughtful speech, showing the historical aspect of the question; he pointed out that a famine in 1860 had led to a Commission, which reported in favour of the Permanent Settlement, and it was approved in a Despatch from the Secretary of State in 1862. There, however, it had remained. Mr. S. Subramania Iyer seconded, and said that, "in an inconsiderate moment," he had invested his savings in land fifteen years before; he found that, practically, all improvements were taxed, so he told his agent not to spend a rupee in improving the land; the revisions prevented improvements being made, and no recourse to the Courts against the secret orders of the Settlement Department could be made. Munshi Sadar-ud-din Ahmed, supporting, gave an instance of a revision by Mr. Colvin—later the Sir Auckland Colvin who so strongly objected to the Congress—in which the Government Revenue assessment made by him on a village exceeded the total gross produce of the village. The poor Zemindar, finding Mr. Colvin obdurate to all prayers, presented a petition, saying that his aged father, before his death, had foretold the coming of a Settlement Officer "in whose time the people would be so miserable and poverty-stricken that in their homes would neither be heard the sound of the grinding-mill, nor the glimmer of the lamp be seen, and that when this came to pass the best thing that he could do would be to give up all his rights and interests in his village to the Government, and become a mendicant". He therefore begged Mr. Colvin to put his own name in all the Revenue papers. Many others spoke from their own experience, and complained of the ignorance of the Settlement Officers. "No civil suit will lie—there is no remedy and no justice." One man said he was cruelly over-assessed, and on asking the officer to visit his fields and hear him on the spot, he was told by the officer that he " had no time for that sort of thing. No, they have no time for anything but to extort money out of the poor." And so the sad story went on ; in the old times the land assessment covered everything, but now :

" There is the same amount of water in the pot, but there are now six holes through which it runs out, when before there was but one."

" We had our cattle in plenty, lots of grazing free, and salt to keep them healthy—now the land is all taken up by the Forest Department and we have no grazing, and if the starving herds stray where there is food, they are run into the pound and we are fined."

" We had plenty of wood for our houses, our ploughs, for every agricultural purpose ; now it is all under the lock and key of the Forest Department, and if we touch it without leave we are run in, and if we want a stick we have a week's running about from one official to another before we get it, and we have to pay, pay, pay. We had arms, and we could shoot or destroy the wild beasts that ravage our crops, but now we have an Arms Act that allows a basket full of arms to every negro rascal who lands on our shores, but takes good care that we poor cultivators, who need them to protect our subsistence from wild animals, are practically debarred from any."

The peasants are still growing poorer and poorer under these conditions, while Land Revenue rises. Will none have pity ?

The Resolution was carried unanimously.

Mr. D. E. Wacha moved Resolution VIII, which was seconded, and carried unanimously. Thanks to Mr. Bradlaugh, this Resolution was successful.

Resolution IX was eminently reasonable, and absolutely necessary to the good government of India, but the House of Commons has, since India was taken over by the Crown, lost all interest in Indian affairs. Mr. W. C. Bannerji proposed and Mr. Shurf-ud-din seconded. Pandit Madan Mohan Malaviya spoke earnestly and effectively:

In the year 1883, the House of Commons passed a resolution to the effect that in the opinion of that House it is necessary that early steps be taken to reduce the expenditure of India. Lord Kimberley, our then Secretary of State, in his despatch, dated the 8th of June 1883, urged the Government of India to take the subject of the reduction of expenditure into their earliest consideration. Lord Randolph Churchill, our next Secretary of State, later on, said that "the financial position of India was very grave indeed, and required the most careful consideration, and the exercise of the most rigid economy was necessary in his opinion, in order to avoid bankruptcy". But the withdrawal of Parliamentary control seems to have emboldened the present Under-Secretary to take up a very different attitude. When complaints were made on the occasion of the last debate on the Indian Budget in the House of Commons, of the ever-growing increase of expenditure in India, Sir John Gorst met them boldly by saying that "expenditure has increased, it ought to increase, and it ought not to be diminished". And he tried to justify this view by asserting that the wealth and prosperity of the country was increasing. Now, gentlemen, no one would be more delighted than ourselves to know that the country was really growing in wealth and prosperity. But unhappily the stern reality of facts forbids us from consoling ourselves with such pleasing fancies. We look wistfully in all directions; we go deep into the Muffasal, we see our brethren in their homes and huts as they actually live; and far from seeing any indications of that increasing prosperity which Sir J. Gorst said he discerned at that distance, we find the people growing poorer and less and less able to maintain themselves, their wives and children, than they were before. And we therefore say, gentlemen, that the increase of expenditure is under existing circumstances not only unjustifiable, but positively sinful. The increase of public expenditure would undoubtedly be welcome if it followed upon an increase of wealth and prosperity among the people. There has been a large increase of revenue in England during the past quarter of a century. But it has followed an enormous growth of wealth and commerce in England and no one complains much of it. But in India public expenditure goes on increasing, while the condition of the people is deteriorating day by day. One simple but incontrovertible proof of this lies in the fact that almost all the recent additions to the revenue of the Government have been screwed out of the first necessities of the Indian people. To take only the most recent instances: increased expenditure has been met by enhancing the duty on salt, a thing necessary alike to man and cattle; by taxing the poor man's oil, as petroleum has rightly been called; by imposing a double tax on the famishing ryots of the North-Western Provinces and Oudh; and by misappropriating the Famine Insurance Fund, a fund especially created and promised by three Viceroys to be religiously set apart for meeting difficulties in times of scarcity and famine.

The Resolution was carried unanimously.

The Resolution of thanks to Lord Reay, Governor of Bombay (X), was moved by Mr. J. U. Yajnik, ex-Sheriff of Bombay, and he bore witness to the fact that Lord Reay's nominations reflected the wish of Indians; he had appointed Messrs. Ranade, Dadabhai Naoroji, Telang, Dayaram Jethmal, Pherozeshah Mehta, and others; "never before had such wisdom and impartiality been shown". It was supported by the Hon. Mr. C. Sankaran Nair, who wished other Provinces the good fortune enjoyed by Bombay,

Mr. H. A. Wadia, who wished Lord Reay would return as Viceroy, and others, and carried with acclamation.

Mr. Eardley Norton moved Resolution XI, because, owing to a mistake, the Subjects Committee had died prematurely; and Resolution XII re-elected Mr. A. O. Hume as General Secretary.

Resolution XIII dealt with organisation, and the number of delegates at future Congresses was limited to 1,000. In answer to an appeal for the Rs. 45,000, over Rs. 9,000 was paid in cash, and Rs. 56,226 promised within half an hour. The resolution was then passed, and Nos. XIV and XV—the latter thanking Sir William Wedderburn for coming from England for the Congress—were quickly carried. Then, the Fifth Congress, with a vote of thanks to the Reception Committee, dissolved.

RESOLUTIONS

I. Resolved—That an address be presented to Mr. Charles Bradlaugh, M.P., on behalf of this Congress here assembled, and that Messrs. Adam, Pherozeshah Mehta, and W. C. Bannerji are appointed a Committee to settle the wording of the said address.

Representation

II. Resolved—That the following skeleton scheme for the reform and reconstitution of the Council of the Governor-General for making Laws and Regulations, and the Provincial Legislative Councils, is adopted, and that the President of this Congress do submit the same to Charles Bradlaugh, Esq., M.P., with the respectful request of this Congress that he may be pleased to cause a Bill to be drafted on the lines indicated in this skeleton scheme and introduce the same in the British House of Commons:

Scheme

(1) The Imperial and Provincial Legislative Councils to consist respectively of Members not less than one half of whom are to be elected, not more than one-fourth to sit *ex-officio*, and the rest to be nominated by Government.

(2) Revenue districts to constitute ordinarily territorial units for electoral purposes.

(3) All male British subjects above 21 years of age possessing certain qualifications and not subject to certain disqualifications (both of which will be settled later) to be voters.

(4) Voters in each district to elect representatives to one or more electoral bodies, according to local circumstances, at the rate of 12 per million of the total population of the district, such representatives to possess certain qualifications and not to be subject to certain disqualifications, both of which will be settled later.

(5) All the representatives thus elected by all the districts included in the jurisdiction of each electoral body, to elect members to the Imperial Legislature at the rate of 1 per every five millions of the total population of the electoral jurisdiction, and to their own Provincial Legislature at the rate of 1 per million of the said total population, in such wise that whenever the Parsis, Christians, Muhammadans or Hindus are in a minority, the total number of Parsis, Christians, Muhammadans or Hindus, as the case may be, elected to the Provincial Legislature, shall not, so far as may be possible, bear a less proportion to the total number of members elected thereto, than the total number of Parsis, Christians, Hindus or Muhammadans, as the case may be, in such electoral jurisdiction, bears to its total population. Members of both Legislatures to possess certain qualifications and not to be subject to certain disqualifications both of which will be settled later.

(6) All elections to be by ballot.

XI. Resolved -That the Subjects Committee be instructed to settle the questions (left open in the skeleton scheme for the reconstruction of the Councils, embodied in Resolution II), of the qualifications requisite for, and the disqualifications which should debar from, becoming

(*a*) a Voter;
(*b*) a Representative;
(*c*) a Member of a Provincial Legislative Council; and
(*d*) a Member of the Imperial Legislative Council; and to submit their Report thereon to Charles Bradlaugh, Esq., M.P., for the purposes of the Bill which he has been requested to have drawn.

Confirmation of Previous Resolutions

III. Resolved—That this present Congress does hereby ratify and confirm the resolutions passed by previous Congresses as to

(*a*) the urgent necessity for the complete separation of executive and judicial functions, such that, in no case, shall the two functions be combined in the same officer;

(*b*) the expediency of extending into many parts of the country, where it is not at present in force, the system of trial by jury;

(*c*) the necessity of withdrawing from the High Courts the powers, first vested in them in 1872, of setting aside verdicts of acquittal by juries;

(*d*) the necessity of introducing into the Code of Criminal Procedure, a provision enabling accused persons, in warrant cases, to demand that instead of being tried by the Magistrate, they be committed to the Court of Sessions;

(*e*) the highly unsatisfactory character of the existing system of Police Administration in India, and the absolute necessity of a fundamental reform therein;

(*f*) the expediency of both establishing Military Colleges in India, whereat the Natives of India, as defined by statute, may be educated and trained for a military career as officers of the Indian Army, and of authorising, under such rules and restrictions as may seem necessary, such a system of volunteering for the Indian inhabitants of the country, as may qualify them to support the Government in any crisis;

(*g*) the extremely unsatisfactory character of the Income Tax Administration, especially as regards incomes below Rupees one thousand, and the expediency of raising the taxable minimum to this amount;

(*h*) the extreme importance of increasing, instead of diminishing, as the present tendency appears to be, the public expenditure on education in all its branches, and the necessity, in view to the promotion of one of the most essential of these branches, the technical, of the appointment of a mixed Commission to enquire into the present industrial condition of the country;

(*i*) the impolicy and injustice involved in the late increase of the Salt Tax in a time of profound peace, and the urgent necessity for an immediate reduction of this tax, and the reimposition, to balance the deficit thus caused, of light *ad valorem* import duties;

(*j*) the necessity for the reduction of, instead of the continual increase to, the military expenditure of the country.

Temperance

IV. Resolved—That this Congress hereby tenders its sincere thanks to Messrs. Caine and Smith, and the members who voted with them, in connection with the debate on the Indian Excise Question in the House of Commons; and while fully appreciating what has been done by some of the local Governments towards the improvement of their systems of Excise and Abkari, desires to express the earnest hope that no further time may be lost in giving full effect to the Resolution of the House of Commons.

Public Service

V. Resolved—That this Congress, while thanking Her Majesty's Government for raising the age for the Indian Civil Service Competitive Examination from 19 to 23, does hereby put on record an emphatic expression of the universal disappointment which has been created by the rest of that Government's orders in regard to the Public Service Question (the net result of which orders is to place the people of India in a worse position than they previously held), and reiterates the National conviction that no real justice will be done to India, in this matter, until the simultaneous holding in India and in England, of all Examinations for all Civil branches of the Public Service in India, at present held only in England, be conceded.

Military

VI. Resolved---That in view of the loyalty of the people, the hardships that the Arms Act, (XI of 1878), as at present administered, entails, and the unmerited slur which it casts upon them, the Government be moved so to modify the rules made under this Act that all restrictions as to the possession and bearing of arms shall apply equally to all persons residing in or visiting India: that licences to possess and bear arms shall be liberally and generally distributed wherever wild animals habitually destroy human life, cattle or crops, and that these and all licences issued under the rules shall be granted once for all, shall operate throughout the Provincial jurisdiction within which they are issued, be only revocable on proof of misuse, and shall not require yearly or half-yearly renewals.

Permanent Settlement

VII. Resolved—That the Government be urged to take the subject of a Permanent Settlement once more under consideration in view to practical action thereon, such that fixity and permanency may be given to the Government Land Revenue demand without further delay, at any rate in all fully populated and well cultivated tracts of country.

Silver Duties

VIII. Resolved—That in view of the fall that has already occurred in the price of silver and in the exchange value of the Indian Rupee, it is impolitic on the part of the British Government to maintain any hindrances whatever to the consumption of silver for manufacturing purposes; and that this Congress strongly urges upon Her Majesty's Government that, not only as an act of justice to India (a matter which has been repeatedly brought to the notice of Her Majesty's Ministers) but also as an act of expediency in the interests of Her Majesty's British as well as Indian subjects, the plate duties should be immediately abolished, and hall-marking be made a voluntary institution.

Grievances before Supply

IX. Resolved—That this Congress respectfully expresses the earnest hope that, in the interest of the people of India, the House of Commons will forthwith restore the right, formerly possessed by members of that Honourable House, of stating to Parliament any matter of grievance of the natives of India before Mr. Speaker leaves the Chair for the presentation in Committee of the Indian Budget statement, and earnestly trusts that the House of Commons will, in future, take into consideration the Annual Indian Budget statement at such a date as will ensure its full and adequate discussion, and further authorises the President, Sir William Wedderburn, Bart., to sign a Petition in the name and on behalf of this Congress for presentation to the House of Commons in accordance with the terms of this Resolution.

Congress Constitution

XIII. Resolved—

(*a*) That, in view of the large number of delegates this year assembled and the probability, arising from past experience, of their number continuing to increase year by year, henceforth the number of delegates to be allowed from each Congress circle be limited to five per million of the total population of the circle: the Standing Committee of each circle allotting the number which their jurisdiction, as a whole, is entitled to elect, amongst their several electoral divisions, as may seem most expedient.

(*b*) That from the date of Mr. Hume's departure for England, the Hon. Pandit Ayodhyanath be appointed Joint General Secretary, and that Rs. 5,000 be assigned for the payment by him of such Assistant Secretaries as he may find it necessary to employ, clerical assistance, postage, telegraphs, and printing, and further that Mr. W. C. Bannerji be appointed Standing Counsel for Bengal, Mr. Pherozeshah Mehta, Standing Counsel for Bombay, and Mr. Ananda Charlu, Standing Counsel for Madras, to the Joint General Secretary.

(*c*) That the tentative rules for the constitution and working of the Congress which were first considered at Madras, and in regard to which various addenda have from time to time been circulated, be thoroughly considered during the coming year by the several Standing Congress Committees, and definitely dealt with by the Congress at its next session.

(*d*) That this Congress does hereby confirm the appointment of Sir W. Wedderburn, Bart., and Messrs. W. S. Caine, M.P., W. S. Bright Maclaren, M.P., J. E. Ellis, M.P., Dadabhai Naoroji and George Yule, as a Committee (with power to add to their number) to guide and direct the operations and control the expenditure of the National

Congress Agency in England, and does further tender its sincere thanks to these gentlemen, and to Mr. W. Digby, C.I.E., the Secretary, for the service which they are rendering to India.

(*e*) That this Congress does formally appoint Mr. George Yule, Mr. A. O. Hume, Mr. Adam, Mr. Eardley Norton, Mr. J. E. Howard, Mr. Pherozeshah Mehta, Mr. Surendranath Bannerji, Mr. Mano Mohan Ghose, Mr. Sharf-ud-din, Mr. N. Mudholkar, and Mr. W. C. Bannerji to represent its views in England, and press upon the consideration of the British Public the political reform which the Congress has advocated.

(*f*) That a sum of Rs. 45,000 be raised for the expenses of the Congress Work in this country and in England during the ensuing year, and that the different Standing Committees do send their respective apportioned amounts to the General Secretary, the one half in three, and the balance in six months.

Thanks of Congress

X. Resolved—That in view to his approaching departure, this Congress puts on record an expression of the high sense entertained, not only in the Bombay Presidency but throughout India, of the ability, integrity and impartiality that have characterised Lord Reay's administration, as also of the gratitude which the whole country feels to be his due for the sympathy that he has ever extended to Indian aspirations and efforts.

XV. Resolved—That the Fifth Indian National Congress hereby tenders its heart-felt thanks to its President, Sir William Wedderburn, as well for his ready sacrifice of personal and political considerations involved by his journey from England to India, as for that courtesy, impartiality and never failing sympathy, which characteristics of his long and honourable career as an official of this country, have marked his control of the proceedings of this assembly.

Formal

XIV. Resolved—That the Sixth Indian National Congress do assemble at some City in Bengal, the exact place to be fixed hereafter, on the 26th of December, 1890.

XII. Resolved—That Mr. A. O. Hume, C.B., be re-elected General Secretary of the National Indian Congress for the ensuing year.

CHARLES BRADLAUGH, M.P.

The presentation of the Congress address to Mr. Charles Bradlaugh, M.P., took place on the same evening, December 28th, at 7 p.m. The table on the platform—18 feet by 4½ feet—was piled up from end to end with addresses in caskets of Indian work, rugs, mats, carvings, sent from every part of India, brought in many cases by poor men, who had come hundreds of miles to give them. Characteristically, he would not accept valuable gifts, such as a splendid Kashmir shawl. Mr. Pherozeshah Mehta was voted to the chair, and made a brief speech, voicing India's love and gratitude for "the high and unselfish endeavours" of one who was a stranger to them, to promote India's "welfare, its prosperity and its best interests".

Sir William Wedderburn read the address of the Congress:

To Charles Bradlaugh, Esq., Member for Northampton in the Parliament of Great Britain and Ireland.

Sir,—On behalf of the Fifth Indian National Congress, assembled at Bombay, we beg to offer you our united and most heartfelt welcome, and through you we desire to convey our thanks to the electors of Northampton who have permitted you to espouse the cause of India.

You come to us a stranger in person, not repute. For your disinterested advocacy of the claims (founded on the unanswerable demands of human progress and the solemn promises of their Queen) preferred by millions—whose appeals for justice have evoked a widespread response since you aroused the people of Great Britain into a sympathetic recognition of India's needs—will enshrine your name for all time in the proudest and most imperishable of human homes, the hearts and traditions of a loving and a grateful race.

Brilliant as was the tribute of national respect which your illness elicited from the fellow-countrymen who for long years had been the daily spectators of your labours and your triumphs in England, you have won, Sir, in the mental distress and prayerful anxiety with which the population of India followed you in the tribulation of your sickness, a homage the more unique and tender that it is not matched in the recorded history of any living statesman. They have appreciated the unflinching courage with which, throughout your political career, you have confronted error and have championed truth. You have enchained their admiration by your inalienable fidelity to the popular cause.

Proud in your possession of such qualities, and thankful for your efforts in our cause, we trust that you may be spared to complete the great work you have begun, and to read the vindication of your generous interpretation of our political aspirations, as well in the ever closer union of India and of England, as in the quickened vigour and expanding energies of a country regenerated by the partial redemption of pledges too long permitted to remain unfulfilled.—We have, etc.

In reply, Mr. Bradlaugh said:

Sir William, and Delegates of the Indian National Congress, I thank you not so much for myself, for I have not yet deserved the tribute you pay me. I thank you for my Electors, without whom I should not have the right to do all the work I do. And in their name, and because I believe that their example will be followed by other constituencies, I feel grateful to you, and only do not translate my gratitude into words because no words can express what I feel.

A few of the caskets only were taken up, as specimens of all, and a few of the articles of Indian manufacture were presented, and a list of some of the places, sending addresses and gifts, was read. An hour was occupied in even this slight summarising, for, as the Report says, "there was scarcely a town of any size" from which an address had not been sent. Mr. Bradlaugh then rose and said :

Friends, fellow-subjects, and fellow-citizens! I address you as friends, for the greeting you have given me entitles me to use the same language to you as I would use to those at home, and you have made me feel since I have been in Bombay that the word "home" has a wider significance than I had given it. I have learned that if I have only a little home, I have a larger one in your sympathies and in your affections, and, as I trust to deserve by future work, in your love. I address you as fellow-subjects; we are here loyal to one rule with the best of loyalty. That is no real loyalty which is only blind submission. Real loyalty means that the governed help the governors by leaving little for the Government to do. Real loyalty means that the claim of right is made with the consciousness of duty; and I feel proud to be a fellow-subject with you in the hope that the phrase fellow-citizens may grow into a reality even before my life-time ends. I pray your indulgence to-night, for it is the first speech I have made since I looked into the blackness of the grave, and I am not sure how far I can trust my tongue to interpret what I would wish to say. Of one thing I am sure, you have overrated alike my work and my ability. (*No, No.*) I pray you, be as indulgent to me as you have been generous; and if you disagree with what I say, let me say it in my own poor fashion, so that you may find at least my meaning clear to you. I am only here as a visitor by your courtesy, a member of a great assembly, the Mother of Parliaments in the world, of which I am one of the poorest members; and as to any force that I may have had in advocating the cause of those to whom I belong at home, let me say I was sorry to hear that I was thanked for my work in the popular cause. For whom should I work, if not for the people? Born of the people, trusted by the people, I will die of the people. And I know no geographical or race limitations. If the Nationality—pardon the word—to which I am proud to belong has raised its Empire, the rule carries with it the duty on the part of every citizen to recognise that which I recognise in you, a lawful constitutional association for the assertion of your just claims and for the advancement of your homes and interests.

I will ask you not to expect too much. One man is only a water-drop in the ocean of human life: you are the breeze driving the water-drop on the western side of the seas and, by your encouragement, adding others to it, and giving it a force that shall wash it into the old rock of prejudice that hindered, you will make those on the other side hear, as I have heard, the clear English sounds, which show that you share our language, our traditions, and our hopes, and are willing to work with us and to make common cause with us.

Not only do not expect too much, but do not expect all at once. Great as this assembly is in its suggestiveness, by its delegates travelling hundreds and thousands of miles, you are yet only the water-drop of the two hundred and ten millions whom you number under our Empire, yours and mine—not mine against yours, not English against Indian, but our common Empire for common purposes. Don't be disappointed if, of a just claim, only something is conceded. It is new, but shall be every day coming; it is new, but you have those who stand in the House of Commons to plead for you; not I alone, but members as devoted to you as I can possibly be; and I hope soon to see added to their ranks, with the authority of his knowledge and of the position which his presiding here has given him—Sir William Wedderburn. I would remind you, as an encouragement to you to be patient, that in England great reforms have always been slowly won. Those who first enterprised them were called seditious, and sometimes sent to gaol as criminals; but the speech and thought lived on. No imprisonment can crush a truth; it may hinder it for a moment, it may delay it for an hour, but it gets an electric elasticity inside the dungeon walls, and it grows, and moves the whole world when it comes out. Your presence here to-day confutes and answers in anticipation one sneer that I have heard spoken within the walls of Parliament. It is said: "There is no Indian Nation, there can be no Indian National Congress; there is no Indian people, there are only two hundred millions of diverse races and diverse creeds." The lesson I read here is that this Congress movement is an educational movement, hammering upon the anvil of millions of men's brains, until it welds into one common whole men whose desire for political and social reforms is greater than all distinctions of race and creed.

It will be my duty, as it is my right, to present to Parliament directly I get back, on the very day of its opening, the claim you make to have the Bill considered. On the second day the Bill will be introduced. For so much I can answer; but I can answer for nothing more. I think it is possible the Government may introduce some Bill themselves. If they do, it will take precedence of, but it will not avoid, the one you have charged me with; because the Government Bill, in Committee, will come under the discussion of Parliament on every one of the propositions that you desire in the Bill you have charged me with. It is not easy work. There are differences; and I have been glad to see that you can meet and discuss differences as you have done. You have shown that you can meet together and listen to one another, and that you are worthy of public trust, and the right of electing and being elected, to help to make the laws which you so discuss.

Then you may take it that on your own Bill, or the Government Bill, this decision of the House of Commons will be taken. You can help that decision; you have a constitutional right, not of coming into the House and being heard yourselves, but of sending your petitions there from every division, from far off Sindh, from every part; and I would ask you, if you want to make me really your mouthpiece in that House, send signatures to petitions which you understand, by the thousand, by the hundred thousand, by the million, if you can, so that India's people may kneel—and there is no shame in kneeling—on the threshold where the Mother of Parliaments sits, and ask that she may do the same justice to those six, seven or eight thousand miles away that she has done to those who can assemble and make themselves heard with the living voice.

We—you will permit me to say "we" although I am only a guest—are here engaged in no seditious movement. We are not even seeking (though if we did, there would be no great crime in the high endeavour) to transplant the democratic Institutions of England to this land. We are only seeking in the hill which is hard to climb, to carve steps in which the strongest may stand, and through coming generations help the weaker brethren to higher posts. It is said that there are many who stand aloof from this movement. I, looking at you, wonder that in its infancy so many have joined in it. It is said that there are influential men of this party and of that who have not yet come. Oh! but the sun's rays grow as the sun rises. You are the dawn; I see the day; and I do not count the rays which are yet below the horizon, but I take account of the gilding of the clouds from the rays that I see.

I feel that I should like to have the title that some have given me in sneer, and some in hearty meaning, of "Member for India". Dead men, whose measure I cannot hope to cope with, have partly held that title. But I should love to hold it, not simply by great efforts made on great occasions, but by simple doings whenever there is injustice to be touched. I know how little one can do, but *little* though one man can do, I will tell you *what* he can do. When, after rain and storm, the waters have gathered, one man may make a little boring through which the water begins to percolate that washes all away; and I will try to be that one man, leaving greater ones than I can ever be to swim on the tide when the water flows.

I am here, because I believe you loyal to the law which I am bound to support. I am here, because I believe you wish, as we in England have done, to win within the limits of the Constitution the most perfect equality and right for all. I have no right to offer advice to you; but if I had, and if I dared, I would say to you, men from lands almost as separate, although within your own continent, as England is from you; I would say to you, men with race traditions and caste views and religious differences; that in a great Empire like ours, all we have the right to is equality before the law for all, equality of opportunity for all, equality of expression for all, penalty on none, favoritism to none; and I believe that in this great Congress I see the germ of that which may be as fruitful as the most hopeful tree that grows under your sun.

I am glad to see that you have women amongst you, glad, although they are few; glad, for they are your mothers and teach your children; glad, for in our land the wives may count through their husbands, and great thoughts and great endeavours are not made less because the man turns to the woman for counsel in his hour of need, and thus makes the woman stronger than the man.

I fear I have already spoken to you too long, if not for you, at any rate, for myself. I beg you—the most eloquent whom I have heard among you—to put into your own words and your own thoughts what you would have me say of hope for you; and let that be said. One thing be sure of: I will only advocate the right. I must judge the right I advocate, and I may not always judge it as you do; but as long as you let me speak for you, I will only speak that which seems to me to be right and true. In this movement no force save the force of brain; no secret union; all open, frank, before the Law. So far as one man may, and so far as one man's speech can do, English liberty shall put itself on the side of yours. This is the first, and it may be the last, speech that I may ever make to you; but let me beg of you to think, and let me think, that you are listening, and that, if I do rightly, you will be generous with me in your judgment; and that even if I do not always plead with the voice that you would speak with, you will believe that I have done my best, and that I meant my best to be greater happiness for India's people, greater peace for Britain's rule, greater comfort for the whole of Britain's subjects.

The whole speech was punctuated with cheers which we have omitted; we have only inserted one cry, where it was needed to explain the words which followed. The speech was closed with tumultuous applause—his first speech in India, and alas! his last.

CHAPTER VI

THE Sixth Congress met at Calcutta in the Tivoli Gardens, in a big temporary Hall—into which 8,000 people managed to crowd themselves—on December 26th, 1890, and it sat for four days, the 26th, 27th, 29th, and 30th December, the Congress Hall being lent on the 28th to the Social Conference. The list shows the names of 677 delegates made up as follows:

Bengal	377
N. W. P. and Oudh	148
Panjab	18
Bombay	47
Berar, C. P., and Secunderabad	29
Madras	58
	677
Without Certificates	25
	702

The limitation of the numbers of delegates, decided by the previous Congress, had been carried out; at 5 delegates per million of population, (see Resolution XIII [*a*] 1889). 995 delegates should have been elected; a little over 1,000 were elected, as a matter of fact, but only 702 attended, of whom 25 did not register with the required certificates, and so their names were omitted. But that the popular interest was undiminished was shown by the packing of the Hall, the largest that had yet been erected, 7,000 visitors attending on the first day, and the number being never less than 4,000. The Report says that many of these came from other Provinces, and would have been counted as delegates but for the enforcement of the demand for certificates of election. The feeling of resentment against the wrongs under which India was suffering had increased considerably, and it is well to recognise the long growth of this feeling until it developed into the "unrest," which formed so prominent a feature of the first decade of the twentieth century, and finally gave birth to a party which sought, in despair, the breaking of the English connexion. Only the concession of the reforms of 1910 revived the hopes of the Constitutionalists, and enabled them to remain firm in their declared creed of Self-Government within the Empire. In 1890, there was angry opposition in India to the trans-frontier policy then in favour, and especially to the cruel invasion of Afghanistan, which caused so much misery. The official report of the Congress of 1890 concluded with the following indictment:

Although our present Viceroy seems not only desirous of seeing and judging for himself, but thoroughly imbued with the true spirit of Liberalism; although in every Province there remain still some faithful few, who deprecate and deplore all the evil that is on foot; although throughout Great Britain signs appear that, here and there, her people are commencing to realise the grave responsibility in regard to India which has devolved upon them, the administration of India still remains, alas! as a whole, "linked with some virtues but a thousand crimes". Millions of educated and patriotic men (than whom no more loyal or loving subjects are numbered in the vast Empire that owns the sway of our beloved Queen-Empress) are treated as political helots to gratify the class prejudices and *amour propre* and fill the pockets of a handful of bureaucrats, the average men amongst whom are, positively, less qualified for rule, *in India*, than a very considerable proportion of those whom England permits them to misgovern.

India's people, free-born British subjects, are denied the smallest fraction of those fundamental political privileges which, as British citizens, are their inherent birthright.

Ninety-five per cent of all the most important and responsible offices in the country are monopolised by Europeans, on salaries fully double of those that would secure quite as, in many cases far more, competent Indians for the majority of these posts.

One-fifth of the entire population tremble on the verge of starvation, to perish by millions whenever the smallest natural calamity of drought or flood increases by one iota the insecurity of their position, and the money wrung from our pauper population, by the cruel taxation of the first necessaries of life—the money which is all our Government has had to show for the 20 odd millions who in recent years have succumbed to famine and its consequences—is ruthlessly squandered in bloodshed, and in wicked, and idiotically mismanaged, aggressions on feebler neighbours, to gratify the ignoble cravings for personal distinctions and titles of individual members of a Simla cabal.

Almost every indigenous art and industry has been crushed, and agriculture, the one art on which now depend nearly 90 per cent of the population, is slowly deteriorating under a grasping rack-renting system of temporary settlements and, with it, our crops and our cattle.

The masses are being persistently demoralised; despite the distinct orders of the House of Commons, an iniquitous system of excise, calculated to stimulate drunkenness and all its attendant crimes and vices, is still retained, only slightly and superficially reformed in some Provinces, in all its original iniquity in others.

Under a barbarous and obsolete system, miscalled Justice, Executive and Judicial, Fiscal and Police powers are so combined in one functionary, that powers professedly granted for one purpose are practically utilised in furtherance of others, for which no civilised Government in the world would, nowadays, dare to confer them.

There is practically no justice in India for the poor against the rich, or the non-official against the official, and the police, who should be the protectors of the poor and the honest, are their terror and their worst oppressors.

What wonder, if some of us, who come of sterner sires, at times, despairing of justice at the hands of man, cry out in bitterness of heart: "How long, O Lord, how long?" But the patient East, sublime in its resignation and charity, longs only to forgive and to forget the *past*, and prays only for justice, however tardy, in the *present*; and wrongs that long since would have roused Teutonic or Gallic nations to frenzy, tolerated in remembrance of the civic peace and order, education and other benefits, unquestionably conferred by England, awaken in the mind of India's people (far truer Christians, though they know it not, than that proud Nation which permits all this evil, and is answerable for it, before God and man) only the mild reproaches embodied in the words with which we headed this article:

Of course we have to submit resignedly to this ruinous, this unprincipled trans-frontier policy of the Government until we succeed in awakening the conscience of our British fellow-subjects. We are British subjects, now, of our own free choice; we have thrown in our lot with England for better and for worse, and it is this which enhances England's sin in permitting the continuance of this hateful policy. Will our British brethren never awake?

Alas! No mortal can reply—their slumber has been long—but they may yet awake.

At 2 p.m. the Chair was taken by Mr. Mano Mohan Ghose, the Chairman of the Reception Committee, who, after defending the Congress from the various attacks made on it, and defining its position, called on Sir Romesh Chandra Mittra to propose the President, and he moved the election of Mr. Pherozeshah M. Mehta; it was seconded by Nawab Shamshoodowla, supported by Mr. Ananda Charlu and Nawab Ghulam Rubbani, and carried by acclamation.

Mr. Pherozeshah M. Mehta, taking the presidential chair and saying, truly, that it was the highest honour that India had to give, began by vindicating the right of the Parsi as a true son of India, after thirteen centuries of home in the Motherland. He welcomed Mr. Caine as one of the elected delegates and thanked him for his work, and then, after warm words of gratitude to Mr. Bradlaugh for the untiring energy, the indefatigable care, the remarkable ability, with which he had worked for India in the House of Commons, he turned to the consideration of his Bill, and of its result, Lord Cross' India Councils Bill. In a few scathing words he disposed of Lord Salisbury's absurd view that "Government by representation .... did not fit eastern traditions or eastern minds," and quoted Mr. Chisholm Anstey, "that the East is the parent of Municipalities. Local Self-Government, in the widest acceptation of the term, is as old as the East itself." Mr. Bradlaugh had fought to substitute election for nomination in Lord Cross' Bill; when that Bill was thrown out, he had introduced another, on similar lines, and this was to be laid before Congress, and should have its unanimous support. He referred to the service rendered by the Congress Deputation to England, and concluded with a singularly fine and poignant appeal to England's love of liberty; the Congress was, indeed, not the voice of the masses, but it was the duty of their educated compatriots to interpret their grievances and offer suggestions for their redress.

History teaches us that such has been the law of widening progress in all ages and all countries, notably in England itself. That function and that duty, which thus devolve upon us, is best discharged, not in times of alarm and uneasiness, of anger and excitement, but when the heart is loyal and clear and reason unclouded. It is, I repeat, the glory of the Congress that the educated and enlightened people of the country seek to repay the debt of gratitude which they owe for the priceless boon of education by pleading, and pleading temperately, for timely and provident statesmanship. I have no fears but that English statesmanship will ultimately respond to the call. I have unbounded faith in the living and fertilising principles of English culture and English education.

True, the Anglo-Indian officials were against them. But they, after all, were Englishmen, and must at last feel that they must work with England's policy. A choice had been offered to England, a blessing and a curse.

All the great forces of English life and society, moral, social, intellectual, political, are, if slowly, yet steadily and irresistibly, declaring themselves for the choice which will make the connexion of England and India a blessing to themselves and to the whole world for countless generations. . . . I appeal to all true Englishmen—to candid friends as to generous foes—not to let this prayer go in vain.

The Subjects' Committee was then elected and ratified by the Congress, and the meeting adjourned.

On the 27th December, Resolution I was proposed by Mr. Lal Mohan Ghose, who defended its moderation, and the proposal was seconded by Mr. Ananda Charlu. Mr. C. V. Nayadu supported, and told of his experiences in England, where, as a member of the "Paddington Parliament," he had carried the Bill. Pandit Madan Mohan Malaviya quoted Mr. Gladstone to the effect that it often happens that a Nation was given the duty of working out some great principle; to England was given the spreading of the principle of representation, and she had worked so successfully that "now the man would be deemed mad," said Mr. Gladstone, "who should denounce the system of popular representation". Yet in India such men were found, and to India the system was denied.

Many others spoke in support. Pandit Bishan Narayan Dhar, speaking against separate electorates, asked the Government if they would follow the noble policy of Akbar, a policy of ignoring religious differences, or were they going to lay stress on them, as did Sir John Strachey who said: "The truth plainly is that the existence side by side of these hostile creeds is one of the strong points in our political position in India."

The Resolution was carried unanimously.

The "Omnibus Resolution" was proposed by Mr. Kali Charan Bannerji, who described himself as "an old driver of your omnibus"; it was the same from (*a*) to (*h*) as that of the previous year, (*i*), on the Salt Tax, was transferred to a separate Resolution (V), and (*j*) took its place; then (*j*) on simultaneous examinations, was put in from the end of Resolution V of 1889, and Resolution VI, on the Arms Act, was also transferred to the omnibus as (*k*). On the Army and the Arms Act the official Report remarks that "even the Russian Government with all its despotic traditions is not so exclusive" as the British, and that "had this same idiotic policy [the Arms Act] been pursued for the 25 years prior to the Mutiny, 1857 would have seen the end of British rule here. It was the people—the armed people accustomed to handle weapons—who rallied to the British Standards in those dark days of danger and distress, and saved the British Empire in the East." Munshi Sadar-ud-din Ahmed said:

The Emperors of old had confidence in the bravery and faithfulness of the people, and never deprived them of arms, and derived considerable assistance from the people in return. The martial spirit of the people of the country raised the descendants of Taimur, Akbar in particular, to the highest pitch of supremacy and power. If the people of India with arms in their hands and bullets in their pockets could remain subject to the Muhammadan's Empire and accepted its supremacy, does it stand to reason that they would rebel against so just and civilised a Government as that of the British people? The peace and prosperity of a people are among the first requisites of sovereignty, and these cannot be secured unless the rulers and the ruled repose mutual confidence in each other. The confidence of the people is dependent on the non-interference of the sovereign with the privileges of the people and their right to do such lawful acts as they please. At any rate arms are the sole protectors of life and property; and their deprivation causes disappointment and dejection which knows no bounds. . . .

No Emperor ever feared the sword of his subject, nor ever emasculated a brave nation by force. The natives of India belong to a race which opposed Alexander and turned him back beyond the Indus. They are descendants of those brave people who, in the battle of Telaveri, made Shahab-ud-din Ghori taste the efficacy of a sword, and made him retreat headlong with his army for upwards of forty miles. To convert such brave and faithful people into protectors of the Throne and guards of the State is to invigorate and strengthen the foundations of the Government. You must have read in history that when Nadir Shah once summoned the Nawab of Furrukabad to Delhi for an interview, and the Nawab replied that he could not come without his armour and weapons, Nadir said: "Go and tell him he may come with his artillery." What a revolution! There was a time when the Emperors of old were not afraid of the arms of their enemies; a time has now come when we, unfortunate though loyal and faithful, subjects are distrusted even by our own Government.

Resolution III drew attention to the annual scandal of the discussion of Indian questions before empty benches in the House of Commons, and was moved by Mr. Caine, seconded by Mr. R. D. Mehta, supported by Mr. Yule and carried. Then Resolution IV, another effort to reform the Excise Administration, was ably proposed by Mr. D. E. Wacha, in an argumentative speech, and vehemently seconded by Lala Murlidhar, who said the East had given the

West mathematics, astronomy and other sciences, and the West had given the East in exchange—liquor. "Even our Muhammadan rulers hated and held the liquor traffic accursed. It has been left to our Christian rulers to love it, pet it, stimulate it, and make money by crores out of it." Needless to say the Resolution was carried unanimously, and the Congress adjourned to Monday, December 29th.

On the third day, Mr. Pringle Kennedy opened the proceedings by moving Resolution V, for the reduction of the salt-tax; in seconding the resolution, Mr. D. E. Wacha sharply criticised the wasteful military expenditure which depleted the resources of Government, and showed that the annual consumption of salt per head in India was about 10 lb. per annum, whereas the average for Europe was 26 lb. varying from 80 lb. in England (including much salt used in manufacture), and 50 lb. in France to 14 lb. in Austria. Mr. G. K. Gokhale supported the resolution, saying that the enhancement of the tax by an executive order in 1888 was unjust and impolitic, and the consequences had been disastrous. Unjust, because in 1886 the Income Tax Act had been brought forward on the ground that the masses were paying more than their due share of taxation, and yet it was on them that a new burden was laid. It was impolitic, because the raising deprived the Government of any financial reserve. The consequence was that the people had used in 3 years 26 lakhs of maunds less than they would have used at the previous price, and this was taken from the very poorest, those who lived always on the borderland of famine:

> When you call to mind the thin emaciated figures of these unhappy, miserable, brethren, who have as much right to the comforts of this, God's, earth as you or I or any one else; when you remember that the lives of these brethren are so uniformly dark and miserable, that they are hardly cheered by a single ray of hope, or relieved by a single day of rest; when, further, you remember that a person does not generally trench upon his stock of necessaries before he has parted with every luxury, every single comfort that he may allow himself; when you recall all these things, you will clearly understand what grievous and terrible hardship and suffering and privation this measure of enhancement, which has curtailed the poor man's consumption of salt by thirty-six lakhs of maunds, has really entailed. We are appealing in the present instance to the Government of India to reduce the duty on salt from two rupees eight annas to two rupees per maund. My friend Mr. Wacha has shown that the state of the finances permits of such reduction. We are appealing to the sense of justice of the Government of India. We are appealing to their statesmanship, to their righteousness, and I will even go further and say, to their mercy. The past is in the past and no one can recall it; but this much can surely be done—further evil and misery from this source can be averted.

An amendment was proposed, but only two hands, those of the proposer and seconder, were held up for it, and, after several other speeches, the Resolution was carried *nem. con.*

The Permanent Settlement of Land came up again, moved by Mr. R. N. Mudholkar and seconded by Mr. R. Sabapati Pillai; supported by many speakers, it was unanimously carried.

The day concluded by passing a Resolution of protest against an Order issued by the Bengal Government, forbidding any official to attend the Congress even as a spectator. Mr. Mano Mohan Ghose proposed and Mr. Yule seconded it, and the President put it, remarking scornfully that the matter was of very little importance to the Congress, but as, if the order was not issued by some subordinate official, it would involve grave discredit to the Government, they might give the Government the "opportunity of extricating themselves from the undignified and ludicrous position, if not worse, in which these precious orders apparently place them". Which was done, and the Congress adjourned. (The Resolution effected its object, for the Viceroy, Lord Lansdowne, answered that the Government order, which had been misunderstood, had nothing to do with the Congress, that the Congress was a perfectly legitimate movement, and that while officials could not take active part in political movements, they should not impede them, nor put pressure on others either to help or hinder them.)

On the re-assembly of the Congress for its fourth day's work, the Hon. Pandit Ayodhyanath in moving Resolution VIII, a vote of thanks to Mr. Charles Bradlaugh and others, referred to Mr. Gladstone's promise to support Mr. Bradlaugh's motion in the House of Commons, and to Lord Salisbury's rude reference to Mr. Dadabhai Naoroji as a "black man". After many had spoken, the Resolution was unanimously carried. The ninth Resolution, also of thanks, was carried, and then it was resolved that the Congress should meet either in Madras or Nagpur.

Mr. Norendranath Sen then proposed a Resolution which is not yet carried out, that if it were possible a meeting of the Congress should be held in London in 1892, so as to bring the Indian question before the British Democracy as no small deputation could do. Mr. Saligram Singh, in seconding, thought that if suitable arrangements could be made for the voyage, no serious objection would be made by the orthodox, and Mr. Viraraghavachari said that as far as Madras was concerned, no orthodoxy would be allowed to stand in the way of their political advancement. A very long discussion arose, and even very orthodox delegates declared that they would go for the sake of the country, although it might give great pain to those they loved and revered.

A Resolution on finance was then passed; Mr. Hume was re-elected Secretary, and Pandit Ayodhyanath, Joint General Secretary for the ensuing year; and a deputation to England was appointed. One of the lady delegates, Mrs. Kadumbini Ganguli, was called on to move the vote of thanks to the Chairman, the first woman who spoke from the Congress platform, a symbol that India's freedom would uplift India's Womanhood. The President spoke a few words of thanks to the Reception Committee and others who had helped, and the Sixth Congress dissolved.

RESOLUTIONS.

Representation

I. Resolved—That this Congress, having considered the draft Bill recently introduced into Parliament by Mr. Charles Bradlaugh, entitled "An Act to amend the Indian Councils Act of 1861," approves the same as calculated to secure a substantial instalment of that reform, in the Administration of India, for which it has been agitating, and humbly prays the Houses of Parliament of the United Kingdom of Great Britain and Ireland to pass the same into law; and further that its President, Mr. Pherozeshah Mehta, is hereby empowered to draw up and sign, on behalf of this assembly, a petition to the House of Commons to the foregoing effect, and to transmit the same to Mr. Charles Bradlaugh for presentation, thereto, in due course.

Confirmation of Previous Resolutions

II. Resolved—That this present Congress does hereby ratify and confirm the resolutions passed by previous Congresses as to—

(*a*) to (*h*) the same as in Resolution III of the Congress of 1889.

(*i*) was made Resolution V of 1890, and (*j*) of 1889 took its place.

(*j*) is from Resolution V of 1889.

(*k*) was Resolution VI of 1889, very slightly modified in the preliminary words which ran: The expediency of so modifying the rules made under Act XI of 1878 (the Arms Act) that all restrictions, etc.

Grievances before Supply

III. Resolved—That this Congress respectfully expresses the earnest hope that in the interest of the people of India, the House of Commons will forthwith restore the right, formerly possessed by members of that Honourable House, of stating to Parliament any matter of grievance of the natives of India before Mr. Speaker leaves the Chair for the presentation in Committee of the Indian Budget statement, and earnestly trusts that the House of Commons will, in future, take into consideration the Annual Indian Budget statement at such a date as will ensure its full and adequate discussion, and further authorises its President to sign a Petition, in the name and on behalf of this Congress, for presentation to the House of Commons, in accordance with the terms of this Resolution.

Temperance

IV. Resolved—That, while recognising the action taken, in response to its previous prayers, in the matter of Excise Reform by H. M.'s Secretary of State for India and the Supreme Government here, and noting with pleasure the increase to the import duty on spirits, the taxation imposed on Indian-brewed malt liquors, the decision of the Bengal Government to abolish the outstill system, and the closing of over 7,000 liquor shops by the Madras Government in 1889-90, this Congress regrets that it is still necessary to urge the Government of India to insist on *all* Provincial administrations carrying out in their integrity the policy in matters of Excise enunciated in paras 103, 104 and 105 of the Despatch published in *The Gazette of India* of March 1st, 1890, especially as to subsection 4 of para 103, *viz.*—

"That efforts should be made to ascertain the existence of local public sentiment, and that a reasonable amount of deference should be paid to such opinion when ascertained."

Salt Tax

V. Resolved—That the condition of the Finances of India having materially improved, and those special circumstances on which the Government relied to justify the recent enhancement of the Salt Tax having practically ceased to exist, this Congress considers it essential that the enhancement referred to should be remitted at an early date, and empowers its President to submit a special memorial on the subject in its name and on its behalf to H. E. the Viceroy in Council.

Permanent Settlement

VI. Resolved—That having reference to the expectations created throughout the country by the Despatch of Her Majesty's Secretary of State in 1862, the principles of which were re-affirmed in a subsequent Despatch of 1865, promising the extension of a Permanent Settlement to all temporarily settled tracts in which certain conditions have long since been fulfilled, this Congress respectfully submits that the Government of India is now in honour bound to take up this question of Permanent Settlement, without further delay, in view to practical action thereon such that fixity and permanency may be given to the Government Land Revenue demand, as explicitly promised by Her Majesty's Secretary of State more than a quarter of a century ago.

An Enquiry

VII. Resolved—That this Congress, having observed with surprise a notice, apparently official, in various Calcutta newspapers which runs as follows :

THE CONGRESS

The Bengal Government having learnt that tickets of admission to the visitors' enclosure in the Congress pavilion have been sent to various Government officers residing in Calcutta, has issued a circular to all Secretaries, and heads of departments subordinate to it, pointing out that under the orders of the Government of India the presence of Government officials, even as visitors at such meetings is not advisable, and that their taking part in the proceedings of any such meetings is absolutely prohibited:

And having also considered a letter addressed by the Private Secretary of His Honour the Lieutenant-Governor of Bengal to the Secretary of the Reception Committee, of which the following is an exact copy:

BELVEDERE,
26th December, 1890

Dear Sir,—In returning herewith the seven cards of admission to the visitors' enclosure of the Congress pavilion, which were kindly sent by you to my address yesterday afternoon, I am desired to say that the Lieutenant-Governor and the members of his household could not possibly avail themselves of these tickets, since the orders of the Government of India definitely prohibit the presence of Government Officials at such meetings.

Yours faithfully,
P. C. LYON,
Private Secretary

J. Ghosal, Esq., Secretary,
Congress Reception Committee

authorises and instructs its President to draw the attention of His Excellency the Viceroy to the declaration embodied in these papers that Government servants are prohibited from attending any meetings of this Congress even as spectators, and to enquire, most respectfully, whether His Honour the Lieutenant-Governor of Bengal has, or has not, correctly interpreted the orders of the Government of India.

Thanks of Congress

VIII. Resolved—That the best thanks of this Congress be tendered to Mr. Charles Bradlaugh, M.P., for the invaluable services rendered by him during the past year, as also to Sir W. Wedderburn, Mr. W. S. Caine, Mr. J. Bright Maclaren, M.P., Mr. J. Ellis, M.P., Mr. George Yule, and Mr. Dadabhai Naoroji for the unselfish zeal and ability with which they have presided over the British Agency of the Congress; further that they put on record an expression of their high appreciation of the manner in which Mr. Digby, C. I. E., Secretary of the Agency, and Messrs. Surendranath Bannerji, R. N. Mudholkar, W. R. Bannerji, Eardley Norton, and A. O. Hume, delegates to England, respectively, discharged the onerous duties imposed upon them, and of their gratitude to all those members of the British public who so kindly welcomed and so sympathetically gave audience, in over fifty public and a far larger number of private meetings, to one or more of these delegates.

IX. Resolved—That a vote of thanks be recorded to Kumar Debendra Mullick and Brothers, Proprietors of the Tivoli Gardens, Mr. N. C. Bose and Babu Bhupendranath Bose, Proprietors of Mohan Bagan Villa, and to the Hon. Sir Romesh Chandra Mitra, Mr. T. N. Palit, Babus Janaki Nath Roy, Gopi Mohan Roy, Harendra Nath Roy, Kissori Mohan Roy, Ramanath Ghose, and Jamadar Ghasiram, owners of houses kindly lent for the use of delegates.

Congress Work

XI. Resolved—That provisional arrangements be made to hold a Congress, of not less than 100 delegates, in England, all things being convenient, in 1892, and that the several standing Congress Committees be directed to report, at the coming Congress, the names of the delegates that it is proposed to depute from their respective circles.

XII. Resolved—That of the Funds now in the Joint General Secretary's hands and about to be received, a further sum of twenty thousand rupees be added to the Permanent Fund and placed in fixed deposits, and that the rest of the funds accruing on account of this current year, 1890, be held by him available for the immediate purposes of the British Committee of the Indian National Congress, but to be replaced as the subscriptions for 1891 are received, and, ultimately, also added to the Permanent Fund.

XIII. Resolved—That a sum of Rs. 40,000, exclusive of individual donations, is assigned for the expenses of the British Committee of the Congress and Rs. 6,000 for the General Secretary's Office and Establishment, and that the several circles and districts do contribute as arranged in Committee.

XV. Resolved—That this Congress does formally appoint Messrs. G. Yule, Pherozeshah Mehta, W. C. Bannerji, J. Adam, Mano Mohan Ghose, A. O. Hume, Kali Charan Bannerji, Dadabhai Naoroji, D. A. Khare, and such other gentlemen as may volunteer for the duty with the sanction and approval of the Standing Congress Committees of their respective circles, to represent its views in England, and press upon the consideration of the British Public the political reforms which the Congress has advocated.

Formal

X. Resolved—That the Seventh Indian National Congress do assemble on the 26th December, 1891, at either Madras or Nagpore, as may be hereafter settled, in consultation between the Madras, Central Provinces and Berar Committees, and the Joint General Secretary.

XIV. Resolved—That Mr. A. O. Hume and Pandit Ayodhyanath are re-elected General and Joint-General Secretaries for the ensuing year.

CHAPTER VII

NAGPUR had the honour of welcoming the Seventh National Congress on the 28th, 29th and 30th of December, 1891, and 812 delegates met in a very beautiful Pavilion, in the Lall Bagh. It held just 4,000 chairs and was packed in every part. The delegates were distributed as follows:

Bengal	73
N. W. P. and Oudh	56
Panjab	5
Bombay (135) and Sindh (2)	137
Berar, C. P. and Secunderabad	480
Madras...	61
	812

At 2 p. m., the Chairman of the Reception Committee—Chairman also, as it happened, of the Nagpur Municipality—Mr. C. Narayanaswami Nayadu, welcomed the delegates; he spoke warmly of India's "love of the British people to whose advent here India owes her rebirth," and he bore testimony to the cordial way in which the Chief Commissioner of the Central Provinces, Mr. A. P. Macdonnell, had signified that, so far as he was concerned, any official who wished to do so could attend the Congress.

Pandit Ayodhyanath proposed and Mr. Pherozeshah Mehta seconded, the election of Rao Sahab P. Ananda Charlu as President, who, on taking the Chair, alluded to two others who had also been suggested as President, one of whom, Pandit Ayodhyanath, had preferred that the Presidency should go to Madras, and the other, Dewan Bahadur S. Subramania Iyer, had been raised to the Bench of the High Court, Madras, and was thus precluded from taking part in the Congress. His next reference was to the irreparable loss sustained by India in the death of Mr. Charles Bradlaugh, M.P., "an embodiment of universal benevolence"; what it meant to India was shown by Lord Cross immediately dropping even his feeble measure of reform, and the renewed indifference of the British Government, which had already lasted for nearly twenty years, until India was almost on the verge of revolt. The deaths of Sir T. Madhava Rao and Dr. Rajendralal Mitra were also mournfully recorded. The President, after alluding to the approaching departure of Mr. A. O. Hume, urged on the attention of the Congress the meeting in London, as proposed the previous year, and their duty to spread the knowledge of the work of the Congress among the masses.

The Subjects Committee already elected by the delegates was then ratified by the Congress, and Mr. Surendranath Bannerji brought up Resolution I, appointing a Committee to consider and report on a momentous question, whether the Annual Sessions of the Congress should be discontinued until after the proposed Session had been held in England. He spoke passionately in favour of maintaining the regular Sessions while also holding one in England, and the resolution was seconded and carried. The Congress then adjourned.

On meeting on December 29th, Mr. Gladstone's 82nd birthday, the Congress gave three cheers for him before settling down to business. Then Mr. Surendranath Bannerji, who moved Resolution II, insisted on the value of the Congress in bringing about reforms, pointing to the demand of the Congress for Legislative Councils in the N. W. P. and the Panjab, and the establishment of the first, and to some other hoped for changes. He urged that India was not well governed, but "it is not the men who are to blame; it is the system; it is the bureaucracy, the autocratic despotism, that has been established, that must be arraigned before the bar of public opinion in India and throughout the civilised world. . . . It is a despotism, tempered by a free press and the right of public meeting." [Both of these have since been taken away.]

What is the financial position of the Government of India? It may be briefly summed up. It is a position of ever recurring deficits diversified by an ever-increasing debt. . . . . . England has educated us, and has awakened in our minds ambitions which she is bound to satisfy. . . The policy of the Government is not a policy of conciliation, I am sorry to say. At times it is an irritating policy. Take the case of the volunteers. We are excluded from enrolment as volunteers. Armenians, Negroes, West African Mulattoes, and nondescripts of humanity who infest the back slums of Calcutta—these are all eligible as volunteers, these are our martial heroes, these are the defenders of our hearths and homes. These are invidious distinctions, and I am sure that they must disappear before the irresistible might of constitutional agitation. They are opposed to the spirit of British law; they are opposed to the spirit of that law which is higher than all human laws, the law of nature, which is engraved on the hearts and consciences of the people of this country.

All this is entirely true; the words were spoken in 1891; this is the year of grace 1915.

The Resolution was briefly seconded by the Rev. Mr. R. C. Bose and carried by acclamation.

Mr. Pringle Kennedy then moved Resolution III, which with Resolutions IV, V, VI, VII and VIII, really, though they were separately moved and carried, constituted a sort of "omnibus Resolution". Mr. Kennedy made a remarkably good speech, on "peace, economy, and reform," urging that instead of a "scientific frontier," they should remember the words of Lord Derby in 1878, when an invasion of India was feared: "A full treasury, a prosperous and contented people—these are the real defences of the country." He pleaded for the people in words as pitifully true in 1915 as in 1891, saying that millions

> have not, from year's end to year's end, a sufficiency of food. From one day to another they do not know, what every one of us knows every day of his life, what it is to have their stomachs full.

Mr. Mudholkar seconded, saying that there was "acute, widespread, growing poverty," and quoted Sir William Hunter, who said that fully 40 millions of people in India went through life with insufficient food, and Sir Charles Elliot, who declared: "I do not hesitate to say that half the agricultural population do not know from one year's end to another what it is to have a full meal." He gave the records of some famines—in 12 years, 12 million people had died. The average income of the Indian was put down by Government at Rs. 27, while that of the Englishman was Rs. 570. And this is an *average*; some have enormous incomes; to what then do the incomes of the peasants fall?

Lala Murlidhar, speaking in Urdu, made an impassioned speech; the hag Poverty, he said, brought forth a brood, wretchedness, misery, degradation, famine, pestilence, crime; all were to blame for this, people and Government:

> You, you, it seems, are content to join with these accursed monsters in battening on the heart's blood of your brethren (*cries of No, No*). I say *Yes*; look round: What are all these chandeliers and lamps, and European-made chairs and tables, and smart clothes and hats, and English coats and bonnets and frocks, and silver-mounted canes, and all the luxurious fittings of your houses, but trophies of India's misery, mementoes of India's starvation! Every rupee you have spent on Europe-made articles is a rupee of which you have robbed your poorer brethren, honest handicraftsmen, who can now no longer earn a living. Of course I know that it was pure philanthropy which flooded India with English-made goods, and surely, if slowly, killed out every indigenous industry—pure philanthropy which, to facilitate this, repealed the import duties and flung away three crores a year of a revenue which the rich paid, and to balance this wicked sacrifice raised the salt tax, which the poor pay; which is now pressing factory regulations on us, to kill, if possible, the one tiny new industrial departure India could boast. Oh, yes, it is all philanthropy, but the result is that from this cause, amongst others, your brethren are starving.

Not 30 years ago wheat sold for $1\frac{1}{2}$ maunds and gram for 2 maunds for the rupee, for our grain was not exported to foreign lands. Now it is six times as dear, and six times as hard for the poor to fill their bellies, because our philanthropists have conjured up the phantasm of free trade to drain our granaries. Free trade, fair play between nations, how I hate the sham. What fair play in trade can there be between impoverished India and the bloated capitalist England? As well talk of a fair fight between an infant and a strong man—a rabbit and a boa-constrictor. No doubt it is all in accordance with high economic science, but, my friends, remember this—this, too—is starving your brethren.

And our good Government is so grieved at the decay of all native industries, so anxious that we should once more be in a position to supply ourselves and find work here for our people, that they have established, I believe, nearly one dozen technical schools, amongst 300 millions of people.

He complained bitterly that Indians might not manage their own finance, though Akbar trusted his finance to Hindu ministers, who always had large surpluses and money to spare.

Mr. D. E. Wacha took up the growing military expenditure, and showed that the peasantry were being ruined by the revenue system of British India. Between 1864 and 1885 the military expenditure had increased by five crores. In 1869 it stood at 14 crores. Since 1885-86 to 1890-01 it had increased 54 crores, and it continued to increase.

Our readers will remember that Mr. Gokhale's Bill for Education was rejected as involving an expenditure of "between 5 and 10 crores annually".

Pandit Madan Mohan Malaviya remarked that Indian soldiers had gone outside India, and had shed their blood for the Queen wherever she wished, but they could only be Subedar and Resaldar Majors, subject, after 25 years of service, "to the sub-lieutenant who joined yesterday". It was said they spoke with bitterness and warmth: "It is the man who is being flogged who cries out, not the mere bystanders." Mr. K. G. Deshpande dealt with the frequent land assessments, showing their ruinous effect on the peasantry, and the absurdity of arguing from the rise in prices for peasants, who cultivated not to sell, but to eat. Others followed, one land-holder saying that in his district a new settlement had recently been made which in one sub-district had enhanced the revenue 66, in another 99, in a third 116 per cent. In a few villages the revenue had been raised 300 to 1,500 per cent. The peasants were being destroyed. The President summed up the discussion caustically:

> The result of the whole argument is that there are facts and figures of a very telling character impaling us on the horns of a dilemma: either, if we believe the authorities, to submit to Russian aggression, or, if we look to facts, to calmly look on when millions upon millions of our countrymen die of famine every decade. That is the sum and substance of the whole of what has been said. We call upon the Government to take away the one horn of that dilemma, which is based on undeniable facts and is goring us even now, and leave us, if needs be, exposed to that other shadowy and still very distant horn, in which, sooth to say, we have no belief.

The Resolution was unanimously carried.

Mr. B. G. Tilak moved Resolution IV, urging that the question: As the British Government defends you, why want arms? was easily answered. The Government undertakes to defend 250 millions of people against wild beasts and the wild bear of the north. As their own returns show, they do not defend the people against wild beasts, and as for the northern enemy they would doubtless do their best when the time came, but meanwhile their preparations were crushing the life out of the country. They did not wish the people starved to death, because the Russians might make a raid 25 years hence.

Mr. Ali Muhammad Bhimji remarked that the German soldier cost Rs. 145, the French Rs. 185, the English in England Rs. 285, but in India Rs. 775. The income per head in England was £42, in France £23, in Germany £18, in India £1. 10s. Others followed and the Resolution was carried.

Resolution V, for simultaneous examinations, was proposed, seconded and carried, and Resolution VI on Taxation and Excise was also carried. On Resolution VII, on the Judicial and Police Administration, the President gave a case which should be placed on record: a magistrate was determined to convict an accused, and his prejudice was so marked that the case was sent to the Sessions; the last sentence in his order ran: "I am perfectly satisfied as to the guilt of the accused; I was prepared to convict him and pass sentence on him, but my hands have been tied." The Sessions Court, after hearing the case for the prosecution, acquitted the accused honorably, without calling on him for any defence.

Mr. Herambo Chandra Maitra, in moving Resolution VIII on education, declared that they would not allow the Government to assert, uncontradicted, that it was anxious to promote primary education, while doing nothing for it, and trying to withdraw from higher education. If the educated were a "microscopical minority," who but the Government were to blame? He concluded with a fine appeal:

It is hard upon three score years ago that this great problem formally forced itself on the consideration of the British Nation: "Shall we for ever retain these Indians, whose destinies God has confided to our charge, ignorant and as slaves, or shall we educate and raise them to be fit and anxious to join, as free men, in the administration of their own country?" Day after day, in both Houses of Parliament, the great debate was carried on, until the Nation, through its peers and representatives, decided for the latter and nobler course. For years this decision was honestly acted up to, and Lord Derby's (then Lord Stanley's) despatch of 1859 and John Stuart Mill's famous despatch of 1854, remain proofs of the honesty of purpose of the British Nation. But ever since the Congress arose to advocate and vindicate the cause of constitutional freedom, and threaten the autocratic powers and exclusive privileges of the great Indian bureaucracy, this latter, alarmed for these its cherished possessions, has begun to crave for a retrogade movement into the policy which their nobler countrymen, 60 years ago, indignantly repudiated.

It is too late, my friends—too late; the seed has been sown broadcast, has germinated, is germinating everywhere; in vain you try now everywhere to repress and discourage higher education by every insidious means. You may delay, but you cannot destroy. You may earn hatred, you cannot secure the enslavement of those who now know that they are free British subjects. It is too late; put aside this folly, accept the inevitable and foreseen results of the policy your nobler predecessors deliberately adopted. Abstain from discouraging, as you now are discouraging, education ; be true to the higher and better impulses of a Briton's heart ; be true to the edicts of your senates, the orders of our Queen-Empress ; stimulate, heart and soul, as in days gone by, education of all kinds and of every grade, and then, in lieu of a Frankenstein monster ever on the alert to destroy you, you will find in the educated generations that will rally round you, not indeed the servile sycophants that ignorance might have furnished you, but true, loyal and capable colleagues, whose foremost aim and chief glory it will be to labour on equal terms, side by side with you, to secure the safety, honour and welfare of our common Sovereign and all her dominions.

Mr. G. K. Gokhale seconded, not as thinking that anything would come from a Commission, but Commission Reports were useful to students. Education meant the growth of the section which worked to secure the happiness and contentment of the people. "Truly in the happiness and contentment of India's people lie England's glory and England's strength ; and in England's sense of honour and justice lie, at this critical period, all our hopes and all our aspirations."

With the passing of this Resolution the Congress adjourned.

The third day opened with a Resolution which recited a telegram from General Booth and proposed the reply drafted by the Subjects Committee, which was unanimously adopted by the Congress and carried as Resolution IX.

Mr. W. C. Bannerji then brought up the report of the Committee appointed by Resolution I, recommending that the Congress should continue its annual sittings and this, seconded by Pandit Ayodhyanath, was carried as Resolution X.

Mr. Peter Paul Pillai moved Resolution XI on the Forest Laws, and depicted the injury to agriculture caused by them in the Madras Presidency to which he belonged :

> With a single stroke of the legislators' pen, the Forest Laws have extinguished the communal rights of the ryot—rights which have been enjoyed from time immemorial—rights recognised and respected by former Governments, and even by the British Government in former times. . . . . By the extinction of communal rights village society has been revolutionised . . . . Under pressure of necessity they are driven to infringe the all-embracing Forest Laws and thus stand liable to criminal prosecution. For petty infringements of these vexatious forest ordinances, thousands of criminal prosecutions take place in my district.

As a matter of fact the Forest Laws have done more to alienate the peasantry from British rule than any other thing ; the Salt Tax is bad ; the Assessment Settlements are cruel ; but the Forest Laws sting at every point, and the unhappy peasant, doing as his forefathers have done for countless generations, finds himself haled up as a criminal. Mr. Pillai showed that the Government had realised in 1890 a lakh and a half from pasture fees, and three and a half lakhs as penal fees by impounding cattle for trespass on the confiscated communal lands. In one district, North Arcot, during January to September, 1891, 300,000 cattle perished for want of pasture over and above the normal mortality. Mr. Pillai recounted a number of other grievances, and said—he was an

Indian Christian—that all appeals to press and Government having failed, their only hope was in the Congress.

Among other speakers was Mr. S. B. Bhate, who said that in his district the cattle were starving because of the forest administration, which would not even open the old grazing land temporarily, and peasants were giving their cattle away, and selling 10 or 12 for a rupee. Mr. Nunbkar spoke, "an original inhabitant," he said, "of a poor hilly village in a poor district ". Forests, jungles, wilds, gave things men wanted, fuel, wood, grass, stones, earth, leaves, bark, roots ; all had been taken from them, not by God, but by avaricious men. For hundreds of generations they had enjoyed these unchallenged, and now they were deprived of what nature gave them. Forests were blessings in the days of Hindu and Muhammadan rulers ; now they were curses. His land was on the hills, but he could not use forest, brush, scrub, though they were his own. He might not use leaves from his own trees, though he had grown them. Where might his cattle graze ? The forest reserves were not fenced, and cattle trespassed, and the owners were fined. A villager, having no doctor, tried to gather medicinal herbs, he was fined ; the herbs were all in the forests. Nothing could add to the pathos of the simple recital of the facts among which the speaker lived. The Resolution was, of course, unanimously passed.

Resolutions followed of thanks to friends living in this world, of grief and gratitude to Charles

Bradlaugh, lost to India's cause. Several voiced their deep and abiding sorrow, and all stood in silent reverence till the Resolution was declared carried.

Resolution XV postponed the holding of a Congress in London as a General Election was impending. Funds were voted to the British Committee, Mr. A. O. Hume and Pandit Ayodhyanath were elected General and Joint General Secretaries, the invitation to Allahabad for the next Session of the Congress was accepted, and a vote of thanks to the President was passed. Thus ended the Seventh National Congress.

No one who reads these records of Congress work can fail to recognise the single eye to the freedom, prosperity, and happiness of the Motherland ever shown by the Congress. The intense sympathy with the sufferings of the masses, the effort to gain primary education for them, the protest against the laws and administration that were reducing the peasantry to hopeless poverty, these were all close to the heart of the Congressman. Never was there a falser accusation than that which tried to divide the Voice of India from the inarticulate masses whose sufferings it proclaimed, by calling the Congress a movement merely of discontented educated men, wanting place and power.

RESOLUTIONS

I. Resolved—That a Committee be appointed to consider and report, on or before the morning of the 30th instant, whether, or not, it is advisable to discontinue the Annual Sessions of the Indian National Congress until after the British Session, and, if not, under what regulations, as to numbers of delegates, localities for assemblage, and the like, future Congresses shall be held. The Committee to be composed as follows:

EX-OFFICIO MEMBERS:

The President.
The Chairman of the Reception Committee.
The General Secretary.
The Joint General Secretary.
The Standing Counsels to the Congress.

ORDINARY MEMBERS:

Messrs. Surendranath Bannerji.
Viraraghava Chariar.
Hafiz M. Abdul Rahim.
Gangaprasad Varma.
Pringle Kennedy.
Guruprasad Sen.
D. E. Wacha.
M. B. Namjoshi.
Hamid Ali Khan.
Vishnu Moreshwar Bhide.

Messrs. Murlidhar.
Mudholkar.
Deo Rao Vinayak.
Gopal Rao Bhide.
Bipin Krishna Bose.
Daji Abaji Khare.
Madan Mohan Malaviya.
Saligram Singh.
Sankara Nair.

Representation

II. Resolved—That this Congress reaffirms the conclusion arrived at by all previous Congresses, *viz.*, that India can never be well or justly governed, nor her people prosperous or contented, until they are allowed, through their elected representatives, a potential voice in the Legislatures of their own country, and respectfully urges the people of Great Britain and Ireland, whose good will towards India it gratefully recognises, to permit no further delay in the concession of this just and necessary reform.

III. Resolved—That this Congress, concurring in the views set forth in previous Congresses, affirms—

That fully fifty millions of the population, a number yearly increasing, are dragging out a miserable existence on the verge of starvation, and that, in every decade, several millions actually perish by starvation.

That this unhappy condition of affairs is largely due to—

(*a*) the exclusion of the people of India from a due participation in the administration, and all control over the finances, of their own country, the remedy for which has been set forth in Resolution II; to

(*b*) the extravagant cost of the present administration, Military and Civil, but especially the former; and to (*c*) a short-sighted system of Land Revenue Administration, whereby not only is all improvement in the agriculture of the country, on which nine-tenths of the population depend for subsistence, rendered impossible, but the gradual deterioration of that agriculture assured.

That hence it has become imperatively necessary—

that the cost of the administration be greatly reduced; in the Military branch, by a substantial reduction of the standing army, by the substitution of long term local European troops like those of the Hon. E. I. Company, for the present short term Imperial regiments with their heavy cost of recruitment in England, in transport and of excessive mortality amongst non-acclimatised youths; by the cessation of the gigantic waste of money, that has gone on now for several years, on so-called Frontier Defences, and by a strict economy in the Commissariat, Ordnance and Store Departments; and in the Civil branch, by the wide substitution of a cheaper indigenous agency for the extremely costly imported Staff; and that measures be at once taken to give, as was promised by the British Government thirty years ago, fixity and permanence to the Land Revenue demand and thus permit capital and labour to combine to develop the agriculture of the country, which, under the existing system of temporary settlements, in recent times often lasting for short periods, in some cases only extending to 10 and 12 years, is found to be impossible; and to establish Agricultural Banks.

That this Congress does most earnestly entreat the people of Great Britain and Ireland not to permit any further sacrifice of life by the shortcomings of the existing, doubtless well-intentioned, but none the less unsatisfactory, administration, but to insist, and speedily, on these reforms.

Military

IV. Resolved—That this Congress, concurring with previous Congresses, is of opinion that, to ensure the adequate protection and efficient defence of the country, it is desirable that the Government should conciliate Indian public opinion and encourage and qualify the Indians to defend their homes and their Government—

(*a*) by so modifying the rules under the Arms Act, as to make them equally applicable to all residents in, or visitors to, India, without distinction of creed, class or colour; to ensure the liberal concession of licences wherever wild animals habitually destroy human life, cattle or crops, and to make all licences, granted under the revised rules, of lifelong tenure, revocable only on proof of misuse, and valid throughout the Provincial Jurisdiction in which they are issued;

(*b*) by establishing Military Colleges in India, whereat natives of India, as defined by Statute, may be educated and trained for a military career, as *commissioned or non-commissioned* officers (according to capacity and qualifications) of the Indian army ;

(*c*) by organising, throughout the more warlike races of the Empire, a system of Militia service ; and

(*d*) by authorising and stimulating a widespread system of Volunteering, such as obtains in Great Britain, amongst the people of India.

Taxation and Excise

V. Resolved—That as one step towards ensuring the wider employment of Indians in the administration of the country, and as a matter of simple justice to the people of India, this Congress, agreeing with previous Congresses, declares it to be essential that all examinations for any and all of the Civil branches of the Public Service in India, which at present are held only in England, should henceforth be also held simultaneously in India.

VI. Resolved—That this Congress concurs with its predecessors in strongly advocating—

(*a*) the reduction of the salt tax, by at least the amount of its latest enhancement ;

(*b*) the raising of the income tax taxable minimum from Rs. 500 to Rs. 1,000 ;

(*c*) persistent pressure by the Government of India on all Provincial Administrations, to induce them to carry out, in its integrity, the excise policy enunciated in paras 103, 104 and 105 of the despatch, published in *The Gazette of India*, of March 1st, 1890, and the introduction of a simple system of local option in the case of all villages.

Law and Police

VII. Resolved—That having regard to the unsatisfactory character, in many respects, of the Judicial and Police Administration, this Congress concurs with its predecessors in strongly advocating—

(*a*) the complete separation of Executive and Judicial functions, such that in no case shall the two functions be combined in the same officer ;

(*b*) the extension in many parts of the country, where it is not at present in force, of the system of trial by jury ;

(*c*) the withdrawal from High Courts of the powers, first vested in them in 1872, of setting aside verdicts of acquittals by juries ;

(*d*) the introduction, into the Code of Criminal Procedure of a provision enabling accused persons, in warrant cases, to demand that instead of being tried by the Magistrate they be committed to the court of sessions;

(*e*) the fundamental reform of the Police Administration, by a reduction in the numbers and an increase in the salaries, and in the qualifications of the lower grades, and their far more careful enlistment, and by the selection for the higher posts of gentlemen of higher capacities, more in touch with the respectable portions of the community, and less addicted to military pretensions, than the majority of the existing Deputy Inspectors-General, Superintendents and Assistant Superintendents, of Police.

Education

VIII. Resolved—That this Congress, concurring with previous Congresses, affirms the importance of increasing (instead of diminishing, as appears to be the present policy of the Government) the public expenditure on all branches of education, and the expediency, in view to the promotion of one of the most essential of these branches, the technical, of appointing a mixed Commission to enquire into the present industrial condition of the country.

General Booth

IX.

Read the following telegram from General Booth:

"May I be allowed to commend to the attention of the Congress, the claims of the millions of India's starving poor, and to urge the consideration of some scheme by which these destitute multitudes can be placed upon the waste lands of the country, in such an organised and befriended manner as will enable them to gain for themselves, those necessaries of a healthy existence which, in their present circumstances, are denied; praying for the blessing of God upon the labours of the Congress, yours, in sympathy with every effort for the amelioration of the miseries of mankind."

Resolved—That the following telegram be despatched in reply to General Booth:

"The Congress, having received and considered your kindly message, thank you cordially for the same. No possible scheme of internal immigration can perceptibly relieve the fifty to sixty millions of half-starving paupers, whose sad condition constitutes the primary *raison d'être* of the Congress. It is only by modifying the adverse conditions out of which this widespread misery arises, and by raising the moral standard of the people, that any real relief is possible. As regards the first, the Congress programme now embodies all primarily essential reforms ; as regards the second, in every Province and in every caste, associations, public or private, are working with a yearly increasing earnestness. Many good missionaries are labouring in the same field, and we have to thank you that your Army too is now engaged in the good work of elevating our masses. May your efforts and ours, in both directions, be crowned with success. Congress, including men of many creeds, welcomes cordially all who seek to benefit our suffering brethren."

Congress Work

X.

Read the Report of the Committee appointed, under Resolution I, which runs as follows:

" Your Committee have considered the matter referred to them and have also consulted, informally, various members of the Subjects Committee and other delegates. They are clearly of opinion that it is not advisable to discontinue the Annual Session of the Indian National Congress until after the British Session, and that future Congresses should be held under the same regulations as heretofore."

Resolved—That the Annual Sessions of the Congress in India continue to be held until all necessary reforms have been secured.

XV. Resolved—That in view of the General Election now impending in England, and in accordance with the recommendation of our British Committee, the provisional arrangements, set on foot in pursuance of the Resolution passed at the Calcutta Congress of 1890, for holding, all things being convenient, a Congress of not less than 100 Delegates in England in 1892, be now suspended until after such General Election.

XVI. Resolved—That a sum of Rs. 40,000, exclusive of individual donations, is assigned for the expenses of the British Committee of the Congress, and Rs. 6,000 for the General Secretary's office and establishment, and that the several circles do contribute as arranged in Committee for the year 1892.

Forest Laws

XI. Resolved—That having regard to the very serious discontent created, especially in Peninsular India, by the practical administration of the Forest Laws, the Government of India be most respectfully, but earnestly, entreated to investigate this carefully, and endeavour to mitigate its harshness and render it less obnoxious to the poorer classes.

Thanks of Congress

XII. Resolved—That this Congress hereby tenders its most grateful acknowledgments to Sir W. Wedderburn, and the members of the British Congress Committee, for the services rendered by them to India during the past year, and respectfully urges them to widen henceforth the sphere of their usefulness, by interesting themselves, not only in those questions dealt with by the Congress here, but in all Indian matters submitted to them, and properly vouched for, in which any principle accepted by the Congress is involved.

XIII. Resolved—That this Congress puts on record an expression of the gratitude felt, throughout India, for the signal services rendered by the late Mr. Charles Bradlaugh to that country's cause, and of the deep and universal sorrow which his untimely death has engendered; and that a copy of this Resolution, signed by the President, be transmitted through the British Committee for presentation to Mrs. Bradlaugh Bonner.

XIV. Resolved—That this Congress, hereby, puts formally on record its high estimate and deep appreciation of the great services which Mr. Dadabhai Naoroji has rendered, during more than a quarter of a century, to the cause of India; that it expresses its unshaken confidence in him and its earnest hope that he may prove successful, at the coming elections, in his candidature for Central Finsbury, and, at the same time, tenders, on behalf of the vast population it represents, India's most cordial acknowledgments to all in England, whether in Central Finsbury or elsewhere, who have aided, or may aid him, to win a seat in the House of Commons.

Formal

XVII. Resolved—That Mr. A. O. Hume and Pandit Ayodhyanath are re-elected General and Joint-General Secretaries for the ensuing year.

XVIII. Resolved—That the Eighth Indian National Congress do assemble on the 26th December, 1892, at Allahabad.

CHAPTER VIII

The Eighth National Congress met at Allahabad on December 28, 1892, in the same place as the Fourth, in Lowther Castle and its grounds, but these were now lent by the Maharaja of Darbhanga instead of being leased, hot-foot, to secure an abiding-place against the efforts of the official elements in Allahabad. The Maharaja had been a warm supporter of the National Movement, and, as he had become possessed of Lowther Castle, he gladly placed it at the disposal of the Congress. There was raised the Pavilion for the Congress, holding 3,500 chairs, to accommodate the delegates and the expected visitors.

The country was represented as follows:

Madras	38
Bombay	77
C. P., Berar and Secunderabad	63
Bengal	105
N. W. P. and Oudh	323
Panjab	19
	625

The Chairman of the Reception Committee was Pandit Bishambharnath, whose health was very weak, but who succeeded in delivering a short but admirable speech. After welcoming the delegates, he made a touching reference to the loss the movement had sustained in the passing away of that sterling patriot, Pandit Ayodhyanath, and then said a few strong words for the Congress :

> Every true Englishman, with whom the love of liberty is an instinct, must rejoice in his heart to witness that that proud day in the history of the British occupation of India has come, when the children of the soil have learnt to stand upon their feet, and are now claiming their just rights in a constitutional manner. Both posterity and the history of our movement when written calmly, will, I am convinced, accord a just appreciation to its legitimate aims and reasonable objects. They not only err, but sin, and sin criminally too, who insinuate that this movement is calculated to sap and undermine the foundation of constituted authority .... We are now at the fag-end of the 19th century, and live under the ægis of a rule which recognises only lawful agitation by constitutional means. Hence the necessity of our resorting to such a course. Whether such agitation is a blessing or a curse of the present civilisation, I do not propose to discuss here. We must go on, and go on vigorously, and not cease to agitate until we reach the goal of our ambition.

Mr. P. Ananda Charlu proposed, Mr. D. E. Wacha seconded, the election of Mr. W. C. Bannerji as President. It was put and unanimously carried, and he took the chair. A telegram from the Maharaja of Darbhanga was read, which welcomed the delegates to Lowther Castle, and expressed his pleasure "that the first use of this property, since my acquiring it, has been for Congress purposes".

Mr. Bannerji, in delivering his Presidential Address, referred to the reasons for the non-interference by the Congress with social questions, and then said a few words on the loss the movement had sustained in the passing of Pandit Ayodhyanath and Mr. George Yule, who had been respectively the President of the Reception Committee and of the Congress, when the Congress met in Allahabad in 1888. He alluded to the passing of Lord Cross' India Councils Bill, the value of which depended on the Rules framed to give effect to it, and then congratulated the Congress on the election to Parliament of Mr. Dadabhai Naoroji by the Central Finsbury constituency—a noble and generous recognition of the claim of India to make her voice heard. He spoke warmly against the withdrawal of grants for higher education, and scathingly against the withdrawal of trial by jury in seven of the districts of Bengal in serious cases.

In closing, the President made a powerful appeal on the right of Indians to be heard, in answer to some who had said that an agitation of theirs might be disregarded because "it was only a 'native' agitation".

> Is our voice not to be listened to because, forsooth, to that voice has not been added the voice of our European fellow-subjects? We would welcome, welcome with open arms, all the support which we can get from our European fellow-subjects . . . . . But, apart from that, why is our voice to be despised? It is we who feel the pinch; it is we who have to suffer; and when we cry out, it is said to us: "Oh, we cannot listen to you; yours is a contemptible and useless and a vile agitation, and we will not listen to you." Time was when we natives of the country agitated about any matter, with the help of non-official Europeans, the apologists of the Government used to say triumphantly: "This agitation is not the agitation

of the natives of the country, but has been got up by a few discontented Europeans ; don't listen to them, it is not their true voice ; it is the voice of these Europeans." And now we are told : "Don't listen to them ; it is their own voice, and not the voice of the Europeans."

The Subjects Committee, elected by the delegates was then submitted to and approved by the Congress. A telegram was sent to Mr. Dadabhai Naoroji, congratulating him on his election to the House of Commons and thanking the electors of Central Finsbury, and the Congress adjourned.

The meeting of December 29th began by sending a congratulatory telegram to Mr. Gladstone on his 83rd birthday, and then the President read out the rules for the conduct of business.

The first Resolution, accepting the India Councils Bill, but regretting that it did not formally recognise the right of the Indian people to elect their representatives, was moved by Rai Bahadur Ananda Charlu, who emphasised the regret. He quoted Mr. Gladstone, who looked forward to "not merely a nominal, but to a real living representation of the people of India," and Lord Salisbury, who said :

> If we are to do it, and if it has to be done, let us do it systematically . . . . taking care that the machinery to be provided shall effect the purpose of giving representation, not to accidentally constituted bodies, not to small sections of the people here and there, but to the living strength and vital forces of the whole community of India.

Mr. Surendranath Bannerji seconding, alluded to the statement (often heard since) that the Congress movement was discredited and enthusiasm on the wane, and remarked that this very Act was due to the Congress, and pointed to other signs of progress. Mr. Gladstone had spoken in 1892 of representative institutions as the "consecrated possessions ... entrusted to the care and the guardianship of the English people".

We appeal to Mr. Gladstone, we appeal to his colleagues, to admit us into this inestimable legacy of the Anglo-Saxon race. Wherever floats the flag of England, Self-Government is the order of the day. Wherever Englishmen have gathered together in their Colonies, be they in the frigid zones of the north, or amid the blazing heat of the Equator, or in those distinct tracts watered by the southern seas, Self-Government again is the order of the day. We are not Englishmen, or men of English race or extraction, but we are British subjects, the citizens of a great and free Empire; we live under the protecting shadows of one of the noblest Constitutions the world has ever seen. The rights of Englishmen are ours, their privileges are ours, their Constitution is ours. But we are excluded from them. How long is this exclusion to last? That will depend very much upon ourselves. If we are true to the traditions of the Congress, and loyal to the noble teachings of our great Chief, who, though not present in body is present in spirit with us—if we live up to the exalted standard of his noble life, if we consecrate our efforts by the spirit of self-sacrifice, if we are unsparing in our pecuniary sacrifices, unremitting in our personal efforts, then the great God who presides over the destinies of fallen Nations will, in His own due time, pour down upon us, in plentiful abundance, His choicest blessings; and though we may receive a temporary check, and the flag we now hold aloft may drop from our sinking hands, I am confident that in the near future there will rise up others, who, more fortunately situated than ourselves, will carry that standard to victory, and establish in this luckless land those principles of liberty, which, while they will serve to weld together the diversified elements of our common Nationality, will at the same time place the Empire of Britain in this country upon the only unchangeable basis upon which it can rest, the love, the gratitude, and the contentment of a vast and immeasurable population.

The Resolution was supported by Raja Rampal Sinha, Mr. M. B. Namjoshi, Mr. Uma Shankar, Hafiz Muhammad Abdul Rahim and Moulvi Wahab-ud-din, and carried unanimously.

The second Resolution expressed the deep regret of the Congress with the resolution of the Government of India on the Report of the Public Service Commission, narrowing even the proposals made by that Commission. It was proposed by Mr. G. K. Gokhale, who pointed out that the Report of the Commission actually put Indians in a worse position than they were in before. They had had by the rules of 1879 "one-sixth of the whole recruitment" each year, and as there were 600+150 posts, reserved and unreserved, Indians would have had 125 posts. But, by a juggle, they had only 108 set apart for them. These 108 should have been incorporated in the Provincial Service, created by the Commission for Indians only. But the Secretary of State managed to have 93 or 94 of these kept on a separate list, and would appoint to them under the Act of 1870. Mr. Gokhale drily said that he was not sure that the discretion of Government would not be abused. Thus India lost the certainty of the 108, or 93, appointments, and they were made discretionary. The number recommended was reduced, the highest were withheld, and a large and perilous discretion has been reserved by Government to itself which is almost sure to be abused. And all this as the outcome of the labours of a Commission solemnly appointed to do full justice to our claims for larger and more extensive employment in the higher grades of the Public Service !

On simultaneous examinations Mr. Gokhale spoke forcibly and indignantly :

Unfortunately the fact cannot be gainsaid, that of late our rulers have been showing a disposition to regret the promises given us in the past ; and I should not be surprised if they one day turned round and said that these promises were never intended to be carried out. In that case I say it would be well for them to openly and publicly fling into the flames all these promises and pledges as so much waste paper, and tell us once for all that, after all, we are a conquered people, and can have no rights or privileges. That the Government has, of late, been pursuing a policy of retrogression is clear to every one. Turn whichever way we may, we find that a change, and a change for the worse, is coming over the spirit of the Government. Whether you consider the Jury Notification in Bengal, or the curtailment of educational grants, or the treatment accorded to Municipalities, you cannot help feeling that Government is treating us with increasing jealousy and mistrust every day. And unless this régime of distrust is soon changed, unless the policy of Government is inspired by more sympathetic feelings, darker days cannot but be in store for this poor country.

The warning was disregarded. Mr. Gokhale was looked on as an enemy, and followed by police spies, instead of being looked on as a friend, warning the Government of dangers which he, as an Indian, knew to exist, but to which the Government were blind. When, out of despair, anarchism was born, his words were remembered—too late.

Pandit Madan Mohan Malaviya seconded the Resolution, and after giving some figures to "show the great and inordinate drain of India's money because of the inordinate employment of Europeans in the higher ranks of the Public Service," that was "at the bottom of the increasing poverty of the people of this country," went on to support Mr. Dadabhai Naoroji in pressing upon the attention of Parliament the injustice done to India by the refusal of simultaneous examinations in India and England for the Indian Civil Service. The examinations ought really to be held only in India, since the Service was Indian.

> It is singularly unjust to compel the people of this country to go 10,000 miles away from their country to pass an examination to qualify themselves for service in their own country. No other people labour under such an awful disadvantage. Must we alone be subjected to it because we are the subjects of a strong Power like England? England, we know, has got the strength of a giant, but she should not use it as a giant in enforcing unfair terms and conditions against a people placed by Providence under her care, but should allow her nobler instincts to guide her in this matter as they have guided her in many others, and see that we are governed practically, and not merely theoretically, in consonance with those noble principles of justice and good government which her honoured Sovereign and her statesmen have laid down for the purpose, and which guide her in the conduct of her own affairs. We pray only for a fair field and no favour.

Mr. Gokhale and Pandit Madan Mohan spoke in 1892. Twenty-three years have passed, and this little concession has not been made! Still India's sons must travel 10,000 miles on the chance of entering the Indian Civil Service in a competitive examination for the number of posts open every year, for the privilege of employment in their own country. And in the face of this, a concession that would cost England nothing, and would not touch the fundamental injustice of her autocracy here, we are asked not to raise any controversial question now, but to trust to her good-will that after the War she will give us Self-Government.

The Resolution was supported by Mr. Janardana Raghunath Nimkar, Moulvi Umrao Mirza Hairat, and Rai Jotindranath Chaudhuri—who said very pertinently:

> To serve one's own country is a right inalienable from its people. So in this view I look upon all those appointments which can be safely given to the natives of the soil and which are filled by foreigners, as so many appointments robbed from the people to whom they belong by natural right, specially in India, where we Indians are most cruelly debarred from all the higher employments.

Munshi Roshan Lal pointed out the caste difficulty, which the Government knew very well, and which, with the expense incurred by the journey and stay in England, made the nominal opening of the Service to Indians of very little value to them. The Resolution was carried unanimously.

Mr. R..N. Mudholkar moved the third Resolution on the then already well-worn subject of the separation of judicial and executive functions, which has since been moved and carried 22 times in vain. Mr. Mudholkar gave his own experience with men who were civil judges, criminal judges, and revenue officers rolled into one, whose courts travelled and had to be followed by the unlucky litigants or accused persons, and who, being busy men, had no time to study intricate laws, and who were not to be blamed for their ignorance—which caused them to give unjust decisions—nor for their incompatible functions—which led them to give biassed decisions. He quoted the Judges of the Calcutta High Court, who said:

> It not unfrequently happens that the chief executive Magistrate practically becomes the prosecutor and may frequently become the Judge, though he may have formed a strong opinion on the case behind the back of the accused, without having had the opportunity of hearing his explanation or defence.

It may be remembered that a striking case of this was mentioned in the last chapter.

Mr. Ambikacharan Mozumdar seconded the Resolution, and described the condition of things in Bengal, where the Lieut.-Governor over-rode the Codes, and insisted on improper methods, which upset the administration of justice. He mentioned some striking cases of abuse of processes of law by executive officers.

Mr. Hun Chandra Rai, supporting, said, very truly, that the interference of District Officers with the subordinate Magistracy, by referring cases to them with "almost plain directions as to how they are to be decided. . . . has brought about a widespread feeling of alarm, which it is in the interests of good Government instantly to allay". Mr. K. G.

Natu, Rao Sahab Deva Rao Vinayak and Mr. Murlidhar further supported, and the Resolution was carried unanimously.

Mr. D. E. Wacha moved Resolution IV on the Currency question, remarking that the Congress delegates

> earnestly desire at this critical juncture, when some action on the part of Government is reported to be imminent, that it will refrain from either taking a leap in the dark, or adopting precipitately a measure which might eventually prove to be infinitely worse in its consequences than the evils to be witnessed at present.

Mr. Wacha dealt at length with the matter with a clarity all his own, explaining the effects of the demonetisation of silver by Germany in 1873, the bearing of the " Home (foreign) Charges " on India, the Sherman Act of 1890, the effect on India of a gold standard as jeopardising the interests of the masses. Captain Banon and Professor Bhagiratha Prasad followed, and the unanimous passing of the Resolution brought the second day to its close.

On the third day, Mr. G. S. Khaparde brought in the " Omnibus Resolution," No. V, including, this year, Salt Tax, Income Tax, Excise, claim to committal to Quarter Sessions, Police, Arms, Military Colleges, Militia and Volunteering. He was followed by the Rev. T. Evans, Mr. Oudh Behari Lal, Munshi Sheikh Husain, Mr. B. S. Sahasrabuddhe, and Munshi Abdul Qudir, and the Resolution was then carried.

Mr. Guruprasad Sen, in moving the sixth Resolution, demanding the withdrawal of the Jury Notification in Bengal and the extension of the Jury system, gave a mass of facts and figures in support of his motion. Mr. Baikunthanath Sen seconded, and glancing at the history of the Jury system, dwelt on the scandal of suddenly abolishing a vested right, enjoyed for 30 years, by a sudden fiat of a Lieut.-Governor.

Mr. Lakshminath Bezbarua, from Assam, said they had enjoyed it for 60 years, and needed it specially, because of the raw and inexperienced Civilians who administered justice in a lawless manner. Six other delegates spoke, and the Resolution was carried.

Mr. D. E. Wacha moved and Pandit Madan Mohan Malaviya seconded Resolution VII, which pointed out that England should bear part of the cost of the military expenditure caused by Imperial policy which related, not to the defence of India, but to Britain's relations with the great European Powers. It was carried.

Then Mr. Brajendranath Seal made an eloquent and informing speech, moving Resolution VIII, which deprecated the diminution of grants for higher education, and urged increased expenditure on all branches of education. He brought abundant arguments to his thesis, and ridiculed the idea that there were too many graduates, who, finding no outlet, sowed discontent. England had 22,000 University students out of a population of 27 millions, India 15,000 out of a population of 220 millions.

Mr. Heramba Chandra Maitra seconded, Messrs. K. V. Joshi and Hari Prasad Chatterji supported, and the Resolution was carried unanimously.

The sore poverty of India and the remedies therefor were the subject of Resolution IX, reaffirming Resolution III of 1891; it was moved by Mr. Baikunthanath Sen, seconded by Mr. Peter Paul Pillai, supported by four other speakers, and carried unanimously. Resolution X took up the harshness of the administration of the Forest Laws, Mr. Karandikar moving and Mr. P. Keshava Pillai seconding, the latter recounting the grievances he has been struggling to remedy ever since. The Resolution passed, but the grievances still remain.

Then Mr. A. Nandy moved—Resolution XI—for a Committee of four delegates, to draw up a petition to Parliament against the results of the Public Service Commission, and this, seconded by Mr. Kali Prasanna Kavyavisharada, was carried. One thing mentioned by the mover, an Indian Christian, may be put on record. Sir Auckland Colvin had admitted that some grievances might exist:

> But what was the advice Sir Auckland Colvin gave for the redress of these grievances? 99 out of 100 Englishmen would have said: "Agitate, and agitate strongly, till you attain your object." Not so the ex-Lieut.-Governor. He expressed a pious horror of agitation, and stigmatised in bitter terms what he called the professional agitator, but wound up by advising his hearers, if they had a grievance, to do what?—to lay them before the District Magistrate!

If the Magistrate failed, there was the Commissioner, and lastly the Local Government. Still Government officials detest agitation, and some Indians, even, are afraid of it.

Mr. Kanhaya Lal and Mr. Murlidhar moved and supported Resolution XII, asking for a Legislative Council for the Panjab. Carried. Then came Resolution XIII, thanking the British Committee and Mr. Digby, and Resolution XIV, protesting against State-regulated immorality in India. Resolution XV postponed the English Session of the Congress until after that of 1893, and Resolution XVI appointed Mr. Dadabhai Naoroji as India's representative in Parliament, and thanked the electors of Central Finsbury for sending him thither. Resolutions XVII and XVIII dealt with Congress finance, and XIX re-elected Mr. A. O. Hume and gave him Rai Bahadur P. Ananda Charlu as Joint Secretary. Resolutions XX, XXI and XXII fixed the next Congress at Amritsar, thanked the Maharaja of Darbhanga for the loan of Lowther Castle, and confirmed the appointment of Pandit Bishambharnath as one of the Trustees of the Permanent Fund. With a few words from the President, and the usual vote of thanks, the Eighth Congress dissolved.

RESOLUTIONS

Representation

I. Resolved—That this Congress, while accepting in a loyal spirit the Indian Councils Act recently enacted by the Parliament of Great Britain, as explained by the present Prime Minister, with the assent of the then Under-Secretary of State for India—that it is intended by it to give the people of India *a real living representation* in the Legislative Councils—regrets that the Act itself does not, in terms, concede to the people the right of electing their own representatives to the Council, and hopes and expects that the rules, now being prepared under the Act, will be framed on the lines of Mr. Gladstone's declaration in the House of Commons, and will do adequate justice to the people of this country; further, that it prays that these rules may be published in the official Gazettes, like other proposed legislative measures, before being finally adopted.

Public Service

II. Resolved--That this Congress hereby places on record its deep regret at the resolution of the Government of India on the report of the Public Service Commission, in that—

(*a*) Whereas, if the recommendations of the Public Service Commission had been carried out in their integrity, the posts proposed to be detached from the schedule of the Statute of 1861 would have formed part of an organised Service, specially reserved for the Natives of India, the resolution of Government leaves these posts altogether isolated, to which appointment can be made only under the Statute of 1870;

(*b*) Whereas, while 108 appointments were recommended by the Public Service Commission for the Provincial Service, 93 such appointments only have actually been thrown open to that Service: the number to be allotted to Assam not having yet been announced;

(*c*) Whereas, while a Membership of the Board of Revenue and a Commissionership of a Division, were recommended for the Province of Bengal and some other Provinces, the Government has not given effect to this resolution;

(*d*) Whereas, while one-third of the Judgeships were recommended to be thrown open to the Provincial Service, only one-fifth have been so thrown open.

And this Congress, again, distinctly puts on record its opinion, that full justice will never be done to the people of this country, until the open Competitive Examination for the Civil Service of India is held simultaneously in England and in India.

XI. Resolved—That Mr. W. C. Bannerji, Mr. P. M. Mehta, Mr. Surendranath Bannerji, and Rai Bahadur Ananda Charlu, be appointed a Committee to prepare a petition on the line indicated by the petition printed at foot, and that the President be authorised to sign it, on behalf of this Congress, and send it to Mr. Dadabhai Naoroji, M.P., for presentation to the House of Commons.

To

The Honourable The Commons of Great Britain and Ireland in Parliament assembled.

The humble petition of the President and Members of the Eighth Indian National Congress, held at Allahabad, on the 28th, 29th and 30th of December, 1892

Respectfully Showeth,

(1) That in conformity with a resolution adopted at the Eighth Indian National Congress, your humble petitioners beg to bring to the attention of your Honourable House, the deep disappointment which prevails in all parts of Her Majesty's Indian Empire at the orders passed upon the labours of the Public Service Commission.

(2) That the Commission was instructed by the Government of India to submit a scheme which might reasonably be expected to possess the elements of finality and to do full justice to the claims of the Natives of India to higher and more extensive employment in the Public Service. Neither object has been secured by the labours of the Public Service Commission. The Statutory Service, under which appointments had been made, has been abolished, and nothing has been done to secure to the people the full enjoyment of the boon conferred upon them by the Act of 1870. The Government of India, in their resolution appointing the Commission, observed: "That the Statute of 1870 is one of remarkable breadth and liberality, and it empowers the Government of India and the Secretary of State, acting together, to frame rules under which Natives of India may be admitted to any of the offices hitherto reserved for the Covenanted Civil Service." But the result of the Commission's enquiry has been a reduction in the number of offices open to Indians.

(3) That in respect, likewise, to simultaneous examinations in England and in India for appointment in the Civil Service, the Report of the Commission, endorsed by the Government of India, has given no satisfaction whatever. The weight of the evidence taken by the Commissioners was distinctly in favour of simultaneous examinations. Among the witnesses examined, there was a very large preponderance of those who were in favour of simultaneous examinations.

(4) That the disappointment which is everywhere felt at the resolution of the Government of India on the Public Service Commission, is of such a character that this Congress has felt constrained to lay the matter before the Honourable House, and to pray that it will direct the Government of India to give full effect to the Act of 1870, in the matter of appointing Natives of India to the Public Service of their country.

Legal

III. Resolved—That this Congress, seeing the serious mischief arising to the country from the combination of Judicial and Executive functions in the same official, once again puts on record its deliberate and earnest conviction that a complete separation of these functions has become an urgent necessity, and that, in its opinion, it behoves the Government to effect this separation without further delay, even though this should, in some Provinces, involve extra expenditure.

VI. Resolved—That this Congress views with the deepest concern and alarm the recent policy of Government with respect to trial by Jury, and particularly the action of the Governments of Bengal and Assam in withdrawing the right of trial by Jury in the majority of serious offences, and most respectfully, but firmly, protests against such policy and action as retrograde, reactionary, and injurious to the best interests of the country, and prays that the same may be reversed by the Government of India, and failing that, by the Government in England; and that, as prayed for in resolutions of previous Congresses, the right of trial by Jury be extended to those parts of the country where it is not now in force, it being the only safeguard for the people in the present unsatisfactory condition of the administration of Criminal Justice in British India.

Currency

IV. Resolved—That having regard to the diversity of opinion that prevails on the Currency Question, and the importance of the question itself, this Congress desires to express its earnest hope, that unless its hands are forced by the action of any Foreign Power, necessitating a change in the currency, or the standard, which might prove injurious to the interests of the country, the Government of India will refrain from taking any steps, until the labours of the Brussels Conference have been completed: and, further, that the Government will lay before the Public, for discussion, the proposals which Lord Herschell's Committee may recommend, before definite action, if any, is resolved upon.

Confirmation of Previous Resolutions

V. Resolved—That this Congress concurs with its predecessors in strongly advocating—

Taxation

(*a*) The reduction of the salt duty by at least the amount of its latest enhancement;

(*b*) The raising of the Income-tax taxable minimum from five hundred to one thousand;

Excise

(*c*) Persistent pressure by the Government of India on all Provincial Administrations, to induce them to carry out, in its integrity, the Excise policy enunciated in paragraphs 103, 104, 105 of the Despatch, published in *The Gazette of India* of March, 1890, and the introduction of a simple system of local option in the case of all villages;

Legal

(*d*) The introduction into the Code of Criminal Procedure of a provision enabling accused persons in warrant cases, to demand that instead of being tried by the Magistrate they may be committed to the Court of Sessions;

Police

(*e*) The fundamental reform of the Police administration, by a reduction in the numbers and an increase in the salaries and in the qualifications of the lower grades, and their far more careful enlistment; and by the selection for the higher posts of gentlemen of higher capacities, more in touch with the respectable portions of the community, and less addicted to military pretensions, than the majority of existing Deputy Inspectors-General, Superintendents, and Assistant Superintendents of Police are;

Military

(*f*) A modification of the rules under the Arms Act, so as to make them equally applicable to all residents in, or visitors to India, without distinction of creed, caste or colour; to ensure the liberal concession of licences wherever wild animals habitually destroy human life, cattle or crops; and to make all licences, granted under the revised rules, of life-long tenure, revocable only on proof of misuse, and valid throughout the Provincial jurisdiction in which they are issued;

(*g*) The establishment of Military Colleges in India, whereat natives of India, defined by statute, may be educated and trained for a military career as Commissioned or Non-commissioned Officers (according to capacity and qualifications) of the Indian Army;

(*h*) The organising throughout the more warlike races of the Empire of a system of Militia service; and

(*i*) The authorising and stimulating of a wide-spread system of Volunteering, such as obtains in Great Britain, amongst the people of India.

Military

VII. Resolved—That having regard to the fact that the abnormal increase in the annual Military Expenditure of the Empire since 1885-86 is principally owing to the Military activity going on beyond the natural lines of the defences of the country, in pursuance of the Imperial policy of Great Britain in its relation with some of the Great Powers of Europe, this Congress is of opinion that, in bare justice to India, an equitable portion of that expenditure should be borne by the British Treasury, and that the revenues of India should be proportionately relieved of that burden.

Education

VIII. Resolved—That this Congress is emphatically of opinion, that it is highly inexpedient in the present state of Education in the country, that Government grants for High Education should in any way be withdrawn, and, concurring with previous Congresses, affirms in the most emphatic manner, the importance of increasing the public expenditure on all branches of Education, and the expediency, in view to the promotion of one of the most essential of these branches, *i. e.*, the technical, of appointing a mixed Commission to enquire into the present industrial condition of the country.

Poverty and Permanent Settlement

IX. Resolved—That this Congress emphatically re-affirms Resolution III of the Congress of 1891, and having regard to the fact that fully fifty millions of the population, a number yearly increasing, are dragging out a miserable existence on the verge of starvation, and that in every decade several millions actually perish by starvation, deems it imperatively necessary that the cost of administration, especially in the military branch of the Public Service, should be greatly reduced, and that measures should at once be taken to give, as was promised by the British Government over thirty years ago, fixity and permanence to the land revenue demand, and thus permit capital and labour to combine to develop the agriculture of the country, which, under the existing system of temporary settlements, in recent times often lasting for short periods, in some cases only extending to ten and twelve years, is found to be impossible; and to establish Agricultural Banks. And this Congress, again, most earnestly entreats the people of Great Britain and Ireland, not to permit any further sacrifice of life owing to the shortcomings of the existing, doubtless well-intentioned, but none the less unsatisfactory, administration, but to insist, and, that speedily, on the reforms, then and now, so earnestly advocated.

Forest Laws

X. Resolved—That this Congress entirely adopts Resolution XI of the Congress of 1891, and reiterates its prayer, that having regard to the very serious discontent created, particularly in Peninsular India, by the practical administration of the Forest Laws, the Government of India do investigate this matter carefully, and endeavour to mitigate the harshness of such administration, and render it less obnoxious to the poorer classes.

Legislative Council (Panjab)

XII. Resolved—That this Congress, in concurrence with the first Congress held at Bombay in 1885, considers that the creation of a Legislative Council for the Province of the Panjab is an absolute necessity for the good government of that Province, and, having regard to the fact that a similar Council has been created for the United Provinces, hopes that no time will be lost in creating such a Council.

Thanks of Congress

XIII. Resolved—That this Congress hereby tenders its most grateful acknowledgments to Sir W. Wedderburn and the members of the British Congress Committee, for the services rendered by them to India during the past year, and entirely approves and confirms the re-construction of the British Committee of the Congress which has been effected by them, as also the new arrangements which they have made in regard to their office establishment, and the journal *India*; and that this Congress also tenders its thanks to Mr. W. Digby, C.I.E., for the services which he rendered to the cause during his tenure of office as Secretary to the British Committee.

XVI. Resolved—That this Congress most respectfully and cordially tenders, on behalf of the vast population it represents, India's most heartfelt thanks to the electors of Central Finsbury for electing Mr. Dadabhai Naoroji their member in the House of Commons; and it again puts on record its high estimate and deep appreciation of the services which that gentleman has rendered to this country, reiterates its unshaken confidence in him, and looks upon him as India's representative in the House of Commons.

XXI. Resolved—That this Congress hereby tenders its best thanks to His Highness the Maharaja of Darbhanga, for having so kindly lent his Castle and grounds for the holding of this Congress.

Prostitution

XIV. Resolved—That this Congress is thankful that the House of Commons is vigilant in regard to the recent purity legislation by the Government in India, and desires, once again, to enter its protest against all State-regulated immorality in India.

Congress Work

XV. Resolved—That, regard being had to the present political situation in England, the provisional arrangements set on foot, in pursuance of the resolution passed at the Calcutta Congress, 1890, for holding—all things being convenient—a Congress of not less than one hundred delegates in England in 1892, be now suspended, until after the session of the Congress in 1893.

XVII. Resolved—That this Congress hereby empowers the Trustees of the Congress Permanent Fund—now locked up in the "New Oriental Bank Corporation, Ld.," at present in liquidation—

to send, at least, five hundred pounds out of it to the British Committee, to be recouped by subscriptions from the Standing Congress Committees.

XVIII. Resolved—That, regard being had to the representations received from the British Committee, this Congress is of opinion, that a sum equivalent in Rupees to two thousand eight hundred pounds sterling, be allotted for the expenses of the British Committee, for the year 1892-93; that deducting the money which has been received up to now, the balance be allotted amongst the different Standing Congress Committees, in accordance with arrangements come to with them; and that the sum be remitted to England as soon as practicable.

Formal

XIX. Resolved—That this Congress re-appoints Mr. A. O. Hume, C. B., to be its General Secretary, and appoints Rai Bahadur P. Ananda Charlu, to be its Joint-General Secretary for the ensuing year.

XXII. Resolved—That this Congress confirms the appointment of Pandit Bishumbharnath, in place of the late Pandit Ajodhyanath, as one of the Trustees of the Congress Permanent Fund.

XX. Resolved—That the Ninth Indian National Congress do assemble on such day after Christmas, 1893, as may be determined upon, at Amritsar.

CHAPTER IX

The Ninth National Congress met at Lahore—not at Amritsar as chosen by the preceding Congress—on December 27, 28, 29 and 30, 1893. The pavilion was raised on a piece of vacant ground, and contained 4,000 seats, which were not able to accommodate all who crowded to attend. The delegates numbered 867, and, as sent by Provinces, were as follows:

Bengal	59
N.W.P. and Oudh	133
Panjab	481
Bombay (77) and Sindh (47)	124
C.P. and Berar	39
Madras	31
	867

The first sitting began on December 27 at 2 p.m. as usual. The Chairman of the Reception Committee, Sardar Dayal Singh Majithia, was suffering from a violent attack of rheumatism, and handed his address to Mr. Harkishan Lal to read. After characterising the Congress as "the greatest glory of the British Rule in this country," he paid a tribute of thanks to Sir Dennis Fitzpatrick and the officials who had put no hindrance in the way of their preparations, and said that the martial races of the Panjab were in full sympathy with the Congress movement.

> The wand of the magician has touched our eyes. The history and literature of England have permeated our minds, the great heritage of our western Aryan brethren has descended on us, collaterally, as it were, and we are allowed at times, grudgingly it may be, to have a share in it. We happily live under a Constitution whose watchword is freedom, and whose main pillar is toleration. We look back complacently on our past history, and glory in it. Can we then in the midst of this National upheaval remain quiescent and indifferent?

Rai Bahadur Ananda Charlu moved, and Moulvi Muhurram Ali Chiste seconded, the proposal that Mr. Dadabhai Naoroji, M.P., should be the President of the Congress, and the whole pavilion was shaken with the welcome the delegates offered to the first Indian elected to the House of Commons.

After expressing his thanks to the Congress, the President referred feelingly to the passing away of their staunch supporter Justice Kashinath Trimbak Telang, "one of the most active founders of the Congress," and "its first hard-working Secretary in Bombay". Even after he had become a Judge, he always helped with advice. He then read a message to the Congress from his English constituents, expressing their gratification with his work in the House of Commons, and spoke of the small approach to representation granted in the Councils and the concession of the right of interpellation. He pointed out that it would be "the height of unwisdom" for the Ruling Authorities to alienate the educated Indians, and to

> drive this force into opposition instead of drawing it to their own side by taking it into confidence and thereby strengthening their own foundation. This Congress represents the aristocracy of intellect and the new political life created by themselves, which is at present deeply grateful to its creator. Common sense tells you—have it with you instead of against you.

Mr. Naoroji spoke of the formation of an Indian Parliamentary Committee in the House of Commons —a body sorely needed now—and expressed his belief "that our faith in the instinctive love of justice and fair play of the people of the United Kingdom is not misplaced," even though he added that "we are to all intents and purposes under an arbitrary rule". The poverty of India was "the rock ahead," and it was due to the system of Government, not to the officials, though they, unfortunately, took criticisms of the system as personal attacks. As the Duke of Devonshire said, the Anglo-Indian official "is not a person who is distinguished by an exceptionally calm judgment". Lord Cromer's average income of the Indian as Rs. 27 per head included the rich and the incomes of European planters, manufacturers and mine-owners, and the poor had a much lower average; he put it at Rs. 20. This poverty was the greatest danger. If India were allowed to enjoy the fruits of the people's labours, then

> Britain may defy half a dozen Russias. Indians will then fight to the last man and the last rupee for their share, as patriots, not as mercenaries. The rulers will only have to stamp their foot, and millions will spring up

to defend the British Power and their own hearths and homes. . . . Were we enemies of British rule, our best course would be not to cry out, but remain silent, and let the mischief take its course till it ends in disaster as it must. But we do not want that disaster, and we therefore cry out, both for our own sake and for the sake of the rulers. This evil of poverty must be boldly faced and remedied.

It has not been faced; it has not been remedied. And the words spoken are as true in 1915 as in 1893. Mr. Naoroji concluded:

The day, I hope, is not distant when the world will see the noblest spectacle of a great Nation like the British holding out the hand of true fellow-citizenship and of justice to the vast mass of humanity of this great and ancient land of India, with benefits and blessings to the human race.

He said in the course of his speech: "I shall hope as long as I live." He is now in his 91st year. May his hope be realised ere he passes away.

The names of the Subjects Committee were read out and approved, and the Congress adjourned.

On the second day, Mr. R. N. Mudholkar moved the first Resolution, dealing with the unsatisfactory results of the Councils Act of 1892. He pointed out that some success had indeed been gained, but less than they wished. Since 1887 reform had been asked for by the Government of India, and in three sessions Bills were brought into Parliament; in 1892 an Act was passed, as the Conservative Government feared that its successor would bring in a more liberal measure. That Act did not give the right of election, but allowed the Viceroy to make rules, to be approved by the Secretary of State, and in these there was "a sort of a right of election"; also the right of interpellation was granted, but no discussion of the answers; and the submission of the Budget to the Council, without any right to vote thereon. Mr. G. K. Gokhale, in seconding, said :

> Gentlemen, in regard to these Rules [framed for the Presidency of Bombay to give effect to the Act], I will not say that they have been deliberately so framed as to defeat the object of the Act of 1892, but I will say this, that if the officer who drafted them had been asked to sit down with the deliberate purpose of framing a scheme to defeat that object, he could not have done better.

After this opening, Mr. Gokhale proceeded to prove his case, showing how the Government of Bombay—the section assigned to him—having 6 seats to dispose of, gave one each to the European Chambers of Bombay and Karachi and none to the Indian Mercantile Community, one each to the Sardars of the Deccan and the Zemindars of Sindh, land-holders much under the thumb of the Government—Sindh having thus two members—but the Central Division of the Presidency, containing Poona and Satara, had none. Four seats out of the six were thus secured for the Government.

Pandit Bishen Narayan Dhar dealt with the Rules for the N.W.P., and Mr. Baikunthanath Sen with those for Bengal. Mr. T. Kemchand said that Sindh's two members were unjustly allotted. The Central Provinces were particularly unfortunate, said Mr. Keshava Vinayak Joshi. Rai Bahadur

C. Jambulingam Mudaliar explained the grievances of Madras. The Resolution was carried.

Then Resolution II, asking for a Legislative Council for the Panjab, was passed, and the "Omnibus Resolution" followed as No. IV. Dr. Bhadurji next moved resolution V, which asked for the reconstruction of the Indian Civil Medical Service quite apart from the Military. He gave a very full and detailed account of the grievances of Indian doctors, as regarded their colleges, their pay, and their prospects, being allowed much more than his time because the subject was a new one. Dr. M. M. Bose, Dr. Bhalchandra Krishna and Dr. Bhugatram Sawhuy followed, and the motion was carried, the Congress thereupon adjourning.

The third day of the Congress opened on a joyous note; after the usual birthday telegram to Mr. Gladstone, Resolution V was moved by the Hon. Mr. Surendranath Bannerji, thanking the House of Commons for carrying a Resolution in favour of simultaneous examinations. He gave a long list of broken pledges for which he arraigned "the Government of India before the Bar of British and Indian public opinion—before the Bar of civilised humanity in all parts of the globe; for the history of the Civil Service question is one unbroken record of broken promises". It shows, however, the strength of the Indian Civil Service, that despite all the broken promises and the Resolution of the House of Commons, examinations for the I.C.S. are still held in England only. Mr. Hamid Ali Khan seconded the resolution on behalf of his co-religionists, and was followed by Raja Rampal Singh in a breezy speech; he pointed out that after 35 years there were 20 Indians in the I.C.S. and between 900 and 1,000 Europeans; he had been asked by an Englishman which Government he thought the better, English or Muhammadan; he had answered that the English was the better for security, education and railways, but for the wealth of India the Muhammadan, for the Muhammadans became Indians, and the riches stayed in the country, while the English carried the wealth of the country away. He remarked that English Civilians made India their happy hunting ground; they came and "return to England with our money". Munshi Roshan Lal met the objection that simultaneous examinations would make the I.C.S. "the monopoly of the Bengali Babu". If so, where was the objection, in view of Her Majesty's Proclamation? Let the Bengalis fill it if they could; they would have only the same chance as men of other Provinces, whom he believed to be their equals. Mr. C. Venkata Raman Naidu further supported, and the resolution was carried.

Mr. Kalicharan Bannerji proposed Resolution VI, which asked that the Secretary of State should order schemes for the separation of judicial and executive functions to be prepared by Committees appointed for this purpose. He showed the need by a shocking case that had just occurred, in which four men were sentenced to death and three to transportation for life, after a trial in which rules of law were disregarded and the magistrate acted as a prosecutor and judge combined. The Hon. Mr. N. Subbarao Pantulu seconded, and mentioned a case in the Madras Presidency which showed that under present conditions, justice was not done. Mr. Ambikacharan Mozumdar showed that by the efforts of that great agitator Raja Ram Mohan Rai the functions had been separated, but that they were re-united in 1858. He proceeded to make a magnificent speech, exhausting the subject, which should be carefully studied, for in 1915 the scandal still continues.

Resolution VII, a protest against "State-regulated Immorality in India," was moved by Mr. D. E. Wacha, seconded by the Hon. Mr. C. C. Mitra and carried.

Then Pandit Madan Mohan Malaviya moved Resolution VIII, on the perennial starvation of the peasantry, and begged members of the House of Commons, if they would not accept the statistics which proved that the poverty of the country was increasing, to come over to India, visit the villages, and see in what misery the people live. Let them ask the people what the country was before the Mutiny:

> Where are the weavers, where are those men who lived by different industries and manufactures, and where are the manufactures which were sent to England and other European countries in very large quantities year after year? All that has become a thing of the past: every one sitting here is clothed in cloth of British make—almost every one—and wherever you go, you find British manufactures and British goods staring you in the face. All that is left to the people is to drag out a miserable

existence by agricultural operations, and make infinitesimal profit out of the little trade left to them. In the matter of the Services, in the matter of trade, our people are not enjoying one-hundredth part of the profit and gain which they used to enjoy fifty years ago. How then is it possible for the country to be happy?

He then gave a number of figures and quotations to prove his contention. Pandit Gopinath seconded, and Mr. Ambikacharan Maitra, Mr. Muhammad Ali Bhimji and Moulvi Mohurram Ali Chiste supported the motion, and it was unanimously carried.

Once more the harshness of the administration of the Forest Laws was brought up—Resolution IX—and instances of injustice were given; Pandit Meghan Ram showed how the Rules framed by the Panjab Government were specially cruel and unjust, "very arbitrary and unworthy of a civilised Government". An owner or occupant of land was made liable for an accidental fire caused by any one on his land, and might be "treated," said the Rule, "as if he had been guilty of the infraction of the Rules". The hill-men, again, used grass and wood: "it is their life and the life of their cattle"; they were prevented from taking them. In their severe climate, they had kept fires going night and day; now they could not even cut down their own trees for warmth. The Resolution was carried, but the Forest Laws remain.

On the fourth day, Mr. Peter Paul Pillai opened the proceedings by moving Resolution X, asking the Government to fulfil their thirty years' old promise to grant Permanent Settlement, and drew attention to the alarm caused by its interference with that in Bengal and Bihar, declaring that "such tampering with solemn public pledges" was "a National calamity". He complained bitterly of the breach of the terms of sanads granted by Government, and commented in terms none too severe on the dishonour of such breaking of faith with the public. Mr. Baikunthanath Sen seconded, and then Sheikh Wahab-ud-din spoke strongly as to the Panjab. Their Province had been annexed by the British Empire 43 years before, and they were fiscally and physically stronger then. The people had become poorer and poorer, and peasant and gentleman had scarcely any margin to support their families or provide for the future. Mr. B. G Tilak pointed out that in Bombay the increase in 30 years had sometimes amounted to 30 per cent. Sardar Gurucharan Singh showed how in the Panjab the failure of a crop meant ruin to the cultivator:

> The family is broken up, their cattle are sold for debts, the breadwinner of the family either dies of a broken heart, or lingers in the dark recesses of a Civil Gaol under the decree of the money-lender. If he has any son, the poor youth leaves home in despair and joins the army, where he ends his days at a handsome salary of Rs. 7 a month.

These are the conditions which have afforded materials for revolutionary plots; people who are starving and in despair lend a ready ear to suggestions of revolt. Mr. K. V. Joshi brought evidence from the Central Provinces, where the enhancement had been in some cases from 200 to 300 per cent, and where he had found the people so poor that they were living on mowra flowers and the seeds of tamarinds.

Resolution XI, moved by Mr. D. A. Khare, regretted that Government had not carried out its pledges of 1862, 1865, 1882, and 1884. In addition to these, he quoted Lord Reay's solemn promise that improvements made by the holder should not be taxed, and the breaking of the promise in the then recent settlement in the Penwall Taluq. In another case a petition was presented, and a year passed and the Commissioner gave no answer. The petitioners applied to the Government of Bombay; the petition was returned because a copy of the order was not attached. The local officer had written no order. The petition dropped. Mr. G. S. Khaparde seconded, Mir Nisar Ali Shohrat supported, and the motion was carried.

Resolution XII was a long and important one on Education, urging increased expenditure, an enquiry into the industrial condition of the country with a view to technical education, the reduction of fees to meet the means of parents and their remission to the very poor, and pointing out that equal care should be directed to physical as to mental development. Mr. M. B. Namjoshi moved it, and asked for free and compulsory education, citing the example of the Gaekwar. Mr. Nibaran Chandra Das seconded, Bakshi Ram Labkaye supported, and then Lala Lajpat Rai took up the question in a vigorous speech. He specially urged technical education, as that would increase the wealth of the country.

It is 30 or 35 years that the Department of Public Instruction has been started here; but do you know what progress has been made since then? One of the two Government Colleges has been abolished: I mean the

Delhi Government College. The fees in Government Colleges have been this year raised from Rs. 2 to Rs. 12 per mensem, and they have also been raised in schools. The bravery of the Panjabis, the Sikhs and the Rajputs on the fields of Egypt, Abyssinia and Afghanistan has been rewarded by shutting the doors of higher education and the benefits of civilisation on their children.

Mr. S. K. Nair seconded, contrasting the policy of Japan with that of Britain as regarded technical education.

Resolution XIII regretted the despatch of the Secretary of State, saying that the Executive might have to review "judicial errors," a dangerous doctrine, threatening the independence of the Courts. Rai Bahadur P. Ananda Charlu moved it and Mr. Kalicharan Bannerji seconded, pointing out that the despatch put might above right. Rai Jotindranath Chaudhuri followed, and Pandit Mohan Lal made a powerful speech, showing how English Judges had vindicated the independence of their Courts against both King and Parliament. After the motion was carried, Mr. D. E. Wacha moved Resolution XIV, against the stoppage of silver coinage, showing the evils resulting, and pointing out that

> the hard-working labourers, the overtaxed peasantry, are being impoverished in order that Government officials and usurers may fatten at their expense. . . . It robs the ryots; it entails an additional burden on them in order to actually compensate a microscopic minority already in receipt of salaries which find no parallel in any part of the civilised globe.

Mr. R. P. Karandikar seconded, and the Resolution was carried.

Then followed a protest against the exchange compensation allowance to Europeans and Eurasians—Resolution XV—that the Viceroy had called the "crime of the 26th of June," moved by the Hon. Mr. Surendranath Bannerji, who charged "the Government of India with trifling with the interests of the people and having been guilty of injustice to the interests committed to its care by granting this absurd allowance to its non-domiciled Europeans. It is a grave charge, but I make it deliberately." The Government, he pointed out, never had funds for reforms. No money to improve the police, no money to separate judicial and executive functions, no money for sanitation.

But when it comes to a question of granting compensation to the Services, then Government is as rich as the richest Government in the world; and from whom is this money taken? You heard yesterday the story of India's poverty related in graphic and earnest language by Pandit Madan Mohan; you heard on the highest official authority that 20,000,000 of people had died of starvation in the last few years; you heard that 40,000,000 live on one meal a day; and now these 40,000,000 people will be burdened with additional taxation. They will be stinted of their food, of their rice and of their salt, in order that the highly paid officials of the Government may be provided with their usual brandy, beef and champagne. I think it is an unutterable shame..... We are the children of the soil; we are the helots of the land, the hewers of wood and the drawers of water, and we exist for the Services, the gods of the bureaucracy. Illustrious men of Bombay, men of the Panjab, men of northern India, men of Bengal, let us combine, let us take a firm stand, and let us not rest till we have succeeded in convincing these gods of their iniquities; let us not rest till we have disenchanted them of the illusion under which they labour, namely that the country is theirs and not ours. The country is ours and theirs ; and India is for England and also for India ; primarily for India and secondarily for England.

Mr. W. A. Chambers seconded the motion in a strong speech, denouncing the compensation as neither Christian, nor righteous. Mr. D. E. Wacha supported with some telling statistics.

Resolution XVI was a request to the Government to put an end to forced labour, moved by Lala Dharm Das Sari and seconded by Lala Kanakya Lal in an impassioned speech. He pointed out that forced labour was slavery, and England put down slavery in Africa, but winked at it in India. It was forbidden, but officials used it.

Resolution XVII thanked Lord Northbrook for pleading in Parliament for the reduction of the Home (Foreign) Charges. It was moved by Mr. G. K. Gokhale, who remarked that the statements made in the debate on Lord Northbrook's motion furnished an indictment, if the Government were ever put on its trial ; it was admitted that burdens justly belonging to England were thrown on India, and the Duke of Argyll said the grievance should be removed before India heard of it, as though Mr. Wacha had not protested against it from the Congress platform ! Home Charges had increased from £7 millions to £16 millions in 30 years. With part of this the House of Commons had nothing to do, but it could deal with the India Office and the Army. The former might pass, for although it paid liberally its " respectable and at the same time useless and mischievous old gentlemen," the item was comparatively small. But the "Home Military Charges" had risen from £2 millions to over £5 millions, and the recruits which cost the War Office £19 per head were charged to India at £105 per man. When England borrowed Indian troops, she forgot to pay for them; when India borrowed English troops, she paid all ordinary and extraordinary expenses.

Mr. D. B. Chakradev seconded, and the Resolution was carried.

Resolution XVIII asked for the raising of the Chief Court of the Panjab to a High Court: Resolution XIX thanked the electors of Central Finsbury, and Resolution XX assigned Rs. 60,000 for the British Committee and *India*. Resolutions XXI, XXII and XXIII followed, thanking Sir William Wedderburn and the British Committee, re-appointing Mr. A. O. Hume as General Secretary, and fixing on Madras as the meeting-place of the next Congress. Then a vote of thanks to the President was carried, and with a few words from him, the Ninth Congress was dissolved.

RESOLUTIONS

Representation

I. Resolved—That this Congress while tendering its most sincere thanks to His Excellency the Viceroy for the liberal spirit in which he has endeavoured to give effect to the Indian Councils' Act of 1892, regrets to have to put on record the facts, that, alike in the Rules of the Government of India and in the practice of most of the Local Governments, notably in that of the Government of Bombay, material alterations are necessary if real effect is to be given to the spirit of this Act, and, that the Panjab, one of the most important Provinces in the Empire, is still denied the right to be represented, either in the Viceroy's or in any Local Council.

Legislative Council and High Court (Panjab)

II. Resolved—That this Congress, in concurrence with the first Congress held at Bombay in 1885 and other subsequent Congresses, considers that the creation of a Legislative Council for the Province of the Panjab is an absolute necessity for the good government of that Province, and, having regard to the fact that a similar Council has been created for the United Provinces, hopes that no time will be lost in creating such a Council.

XVIII. Resolved—That in the opinion of this Congress, the time has now come to raise the status of the Chief Court of the Panjab to that of a Chartered High Court, in the interest of the administration of justice in that Province.

Confirmation of Previous Resolutions

III. Resolved—That this Congress concurs with its predecessors in strongly advocating—(repeats exactly Resolution V of 1892, Eighth Congress).

Civil Medical Service

IV. Resolved—That this Congress is of opinion that the time has arrived when, in the interest of public medical education and the advancement of medical science and of scientific work in this country, as also in the cause of economic administration, the Civil Medical Service of India should be reconstructed on the basis of such services in other civilised countries, wholly detached from and independent of the Military service, so as to give full effect to the educational policy of Government, which is to encourage education for its own sake in every branch, and to raise a scientific medical profession in India by throwing open fields for medical and scientific work to the best talent available and indigenous talent in particular.

Legal

VI. Resolved—That this Congress having now for many successive years vainly appealed to the Government of India to remove one of the gravest stigmas on British rule in India, one fraught with incalculable oppression to all classes of the community throughout the country, now hopeless of any other redress, humbly entreats the Secretary of State for India to order the immediate appointment, in each Province, of a Committee (one half at least, of whose members shall be non-official natives of India, qualified by education and experience in the workings of the various Courts to deal with the question) to prepare each a scheme for the complete separation of all Judicial and Executive functions in their own Province with as little additional cost to the State as may be practicable, and the submission of such schemes, with the comments of the several Indian Governments thereon, to himself at some early date which he may be pleased to fix.

Prostitution

VII. Resolved—That this Congress having considered the Report of the Parliamentary members of the India Office Committee on the subject of the Rules, Orders and Practices in Indian Cantonments with regard to prostitution and contagious disease, hereby endorses their conclusions:

1. That the system and incidental practices described in that Report and the statutory rules, so far as they authorised or permitted the same, did not accord with the plain meaning and intention of the resolution of the House of Commons of June 5th, 1888; and
2. That the only effective method of preventing these systematic malpractices is by express legislation.

Poverty

VIII. Resolved—That this Congress, concurring in the views set forth in previous Congresses, affirms:

That fully fifty millions of the population, a number yearly increasing, are dragging out a miserable existence on the verge of starvation, and that in every decade, several millions actually perish by starvation.

And humbly urges, once more, that immediate steps be taken to remedy this calamitous state of affairs.

Forest Laws

IX. Resolved—That having regard to the very serious discontent created, especially in Peninsular India and in certain hilly tracts in the Panjab, by the practical administration of the Forest Laws, the Government of India be most respectfully, but earnestly, entreated to investigate this matter carefully and endeavour to mitigate its harshness and render it less obnoxious to the poorer classes.

Permanent Settlement

X. Resolved—That this Congress having on many previous occasions urged on the Government of India the necessity for giving, as was promised by the British Government over thirty years ago, fixity and permanence to the Land Revenue demand, wherever this has not already been conceded, desires now to reiterate emphatically this recommendation and to call attention to the profound alarm which has been created by the action of Government in interfering with the existing permanent settlement in Bengal and Behar (in the matter of the survey and other cesses) and with the terms of the sanads of the permanently settled estates in Madras, and deeming such tampering with solemn public pledges, no matter under what pretences, a national calamity, hereby pledges itself to oppose, in all possible legitimate ways, any and all such reactionary attacks on permanent settlements and their holders.

XI. Resolved—That this Congress regrets extremely that the Government of India have not only failed to carry out the pledges for a permanent settlement in the Provinces in which it does not exist (given by the Secretary of State in his despatches of 1862 and 1865) but have also failed to give effect to the policy of granting a modified fixity of tenure and immunity from enhancements, laid down in 1882 and 1884 by the Government of India, and approved by the Secretary of State.

Education

XII. Resolved—That this Congress is of opinion that it is inexpedient in the present state of Education in the country, that Government grants for High Education should in any way be withdrawn, and concurring with previous Congresses, affirms in the most emphatic manner, the importance of increasing the public expenditure on all branches of Education, and the expediency (in view to the promotion of one of the most essential of those branches, *i.e.*, the technical,) of appointing a mixed Commission to enquire into the present industrial condition of the country; and looking to the great poverty of many classes of the community, strongly recommends, that in all classes of Government or Municipal Schools and Colleges, all fees shall be reduced in proportion to the means of parents and relations and remitted wholly in the case of very poor students; and, focussing the universal opinion of the Indian Community that undue stress is being laid at present upon mere mental development, this Congress earnestly recommends that henceforth, in all grades and classes of Schools and Colleges, at least equal attention should be devoted to the physical development of the students.

Executive and Bench

XIII. Resolved—That this Congress regrets to notice that the Secretary of State for India in his recent despatch to the Government of India has enunciated the doctrine that occasions may arise in which it may be the duty of the Executive Government to criticise Judicial errors, the Congress being of opinion that such criticism is calculated to shake the confidence of the people in the independence of Judicial tribunals.

Monetary

XIV. Resolved—That this Congress places on record its deep regret at the recent hasty legislation of the Government of India closing the Indian mints against the private coinage of silver, whereby the people of this country have been subjected to further indirect taxation of a burdensome and indefinite character, and some of the most important trades and industries, notably the Mill industry, have been seriously disorganised and injured.

XV. Resolved—That this Congress records its emphatic protest against the Exchange Compensation Allowance granted to the undomiciled European and Eurasian employees of Government, involving an annual expenditure of over a crore of Rupees, and to the Banks, to the extent of £131,000, at a time when the financial situation of the country is far from satisfactory and the country is threatened with additional taxation.

Forced Labour and Supplies

XVI. Resolved—That the Government of India be moved, once for all, to put a stop, by new and express legislation, (the existing provisions of the Penal Code having proved inoperative) to the existing oppressive system of forced labour (known as *Begar*) and forced contributions of supplies (known as *Rasads*), which, despite numerous Resolutions of the Government of India, are still prevalent through India.

Thanks of Congress

V. Resolved—That this Congress desires to thank the British House of Commons for their just and wise vote in regard to Simultaneous Examinations in England and in India, and most earnestly prays that august body to insist upon their orders being given prompt effect to by the Secretary of State for India and the Government of India.

XVII. Resolved—That this Congress tenders its most sincere thanks to Lord Northbrook for his powerful advocacy of India's claim to have her burden of Home Charges reduced, and respectfully entreats the House of Commons to appoint at an early date a Committee of their Honourable House to arrive at some equitable settlement of the matter.

XIX. Resolved—That this Congress tenders its best thanks to the Electors of Central Finsbury, both for their kindly sympathy in its objects and for having so generously accorded to it the valuable services of their honoured member Mr. Naoroji, who is destined, the Congress hopes, long to represent both Central Finsbury and India in the British House of Parliament.

XXI. Resolved—That this Congress hereby tenders its most grateful acknowledgments to Sir W. Wedderburn and the members of the British Congress Committee for the services rendered by them to India during the past year.

Congress Work

XX. Resolved—That a sum of Rs. 60,000 be assigned for the expenses of the British Committee and the cost of the Congress Publication, *India*, and that the several circles do contribute as arranged either now, or hereafter in Committee, for the year 1894.

Formal

XXII. Resolved—That this Congress re-appoints Mr. A. O. Hume, C.B., to be its General Secretary for the ensuing year.

XXIII. Resolved—That the Tenth National Congress do assemble on such day after Christmas Day, 1894, as may be later determined upon, at Madras.

CHAPTER X

The Congress of 1894 marked the close of the first decade of its work, and it came back to Madras, after seven years, to find the fair city stronger than ever in her devotion to the work. Rs. 40,000 had been collected by the Reception Committee before the Congress met, and 1,163 delegates gathered in the huge pandal which gave accommodation to nearly 5,000 people. The delegates from Madras Presidency of course headed the list:

Madras...	947
Bombay (128) Sindh (4)	132
C. P., Berar and Secunderabad	37
Bengal ...	30
N. W. P. and Oudh ...	13
Panjab ...	4
	1,163

Madras is so far south that it is difficult for delegates to reach her, but she is one of the best, perhaps the best, organised circle.

December 26th was the first day of the Congress, and the Hon. Mr. P. Rangiah Naidu, as the Chairman of the Reception Committee welcomed the delegates, and remarked that as their influence grew, opposition grew also, and pointing as proof to the Parliamentary Blue Book on Simultaneous Examinations, showing the "straining of the relations between educated Indians and the officials," who cried down the men educated in the schools and colleges founded by the British, characterising "them as a class of disloyal men, devoid of influence with their own countrymen and incapable of discharging any responsible public duty". He described the evils which arose from the class of Englishmen who came to India merely to earn their living and had no permanent stake in the country, but who influenced opinion. "An absentee Government involves a frightful strain on the country's financial resources, an overgrown military system absorbs one-third of the net revenue, the Free Trade principles thrust on us have destroyed the old industries, the population has grown in advance of the food supply, and poverty is increasing from year to year." After offering warm thanks to Colonel Moore, the Chairman of the Madras Municipality, for much kindly help, he called on the Congress to elect its President.

Raja Sir Savalai Ramaswami Mudaliar proposed, and Raja Rampal Singh seconded, the election of Mr. Alfred Webb, M.P., an Irishman.

In taking the chair, the President glanced at the past of the Congress, and mentioned the death of Mr. Charles Bradlaugh, M.P., than whom "you never lost a better nor an abler friend. Few men were ever so sincerely mourned by a larger proportion of the human race." There spoke the gratitude of an Irishman to Ireland's true friend. Mr. Webb pointed to the figures of Indian taxes spent abroad, "25 per cent of your total expenditure. No country could permanently afford such a drain." He urged the well-worn arguments on taxation, on agriculture, on representation; and concluded by declaring that the Congress was "in truth the greatest combined peaceful effort for the good of the largest number of the human race that history has recorded".

At the conclusion of Mr. Webb's speech, a generous gift of Rs. 10,000 to the Congress funds from the Raja of Ramnad was announced, the Subjects Committee was confirmed, and the Congress adjourned.

The work of the second day began with the reading of the rules for the conduct of business, and Mr. D. E. Wacha moved Resolution I, protesting against the injustice of imposing excise duties on cotton goods, crippling the infant mill industry of India and sacrificing the interests of India to those of Lancashire. He praised the Government of India for its resistance to the Excise Bill, and blamed the Secretary of State. The tax was unjust, and it was also impolitic, for it retarded industrial development. He lamented the helplessness of the Government of India, remarking that it might as well cease to exist if it was merely "the registrar of the ukases of the great autocrat for the time being at Westminster". The Hon. Mr. A. Sabapati Mudaliar seconded the Resolution and it was carried.

Resolution II, moved by Mr. Baikunthanath Sen, who had seconded a similar one in 1893, expressed the alarm caused by the breach of the Government pledges as to settled estates, and its interference with the permanent settlement in Bengal and Bihar. The Hon. Mr. Natu seconded, and pointed out how Bombay was being ruined by resettlements, the increase in six Taluqs in the Ratnagiri and Albag Districts being 1,200 per cent. The entire assessment in Bombay was increased by 12 lakhs. An amendment was moved but there was no seconder, and the Hon. Mr. Kalyanasundram Iyer supported the resolution, pointing out that in a country where 80 per cent of the population cultivated the land, there was really no unearned increment to be claimed by the State. Mana Vikrama Raja spoke for Malabar, where Hindu rulers had imposed no taxation, and there had been much trouble over the question, for a permanent settlement had been granted in 1803 and 1805, and any interference was a breach of faith. Four other speakers followed, and the Resolution was carried.

Mr. Seymour Keay, M. P. moved Resolution III on remedying the poverty of India, and said that after 32 years of close intercourse with the Indian masses, he was obliged to recognise as a cause the enormous cost of an alien Government. Some of them had tried to force an enquiry in the House of Commons into the state of the masses, and their power to sustain the enormous cost of Government. He showed how the Secret Department of the Government of India had been used to obtain figures to controvert statements that had been made, and how they had forced Sir John Gorst to put the Blue Books in their hands. He then gave many figures from these,[1] and finally declared that India's only hope lay in bringing the facts before the English Parliament and people:

> Once inform them of the truth, and I say, and I say it with all assurance, that the great heart of the English Nation will grant you both speedy and effective remedy.

Alas! how often we have heard that, but the great heart does not respond. But I believe that an agitation in Britain, based on facts and figures would move the British Democracy. Successive British Governments have long known it, but they will not see. We *must* reach the Democracy. It *will* be reached by the little book mentioned below, and by the English Division of the Home Rule League.

Mr. Nandi seconded the Resolution and pointed out that the highest officials were kept in ignorance of facts, and even when on tour the addresses presented to them contained the views of the officials, not of the people supposed to present them; hence they inevitably lived in a roseate atmosphere, and were angry with any who spoke of the facts. Here and there a conscientious officer mentioned the facts. Mr. H. C. Irwin, of the Bengal Civil Service, writing of the poverty of Oudh said: "While the millions suffer from chronic hunger, it would be as easy to make a pyramid stand upon its apex as to regenerate them by ornamental legislation, or by anything but

[1] A number of these are given in my little book, *India—a Nation*, in Jack's People's Books. Let us see the effect.

putting them beyond the ceaseless pressure of physical want." He sternly added that Oudh had been annexed on the plea of the degradation of the cultivators; let it not be said that with "all the means in our hands of raising the peasantry of Oudh from the squalid poverty and debasement which for centuries past have been their lot, we ignobly suffered them to perish". Lala Murlidhar supported, sarcastically saying that as it was "easier for a camel to pass through the eye of a needle than for a rich man to enter into the kingdom of heaven," the people of India should surely be happy, since "the doors of heaven have been opened to you while they have been shut against all the people of Europe". The poor need not fear thieves. As for facts and figures:

> Go and see those figures in houses and see their squalid condition, pale and miserable, with no food to eat, and with no drink to take, and with no salt. Well, then, is not that the condition of anchorites and holy people? What do you want more? Why do you ask the Government for this or that? . . . You are an ungrateful people. Really you are. You ask to be admitted to the Government of your country. Why should you have all this botheration? Numerous troops have been provided to protect you and your lives. Numerous civil officials have taken the care off your shoulders. Then what do you want more?

Mr. Vishnupada Chatterji followed with further quotations from Government authorities, and after a Telugu speech from Mr. Parthasarati Naidu, the resolution was carried.

Mr. Eardley Norton was called on to move Resolution IV, asking for the abolition of the India Council, without which the re-constitution of the Legislative Councils was useless. "At present we stand sandwiched between officials in India and officials in Europe." The Council members

> were swayed by the same official interest, trained in the same official career, steeped in the same official prejudices as the men out here, who, also with the best of intentions, are resolutely endeavouring to thwart and obstruct your moral, material and political reforms.

He quoted some striking opinions of English statesmen on the way in which the Council and the Secretary of State worked; no one seemed to know which was the real power:

> If the Secretary of State is to be controlled by the Council, then abolish the Secretary of State. If the Council is to be controlled by the Secretary of State, then abolish the Council. The dual existence is useless, dangerous, expensive, obstructive.

He gave instances of commercial incapacity, such as sanctioning the Calcutta and S. E. Railway against Lord Canning's protest, guaranteeing interest at 5 per cent, and when it was practically bankrupt, buying it at half a million sterling. 5 per cent interest was guaranteed on a million sterling for the Madras Irrigation Company, and as the work never paid its expenses, it was purchased for India at par. It bought at Rs. 1,000 per share the shares of the Elphinstone Land and Press Company, selling in the market at Rs. 339. A Council of twelve members so incapable, at £ 1,200 a year each, was dear. Then politically, Mr. Gladstone had remarked:

> Suddenly in the dark, in the privacy of the Council Chamber, I believe in answer to a telegram, without the

knowledge of Parliament without the knowledge of the country, a law was passed, totally extinguishing the freedom of the native press. I think a law such as that is a disgrace to the British Empire.

What would Gladstone have said of the deeper disgrace of the Press Act of 1910? After a caustic review of the expenses of the India Council, including the wages of 28 housemaids, 1 housekeeper and 3 charwomen, Mr. Norton gave way to Mr. R. N. Mudholkar, who seconding the Resolution remarked that the Council was supposed to protect Indian interests, but it had failed and egregiously. The Resolution was passed, and an invitation from the Cosmopolitan Club for the 29th December was extended to the Congress.

The third day, the 28th December, began with Resolution V, asking for a Select Committee of the House of Commons to enquire into Indian finance, and Rai Bahadur C. Jambulingam Mudaliar gave some striking facts to prove the need for enquiry. He specially thanked Mr. Westland, the Financial Secretary to the Government of India, whose sophistry and bad logic had attracted exceptional attention to the Indian Budget, and exposed Sir Richard Temple's fatuous statements. Mr. H. Morgan-Browne seconded, and took up the question of the Famine Insurance Fund, quoting the solemn promise of the Government that the money raised by the new taxation should be devoted wholly to Famine Relief and Insurance, and yet out of 24 crores of rupees thus raised only 16 crores had been used as promised. He touched on the Exchange Compensation, on the "Stores," one of the meanest and most corrupt departments; India was made to pay Rs. 120,000 for a ball in Constantinople, on the ground that it was well for India to be on good terms with the Sultan of Turkey—by means of a ball, outraging Oriental and Musalman views of decency!

Mr. G. Subramania Iyer urged that there was no responsible authority to control Indian administration and remedy its defects, and the interests of India suffered. Sir William Hunter in *The Times* impugned the honesty of the Government of India, and where such accusations were made enquiry was needed. After two other speeches the Resolution was carried.

The Hon. Mr. Surendranath Bannerji was then called on to move Resolution VI, on the evergreen subject of Simultaneous Examinations, and laid special stress on the way in which the promises of equal treatment had been broken. He concluded with a glowing picture of the land of promise on which their eyes were fixed,

> where their fetters will fall off, their badge of political slavery will disappear. . . . . where under the fostering influence of free political institutions, they will develop a civilisation the noblest which the world has ever seen, the emblem of indissoluble union between England and India, a civilisation fraught with unspeakable blessings to the people of India, and unspeakable renown to the English name.

The Hon. Raja Rampal Singh seconded, and was followed by Mr. R. Venkata Subba Rao, Moulvi Hafiz Abdul Rahim, Mr. M. V. Joshi, and Professor G. K. Gokhale. The last-named pointed out that the idea of an "irreducible minimum of Europeans in the Service" had now been boldly put forward for the first time. The Secretary of State and the Government now said that the highest posts must "for all time to come be held by Europeans". That meant

> that the present arrangement should be perpetuated and is, in fact, an attempt to keep us always under as a subject race. Gentlemen, is it not plainly our duty as men not to allow this barefaced attempt to succeed? . . . Let our opponents put themselves into our position, and then say what they would feel. I believe they will allow that it is not wrong to love one's country. I believe they will allow that it is not wrong to have a high ideal for one's country. And then I believe they will allow that it is not wrong for us to be dissatisfied with our present condition. Well, gentlemen, the pledges of equal treatment which England has given us have supplied us with a high and worthy ideal for our Nation; and if these pledges are repudiated, one of the strongest claims of British rule to our attachment will disappear.

Mr. Gokhale was followed by Mr. Ghulam Ahmed Khan and Mr. Seymour Keay, who remarked that the Blue Book had "not a hint or whisper in it of any admission that the natives of India have even the faintest right to live on their own soil, much less that they have any preferential claim over the other subjects of the British Empire to administer in their own country". The Resolution was then carried unanimously.

The Hon. Mr. N. Subba Rao moved Resolution VII on the recruitment for the Judicial Service, and complained of the system which made men judges without any sufficient training in law. These gentlemen then supplied some of the Judges of the High Court, so that "litigation has become a question of gambling, and no one can be sure, notwithstanding he has a good case, that that would be the view which would prevail in the Courts". Mr. K. G. Natu seconded, Mr. A. R. Krishna Iyer supported, and the Resolution was carried.

Resolution VIII on the Medical Service was moved by Dr. Bahadurji, who proved by definite figures and facts the gross injustice done by the privileged position of the members of the I.M.S. to the Subordinate Medical Service, though some of the latter had passed higher educational tests than the men of the I.M.S. The latter rose from Rs. 500 to Rs. 2,500, while the former rose from Rs. 100 to Rs. 200. He also urged :

> Then there are two other enlistments for the subordinate service—one military and the other civil—the former being open to Christians only. But see what difference the element of religion makes in the treatment accorded to the two classes. John, the Christian, and Pandu, the non-Christian, both seek admission to their respective services. John, the Christian, need not know more than the High School fourth standard, reading, writing, and sums, but Pandu, the non-Christian, must pass a much higher test. They both go through the same professional course and examination. If anything, Pandu has to undergo a severer examination. John, the Christian, then begins as a Military Apothecary, and works under the regimental Surgeons. His salary ranges from Rs. 50 to Rs. 450. He may, however, be promoted to the uncovenanted grade and given even Rs. 750 by being found a post in the Civil Department. His new designation is Assistant Surgeon, I.M.S., and he rises from the rank of Lieutenant to that of

Major. But Pandu, the non-Christian, begins as a Hospital Assistant and dies a Hospital Assistant. His work is as vast as it is responsible. He practises medicine, surgery and midwifery. He it is who really dispels the ignorance and prejudice of the masses in regard to the western system of medicine. He treats a thousand times more cases in a month than the highest officer of a hospital does in a year. On his judgment, intelligence and integrity depend the lives of his fellow citizens in the Muffasal, questions of life and death turning upon the nature of his evidence in medico-legal cases. But, alas ! the respectability and responsibility of this most important servant of the State are in an inverse ratio, and that too in very abnormal proportions. One feels almost ashamed to say that the non-Christian Pandu, who does such responsible and excellent work for the Government is paid no higher salary than is paid to a senior punka-walla in the hospital, or a cook or a coachman. The scale of his pay is Rs. 16 to Rs. 80 odd.

The Resolution was seconded by Rai Bahadur P. Ananda Charlu, supported by Dr. M. G. Desmukh and carried.

The last Resolution of the day was No. IX, on Legislative Councils, proposed by Pandit Madan Mohan Malaviya, seconded by Bakshi Jaishi Ram, supported by three others and carried.

The President announced the sad and unexpected death of the Maharaja of Mysore, just before the Congress adjourned, and on the following day, December 29th, the first business done was the passing in silence of a resolution of grief for his loss.

The last day of the Congress was, as usual, crowded, no less than 18 resolutions being crushed into it. The Hon. Mr. Setalvad proposed Resolution XI, the extension of trial by jury, the restoring of finality to the verdicts given by juries as before 1872, and the removal of the Government's power to appeal against acquittals—that scandalous peculiarity of Indian law. Mr. K. N. Desmukh seconded, and Mr. Ambika Charan Mozumdar made a splendid and argumentative speech in support, full of facts. The effect, he said finally, of the law was to divide the population into two castes, European Brahmanas and Indian Shudras, and after pointing out that the place where a murder was committed decided whether the accused should "be dealt with as a true citizen or as bondsman," he finished with a passionate appeal:

> Sir, we are judged without evidence, and condemned without trial! Alas, we seem to be nobody's care. Even the Viceroy, whom we loyally welcome as a hereditary ruler, in his anxiety to accentuate the invidious distinction of colour, has lost no time in issuing on his own motion confidential circulars to protect the rights of those who virtually need no protection. But though the people have been long crying for help in this and other connections, the Gods are asleep, and there is no response to their call. Is the race of British philanthropists extinct? And have the mighty builders of this vast Empire left no heritage of broad and noble ideals of justice for their successors? We are not appealing to Jews or Cossacks, but to those for whom they proudly say Milton wrote and Sydney died, and for whom the Magna Carta was obtained; and, in making our present appeal, we are asking not only for the protection of our life, liberty, and property, but also for the vindication of the honour and dignity of the great British Constitution.

The Resolution was carried.

Resolution XII, the familiar separation of Judicial and Executive functions, was moved, seconded, supported and carried, and once more the status of a High.

Court was claimed for the Panjab (No. XIII). No. XIV was on Military Expenditure, and was moved and seconded by two powerful speakers—the Hon. Mr. C. Sankaran Nair and Mr. D. E. Wacha. Being carried, it was followed by Resolution XV on Education, and then came the Omnibus, driven this time by Pandit Bishan Narayana Dhar. Four other speakers were the horses drawing it to victory.

Resolution XVII protested against the further powers conferred on magistrates as most arbitrary, dangerous and unwise, and was carried after two short speeches by Messrs. R. N. Mudholkar and M. B. Namjoshi. Resolution XVIII thanked the Government of India for its circular in October 1894, declaring that fiscal interests must be subordinated to the needs of the ryots in the management of forests, a good result of the three preceding Sessions of the Congress.

A Government of India Notification of June, 1891, depriving the Press of liberty in territories under British administration in Feudatory States, formed the subject of the next Resolution (No. XIX), moved by Mr. P. Ramachandra Pillai, one of the delegates from Secunderabad, a place affected by the Notification, which ran as follows:

> Whereas some misapprehension has hitherto existed as to the regulations in force in territory under the administration of the Governor-General in Council, but beyond the limits of British India, with reference to newspapers published within such territory, the Governor-General in Council has been pleased to make the following order:

1. No newspaper or other printed work, whether periodical or other, containing public news or comments on public news shall, without the written permission for the time being in force of the Political Agent, be edited, printed, or published, after the 1st day of August 1891, in any local area administered by the Governor-General in Council but not forming part of British India.

2. If after the day aforesaid any person shall without such permission as aforesaid edit, print, or publish any such newspaper or other work as aforesaid in any such local area as aforesaid the Political Agent may by order in writing;

(*a*) require him to leave such local area within seven days from the date of such order;

(*b*) and prohibit him from re-entering such local area without the written permission of the Political Agent.

3. If any such order as is mentioned in the last foregoing paragraph be disobeyed, the offender shall be liable to forcible expulsion from such local area in pursuance of an order to be made in writing by the Political Agent.

It may be noted that at the present time (September, 1915) Sir Hugh Daly, Resident in Bangalore, has, under this, stopped an English paper which has existed there for many years. Mr. G. Subramania Iyer, then Editor of *The Hindu*, seconded, and the Resolution was carried.

Resolution XX brought up the consideration of the Water-cess, varying in amount at the will of the Government, and urged that it should be levied on some fixed principle. It was effectively moved by Mr. G. Venkataratnam, seconded by Mr V. V. Avadhani, supported by Mr. S. B. Sankaram and carried.

A protest Resolution (No. XXI) against the disfranchisement of Indians in S. Africa—the first of many protests, was moved from the Chair and carried. Resolution XXII nominated a deputation to Lord Elgin, the Viceroy, and Mr. Fowler, the Secretary of State, to present to them some of the Congress resolutions. Resolutions XXIII and XXIV, on the grant to the British Committee and conveying the thanks of the Congress for their work; Resolution XXV, re-appointing Mr. A. O. Hume as General Secretary; Resolution XXVI, fixing the next meeting of the Congress at Poona, were carried. The President then moved an important Resolution (No. XXVII) for shaping a Constitution for the Congress, and requested the Standing Congress Committee of Poona to draft and circulate draft rules among the remaining Standing Committees for report, the whole to be considered by the next Congress.

A vote of thanks was then passed to the President, and with his brief reply the Tenth Congress closed.

RESOLUTIONS

Excise Duty

I. Resolved--

(*a*) That this Congress respectfully enters its emphatic protest against the injustice and impolicy of imposing excise duty on Cottons manufactured in British India, as such excise is calculated to cripple seriously the infant Mill Industry of this country.

(*b*) That this Congress puts on record its firm conviction that in proposing this excise the interests of India have been sacrificed to those of Lancashire, and it strongly deprecates any such surrender of Indian interests by the Secretary of State.

(*c*) That in case the Excise Bill becomes law this Congress earnestly prays that the Government of India will without delay seek the sanction of the Secretary of State to exercise the powers which the Bill confers on Government to exempt all Cottons from "twenties" to "twenty-fours" from the operation of the Act.

(*d*) That the President be authorised to telegraph the above Resolution to the Government of India and to the Secretary of State.

Permanent Settlement

II. Resolved—

(*a*) That this Congress desires to express the profound alarm which has been created by the action of Government in interfering with the existing Permanent Settlement in Bengal and Behar (in the matter of Survey and other cesses) and with the terms of sanads of permanently settled estates in Madras; and, deeming such interference with solemn pledges a national calamity, hereby pledges itself to oppose in all possible legitimate ways all such re-actionary attacks on Permanent Settlements and their holders, and resolves to petition Parliament in that behalf.

(*b*) That this Congress regrets extremely that the Government of India have not only failed to carry out the pledges (given by the Secretary of State in his despatches of 1862 and 1865) for Permanent Settlement in the Provinces in which it does not exist, but have also failed to give effect to the policy of granting modified fixity of tenure and immunity from enhancements laid down in 1882 and 1884 by the Government of India and approved by the Secretary of State; and this Congress hereby entreats the Government of India to grant a modified fixity of tenure and immunity from enhancement of land-tax for a sufficiently long period of not less than sixty years, so as to secure to landholders the full benefits of their own improvements.

Poverty

III. Resolved—That this Congress, concurring in the views set forth in previous Congresses, affirms:

That fully fifty millions of the population, a number yearly increasing, are dragging out a miserable existence on the verge of starvation, and that, in every decade, several millions actually perish by starvation.

And humbly urges, once more, that immediate steps be taken to remedy this calamitous state of affairs.

India Council

IV. Resolved—That this Congress considers the Abolition of the Council of the Secretary of State for India, as at present constituted, the necessary preliminary to all other reforms; and suggests that in its place a Standing Committee of Members of the House of Commons be appointed.

Finance

V. Resolved—That this Congress, while thanking Her Majesty's Government for the promise they have made to appoint a Select Committee of Members of Parliament to enquire into the financial expenditure of India, regards an enquiry with so limited a scope as inadequate, and is of opinion that if the enquiry is to bear any practical fruit it must include an enquiry into the ability of the Indian people to bear their existing financial burdens, and into the financial relations between India and the United Kingdom.

XIV. Resolved—That having regard to the fact that the embarrassed condition of the finances of the country has been giving cause for grave anxiety for some years past, this Congress records its firm conviction that the only remedy for the present state of things is a material curtailment in the expenditure on the Army Services and other Military Expenditure, Home Charges, and the cost of Civil Administration, and in view of the proposed appointment of a Parliamentary Committee to investigate the subject, this Congress strongly recommends that the Standing Congress Committees of the several Presidencies and Provinces should, so far as practicable, make arrangements to send to England at least one well-qualified delegate from each Presidency or Province to urge such reduction before the Committee.

Public Service

VI. Resolved—

(*a*) That this Congress expresses its deep sense of disappointment at the despatch of the Secretary of State supporting the views of the Government of India on the question of Simultaneous Examinations, and this Congress hereby places on record its respectful but firm protest against the despatch, as, among other things, introducing a new principle inconsistent with the Charter Act of 1833 and the Proclamation of the Queen of 1st November 1858 (the solemn pledges contained in which the Secretary of State and the Government of India now seek to repudiate) by creating a disability founded upon race, for the despatch lays down that a minimum of European officials in the Covenanted Service is indispensable.

(*b*) That in the opinion of this Congress the creation of the Provincial Service is no satisfactory or permanent solution of the problem, as this Service, constituted as it is at present, falls short of the legitimate aspirations of the people, and the interests of the subordinate Service will not suffer by the concession of Simultaneous Examinations.

(*c*) That no attempt has been made to make out a case against the holding of Simultaneous Examinations for the recruitment of the Engineering, Forest, Telegraph and the higher Police

Service Examinations, and the Congress regrets to notice that the despatches of the Secretary of State, the Government of India, and the various local Governments are absolutely silent with regard to this aspect of the Resolution of the House of Commons.

(*d*) That this Congress respectfully urges on Her Majesty's Government that the Resolution of the House of Commons of 2nd June, 1893, on the question of Simultaneous Examinations should be speedily carried out as an act of justice to the Indian people.

Legal

VII. Resolved—That this Congress views with great dissatisfaction the system of recruiting the higher Judicial Service of the country, and is of opinion that provision should be made for proper Judicial training being given to persons who are appointed to the post of District and Sessions Judge, and that the higher Judicial Service in Bengal, the N.W.P. and Oudh, Bombay and Madras, and the Judicial Service generally in other parts of the country, should be more largely recruited from the legal profession than is now the case.

XI. Resolved—

(*a*) That, in the opinion of this Congress, the time has now arrived when the system of trial by Jury may be safely extended, in cases triable by Sessions Courts, to many parts of the country where it is not at present in force.

(*b*) That, in the opinion of this Congress, the innovation made in 1872 in the system of trial by Jury, depriving the verdicts of Juries of all finality, has proved injurious to the country, and that the powers, then, for the first time, vested in Sessions Judges and High Courts, of setting aside verdicts of acquittal, should be at once withdrawn.

(*c*) That in the opinion of this Congress it is extremely desirable that the power at present vested in Government to appeal against acquittals be taken away.

XII. Resolved—That this Congress having till now vainly appealed for many successive years to the Government of India, and also to the Secretary of State, to remove one of the gravest defects in the system of administration and one fraught with incalculable oppression to all classes of people throughout the country, and having noted with satisfaction the admission of the evil by two former Secretaries of State (Lord Kimberley and Lord Cross), and being of opinion that the reform is thoroughly practicable, as has been shown by Messrs. R. D. Dutt, M. M. Ghose and P. M. Mehta, entreats the Government of India to direct the immediate appointment in each Province of a Committee (one-half at least of whose members shall be non-official natives of India, qualified by education and experience in the workings of various Courts to deal with the question) to prepare a scheme for the complete separation of all Judicial and Executive functions in their own Province with as little additional cost to the State as may be practicable, and the submission of such schemes, with the opinions of the several Governments thereon, at an early date.

XIII. Resolved—That this Congress reaffirms the opinion of the preceding Congress that the time has now come to raise the status of the Chief Court of the Panjab to that of a Chartered High Court in the interests of the administration of justice in this Province.

XVII. Resolved—That this Congress hereby empowers its President to convey to the Government of India its opinion that the powers proposed to be conferred on District Magistrates by amendments and additions to section 15 of Police Act V of 1861, with respect to the levy of the costs of punitive police and of granting compensation, are of a most arbitrary, dangerous, and unprecedented character.

Medical Service

VIII. Resolved—

(*a*) That this Congress is of opinion that the present constitution of the Higher Civil Medical Service is anomalous, indefensible in principle, injurious in its working, and unnecessarily costly; that the time has arrived when in the interests of Public Medical Education, and the advancement of Medical Service and of scientific work in the country, as also in the cause of economic administration, the Civil Medical Service of India should be reconstructed on the basis of such Service in other civilised countries, wholly detached from and independent of the Military Service.

(*b*) That the very unsatisfactory position and prospects of Members of the Subordinate Civil Medical Service (Assistant-Surgeons and Civil Hospital Assistants) compared with members of similar standing in other departments of the Public Service, require thorough investigation and redress, and prays that Government will grant for the purpose an open enquiry by a mixed Commission of official and non-official members.

(*c*) That whilst this Congress views with satisfaction the desire of the Imperial Government to reorganise the Chemical Analyser's department with a view to its administration as an independent scientific department, it earnestly hopes that Government will not fail to recognise the responsible and meritorious work of Assistants, or as they in reality are, Government Chemical Analysers, and place them on the footing of Specialists.

Legislative Councils and Rules

IX. Resolved—

(*a*) That this Congress, in concurrence with the preceding Congresses, considers that the creation of a Legislative Council for the Province of the Panjab is an absolute necessity for the good Government of that Province, and having regard to the fact that a Legislative Council has been created for the N. W. Provinces, urges that no time be lost in creating such a Council for the Panjab.

(*b*) That this Congress, in concurrence with the preceding Congress, is of opinion that the Rules now in force under the Indian Councils Act of 1892 are materially defective, and prays that His Excellency the Viceroy in Council will be pleased to have fresh Rules framed in a liberal spirit, with a view to a better working of the Act and suited to the conditions and requirements of each Province.

Vote of Sympathy

X. Resolved—That this Congress wishes to express its respectful condolence and sympathy with the Royal Family of Mysore in their recent sad and sudden bereavement, and at the same time to testify to its deep sense of the loss which has been sustained in the death of the Maharaja of Mysore, not only by the State over which he ruled with such wisdom, ability and beneficence, but also by all the Indian peoples, to whom his constitutional reign was at once a vindication of their political capacity, an example for their active emulation, and an earnest of their future political liberties.

Education

XV. Resolved—That this Congress is emphatically of opinion that it is inexpedient in the present state of Education in the country that Government grants for Higher Education should in any way be withdrawn, and, concurring with previous Congresses, affirms in the most emphatic manner the importance of increasing public expenditure on all branches of Education and the expediency of establishing Technical Schools and Colleges.

Confirmation of Previous Resolutions

XVI. Resolved—That this Congress concurs with its predecessors in strongly advocating —previous (*a*)—(*i*)

(*j*) The discontinuance of the Exchange Compensation allowance granted to undomiciled European and Eurasian employees of Government, involving an annual expenditure of over a crore of rupees while the Exchequer is in a condition of chronic embarrassment.

(*k*) The giving effect to the Report of the Parliamentary members of the India Office Committee on the subject of the Rules,

Orders, and Practices in Indian Cantonments, with regard to prostitution and contagious disease, and the endorsing of their conclusions:

(I) That the system and incidental practices described in that Report, and the statutory rules, so far as they authorised or permitted the same, did not accord with the plain meaning and intention of the Resolution of the House of Commons of June 5th, 1888; and

(II) That the only effective method of preventing these systematic malpractices is by express legislation.

Forest Administration

XVIII. Resolved—That this Congress records its deep-felt gratitude to the Government of India for its circular resolution No. 22/F, published in the Supplement to *The Gazette of India*, dated 20th October, 1894, and its high appreciation of the generous principle, which it enunciates, of subordinating fiscal interest to the needs and agricultural interests of the ryot population in the management of forests.

And would further represent that in forests falling under classes 3 and 4 of the said resolutions, fuel, grazing concessions, fodder, small timber for building houses and making agricultural implements, edible forest products, etc., may be granted free of charge in all cases, under such restrictions as to quantity, etc., as the Government may deem proper; and that wherever hardship may be felt, under present conditions, the policy of the said Resolution may be carried out with reference to existing Forest areas, and the existing Reserve boundaries so adjusted as to leave a sufficiently large margin to facilitate the enjoyment by the agricultural population of their communal rights without molestation and annoyance by the minor subordinates of the Department.

Coercion of the Press

XIX. Resolved—That this Congress, being of opinion that the Government of India Notification of 25th June, 1891, in the Foreign Department, gagging the Press in territories under British administration in Native States, is retrograde, arbitrary, and mischievous in its nature, and opposed to sound statesmanship and to the liberty of the people, most respectfully enters its emphatic protest against the same and entreats its cancellation without delay.

Water-Cess

XX. Resolved—That this Congress views with apprehension the arbitrary policy of the Government of India with regard to the imposition of water-cess, introducing as it does a disturbing element in taxation, and suggests that the imposition of the said cess be regulated by certain defined principles affording security to the rights of landowners and of persons investing money in land.

South Africa

XXI. Resolved—That this Congress earnestly entreats Her Majesty's Government to grant the prayer of Her Majesty's Indian subjects, resident in the South African Colonies, by vetoing the Bill of the Colonial Government disenfranchising them.

Deputations

XXII. Resolved—That a deputation consisting of the following gentlemen be appointed for the purpose of presenting Resolutions numbered 1, 2, 3, 6, 7, 8, 9, 11, 12, 13, 14, 15, 16, 17, 18, 19, 20 and 21 to His Excellency Lord Elgin; and that the British Committee of the National Congress be requested to arrange a similar deputation to wait upon the Secretary of State for India in London.

From Bengal and Behar:—His Highness the Maharaja Bahadur of Durbhanga, Sir Romesh Chandra Mitra, *Kt*., Hon Mr. W. C. Bannerji, Hon. Mr. Surendranath Bannerji, Mr. J Ghosal, Babu Saligram Singh, Mr. Shuref-ud-din, Rai Jotendranath Chaudhuri and Babu Baikunthanath Sen.

From the North-West Provinces:—Hon. Raja Rampal Singh, and Hon. Babu Charu Chandra Mitra.

From Oudh:—Sheikh Raja Hussein Khan, Mr. Hamid Ali Khan and Babu Gokal Chand.

From the Panjab:—Sardar Dayal Singh Majithia, Mr. Kali Prasanna Rai, Mr. Jussawala, Shaik Umar Bunksh, Lala Murlidhar and Bakshi Jaishi Ram.

From Bombay:—Hon. Mr. P. M. Mehta, C.I.E.

From the Central Provinces:—Hon. Mr. G. M. Chitnavis and Rai Bahadur C. Narainswami Naidu.

From Poona:—Rao Bahadur V. M. Bhide, Mr. S. B. Bhate, Mr. N. B. Mule and Mr. P. L. Nagpurkar.

From Berar:—Rao Sahab Deorao Vinayek.

From Madras:—Manivikram, Raja of Calicut, Hon. Mr. Sabapati Mudaliar, Rai Bahadur P. Ananda Charlu and Mr. G. Subramania Iyer.

Congress Work

XXIII. Resolved—That a sum of Rs. 60,000 be assigned for the expenses of the British Committee and the cost of the Congress publication, *India*, and that the several circles do contribute as arranged, either now, or hereafter in Committee, for the year 1895.

Thanks of Congress

XXIV. Resolved—That this Congress hereby tenders its most grateful thanks to Sir W. Wedderburn and the other members of the British Congress Committee for the services rendered by them to India during the present year.

Formal

XXV. Resolved—That this Congress reappoints Mr. A. O. Hume, C.B., to be its General Secretary for the ensuing year.

XXVI. Resolved—That the Eleventh Indian National Congress do assemble on such day after Christmas Day, 1895, as may be later determined upon, at Poona.

Congress Constitution

XXVII. Resolved—That this Congress is of opinion that the time has come when the Constitution of the Congress should be settled, and rules and regulations laid down as to the number of Delegates, their qualifications, the localities for assemblage, and the like, and with this view the Congress requests the Standing Congress Committee of Poona to draw up draft rules and circulate them among the different Standing Congress Committees for their report; these reports, together with the draft rules and the report thereon to be laid before the next Congress for its consideration.

CHAPTER XI

THE second decade of the life of the National Congress opened at Poona, the great capital city of Maharashtra, on December 27, 1895, and it sat for three days, December 27, 28 and 30, the 29th being omitted, as a Sunday. No less than 1,584 delegates were present, and there was a huge crowd of visitors. The delegates were distributed as follows:

Bombay (1,246), Sindh (11)	1,257
Berar, C. P.	131
N. W. P. and Oudh	24
Bengal	51
Panjab	3
Madras	118
	1,584

The proceedings of the Congress opened as usual with the welcome address of the Chairman of the Reception Committee, Rao Bahadur V. M. Bhide, a noble and venerable man of seventy years of age, who, after a word of welcome, asked Professor G. K. Gokhale—"as I am a very old man"—to read his speech. At Poona it was, he said, that Mr. A. O. Hume had first discussed the scheme of the Congress with his Indian friends; Poona had been first chosen for its gathering, though the meeting had to be transferred to Bombay; and it was fitting that its second ten years' cycle should begin there. The speech was a particularly fine one, commencing with a reminder that a hundred years before Poona had been the centre of a Confederacy which held together the continent of India from the Himalayas to Cape Comorin, from Dwaraka to Cuttack, and vindicating India's Nationhood. Met there were they, he said, to "do all that is in their power to build up the great Indian Nation, which has been their aspiration by day and dream by night, and which, if not fulfilled before their eyes, will certainly be accomplished in the near future". It was for them to justify those hopes and aspirations, "to realise the dream of a united and federated India". The Hon. Mr. Surendranath Bannerji had been chosen as President, a man who "joins in himself all that is good and enlightened in young and in old India," holding "the foremost place in the hearts of what may well be called the hope and blossom of coming years—the hearts of many thousands of students".

The Hon. Mr. P. Ananda Charlu proposed, Dr. K. N. Bahadurji seconded, and Mr. R. N. Mudholkar supported the election of the Hon. Mr. Surendranath Bannerji, and it was carried by acclamation.

Mr. Surendranath Bannerji, after a few graceful words of thanks, referred to a difference that had arisen as to the Social Conference—put an end to by the tolerant and wise action of Mr. Justice Ranade—and said that the Congress was not of one social party rather than another:

> It is the Congress of United India, of Hindus and Muhammadans, of Christians, of Parsis and of Sikhs, of those who would reform their social customs and those who would not. Here we stand upon a common platform—here we have all agreed to bury our social and religious differences, and recognise the one common fact that being subjects of the same Sovereign and living under the same Government and the same political institutions, we have common rights and common grievances. And we have called forth this Congress into existence with a view to safeguard and extend our rights and redress our grievances.

The President then earnestly besought the delegates, to shape a Constitution for the Congress. In 1887 the Congress appointed a Committee to consider what rules, if any, should be framed. They reported, and a Resolution was passed to circulate the suggested rules to the Standing Congress Committees who were to work on them and report to the next Congress of 1888. That was passed in Madras, and nothing was done till the Congress returned to Madras in 1894, although at Lahore, in 1893, a wish for a Constitution was expressed. In 1894, the Standing Committee at Poona was requested to draw up and circulate rules; they drew them up, at the last moment, and sent them round, but there were no reports from the other Standing Committees. Let them form a Committee to frame rules and report on the last day, not circulating them to the Committee: "That is the old plea for inaction. We shall not have any rules at all if we are to repeat the hapless experiment of former years."

Turning to National affairs, the President pointed out the utter inadequacy of the Councils Act of 1892; for instance, Bengal, with a population of 70 millions, had 7 elected members. The right of interpellation had been usefully exercised. The members were allowed to talk about the Budget, but might not move any resolution thereon. He then discussed the tremendous increase of the military expenditure due to the frontier and other wars carried on by the Government. The whole policy was both wrong and ruinous. "Let me tell the Government of India, in your name, that the true scientific frontier against Russian invasion does not lie in some remote inaccessible mountain, which has yet to be discovered, nor is it to be found in the House of Commons, as some one said; but it lies deep in the heart of a loyal and contented people."

Having considered other points of expenditure and the woeful poverty of the people, the President touched on import duties, the exchange compensation allowance, the question of industries, and the then sitting Royal Commission to enquire into Indian expenditure. He spoke bitterly of the exclusion of Indians from the higher branches of the Services, especially the Army, "this ostracism of a whole people," and quoted Sir Henry Lawrence: "If Asiatics and Africans can obtain honourable position in the armies of Russia and France, surely Indians, after a tried service of a century under England's banner, are entitled to the same boon, nay, justice." He reviewed many other matters in the field of Indian politics, and urged that they should be made party questions in the English Parliament. After expressing gratitude for the improvements so far made, the President concluded:

> Nevertheless we feel that much yet remains to be done, and the impetus must come from England. To England we look for inspiration and guidance. To England we look for sympathy in the struggle. From England must come the crowning mandate which will enfranchise our peoples. England is our political guide and our moral preceptor in the exalted sphere of political duty. English history has taught us those principles of freedom which we cherish with our life-blood. We have been fed upon the strong food of English constitutional freedom. We have been taught to admire the eloquence and genius of the great masters of English political philosophy. We have been brought face to face with the struggles and the triumphs of the English people in their stately march towards constitutional freedom. Where will you find better models of courage, devotion, and sacrifice; not in Rome, not in Greece, not even in France in the stormy days of the Revolution—courage tempered by caution, enthusiasm leavened by sobriety, partisanship softened by a large-hearted charity—all subordinated to the one predominating sense of love of country and love of God. . . . The noblest heritage which we can leave to our children and our children's children is the heritage of enlarged rights, safeguarded by the loyal devotion and the fervent enthusiasm of an emancipated people. Let us so work with confidence in each other, with unwavering loyalty to the British connection, that we may accomplish this great object within a measurable distance of time. Then will the Congress have fulfilled its mission—justified the hopes of those who founded it, and who worked for it—not, indeed, by the supersession of British rule in India, but by broadening its basis, liberalising its spirit, ennobling

its character, and placing it upon the unchangeable foundations of a nation's affections. It is not severance that we look forward to—but unification, permanent embodiment as an integral part of that great Empire which has given the rest of the world the models of free institutions—that is what we aim at. But permanence means assimilation, incorporation, equal rights, equal privileges. Permanence is incompatible with any form of military despotism, which is a temporary makeshift adapted to a temporary purpose. England is the august mother of free Nations. She has covered the world with free States. Places, hitherto the chosen abode of barbarism, are now the home of freedom. Wherever floats the flag of England, there free Governments have been established. We appeal to England gradually to change the character of her rule in India, to liberalise it, to shift its foundations, to adapt it to the newly-developed environments of the country and the people, so that, in the fulness of time, India may find its place in the great confederacy of free States, English in their origin, English in their character, English in their institutions, rejoicing in their permanent and indissoluble union with England, a glory to the mother-country, and an honour to the human race. Then will England have fulfilled her great mission in the East, accomplished her high destiny among Nations, repaid the long-standing debt which the West owes to the East, and covered herself with imperishable renown and everlasting glory.

The speech was an exceptionally fine one, both for matter and manner, keeping throughout a high level of sustained eloquence, and it was enthusiastically cheered. The Subjects Committee was approved, and the Congress adjourned.

On the second day, Mr. Ghosal moved, and Mr. Jaishi Ram seconded Resolution I, which ordered that the draft rules framed by the Poona Council should be circulated, with instructions to report to the General Secretary and Standing Counsel three months before the next Congress, and it was carried unanimously.

Mr. Baikunthanath Sen moved Resolution II, stating the opinion that the enquiry on Expenditure could not be satisfactory unless evidence were given other than official and Anglo-Indian. The value of the Commission did not lie in the examining of accounts, but in an enquiry into the policy, which was at the root of the expenditure. This view was supported by the seconder, the Hon. Mr. Jambulingam Mudaliar, who pointed out that enquiry should be made into the enormous Home (Foreign) Charges, and the purchase of all stores in England, instead of developing manufactures here; also into the trans-frontier warfare and the scientific boundary search. Why should the enquiry be heard in camera, like an indecent divorce suit? there was nothing private about it. Pandit Madan Mohan Malaviya spoke of the joy with which India had welcomed direct Government by the Crown, believing that the transfer meant a share in free institutions and an improvement of the condition of the people. But the bureaucracy which ruled them forced them to doubt if they were right in their joy. Far more attention was paid to India, there was a keener desire to see that no injustice was done, and the interests of the people were more considered, before the Crown took over the Government. When the East India Company applied for the renewal of their charter every 20 years, a Parliamentary Committee enquired into their administration and reforms were made. But since the Crown took things over, there had been no such enquiry. They said to England:

> If you do not think us fit to govern ourselves; if you think we cannot understand our own finances, and say what we can and what we cannot spend, considering what our means are; if you think you are better judges of it, pray devote a little time and attention to the consideration of these matters. If you cannot find time to do so, permit us, pray, to do it. Why make us suffer by reason of your inability to attend to our concerns, and by preventing us from attending to them, from doing what we are most anxious to do, not only in our own interests but in the interests of the Government as well?

The eloquent speaker concluded:

> I ask English gentlemen, I ask the people of England, to seriously consider the position in which India is placed. That position is simply this. Educated Indians, representing the cultured intelligence of the country, have been praying for an enquiry, a full and fair enquiry, into the administration of this country during the last forty years. We have impeached that administration on almost every conceivable ground. We charge the Government of England, with having saddled us with an unnecessarily costly expenditure on the Civil Service of India; we charge them with having forced upon us a crushingly heavy military expenditure; we charge them with indulging in a great waste of India's money beyond the borders of India; we charge them with want of fairness in their dealings with India in the matter of the Home Charges; nay more, we charge them—the Government of India, the Government of England and the people of England with them—with being responsible, by reason of their neglect to adequately perform their duty towards India, for the loss of millions of lives which are lost in every decade from starvation, largely the result of over-taxation and inefficient administration.

We charge the people of England, because as some one has said,

> Hear him, ye senates, hear this truth sublime,
> He who allows oppression shares the crime.

If the English Parliament, if the people of England, who have solemnly taken upon themselves the duty of governing India, by reason of their neglect to do that duty properly, allow any loss of life to occur in India which they could prevent, they are surely answerable before God and man for that loss of life. In the face of such an impeachment, does it become the great English people and the English Parliament to give us a lame Commission, to enquire imperfectly into one branch only of this administration? Would it not become them rather to stand up, like true Englishmen, and say: "We shall face all these various charges, and either prove them to be untrue, or admit that they are true and make amends for them." The charges are not of a light nature nor are they lightly made, and if the English people do not care to enquire into them in the interests of their Empire, if they care not to do so in the interests of suffering humanity, if they do it not, even as a matter of duty, let them do it at least for the sake of the honour of England, which, I hope and trust, is still dear to every Englishman.

The Resolution was then carried.

Finance was still to the fore, and Resolution III dealt with Civil and Military expenditure. If the Commission would not go into policy, the Congress would, and Mr. Wacha pointed out that Sir James Westland had seriously misrepresented the facts by saying that the increase was due to the exchange, and that General Sir Henry Brackenbury had joined him by saying that, out of 62 lakhs of increase, 57½ were due to the fall in exchange. Mr. Wacha gave the official figures, proving the inaccuracy of the statement beyond possibility of dispute.

Munshi Shaik Hussain seconded, Mr. S. K. Nair and Dr. K. N. Bahadurji supported, and The Resolution was carried unanimously.

Resolution IV, the perennial separation of Judicial and Executive functions, was moved, this year by Mr. Mano Mohan Ghose. He added to the arsenal a statement by Mr. James, a Commissioner, in which he said that the union was "the mainstay of the British power in India"—a sorry confession. The Hon. Mr. C. Setalwad seconded, four other delegates supported, and it was carried.

Mr. W. C. Bannerji, in proposing the extension of the Jury system (Resolution V), made a new point in urging that a judge, translating in his mind the vernacular of a rustic witness, was too engrossed with the language to properly attend to the witness; Indian jurymen, understanding the language, would watch the demeanour of witnesses and would distinguish truthful speech from false. He feared that the strange changes which were being introduced into criminal procedure would shake the faith of the people in the administration of justice. Mr. Venkatasubba Iyer seconded, and Mr. Venkatrao Gutikar, in supporting, pointed to the practical identity between the Panchayat and the Jury, and the Marathi proverb: "The Five are the Voice of God." Sir Thomas Munro, in 1825, noted that the jury system was likely to succeed in India, because the Indians were accustomed to sit on Panchayats, and were "in general sufficiently expert in examining and weighing evidence ". The Resolution was carried, after three more speeches.

Mr. Seymour Keay, in an able and fiery speech, moved Resolution VI, on the gagging of the Press at the will of the Resident in Indian States (see Notification in Chapter X). In the State of Hyderabad several presses had been ruined, and in that State, bigger than the United Kingdom of Great Britain and Ireland, there was " not even a rag of an English newspaper published ". Mr. Ramachandra Pillai from Secunderabad seconded, and Mr. V. V. Modak spoke of what had occurred in Mysore, and Mr. A. L. Desai in Kathiawar. The Resolution was passed.

Mr. Kalicharan Bannerji, with great courage, brought up Simultaneous Examinations once again (Resolution VII), complaining that the deafness of the Government reminded him of the Bengali bogey, " khaun khutla," the cutter off of ears, only it was the Government whose ears were cut off. Three other speakers followed and the Resolution was passed.

The last Resolution on this day was the eighth, declaring that if England continued to use Indians in trans-frontier expeditions England should share the expense. This indubitably just proposal was moved by Mr. H. A. Wadia, in a very vigorous and sensible speech, condemning the " forward policy " advocated by Lord Roberts, Mr. Curzon and the brothers Younghusband. It was evil in policy and illegal in practice, for no right existed to use Her Majesty's forces beyond the frontiers, without the sanction of Parliament. Asia was swept off the surface of the globe, and Europe was advancing North and South and East; "all that remains of the living Orient" was contained in Japan; Russia and France threatened England in India! Mr. D. G. Padhye seconded, Mr. W. A. Chambers supported, and with the passing of the Resolution, and a telegram to Mr. Gladstone on his 87th birthday, the Congress adjourned to December 30.

The opening of the Congress on the third day was particularly interesting in view of subsequent events, for it asked the British to protect the Indians in South Africa, and Mr. G. Parameshvaram Pillai dealt specially with the disabilities imposed on them in the South African Republic—then existing. Mr. Ali Muhammad Bhimji asked if, in view of Her Majesty's Proclamation, it could be contended that the competition of coloured traders with white ones was to be stopped by disqualifying the former? Mr. J. M. Samant declared that the Act disfranchising Indians in South Africa was an insult to the whole Nation, but that the only hope of redress lay in appealing to Englishmen in England, "whose sense of Justice is not perverted and not contaminated by the slavery-producing atmosphere of Africa, or the tyranny-producing atmosphere of India". Mr. Vithal Laxman complained that while Englishmen kept the peace in territories subject to them, "their idea of justice becomes changed and one-sided. . . when the question of race comes, justice is set aside or is at least one-sided". The Resolution was carried.

The tenth Resolution, moved by Mr. R. N. Mudholkar, dealt with agricultural indebtedness, and urged that measures should be taken to lessen this indebtedness without depriving the ryot of his right to dispose of land if he chose. Mr. R. P. Karandikar dealt specially with the rigidity of the revenue system. The Resolution was carried.

Then followed Mr. V. R. Natu with Resolution XI, which asked that members, in making interpellations, might be allowed to preface a question with a short explanation, and the proposal was seconded by Mr. N. V. Gokhale, supported by Mr. P. S. Sivaswami Aiyar, and carried.

Resolution XII was on the Medical Service, and was again introduced by Dr. K. N. Bahadurji, and as readers do not need as much repetition as is necessary for Governments, it is sufficient to say that it was seconded by the Hon. Mr. B. G. Tilak—whose speech, being in Marathi, is not reported—supported by three other delegates, and carried.

Resolution XIII, on the danger of the method proposed by Government for suppressing law-touts, was moved by the Hon. Mr. N. Subbarau Pantulu, seconded by Rai Jotindranath Choudhuri, supported by Mr. M. V. Joshi and two others, and passed.

Mr. M. N. Samarth moved Resolution XIV, on fixity of land tenure, and ably summarised the arguments of an immense question in the very short time at his disposal. Mr. G. Venkataratnam seconded, and Mr. B. G. Tilak and another supported.

Mr. Pandurang Bapuji, an agriculturist from Berar, made a poignant speech, telling how the ryots of his Province lived; the Survey officer reported they were happy, and though a few District officers, to their honour, reported against the proposal, the assessment was raised. He said :

I give the following information from the Berar Revenue Report for the year 1894-95. Out of the entire Berar soil nearly 77 lakhs of acres are brought under cultivation. Population of Berar is about 28 lakhs and a half. Two acres and a half, therefore, of the land under cultivation, are used up by each individual. Javaree and cotton are the common crops. These two crops find place in sixty-eight out of a hundred acres of land under cultivation. During the year under report, one acre yielded 107 seers of javaree. The same area produced 44 seers of cotton. In the market javaree was selling at 21½ seers per rupee, while cotton was selling at 9 seers a rupee. It is thus clear that the entire produce of the 2½ acres of land which could be appropriated by a single individual was worth about 12½ rupees. Now the total amount of land-revenue in Berar is a little above 72 lakhs of rupees. Each individual has thus to pay to the Government about Rs. 2-8-0. Deducting this amount from the value of the produce at his command, he finds only 10 rupees, out of which he has still to defray the expenses incident to cultivation. This mode of looking at things gives us an idea of how the cultivator lives. Upon the trash of some 7 or 8 silver pieces he is doomed to live one long year, shifting as best he can, through varied seasons, and battling with risks and dangers that human life is liable to meet with. It is better to imagine than realise the keen pain and anguish which is the lot of the cultivating classes. This situation is not a whit altered. It is the same all the years of their life. 80 per cent of the Berar population live upon the soil. I ask you, ladies and gentlemen, whether you really think, with these facts before you, that the Berar people are happy and wealthy!

Are they not steeped, over head and ears, in deep misery and woe? The Government expends annually between 40 and 50 rupees on account of the maintenance of a single convict. The lawless and most dangerous foes of human peace and safety are circumstanced five times better than the peace-loving and. law-abiding subjects. It is strange how such a state of things can be tolerated by the benign and most impartial British Government. Now, these observations apply to the state of things as it once existed, while the old assessment rates were in force. I leave it, ladies and gentlemen, to you to conceive how cheerfully the contemplation of enhancement on the part of the Government would be welcome to the impoverished ryot!

Mr. Bhagirath Prasad, from the Central Provinces, further supported, and the Resolution was passed.

The same gentleman moved Resolution XV, protesting against the retrograde policy of the Government in nominating a member for the C. P. to the Supreme Council without any consultation with the Provinces he was supposed to represent. The Resolution was seconded and carried.

Resolution XVI, against the Exchange Compensation, was moved by Mr. Ambikacharan Mozumdar in a characteristically fine speech; he concluded by saying that "there ought to be reason in all things—even in the administration of India," and that "if from Pay to Pension, from Pension to Compensation, is to be the established order of financial progress of the Government, all that we Indians can say is, call it by any name you please, our legal phraseology has but one expression for it: it is illegal gratification". Mr. A. C. Parthasarathi seconded and, after two other speeches, the Resolution was carried.

Resolution XVII thanked the Government for recognising the grievances of third class railway passengers, and asked them to proceed from recognition to redress. Resolution XVIII repeated the protest against Forest Grievances, and XIX was against the Salt Tax. Professor G. K. Gokhale, in moving, compared the prosperous Manchester merchant with

> the starving, shrunken, shrivelled up Indian ryot, toiling and moiling from dawn to dark to earn his scanty meal, patient, resigned, forbearing beyond measure, entirely voiceless in the Parliament of his rulers, and meekly prepared to bear whatever burdens God and man might be pleased to impose upon his back.

Mr. A. D. Upadhye seconded, saying that while they could do, at a pinch, without cloth or hut, they could not do without salt; a basket of salt which cost 1 pice (¼th of an anna, or of a penny) cost 5 annas in British India. "What enormous crime have we committed that all should be put to this unbearable punishment of going without enough salt from year's end to year's end ? " he concluded.

The twentieth Resolution was on Education, repeating previous demands and was carried. The twenty-first, supporting import duties on cotton, was moved by Mr. Wacha, "the fire-brand of Bombay," speaking out of full knowledge, seconded by the Hon. Mr. P. Ananda Charlu in three sentences, and supported by Mr. Tulsi Ram, representing the hand-weavers of Madura, and by one other speaker, and carried.

The Omnibus (No. XXII) was driven this year by Mr. Ali Muhammad Bhimji, seconded by

Mr. N. M. Samarth, and supported by Rai Sangavani, who said he was an orthodox Hindu devotee, retired from the world, but he offered up to God "a meek and suppliant heart, devoted to the interests of my country and to the salvation of my race". Verily, a devotee of the ancient type, "intent upon the welfare of the world". Others supported, and the Resolution was carried.

The hour was late, and Resolutions XXIII to XXVI were rushed through, passing the grant to the British Committee, thanking it, appointing Mr. A. O. Hume and Mr. D. E. Wacha as General Secretary and Joint General Secretary—the omission of this last officer in the previous year had not worked well—and fixing Calcutta for the meeting of the Congress in 1896.

A vote of thanks to the Chair, and a few eloquent words from the President—especially urging the young to carry on the work to "be entrusted to your care and to your keeping"—closed the meeting, and the Eleventh Congress rose.

RESOLUTIONS

Congress Constitution

I. Resolved—That the draft rules in regard to the constitution and working of the Indian National Congress, as framed by the Poona Congress Committee in accordance with the resolution, in that behalf, of the last Congress, be circulated by the Poona Committee to all the Standing Congress Committees, with instructions to report to the General Secretary and the Standing Counsel at least three months before the next Congress.

Finance

II. Resolved—That this Congress is of opinion that the enquiry by the Expenditure Commission will not be satisfactory to the people of this country, nor be of any practical advantage to the Government, unless the lines of policy which regulate expenditure are enquired into, and unless facilities are afforded and arrangements made for receiving evidence other than official and Anglo-Indian. And this Congress also feels that the enquiry would, in all probability, yield better results, if the proceedings were conducted with open doors.

III. Resolved—That this Congress again records its firm conviction that in view of the embarrassed condition of the finances of the country, the only remedy for the present state of things is a material curtailment in the expenditure on the Army Services and other military expenditure, Home Charges and the cost of Civil Administration; and it notices with satisfaction that expert opinion in England has now come over to the view of the Indian Parliamentary Committee that growth in military expenditure is a more potent cause of Indian financial embarrassment than the condition of exchange.

VIII. Resolved—That in view of the great extensions of the British power on the North-West and North-East of the proper frontiers of India into regions not contemplated by Parliament when it passed Section 56 of the Government of India Act, the Congress is of opinion that over and above the sanction of Parliament necessary before the revenue and forces of India are employed outside the frontiers of India, the interests of India absolutely demand that the expenses of all such expeditions should be shared between England and India. Without some such additional guarantee, the forward Military policy will involve India in hopeless financial confusion.

Legal

IV. Resolved—That this Congress again appeals to the Government of India and the Secretary of State to take practical steps for the purpose of carrying out the separation of Judicial from Executive functions in the administration of justice.

V. Resolved—That this Congress views with alarm the constant changes that are being made and threatened on the subject of trial by Jury in this Country, and, regard being had to the fact that no demand for any such change has been made by any portion of the population of British India, trusts that the Bill now before the Supreme Legislative Council on the subject will not be further proceeded with; and this Congress, reaffirming resolutions passed by former Congresses, also trusts that trials by Jury will be extended to districts and offences to which the system at present does not apply and that their verdicts should be final.

Coercion of the Press

VI. Resolved—That this Congress, being of opinion that the Government of India Notification of 25th June, 1891, in the Foreign Department, gagging the Press in territories under British administration in Native States, is retrograde, arbitrary and mischievous in its nature and opposed to sound statesmanship and to the liberty of the people, again enters its emphatic protest against the same and urges its cancellation without delay.

Public Service

VII. Resolved—That this Congress, concurring with previous Congresses, again records its deep regret that the labours of the Public Service Commission have practically proved void of any good results to the people of this country, and repeats its conviction that no satisfactory solution of the question is possible, unless effect is given to the resolution of the House of Commons of June, 1893, in favour of holding the competitive examinations for the Indian Civil Services simultaneously in India and England.

South Africa

IX. Resolved—That the Congress deems it necessary to record its most solemn protest against the disabilities sought to be imposed on Indian settlers in South Africa, and it earnestly hopes that the British Government and the Government of India will come forward to guard the interests of these settlers in the same spirit in which they have always interfered, whenever the interests of their British-born subjects have been at stake.

Land Tenure

X. Resolved—That, in the opinion of this Congress, any proposal to restrict the right of private alienation of lands by legislation as a remedy for the relief of agricultural indebtedness will be a most retrograde measure, and will, in its distant consequences, not only check improvement but reduce the agricultural pepulation to a condition of still greater helplessness. The indebtedness of the agriculturist classes arises partly from their ignorance and partly from the application of a too rigid system of fixed revenue assessments which takes little account of the fluctuating conditions of agriculture in many parts of India; and the true remedy must be sought in the spread of general education and a relaxation of the rigidity of the present system of revenue collections in those parts of the country where the Permanent Settlement does not obtain.

XIV. Resolved—That this Congresses express its firm conviction that in the interests of the country it is absolutely necessary that there should be greater fixity in the tenure on which land is held in the temporarily settled districts than exists at present, and that

Government should impose on its own action restrictions against enhancement or assessment similar to those which it has deemed necessary in the interests of tenants to impose upon the rights of private landlords in permanently settled estates.

Interpellation

XI. Resolved—That this Congress notes with satisfaction that the right of interpellation, vested in non-official members of the Legislative Councils, has, on the whole been exercised in a spirit of moderation, which has secured the approval of the authorities here and in England; and the Congress, being of opinion that the practical utility of interpellations would be greatly enhanced, if the members putting them were allowed to preface their questions by a short explanation of the reasons for them, urges that the right to make such explanations ought to be granted.

Medical Service

XII. Resolved—

(*a*) That this Congress notices with satisfaction that its views in regard to the urgency and lines of reform in regard to the condition of the Civil and Military Medical Services of the country are being endorsed in influential Medical and Military circles, and that in the interests of the public, Medical Science and the profession, as also in the cause of economic administration this Congress once again affirms (1) that there should be only one Military Medical Service with two branches, one for the European army and the other for Native troops, worked on identical lines; (2) that the Civil Medical Service of the Country should be reconstituted a distinct and independent Medical Service, wholly detached from its present Military connection, and recruited from the open profession of Medicine in India and elsewhere, with a due leaning to the utilisation of indigenous talent, other things being equal.

(*b*) That this Congress further affirms that the status and claims of Civil Assistant Surgeons and Hospital Assistants require thorough and open enquiry with a view to the redressing of long standing anomalies and consequent grievances; and the Congress notices with regret that in their recent scheme of the reorganisation of the Chemical Analyser's department, the oft-admitted claims of Assistant Chemical Analysers have been apparently overlooked by Government.

Legal Practitioners

XIII. Resolved—That this Congress, while fully sympathising with any genuine effort which the Government may make for the suppression of law-touts, views with grave alarm those provisions of the Bill to amend the Legal Practitioners' Act, now pending the consideration of the Supreme Legislative Council, which propose to invest District Judges and Revenue Commissioners with the power of dismissing legal practitioners and, in cases coming under the Act, to throw the entire burden of proving their innocence upon the latter; and this Congress, being of opinion that the provisions of the Bill are calculated to prejudicially affect the independence of the Bar and to lower the position of legal practitioners in the eyes of the public without, in any way, helping to suppress law-touts or to further the ends of justice, urges that it should be dropped.

Representation

XV. Resolved—That this Congress puts on record its emphatic protest against the retrograde policy that the Government of India have this time followed in nominating a gentleman for the Central Provinces to the Supreme Legislative Council without asking Local Bodies to make recommendations for such nomination and earnestly hopes that Government will be pleased to take early steps to give to the Central Provinces the same kind of representation that it has already granted to Bengal, Madras, Bombay and the N. W. Provinces.

Exchange Compensation

XVI. Resolved—That this Congress repeats its protest of the last two years against the grant of Exchange Compensation allowance to the undomiciled European and Eurasian employees of Government, involving now an annual expenditure of over a crore and a half of rupees.

Third Class Passengers

XVII. Resolved—That this Congress, while thanking the Government of India for recognising the grievances of third class Railway Passengers, from whom the largest portion of railway revenue is derived, in their recent resolutions on the subject, desires to express its hope that Government will take effective steps to bring about an early redress of those grievances.

Forest Administration

XVIII. Resolved—That this Congress is of opinion that the action of the Forest Department, under the rules framed by the different Provincial Governments, prejudicially affects the inhabitants of the rural parts of the country by subjecting them to the annoyance and oppression of forest subordinates in various ways, which have led to much discontent throughout the country. The objects of forest conservancy, as announced in the resolution of 1894, are declared to be not to secure the largest revenue but to conserve the forests to the interest chiefly of the agricultural classes and of their cattle. The existing set of rules subordinate the latter consideration to the former and an amendment of the rules with a view to correct this mischief is, in the opinion of the Congress, urgently called for.

Thanks of Congress

XIX. Resolved—That this Congress tenders its thanks to the Secretary of State for India for his promise of September last to take an early opportunity to reduce the Salt Duty, and, concurring with previous Congresses, once more places on record its sense of the great hardship which the present rate of salt taxation imposes upon the poorest classes of the country—a hardship which renders it incumbent on Government to take the first opportunity to restore the duty to its level of 1888.

XXIV. Resolved—That this Congress hereby tenders its most grateful thanks to Sir W. Wedderburn and the other members of the British Congress Committee for the services rendered by them to India during the present year.

Education

XX. Resolved—That this Congress is emphatically of opinion that it is inexpedient in the present state of Education in the country that Government grants for Higher Education should in any way be withdrawn, or that fees in educational institutions, wholly or partially supported by the State, should be increased, and concurring with previous Congresses, affirms in the most emphatic manner the importance of increasing public expenditure on all branches of Education and the expediency of establishing Technical Schools and Colleges.

Excise Duty

XXI. Resolved—That this Congress is of opinion that the objection taken by Lancashire manufacturers to the exemption of Indian yarns below "twenties" from excise duty is not well-founded, and trusts that the Government of India will stand firm in its policy of levying import duties for revenue purposes, as such levy does not conflict in any way with principles of free trade.

Confirmation of Previous Resolutions

XXII. Resolved—That this Congress concurs with its predecessors in strongly advocating: (previous (a) comes in XIX; previous (b) (c) (d) are repeated, becoming (a) (b) (c); previous (e) is omitted; previous (f) (g) (h) (i) become (d) (e) (f) (g); previous (j) and (k) are omitted;) finally, a new item is added:

(h) The regulations of the imposition of the Water-cess by certain defined principles affording security to the rights of land-owners and of persons investing money in land.

Congress Work

XXIII. Resolved—That a sum of Rs. 60,000 be assigned for the expenses of the British Committee and the cost of the Congress publication, *India*, and also for the expenses of the Joint-General Secretary's office, and that the several circles do contribute as arranged, either now, or hereafter in Committee, for the year 1896.

Formal

XXV. Resolved—That this Congress reappoints Mr. A. O. Hume, C. B., to be its General Secretary, and appoints Mr. D. E. Wacha to be its Joint General Secretary for the ensuing year.

XXVI. Resolved—That the Twelfth Congress do assemble on such day after Christmas Day, 1896, as may be later determined upon, at Calcutta.

CHAPTER XII

CALCUTTA had been chosen for the holding of the Twelfth National Congress, and it opened its four days' sitting on December 28th, 1896. The delegates numbered 790, the premier place being, of course, taken by the Presidency in which the Congress had its temporary home. The delegates were distributed as follows:

Bengal	605
N. W. P. and Oudh	60
Panjab	7
C. P., Berar, Secunderabad and Rajputana	31
Bombay	52
Madras...	28
London	1
	784

The Congress was welcomed by Dr. Rash Behari Ghose, for the President of the Reception Committee, Sir Romesh Chandra Mitra, was, unfortunately, too ill to be present. Dr. Rash Behari, however, read the speech which Sir Romesh had prepared, and which opened with the expression of his belief that, despite all the difficulties surrounding their work, "British Justice vivified by British magnanimity" would ensure its ultimate triumph. Difficulties of Government were always great; how much greater were they when the "Government is a Government by foreigners, alien in manners and customs, sentiments and feelings to the subject race". Hence the need for the Congress, which showed the Government how India was feeling: "We offer help, but no menace, to the Government." He regretted the hostility and the suspicion of many of the ruling body, who claimed to know their thoughts better than they knew them themselves. As to the absurd statement that the Congress did not represent the masses, "it presupposes that a foreign administrator in the service of the Government knows more about the wants of the masses than their educated countrymen". In all ages it had been true "that those who think must govern those who toil," and could it be "believed that this natural order of things does not hold good in this unfortunate country?" The masses were not familiar with western methods, and the educated Indians alone could explain these to them. No foreigner could "touch the inner life of the people". The times were difficult. The land was suffering from famine; "what is called the plague" had appeared in Calcutta. Famine was a recurring trouble, and there was a widespread idea that the country was being "impoverished by excessive taxation and by over-assessment in the districts that are not permanently settled". A feeling reference was made to the passing away of Mr. Mano Mohan Ghose, and a few words of deep admiration for the Queen-Empress, who had just overpassed the limits of any previous reign, closed the address.

The President of the Congress, the Hon. Mr. Muhammad Rahimatullah Sayani, was then proposed by the Hon. Pandit Bishumbarnath, seconded by the Hon. Rao Bahadur P. Ananda Charlu, and elected with enthasiasm.

The President referred to the origin of the Congress as due to the fact that there was a consensus of opinion amongst educated Indians that the political condition of the country needed vast improvement, and that there were serious grievances and disabilities to be removed:

> They keenly felt the desire for wholesome reform, and discussed with freedom and candour their political condition, which they considered to be degrading. Their intellectual attainments recoiled against what they considered to be political subservience; their educated notions revolted against political disabilities; and their hearts aspired to attain a higher National ideal of citizenship under the beneficent rule of the British, which they highly appreciated. It was an ideal worthy to be encouraged and fostered by all right-minded and justice-loving Englishmen, and took complete hold of them.

He then analysed the declarations of the Congress leaders, noted the subjects dealt with in the discussions, and showed how from the Act of 1813 onwards, England had recognised the duty of fostering education in India, giving extracts to prove that free institutions were promised, and that the Congress was therefore bound to win, "if the people of India are true to themselves".

> In fact, a more honest or sturdy Nation does not exist under the sun than this English Nation; and there ought to be no doubt whatever as to the ultimate concession of our demands, founded as such demands are on reason and justice on the one hand, as on the declared policy and the plighted word of the people of England on the other.

The President then considered the views of Musalmans in relation to the Congress, and controverted their objections, and then proceeded to consider the condition of India, its heavy taxation, contrasted the differences between the financial treatment of Indians and English, and quoted many passages from eminent Englishmen to show the poverty and over-taxation of India, the ruinous drain upon her resources, the need for change, and the sad results financially of a century of British rule. He then proceeded to deal with the famine, and condemned the payment of the land revenue in cash as having a pernicious effect on the ryot, whereas payment in kind always left him food enough for himself and his family. He pointed out that the evidence which was being given before the Royal Commission on Expenditure justified the position taken up, but complained that the discussion of budgets in Legislative assemblies was purely academic, since the most pungent criticism had no effect.

The President concluded with a few words on the deaths of some Congressmen during the year, and on the 60 years Jubilee of the Queen-Empress in the coming June. The Subjects Committee, as elected, was approved, and the Congress adjourned.

The first Resolution conveyed the congratulation and hope for long life to the Queen-Empress, moved by the Maharaja of Natore, seconded by Prince Zaigam-ud-Dowlah, supported by Sardar Shrimant Shri Vasudev Rao Harihur, and carried by acclamation. Then came the second Resolution, of thanks to Sir William Wedderburn and to the British Committee, welcoming to the Congress its delegate Mr. W. S. Caine. Mr. Caine, in replying, dealt with the Expenditure Commission, and finance in India. Not inappropriately he asked the Congress Standing Committee to be more regular in its payments for the support of the work in England.

Resolution III brought up the separation of Judicial and Executive functions, moved by Mr. J. P. Goodridge, C. S., seconded by Mr. N. N. Ghose, supported by three other speakers, and carried.

Resolution IV introduced a new and important question—the proposal to give greater fiscal responsibility to the Provincial Governments, only a fixed contribution to be levied by the Supreme Government on each. It was moved by the Hon. Mr. Bal Gangadhar Tilak in a short but effective speech, in which he described the arrangement between the Supreme Government and the Local Governments being like that between an intemperate husband and his wife, that when the first had indulged all his extravagant habits, he asked his wife to surrender all her savings. As the Congress was taking up the subject for the first time, it should confine itself to the main principle, limiting the power of the

Supreme Government to draw on Provincial resources to a fixed amount, levied on a definite and just basis.

Rai Yatindranath Choudhuri seconded, and dealt with his own Province, Bengal, showing how unfair a proportion of revenue was taken by the Supreme Government, and how every five years it appropriated the Provincial savings, gained by careful administration, thus making important public works of utility impossible of execution. Mr. G. Parameshvaram Pillai emphasised the hardships of the system, and Pandit Madan Mohan Malaviya urged that the progress and happiness of the people depended far more on good Provincial administration than on the doings of the Supreme Government, and that the former was sacrificed to the latter. If the latter appropriated the funds of the former, it should also assume its responsibilities. He showed how the Government of his own Province was crippled, and education, specially, suffered. The Resolution was carried.

After this excursion into the new, the Congress returned to its old demand for Simultaneous Examinations in Resolution V, and not even Mr. G. Subramania Iyer, the mover, could find new arguments for it. Professor D. G. Padhye seconded it, and two more delegates supported it, and then it achieved its annual passing. Even now, in 1915, this minute concession remains ungranted.

The Hon. Mr. A. M. Bose proposed Resolution VI, which was, as he said, brand-new, for it protested against the new injustice just perpetrated in the scheme for re-organising the Educational Service, as being calculated to exclude Indians from the higher grades of that Service. It would be an astounding thing, were we not so habituated to it, that Indians should be systemically kept out of the higher and better paid positions *in their own country*, and that this should be done as a matter of course. Mr. Bose asked indignantly if the cause of progress in India was "not only not to advance but to be put back? Is the future to be worse than the past?" The scheme, dealt with for the first time, divided the superior Educational Service into two—the higher, the Indian Educational Service to be filled by persons appointed in England, and the lower, the Provincial E. S. to be filled in India. Before 1880, in Bengal, both Indians and Europeans in the higher Service received the same pay: both began on Rs. 500 p. m. In 1880 the pay for Indians was reduced to Rs. 333, and in 1889 to Rs. 250, although the Indians had graduated in an English University. The highest pay for the Indian now was to be Rs. 700, however long he might serve, while the Englishman had Rs. 1,000 at the end of 10 years. These invidious distinctions caused the most brilliant Indians to refuse to enter the Service. The new scheme further barred Indians out of Principalships of certain Colleges, reserved for Englishmen. The year of Her Majesty's Jubilee should not have been selected for this retrograde policy. He appealed to the Congress to protest against this policy of exclusion, and to fight against it, and then "this attempt to fix on the brows of the people of this ancient land a new stigma and a new disability shall fail, as it deserves to fail ".

The Hon. Rai Bahadur P. Ananda Charlu seconded the Resolution formally, and, supported by three other speakers, it was carried.

Resolution VII, on the extension of the Jury System, was moved by Mr. Hem Chandra Rai in a very short speech, in which he quoted the opinion of Sir Cecil Beadon as long ago as 1867, that the system should be universally adopted, as it would prove of "decided benefit to the Courts," and would increase public confidence. Mr. R. P. Karandikar said a few words only in seconding, and the Resolution was carried.

Another long and vainly urged reform, that of the Salt Tax, was moved as Resolution VIII by Mr. R. D. Nagarhar, seconded by M. S. Ramaswami Gupta, and carried, whereupon the Congress adjourned.

The third day opened with telegrams of sympathy and adhesion, and then Mr. G. Parameshvaram Pillai was called on to move Resolution IX, protesting against the disabilities inflicted on Indians in South Africa, and calling on the Governments of Her Majesty and of India to protect them. He spoke strongly and bitterly as was natural, after describing the infamous Act passed in Natal, which compelled Indians who had gone thither either to renew the indenture whenever it expired, or to pay nearly half their annual earnings to the State. The Government of India had agreed "to this monstrous measure," which would convert a large class of industrious people into hereditary bondsmen. Strange was the position of Indians:

> In India, we are permitted to become members of the Imperial Legislative Council. In England, even the doors of that august assembly, the House of Commons, are open to us. But in South Africa, we are not permitted to travel without a pass, we are not allowed to walk about in the night, we are consigned to locations, we are denied admission to the first and second classes on railways, we are driven out of tramcars, we are pushed off footpaths, we are kept out of hotels, we are refused the benefit of the public paths, we are spat upon, we are hissed, we are cursed, we are abused, and we are subjected to a variety of other indignities which no human being can patiently endure.

He pointed out that Indians were urged to show enterprise and go out into the world, and this was the result. They had better remain here, if the Government would not protect them, "till the merciful hand of pestilence or famine relieves an overburdened Empire of its surplus population".

Mr. V. N. Apte seconded, saying that they were told that England's mission was to raise all fallen and downtrodden races. Who would believe it in the face of South Africa? Mr. R. D. Mehta supported, and the Resolution was carried.

Resolution X brought up the grievances of the Medical Services, moved by Dr. Nilratan Sarkar, who with Dr. Golab Chandra Bez Barna, and Dr. P. C. Nandi, recounted and urged the facts which Dr. Bahadurji had laid before the previous Congress. It was carried.

Resolution XI was the Omnibus, and it was proposed by Mr. Ali Muhammad Bhimji, and seconded by Dr. Nibaran Chandra Das. It attracted four other supporters and was passed.

Then the grim spectre of famine stalked into the Congress with Resolution XII, and the Hon. Mr. Surendranath Bannerji undertook the sad task of moving it. Had the Government accepted the policy urged upon them by the Congress, there would have been no famine. Lord Elgin, the Viceroy, had spoken of the prosperity of the Central Provinces, but what was their state, as described by eye-witnesses? Consider the rise of the death-rate during the last two years, from 25 to 97 in one case, from 44 to 138 in another, from 36 to 140 in a third. The Chief Commissioner spoke of famines as "visitations of Providence," but they came through the blunders of our Rulers. The speaker proved from figures how much better off Indian labourers were in the time of Akbar than now, and famines were Nature's reminders to Government to mend their ways.

The resolution was seconded by the Hon. Rai Bahadur P. Ananda Charlu, who enquired after Lord Lytton's Famine Fund. The failure of one monsoon had reduced the country to starvation. Nine other speakers followed, giving details of relief-work, and pointing to the causes of famine in the drain, the over-taxation, the lavish expenditure, the destruction of industries, the many evils against which the Congress was ever protesting.

Resolution XIII dealt with the normal poverty of India, so closely related to the famines; people normally half-starved have little resistance power when complete starvation comes. Mr. R. N. Mudholkar moved it, urging Permanent Settlement, Agricultural Banks, raising of minimum for Income-Tax, and Technical Education. Mr. N. M. Samarth pointed to the danger, showing the riots which were breaking out, from the desperation of the people. He laid stress on the insufficiency of the food-grains in the country, the growing poverty of the people, and the mistaken policy of the Government. An amendment was proposed, and the Congress adjourned, but it was next day withdrawn, and the Resolution carried.

The fourth day opened with eleven resolutions still to dispose of, but the hardened Congressman is accustomed to rush his last fences. Mr. Kalicharan Bannerji led off with Resolution XIV, asking for Teaching Universities in particular, and improvements in the Universities in general. He pointed out that the Universities afforded no post-graduate facilities for teaching or study, and noted that the successes of Professor J. C. Bose and Dr. Roy had been won in despite of disabilities and discouragements. The Acts of Incorporation fettered their Universities, and they could not do as they would. Government said the matter was not urgent; he prayed the Congress to make it so.

Mr. Shivaram Mahadeva Pranjapi seconded the Resolution very briefly, but made a good point: "What is this Congress? It is a Congress of the Educated. Education is the Soul of the Congress." The Resolution was carried.

Mr. Jogendra Chandra Ghose proposed Resolution XV, asking for the Repeal of the Inland Emigration Act. He spoke of the miseries of the coolies in the Assam Tea Gardens that he had seen, and said that he had seen men and women jump off the steamers into the Brahmaputra to escape. In 1886, the Chief Commissioner of Assam had said "that in remote and unhealthy tracts the planters cannot do without a Penal Act". So an Act had been passed punishing with imprisonment a man who, after registration, refused to go, or who deserted, or refused to work. Recruiters enlisted the coolies, sometimes kidnapped them, constantly cheated them. In the gardens both men and women were beaten. The death-rate of coolies under the Act was more than twice that of non-Act coolies. There was no difficulty in getting labour at fair wages, and the wages under the Act were unfairly low.

Mr. Bepin Chandra Pal seconded, saying the Act was not needed except for out-of-the-way and unhealthy places, and none had a right to force the coolies to these. Mr. Rajani Kanta Sarkar was surprised that the British, who had abolished slavery, allowed this disgraceful Act on the Statute Book. Its provisions were barbarous, and the coolies so dreaded them that one man, not long before, had cut his throat, as he was being marched in a gang to the railway station. The Resolution was carried.

Resolution XVI asked that the Executive Councils of the Governments of Bombay and Madras might have three members instead of two. Mr. G.

Parameshvaram Pillai who moved, pointed out that a sympathetic Governor was often over-ruled by the two civilian Councillors. If there were three, and the third a non-civilian, the Governor and the non-civilian could vote against the civilian pair, and the Governor's casting vote would decide. The Resolution was seconded by Mr. Ali Muhammad Bhimji and carried.

Mr. G. Subramania Iyer moved Resolution XVII, which protested against the Government policy of short settlements of Land Revenue, and asked that at least 60 years should separate revisions. The Government had promised that Permanent Settlements should everywhere be introduced, but the promise remained unfulfilled. Mr. J. P. Goodridge seconded, speaking from his own experience as a Settlement Commissioner, and said that the present policy involved a breach of faith, and was economically indefensible. The Resolution was carried.

Mr. S. P. Sinha moved the eighteenth Resolution, stating that it was desirable that no Chief should be deposed without trial before a Public Tribunal, satisfactory to the British Government and the Indian Chiefs. A Chief had no safeguard against an oppressive Resident. He might be deposed without trial. He had no appeal to the House of Commons. Such depositions caused disquiet and were impolitic. Mr. Caine seconded, and said that the only thing he could discover as the reason for the late deposition of the Maharaja Rana of Jhallawar was "a petty dispute between a proud and sensitive Prince and an exceedingly foolish Resident". He did not know if the deposition were justified or not, for the facts were concealed.

Resolution XIX asked that the Central Provinces might have an elected instead of a nominated member in the Supreme Legislative Council. It was carried.

Resolution XX expressed the satisfaction of the Congress over the delegation of Mr. D. E. Wacha to give evidence before the Royal Commission on expenditure, and was moved by the Hon. Pandit Bishambharnath, who called him "our Indian Fawcett". The Resolution was seconded by Mr. G. K. Gokhale, who said that he wanted "to pay my own humble tribute of admiration of Mr. Wacha for the splendid work he has been doing all these recent years". He spoke of their admiration "for his unflagging energy, for the painstaking character of his work, and, above all, for the indomitable courage which always characterises him" and for his unrivalled grasp of financial questions. The Hon. Raja Rampal Singh and Mr. Caine also bore testimony to Mr. Wacha's great capacity.

Mr. W. C. Bannerji, in Resolution XXI, voiced the Congress' continued confidence in Mr. Dadabhai Naoroji, and hoped that he would be re-elected to the House of Commons; the Resolution was seconded and carried.

Then came the final Resolutions, voting Rs. 60,000 to the British Committee, re-appointing Mr. A. O. Hume and Mr. D. E. Wacha as General and Joint General

Secretaries, and fixing on Amraoti as the place of meeting for the Thirteenth Congress.

The Congress rose after a warmly proposed and seconded vote of thanks, and the presentation of a gold watch and chain to the President by his Muhammadan admirers, and his speech in reply.

Thus ended the Twelfth National Congress, 1896.

RESOLUTIONS

The Queen-Empress

I. Resolved—That this Congress desires to place on record its humble congratulations on Her Gracious Majesty, the Queen-Empress, having attained the sixtieth year of her reign, the longest and the most beneficent in the annals of the Empire—a reign associated with the most important advances in human happiness and civilisation. The Congress expresses the hope that Her Majesty may long be spared to reign over her people.

Thanks of Congress

II. Resolved—That this Congress desires to convey to Sir William Wedderburn and the other members of the British Committee its most grateful thanks for their disinterested services in the cause of Indian Political Advancement and accords its hearty welcome to Mr. W. S. Caine as the Delegate of the British Committee to this Congress.

Legal

III. Resolved—That this Congress notices with satisfaction the support of public opinion both in England and in India, which the question of the separation of Judicial from Executive functions in the administration of justice has received; and this Congress once again appeals to the Government of India and the Secretary of State, to take practical steps for speedily carrying out this much-needed reform. In this connection, the Congress desires to record its deep regret at the death of Mr. Mano Mohan Ghose, who made this question the subject of his special study.

VII. Resolved—That this Congress having regard to the opinion of the Jury Commission as to the success of the system of Trial by Jury, and to the fact that with the progress of education a sufficient number of educated persons is available in all parts of the country, and concurring with previous Congresses, is of opinion that Trial by Jury should be extended to districts and offences to which the system at present does not apply, and that the verdicts should be final

XVIII. Resolved—That in the opinion of this Congress it is desirable that in future no Indian Prince or Chief shall be deposed on the ground of mal-administration or misconduct until the fact of such mal-administration or misconduct shall have been established to the satisfaction of a Public Tribunal, which shall command the confidence alike of Government and of the Indian Princes and Chiefs.

Provincial Finance

IV. Resolved—Considering that the Local Governments are entrusted with all branches of administration, excepting Army expenditure, superior supervision and control here and in England, and the payment of interest on debt, this Congress is of opinion that the allotments made to the Provincial Governments on what is called the Provincial Adjustments are inadequate, and that in view of the revision of the Quinquennial Provincial Contract, which is to take place in 1897, the time has arrived when a further step should be taken in the matter of financial decentralisation, by leaving the responsibility of the financial administration of the different Provinces principally to the Local Governments, the Supreme Government receiving from each Local Government only a fixed contribution levied in accordance with some definite and equitable principle, which should not be liable to any disturbance during the currency of the period of contract, so as to secure to Local Governments that fiscal certainty, and that advantage arising from the normal expansion of the revenues, which are so essential to all real progress in the development of the resources and the satisfactory administration of the different Provinces.

Public Service

V Resolved—That this Congress, concurring with previous Congresses, again records its deep regret that the labours of the Public Service Commission have practically proved void of any good result to the people of this country, and repeats its conviction that no satisfactory solution of the question is possible unless effect is given to the Resolution of the House of Commons of the 2nd June, 1893, in favour of holding the competitive examinations for the Indian Civil Services, *viz*, Civil, Medical, Police, Engineering, Telegraph, Forest, and Accounts, both in India and in England. This Congress would once again respectfully urge on Her Majesty's Government that the Resolution of the House of Commons should be speedily carried out as an act of justice to the Indian people and as the only adequate fulfilment of the pledges made to them.

VI. Resolved--That this Congress hereby records its protest against the scheme reorganising the Educational Service which has just received the sanction of the Secretary of State, as being calculated to exclude Natives of India, including those who have been educated in England, from the superior grade of the Education Service to which they have hitherto been admitted; for in the words of the Resolution:—" In future Natives of India who are desirous of entering the Education Department will usually be appointed in India, and to the Provincial Service." The Congress prays that the scheme may be so recast as to afford facilities for the admission of Indian graduates to the superior grade of the Educational Service.

X. Resolved--(*a*) That this Congress notices with satisfaction that its views in connection with the urgency and the lines of reform in regard to the condition of the Civil and Military Medical Services of the country have been endorsed in influential Medical and Military circles; and in the interests of the public, the Medical Science and the profession, as also in the cause of economic administration, this Congress once again affirms: (1) that there should be only one Military Medical Service with two branches, one for the European army and the other for native troops, worked on identical lines, and (2) that the Civil Medical Service of the country should be reconstituted as a distinct and independent Medical Service, wholly detached from its present Military connection, and recruited from the open profession of Medicine in India and elsewhere, with due regard to the utilisation of indigenous talent, other things being equal.

(*b*) That the Congress further affirms that the status and claims of Civil Assistant Surgeons and Hospital Assistants require thorough and open enquiry with a view to the redressing of long-standing anomalies and consequent grievances.

XVI. Resolved—That having regard to the wisdom of the policy of appointing to the Governorships of Madras and Bombay, statesmen from England to the exclusion of the Services in India, and in view to the utilisation by those Governors of the power of giving when necessary a casting vote allowed them by law, this Congress is of opinion that it is desirable that the Executive Governments of those Provinces should be administered by the Governors with Councils of three members and not of two members as at present, and that one of the three Councillors must be other than a member of the Indian Civil Service; and in view to carrying out the object without additional cost, this Congress would suggest that the officers commanding the forces of those Presidencies be declared members of the respective Councils, as the Commanders-in-Chief of Madras and Bombay were, before the Madras and Bombay Armies Act of 1893 was passed.

Salt Tax

VIII Resolved—That this Congress once again places on record its sense of the great hardship which the present rate of Salt Tax imposes upon the poorest classes of the country, a hardship which renders it incumbent upon the Government to take the earliest opportunity to restore the duty to the level of 1868

South Africa

IX. Resolved—That this Congress once again deems it necessary to record its most solemn protest against the disabilities imposed on Indian settlers in South Africa, and the invidious and humiliating distinctions made between them and European settlers, and appeals to Her Majesty's Government and the Government of India to guard the interests of Indian settlers and to relieve them of the disabilities to which they are subjected

Confirmation of Previous Resolutions

XI. Resolved—That this Congress concurs with its predecessors in strongly advocating :—

Excise

(*a*) Persistent pressure by the Government of India on all Provincial Administrations to induce them to carry out in its integrity the excise policy enunciated in paragraphs 103, 104 and 105 of the Despatch published in *The Gazette of India* of March, 1890, and the introduction of a simple system of effective local option.

Legal

(*b*) The introduction into the Code of Criminal Procedure of a provision enabling accused persons in warrant cases to demand that instead of being tried by the Magistrate, they may be committed to the Court of Sessions.

Military

(*c*) A modification of the rules under the Arms Act so as to make them equally applicable to all residents in, or visitors to, India without distinction of creed, caste or colour, to ensure the liberal concession of licences wherever wild animals habitually destroy human life, cattle or crops, and to make all licences, granted under the revised rules, of life-long tenure, revocable only on proof of misuse, and valid throughout the Provincial jurisdiction in which they are issued,

(*d*) The establishment of Military Colleges in India, whereat Natives of India, as defined by Statute, may be educated and trained for a military career, as Commissioned or non-Commissioned officers (according to capacity and qualifications) in the Indian army ;

(*e*) The authorising and stimulating of a widespread system of volunteering, such as obtains in Great Britain, amongst the people of India.

Compensation

(*f*) The discontinuance of the grant of Exchange Compensation Allowance to the non-domiciled European and Eurasian employees of Government.

India Council

(*g*) The abolition of the Council of the Secretary of State for India.

Provincial Council and High Court (Panjab)

(*h*) The establishment of a High Court of Judicature and a Provincial Legislative Council in the Punjab.

Coercion of the Press

(*i*) The withdrawal of the Government of India Notification of 25th June, 1891, in the Foreign Department, gagging the Press in Territories under British administration in Native States, as being retrograde, arbitrary and mischievous in its nature and opposed to sound statesmanship and to the liberty of the people.

Poverty, Famine, and Remedies

XII. Resolved--That this Congress deplores the out-break of famine in a more or less acute form throughout India and holds that this and other famines which have occurred in recent years are due to the great poverty of the people, brought on by the drain of the wealth of the country which has been going on for years together, and by the excessive taxation and over-assessment, consequent on a policy of extravagance, followed by the Government both in the Civil and the Military departments, which has so far impoverished the people that at the first touch of scarcity they are rendered helpless and must perish unless fed by the State or helped by private charity. In the opinion of this Congress the true remedy against the recurrence of famine lies in the adoption of a policy, which would enforce economy, husband the resources of the State, foster the development of indigenous and local arts and industries which have practically been extinguished, and help forward the introduction of modern arts and industries.

In the meantime the Congress would remind the Government of its solemn duty to save human life and mitigate human suffering (the provisions of the existing Famine Code being in the opinion of the Congress inadequate as regards wages and rations and oppressive as regards task work), and would appeal to the Government to redeem its pledges by restoring the Famine Insurance Fund (keeping a separate account of it) to its original footing, and to apply it more largely to its original purpose, *viz.*, the immediate relief of the famine-stricken people.

That in view of the fact that private charity in England is ready to flow freely into this country at this awful juncture, and considering that large classes of sufferers can only be reached by private charity, this Congress desires to enter its most emphatic protest against the manner in which the Government of India is at present blocking the way, and this Congress humbly ventures to express the hope that the disastrous mistake committed by Lord Lytton's Government in the matter will not be repeated on this occasion.

XIII. Resolved—That this Congress once again would desire to call the attention of the Government to the deplorable condition of the poorer classes in India, full forty millions of whom, according to high official authority, drag out a miserable existence on the verge of starvation even in normal years, and the Congress would recommend the following amongst other measures for the amelioration of their condition:

(1) That the Permanent Settlement be extended to those parts of the country where it does not exist at the present time, and restrictions be put on over-assessments in those parts of India where it may not be advisable to extend the Permanent Settlement at the present time, so as to leave the ryots sufficient to maintain themselves.

(2) That Agricultural Banks be established and that greater facilities be accorded for obtaining loans under the Agricultural Loans Act.

(3) That the minimum income assessable under the Income-tax Act be raised from five hundred to one thousand.

(4) That technical schools be established and local and indigenous manufactures fostered.

Education

XIV. Resolved—That the time having come when greater facilities are imperatively required for Higher Education and the proper development of the Indian intellect than what are at present offered by examinations alone, this Congress is of opinion that the Acts of Incorporation of the Universities of Calcutta, Madras and Bombay should be amended so as to provide for the introduction of teaching functions and for a wider scope of learning, and so as to suit generally the requirements of the present day.

Migration

XV. Resolved—That having regard to the facility of intercourse between all parts of India and Assam, this Congress is of opinion that the time has now arrived when the Inland Emigration Act I of 1882, as amended by Act VII of 1893, should be repealed.

Permanent Settlement

XVII. Resolved—That this Congress enters its emphatic protest against the policy of Government, in Provinces where the Settlement of Land Revenue is periodical, to reduce the duration of the Settlement to shorter periods than had been the case till now, and prays that the Settlement should be guaranteed for long periods, at least for sixty years.

Representation

XIX. Resolved—That this Congress puts on record its emphatic protest against the retrograde policy of tho Government of India followed last year in nominating a gentleman for the Central Provinces to the Supreme Legislative Council without asking local bodies to make recommendations for such nomination, and earnestly hopes that Government will be pleased to take early steps to give to the Central Provinces the same kind of representation that it has already granted to Bengal, Madras, Bombay and the North Western Provinces.

Expenditure Commission

XX. Resolved—That this Congress desires to place on record its sense of satisfaction at the delegation by the Bombay Presidency Association of Mr. Dinshaw Eduljee Wacha, Joint General Secretary of the Congress, to give evidence before the Royal Commission on Expenditure, and the Congress has full confidence that Mr. Wacha will give accurate and adequate expression to its views on the questions which form the subject of enquiry.

Parliamentary Representation

XXI. Resolved—That this Congress again expresses its full and unabated confidence in Mr. Dadabhai Naoroji as the representative of the people of India, and hopes that he will be re-elected by his old constituency of Central Finsbury or any other Liberal constituency.

Congress Work

XXII. Resolved—That a sum of Rupees sixty thousand be assigned for the expenses of the British Committee and cost of the Congress Publication, *India*, and also for the expenses of the Joint General Secretary's Office, and that the several circles do contribute as arranged, either now, or hereafter in committee, for the year 1897.

Formal

XXIII. Resolved—That this Congress reappoints Mr. A. O. Hume to be General Secretary, and Mr. D. E. Wacha to be Joint General Secretary for the ensuing year.

XXIV. Resolved—That the Thirteenth Congress do assemble on such day after Christmas Day, 1897, as may be later determined upon, at Amraoti, Berar.

CHAPTER XIII

THE 27th, 28th and 29th of December, 1897, saw the Thirteenth National Congress in meeting assembled at Amraoti, Berar. 692 delegates had answered to the call in that terrible year of distress. The number was smaller than usual, but the officials put every possible difficulty in the way of holding the Congress —partly because of the wild outburst of suspicion and hatred which followed the murders of Mr. Rand and Lieutenant Ayerst, and partly because of the quarantine established in the first fear of the plague. There was even doubt if the officials would allow the Congress to be held, but the steadfastness of the Reception Committee and the care they took in their arrangements finally triumphed. The delegates were distributed as follows :

Berar, C. P. and Secunderabad	593
Madras	38
Bengal	33
Bombay	17
N. W. P. and Oudh	10
Panjab	1
	692

The Congress was welcomed by Mr. Khaparde, Chairman of the Reception Committee, and he opened with a brief account of the saddest year that India had known for long: famine had ravaged the land; plague had appeared in a form unknown for centuries; a ruinous frontier war had hampered finances; floods, fires, and earthquakes had added their terrors. Government and people were united in their efforts to relieve the distress caused by so many natural catastrophes, when two "deplorable murders," committed at Poona, roused the distrust of the Government, a panic over a supposed widespread conspiracy arose, State prosecutions began, and "unexpected deportations" with a proposal to amend criminal procedure. Under such circumstances they met; the only bright spot in the year was the Jubilee of her who gave the Magna Carta of 1858. He called on the Hon. Mr. Surendranath Bannerji to propose the President of the Congress.

Mr. Bannerji, in a few words, noting the gravity of the times owing to the reactionary tendency of the Government, and the need for a statesman to guide their deliberations, proposed the Hon. Mr. C. Sankaran Nair, "an honoured and illustrious leader of the Congress movement".

Mr. M. V. Joshi seconded, saying that they needed that year, especially, in their President unswerving devotion to the Congress, unquestionable loyalty, and unblemished personal character. These they found in the President proposed. Pandit Madan Mohan Malaviya and Mr. C. H. Setalwad supported, and the Resolution was carried with great enthusiasm.

The President opened his speech with a few graceful words of reference to the Jubilee of the Queen-Empress, and then passed on to the cry of sedition suddenly raised by a section of the Anglo-Indian Press against the whole class of educated Indians. He pointed out the impossibility of a class brought up on the English classics by English professors, studying English history, reading English books, newspapers, journals, not acquiring "English conceptions of duty, of rights, of brotherhood". They knew that class and race divisions, degradation and misery, had been cured in England by free institutions, and they believed that similar results would follow them here. To deny India representative institutions would be to ignore the principles, for which the noblest names in England's history had toiled and bled. She could not close the schools, nor prevent her papers circulating, with denunciations of tyranny in them. Mr. Chamberlain had been holding up to admiration Wallace, whose head was stuck up as that of a traitor, Bruce, guilty of a foul murder, Emmet and other Irish leaders, executed for treason by the English Government. "It is impossible to argue a man into slavery in the English language." Therefore they wished for the continuance of British rule, that India might take her place in the Confederacy of the free English-speaking Nations of the world.

The President, gratefully recognising the magnificent aid sent to starving India by Great Britain and other countries, said they could not shut their eyes to the need of turning the energy, which sought to relieve, to a removal of the causes of famine. "At the root of these famines is the great poverty of India." In Madras in a favourable season there was no grain for 5 millions out of a population of 28 millions. Was that to continue? Permanent Settlement and Retrenchment were two of the necessary reforms. Much of the expenditure was due to the idea that the English were a superior race, holding India by the sword. "To us this idea is hateful, and therefore we insist upon equality before law and Government... These distinctions... cast a slur on our loyalty, accentuate race prejudices in a most invidious form, and relegate Indians to the position of an inferior race, and silently ensure the emasculation of our manhood." The Colonies justified their bad treatment by

> our degraded position in our own country..... On this race question no concession is possible. No compromise can be accepted so far as it lies in us. We must insist on perfect equality. Inequality means race inferiority, national abasement. Acquisition, therefore, of all civil rights conferred on Englishmen, removal of all disabilities on Indians as such—these must be our aim.

The President then referred to the distress and anger caused by the plague measures in Poona, the forcible intrusion of soldiers into the ladies quarters in Hindu and Muhammadan homes, and their entry into family temples. Mr. Natu, a leading Poona Sardar, had sent formal written complaints to Government, appealing to them to interfere. The outrages went on, and the President of the Plague Committee was murdered. The Anglo-Indian Press attacked the Vernacular Press and the educated Indians, "a gagging Act was loudly demanded, the policy of imparting education to the Indians was questioned, the Press in England was worked, and the Europeans were thrown into a panic". The result was lamentable. The brothers Natu were arrested and kept in prison without trial, Mr. Tilak and the Editors of two Vernacular papers were prosecuted. Mr. Tilak was tried by a judge and a jury of 6 Europeans and 3 Indians, and was, of course, convicted by 6 votes to 3, and was treated as an ordinary criminal. Government had not answered the question as to the foundation of the complaints made. But India was asking it, and posterity would ask it. To try to stop progress "may compel underground passages or its overflow".

> Shall we be content to have India as it is, or shall we go on and do all in our power to lift it to a higher level? Years of subjection, nay, we may even say servitude, have sapped the strength of the Indian Nation, dwarfed its growth, and stripped it of all that was grand and noble in it, and if India is ever to occupy a better position than she fills at the present moment and take her proper place in the scale of Nations, it must be entirely due to the zealous efforts of her educated and enlightened men.

The warnings of the speaker as to the results of repression were unheeded, and progress was driven underground. Mr. Tilak was embittered, but not terrified, and took his place among the martyrs of liberty. The birth of the Extremist party may be dated from the plague outrages in Poona, the answer to the just appeals by the Natu Sardars for investigation by imprisonment without trial—since a trial would have proved the truth of their complaints —and the unwise Press prosecutions.

The Subjects Committee was approved and the Congress adjourned.

On the second day, the regular business began with a protest against the frontier policy, and a request that, if the Imperial policy required these trans-frontier excursions, the British Exchequer should bear most of the cost. Mr. D. E. Wacha moved Resolution I, embodying these views, and as he said, the subject had really been threshed out. They had protested annually against the military expenditure incurred by frontier wars. The Resolution was seconded by Mr. G. Subramania Iyer and carried.

Resolution II was closely knit with the first, and asked the British Parliament, in view of the distress caused by famine and plague, to make a substantial contribution to the cost of the War then going on. Mr. Baikunthanath Sen, in moving it, urged that India was living from hand to mouth, and that the famine had dislocated her finances; moreover the evidence laid before the Expenditure Commission justified the hope that Britain would bear her share. Mr. Jaishi Ram seconded, and the Resolution was carried with the addition that a petition embodying the two resolutions should be sent to Parliament.

Pandit Madan Mohan Malaviya moved Resolution III, which, as he said, crystallised the expressions of opinion uttered at previous Congresses, on the right to vote on Budgets, the reduction of Military and Civil Expenditure, and a sharing between Britain and India of all costs incurred in their common interests. India had to pay for the annexation of Burma, for foreign wars; let there be direct Indian representation on the India Council to vote against these charges. Mr. Hirendranath Datta, in seconding, said that some good had come out of the Expenditure Commission, since its members had become convinced of the poverty of India, and this should lead to the establishment of an effective control over Indian finance. The Resolution was further supported and carried.

A wise innovation was adopted, by the Omnibus Resolution, No. IV, being moved from the Chair, as having been thoroughly discussed at previous Congresses; for the same reason, Resolution V on the Public Service Commission, and Resolution VI, on gagging the Press in the Feudatory States, were put and carried. The same procedure might well have been adopted with Resolution VII on Permanent Settlement, which was, however, moved in a very long speech by Mr. John Adams, seconded by the Hon. Mr. D. S. Garvel, supported by three other speakers, and carried.

Mr. J. Choudhuri moved Resolution VIII, another very old stager, the separation of Judicial and Executive functions, and Mr. C. H. Setalwad in seconding usefully pointed out that both the Hon. Mr. Pherozeshah Mehta and Mr. Dutt had formulated schemes which showed that no additional expenditure need be entailed by carrying out the reform. The Resolution was carried, as was Resolution IX, moved from the Chair, on the cause of famine being only removable by a policy of retrenchment and reform.

With this the Congress adjourned.

On the third day, the President opened the proceedings by putting from the Chair Resolution X, expressing thanks to Great Britain, the Colonies, the United States and other countries for help given to relieve the famine, and also for the services rendered in India by English and Indians.

Gratitude was right and fitting, but the heart aches that the India, "the droppings of whose soil fed distant Nations" in the 18th century, should at the end of the 19th be a beggar asking, at the doors of happier Nations, for bread.

Resolution XI, asking for three members instead of two in Executive Councils, and one of them a non-official, was moved by the Hon. Mr. N. Subba Rau. He pointed to the necessity for placing an Indian in each Executive Council, and commented on the fact that men like Dewan Bahadur Srinivasa Raghava Iyengar should have to go to Baroda, and Sir T. Madhava Rao successively to Travancore, Baroda, and Indore, being shut out of high service in British India.

Mr. N. C. Kelkar seconded, and the Resolution was carried.

Resolution XII was moved by the Hon. Mr. Surendranath Bannerji, and dealt with the exercise by

Government of the special powers given by the Regulations of 1818, '19 and '27, and urged the Government of Bombay either to try or release the Sardars Natu, whom they had kept in custody for five months. (This terrible power is exercised in India still, the old *lettres de cachet* of Bourbon times, and anyone suspected by Government may be, and too often is, suddenly swept out of sight, disappears, and there is no redress.) Mr. Surendranath Bannerji, as was fitting, spoke warmly :

> We regard the quartering of the Punitive Police at Poona as a mistake. We regard the imprisonment of Mr. Tilak and of the Poona Editors as a still greater mistake. For Mr. Tilak my heart is full of sympathy. My feelings go forth to him in his prison house. A Nation is in tears. . . . . Englishmen have won for themselves the Magna Carta and the Habeas Corpus. The principles which underlie those concessions are embalmed in their glorious constitution. The constitution, I have no hesitation in saying, is ours by birthright ; born British subjects, we are entitled to the privileges of British subjects. Who will filch away these rights from us ? We are resolved, and this Congress will take the pledge, you and I will enter into a solemn League and Covenant. Let it go forth from this hall, let it impregnate the public mind of India, we are resolved, by every constitutional means that may be available to us, to assert under the Providence of God our rights as British subjects, not the least important of which is the inestimable right of personal liberty.

Brave and true words, but as fruitless in 1897 as in 1915, and to remain fruitless until they ring from one end of India to the other. Now, as ever, is it true, that only

> They have rights who dare maintain them.

Rightly did the eloquent speaker say :

> Brother delegates, security of life and property are the great foundations upon which rests the vast, the stupendous, the colossal fabric of British rule in India. What becomes of these inestimable blessings if at any moment your property may be confiscated, and you may be arrested, kept in custody for months together, without a trial and without a word of explanation? What becomes of the boasted vaunt of the boon of personal liberty and personal security under British rule under these circumstances?

Mr. R. K. R. Cama seconded the Resolution, and quoted a remarkable statement of Lord George Hamilton: "In India, almost without warning, an apparently peaceful population might suddenly become as dangerous as criminal lunatics, with but one object before them—to murder the class alien to them." This wicked statement, made in the House of Commons by Lord George Hamilton, Secretary of State for India, is one more proof of the profound ignorance of India which seems to be the qualification for the Secretaryship. If the shameful slander were as true as it is false, even a criminal lunatic has to be brought to trial, not kept indefinitely in prison, untried. Messrs. P. Kesava Pillai, Alfred Nandi, and V. K. Kale further supported, and the Resolution was unanimously carried.

Resolution XIII, brought up by Mr. W. C. Bannerji, protested against the proposed changes in the law of sedition, as dealing an irreparable blow to liberty of speech and the freedom of the press. He moved it in an argumentative and powerful speech, showing the unfairness, in matters called seditious, of trying an Indian before an English jury, who might not even know the language of the accused, or by District Magistrates, officers of the Government threatened by the sedition. He thought the proposals would be forced into law, and he said:

> We must go before the British public. We must explain to them how the agents they have sent to govern the country on their behalf and in their name are dealing with the people, that is, dealing in a manner wholly unworthy of the British name and the British love of freedom. And if we can convince them that we are right, I have no doubt that the British Nation will rise in their wrath, and free us from the trammels which Lord Elgin and his councillors are forging for us.

Mr. Mudholkar seconded, in an able speech, pointing to the danger of the loose form of words employed, urging that the measure was retrograde and most mischievous. Pandit B. Narrain Dhar quoted a minute recorded by Lord Hobhouse in 1876, in which he pointed out that any attempt towards even-handed justice was met by the Anglo-Indian press with "outcries and menaces, compared to which the complaints of the native newspapers are gentle murmurs". Similarly, Sir James Fitzjames Stephens, asked by certain "Native Associations" how they could tell whether they were infringing the law, said: "Go to the English newspapers; whatever they say, you may say; that anybody should want to be more offensive than they, is inconceivable."

Mr. A. C. Mozumdar was astonished that the petty calumnies of newspapers, poisoning against Indians the mind of the Government, had been so successful as to lead the State itself to charge them with sedition.

> Born of a people whose ancestors often sacrificed their own children for the supposed welfare of their Kings, we disdain to learn lessons of loyalty from those whose liberties are bathed and consecrated in royal blood.

After two other speakers had addressed the Congress, the Resolution was carried.

Mr. John Adam moved Resolution XIV, against the proposed increase of the powers of the Police, and analysed at great length the provisions of the Criminal Procedure Bill then pending. Three other speakers followed and the Resolution was carried.

After a brief recess, a telegram was sent to Mr. Gladstone on his completion of his 89th year, and then Resolution XV, thanking the Government for giving a Legislative Council to the Panjab, and regretting its limitations, was put from the Chair and carried.

Resolution XVI pointed out that legislation for Berar was passed by the Executive, and requested it might be passed in the Supreme Legislative Council. No. XVII asked for the extension of the scope of the Famine Commission to enquire into the causes and prevention of periodical famines. Mr. Ramanjalu Naidu moved it, noticing the Madras famines of 1854, '65, '76, '77-'78, '91 and '97. Nothing had been done to prevent these recurrences. Fourteen times as much was spent on railways as on irrigation, while if the money invested in railways were used for irrigation, famine would disappear. Professor A. S. Sathe seconded, urging that the root of the recurring famines must be found and destroyed. It was the result of a century's bungling. Railways helped English trade; irrigation helped the ryot. The Resolution was carried.

Resolution XVIII expressing confidence in Mr. Naoroji was moved by the Hon. Rai Bahadur P. Ananda Charlu, seconded by Mr. Motilal Ghose and carried. Resolutions XIX and XX, the usual thanks to Sir William Wedderburn and the British Committee and the yearly grant, and the re-appointment of Mr. A. O. Hume and Mr. D. E. Wacha were moved from the Chair and carried, and Resolution XXI fixed the meeting of the next Congress in Madras.

The final Resolutions, XXII thanking the Reception for the success of its singularly difficult work, and XXIII the vote of thanks to the Chair, were enthusiastically carried, and the President, with a few kindly words of recognition, declared the Thirteenth National Congress dissolved.

RESOLUTIONS

Military

I. Resolved—That this Congress expresses its deep and earnest conviction that the present Frontier policy of the Government of India is injurious to the best interests of the British Empire in general, and this country in particular, as it involves frequent Military expeditions beyond the present limits of the British Indian Empire and causes great loss of valuable lives and public money: it therefore entreats the British Nation to put a stop to this aggressive policy and to lay down, that, if such expeditions are found necessary, they being for Imperial purposes, the major portion of their expenses should be defrayed by the British Exchequer.

II. Resolved—That in view of the fact that the calamities of famine and plague have dislocated the already seriously embarrassed finances of this country, and crippled its limited resources, and that the Military operations carried on beyond the North West Frontier are for the protection of Imperial interests, this Congress prays that the British Parliament will, pending the settlement of the principle on which the Military charges are to be apportioned between Great Britain and India, be pleased to make a substantial contribution to the cost of the present War.

II. A. Resolved—That this Congress authorises the President to submit a petition to Parliament, embodying the prayer contained in Resolutions I and II under his hand on its behalf.

Expenditure Commission

III. Resolved—That this Congress rejoices that the "Royal Commission on Indian Expenditure" was pleased to decide to admit the public to its proceedings, and further desires to express its grateful acknowledgments for the opportunity afforded by the Honourable Commission to representative Indian witnesses, to state fully the case on behalf of India. With regard to the three divisions of the reference, the Congress desires most respectfully to submit the following prayers for the favourable consideration of the Honourable Commission:

(I) As regards the machinery to control Indian Expenditure it is prayed

(1)—that the non-official members of the Viceroy's Council may be made more directly representative of the Indian people, and that they may have the right to move amendments and divide the Council upon the Provisions of the Budget; (2) That a sufficient number of representative Indians of position and experience may be nominated to the Council of the Secretary of State on the recommendation of the elected members of the Viceroy's and Local Legislative Councils; and (3) that each year a Select Committee of the House of Commons may be appointed to enquire into, and report upon, the financial condition of India;

(2) As regards the progress of Expenditure, it is prayed that the Military and other unproductive expenditure be reduced, that larger amounts be spent in promoting the welfare and progress of the people, and that a large saving and more efficient administration may be obtained, by the substitution, as far as practicable, of Indian for European agency, in the higher grades of the Public Service; and

(3) As regards apportionment of charges, it is prayed that the Imperial Treasury may bear a fair proportion of all expenditure, in which the common interests of India and the rest of the Empire are involved; and that especially the expense of the present war beyond the frontier may be largely borne by the Imperial Exchequer. Lastly, that it be an instruction to the President to submit a

copy of this Resolution, under his own signature to the Chairman of the Royal Commission with the least practicable delay.

Confirmation of Previous Resolutions

IV. Resolved—That this Congress concurs with its predecessors in strongly advocating: (1896: (*a*) (*c*) (*g*); (*h*) omitting Provincial Council, which had been granted.)

And this Congress, concurring with its predecessors records its protests: (1896 (*a*)—(*d*) VI, VIII, IX, XIX.)

And this Congress, also concurring with its predecessors, expresses its firm conviction:

(*a*) (1896 X) That in the interests of the public, the Medical Science, and the Profession, as also in the cause of economic administration, (1) there should be only one Medical Military Service, with two branches, one for the European Army and one for Native Troops, worked on identical lines; (2) the Civil Medical Service of the country should be reconstituted as a distinct and independent Medical Service, wholly detached from its present Military connection, and recruited from the open profession of medicine in India and elsewhere, with due regard to the utilisation of indigenous talent, other things being equal; and (3) there should be a thorough, open enquiry into the status and claims of Civil Assistant Surgeons and Hospital Assistants with a view to the redressing of long-standing anomalies and consequent grievances.

(*b*) (1896 XIV).

(*c*) (1896 XV).

(*d*) (1896 XVIII).

(*e*) (1896 VII).

Public Service

V. Resolved—That this Congress concurring with previous Congresses, again records its deep regret that the labours of the Public Service Commission have practically proved void of any good result to the people of this country, and repeats its conviction that no satisfactory solution of the question is possible, unless effect is given to the Resolution of the House of Commons of the 2nd June, 1893, in favour of holding the competitive examinations for the Indian Civil Services, *viz.*, Civil, Medical, Police, Engineering, Telegraph, Forest, and Accounts, both in India and in England. This Congress would once again respectfully urge on Her Majesty's Government that the Resolution of the House of Commons should be speedily carried out, as an act of Justice to the Indian people, and as the only adequate fulfilment of the pledges made to them.

XI. Resolved—That, having regard to the wisdom of the policy of appointing to the Governorships of Madras and Bombay, statesmen from England, to the exclusion of the Services in India, this Congress is of opinion that it is desirable that the Executive Government of those Provinces should be administered by the Governors with Councils of three Members and not of two Members, as at present, and that one of the three Councillors should be other than a member of the Indian Civil Service.

Coercion

Press

VI. Resolved—That this Congress being of opinion that the Government of India Notification of 25th June, 1891 in the Foreign Department, gagging the Press in Territories under British administration in Native States, is retrograde, arbitrary, and mischievous in its nature, and opposed to sound statesmanship and to the liberty of the people, again enters its emphatic protest against the same, and urges its cancellation without delay.

Lettres de Cachet

XII. Resolved—That this Congress respectfully deprecates the exercise by the Government of the extraordinary powers vested in them by Bengal Regulation III of 1818, Madras Regulation II of 1819, and Bombay Regulation XXV of 1827 at a time of peace and quiet, and submits that such powers should be exercised only under such limitations as will ensure their being put in force with the utmost circumspection and care and under a sense of the highest responsibility by the Government.

(*a*) This Congress therefore urges that none of these Regulations should be put into force except after notification by the Local Government concerned that the circumstances contemplated by the preamble of the Regulations exist in its Province or in some definite area within the Province, and that it intends, if necessary, to exercise the powers vested in it; and further that in no case should such powers extend to keeping a person arrested under them in custody for a period of longer than three months without his being brought to trial before a Court of Justice.

(*b*) That this Congress, while feeling that the Government of Bombay must have acted under a sense of responsibility in arresting the Sardars Natu under Bombay Regulation XXV of 1827, is yet of opinion, that, five months having now elapsed from such arrest, it is the duty of the Government, in the interests of Justice, and also to allay the disquiet and uneasiness which has been created in the minds of the people at large by the arrest, to bring them—the Sardars Natu—to trial without delay, or, if the Government have no sufficient evidence against them to place before a Court of Justice, to release them.

Sedition

XIII. Resolved—That this Congress views with alarm and anxiety the changes proposed in the existing law of sedition as defined in Section 124a, and of circulating false reports as defined in Section 505 of the Indian Penal Code, and is of opinion that Section 124a of the Indian Penal Code requires amendment, not in the direction of greater stringency but in that of greater freedom, and if the law of sedition in India is to be made the same as it is in England, the administration of it ought to be safeguarded substantially in the same way as it is there, *viz.*, that the trial of accused persons must always be by jury, at least one half of whom should be persons of the same nationality as the accused, and that their verdict should be unanimous. And this Congress strongly protests against cases of sedition being made triable by Magistrates and not by Courts of Sessions and High Courts exclusively, as heretofore, and against the proposal to invest District Magistrates with the power of calling upon persons who, in their opinion, disseminate disaffection, to find sureties of good behaviour for twelve months. This Congress is further of opinion that the changes in the law now proposed, will be altogether at variance with the pledges given by Sir James Fitz-James Stephen when passing Section 124a of the Indian Penal Code through the Council, and will deal an irreparable blow to liberty of speech and freedom of the Press, thus retarding the progress of the country and creating terror instead of confidence in the minds of the people.

That a copy of this Resolution be submitted to the Legislative Council by the President.

Criminal Procedure

XIV. Resolved—That this Congress desires to record its protest against the Criminal Procedure Bill of 1897 now pending before the Imperial Legislative Council, as being a retrograde and reactionary measure, which will add to the already large powers of the Police, invest Magistrates with a discretionary authority which they do not now possess, and curtail the powers of the High Courts, all to the extreme prejudice of accused persons.

Permanent Settlement

VII. Resolved—That this Congress enters its emphatic protest against the policy of the Government in Provinces where the settlement of land revenue is periodical in reducing the duration of the Settlement while enhancing its amount, and expresses its firm conviction that, in the interests of the country it is absolutely necessary that the land revenue in such Provinces should be permanently settled.

Legal

VIII. Resolved—That this Congress notices with satisfaction the support of public opinion both in England and in India which the question of the separation of Judicial and Executive functions in the administration of justice has received; and this Congress once again appeals to the Government of India and the Secretary of State to take practical steps for carrying out the much needed reform.

Famine

IX. Resolved—That this Congress is glad to note that the Government of India has appointed a Famine Commission and hopes that the Commission will institute a searching enquiry into the matter. At the same time the Congress once again desires to repeat its conviction that famines are due to the great poverty of the people, brought on by the drain of the wealth of the country which has been going on for years together, and by the excessive taxation and over-assessment consequent on a policy of extravagance, followed by the Government both in the Civil and Military Departments, which have so far impoverished the people that, at the first touch of scarcity, they are rendered helpless and must perish, unless fed by the State, or helped by private charity. In the opinion of this Congress the true remedy against the recurrence of famine lies in the adoption of a policy which would enforce economy, husband the resources of the State, foster the development of indigenous and local arts and industries, which have practically been extinguished, and help forward the introduction of modern arts and industries.

XVII. Resolved—That this Congress prays that the scope of the Famine Commission appointed by the Government of India be extended, so as to include an enquiry into the causes of periodical famines and the remedies for the prevention of the same.

X. Resolved—That this Congress expresses its heart-felt gratitude to the British public and to the peoples of the British Colonies, the United States of America and other foreign countries for the generous aid afforded by them to the starving millions of this country, during the late dreadful visitation of famine, and also wishes to place on record its high appreciation of the services which many men, and women—English and Indian—residing in this country rendered, and the pecuniary help they gave for the relief of those afflicted by that calamity.

And that it be an instruction to the various Congress Committees to raise a sum of a thousand pounds, to be sent to the Lord Mayor of London on behalf of the Congress, in order that he might be pleased to put some memorial in some conspicuous part of London expressing the gratitude of the people of India for the help rendered them during the time of the last famine.

Legislative Council (Panjab)

XV. Resolved—That this Congress, while thanking the Government for granting the boon of a Legislative Council to the Panjab, places on record its regret that they have not extended to the Councillors the rights of interpellation, and to the people the right of recommending Councillors for nomination, such as are enjoyed by the Councillors and people in the other Provinces.

Berar Legislation

XVI. Resolved—That the Province of Berar, though not a part of British India, is administered by the Governor-General-in-Council in the same way as any portion of British India, but the important work of legislating for the Province is performed by the Executive instead of by the Legislative Council, resulting often in unsuitable and inconvenient legislation. This Congress therefore humbly prays that so long as Berar is administered by the Governor-General-in-Council all laws and orders having the force of law, intended for Berar, should be enacted by the Supreme Legislative Council, in the same way as those for British India proper.

Parliamentary Representation

XVIII. Resolved—That this Congress again expresses its full and unabated confidence in Mr. Dadabhoi Naoroji as the representative of the people of India, and hopes that he will be re-elected by his old Constituency of Central Finsbury or any other Liberal Constituency.

Thanks of Congress and Congress Work

XIX. Resolved—That this Congress desires to convey to Sir Willam Wedderburn and the other members of the British Committee its most grateful thanks for their disinterested services in the cause of Indian political advancement.

And that a sum of Rs. 60,000 be assigned for the expenses of the British Committee and cost of Congress publication, *India*, and also for the expenses of the Joint General Secretary's Office, and that the several circles do contribute as arranged, either now or hereafter in Committee, for the year 1898.

Formal

XX. Resolved—That this Congress re-appoints Mr. A. O. Hume, C.B., to be General Secretary and Mr. D. E. Wacha to be Joint General Secretary for the ensuing year.

XXI. Resolved—That the Fourteenth Indian National Congress do assemble on such day after Christmas Day, 1898, as may later be determined upon, at Madras.

CHAPTER XIV

THE Fourteenth Session of the National Congress was held in Madras, on December 29th, 30th and 31st, 1898. The clouds were gathering on the political horizon, coercion was showing its hideous face, ensuring the growth of secret conspiracy, and alienating from the Government, which confessed its weakness by employing it, all that was best and noblest in the land. The famine and the plague had exercised a depressing influence in the country, and the dislike shown to the vivifying influence of English education had increased. The number of delegates fell to 614, distributed as follows:

Madras	519
Berar, C. P. and Hyderabad	18
Bombay	27
N. W. P.	11
Bengal and Assam	38
Panjab	1
	614

The Congress met on December 29th, and was welcomed by the Chairman of the Reception Committee, the Hon. Mr. N. Subbarau Pantulu, who, after a few words referring to the loss of Mr. Gladstone, the Maharaja of Darbhanga and Sardar Dayal Singh—two towers of strength to the Congress—dwelt on the value of the Congress as an interpreter of the Indian mind to the British Government and to England. He complained of the attitude to the Indians of the officials, who saw conspiracy where there was none, who narrowed personal liberty in times of peace, brought in laws against sedition, and made distinctions between the British-born and the Indian subjects of the Queen-Empress. He pointed out that the function of the Services was not to shape the policy of the State, but only to carry it out when declared, and that their inroads on Government should be checked.

The Hon. Rai Bahadur P. Ananda Charlu, C.I.E., proposed Mr. Ananda Mohan Bose as President, Mr. R. N. Mudholkar seconded, Mr. John Adam and Mr. Jaishi Ram supported, and the election was carried by acclamation.

The President opened his speech with a very beautiful tribute to Mr. Gladstone, who had passed away during the year, and then said a few words on the arrival of the new Viceroy, Lord Curzon, who had landed at Bombay on that day, expressing a hope—not destined to be realised—that when he left the country, he might carry with him some of the love that followed Mr. Gladstone on leaving the world. He then turned to the unfortunate tendency which was showing itself, which would become disastrous if not checked. However slow progress towards freedom was in this country, it had at least been almost continuous.

Twenty years before, they had a brief reaction, in the Vernacular Press Act of Lord Lytton,. but it was quickly withdrawn; now they had had two years of re-action, a reversal of the wise and beneficent policy of the past. In the Educational Service, Indians had been admitted to the highest grades on exactly the same terms as Englishmen; about twenty years ago, their pay was reduced, but the highest grades were still open to them. In 1896, the year of the Diamond Jubilee, they were excluded from some of these appointments for the first time, their status lowered, and their pay further reduced. In this same year, the Engineering College of Roorkee was closed to Asiatics of pure descent, whose domicile was in one of the three Presidencies.

It is quaint to notice in this that Asiatics of impure descent were not excluded! To give privileges to illegitimacy is peculiar to the Government of India.

The next great wrong was the imprisonment of the brothers Natu, who had been lying for 18 months in prison without trial. England pointed at Russia with scorn for similar deeds, and everyone felt his personal liberty insecure where such measures were allowed. Again, there was the new law of sedition, and the changes in the Criminal Procedure Code, which put public speakers and editors of newspapers on a level with rogues and vagabonds, liable to be called on to furnish security for good behaviour, and allowed a District Magistrate, the head of the police, to try cases of sedition. Many other retrograde measures had been passed, among them the

Calcutta Municipal Bill, which proposed to take away almost all power from a Corporation which had used its powers with marked success, thus striking a severe blow at Local Self-Government. The President then criticised the Frontier policy of the Government, crippling by its cost every internal reform. What was to be the future policy of the Government—backward or forward ?

> Are we to march backwards into the methods of despotism, to the weapons of coercion, to the policy of distrust ? or we are to march onwards in the path which was traced out by those noble Englishmen who have been the founders, the consolidators, the saviours of the Empire, the path which leads to advancing and not to receding freedom, to greater trust in the people, to rights enlarged and not to concessions withdrawn ?

Alas ! the first alternative has been chosen, despite the one item of the Council Reforms, with much of their value juggled out of them by the policy of distrust.

In a letter received by him while in England, the President said, from a gentleman who had taken no part in politics, the following occurred : "Are you a friend to British Rule ? try your best to induce the authorities to withdraw the suicidal policy of Government. If you are an enemy, well, my advice is keep quiet and let things take their course." Mr. R. C. Dutt had lately said that he could hardly remember any time "when the confidence of the people of India in the justice and fair play of English rulers was so shaken, as it has been within the last two years".

The President eloquently urged on the British to give up coercion, and to find the path of safety, of honour, of mutual advantage, and the truest and most abiding glory, in going forwards in fearless confidence, trusting the people, extending the bounds of freedom, not forging new fetters but gradually removing those that exist, not taking away but adding to the rights of the people, helping on the cause of India's regeneration with the passionate longing and the loving ardour that come from the consciousness of a duty and a solemn responsibility from on high. The educated classes of India are the friends and not the foes of England, her natural and necessary allies in the great work that lies before her.

The President further touched on various reforms, and suggested the direct representation of India in Parliament; urged that the Congress should work continuously throughout the year, and choose special items to press each year. He concluded with a noble peroration on "God and the Motherland," and sat down amidst enthusiastic applause.

The Subjects Committee was then approved and the Congress adjourned.

On the second day, December 30th, the first three Resolutions, expressing grief for the deaths of Mr. Gladstone, the Maharaja of Darbhanga and Sardar Dayal Singh were moved from the Chair and passed by the audience standing up in solemn silence.

The Hon. Mr. C. Jambulingam Mudaliar moved Resolution IV, a protest on the law of sedition which had been passed in the Supreme Legislative Council against the stubborn opposition of the non-official members and an unprecedented agitation in the country. He traced the history of laws against sedition, and the introduction of the words "hatred and contempt," which included all criticism of Government, since criticism implied that the action criticised was against sound reason or common sense; also Indian Native subjects, not Eurasian or Anglo-Indian, might be punished on return home for words spoken abroad. The effect of this and of the "good behaviour" clauses was that an Empire which had been consolidated "by confidence and goodwill has been converted into a Government of suspicion and distrust. . . . A permanent bitterness of feeling has taken root over the land, over its whole length and breadth." He concluded with a hope that the new Viceroy would repeal "the iniquitous legislation of his predecessor". Mr. Tarapadu Bannerji seconded, and the Resolution was supported by Pandit K. P. Kavyabisharad and Mr. T. Venkatasubba Iyer, and carried.

Resolution V welcomed Lord Curzon and expressed a hope that he would govern according to the best traditions of British rule; it was moved by the Hon. Mr. Surendranath Bannerji, who, referring to speeches delivered in England by the new Viceroy, said that these speeches inspired a hope that Lord Curzon's name might be linked with those of Bentinck, Canning and Ripon. Such was the friendly feeling which Lord Curzon changed into bitter hatred. The Resolution was seconded by Nawab Syed Muhammad Bahadur, supported by the Hon. Rai Bahadur P. Ananda Charlu and the Hon. Mr. D. S. Garud, and carried.

Resolution VI, on Permanent Settlement, was moved by Mr. G. Venkataratnam, who showed how the promises of Government as regards the land had been treated as waste paper, and pointed out that the ryotwari tenure had been so changed as to have lost its valuable characteristics. Mr. M. R. Bodas seconded, and dealt with the retrograde land policy in Bombay, shown by the legislation. The Khots were being forced to give up their villages, because the assessments they were compelled to pay to the Government were far higher than the rents they received from their tenants. A Khot who received Rs. 700 for a village had to pay Rs. 2,000, and so the Khots gave up the villages and the Government attached them. By legislation the Government were confiscating private property enjoyed for long, and under sanads from Musalman Emperors. The Resolution was carried.

Resolution VII dealt with the Frontier policy of the Government, and was moved in a spirited speech by Mr. G. Subramania Iyer, who condemned "this mischievous and dangerous Frontier policy .... a policy prompted by that spirit of aggression abroad and repression at home which has prevailed for some time". All improvements at home were starved for want of the funds wasted in foolish aggression. If the wars were made for Imperial purposes then let Britain pay the cost, and leave Indian money to be spent on Indian needs. Mr. Charu Chandra Ghose seconded, quoting English opinion, civil and military, against the forward policy, and asking the Government to return to the policy of Lord Lawrence and Lord Ripon, and find a scientific frontier in the hearts of a loyal and contented people. The Resolution was carried.

Mr. W. A. Chambers, in moving Resolution VIII, against the establishment of Secret Press Committees, said that, as an Englishman, he could not understand such an institution being established in any country administered by his countrymen. He gave as an example an article published in the Bombay Presidency, which had drawn down on the Editor a letter from his Magistrate; the article and letter were sent to Sir William Wedderburn, and came into his own hands. He took them to the Editor of a large London paper, who characterised the article as innocent, and the letter as "monstrous". He said to the Editor: "This is the sort of thing that is taking place, not in Russia, not in Germany, but in a country for whose Government you and I are responsible." In his own paper, he had always been ready to correct any mistake he had unwittingly made, and all Indian Editors would do the same if treated with courtesy and candour. Mr. N. C. Kelkar seconded, and asked for the indignant vote of the Congress against "the hateful institution of the Press Committees, which are only a thinly veiled Press censorship, and as such a distinct disgrace to British Rule in India". They were part of the re-actionary policy adopted by the Government, the natural sequel of the amendments to the criminal law. The Resolution was carried.

Resolution IX continued the protest against re-action, this time with regard to Local Self-Government, by the introduction of the Calcutta Municipal Bill and the Bombay City Improvement Trust. Mr. G. S. Khaparde moved it, remarking that Lord Ripon inaugurated a policy of Local Self-Government, but the executive officers spoiled it in carrying it out. To Calcutta they gave a "Master-Servant," in the shape of an appointed Chairman who controlled everything, and to Bombay a "Servant-Master," a Municipal Commissioner who acted as a paid Secretary but did not take his orders from his employers; thus, he declined on one occasion to produce the records of the Municipality for the inspection of the Municipality! Mr. Khaparde made a thorough and witty exposure of the devices of the officials to make Self-Government a sham. Mr. J. Choudhuri seconded, remarking that the fault of the Calcutta Corporation was that they did too much and wore out their official chairman. The Lieutenant-Governor complained "that they were over-zealous, they did their duties with a great amount of self-sacrifice and zeal, and that the Commissioner could not keep pace with them". Mr. B. S. Sahasrabuddhe supported, and noted that in Poona the number of nominated members had been increased, and the candidates rejected by the people had been nominated by the Government. The Resolution was carried.

Resolution IX, in favour of the separation of Executive and Judicial functions, was put from the Chair and carried.

Resolution X, for the reorganisation of the Civil and Military Medical Service, so closely associated with the name of Dr. Bahadurji, was moved by Dr. Nilratan Sirkar, seconded by Dr. T. M. Nair, and carried, with a rider expressing grief at the loss sustained by the Congress and the country in the untimely death of Dr. K. N. Bahadurji.

Mr. G. Parameshvaram Pillai moved Resolution XII, protesting against the disabilities inflicted on Indians in South Africa, showing how they were becoming greater as time went on. In 1894, they were deprived of the franchise in Natal, the disabilities of Indians in their own country being carried over to Natal. In 1897, the law compelled them "to choose between perpetual bondage and an odious poll-tax". Mr. Gandhi had begun his agitation —none knew then how far it would go—and three additional disabling Acts had been passed, in which Indians were not named, the Colonists being ashamed openly to take so unfair a course, but the Prime Minister of Natal, Mr. Harry Escombe, was not ashamed to say that "no Government dreamt of applying the law to Europeans. . . . The object, however, was to deal with Asiatics. Some people said they liked an honest straightforward course. When a ship was heading against a wind she had to tack, and by-and-bye she reached her goal. When a man met difficulties he fought against them, and, if he could not knock them over, he went round them, instead of breaking his head against a brick wall." The Transvaal Republic was restricting them to "locations," and these were assigned to them outside the towns, where refuse was shot, and they had "to reside in these places amongst dung-heaps". In some Colonies they might not walk on footpaths, nor travel in 1st or 2nd class railway carriages, nor possess native gold, nor be out after 9 p.m., nor travel without passes. The Viceroy, Lord Elgin, consented to the cruel Natal law, which 11 years before, had been declared to be "a grievous wrong," to which the Government of India would never consent. The Secretary of State for the Colonies, Mr. Joseph Chamberlain, had promised help, but had never given it. The Secretary of State for India, Lord George Hamilton had "characterised us as a nation of savages," so no help could be looked for from him.

> I think it is a standing disgrace . . . . a shame and a scandal that we, Her Majesty's beloved subjects, who are competent enough to compete with her English subjects in Great Britain and enter the House of Commons, should be treated as an inferior order of beings, fit only to be hewers of wood and drawers of water to the domineering white population in the Colonies.

The Resolution was seconded by Mr. R. D. Nagarhar, supported by Mr. Ramesan and carried. The Congress then adjourned.

The third day, December 31st, began with the reading of a telegram of thanks from Lord Curzon to the Congress "for their cordial message of welcome". It is pathetic to read of Lord Curzon expressing the hope that, when he left India, some one present at his arrival might be able "to testify that during my time I have done something, if it even be but little, for this land which, next to my own country, is nearest to my heart". Who then imagined that in 1905, Mr. Gokhale, as President of the Congress, would declare that Lord Curzon's rule had been the worst India had suffered under since that of Aurungzeb ?

After the reading of other telegrams, Resolution X was moved by Mr. D. E. Wacha, on what may be called his own subject, the Indian Currency question. He said that few realised how much each person was affected by alterations in the currency, for the subject was highly technical and difficult of apprehension. The Amended Coinage Act of 1893, closing the mints to the free coinage of silver, passed in half an hour by the Simla Legislature, without any representative of India being summoned, was the starting point of a wrong course. It was the Home (Foreign) Charges that were the disease, not the currency. Then came attempts to fix exchange value and to prop it up by the Gold Bill. Frontier policy, famine and plague exhausted the cash balances. Mr. Wacha analysed the financial conditions, and showed that unwise policy, not currency, was the root of Indian distress. Mr. G. Subramania Iyer seconded, pointing out that Government looked only to exchange, Anglo-Indian merchants only to trade ; none considered the people. Taxes were levied in silver, and the ryot would have to sell 60 per cent more of his produce to gain the inflated value of the rupee. He did not regard the great flow of English capital into the country as an advantage, for it increased the "drain"; Indian capital should be invested here, and then the gain would be real. The Resolution was carried.

Resolution XIV, on the composition of the Executive Councils of Bombay and Madras, was again brought up; Mr. V. Krishnaswami Iyer proposed, Professor Paranjpe seconded it, and it was carried.

In Resolution XV the demand for the repeal of the three objectionable Regulations of 1818, '19 and '27 was once more urged—they still flourish!—this time by Mr. P. R. Sundara Iyer. There was nothing new to be said about it by him, or by Mr. John Adam the seconder, or by Rai Nalinaksha Basu Bahadur, the supporter, and it was once more passed. Then the President put Resolutions XVI and XVII, on Simultaneous Examinations and the Press Gagging Act respectively, and they were carried. Mr. R. N. Mudholkar proposed Resolution XVIII, in favour of Technical Education; it was seconded by Mr. M. Baikunthanath Sen, supported by four other speakers and carried.

The Hon. Mr. Ratnasabhapati Pillai moved Resolution XIX, on the Constitution and working of the Congress, asking the Standing Committee to form Provincial Committees, and appointing a Committee to consider the draft Constitution circulated by the Reception Committee of Madras, and submit a definite scheme to the next Congress, to be the first subject of discussion. The Hon. Mr. Surendranath Bannerji seconded, Mr. Ashvini Kumara Dutt and Mr. M. V. Joshi supported, and the Resolution was carried.

Resolution XX, the Omnibus, had passengers (*a*) to (*g*) despite those put from the Chair; it was moved by Mr. Grubb, seconded by Mr. John Adam, supported by Messrs. Habibulla Sahab, and A. C. Parthasaradhi Naidu, and carried. Resolution XXI, thanking the Government for granting a Legislative Council for the Panjab and regretting that its powers were smaller than those of other Provinces, and Resolution XXII, on Legislation for Berar, were put from the Chair.

Then Mr. V. C. Desikachariar moved Resolution XXIII, asking that plague expenditure should come out of Government and not out of local funds; it was seconded by Mr. G. B. Phansalkar, and carried. Resolution XXIV, renewing the expression of confidence in Mr. Dadabhai Naoroji, was moved, seconded and carried. The President put from the Chair Resolution XXV, the annual vote of thanks to Sir William Wedderburn and the British Committee, and the funds for the latter, and also Resolution XXVI, reappointing Messrs. A. O. Hume and D. E. Wacha as General and Joint General Secretaries. Resolution XXVII accepted the invitation of Lucknow for the next Session of the Congress, and Resolution XXVIII moved by Mr. Bhupendranath Basu, thanked the Reception Committee and the Volunteers.

The last Resolution, No. XXIX, conveying a vote of thanks to the President, was moved by Mr. G. Subramania Iyer and unanimously passed. The President acknowledged it, in an eloquent and touching speech, and the Fourteenth National Congress was dissolved.

RESOLUTIONS

The Grief of Congress

William Ewart Gladstone

I. Resolved—That this Congress records its profound regret at the irreparable loss that the British Empire and the civilised world at large have sustained by the death of Mr. W. E. Gladstone, the greatest statesman of modern times, and a warm and genuine friend of humanity, and desires to express its sense of gratitude for the sympathy which he uniformly evinced towards the efforts of the Indian people in securing a more liberal and progressive Government in India; and that a copy of the foregoing resolution be forwarded to his son, Mr. Herbert Gladstone.

Maharaja of Darbhanga

II. Resolved—That this Congress deeply mourns the great loss the country has suffered by the sad and untimely death of the late Maharaja of Darbhanga, Sir Lakshmessur Singh Bahadur, G.C.I.E. The Congress places on record its high appreciation of his ready and enlightened public spirit and his liberal and catholic benefactions, and desires to give expression to its feeling of gratitude for the generous and unfailing support which the Congress movement received at his hands; and that a copy of the foregoing resolution be forwarded to Maharaja Rameshwar Singh, the brother of the deceased Maharaja.

Dayal Singh

III. Resolved—That this Congress expresses its profound grief for the great loss which the people of the country in general and those of the Panjab in particular have sustained by the death of the late Sardar Dayal Singh of Lahore, and places on record its high appreciation of the public spirit and the liberal support he gave in furtherance of the progressive movements which tended to ameliorate the condition of the Natives of India.

[See also (*c*) of Res. XI.]

Coercion

Criminal Procedure

IV. Resolved—That this Congress regrets, that, in despite of its protest at its last sitting and the protest of many public bodies and eminent men, English and Indian, the amendments proposed in the Indian Penal Code, and the Criminal Procedure Code, which are calculated to unduly enlarge the powers of the Police and of the Magistracy, to fetter the freedom of the Press and to restrict liberty of speech, have been carried through the Imperial Legislative Council, and urges their repeal.

Press

VIII. Resolved—That this Congress is strongly of opinion that the establishment of Secret Press Committees in certain parts of India is highly objectionable and inconsistent with the spirit of British administration.

XVII. Resolved—That the Government of India Notification of 25th June, 1891, in the Foreign Department, gagging the Press in territories under British administration in Native States, is retrograde, arbitrary and mischievous in its nature, and opposed to sound statesmanship and to the liberty of the poeple, and ought to be cancelled without delay.

Lettres de Cachet

XV. Resolved--That this Congress respectfully urges upon the Government the necessity of repealing Bengal Regulation III of 1818, Madras Regulation II of 1819, and Bombay Regulation XXV of 1827, inasmuch as the principle and provisions thereof are contrary to the traditions and sense of justice of the Government of Her Most Gracious Majesty, and indeed of all civilised Governments, and inasmuch as they are a standing menace to the liberty of the subject.

Lord Curzon

V. Resolved—That this Congress accords a respectful welcome to Lord Curzon, notes with gratitude His Lordship's words of sympathy for the people of India, and trusts the policy of progress and confidence in the people which has characterised the best traditions of British rule in this country will be followed during his Lordship's tenure of office in India, and authorises the President to wire the foregoing resolution to His Lordship at Bombay.

Permanent Settlement

VI. Resolved—That this Congress regrets extremely that the Government of India have failed not only to carry out the pledges (given by the Secretary of State in his despatches of 1862 and 1865) for Permanent Settlement in the Provinces in which it does not exist, but also to give effect to the policy of granting the modified fixity of tenure and immunity from enhancement laid down in 1882 and 1884 by the Government of India, and this Congress hereby entreats the Government to grant a modified fixity of tenure and immunity from enhancement of land-tax for a sufficiently long period of not less than sixty years, so as to secure to land-holders the full benefit of their own improvements.

Military

VII. Resolved—That this Congress expresses its deep and earnest conviction that the Frontier policy pursued for some years past by the Government of India is injurious to its best interests, inasmuch as it involves this country in frequent military expeditions beyond its natural limits and the practical starvation of the civil administration; and that, as long as the policy is not radically reversed, and a return made to the older and the only safe policy of keeping within the statutory limits of the country, all declarations, no matter however confidently made, about the cessation of frontier troubles and the friendly attitude of frontier tribes, are entitled to little weight, as evidenced by the occurrences of the last few weeks in the Swat Valley which necessitated the holding in readiness of a considerable body of troops imposing fresh burdens on the Exchequer; and that of all the expenditure which these military expeditions may involve, an adequate share should be borne by the British Exchequer.

Local Self-Government

IX. Resolved—That this Congress expresses its deep sense of disapproval of the reactionary policy of Government with regard to Local Self-Government recently inaugurated by the introduction of the Calcutta Municipal Bill into the Bengal Legislative Council, the creation of the Bombay City Improvement Trust without adequate popular representation, and its action in other directions.

Legal

X. Resolved—That this Congress notices with satisfaction the support of public opinion both in England and in India, which the question of the separation of Judicial from Executive functions in the administration of justice has received; and this Congress once again appeals to the Government of India and the Secretary of State to take practical steps for speedily carrying out this much-needed reform.

Public Service

XI. Resolved—(*a*) That this Congress is of opinion that the present constitution of the Higher Civil Medical Service is anomalous, indefensible in principle, injurious in its working, and unnecessarily costly; that the time has arrived when, in the interests of the public, medical education and the advancement of the medical service and scientific work in the country, as also in the cause of economic administration, the Civil Medical Service of India should be reconstructed on the basis of such Service in other civilised countries, wholly detached from and independent of, the Military Service.

(*b*) That whilst this Congress views with satisfaction the action of the Imperial Government in throwing open 19 Civil Surgeoncies to be filled up by promotion from the ranks of Civil Assistant Surgeons, it deplores nevertheless the unsatisfactory position and prospects of members of the Subordinate Civil Medical Service (Civil Assistant Surgeons and Civil Hospital Assistants) compared with the members of similar standing in other departments of the Public Service, and prays that Government will grant an open inquiry into the present constitution of the Subordinate Civil Medical department by a mixed commission of official and non-official members.

(*c*) That in this connection the Congress desires to place on record its sense of loss the Congress and the country have sustained by the untimely death of the late Dr. K. N. Bahadurji, of Bombay, the last years of whose life were devoted to the promotion of the reform of the Medical Services in this country.

XIV. Resolved—That, having regard to the wisdom of the policy of appointing to the Governorships of Madras and Bombay statesmen from England to the exclusion of the Services in India, this Congress is of opinion that it is desirable that the Executive Governments of those Provinces should be administered by Governors with Councils of three and not of two members, as at present, and that one of the three Councillors should be a Native of India.

XVI. Resolved—That this Congress again records its deep regret that the labours of the Public Service Commission have practically proved void of any good result to the people of this country, and urges the desirability of holding the competitive examinations for the Indian Civil Services, *viz.*, Civil, Medical, Police, Engineering, Telegraph, Forest and Accounts, both in India and in England, in accordance with the Resolution of the House of Commons of the 2nd June, 1893. This Congress further points out that in regard to the employment of Indians in the higher ranks of the Postal, Salt, and Abkari and Forest Services, the recommendations of the Public Service Commission have not been adequately carried out, and prays that in all ranks of the said Services more educated Indians should be employed.

South Africa

XII. Resolved—That this Congress deplores the invidious and humiliating distinctions made between Indian and European Settlers in South Africa, a prominent instance of which is afforded by the recent decision of the Transvaal High Court restricting Indians to "locations," and appeals to Her Majesty's Government and the Government of India to guard the interests of Indian settlers, and to relieve them of the disabilities imposed on them.

Monetary

XIII. Resolved—(*a*) That, having regard to the fact that the principal cause of the loss by exchange is the steady growth in the demands on India for expenditure in England, this Congress is of opinion that any artificial device for meeting that loss either by changing the currency at a heavy cost or contracting the internal currency must add to the pressure of India's monetary resources and to her trading disadvantage.

(*b*) That the only real relief lies in carrying out practically the principle, affirmed by competent authorities, of England bearing an equitable share of that expenditure.

(*c*) That the Congress regrets that, save Mr. Romesh Chandra Dutt and Mr. Merwanji Rastamji, competent and qualified Indian representatives have not yet been invited as witnesses to represent the Indian view of matters on the subject which now engages the attention of the Currency Committee of which Sir Henry Fowler is the President.

(*d*) That the President be authorised to request Sir William Wedderburn, Chairman of the British Congress Committee, to communicate this Resolution to Sir Henry Fowler, Chairman of the Currency Committee in London.

Education

XVIII. Resolved—That this Congress places on record its deep conviction that the system of technical education now in vogue is inadequate and unsatisfactory, and prays that, having regard to the poverty of the people and the decline of indigenous industries, the Government will introduce a more elaborate and efficient scheme of technical instruction, and set apart more funds for a better and more successful working of the same.

Congress Work

XIX. Resolved—(*a*) That all the Standing Congress Committees be requested to form Central Committees in their respective Provinces, for the appointment of agents and adoption of other measures, for furthering the objects of the Congress, such Central Committees submitting annually at the meeting of the Congress a report of the work carried out in their Provinces during the year.

(*b*) That the Standing Congress Committees at Madras, Bombay, Nagpur, Amraoti, Calcutta, Allahabad and Lahore be requested to take measures to give early effect to this Resolution.

(*c*) And further that a Committee consisting of the following gentlemen, exclusive of the President and ex-Presidents now in India, who shall be *ex officio* members, be appointed to consider the draft constitution circulated by the Reception Committee of Madras and submit a definite scheme to the next Congress, and that this do form the first subject of discussion at the next meeting of the Congress :

(1) Mr. Aswini Kumara Dutt, Bengal.
(2) Mr. D. E. Wacha, Bombay.
(3) Mr. Jaishi Ram, Panjab.
(4) Mr. Ganga Prasad Varma, Oudh.
(5) Pandit Madan Mohan Malaviya, North-West Provinces.
(6) Mr. Raghunath Pandurang Karandikar of Satara.
(7) Mr. Bapu Rao Dada, Central Provinces.
(8) Mr. G. Subramania Iyer, Madras.
(9) Mr. R. N. Mudholkar, Berar, to act as Secretary to the Committee.

Confirmation of Previous Resolutions

XX. Resolved—(I) That this Congress concurs with previous Congresses in strongly advocating—[1897 (*a*)—(*g*)].

That this Congress, concurring with previous Congresses records its protest: [1897 (*a*) (*b*) (*d*)].

And that this Congress, concurring, etc. [1897 (*b*) (*c*) (*d*) (*e*) as (*a*) (*b*) (*c*) (*d*) and (*e*)] That this Congress is of opinion that it is desirable in the interests of the people of this country that the Criminal Procedure Code should be so amended as to confer upon the accused persons, who are Natives of India, the right of claiming, in trials by Jury, before the High Court and in trials with the aid of assessors, that not less than half the number of the Jury, before the High Court, and in trials with the aid of assessors, that not less than half the number of the Jury or of the assessors shall be Natives of India.

(*f*) That the action of the Forest Department, under the rules framed by the Different Provincial Governments, prejudicially affects the inhabitants of the rural parts of the country by subjecting them to the annoyance and oppression of Forest subordinates in various ways, which have led to much discontent throughout the country: that though the objects of forest conservancy, as announced in the Resolution of 1894, are declared to be, not to secure the largest revenue, but to conserve the forests in the interest chiefly of the agricultural classes and of their cattle, the existing set of rules subordinates the latter consideration to the former, and an amendment of the rules with a view to correct this mischief is, in the opinion of the Congress, urgently called for.

(*g*) That the minimum income assessable under the Income-Tax Act, be raised from five hundred to one thousand.

Legislative Council (Panjab)

XXI. Resolved—That this Congress, while thanking the Government (as in Resolution XV, 1897.)

Berar Legislation

XXII. Resolved—That the Province of Berar, though not a part of British India, (as in Resolution XVI, 1897.)

Plague Expenditure

XXIII. Resolved—That the adoption of measures against the plague being a matter of imperial concern and recognised as such, this Congress is of opinion that the expenditure incurred in connection thereof should be borne by the Government and not charged to the funds of the local bodies.

Parliamentary Representation

XXIV. Resolved—That this Congress again expresses its full and unabated confidence in Mr. Dadabhai Naoroji as the representative of the people of India, and hopes that he will be re-elected by his old Constituency of Central Finsbury or any other Liberal Constituency.

Thanks of Congress and Congress Work

XXV. Resolved—That this Congress desires to convey to Sir William Wedderburn and the other members of the British Committee its most grateful thanks for their disinterested services in the cause of Indian political advancement.

And that a sum of Rs. 60,000 be assigned for the expenses of the British Committee and the cost of the Congress publication *India*, and also for the expenses of the Joint General Secretary's Office, and that the several circles do contribute, as arranged, either now or hereafter in Committee, for the year 1899.

Formal

XXVI. Resolved—That this Congress re-appoints Mr. A. O. Hume, C. B., to be General Secretary, and Mr. D. E. Wacha to be Joint General Secretary for the ensuing year.

XXVII. Resolved—That the Fifteenth Indian National Congress do assemble, at Lucknow, on such day after Christmas Day in 1899, as may be later determined upon.

CHAPTER XV

In the ebb and flow of Anglo-Indian feeling against the National Congress, efforts to embarrass it were at first made in Lucknow, but these were put an end to by the wise and liberal action of the Lieutenant-Governor, Sir Antony MacDonnell, who in this matter showed a liberality which he has since, unhappily, left behind. A very good feature was the presence of no less than 300 Muhammadan delegates from Lucknow alone. The Pandal, erected in the Shahmina ground, accommodated some 4,000 persons, and was fully crowded when the Congress met. The President elect, Mr. Romesh Chandra Dutt, had a splendid reception on his arrival on the evening before the date fixed for the Congress, and on the 27th of December, 1899, 740 delegates assembled in the Pandal. They were distributed as follows:

N. W. P. and Oudh	603
Bengal and Assam	57
Panjab	26
Bombay and Sindh	36
Berar, C. P. and Secunderabad	6
Madras	12
	740

The Chairman of the Reception Committee, Mr. Bansi Lal Singh, welcomed the delegates, and then handed his written speech to Pandit Bishan Narayan Dhar to read, being himself in feeble health. After thanking the Lieutenant-Governor for his help, he deprecated the attitude of the officials towards educated Indians, and the re-actionary policy of the Government. "You are foreigners in the country," he said to the hostile officials. "You do not and, from your exclusive way, cannot know the mind of the people, and the people do not know your mind."

> But you have, by your educational policy, which has immortalised the names of Bentinck and Macaulay, created a considerable class of men, filled with your ideas and aspirations, conversant with your manners and customs, attached to your rule by every tie of duty and interest, who are desirous of acting as interpreters between you and the people placed under your care, and, in order to carry out this object, adopt those methods of constitutional agitation which you yourselves have taught them.

After touching on the question of Congress organisation, the Chairman called on the assembly to elect their President.

The Hon. Pandit Bishambarnath proposed, Nawab Bagar Ali Khan seconded, Mr. Wacha and others supported the election of Mr. Romesh Chandra Dutt, C.I.E., as President, and he took the Chair amid great acclamations.

The President began by delivering a message from Mr. A. M. Bose, the last President, and reading a letter from Mr. W. S. Caine, in which he said of the Indian people: "My belief in their future as a great

Self-Governing portion of the British Empire, and my conviction of their natural capacity for Self-Government deepens and strengthens every year." After referring to the passing away of Dr. Romesh Chandra Mitra, he touched on "the creed of the Congress," and then noted that he was in London at the Queen's Jubilee and saw the procession of the representatives of the British Empire, including India, and he heard it remarked that, while every Self-Governing Colony was prosperous and happy, India was suffering from famine, and "doubts were expressed if British Rule in India had been altogether a blessing for the poor cultivators and labourers of India". He then condemned the Sedition Law of 1898, and urged that there was no better way of creating sedition than by suppressing free discussion, newspapers and meetings. Educated India, while loyal to the British rule, sought "a large measure of Self-Government" and a "position among the modern Nations of the earth". He grieved over the withdrawal of Self-Government from Calcutta by the Municipality Act, passed in the first year of Lord Curzon's administration; he believed the Viceroy had good intentions, but he did not know the Indian side of the question. Turning to the famine then prevailing, he urged that the cause of famine was not increase of population—Germany and England increased faster—nor was it the fault of the peasant, the most frugal and provident cultivator on the face of the earth; if he borrowed at high interest, it was because he had nothing to eat; the cause of famine was the heavy assessment, and the destruction of village industries by free competition with English machinery. One-sixth of the gross produce of the land was its proper rent, shown by the experience of thousands of years. Famines would cease were this the assessment. The President passed rapidly over other causes of poverty, the Military and Civil Services, etc., the Indians being virtually foreigners in their own country, so far as control over its administration was concerned, and then he dealt with administration problems. The country which had organised village Self-Government and carried it on for 3,000 years was now virtually ruled through the police, "the hated link" between the District officers, and the people. He pointed out the deficiencies in Municipalities, District Boards, Provincial Legislative and Executive Councils, and finally urged that no country could be well governed if the hands of its people were tied up. To prevent distress and disasters it was necessary to concede Self-Government, for that only could consolidate British Rule in India.

The President closed his speech by announcing the release of the Natu brothers, and called for the names of the members of the Subjects Committee. The list was handed in and confirmed, and the Congress rose for the day.

The second day's business began with the presentation by Mr. Mudholkar of the Report of the Committee appointed by the previous Congress to consider the draft constitution and to submit a definite scheme. Mr. Mudholkar said that the only new thing was the creation of a Central Body to control and carry on Congress work during the year. The discussion on the Report was adjourned to the next day, to give the delegates time for consideration.

Mr. Ambikacharan Mozumdar then moved Resolution I, the separation of Executive and Judicial Functions, a subject worn threadbare, but, necessarily, brought up for the fifteenth time. Mr. Agashe seconded, Mr. S. Sinha, Munshi Nasir-ud-din Ahmed, Pandit Sham Narayana, Mr. A. C. Parthasarathi Naidu, and Mr. Abdul Rahim all supported it. Needless to add that the Resolution was carried.

Rai Sahab Lala Murlidhar introduced Resolution II, on the Panjab Land Alienation Bill, and urged that to forbid the proprietor to sell his land was to worsen his position, as he would not be able to borrow in order to cultivate it. Lala Kannaihia said that the land had always belonged to the people; the King had a right to a share in the produce but not to the land, and the revenue was a tax, not a rent. Mr. Phansalhar supported—the Act reduced the value of land to its proprietor—as did Nawab Hashmat Husain, and the Resolution was carried.

Resolution III, asking that Britain would contribute to the cost of maintaining the large British forces in India, was moved by Miss Garland, a delegate sent by the British Committee. She urged that the forces in India were unnecessarily large, so far as India was concerned, and that if so many troops were kept here because India was a convenient military base for Imperial purposes, then England should bear part of the cost, and the money saved in

India could be used for Indian reforms. She then spoke on behalf of the British Committee on the general situation.

The Hon. Mr. Baikunthanath Sen seconded, pointing out that as 10,000 men had been removed from India for foreign service, it was evident that they had more men than were needed. Messrs. Patvardhan, and Hari Ram Panday, and Pandit Gyaneshvara Shastri supported, and the Resolution was carried.

Mr. D. E. Wacha moved Resolution IV, against the introduction of a gold standard into India. He said that the question of currency reform had been discussed thrice before in the Congress. Lord Curzon thought that gold would flow into India from all gold-producing countries, so that every ryot in the country would become prosperous, and the fifty millions who go without one full meal a day would be happy. The root of India's poverty was the yearly drain of from 30 to 40 millions which should remain and fructify in the country. If more foreign exploiters flowed in, the profits would go abroad. Only indigenous wealth was fruitful. The silver value of the rupee had been depreciated while its nominal value was enhanced. Silver had sold at a rupee per tola, but now only at 10 or 11 annas, so silver trinkets, in which the more prosperous stored their savings, had diminished in saleable value.

Mr. Ramaswami seconded, Mr. Sitaram Seth supported, and the Resolution was carried.

Resolution V, on the separation of the Military and Civil Medical Services, was briefly moved by

Dr. Nilratan Sarkar, seconded by Dr. T. M. Nair and carried, whereupon the Congress adjourned.

On the opening of the third day, the President announced that the consideration of the Constitution would be taken up on the morrow, and he called on Mr. S. V. Bhate to move Resolution VI, which declared that the principle embodied in the Foreign Telegraphic Press Messages Bill was opposed to the policy followed by the British Government as to the unrestricted dissemination of useful knowledge and information. Mr. Bhate said that the measure had been proposed ten years before, but was pigeon-holed, and its emergence now was due to the change in the feeling of Government towards Indians. It was intended to prevent news cabled to this country being printed by the vernacular Press. Haji Riaz-ud-din Ahmad said that the Bill was brought in at the instance of a few Anglo-Indian newspapers, and prevented newspapers reprinting Reuter's press cables for 24 hours after their publication in papers which subscribed for them. The Resolution was carried.

Resolution VII, disapproving the re-actionary policy of the Calcutta Municipality Act, was appropriately proposed by Mr. Surendranath Bannerji. He was obliged to say that the hope of the previous Congress, that Lord Curzon would reverse "the policy of repression and reaction which is now in the ascendant in the Councils of the Empire," had not been realised. The Viceroy had lately made a noble speech :

> We cannot bring ourselves to believe that a ruler so sympathetic in his utterances, so generous, so large-hearted

in his views, so keenly appreciative of the situation, will countenance a policy opposed to the best traditions of British rule, repugnant to all that is highest, noblest and truest in British statesmanship..... Read that speech, contrast that speech with the policy. The speech, how noble, how generous, how sympathetic; the policy, how narrow, how illiberal, how un-English.

Mr. Bannerji then went on to speak words as true to-day as they were true then, words of wise warning:

> Sir, who are the men who are bitterly disloyal—the men who say ditto to every measure of Government, who in season and out of season sing the praise of Government, who suffer and suffer in the silence of bitterness of unknown and unknowable sorrow, or those who, like myself, give expression, frank expression, to our grievances, raise the danger signal, and call the attention of Government and press for remedy? Sir, in these days I am perfectly sure the greatest bulwark of all the Governments, be they indigenous or be they foreign, is the contentment, the gratitude and the affection of the people. How is the affection of the people to be won except by the removal of grievances, and how are the people to remove their grievances except by the adoption of constitutional means or the adoption of revolutionary measures? We are the friends of Reform because we are the enemies of Revolution. We have made our choice; let our enemies make theirs. Do they wish to belong to our camp, or do they wish to belong to the camp of revolutionists? There is no intermediary step between Reform and Revolution. For you must enlist yourselves under the banner of Reform, or you must take your place behind the standard of Revolt and Revolution.

True loyalty to the Empire now, as then, consists in open speech on dangerous grievances, for Governments, flattered into error by sycophants—who secretly hate them the more bitterly for their own degradation in the flattery—sleep until the accumulation of hatred rises in furious anger and awakes them, too late. In frank and open speech no danger lurks. Surendranath Babu analysed the Act, and showed how the civic rights of Calcutta had been destroyed. The gulf between rulers and ruled was widening.

> There is reaction in their policy, reaction in opinion, reaction along the entire line, reaction is the order of the day. . . . . They would fain undo the past. They would fain roll back the tide of progress which has set in with such irresistible force. Shall we let them, shall we permit them, to prove false to the noblest traditions of their own race?

Mr. Nazir-ud-din Kamur-ud-din seconded the Resolution, and it was carried.

Resolution VIII protested against the prohibition imposed on managers and teachers in aided Institutions, forbidding them from taking part in political movements or attending political meetings without the consent of the Director of Public Instruction. It was moved by Mr. Kalicharan Bannerji, seconded by Dr. T. M. Nair, supported by three other speakers, and carried.

Mr. G. C. Mitra moved Resolution IX, on the well-worn subject of Local Option. Mr. A. C. Parthasarathi Naidu seconded, and it was supported by Miss Garland, Pandit Ratannath, and Mr. Ram Prasad, and carried, closing the work of the third day.

On the fourth day, the President put from the Chair the Rules of the Congress Constitution, as follows, forming Resolution X:

(1) The object of the Indian National Congress shall be to promote by constitutional means the interests and the well-being of the people of the Indian Empire.

(2) It shall ordinarily meet once a year at such time and in such place as shall have been resolved on by the last preceding Congress. Provided that the Indian Congress Committee, as hereinafter provided for, may, in case of necessity, change the place or time of the Congress, provided also that in case of emergency the Indian Congress Committee may convene an extraordinary session of the Congress at such time and place as may be determined by them.

(3) It shall consist of delegates elected by political associations or other bodies, and by public meetings.

(4) Its affairs shall be managed by a Committee, styled the Indian Congress Committee, consisting of 45 members elected by the Congress, 40 of whom shall be elected upon the recommendations of the different Provincial Congress Committees, and, in the absence of such Committees, by the delegates of the respective Provinces in Congress assembled, in the manner hereinbelow laid down, that is to say :

For Bengal including Assam	8
For Bombay including Sind	8
For Madras including Secunderabad	8
For N. Western Provinces including Oudh ...	6
For Panjab	4
For Berar	3
For Central Provinces	3

The term of office of the members of the Committee shall be the period intervening between two ordinary meetings of the Congress.

(5) The Indian Congress Committee shall meet at least three times a year, once immediately after the Congress, once during the year between the months of June and October, as may be determined upon by the Committee, and once immediately before the Congress, at such place as the Committee may find convenient.

(6) The Indian Congress Committee shall have an Honorary Secretary and a paid Assistant Secretary, with suitable office staff, for which a sum of Rs. 5,000 shall be granted annually, one half of which shall be provided by the Reception Committee of the place where the last Congress is held, and the other half by the Reception Committee of the place where the next succeeding Congress is to be held.

The Secretary to the Indian National Congress shall be the Honorary Secretary of the Committee.

(7) Provincial Congress Committees shall be organised at the capitals of the different Presidencies and Provinces of India for the purpose of carrying on the work of political education, on lines of general appreciation of British rule and of constitutional action for the removal of its defects, throughout the year by organising Standing Congress Committees, holding Provincial Conferences, and by such other means as they may deem proper, in consultation with the Indian Congress Committee, for furthering the objects of the Congress. They shall be responsible agents of the Indian Congress Committee for their respective Provinces, and shall submit annual reports of their work to that Committee.

(8) The nomination of the President, the drafting of Resolutions and all other business in connection with the Congress, shall be done by the Indian Congress Committee. It shall also, subject to the approval of the Congress, frame rules for the election of delegates, the election of speakers, and the conduct of the proceedings of the Congress.

(9) Rules and Bye-laws shall be framed by the Provincial Congress Committees for the election of members, the conduct of their own proceedings, and other matters appertaining to their business. All such rules and bye-laws shall be subject to the approval of the Indian Congress Committee.

(10) A Committee, styled the British Congress Committee, shall be maintained in England, which shall represent there the interests of the Indian National Congress. The amount requisite for the expenses of the said Committee shall be determined and voted by the Congress, and the amount so voted shall be raised by the Indian Congress Committee in such manner as may be determined upon by that body from time to time.

(11) The Indian Congress Committee shall take such steps as they may deem fit to raise a permanent fund for carrying on the work of the Indian National Congress; and such fund shall be invested in the name of 7 trustees, one from each Province in India, to be appointed by the Congress.

The 45 members of the Committee were then chosen. Resolution XI, thanking Sir William Wedderburn and the British Committee, and Resolution XII, asking, as often before, that the Executive Councils of Madras and Bombay should consist of three members instead of two, one of the three to be an Indian, were also put from the Chair and carried.

Resolution XIII, moved by Mr. Mudholkar, urged, as remedies for famine, curtailment of expenditure, development of industries, and the lessening of land assessment. He gave the figures of Mr. Dadabhai Naoroji, and Sir W. Hunter on poverty; he showed that the public debt had increased in 60 years from 26 to nearly 270 crores of rupees. Pandit Madan Mohan Malaviya followed, pleading the cause of the peasant, and urging that "Government ought to foster native industries and native arts". After Haji Shaik Hussain had spoken in Urdu, Mr. Chintamani said that that they were firmly convinced that the costly, extravagant and unnatural system of administration was the root cause of the recurring famines. The poverty of the people was beyond challenge; less than half a million persons were assessed to income-tax in 1897, although every one was assessed who had an annual income of Rs. 500 (£33. 6s). Mr. S. S. Dev supported, and the Resolution was carried.

Munshi Muhammad Sujjad Hussain drove the Omnibus this year, and before it was seconded by Mr. Yatindranath Choudhuri, the President read a telegram of thanks to the Congress from the Natu brothers for the sympathy shown to them. Mr. S. K. Nair, Syed Ali Usat, and Mr. Krishna Badev Varma supported, and the Resolution was carried.

Mr. Ramachandra Pillai moved, and Mr. Maheshvara Prasad seconded our familiar friend of gagging the Press in Indian States as Resolution XV, and Resolution XVI pressed the necessity for Technical

Education and thanked Mr. Tata for his splendid gift.

Resolutions XVII, Panjab Legislative Council restrictions; XVIII, Berar Administration; XIX, plague expenditure; XX, confidence in Mr. Dadabhai Naoroji; XXI, re-election of Mr. A. O. Hume and Mr. D. E. Wacha as General and Joint General Secretaries, were all put from the Chair.

Resolution XXII appointed an Agency in England to co-operate with the British Committee to disseminate information on Indian subjects, a work that has not yet been done effectively. It was carried, and Rs. 3,000 subscribed.

Rai Sahab Lala Murlidhar then invited the Congress to meet in Lahore the following year. Pandit Bishan Narayana Dhar moved the vote of thanks to the President, who responded in a few graceful words.

With these, the Fifteenth National Congress dissolved.

RESOLUTIONS

Legal

I. Resolved—That this Congress notices with satisfaction the support of public opinion, both in England and in India, which the question of the separation of the Judicial from the Executive functions in the administration of justice has received; and this Congress, while thanking Lord Hobhouse, Sir Richard Garth, Sir Richard Couch, Sir Charles Sergeant, Sir William Markby, Sir John Budd Phear, Sir John Scott, Sir Roland K. Wilson, Mr. Herbert J. Reynolds, and Sir William Wedderburn for presenting a petition to the Secretary of State in Council to effect the much-needed separation, earnestly hopes that the Government of India will give their earliest attention to the petition which has been forwarded to them, and will take practical steps for carrying out this much-needed reform.

Land Tenure

II. Resolved—(*a*) That this Congress regrets the introduction into the Supreme Legislative Council of a Bill to amend the Law relating to agricultural land in the Panjab, with a view to restrict alienation of land as proposed in the Bill by sale or mortgage, which is calculated (1 to decrease the credit of the agriculturists and landholders; (2) to make them more resourceless on account of their inability to meet the ever increasing State demands upon their land; and this Congress is of opinion that the provision to give retrospective effect to the Bill is inequitable and unfair.

(*b*) That this Congress recommends that real relief be afforded to the cultivating classes in the following way: that where the Government is the rent-receiver, the rule proposed in 1882, prohibiting any advancement except on the ground of rise in prices, be enforced, and that where private landlords are the rent-receivers, some provision to prohibit undue enhancement of rent be made.

(*c*) This Congress further resolves that a Committee consisting of the President, Mr. Jaishi Ram, Mr. N. Gupta, Mr. Wacha, Munshi Madho Lal, Mr. Mudholkar and Mr. Ikbal Shankar be appointed and empowered to submit a representation to the Government, pointing out the unsuitable nature of many of the provisions of the Bill.

Military

III. Resolved—That whereas it is considered safe and prudent to withdraw large bodies of British troops for service outside the statutory limits of India, this Congress is of opinion that the time has come when the Indian tax-payer should be granted some relief out of the British Exchequer towards the cost of maintaining in India so large a force of European soldiers. This Congress sees no objection to the location of British troops in India as a reserve force for the whole of the British Empire, but is of opinion that the time has come for the transfer of the cost of 20,000 British troops from the Indian to the British Exchequer.

Monetary

IV. Resolved—(*a*) That having regard to the fact that the principal cause of loss by Exchange is the steady growth of the demand on the Indian Exchequer for expenditure in England, this Congress regrets the introduction of a gold standard in India on the recommendation of the Currency Committee for the purpose of preventing the loss by exchange, and is of opinion that the new measure is calculated to increase the gold obligations of India.

(b) That this Congress is further of opinion that the decision accepted by the Government will in effect add to the indebtedness of the poorer classes in India, depreciate the value of their savings in the shape of silver ornaments, and virtually add to their rent and taxes.

(c) That this Congress is further of opinion that the decision accepted by the Government is likely to be prejudicial to the indigenous manufactures of the country.

Public Services

V. Resolved—That this Congress is of opinion that the union of the Military and Civil Medical Services is extravagant, inconvenient, and prejudicial to the interests of the Government as well as of the people, and strongly urges the necessity of the separation of the two Services, by the creation of a distinct Civil Medical Department, recruited by open, simultaneous competition in England and India.

XII. Resolved—That having regard to the policy of appointing to the Governorships of Madras and Bombay statesmen from England to the exclusion of the Services in India, this Congress is of opinion that it is desirable that those Provinces should be administered with the help of Councils of three and not two members as at present, and that one of the three councillors should be a Native of India.

Re-action

VI. Resolved—That it is the opinion of this Congress that the principle embodied in the Foreign Telegraphic Press Messages Bill, now pending before the Supreme Legislative Council, is opposed to the policy followed by the British Government in India as to the unrestricted dissemination of useful knowledge and information, and that no adequate necessity is shown to exist for the passing of the proposed measure in India.

VII. Resolved—That this Congress expresses its disapproval of the re-actionary policy, subversive of local Self-Government, evidenced by the passing of the Calcutta Municipal Act, and by the introduction into the Legislative Council of Bombay of a similar measure, which will have the effect of seriously jeopardising the principles of Local Self-Government.

VIII. Resolved—That this Congress is of opinion that the rules prohibiting managers and teachers of aided institutions from taking part in political movements or attending political meetings without the consent of the Director of Public Instruction, or other authorities, are likely to interfere with the practical and effectual exercise of the rights of British subjects, to withdraw able and influential men from the cause of education, and to restrict private enterprise and organisation for the spread of education in this country. And this Congress hopes that the Madras and Bombay Governments will take steps to remove from the educational rules and the grant-in-aid code the provisions to the effect described above.

Local Option

IX Resolved—That this Congress is of opinion that stringent measures should be taken by the Government in granting licences to retail liquor shops, and that no such shops should be established anywhere in India without taking the sense of the inhabitants of the place

Congress Constitution

X. Resolved—That this Congress adopts the following rules regarding the Constitution of the Congress —(See pp 300, 301.)

MEMBERS OF THE INDIAN CONGRESS COMMITTEE

Appointed by the Congress under the above Resolution

GENERAL MEMBERS

Mr. W. C Bannerji
The Hon Surendranath Bannerji
The Hon. P Ananda Charlu.
The Hon P M. Mehta.
Mr. Mudholkar

BENGAL

Mr A. M. Bose
Mr Kalicharan Bannerji
Mr Bhupendra Nath Bose
The Hon Baikunthanath Sen
Mr. Ambikacharan Mozumdar
Mr J Ghosal.
Mr Aswini Kumar Dutt
Mr. Dipnarain Sinha.

N. W. P. & OUDH ·

The Hon. Pandit Bishambharnath.
Babu Ganga Prasad Varma
Pandit Madan Mohan Malaviya
Mr A Nundy
Mr Bishan Narayan Dhar
Mr. Hafiz Abdur Rahim

BOMBAY:

Mr. D. E. Wacha.
The Hon. G. Chandravarkar.
Mr. W. A. Chambers.
Mr. R. M. Sayani.
Mr. Daji Abaji Khare.
Mr. Chiman H. Setalwad.
Mr. R. P. Karandikar.
Mr. Tahilram Khem Chand.

PANJAB:

Lala Kaniha Lal.
Sirdar Jhenda Singh.
Lala Harkishan Lal.
Mr. Jaishi Ram.

CENTRAL PROVINCES:

Mr. Bapurao Dada.
Mr. Bhagirath Prasad.
Mr. H. V. Kelkar.

BERAR:

Mr. Deorao Vinayak.
Mr. M.V. Joshi.
Mr. G. S. Khaparde.

MADRAS:

The Hon. C. Vijiaraghavachari.
The Hon. C. Jambulingam Mudaliar.
The Hon. G. Venkataratnam.
Mr. C. Sankaran Nair.
Mr. P. Rangia Naidu.
Mr. P. Ramchandra Pillai.
Mr. G. Subramania Iyer.
Mr. V. Ryru Nambier.

Congress Work

XI. Resolved—That this Congress recognises the valuable services of the British Committee in the cause of the people of India, and expresses its unabated confidence in Sir William Wedderburn and the other members of the Committee.

And the sum of Rs. 54,000 be assigned for the expenses of the British Committee and the cost of the Congress publication *India*.

XXII. Resolved—That an agency be appointed in England, for the purpose of organising in concert with the British Congress Committee, public meetings for the dissemination of information on Indian matters, and that funds be raised for the purpose.

Famine

XIII. Resolved—That this Congress while gratefully recognising the endeavours made by the Indian and Provincial Governments to save human life and relieve distress at the present famine, urges the adoption of the true remedy : to improve the condition of the cultivating classes and prevent the occurrence of famine, this Congress recommends the curtailment of public expenditure, the development of local and indigenous industries and the moderating of land assessment.

Confirmation of Previous Resolutions

XIV. Resolved—(I) That this Congress concurs with previous Congresses in strongly advocating—[(1897 (*b*)—(*e*) and (*g*)].

(II) That this Congress concurring with previous Congresses records its protest—[(1897 (*a*) and (*b*)].

(*c*) Against the retrograde policy of the Government of India in nominating a gentleman for the Central Provinces to the Supreme Council without asking local bodies to make recommendations for such nomination, entertaining the earnest hope that the Government will be pleased to take early steps to give to the Central Provinces the same kind of representation that it has already granted to Bengal, Madras, Bombay and the North Western Provinces.

(*d*) Against the labour laws of Assam, *viz.*, the Inland Emigration Act I of 1882, as amended by Act VII of 1893.

(III) This Congress concurring with previous Congresses, expresses its conviction—

(*a*) That having regard to the opinion of the Jury Commission as to the success of the system of trial by jury, and also the fact that with the progress of education a sufficient number of educated persons is available in all parts of the country, the system of trial by jury should be extended to the districts and offences, to which at present it does not apply.

(*b*) That this Congress is of opinion that it is desirable in the interests of the people of this country that the Criminal Procedure Code should be so amended as to confer upon accused persons, who are Natives of India, the right of claiming, in trials by jury before the High Court, and in trials with the aid of assessors, that not less than half the number of the jurors or of the assessors shall be Natives of India.

(*c*) That the action of the Forest Department under the rules framed by the different Provincial Governments, prejudicially affects the inhabitants of the rural part of the country by subjecting them to the annoyance and oppression of Forest subordinates in various ways; and these rules should be amended in the interests of the people.

(*d*) That the minimum income assessable under the Income-Tax Act, be raised from five hundred to one thousand rupees.

(*e*) That no satisfactory solution of the question of the employment of Natives of India in the Indian Civil Service is possible, unless effect is given to the resolution of the House of Commons of June, 1893, in favour of holding the competitive Examinations for the Indian Civil Service simultaneously in India and England.

Coercion

XV. Resolved—That this Congress is of opinion that the Government of India Notification of 25th June, 1891, in the Foreign Department, gagging the Press in Territories under British administration in Native States is retrograde, arbitrary and mischievous in its nature, and opposed to sound statesmanship and to the liberty of the people and ought to be cancelled.

Education

XVI. Resolved—That this Congress places on record its conviction that the system of Technical Education now in vogue is inadequate and unsatisfactory, and prays that, having regard to the poverty of the people and the decline of indigenous industries, the Government will introduce a more elaborate and efficient scheme of technical instruction, and set apart more funds for the successful working of the same. And this Congress desires to express its grateful appreciation of the patriotic and munificent gift of Mr. Tata for the promotion of the higher scientific education and research.

Legislative Council (Panjab)

XVII. Resolved—That this Congress while thanking the Government for granting the boon of a Legislative Council to the Panjab, places on record its regret that they have not extended to the Councillors the right of interpellation, and to the people the right of recommending Councillors for nomination, such as are enjoyed by the Councillors and the people in the other Provinces.

Berar Legislation

XVIII. Resolved—That this Congress is of opinion that so long as Berar is administered by the Governor-General-in-Council, all laws and orders having the force of laws intended for Berar should be enacted by the Supreme Legislative Council, in the same way as those for British India proper.

Plague Expenditure

XIX. Resolved—That the adoption of measures against the plague being an Imperial concern and recognised as such, this Congress is of opinion that the expenditure incurred in connection therewith should be borne by the Government and not charged to the funds of the local bodies.

Parliamentary Representation

XX. Resolved—That this Congress expresses its unabated confidence in Mr. Dadabhai Naoroji as the representative of the people of India, and hopes that he will be re-elected by his old constituency of Central Finsbury or any other Liberal Constituency.

Formal

XXI. Resolved—That this Congress re-appoints Mr. A. O. Hume, C.B., to be General Secretary, and Mr. D. E. Wacha to be Joint General Secretary for the ensuing year.

The Congress accepted the invitation to Lahore for its 16th Session.

CHAPTER XVI

To the far north had the Congress travelled for its Sixteenth Session, and it met at Lahore on December 27th, 28th and 29th, 1900, in the first year of the twentieth century. It met in the Bradlaugh Hall, the Hall built in loving memory of a great Englishman and a great servant of India. 567 delegates had answered to the call, a goodly number for the long journey into the chill of the Panjab in midwinter. But if Panjab winters are cold, Panjab hearts are warm. The delegates were grouped as follows :

Bengal and Assam	38
N. W. P. and Oudh	39
Panjab	421
Bombay (28) and Sindh (29)	57
C. P. and Secunderabad	3
Madras...	9
	567

Rai Bahadur Kali Prasanna Roy was the Chairman of the Reception Committee, and welcomed the delegates warmly, but alluded with grief to the passing away of Sardar Dayal Singh the year before, and of Mr. Jaishi Ram, "the light and life of the

Congress cause in this Province". He rightly claimed the Congress as "the only true interpreter between the rulers and the ruled," and it was necessary that it should reach England, and teach the British people the greatness of their responsibility in taking the Government of 300 millions of people. Hindus had no need to agitate under their own rulers, nor under the Muhammadans, who selected their most trusted counsellors from among Hindus; "But the times have changed, and the alien Government now ruling over us has entirely different ideas and constitutions. The English Government, though democratic at home, is imperialistic and bureaucratic here. So agitation is the rule. If we wish to live upon two meals a day we must conform our ways to theirs, and carry on an agitation with untiring and persistent zeal."

The Hon. Mr. Surendranath Bannerji proposed as President the Hon. Mr. N. G. Chandravarkar, "one of the Judges of Her Majesty's High Court of Bombay". The proposal was seconded by Lala Hans Raj, supported by Moulvi Muhurram Ali Chisti, the Hon. Mr. C. Vijiaraghavachariar, and Mr. Bansi Lal, and carried unanimously.

The President, after a few words of thanks, turned to the consideration of the condition of the country. During the year the country had been suffering a terrible famine, justifying the repeated warnings of the Congress of the increasing poverty of the masses; the Viceroy had said that "the weakness and incapacity for resistance of the people took the Local Government by surprise," but it was the outcome of the long poverty. The necessary changes were not made, the revenue collections remained rigid, the agrarian problem was not faced. The Panjab Land Alienation Act, just passed, tied the ryot to the soil, but did not enable him to live and flourish on it. Both agriculture and industry needed to be helped to improve, and to this should be added economy in administration. The Congress should help the Government with facts, information and practical suggestions, so as to enable it to pursue a large and liberal policy.

The Subjects Committee was then approved, and the Congress adjourned.

On the 28th December, Mr. R. N. Mudholkar moved Resolution I on the Congress Constitution, making slight changes in the number of members in the Indian Congress Committee assigned to each Province; the Resolution was seconded by Mr. V. R. Nambier and carried.

Mr. G. Subramania Iyer moved Resolution II, asking for an enquiry into the economic condition of India, with a view to discover and adopt remedies for the oft-recurring famines. Labourers left India for other countries, and developed the prosperity of other lands by their industry, but they were cruelly ill-used there. Millions of people had died of famine, and millions more were left permanently deteriorated. The causes of such famines should be examined, and remedies adopted.

Mr. R. N. Mudholkar seconded, and gave statistics on the poverty of the people, and showed how the enhancement of the land revenue pressed on the peasantry, yet nothing was done. At least some effort should be made to grapple with the question, after obtaining information. Mr. B. G. Tilak said that some blamed the ryot for his poverty, but the ryot was much the same as he had long been. But if you took away the produce of the land and did not give it back to the land in some form more material than prestige and advice, the country must grow poorer and poorer. That was the Congress view. Moulvi Muhurram Ali Chisti supported in a vigorous speech, and Mr. Joseph Benjamin followed, reporting what he knew of the famine-stricken districts in Gujerat, and of the efforts to collect the revenue against the advice of the Commissioner and the Collector, who had stated that the people could not pay. Mr. Chura Mani, from Hissar, a famine-stricken district in the Panjab, gave testimony that the people borrowed from the money-lenders to pay the Government tax. The Resolution was carried.

Resolution III, on throwing open the higher grades of the Army to Indians, and asking for Military Colleges, was moved by Sardar Man Singh, who pointed to the loyalty, the bravery, the devotion shown by Indian soldiers, fighting her Majesty's battles in Tirah, in Burma, "at present they are shedding their blood in China, for the service of the Empire". Lord Roberts had said that the Panjabi soldiers were as good as the British.

These words were spoken in 1900. We are repeating them in 1915. In other wars since 1900

Indians have shed their blood. They have never failed England in her need. And still they are kept out of the commissioned ranks, and still we are told : "Trust in the gratitude of England."

Sardar Gurcharan Singh followed, on the same old lines—young men of martial races, offered the rank of a Jamadar. He recalled the march of the Sikhs, who marched 580 miles in 22 days under the burning sun of June to the rescue of the hard pressed British at Delhi and arrived, Sir Henry Barnard said, "in perfect order and ready for immediate service," a march to which he believed "there is no parallel on record". The resolution was supported by Sardar Rajendra Singh, Mr. Karandikar, Mr. Krishna Baldeo Varma, and Hafiz Abdul Rahim, and carried.

Mr. S. Sinha moved Resolution IV, on the separation of Judicial and Executive functions, and made a very able speech, reviewing the whole history of the controversy, and concluding by saying that the Government must rest on the affection of the people, and that that could "only be secured by conferring upon them the boon of justice, not the justice which we enjoy to-day, half milk and half water, adulterated justice, but real and righteous British Justice".

The Resolution was seconded by Mr. Chail Behari Lal, supported by Bakshi Ram Lubhaya, Messrs. A Choudhuri, C. Y. Chintamani, Kali Prasanna Kavyabisharad, and carried.

Resolution V condemned the practical exclusion of Indians from several of the Public Services, and was moved by the Hon. Mr. Surendranath Bannerji in a long and eloquent speech. He contrasted the policy of the English Rulers with the policy of the Roman Empire of old, and the policy of the great Akbar.

In the case of Akbar, the grandsons of those who had fought against his grandfather became the captains of his army, the Governors of his provinces, the confidential advisers of their Sovereign. It was a policy of trust and confidence, a policy which was sanctified by the immediate successors of the great Mughal. I am sorry that in the case of the English Rulers of India it is no longer a policy of trust and confidence but a policy largely leavened by mistrust and suspicion. Our fathers, as soon as their intellects were stimulated and their self-respect enhanced by the education which they received at the hands of Englishmen, commenced an agitation against their exclusion from these high offices. Therefore this question comes to us in the light of a heritage. In carrying on this agitation, we are performing an act of filial piety, rendering obeisance to the adored memory of our sires, for what memories in Bengal are more loved or respected than those of Kristodas Pal and Ram Gopal Ghose, or what name excites greater reverence in Bombay than that of Dadabhai Naoroji?

The speaker gave figures of the proportion of Indians in the higher appointments in the Services in Bengal. In the Forest there were 24 high appointments, 2 of which were held by Indians; in the Opium 77, Indians 8; the Customs 33, Indians 2; Preventive Branch of Customs 157, Indians 0; in 100 apprentices to this, 1 Eurasian; in the Survey, Indians 0; Superintendents of Gaols, Indians 0; in the Telegraphs 29 appointments, Indians 4; in the Police 102, Indians 5; Calcutta Police 10, Indians 1; and all this in face of the Proclamation of 1858.

Mr. G. Subramania Iyer seconded, and said that the statements made might be repeated of Madras. The Resolution was supported by Pandit Rambhaj Datta of Lahore, and carried.

Resolution VI, moved by Lala Dwarkadas, regretted the suspension of the right of electing Fellows by the graduates of Calcutta University, and the non-carrying out of the provisions of the Act constituting the Panjab University. Mr. Hem Chandra Rai seconded for Calcutta, Mr. Bepin Behari Bose for Allahabad, and Mr. Rustam Cama for Bombay. The carrying of the Resolution closed the second day's work.

The third day opened with a statement by the President that at the Subjects Committee it was decided to postpone the discussion of the Panjab Land Alienation Act so as to watch its working for a year, since the Hindu and Muhammadan delegates disagreed on it.

The seventh Resolution, thanking Lord Curzon for his famine policy, his regulation as to issuing shooting passes to soldiers, and his proceedings in the Rangoon and O'Gara cases, was moved by Mr. Surendranath Bannerji, who guarded himself from being supposed to approve the Viceroy's policy outside the points named in the Resolution. He warmly blamed that policy with regard to Local Self-Government, Education, and Land Legislation. But in checking outrages on Indians by Europeans and in famine relief, he had done well. Mr. Rustam Cama seconded, and the Resolution was carried.

Resolution VIII on Technical Education, IX on Berar Legislation, X the Omnibus, and XI on a promised annual contribution from the British exchequer to India, were put from the Chair and carried.

Resolution XII, on giving half a day at each Congress to the discussion of educational and industrial problems, was moved by Lala Lajpat Rai in Urdu, and the speech was unfortunately not reported. Mr. Duni Chand seconded, laying stress on the need for practical work, and the Resolution was carried.

Mr. D. E. Wacha shortly moved Resolution XIII, appointing a deputation to wait on the Viceroy, to submit to him a memorial drawing his attention to the Resolutions of the Congress regarding the need of separating Judicial and Executive functions, of dealing with the problem of Indian poverty, and of enquiring into the growing impoverishment of the peasantry. Munshi Murlidhar seconded, and Moulvi Muhurram Ali Chisti supported with equal brevity. The Resolution was carried.

Lala Har Bhagavan Das moved and Mr. Taraknath Mitra seconded, Resolution XIV, that the Panjab be constituted into a Regulation Province. It was carried.

Kumar M. N. Choudhuri moved Resolution XV, asking for legislation against liquor, urging that the placing of cheap liquor within the reach of the poor caused immense evils. Drunkenness which had been a heinous crime had become a pleasant vice, inseparably linked with western civilisation, and

Keshab Chandra Sen had complained that the British Government had brought Shakspere and Milton to them but also brandy bottles. The Excise Commission of 1883 showed the great increase of drunkenness among the labouring class, whose simplicity, innocence and industrious habits were fading away with the increase. Lala Beni Prasad seconded, and the Resolution was carried.

Resolution XVI, congratulating Mr. Caine on his election to Parliament, and Resolution XVII assigning Rs. 30,000 to the British Committee and *India* were put from the Chair and carried.

Resolution XVIII condemned the new Rules restricting the admission of Indians to Cooper's Hill College and Roorki, and was moved by Mr. J. Choudhuri, who pointed out that Cooper's Hill College was built with Indian money, but only two Indians a year might enter it. Indians went to England at a great cost of social sacrifice and money, and were told: "Intellectually you may be our equals; still, so far as the appropriation of the fishes and loaves of your country go, you are not." The Roorki regulation also placed special restrictions on Indians. "The policy pursued by Government with regard to the Cooper's Hill and Roorki appointments is both unjust to us as a Nation, and unworthy of a Government which professes to administer the country in our interests." Mr. A. C. Parthasarathi Naidu seconded, and Mr. S. M. Paranjpe supported; he urged that, after all, Indian buildings were not so bad, before Cooper's Hill existed; they lasted for many hundreds of years. "We Indians and black men can do" these things.

> Our humble aspirations are for preparing our roads and building our bridges, so that Indian bridges and Indian roads may be prepared and built by Indians. We never aspire to go to Southampton and prepare the roads for Southampton. We do not aspire to build bridges over the Thames. If we do not wish to go to England to perform these things, naturally the question may be asked, whether Indians may not be allowed to construct their own roads and their own bridges.

A modest request enough, after all. The Resolution was put and carried.

Resolution XIX, thanking Sir William Wedderburn, Mr. Dadabhai Naoroji and Mr. A. O. Hume for their great services, was put from the Chair and carried amid loud cheers. Resolution XX, on South Africa, was also put from the Chair and carried.

Mr. Thakur Das moved Resolution XXI, asking that qualified Indians might be placed on the Committee to consider the proposal to establish Agricultural Banks; the Resolution was seconded by Pandit Gyaneshvara Shastri, and carried, the latter gentleman remarking, in his two-minutes speech, that it was a "horse-race to-day". Certainly the work went fast.

Resolution XXII, lamenting the loss of Bakshi Jaishi Ram, was put from the Chair and carried unanimously.

Then Pandit Madan Mohan Malaviya moved Resolution XIII, on Permanent Settlement; he said that in the midst of much to admire and to be grateful for in British Rule, the note of distress and poverty was sounding louder and louder. From living and moving among the people, they knew how they existed under the present system. He criticised the answer of the Viceroy to the Madras Mahajana Sabha, pointing out its unfairness in ignoring all the suggestions for remedying poverty made by the Congress. Bengal had escaped famine by its Permanent Settlement, and other Provinces should be given similar relief.

Mr. V. R. Nambier seconded the Resolution, and it was carried.

Mr. Bhupendranath Basu moved Resolution XXIV, criticising the Indian Mines Bill, making a speech full of sound wisdom. Some objected to political agitation and urged them to turn rather towards industrial development. "They say: Dissolve your Congresses and Conferences; shut up your newspapers; and, like dumb beings work out your destiny; devote your whole energy to the consideration of industrial questions." But, said Bhupendranath Babu, industries were doomed without political freedom:

> Where is the country in the world, I ask you assembled delegates and visitors, which would put countervailing duties upon its own produce, in order that foreign producers may be put on terms of equality? I ask you, where is the country that will put a duty upon an article of consumption like sugar, in order that foreign producers and merchants might be benefited? I ask you, again, where is the country that will introduce and undertake factory legislation in order to suppress and repress factories, and make their work difficult? Therefore those who pin their faith upon industry alone must beware.

These arguments are as cogent now as then. Political freedom is the condition of industrial success. The proposed legislation took no notice of the Indian habit of families all working together; ignored the fact that there were no labour disputes, no complaints from either employers or employed. The legislation would ruin a flourishing industry, and the miners asked to be saved from it. Mr. J. Ghosal formally seconded the Resolution, and it was carried.

The President then put from the Chair Resolution XXV, re-appointing Mr. A. O. Hume and Mr. D. E. Wacha to their offices, constituting the Indian Congress Committee, and the Industrial and Educational Committees for 1901, and it was carried. Mr. Bhupendranath Basu invited the Congress to meet in Calcutta in 1901, and, with the President's concluding speech, the Sixteenth National Congress dissolved, and sent its members forth into the new century's work, the century which shall see their labours crowned with success.

RESOLUTIONS

Congress Constitution

I. Resolved—That Rule 4 of the Constitution of the Congress Committee be amended as follows:

" Its affairs shall be managed by a Committee styled the Indian Congress Committee consisting of, besides the *ex-officio* members referred to below, 45 Members elected by the Congress, 40 of whom shall be elected upon the recommendations of the different Provincial Congress Committees, and, in the absence of such Committees, by the delegates of the respective Provinces in Congress assembled, in the manner hereinbelow laid down, that is to say :

For Bengal including Assam 7
" Bombay including Sindh 7
" Madras 7

For N. W. P. including Oudh		...	...	7
„ Panjab	...	...	...	6
„ Berar	...	...	...	3
„ Central Provinces	...	...	...	3

"The *ex-officio* members shall be the President of the Congress and President-elect from the day of his nomination, the Ex-Presidents of the Congress, the Secretary and Assistant Secretary of the Congress, the Chairman of the Reception Committee, the Secretary of the Reception Committee, to be nominated by the Reception Committee.

"The term of office of the Members of the Committee shall be the period intervening between two ordinary meetings of the Congress."

Famine Enquiry

II. Resolved—That having regard to the oft-recurring famines in India, and the manifestly decreasing power of resistance on the part of its population in the face of a single failure of harvest, leading as it frequently does to human suffering, loss of life, destruction of live-stock, disorganisation of rural operations and interference with the legitimate work of the administrative machinery, the Congress hereby earnestly prays that the Government of India may be pleased to institute at an early date a full and independent enquiry into the economic condition of the people of India with a view to the ascertainment and adoption of practicable remedies.

Military

III. Resolved—That having regard to the devoted and loyal services rendered by Indian soldiers in the service of the Empire, the Congress again urges on the Government—

(*a*) The desirability of throwing open to them the higher grades of the Military Service; and

(*b*) The establishment of Military Colleges in India, at which Natives of India, as defined by Statute, may be educated and trained for a military career, as Commissioned or Non-Commissioned Officers, according to capacity and qualifications, in the Indian Army.

Separation of Judicial and Executive Functions

IV. Resolved—That this Congress notices with satisfaction the support of public opinion, both in England and in India, which the question of the separation of the Judicial from the Executive functions in the administration of justice has received; and this Congress, while thanking Lord Hobhouse, Sir Richard Garth, Sir Richard

Couch, Sir Charles Sergeant, Sir William Markby, Sir John Budd-Phear, Sir John Scott, Sir Roland K. Wilson, Mr. Herbert J. Reynolds and Sir William Wedderburn for presenting a petition to the Secretary of State in Council to effect the much-needed separation, earnestly hopes that the Government of India will give their earliest attention to the petition which has been forwarded to them, and will take practical steps for speedily carrying out this much-needed reform.

Public Service

V. Resolved—That the Congress regrets the practical exclusion of natives of India from the higher appointments in the Police, the Public Works, the State Railways, the Opium, the Customs, the Telegraph, the Survey and other Departments, and prays that full justice be done to the claims of the people of India in regard to these appointments.

XVIII. Resolved—That, in the opinion of the Congress, the new 'rules restricting the number of Indians eligible to qualify themselves for employment in the Engineering Branch of the Indian Public Works Department, through the Cooper's Hill College, to a maximum of two only in a year, should be withdrawn as a matter of bare justice to the people of this country, and that the said College should be made available equally for the use of all subjects of Her Majesty; and the Congress is further of opinion that the invidious distinction made between Indians and Anglo-Indians as regards the guaranteed appointments in connection with the College at Roorki should be withdrawn and that these appointments should be made available to all Her Majesty's Indian subjects in all parts of the country.

Election of University Fellows

VI. Resolved—That this Congress regrets the suspension of the privileges accorded to the graduates of a certain standing of the Calcutta University to return Fellows to the University, and the fact that effect is not given to the provisions of the Act constituting the Panjab University with regard to the election of Fellows by the Senate, and is of opinion that it is desirable, in the interests of sound education, to confer the privilege of electing Fellows upon the graduates of Indian Universities where it does not exist, and of extending it where it does exist.

Thanks of Congress

VII. Resolved—That this Congress desires to record its gratitude to H. E. the Viceroy for the benevolence of his famine policy, and for his firm resolve to uphold the interests of order and justice, as evidenced in the regulations recently issued regarding the grant of shooting passes to soldiers and his proceedings in connection with the Rangoon and O'Gara cases.

XI. Resolved—That this Congress, while expressing its grateful acknowledgments for the annual contribution of £ 257,000 promised to be made from the British to the Indian Exchequer in accordance with the recommendations of the majority of the Royal Commission on Indian Expenditure, respectfully desires to point out that for doing adequate justice to the claims of India so far as admitted by that Commission it is necessary that she should be granted the arrears payable on this account for the past many years, and prays that the British Parliament will be pleased to make this grant.

XIX. Resolved—That this Congress begs to record its high and grateful appreciation of the services rendered to this country and the Congress movement by Sir William Wedderburn, Mr. Dadabhai Naoroji, and Mr. A. O. Hume, and to express its regret at the retirement of Sir William Wedderburn from Parliament, where he rendered great and valuable services to this country, and hopes that he may soon return to Parliament to renew his labour of love for the people of India.

Education

VIII. Resolved—That this Congress places on record its conviction that the system of Technical Education now in vogue is inadequate and unsatisfactory, and prays that, having regard to the poverty of the people and the decline of indigenous industries, the Government will introduce a more elaborate and efficient scheme of technical instruction, and set apart more funds for a successful working of the same. And this Congress desires to express its grateful appreciation of the patriotic and munificent gift of Mr. Tata for the promotion of higher scientific education and research.

Berar Legislation

IX. Resolved—That this Congress is of opinion that so long as Berar is administered by the Governor-General in Council, all laws and orders having the force of law, intended for Berar, should be enacted by the Supreme Legislative Council in the same way as those for British India proper.

Confirmation of Previous Resolutions

X. Resolved—(I) That this Congress concurs with previous Congresses in strongly advocating: [1897, (*b*) (*d*) (*e*) (*g*)].

That this Congress, concurring with previous Congresses, records its protest: [1897, (*a*) and (*b*); 1899, (*c*) and (*d*)].

This Congress, concurring with previous Congresses, expresses its conviction: [1899, (*a*) to (*c*)].

Education and Industry

XII. Resolved—That the Congress hereby approves of the suggestion presented by the Indian Congress Committee for the consideration of this Session that at least half a day at each annual Session of the Congress be devoted to the consideration and discussion of the Industrial and Educational problems of the country. Further resolved that annually two Committees be appointed by the Congress, one for Educational and one for Industrial subjects, to consider and suggest means for the Education and Industrial improvement of the country and to assist therein, and that to each Committee a Secretary be annually appointed. These Committees shall divide themselves into Provincial Committees with power to add to their number.

Deputation to the Viceroy

XIII. Resolved—That the following Memorial be submitted to His Excellency the Viceroy in Council by a deputation consisting of the following gentlemen :

Hon. P.M. Mehta.
Hon. W.C. Bannerji.
Hon. Ananda Charlu.
Hon. Surendranath Bannerji.
Hon. Munshi Madho Lal.
Mr. R. N. Mudholkar.
Mr. R. M. Sayani.
Mr. Harkishan Lal.

YOUR EXCELLENCY,

We, on behalf of the delegates assembled at the 16th Session of the Indian National Congress at Lahore in December last, have the honour to submit most respectfully for the consideration of Your Excellency in Council the accompanying Resolutions passed by that assembly, and specially the following questions which have long been before the country, and which, in the opinion of the Congress, now await a speedy solution of a practical and beneficent character.

1. The question of the extreme desirability of separating Judicial from Executive functions has now been so well recognised, and there exists such a strong consensus of opinion on the subject, official and non-official, that your Memorialists are earnestly of hope that the Government will be pleased at an early date to introduce this popular reform in the administration of the country.

2. The increasing poverty of the peasantry in the greater part of the country, and their consequent inability to maintain themselves without State and private benevolence at the very

outset of scarcity or famine, is another pressing problem. Your Memorialists are fully aware of the fact that the serious attention of the Government has been engaged on it, and they trust that some efficacious remedy will be soon found which may greatly contribute to mitigate that severe poverty, and enable the peasantry to better resist the strain which years of bad harvests or scarcity may entail on them.

3. That in view of the condition to which the recent famines have reduced the ryots, the Government will be so good as to cause an exhaustive enquiry to be instituted into their growing impoverishment by means of an independent Commission.

Panjab

XIV. Resolved—That the Congress respectfully urges upon the Government that in its opinion the time has come when the Panjab should be constituted into a Regulation Province.

Liquor Legislation

XV. Resolved—That this Congress views with grave alarm and deep regret the rapid increase in the consumption of intoxicants, specially liquor, in the country, and the Congress is of opinion that the cheap supply of liquor, etc., is alone responsible for this. The Congress, therefore, fervently appeals to the Government of India to pass measures like the Maine Liquor Law of America, and introduce Bills like Sir Wilfrid Lawson's Permissive Bill or the Local Option Act, and impose an additional tax upon intoxicants not intended to be used as medicine. The Congress records its firm conviction that if the Government do not take these practical steps immediately, the moral, material and physical deterioration of those classes, among whom liquor, etc., have obtained a firm hold, would be inevitable; and as intoxicants have already affected the great labouring class, the benevolent intention of the Government to help the growth of the Indian Arts and Industries would bear no fruit. The Congress gives great importance to this question, which, it strongly believes, is intimately connected with the material progress of the country, and emphatically protests against the cheap supply of liquor, etc.

Congratulations of Congress

XVI. Resolved—That this Congress offers its sincere and hearty congratulations to Mr. W. S. Caine on his election to Parliament, and expresses its confidence in him as a trusted friend of the people of India and a promoter of their best interests.

Congress Work

XVII. Resolved—That a sum of Rs. 30,000 be assigned for the expenses of the British Committee and the cost of the publication of *India*.

South Africa

XX. Resolved—That this Congress once more draws the attention of the Indian Government as well as of the Secretary of State for India to the grievances of the British Indians in South Africa, and earnestly hopes that in view of the re-arrangement of the boundaries in that Continent and the incorporation of the late Boer Republics into the British Dominions, the disabilities under which the Indian settlers laboured in those Republics, and as to which Her Majesty's Government owing to their independence in internal matters felt powerless to obtain redress, will now no longer exist, and that the serious inconvenience caused to the settlers in Natal, among others by the Immigration Restrictions and the Dealer's Licences Acts of that Colony, which are manifestly inconsistent with the fundamental principles of the British Constitution as also the Proclamation of 1858, will be materially mitigated, if not entirely removed.

Indians on Committee

XXI Resolved—That the Congress begs to suggest to the Government of India that qualified Indian members, representing the different Provinces, may be nominated to the Committee, recently formed, in connection with the proposal of starting Agricultural Banks in India.

Sorrow of Congress

XXII. Resolved—That this Congress desires to put on record its deep sense of the loss sustained by the death of Bakshi Jaishi Ram, who was one of the staunch supporters of the Congress for many a year and rendered valuable services to it in connection with his own Province

Permanent Settlement

XXIII. Resolved—That while thanking the Government of India for its intention to investigate the question of the incidence and pressure of the land assessment as affecting the well-being and resources of the agricultural population, the Congress respectfully urges upon the Government the desirability of including within the scope of the contemplated investigation the question of periodical settlement of assessments and the necessity repeatedly pointed out by the Congress of making it permanent. This Congress further prays that the Government of India may be pleased to publish the opinions invited from Local Governments and Administrations, on the subject referred to in para 4 of the Resolution of the Government of India (Revenue and Agricultural Department) published in *The Gazette of India* dated 22nd December,

1900, and allow the public an opportunity to make their representations thereon before the Government decides whether further investigation is necessary or not in the terms of the said Resolution.

Indian Mines

XXIV. Resolved—That the Congress respectfully submits that the provisions of the Indian Mines Bill, so far as they impose restrictions on the employment of labour, be omitted, and that the penal provisions thereof may not be put in force for a period of 5 years, and that, in the meantime, mining schools be opened in suitable centres where young men may qualify themselves for employment under the Act.

Formal

XXV. Resolved—(*a*) That this Congress appoints Mr. A. O. Hume, C.B., the General Secretary, and Mr. D. E. Wacha, the Joint General Secretary, for the ensuing year.

(*b*) That the following gentlemen do constitute the Indian Congress Committee for 1901:

EX-OFFICIO MEMBERS

1. The Hon W. C. Bannerji (1885).
2. The Hon. Dadabhai Naoroji (1886).
   The Hon. Budrudin Tyabji (1887).
   (Now Judge, Bombay High Court). (Dead) (1888).
3. Sir William Wedderburn (1889).
4. The Hon. Pherozeshah Mehta (1890).
5. The Hon. Ananda Charlu (1891).
   The Hon. W. C. Bannerji (1892). (Second time).
   The Hon. Dadabhai Naoroji (1893). (Second time).
6. Alfred Webb Esq. (1894).
7. The Hon. Surendranath Bannerji (1895).
8. The Hon. R. M. Sayani (1896).
9. The Hon. C. Sankaran Nair (1897).
10. The Hon. A. M. Bose (1898).
11. R. C. Dutt, Esq. (1899).
    The Hon. N. G. Chandravarkar (1900). (Now Judge, Bombay High Court).
12. D. E. Wacha, Esq., General Secretary.
13. Alfred Nundy Esq., Assistant Secretary.
14. Chairman of the Reception Committee, Calcutta.
15. Secretary of the Reception Committee, Calcutta.
16. President-elect of the Congress for 1901.

GENERAL LIST:

Mr. J. Ghosal.
Pandit Bishambarnath.
Mr. R. N. Mudholkar.
Hon. Vijiaraghavachari.
Mr. W. A. Chambers.

BENGAL:

Hon. Baikunthanath Sen.
Mr. Saligram Singh.
Mr. Ambikacharan Mozumdar.
Mr. Motilal Ghose.
Rai Yatindranath Choudhuri.
Mr. Bhupendranath Basu.
Mr. Prithwis Chandra Roy.

N. W. P. & OUDH:

Hon. Munshi Madho Lal.
Pandit Madan Mohan Malaviya.
Mr. Bishan Narayan Dhar.
Munshi Ganga Prasad Varma.
Mr. S. Sinha.
Pandit Prithwinath.
Hafiz Abdul Rahim.

MADRAS:

Mr. P. Rungiya Naidu.
Mr. G. Subramania Iyer.
Hon. Nawab Syed Muhammad Bahadur.
Mr. P. Ramchandra Pillai.
Mr. V. Ryru Nambier.
Mr. P. Kesava Pillai.
Mr. G. Srinavasa Rao.

BOMBAY:

Mr. Rustam K. R. Cama.
Mr. Daji Abaji Khare.
Mr. C. H. Setalwad.
Hon. Professor G. K. Gokhale.
Mr. Bal Gangadhar Tilak.
Mr. R. P. Karandikar.
Mr. Tahil Ram Khem Chand.

BERAR:

Mr. M. V. Joshi.
Mr. Deorao Vinayak.
Mr. G. S. Khaparde.

CENTRAL PROVINCES:

Mr. Buparoodwada.
Mr. Krishna Rao Vaman.
Mr. Raoji Gobind.

PANJAB:

Rai Bahadur Babu Kali Prasanna Rai, Pleader, Chief Court
Lala Harkishan Lal. Barrister-at-Law.
Rai Sahab Sukh Dyal, Pleader, Chief Court.
Lala Lajpat Rai, Pleader, Chief Court.
Lala Dharam Das Suri, Pleader, Chief Court.
Lala Kanhaya Lal, Pleader, Chief Court.

(e) That the following gentlemen do form the Industrial Committee, with Mr. Harkishan Lal as Secretary, for 1901.

BENGAL:

Hon. Baikunthanath Sen.
Kumar Manmathanath Rai Choudhuri.
Mr. Pulin Bihari Sarkar.
Mr. Radharaman Kar.
Mr. J. Choudhuri.
Mr. Bhupendranath Basu.
Mr. Akhoy Kumar Maitra.
Mr. Gaganendranath Tagore.
Mr. Mohini Mohan Chakravarti.
Mr. Akhoy Kumar Majumdar.
Mr. Kali Prasanna Kavyabisarad.
Mr. Lalit Chandra Sen.
Mr. Pramada Gobinda Choudhuri.
Mr. Tarapada Bannerji.

PANJAB:

Mr. Harkishan Lal.
Mr. Lajpat Rai.
Mr. Balak Ram.
Mr. Dwarka Das.
Mr. Kashi Ram.
Mr. Duni Chand.
Mr. Lal Chand.
Mr. Prabhu Dyal.

BOMBAY:

Professor Gajar.
Mr. J. N. Tata.
Mr. D. E. Wacha.

N. W. P. & OUDH:

Mr. Bansi Lal Singh.
Mr. Ganga Prasad Varma.
Mr. S. Sinha.
Mr. K. P. Basak.
Mr. Bepin Bihari Bose.
Pandit Madan Mohan Malaviya.

CENTRAL PROVINCES:

Mr. Raoji Gobind.

MADRAS:

Mr. C. Sankaran Nair
Mr. G. Subramania Iyer.
Mr. P. Kesava Pillai.
Mr. K. P. Achyuta Menon.
Mr. T. Rangachari.
Hon. P. Ratnasabhapati Pillai.
Hon. V. Venkataratnam.

BERAR:

Mr. D. V. Bhagawat.
Mr. R. N. Mudholkar.
Mr. Deorao Vinayak.
Mr. Ganesh Nagesh.

(*d*) That the following gentlemen do form the Educational Committee, with Mr. Harkishan Lal as Secretary, for 1901.

BENGAL:

Hon. A. M. Bose.
Hon. Surendranath Bannerji.
Dr. Nilratan Sircar.
Mr. Heramba Chandra Maitra.
Mr. Aswini Kumar Dutt.
Mr. Peary Lal Ghosh.
Mr. Raghunath Das.
Mr. Prithwis Chandra Roy.
Mr. Krishna Kumar Mitra.
Mr. Syamacharan Roy.

PANJAB:

Mr. Harkishan Lal.
Mr. Lajpat Rai.
Mr. Balak Ram.
Mr. Ishwar Das.
Mr. Lal Chand.
Mr. Shadi Lal.

BOMBAY:

Hon. Professor G. K. Gokhale.
Mr. Chimanlal H. Setalwad.
Mr Rustam K. R. Cama.
Mr. B. G. Tilak.

N. W. P. & OUDH:

Mr. A. Nundy.
Mr. Madan Mohan Malaviya.
Mr. Bishan Narayan Dhar.
Mr. G. L. Maitra.
Mr. Ganga Prasad Varma.
Mr. Ramananda Chatterji.
Mr. Bepin Bihari Bose.
Mr. K. P. Basak.
Pandit Hari Ram Pande.
Pandit Tej Bahadur Sapru.

CENTRAL PROVINCES:

Mr. S. B. Gokhale.

MADRAS:

Hon. Rai Bahadur P. Ananda Charlu, C.I.E
Hon. C. Vijiaraghavachari.
Hon. Rai Bahadur C. Jambulingam Mudaliar.
Mr. V. Ryru Nambier.
Mr. C. Karunakara Menon.
Mr. V. C. Desikachariar.
Mr. S. Kasturiranga Iyengar.

BERAR:

Mr. M. V. Joshi.
Mr. R. N. Mudholkar.
Mr. G. S. Khaparde.
Mr. D. V. Bhagawat.

CHAPTER XVII

CALCUTTA welcomed the Seventeenth National Congress in a great Pavilion erected in Beadon Square, lent for the occasion by the Calcutta Corporation. The whole square offered a brilliant scene, the Industrial Exhibition having its own separate Pavilion, and both being gay with flags. The Congress Pavilion was beautifully decorated with coloured foliage plants and palms, and was lighted by electricity. 896 delegates were present, distributed as follows:

Bengal	580
N. W. P. and Oudh	89
Panjab	30
C. P., Berar and Secunderabad	44
Bombay (43) and Sindh (8)	51
Madras	102
	896

After the President-elect's procession had made its slow way through the crowd, a song, "Hindustan," composed by Sarola Devi Ghosal was sung by a choir of 58 men and boys, the nearly 400 volunteers joining the chorus with fine effect.

Maharaja Bahadur Jagadindranath Rai Bahadur of Natore, the Chairman of the Reception Committee, welcomed the delegates in a graceful speech, saying that he had only ventured to accept the honour offered to him "because it has been the one great ambition of my life to join the ranks of those who think, those who feel, and those who work for their country". He spoke with deep feeling of the Passing of the Great Queen, whose words were the Magna Carta of India: "That message so full of sympathy for an alien subject race, so noble and liberal in its spirit, so magnificently just in its policy, would alone have won the eternal gratitude and unflinching loyalty of her Indian subjects." The National Congress, the embodiment of India's hopes and aspirations, born in her reign, would for ever link the name of Victoria with the destiny of India. Her Majesty's successor had "won the hearts of his Indian subjects by his charming personality"; might his reign be a continuation of his great mother's. The Speaker then alluded to the plague having come to Calcutta, but the authorities asked them to take it philosophically, instead of harrying them with the fads of science, isolation, segregation and inoculation, and the advice "falls in with our humour". The officials were uncharitable to them, and that kept away title-hunters, but most of the men of rank and wealth supported them. After announcing that they had opened an Industrial Exhibition in connection with the Congress, the first, but, he hoped, a permanent feature in future, he called on

Mr. W. C. Bannerji to propose the President. He proposed Mr. D. E. Wacha, "the life and soul of this movement," and called on the Congress to elect him with acclamation. Rai Bahadur P. Ananda Charlu seconded, Mr. R. N. Mudholkar supported the Resolution, and it was carried with loud applause.

Mr. Dinshaw Edulji Wacha began his address with a touching and heartfelt tribute to Mr. Justice Ranade, who had suddenly passed away on January 17th, 1901, leaving behind him a noble and spotless memory.

He then spoke gratefully of the late Queen-Empress, sadly of the assassination of President McKinley, and grieved over the death of Sir Sheshadri, the great Dewan of Mysore, who proved "that statesmanship is not a monopoly which is confined to one race and one country alone". The President, after an allusion to the new King-Emperor, who on his visit to India had won the hearts of Princes and people, turned to the subject of the famine, reviewing its effect, the aid given, the policy of the Bombay Government, the way in which funds were spent, and ought to be spent, in relief. He pointed out that the peasants who were relieved in famine time were the very same people who paid 47¼ crores a year in taxation, and it was not much to give them back some of it in the time of the periodical famines. He dealt with the causes of famine, and quoted authorities, including Lord Salisbury, in favour of lightening the drain on the cultivator. There ought to be full enquiry into the causes of the present agrarian condition, for recent legislation was disastrous. Irrigation Works were essential, and they should be preferred to railways, which were not an "unmixed blessing". Irrigation increased agricultural wealth, while railways only distributed it. Agricultural Banks were at last recognised as useful, and here he advocated the system adopted in Egypt. The export of grain prevented a sufficient storage in the country. Adverting to the condition of the masses, and the average rate of agricultural wealth per head of the population, the President complained that Government shrank from publishing details which could be examined; the Duke of Argyll had said that "of chronic poverty and of permanent reduction to the lowest level of subsistence, such as prevail only too widely among the vast population of rural India, we have no example in the western world". Improvement was impossible "so long as absenteeism, which is the principal feature of British rule, exists"; the annual extraction of 30 to 40 crores from the country without any hope of return was the greatest obstacle to Indian prosperity.

The fact is India is not free to choose its own administrative agency. Were it free, is there the slightest doubt that the entire administrative agency would be indigenous, living and spending their monies in the country? India, I repeat, is not free, and, therefore, it has no choice in the matter. The governing authorities in the first place have most strangely willed that almost all the higher posts shall be held by men who live a while here, and then retire to their own country. Even another great modern Asiatic power, Russia, is not known to import wholesale Russian agency to carry on the work of administration in the distant provinces of Central Asia! But we are told that the European agency is extremely limited. It counts no more than 17,300 persons. True. But contrast the annual expenditure of 16 crores incurred on their account with the $2\frac{3}{4}$ crores earned by Indians. Did England sit quiet while the Plantagenets were filling all the high offices from France to the great disadvantage of the English themselves? Was not England pauperised when the Papacy was rampant and abstracted millions from it annually, as history has recorded? Would England refrain from complaining, supposing that the position of India and England was to-day reversed?

India was poor, and was "ruled at a cost unheard of in any part of the civilised world".

The President then turned to finance and analysed, with masterly skill, the taxation and expenditure of the country, in which Indians had no voice. There must be industrial development, although improvement would be slow since the root of poverty lay in political causes. "'Insane Imperialism,' to use Mr. Morley's phrase, with its mischievous policy of retrogression and repression is in the ascendant for the moment. But this policy of political insanity, I am firmly of conviction, must sooner or later give way to the former policy of sound liberalism, modified in conformity with the march of time and the irresistible logic of events. . . . Indians have never been slow to recognise the benefits of British rule. But it would be unreasonable to ask them to sing eternally its praises and transform themselves into its unqualified panegyrists. No doubt we have a good Government, but it is not unmixed with many an evil. The desire is that the evil may be purged away, and that in the course of time we may have a better Government."

The Subjects Committee was approved, when the prolonged cheers had ceased, and the Congress rose for the day.

On the second day, the first Resolution was put in three sections from the Chair, expressing grief for the death of the Queen-Empress, tendering homage to the new Sovereign, and lamenting the loss of the Hon. Mr. Justice Ranade.

After two letters had been read, Mr. W. C. Bannerji moved Resolution II, on the maintenance of the British Committee, and guaranteeing a circulation of 4,000 copies of *India*. He made a vigorous speech in support of the Congress, and was followed by the Hon. Mr. P. M. Mehta, unfortunately unreported, the text not having been received back. Rai Bahadur P. Ananda Charlu, Pandit Madan Mohan Malaviya, and Moulvi M. Ali Chisti supported, and the Resolution was carried.

It is interesting to notice that the speakers all defended the Congress from being less enthusiastically supported than before. The complaints made now were made then, when the Congress is now supposed to have been at its best. All movements include croakers, who belittle the present in comparison with the past. The main reason for this perennial depreciation is the fact that they are themselves older and less energetic, and do not realise that the youngers now supply the enthusiasm they have lost.

Mr. Mudholkar moved Resolution III, on Indian poverty. All now agreed that the masses were sinking more deeply into the quagmire of poverty, and the census of 1901 showed that in five Provinces the population had actually decreased from the number reached in 1891. A million people died in the famine in excess of the ordinary mortality, in spite of all the efforts of Government, and if the people were not in abject poverty such a result could not have accrued. The Commission of 1874 found that it was the revenue policy of the Government that was mainly responsible for the degradation of the ryots. In Berar there was a general enhancement of 30 per cent. In the C. P. from 100 to 200 per cent. Where 80 per cent of cultivable land had been brought under cultivation, there should be a Permanent Settlement on the lines laid down by Lord Ripon in 1882.

Mr. G. Venkataratnam seconded, and dealt with Madras. In 1862 the Madras Government declared that "there can be no question that one fundamental principle of the ryotwari system is that the Government demand on the land is fixed for ever". Various promises were made and hopes held out in 1865, 1867, 1868, but the 1862 policy was formally negatived by the Secretary of State in 1883. Things were going steadily from bad to worse.

Mr. G. Subramania Iyer took up the sad story, and gave more figures, remarking that the reason that the ryots could live at all was the "tropical climate where life can linger on the scantiest of subsistence. But is the life's function of the Indian ryot to live and die merely like a brute? Is he not a 'human being, endowed with reason, sentiment, and latent capacity'?" The peasant had sunk to a lower and a lower standard of living. There were

> nearly 200 millions of people living a life of chronic starvation and of the most abject ignorance, grim and silent in their suffering, without zest in life, without comfort or enjoyment, without hope of ambition, living because they were born into the world, and dying because life could no longer be kept in the body.

Mr. B. Pal Choudhuri supported, dealing with Agricultural Banks, and Mr. Guha followed in Bengali, the Resolution being then put and carried.

Dr. Gour proposed, the Hon. Mr. Srinivasa Rao seconded, Messrs. Ambikacharan Mozumdar and Kali Prasanna Kavyabisarad supported the hardy annual of the separation of Judicial and Executive functions, to which we cannot afford more space.

Mr. Kalicharan Bannerji moved Resolution V, asking that eminent Indian lawyers should be added to the Judicial Committee of the Privy Council for Indian Appeals. The "law of the Courts" was not always in accord with the "law of the people," and long establised rules were set aside. Mr. P. S. Sivaswami Iyer seconded it, as an extension of the principle already applied in the High Courts. The Resolution was carried.

Mr. Gandhi moved Resolution VI, on South Africa, as "a petitioner on behalf of the hundred thousand British Indians in South Africa". He told the now familiar tale of Indian grievances, and the Resolution, seconded by Mr. A. Pillai, was carried, and the Congress adjourned.

On the third day, Mr. S. Sinha moved the seventh Resolution, urging various matters of Police Reform, and he dwelt on the admittance of Indians to examination for the Police Service, the recruitment of Inspectors and Sub-Inspectors, and asked for a larger number of Indians in the higher grades. Mr. V. R. Nambier seconded, laying stress on the need for education in the lower grades, and the employment of Indians who understood their own countrymen in the higher. Five other speakers supported, and the Resolution was carried.

Resolution VIII returned to the famine, which brooded over all hearts, and was moved by Mr. G. Subramania Iyer. He dwelt this time on the need for industrial independence, and pointed to the rapid industrial improvement in Japan since 1868. How could India adjust her industrial condition as Japan has adjusted hers to new needs? India must either go forward or perish. He made practical suggestions for founding technical institutions and foreign scholarships, and a careful survey of indigenous industries.

Mr. N. M. Samarth seconded, and Mr. N. K. Ramaswami Aiyar supported, giving histories of past famines and analysing the causes of famine; the Resolution was further supported by Messrs. Jadunath Majumdar and Joseph Benjamin, and carried.

Mr. Surendranath Bannerji moved Resolution IX, demanding the wider employment of Indians in the

Public Services. It was seconded by Mr. Abdul Kasim, and carried.

Mr. Dixit moved Resolution X, on the cost of British troops in India, in a brief speech, and Mr. C. Y. Chintamani seconded with equal brevity. The resolution was supported by Mr. Smedley in a discursive and breezy speech, which he concluded by saying that he believed in Home Rule for Ireland and Home Rule for India. He appealed to the young men to be determined, and ask for Home Rule for India.

> These resolutions seem to me to be making so small a demand, that they will be glad to allow you these little things to keep you off from Home Rule. My last word is: "Go in for Home Rule for India," and the blessing of God rest upon your efforts.

We are taking Mr. Smedley's advice in 1915.

Dr. Sarat K. Mullick moved Resolution XI, approving of the formation of a Cadet Corps for Indian Princes as a step to the establishment of Military Colleges. Moulvi M. Ali Chisti seconded, Mr. K. B. Varma supported, and the Resolution was carried.

Resolution XII dealt with Education, and was moved by Mr. V. R. Pandit, who condemned the small expenditure on Education by the Government. Mr. B. G. Tilak seconded, urging that Education should be made thorough. Mr. A. Choudhuri and Mr. Mahesvara Prasad seconded, and it was carried.

The thirteenth Resolution urged the raising of coolies' wages in Assam and the abolition of the penal legislation affecting them. It was moved by

Mr. Jogendra Chandra Ghose, who, himself an employer of coolie labour, protested against the cruel treatment of the Assam coolies, who died in hundreds, while in three years he had only lost two of his labourers in the Sunderbans, one from cholera and one carried off by a tiger. He pleaded for justice, so that the rule of England might last: "I say this out of my great love for you Englishmen—lest ye forget, lest ye forget."

Mr. Bepin Chandra Pal seconded, urging the repeal of the Penal Labour Law, and combination to defend the coolies. Mr. Lalit Mohan Ghosal having supported, the Resolution was carried.

The medical grievances were again brought up in Resolution XIV, moved by Mr. M. N. Bannerji, seconded by Dr. Nilratan Sarkar, and carried. The fifteenth Resolution urged the needs of agriculture and was very briefly moved, seconded, and supported by Messrs. Yatindranath Choudhuri, Cama, N. K. Ramaswami Aiyar, Moulvi Khoja Muhammad Noor, Dr. Sureshvara Mukerji, and carried.

Resolutions on the Economic Question in India (No. XVI), on Currency Legislation (No. XVII), were carried, but were too complex to be effectively dealt with in the last rush of the Congress. Resolution XVIII asked for the establishment of a Mining College, and Resolution XIX, the Omnibus, was put from the Chair. Resolution XX re-appointed Mr. A. O. Hume and Mr. D. E. Wacha, and Resolution XXI accepted the invitation of the Hon. Mr. P. M. Mehta to the Bombay Presidency.

Then came the votes of thanks to the Reception Committee and the President, and the President's reply, bringing to a close the Seventeenth National Congress.

RESOLUTIONS

The Death of the Queen-Empress

I. Resolved—(*a*) That this Congress desires to express its profound sorrow at the death of Her Majesty, Queen-Empress Victoria, and its sense of the irreparable loss which the Empire has sustained thereby. This Congress recalls with gratitude Her late Majesty's deep personal sympathy with the people of India, as evidenced by her gracious Proclamation and by various other measures and personal acts, conceived in the same spirit of anxious solicitude for the welfare of the people of India.

(*b*) That this Congress tenders its respectful homage to His Gracious Majesty King Edward VII, and under His Majesty's beneficent reign hopefully looks forward to the strengthening of free institutions, the expansion of popular rights, and the gradual but complete redemption of the promises contained in Her late Majesty's Proclamation.

(*c*) That this Congress desires to place on record its deep sense of regret at the great loss that the country has sustained by the untimely death of the Hon. Mr. Justice Ranade.

Work of the Congress

II. Resolved—(*a*) That the Congress is of opinion that it is essential for the success of its work, that there should be a Committee in London, acting in concert with it, and a weekly journal published in London, propagating its views, and this Congress resolves that its British Committee as at present constituted, and the journal *India* as published by it, be maintained and continued, and the cost be raised in accordance with the following scheme:

(*b*) That a circulation of 4,000 copies of *India* be secured by allocating 1,500 copies to Bengal, 700 copies to Madras, 200 copies to the N. W. Provinces, 50 copies to Oudh, 100 copies to the Panjab, 450 copies to Berar and the Central Provinces, and 1,000 copies to Bombay, the rate of yearly subscription being Rs. 8.

(*c*) That the following gentlemen be appointed Secretaries for the Circles against which their names appear, and be held responsible for the sums due for the copies of *India* assigned to their respective Circles: and the money be paid in advance in two half-yearly instalments.

BENGAL·

Mr. Surendranath Bannerji.
Mr. Bhupendranath Basu
Mr. Baikunthanath Sen

BOMBAY

Hon. Mr. P. M. Mehta.
Mr. D E Wacha
Hon. Mr. G. K Gokhale.

MADRAS

Hon Mr Srinivasa Rao.
Mr. Vijiaraghavachari
Mr. V Ryru Nambier
Mr. G Subramania Iyer

BERAR & THE CENTRAL PROVINCES

Mr R N. Mudholkar.

N W. PROVINCES AND OUDH:

Pandit M M Malaviya
Mr. Ganga Prasad Varma
Mr S. Sinha.
Mr. A Nundy

CAWNPORE

Mr Prithwinath Pandit.

PANJAB

Lala Harkishan Lal.

(*d*) That with a view to meet the balance required to defray the expenses of *India* and the British Committee a special delegation fee of Rs. 10 be paid by each delegate in addition to the usual fee now paid by him, with effect from 1902.

Poverty and Remedies therefor

III Resolved—(*a*) That the Congress once again desires to call the attention of the Government to the deplorable condition of the poorest classes in India, full forty millions of whom, according to high official authority, drag out a miserable existence, on the verge of starvation even in normal years, and this Congress recommends the following amongst other measures for the amelioration of their condition—

(2) That the Permanent Settlement be extended to those parts of the country where it does not exist; that restrictions be put on over-assessments in those parts of India where it may not be advisable to extend the Permanent Settlement at the present time, so as to leave the ryots sufficient to maintain themselves on, and that these Settlements of land revenue be guaranteed for longer periods than is the case at present.

(3) That Agricultural Banks be established and greater facilities be accorded for obtaining loans under the Agricultural Loans Act.

(4) That steps be taken to improve the Agriculture of the country and in connection with this. this Congress exhorts all landed proprietors in the country to pay greater attention to the agricultural needs of the country and adopt such measures as are in their power to meet them

(5) That the minimum income assessable under the Income-Tax Act be raised from Rs. 500 to Rs. 1,000.

(6) That the drain of the wealth of the country be stopped, at least in part, by the wider employment of the children of the soil in the Public Services.

VIII. Resolved—That this Congress deplores the recurrence of famine in a more or less acute form throughout India in recent years, and records its deliberate conviction that famines in India are mainly due (1) to the great poverty of the people brought on by the decline of all indigenous arts and industries and the drain of the wealth of the country which has gone on for years; and (2) to excessive taxation and over-assessment of land, consequent on a policy of extravagance followed by the Government both in the civil and military departments, which has so far impoverished the people that at the first touch of scarcity they are rendered helpless and must perish unless fed by the State or helped by private charity. In the opinion of this Congress the true remedy against the recurrence of famine lies in the adoption of a policy which would enforce economy, husband the resources of the State, improve the agriculture of the country, foster the revival and development of indigenous arts and manufactures, and help forward the introduction of new industries.

(*b*) That this Congress rejoices that a "Famine Union" has been formed in London with a branch in Liverpool, consisting of distinguished men from all parties, and this Congress desires to place on record its deep gratitude to the members of the Union for their sympathy with the famine-stricken sufferers in India, and the earnest and eminently practical way in which they have set themselves to the task.

Legal

IV. Resolved—That the Congress once again records its deliberate opinion that the separation of Judicial and Executive functions is necessary in the interests of righteous and efficient administration of justice; the Congress is supported in this opinion by high and distinguished authorities, intimately familiar with the administration of criminal justice in India, such as Lord Hobhouse, Sir Richard Garth, Sir William Markby, Sir James Jardine, Mr. Reynolds and others. This Congress understands that the question is now under the consideration of the Government of India; and having regard to the soundness of the principle involved, the unanimity of public sentiment on the subject, and above all to the numerous instances of failure of justice resulting from the combination of Judicial and Executive functions, this Congress appeals to the Government of India to introduce this much-needed reform, which has been too long delayed partly through the fear of loss of prestige and the weakening of the executive Government, but chiefly on the score of expense, which it is believed will not be heavy and which in any case ought not to be an insurmountable difficulty.

V. Resolved—That this Congress is strongly of opinion that the Judicial Committee of the Privy Council should be strengthened so far as appeals from India are concerned and this Congress respectfully ventures to suggest that Indian lawyers of eminence should be appointed as Lords of the Judicial Committee to participate in the determination of appeals from India.

South Africa

VI. Resolved—That this Congress sympathises with the British Indian settlers in South Africa in their struggle for existence, and respectfully draws the attention of His Excellency the Viceroy to the Anti-Indian legislation there, and trusts that while the question of the status of British Indians in the Transvaal and the Orange River Colonies is still under the consideration of the Rt. Hon. the Secretary of State for the Colonies, His Excellency will be graciously pleased to secure for the settlers a just and equitable adjustment thereof.

Public Service

VII. Resolved—That this Congress notices with satisfaction that the question of Police Reform is now under the consideration of the Government and that it is one of the twelve questions which His Exellency the Viceroy proposes to deal with during the term of his Viceroyalty. The Congress repeats its conviction that no satisfactory reform could be effected unless the Police were re-organised on the following lines :

(1) That the higher ranks of the Police should be recruited more largely than at present from among educated Natives of India as by statute defined, who, being conversant with the language and habits, thoughts, and life of their subordinates, would be in a position to exercise a more effective control over their subordinates than is exercised at present.

(2) That the pay and prospects of the subordinate ranks of the Police should be substantially improved so as to render the Service more attractive to the educated community. This Congress is of opinion that the wider employment of educated Indians in the subordinate ranks of the Police upon higher pay and with better prospects can alone contribute to the efficiency and integrity of the Police.

(3) That the competitive examination held in England for the recruitment of the provincial branches of the Police Service, should be thrown open to natives of India, instead of being confined to candidates of British birth.

IX. Resolved—That the Congress once again records its deep regret that the labours of the Public Service Commission have not produced the results which were anticipated, and this Congress repeats its conviction that no satisfactory solution of the question is possible unless effect is given to the Resolution of the House of Commons of the 2nd of June, 1893, in favour of holding the examinations for the Indian Civil Service simultaneously in England and India.

That, in this connection, this Congress desires to express its profound disappointment at the policy of the Government in respect of the wider employment of Natives of India in the higher offices of the Minor Civil Services, such as the Police, the Customs, the Telegraph, the Forest, the Survey, the Opium, as involving their practical exclusion from these offices, and as being opposed to the terms of the Queen's Proclamation and the recommendations of the Public Service Commission; and this Congress prays that the Government will be pleased to take early steps to remedy the injustice done to the claims of the people of this country.

XIV. Resolved—That this Congress is of opinion that in the interests of the public, the medical service, and the profession, as well as in the cause of economical administration, it is necessary (1) that there should be only one Military Medical Service with two branches—one for the European Army and the other for the Native Troops worked on identical lines; and (2) that the Civil Medical Service of the country should be reconstituted as a distinct and independent Medical Service wholly detached from its present military connection and recruited from the profession of medicine in India and elsewhere, due regard being had to the utilisation of indigenous talent.

That this Congress further affirms that the status and claims of Civil Assistant Surgeons and Hospital Assistants require a thorough and open enquiry with a view to redressing long-standing anomalies and consequent grievances.

Military

X. Resolved—That inasmuch as large bodies of British troops have, with perfect safety and without imperilling the peace of the country, been withdrawn for service outside the statutory limits of British India, this Congress is of opinion that the Indian tax-payer should be granted some relief out of the British Exchequer towards the cost of maintaining in India the present strength of the European Army:—the claims of financial justice to India demand the transfer of the cost of a portion of British troops from the Indian to the British Exchequer.

XI. Resolved—That this Congress desires to express its appreciation of the action of the Government in forming a Cadet Corps consisting of the representatives of Indian Princes and Noblemen, and regards it as the first instalment of a policy which will culminate in the establishment of Military Colleges (as recommended by the Duke of Connaught) at which Natives of India may be educated and trained for a military career, as commissioned and non-commissioned officers in the Indian Army.

Education

XII. Resolved—That this Congress notices with great satisfaction that the subject of Education in all its divisions is receiving the earnest and careful attention of His Excellency the Viceroy, and this Congress trusts that in constituting the proposed Education Commission, His Excellency will be pleased to give adequate representation to Indian interests by appointing a sufficient number of Indian gentlemen to be members of the Commission.

Assam Labour

XIII. Resolved—That this Congress while thanking the Government of India for its benevolent intentions, regrets that immediate effect has not been given to the proposal made by the Government itself to enhance the coolies' wages in Assam, although such a course was strongly insisted upon by the Chief Commissioner, and was imperatively demanded by the plainest considerations of justice to the coolies; and this Congress is further of opinion that the time has come when the Government should redeem its pledge to do away with all penal legislation for labour in Assam.

Agriculture

XV. Resolved—(*a*) That in view of the fact that it is agriculture alone that enables the vast masses of people in the various provinces of India to maintain themselves, and in view of the excessive cost of British rule, this Congress is of opinion that the Government should be pleased to bestow its first and undivided attention upon the department of agriculture, and adopt all those measures for its improvement and development which have made America, Russia, Holland, Belgium and several other countries so successful in that direction.

(*b*) That this Congress begs to draw the special attention of the Government to the recommendations of Dr. Voelsker, who was sent out to India in 1889 to enquire into the condition of Indian agriculture, and prays that early effect may be given to the same.

(*c*) That this Congress further prays that the Government would be pleased to establish a large number of experimental farms all over the country, as well as scholarships to enable Indian students to proceed to foreign countries for the purpose of learning the methods of improving and developing agricultural resources which are in vogue in those countries.

Committee on Industries

XVI. Resolved—(*a*) That the following gentleman do form a Committee to report to the Congress next year whether it is desirable to adopt the following resolutions with or without amendments and alterations :

Mr. B. G. Tilak.
Mr. Madan Mohan Malaviya.
Mr. Bhupendranath Basu.
Mr. J Choudhuri.
Mr. B. Pathak.
Mr. Ranade.
Mr. Ganga Prasad Varma.
Mr. Umar Buksh.
Mr. Harkishan Lal.

(*b*) That in the opinion of this Congress much of the present state of economic depression of the country is owing to want of knowledge of the methods of production and distribution which prevail in foreign countries, and that it behoves our countrymen to adopt means to bring advanced knowledge and exact information within the reach of the people.

(*c*) That one of the most important economic questions that require solution at our hands is the organisation of Capital and Credit in villages, towns, provinces, and the country. This Congress invites the attention of its countrymen to make sustained and extensive efforts to organise capital and remove one of the many difficulties in the way of improvement of our economic conditions.

Finance

XVII. Resolved—That this Congress reaffirms its protest against the Currency Legislation of 1893, in which was artificially enhanced the value of the rupee by over 30 per cent, which indirectly enhances all taxation to that extent, and which, whilst giving the Government large surpluses from year to year owing to this heavy indirect taxation—and that too in times of unexampled distress brought about by famines—affects most detrimentally the wealth-producing institutions of the country, *viz.*, agriculture, plantation, and manufacture. That it is further of opinion that the above-mentioned legislation has alarmingly diminished the power of the peasantry to withstand the attacks of natural calamities, and that the most deplorable consequences may be anticipated to follow from it in course of time.

Mining Industry

XVIII. Resolved—That this Congress notices with satisfaction the rapid progress of the mining industry of India, and in consideration of the fact that the mineral resources of this country are vast and the facilities for acquiring a thorough knowledge of mining engineering in this country are almost nothing, and in view of the fact that the tendency of recent legislation on mining, namely Act VII of 1901, is, that all Indian mines must be kept under the supervision of mining experts, this Congress is of opinion that a Government College of Mining Engineering be established in some suitable place in India after the model of the Royal School of Mines of England, and the Mining Colleges of Japan and the Continent.

XIX. Resolved—(I) That this Congress concurs with previous Congresses in strongly advocating—

(*a*) The raising of the minimum income assessable under the Income-Tax from Rs. 500 to Rs. 1,000. [1900 (*a*) to (*d*)].

(II) That this Congress, concurring with previous Congresses, records its protest—[1900, (*a*) and (*b*)].

(III) That this Congress, concurring with previous Congresses expresses its opinion—

(*a*) That the system of Technical Education now in vogue is inadequate and unsatisfactory, and prays, that having regard to the poverty of the people, the decline of indigenous industries and the necessity of reviving them, as also of introducing new industries, the Government will be pleased to introduce a more elaborate and efficient scheme of technical instruction and set apart more funds for its successful working. [1900, (*a*) and (*b*)].

(*d*) That the action of the Forest Department under the rules framed by the different Provincial Governments prejudicially affects the inhabitants of the rural parts of the country by subjecting them to the annoyance and oppression of Forest subordinates in various ways: and that it is necessary that these rules should be amended so as to remedy the grievances of the people in the matter.

Formal

XX. Resolved—That this Congress re-appoints Mr A.O. Hume, C.B., to be General Secretary, and Mr D. E. Wacha to be Joint-General Secretary, for the ensuing year.

XXI. Resolved—That the Eighteenth Indian National Congress do assemble after Christmas, 1902, on such day and place in the Bombay Presidency as may be later determined upon.

CHAPTER XVIII

THE National Congress, meeting at Ahmedabad, in the Bombay Presidency, on December 23rd, 24th and 26th, 1902, began its work on an earlier date than ever before, in consequence of the Coronation Darbar of the King-Emperor, Edward VII, held on January 1st, 1903, in the Imperial City of Delhi. For the second time an Industrial Conference was held in connection with the Congress, and it was opened on December 15th by H. H. the Gaekwar of Baroda, always devoted to the welfare of India. There were 471 delegates present, of whom no less than 287 came from the Ahmedabad Circle. They were distributed as follows :

Bombay and Sindh	418
Madras	12
Berar, C. P. and Hyderabad	16
United Provinces of Agra and Oudh (formerly N. W. P. and Oudh)	5
Bengal	20
Panjab	0
	471

The Chairman of the Reception Committee, Dewan Bahadur Ambalal Desai, welcomed the Congress to the capital of Guzerat; Guzerat was an industrial and commercial region, and the two terrible famines through which it had just passed had aroused it to seek the reason of such horrors; nearly 25 lakhs of people had died out of a population of less than a crore. They saw one reason in the huge amount of wealth drained out of the country. Many of their people emigrated, and they found that their inferior political position hampered their trade, and that it was therefore necessary to agitate politically. They had many cotton mills, forced to pay the unjust excise duty, and they felt that commercial pursuits without political action were suicidal. Agriculturalists suffered under inelastic revenue conditions, and all asked: "Why are we so poor?" Hence Guzerat turned to the Congress.

The Hon. Mr. P. M. Mehta proposed, the Hon. Mr. S. Nair seconded, and Mr. S. N. Pandit supported the election of the Hon. Mr. Surendranath Bannerji, and he took the Chair amid immense applause.

After alluding to the Congresses previously held in the Bombay Presidency, Mr. Bannerji alluded to the Coronation Darbar to be held at Delhi, and remarked that the 1858 Darbar at Allahabad, that of 1877 at Delhi, that of 1887 at Calcutta, had been marked by declarations of wider liberty to Indians; surely the Darbar of Delhi in 1893 would grant some substantial concession to the people.

The question, however, which concerned them most was the Report of the Universities Commission, which had aroused "alarm, deep, genuine, and all-pervading, felt by all sections of the educated community throughout India, by Hindus and Musalmans alike". "The noblest gift which British rule has conferred upon India is the boon of high education. It lies at the root of all our progress." The President then analysed the Report, pointing out its deficiencies, and condemned the new policy towards the Universities; he, however, put much trust in the Viceroy, who would, he hoped, remedy the points protested against by the Indian community. He then turned to the economic problem, and asked whether it was true, as Mr. Digby asserted, "that India has undergone steady material retrogression under British rule," and declared that behind the economic policy lay the entire problem of Indian administration. A Commission of Enquiry should be issued to settle the question: "Is the country getting poorer day by day?" An enquiry had been held in 1880-81, under Lord Ripon, and a second during the Viceroyalty of Lord Dufferin, but the results of those enquiries were withheld from publication:

Now these enquiries either prove or disprove the allegation that the country is becoming poorer under British rule. If they disprove the allegation, nothing would be more natural than that the rulers of India should hasten, by their publication, to refute a charge which involves so serious a reflexion upon their own administration. If these enquiries do not disprove the charge, nothing would be more natural than that they should keep back the evidence of which they are in possession. To withhold from the public the results of these enquiries and the evidence on which they are based, raises a presumption against the roseate view of the economic situation. The presumption is strengthened by the steady refusal to hold an open enquiry, and it assumes more or less the complexion of definite proof, in view of facts the significance of which cannot be overlooked.

The President then dealt with the terrible recurrence of famines, growing worse as time went on. If such famines happened in Europe, what would be said? "But India is beyond the pale of civilised opinion, and her calamities do not apparently stir the conscience of even the great Nation into whose hands her destinies have been consigned by an all-wise Providence." "Destitution is the root-cause of Indian famines." The people, if they were normally prosperous, could buy food when crops failed:

> But they are absolutely resourceless, sunk in the deepest depths of poverty, living from hand to mouth, often starving upon one meal a day, and they die in their thousands and hundreds of thousands upon the first stress of scarcity, and as the situation deepens they die in their millions and tens of millions, despite the efforts of a benevolent Government to save them.

The President urged that the Government should seek to check the growing destitution by:

> (1) The revival of our old industries and the creation of new ones; (2) the moderate assessment of the land-tax; (3) the remission of taxes which press heavily upon the poor; (4) the stoppage of the drain, and the adoption of the necessary administrative measures in that behalf.

The President then considered Industries, Land-Revenue Assessment, Remission of Taxation, the Drain, and other subjects, and urged that if the people had a voice in the expenditure, economy would result. He said in conclusion:

The triumphs of liberty are not won in a day. Liberty is a jealous Goddess, exacting in her worship and claiming from her votaries prolonged and assiduous devotion. Read history. Learn from it the inestimable lesson of patience and fortitude and the self-sacrificing devotion which a constitutional struggle for constitutional liberty involves. Need I impress these lessons upon a people who have presented to the world the noblest of these virtues? Every page of Indian history is resplendent with the touch of self-abnegation. . . . The responsibilities of the present, the hopes of the future, the glories of the past ought all to inspire us with the noblest enthusiasm to serve our country. Is there a land more worthy of service and sacrifice? Where is a land more interesting, more venerated in antiquity, more rich in historic traditions, in the wealth of religious, ethical and spiritual conceptions, which have left an enduring impress on the civilisation of mankind? India is the cradle of two religions. It is the Holy Land of the East. Here knowledge first lit her torch. Here, in the morning of the world, the Vaidic Rishis sang those hymns which represent the first yearnings of infant humanity towards the divine ideal. Here was developed a literature and language which still excite the admiration of mankind —a philosophy which pondered deep over the problems of life and evolved solutions which satisfied the highest yearnings of the loftiest minds. Here, man first essayed to solve the mystery of life, and the solution, wrapped in the rich colours of the poetic imagination and clothed with the deeper significance of a higher spiritual idea, bids fair, thanks to the genius of the greatest Hindu scientist of the age, to be accepted by the world of science. From our shores went forth those missionaries who, fired with apostolic fervour, traversed the wilds of Asia and established the ascendency of that faith which is the law and the religion of the Nations of the far East. Japan is our spiritual pupil. China and Siberia and the islands of the Eastern Archipelago turn with reverend eyes to the land where was born the Prophet of their faith. Our pupils have out-distanced us; and here are we, hesitating, doubting, calculating, casting up moral results to satisfy ourselves that our gains have been commensurate to our sacrifices. Such indeed has not been the royal road to political enfranchisement. The triumphs of liberty have not thus been won. Japan is an object-lesson which thrusts itself upon the view. Read her history; note her wonderful self-sacrifice, her marvellous power of adaptation, her patience, her fortitude, her indomitable energy and persistency, and let the most ancient of Eastern nations derive inspiration and guidance from the youngest, which has solved the riddle of Asiatic life and has harmonised the conservatism of the East with the progressive forces of the West. . . . . Despotic rule represents a stage of transition, the period of which should not be unnecessarily prolonged. But transition must give place to permanence. All signs point to the conclusion that the period of reconstruction has now arrived. The forces are there; the materials are there; they lie in shapeless masses. Where is the man of genius who will communicate to them the vital spark and transform them into a new and a higher and a grander organisation, suited to our present requirements and fraught with the hopes of a higher life for us and a nobler era for British rule in India? The statesmanship of Mr. Chamberlain, bent upon the work of reconstruction and consolidation in South Africa, will pale before the splendour of this crowning achievement. We plead for the permanence of British rule in India. We plead for the gradual reconstruction of that ancient and venerated system which has given to India law and order and the elements of stable peace. We plead for justice and liberty, for equal rights and enlarged privileges, for our participation in the citizenship of the Empire; and I am sure we do not plead in vain; for the Empire, thus reconstituted and reorganised, will be stronger, nobler, richer far in the love, the gratitude, the enthusiastic devotion of a happy and contented people, rejoicing in their indissoluble union with England, and glorying in the rich promises of steady and uninterrupted progress towards their high destinies, under the protection and guidance of that great people, to whom in the counsels of Providence has been assigned the high mission and the consecrated task of disseminating among the nations of the earth, the great, the priceless, the inestimable blessing of constitutional liberty.

When the cheers evoked by the eloquent speaker had subsided, the Subjects' Committee was approved, and the Congress adjourned.

On the second day, Resolution I, offering homage to the new King-Emperor, and Resolution II expressing sorrow for the passing away of Mr. R. M. Sayani and Mr. Ranga Naidu, were put from the Chair and carried.

Mr. G. Subramania Iyer moved Resolution III, drawing attention to the poverty of the people, and suggesting remedies. He pointed out that there had been a time when the population of India was so flourishing that foreign visitors envied it, and when arts and industries flourished. The East India Company had deliberately sacrificed India to the commercial advantage of England, had discouraged industries and encouraged agriculture, so that India might produce raw materials for the manufacturing industries of England; that policy had destroyed Indian industries, and Government, which had inherited it, should reverse it. What is being done? The gold mines of Kolar are worked by European capital. They yield 20 crores of rupees worth of gold annually, which is taken to another country. When in another 20 or 30 years all the gold is dug up and carried away, what will remain to the people of Mysore but stones? Government ought to protect Indian wealth, not allow it to be carried away. The splendid gift of Mr. Tata for scientific research and training had not been utilised. Further, the capital existing in the country in small amounts should be gathered into banks and used for industrial and agricultural purposes.

The Hon. Mr. Perraju seconded, and dealt with revenue assessment, the ever fruitful source of poverty. Mr. M. K. Patel laid stress on the money-famine in India, and contrasted the beginning of the 18th century, when India exported to England more than a million and a half sterling worth of piece goods, and the end of the nineteenth, when she imported 28 millions worth of manufactured cotton. It is this destruction of her manufactures which has impoverished India. "The Indian Railways and Free Trade have between them ruined our artisan classes." The Hon. Mr. Goculdas K. Parekh also supported, showing how the heavy assessments threw land out of cultivation. The Resolution was carried.

The fourth Resolution thanked the Famine Union in England for its effort to secure an enquiry into the economic condition of typical villages, and endorsed its request. It was moved by Mr. G. Raghava Iyer, and he showed the need for enquiry, in order that an accurate judgment might be formed on reliable facts and figures. He also supported the publication of previous enquiries. Mr. Peter Paul Pillai seconded, pointing to the frequency of famines in India. Mr. V. R. Natu and Mr. Bhaishankar Nanabhai supported, and the Resolution was carried.

Resolution V appealed to Government to secure better treatment for the Indian settlers in South Africa, and Mr. D. P. Thakore gave a graphic picture from his own experience of the constant and intolerable insults to which all Indians were subjected: "the Indian is hated and insulted both in public and private life". Mr. Krishna Iyer seconded, and three Muhammadan residents in South Africa, Messrs. Ghulam Hasan Muakhan, Haji Suleiman and Haji Sumar, having supported, the Resolution was carried.

The sixth Resolution protested against the Currency Legislation of 1893, and was moved by Mr. Vithaldas Damodardas Thakarsey, seconded by Mr. G. Subramania Iyer, and supported by Mr. Sorabji Karaka, who said it had literally killed the mill-industry; it carried.

Mr. N. M. Samarth moved Resolution VI, condemning the new burden imposed on India by increasing the pay of the British soldier, and the suggestion of an increase in the British troops quartered in India; the Resolution was seconded by the Hon. Mr. Srinivasa Rao, supported by Mr. Baikunthanath Sen and carried. Whereon the Congress adjourned.

On meeting for the third day, the Congress found itself face to face with sixteen Resolutions, and the annual race began. Mr. J. Choudhuri moved

Resolution VIII, thanking the Government of India for its circular letter staying action on some of the proposals of the Universities Commission, and raising special objections to the most reactionary of the proposals made. He pointed out that education was regarded in quite a wrong spirit, and protested against the obstacles placed in the way of poor students. Mr. D. G. Padhya remarked that the Universities Commission had been composed of Government representatives more largely than any other, and the whole scheme aimed at the narrowing of the sphere of education in India, and the curtailment of the rights of the Fellows and Faculties had for object the gaining of an official majority in the Senate and Syndicate. Mr. N. B. Ranade drew attention to the injury proposed to be done to the teaching of History, Political Economy and Science, subjects vitally necessary for Indians. Mr. G. M. Tripathi condemned the interference of the State in education, forcing on men who should be gurus, giving freely of their knowledge, the banya system of so much education for so much coin. The poor boys here were more eager for learning than the rich. The Resolution was carried.

Mr. G. Subramania Iyer proposed Resolution IX, asking the Government to support Mr. Tata's Research Institute, and recommending the establishment of similar institutions in different parts of the country. It was seconded by Mr. Krishna Nair, supported by Pandit Madan Mohan Malaviya, and carried.

In Resolution X, the inadequacy of the representation of experienced Indians on the Police Commission was regretted, Mr. S. Sinha pointing out that there were only two Indians outside officials, and of these one was a C. I. E. always seeking to please Englishmen, and the other a Maharaja as yet untried. Unless the grievances of the people touching the Police were placed before the Commission, there would be no reforms. Mr. Krishnamachari seconded, Messrs. N. N. Mitra, M. K. Padhya, S. B. Bhagvat supported, and the Resolution was carried.

Resolution XI was on the separation of the Judicial and Executive Functions, patiently moved by Dewan Bahadur Amhalal Sakerlal, seconded by Mr. Ambikacharan Mozumdar—who said they could not afford to be tired of discussing it as long as the administration tired them by practising it—supported by Mr. Rustam K. R. Cama and Pandit K. P. Kavyabisharad, and carried.

Resolution XII passed a well-merited condemnation on the system of appointing to District Judgeships Covenanted Civilians with little knowledge of law. Mr. Jogendranath Mukerji moved it, giving instances of judicial ignorance. Mr. A. M. Advani, in seconding, added to these, and Mr. Hardeoram Nanabhai Haridas complained that logic and facts were useless before the Assistant Civilian Judge; they had to rely on adjectives. The Resolution was passed.

Once more the reduction of the Salt Tax, that most iniquitous burden on the poor, came up as Resolution XIII, and was moved by Mr. C. Y. Chintamani in a terse and forcible speech, and seconded by Mr. J. V. Desai, who remarked that, in Guzerat, salt cost Re. 0-1-3 per maund, and the duty on that quantity was Rs. 2-8-0. The Resolution was carried. It is astounding that these things should be pointed out so constantly, and no redress should be gained. In a Self-Governed country such grievances would be removed.

Once more the Congress, in Resolution XIV, voiced the grievances of Indians in the Public Services. Mr. G. K. Setna moved, Mr. Abdul Kasim seconded, and it was carried.

Railways were the next example of the exclusion of Indians in the higher branches of the Service, and Mr. Govindrao Apaji Patil moved Resolution XV, remarking that there would be less loss on the railways were it not for the high cost of Europeans, and caustically remarking that Indians might become Assistant Collectors and Collectors, but not Traffic Inspectors. Mr. S. M. Patel seconded, and Mr. M. K. Patel having supported it, the Resolution passed.

Mr. D. E. Wacha brought up the standing grievance of the Excise Duty on Indian-produced cloth in Resolution XVI, saying that he would refer the Congress to his previous speeches on the subject. Seth Mangaldas Girdhardas seconded, and the Resolution was carried.

Resolution XVII, on the Medical Services, asking for the reforms previously demanded, was moved by Dr. A. Erulker Salomon. Dr. Joseph Benjamin seconded, and it was carried.

Mr. N. C. Kelkar moved the eighteenth Resolution, urging Government to throw open the higher grades of the Army to Indians and to establish Military Colleges. These requests had long been lurking in the seclusion of the Omnibus, but now came out once more on their own feet, were seconded by Dr. Joseph Benjamin, and carried.

The President then drove in the Omnibus (No. XIX), and Resolution XX on the British Committee and *India*, and both were carried. Thanks were offered to Sir William Wedderburn and the British Committee in Resolution XXI, and the reappointment of Messrs. A. O. Hume and D. E. Wacha as Secretaries was put from the Chair as Resolution XXII. He also put Resolution XXIII, fixing the Nineteenth Congress at Madras.

A vote of thanks was moved to the President, who acknowledged it in a felicitous and eloquent speech, specially appealing to the younger generation to take up the work of the Congress, and so bring about the realisation of the Nation's hopes.

With his inspiring words ringing in their hearts, the Eighteenth National Congress dissolved.

RESOLUTIONS

Homage to the Crown

I. Resolved—That the Congress begs to tender its respectful homage to His Most Gracious Majesty, King-Emperor Edward VII, on the occasion of the approaching Coronation Darbar to be held at Delhi on 1st January, 1903, and humbly trusts that His Majesty's reign will be an era of peace, prosperity and contentment throughout the Empire and will be marked by the gradual but complete redemption of the pledges contained in Her late Majesty's Proclamation and re-affirmed in His Majesty's gracious Message to the Indian people.

Regret of the Congress

II. Resolved—That this Congress wishes to place on record its great regret at the death of Mr. R. M. Sayani, one of its past Presidents, and of Mr. P. Rangia Naidu, who did valuable services in various capacities to the interests of this country.

Poverty and Remedies

III. Resolved—That the Congress earnestly desires to draw the attention of the Government of India to the great poverty of the Indian people, which, in the opinion of the Congress, is mainly due to the decline of indigenous arts and manufactures, to the drain of the wealth of the country which has gone on for years, and to excessive taxation and over-assessment of land which have so far impoverished the people that at the first touch of scarcity large numbers are forced to throw themselves on State help. And the Congress recommends the following amongst other remedial measures :

(1) That practical steps in the shape of State encouragement be taken for the development and revival of indigenous arts and manufactures and for the introduction of new industries.

(2) That Government be pleased to establish technical schools and colleges at important centres throughout the country.

(3) That the Permanent Settlement be extended to such parts of the country as are now ripe for it, in accordance with the conditions laid down in the Secretary of State for India's Despatches of 1862 and 1867 on the subject ; and that reduction of, and judicial restriction on, over-assessments be imposed in those parts of India where Government may still deem it inadvisable to extend the Permanent Settlement.

(4) That the drain of the wealth of the country be stopped, at least in part, by a much wider employment of the children of the soil in the higher branches of the Public Service.

(5) That Agricultural Banks be established for the better organisation of rural credit and for enabling solvent agriculturists to obtain loans on comparatively easy terms.

Enquiry into Economic Condition

IV. Resolved—That this Congress desires to place on record its grateful appreciation of the efforts which the Famine Union in England is making to secure a detailed enquiry into the economic condition of a number of typical villages in India. In the opinion of this Congress, such an enquiry will in no way prove inquisitorial as apprehended, but will be of the highest value for a proper understanding of the true condition of the Indian Ryot, and will clear up many of the misapprehensions which prevail at present on the subject and which interfere with the adoption of the right remedial measures. That the Congress is of opinion that such an enquiry, following the two severe famines, is highly expedient, inasmuch as it will enable the Government to be placed in possession of economic data of great utility for purposes of comparison. And the Congress hopes that the Secretary of State for India will be pleased to reconsider his decision in the matter.

In this connection the Congress would respectfully urge that the Government of India should be pleased to publish the results of the official enquiries which have been held in the past on this subject, notably the enquiry instituted during the time of Lord Dufferin, extracts from which, alone, have been published.

South Africa

V. Resolved—That this Congress once more urges upon the attention of the Government of India the serious grievances of Indian Settlers in South Africa, and regrets to observe that the Imperialistic spirit of the British Colonies, instead of mitigating the anti-Indian legislation, threatens to impose further disabilities and hardships on His Majesty's loyal Indian subjects there. In view of the admitted loyalty of these Indian settlers and the help rendered by them during the late war, as well as the invaluable help rendered by India to the British Empire at a most critical time, the Congress fervently prays that the Government of India will be pleased to take the necessary practical steps to secure a just, equitable, and liberal treatment of the Indian settlers in South Africa.

In this connection the Congress notes with satisfaction the assurance recently given by the Secretary of State for India, to a deputation that interviewed him on the subject, that early steps are contemplated to relax the stringency of the restrictions at present enforced against the Indian settlers in the territories lately conquered from the Boer Government.

Monetary

VI. Resolved—That this Congress strongly reiterates its protest against the currency legislation of 1893, which has artificially enhanced the value of the rupee by more than thirty per cent, which indirectly enhances all taxation to that extent, and which, whilst giving the Government large surpluses from year to year, affects most injuriously the interests of the agriculturists and other producers of this country.

Military

VII. Resolved—That this Congress enters its most emphatic protest against the fresh permanent burden of £786,000 per annum, which the increase made during the course of the year in the pay of the British soldier would impose on the revenues of India, and views with alarm the recent announcement of the Secretary of State for India, hinting at a possible increase in the near future of the strength of the British troops in the country. In view of the fact that during the last three years large bodies of British troops have with perfect safety been withdrawn for service in South Africa and China, the proposal to increase the strength of the existing British garrison manifestly involves a grievous injustice to the Indian tax-payer, and the Congress earnestly trusts that the proposal will either be abandoned, or else be carried out at the cost of the British Exchequer, which, in fairness should bear, not only the cost of any additional British troops that may be employed, but also a reasonable proportion of the cost of the existing garrison.

XVIII. Resolved—That while thanking the Government of Lord Curzon for opening a military career to a few scions of noble families by the creation of the Cadet Corps, this Congress urges that in view of the loyalty and splendid services rendered by the Indian troops to the British Empire in the late Chinese war and in other wars, Government will be pleased to throw open to the Natives of India higher posts in the Military Services and to establish Military Colleges at which Indians may be trained for a military career as commissioned and non-commissioned officers in the Indian Army.

Education

VIII. Resolved—That this Congress desires to tender its respectful thanks to the Government of India for the Circular Letter recently addressed by them to Local Governments on the subject of the Universities Commission Report—so far as it relates to the proposals for the abolition of Second Grade Colleges and Law classes—which has partially allayed the apprehension in the public mind that due weight might not be attached to public opinion in taking action on the recommendations of the Commission. That this Congress views with the gravest alarm many of the Commission's recommendations, the acceptance of which will, in its opinion, reverse the policy steadily pursued during the last half of a century by the British Government in the matter of higher education, by checking its spread and restricting its scope, and by virtually destroying such limited independence as the Universities at present enjoy.

That in particular the Congress objects most strongly to the following recommendations of the Commission:

(*a*) The abolition of all existing Second Grade Colleges except such as may be raised to the status of a First Grade College, and the prohibition of the affiliation of new Second Grade Colleges.

(*b*) The fixing by the Syndicate of minimum rates of fees for different colleges.

(*c*) The introduction of a rigidly uniform course of studies throughout the country, irrespective of the lines on which the different Universities have so far progressed.

(*d*) The monopoly of legal instruction by Central Law Colleges, one for each Province or Presidency.

(*e*) The virtual licensing of all secondary education by making the existence of all private schools dependent upon their recognition by the Director of Public Instruction.

(*f*) And the officialisation of the Senate and the Syndicate and the practical conversion of the University into a Department of Government.

IX. Resolved—That this Congress considers that the Institute of Research which the private beneficence of Mr. Tata proposes to establish, should receive adequate support from Government, and the Congress is strongly of opinion that similar institutions should be founded in different parts of the country.

Police

X. Resolved—That this Congress records its sense of regret at the inadequacy of the representation on the Police Commission of Indian gentlemen of experience on the subject, and at the limited scope of reference as indicated in the Resolution of the Government of India, and in the opening speech of the President.

This Congress further records its deliberate conviction that the Police will not be rendered efficient unless the following among other reforms are carried out:

(1) That men of adequate qualification are secured for superior offices in the Police Service.

(2) That educated Indians are largely employed in the superior offices in the Police Service.

(3) That the position and prospects of investigating and inspecting officers are improved, so as to attract educated men to the Service.

(4) That the District officer, who is District Magistrate and head of the Police, is relieved of his judicial powers and of all control over the Magistracy.

Legal

XI. Resolved—That this Congress, concurring with previous Congresses, appeals to the Government of India and the Secretary of State, to take early practical steps for the purpose of carrying out the separation of Judicial and Executive functions in the administration of criminal justice, the desirability of which has been frequently admitted on part of Government. In this connection, the Congress regrets to notice that the trend of recent legislation is not only to deprive the Judiciary of its salutary and wholesome power of check and restraint over the Executive, but to invest the Executive with greater and uncontrolled powers.

Civilian Judges

XII. Resolved—That this Congress is of opinion that the present system, under which a very large proportion of the District Judgeships, Joint-Judgeships and Assistant-Judgeships, are filled by Covenanted Civilians without any special legal training and without adequate guarantee of the knowledge of law necessary for the satisfactory discharge of the very important and responsible judicial duties entrusted to them, is injurious to the best interests of efficient judicial administration in the Muffasal, and that it is urgently necessary to devise means to ensure a higher standard of efficiency in the administration of law, by securing the services of trained lawyers for the said posts.

Salt Tax

XIII. Resolved—That the Congress strongly protests against the present high duty on salt, and in view of the fact that the prevalence and spread of many diseases are now traced to the insufficiency of salt consumed by the Indian masses, and that the accounts of the Government of India have now been showing large surpluses year after year, the Congress urges that Government should be pleased to reduce the Salt Tax by at least the amount of its enhancement in 1888.

Public Service

XIV. Resolved—That the Congress, concurring with previous Congresses, again records its deep regret that the labours of the Public Service Commission have practically proved void of any good results to the people of this country, and is strongly of opinion that no satisfactory solution of the question is possible, unless effect is given to the Resolution of the House of Commons of 2nd of June, 1893, in favour of holding the Competitive Examination for the Indian Civil Services, *i.e.*, Civil, Medical, Police, Engineering, Telegraph, Forest, and Accounts, both in England and in India. That the policy of the Government of India in regard to the minor Civil Services practically excludes the Natives of India from higher appointments in them, and is therefore opposed not only to the recommendations of the Public Service Commission but to Royal and Viceregal pledges given to the Indian people from time to time.

XV. Resolved That, in view of the fact that the Railway Administration forms an important branch of the P.W. Department of the Government, the Congress notices with regret that the Natives of India are practically excluded from higher appointments such as Traffic Inspectors, District Traffic Superintendents, Accountants, etc., on State, as well as on guaranteed Railways, and appointments of Rs. 200 and above are, as a rule, bestowed only on Europeans. That the exclusive employment of Europeans in the higher posts results in heavy working charges, the burden of which falls on the Indian tax-payers at whose expense the State railways have been constructed, and who have to bear the ultimate liability of deficits on the Guaranteed Railways. The Congress therefore deems it its duty to urge in the interests of economical railway administration, as also for the purpose of removing legitimate grievance, that Government will be pleased to direct the employment of qualified Indians in the higher branches of the Railway Service.

Cotton Excise Duty

XVI. Resolved—That having regard to the fact, that while cloth manufactured by means of power looms in this country in no way competes with the piece goods imported from Lancashire, the imposition of the Excise duty of 3½ per cent thereon, apart from its tendency to arrest the free growth of the weaving industry, continues to operate as a great injustice to the manufacturers, and imposes serious hardship on the masses of the people who consume the coarser indigenous products. This Congress earnestly prays that the Government will be pleased to take the matter into favourable consideration and repeal the duty at an early date.

Medical

XVII. Resolved—That this Congress is of opinion that in the interests of the Public, the medical science and the profession, as well as to secure economy of administration it is necessary—

(1) That there should be only one Military Medical Service, with two branches—one for the European Army and the other for the Native troops, graduates of the Indian Colleges being employed to the latter with greater economy and efficiency to the State; and

(2) That the Civil Medical Service of the country should be reconstituted as a distinct and independent Medical Service, wholly detached from its present military connection, and recruited from the open profession of medicine in India and elsewhere, due regard being had to the utilisation of indigenous talent. That this Congress, while gratefully acknowledging what has been done to improve the position and prospects of the subordinate Medical Service, is of opinion that the grievances of assistant surgeons and hospital

assistants, compared with members of similar standing in other departments of the Public Service, require thorough redress.

Confirmation of Previous Resolutions

XIX. Resolved—That this Congress concurs with previous Congresses in strongly advocating: (*a*) That with a view• that the Judicial Committee of the Privy Council may enjoy greater respect and confidence it is necessary to reconstitute it on a broader basis and that the time is ripe for the appointment of Indian lawyers of eminence as Lords of the Judicial Committee, to participate in the decision of Indian appeals.

(*b*) That the grant of exchange compensation allowance to the non-domiciled European and Eurasian employees of Government, should be discontinued.

(*c*) That the rules under the Arms Act should be modified so as to make them equally applicable to all residents in, or visitors to, India, without distinction of creed, caste, or colour, to ensure the liberal concession of licences wherever wild animals habitually destroy human life, cattle, or crops, and to make all licences granted under the revised rules, of lifelong tenure, revocable only on proof of misuse, and valid throughout the Provincial jurisdiction in which they are issued.

(*d*) That a widespread system of Volunteering, such as obtains in Great Britain, should be introduced amongst the people of India.

(*e*) That a High Court of Judicature be established in the Panjab.

(*f*) That, inasmuch as the scheme of reorganisation of the Education Service is calculated to exclude Natives of India, including those who have been educated in England, from the superior grade of the Educational Service to which they have hitherto been admitted, the scheme should be recast, so as to afford facilities for the admission of Indian graduates to the superior grade of the Educational Service.

(*g*) That the act of the Secretary of State of India in fixing the limit at two posts beyond which Natives of India cannot compete in the Cooper's Hill College is opposed to the plain words of Act I of 1833, and to Her late Majesty's gracious Proclamation.

(*h*) That the system of trial by jury should be extended to the districts and offences to which at present it does not apply, and that the verdicts of juries should be final.

(*i*) That it is desirable that the Criminal Procedure Code should be so amended as to confer upon accused persons who are Natives of India, the right of claiming in trials by jury before the

High Court, and in trials with the aid of assessors, that not less than half the number of jurors, or of the assessors, shall be Natives of India.

(*j*) That the existing rules, framed by the different Provincial Governments in the matter of the Forest Department are opposed to the Resolution of the Government of India made in 1894, with the object of enunciating the objects of forest conservancy and that an amendment of the rales, in conformity with the above resolution, is urgently called for in the interests of the inhabitants of rural India.

Congress Work

XX. Resolved—That the Congress is of opinion that it is essential for the success of its work that there should be a Committee in London acting in concert with it, and a weekly journal published in London propagating its views, and this Congress resolves that its British Committee, as at present constituted, and the Journal *India* as published by it, be maintained and continued, and the cost be raised in accordance with the following scheme:

That a circulation of 4,000 copies of *India* be secured by allotting 1,500 copies to Bengal, 700 copies to Madras, 200 copies to the N. W. Provinces, 50 copies to Oudh, 100 copies to the Panjab, 450 copies to Berar and the Central Provinces and 1,000 copies to Bombay; the rate of yearly subscription being Rs. 8.

That the following gentlemen be appointed Secretaries for the circles against which their names appear, and to be held responsible for the sums due for the copies of *India* assigned to their respective circles, and the money be paid in advance in two half-yearly instalments:

BENGAL:

Mr. Surendranath Bannerji.
Mr. Bhupendranath Basu.
Mr. Baikunthanath Sen.

BOMBAY:

Hon. Mr. P. N. Mehta.
Mr. D. E. Wacha.
Hon. Mr. G. K. Gokhale.

MADRAS:

Hon. Mr. Srinivasa Rao.
Mr. Vijiaraghavachari.
Mr. V. Ryru Nambier.
Mr. G. Subramania Iyer.

BERAR & THE CENTRAL PROVINCES

Mr. R. N. Mudholkar.

N. W. PROVINCES & OUDH:

Pandit M. M. Malaviya.
Mr. Ganga Prasad Varma.
Mr. S. Sinha.
Mr. A. Nundy.

CAWNPORE:

Mr. Prithwinath Pandit.

PANJAB:

Lala Harkishan Lal.

That with a view to meet the balance required to defray the expenses of *India* and the British Committee, a special delegation fee of Rs. 10 be paid by each delegate, in addition to the usual fee now paid by him, with effect from 1902.

Thanks of Congress

XXI. Resolved—That this Congress tenders its most grateful thanks to Sir W. Wedderburn, and the other members of the British Congress Committee, for the services rendered by them to India during the present year. [And see IV, VIII, and XVIII.]

Formal

XXII. Resolved—That this Congress re-appoints Mr. A. O. Hume, C.B., to be General Secretary, and Mr. D. E. Wacha, to be Joint-General Secretary, for the ensuing year.

XXIII. Resolved—That the Nineteenth Indian National Congress do assemble after Christmas, 1903, at Madras.

CHAPTER XIX

Once more the National Congress met at Madras, in a large pandal holding nearly 6,000 persons, erected in Spring Gardens, Teynampet. The Nineteenth Congress held its sittings on December 28th, 29th and 30th, 1903, and the third Industrial Exhibition was held with it, and was opened, on December 26th, by the young Maharaja of Mysore. The delegates numbered 538, distributed as follows:

Madras	383
C. P., Berar, Secunderabad and Hyderabad...	18
Bengal and Assam	47
Bombay	76
U. P.	8
Panjab	5
Burma	1
	538

We see Burma represented for the first time, but Sindh sent no one this year.

The President of the Reception Committee, Nawab Syed Muhammad Sahab Bahadur, welcomed the delegates, and after announcing the loss the Congress had sustained in the passing away of Lord Stanley of Alderley and the Raja of Ramnad, he urged that Muhammadans and Hindus had common political interests, and must cordially unite for the good of their common country. Some deprecated political agitation, but "politics is the science of social happiness," and in concerning themselves with political work, they were following the example shown them by the British Nation. Impatience of criticism was a common official fault; none the less was it their duty to point out what was needed, and the people must be emancipated from their intellectual and political thraldom. He recalled Lord Ripon's work in laying the foundations of Self-Government, and suggested that a statue should be erected to him.

The Hon. Mr. P. M. Pherozeshah Mehta proposed Mr. Lal Mohan Ghose for formal election as President, paying tribute to his great gifts; Mr. Eardley Norton seconded, the Hon. Pandit M. M. Malaviya supported, and the election was confirmed with deafening cheers.

The President said that though for some years he had not taken an active part in politics, he had been thinking over political problems and had followed with unabated interest the course of events, and perhaps the views thus slowly matured might be more valuable than if he had been speaking all the time. Lord Curzon saw the hand of Providence in the extension of British rule, and said everyone would admit it was for his good. But Providence was too often appealed to both by the governing classes and by the leaders of the masses.

Coming to the case of our own country, although there is not a man amongst us who is not sincerely loyal to the British Government, yet, claiming the undoubted right of British subjects to criticise the acts of the Government, may we not respectfully ask our rulers—and in this connection I make no distinction between the different English political parties—may we not ask whether we are to believe that the policy which many years ago killed our indigenous industries, which even only the other day and under a Liberal administration unblushingly imposed excise duties on our cotton manufactures, which steadily drains our National resources to the extent of something like 20 millions sterling per annum, and which, by imposing heavy burdens on our agricultural population, increases the frequency and intensity of our famines to an extent unknown in former times—are we to believe that the various administrative acts which have led to those results were directly inspired by a beneficent Providence?

The speaker then turned to the very sore subject of Lord Curzon's Delhi Darbar, with its extravagance, the treatment accorded to the Indian Princes—" subjected to a humiliation they had never before known under the British Government"—and the Indian visitors, who returned "with bitter memories of the different treatment received by Indians and Europeans". The growing feeling of dislike to Lord Curzon was intensified by the anger aroused by that unfortunate pageant. The President said:

We are not a Self-Governing Nation. We are not able, like the English people, to change one administration for another by our votes in the polling booths. We have to depend entirely upon the justice of the British Parliament; for unfortunately it is only too true that, as time advances, our Indian bureaucracy, instead of coming into line with popular ideas, seems to grow more and more unsympathetic. Do you think that any administration in England, or France, or the United States, would have ventured to waste vast sums of money on an empty pageant, when Famine and Pestilence were stalking over the land, and the Angel of Death was flapping his wings almost within hearing of the light-hearted revellers? Gentlemen: a year has now rolled by since the great political pageant was held at Delhi against the almost unanimous protests of all our public and representative men both in the press and on the platform. On what ground did they protest? They protested, not because they were wanting in loyalty to the Sovereign, whose coronation it was intended to celebrate, but because they felt that if His Majesty's Ministers had done their duty, and had laid before him an unvarnished story of his famine-stricken subjects in India, His Majesty, with his characteristic sympathy for suffering humanity, would himself have been the first to forbid his representatives in this country to offer a pompous pageant to a starving population. However, our protests were disregarded, and the great tamasha was celebrated, with that utter recklessness of expense which you may always expect when men, no matter how highly placed, were dealing with other people's money, and were practically accountable to no one for their acts.

We are all familiar with the financial jugglery which, by distributing the expenses under various and sometimes under the most unexpected headings, makes it so difficult for ordinary men to find out the total cost of such a pageant. Still, whether you estimate that cost by a few lakhs more or less, it cannot be denied that if even half of the vast sum spent in connection with the Delhi Darbar had been made over for the purposes of famine relief, it might have been the means of saving millions of men, women and children from death by starvation.

The President then discussed the questions of Free Trade and Fair Trade as affecting India, dealing caustically with Mr. Chamberlain's programme, and proceeded to analyse the causes of the increasing poverty of India. Anarchy had been put an end to, but "after all it makes but little difference whether millions of lives are lost on account of war and anarchy, or whether the same result is brought about by famine and starvation". The President next referred to the burden of military extravagance, the maladministration of justice, and the physical ill-treatment of Indians by Europeans and the impossibility of obtaining redress, saying that he was hopeless of obtaining justice where crimes of violence on Indians were committed, unless Parliament would take up the question. *Lettres de cachet* were abolished in France in 1789, but were introduced here in 1818, and were not a dead letter. Lately, they had had a Sedition Act, and this year Lord Curzon had thrown a bombshell into their midst with the Official Secrets Bill, which relieved the prosecution of giving evidence to prove the guilt of the accused, and left the accused to prove his innocence—a reversal of all civilised jurisprudence. The Universities Bill, officialising the centres of learning, came in for trenchant criticism. Then followed a plea for compulsory free primary education, a condemnation of the "retrograde and reactionary Madras Municipal Bill," a pressing of the claims of Indian industries, ending on a glad note of some sympathy shown in England, and the rapprochement between Hindus and Muhammadans.

Thus ended one of the ablest speeches uttered by a President of the National Congress. Readers will do well to note the increasing signs of the coming danger, forced on by Lord Curzon's policy against all the warnings of the Congress. Coercion created unrest; a feeling of general insecurity arose, owing to the odious system of the *lettres de cachet*, under which no man's liberty was safe; men began to despair of improvement, and secret societies were formed. The voice of Congress was disregarded, and its leaders lived under the shadow of arrest. Each year showed growing anger and increasing resentment again the Curzonian rule.

The Congress adjourned for the day, after the Subjects Committee had been approved.

The second day began with the expression of sorrow for the loss sustained by India in the deaths of Lord Stanley of Alderley, Mr. W. S. Caine and the Raja of Ramnad, the Resolution being put from the Chair and passed in silence, standing.

Resolution II, moved by Mr. D. E. Wacha, dealt with the deeply felt wrong of the exclusion of Indians from the higher grades of the Public Service.[1] He

[1] *Survey Department of the Government of India.*—132 Officers salaries from Rs. 300—2,000, only two are Indians on Rs. 300.

Government Telegraph Department.—52 Appointments of Rs. 500 and more, only one Indian.

Indo-British Telegraph.—13 Officers above Rs. 500 salary, not an Indian.

Mint Department.—6 Officers above Rs. 500 pay, not an Indian.

Post Office.—Last year only 1 Indian among the 10 men drawing more than Rs. 500, who was a member of the Civil Service.

Geological Survey.—2 out of the Officers drawing salaries above Rs. 500, an Indian.

Botanical Survey.—None.

In the Foreign Department.—Out of 22 such Officers only 3 are Indians.

Miscellaneous.—There are 22 Officers, of whom there is not a single Indian.

Financial Department.—14 are Indians out of 59 who draw more than Rs. 500 pay.

gave some striking statistics of the various Services, showing how foreigners everywhere kept out Indians, leaving the badly paid offices to the people of the country and monopolising the well-paid, a condition intolerable to the self-respect of the people of any civilised land. "We do not grumble at Europeans having a share of the loaves and fishes, but we do grumble and make it a strong grievance that the bigger and most numerous loaves are deliberately allowed, in defiance of charters, pledges and proclamations, to go to the whites, and smaller and fewer loaves to the blacks."

It is not open to us to suspect the motives of Government, but Government may do so, and castigate us to any extent, as Lord Curzon tried the other day to castigate Mr. Gokhale most wrongfully. It comes to this, that what is mild or inoffensive in the captain becomes choleric and blasphemous in the soldier. So on our part it is blasphemous to attribute motives to Government, but it is not blasphemous for the Government to rave and rant and castigate us to its heart's content. . . . Throughout the whole career of the British Indian Government, not from to-day but from the days of the East India Company, there is this tradition to give a promise to the ear and to break it to the heart, and they faithfully and loyally follow that tradition. In the case of the Public Service Commission, we have found, to our bitter cost and experience, that the same traditional policy has been carried on. Promises were most profusely given to us; a Commission was appointed amid a great flourish; finality was to be given to our legitimate aspirations and our just grievances were to be fairly redressed. It has been so for the last half century. When the practice comes, we find ourselves exactly in the same situation as we were in before the Commission was appointed. This is the tale of our grievances, of our legitimate and fair grievances.

So spake Mr. Wacha in 1903. We have now, in 1915, the Report of another Public Service Commission awaiting publication. The same old story will be repeated. How can it be otherwise when the Commissions are predominantly Anglo-Indian, and when the power and place of the Anglo-Indian depend on his asserting that the Indian is unfit?

Mr. G. Subramania Iyer seconded, showing how Indians had been more and more ousted from positions of influence, giving them no opportunity of developing their powers; where was an Indian Marquis of Ito, or Count Okuma? Europeans were paid large salaries while they gained experience here, and then were given high positions abroad to utilise outside India the experience gained in India.

> They say there should be an irreducible minimum of Englishmen. What does it mean? Slavery is engrained in the skin of our body. If we in our own country are not to be trusted with responsible appointments, if our own Government will not take us into their confidence and place us in offices which will give us responsibility in the administration of our own country, what is it, Gentlemen, but slavery? We are hewers of wood and drawers of water, and nothing more. .... In every department there is a regular retrograde policy being pursued. On the one hand, they go on making promises and giving us hopes and assurances, and on the other hand they go on adopting a backward policy. After a hundred years we have not advanced by one inch, but have gone a long distance backward from where we were.

Mr. Surendranath Bannerji spoke to the resolution, declaring that "we have lost ground, but our cause is one of righteousness and justice," and he felt "confident that the day will come which will mark the ultimate triumph of equality, and of equal principles even in this unhappy land of ours". Messrs. Peary Lal Ghose and Abdul Kasim followed and the Resolution was carried.

Resolution III on the rise of land assessment, was entrusted to Mr. L. A. Govindaraghava Iyer, who pointed out that Permanent Settlement, and where that could not be, longer terms of Settlement would better the condition of the ryot. He showed that more was demanded than the ryot could pay, whereas he ought to be so taxed that he could save in good seasons and so face bad ones. In 1852, the Secretary of State sent out a statesmanlike despatch on Permanent Settlement, but the present-day Government was not politically wise.

The Hon. Mr. Parekh seconded, and the Resolution was supported by Messrs. Peter Paul Pillai, N. Srinivasavarada Chariar, S. Subramaniam, P. R. Sundara Iyer, and carried.

Resolution IV, on South Africa, was moved by Dr. U. L. Desai and seconded by Mr. S. K. Nair. Mr. C. F. Sievwright brought a petition from Indians in Australia, asking to be rescued from the degrading restrictions placed on them. Mr. V. G. Vasudeva Pillai, the first delegate from the newly created Burmese Congress centre, supported, and the Resolution being carried, the Congress rose for the day.

On the third day, Resolution V, on the Universities Bill, was moved by Mr. Surendranath Bannerji, who pointed out that Government was taking control of Higher Education, as it had limited the civil freedom of their Corporations. The new-fangled Imperialism was darkening the prospects of human freedom. Lord Curzon's " name would go down to posterity indissolubly linked with a reactionary and retrograde measure which has been condemned by the unanimous opinion of educated India ". They were told that a body of educational experts met in 1901, and advised changes. They " met in secret, deliberated in secret, resolved in secret, and, I presume, dispersed in secret ". The Senates were against the Bill, and they had public opinion behind them. The Universities were made Government Departments. Private institutions would be checked, private colleges destroyed, the educational area restricted. The Bill made a revolution.

Mr. Ambalal Saharlal Desai seconded the Resolution, and it was supported by Messrs. Hariprasad Chatterji, R. N. Mudholkar, G. Subramania Iyer, Pandit Madan Mohan Malaviya and Mr. Choudhuri, all voicing protest and condemnation. The Resolution passed, and the results of that reactionary and mischievous measure have fully justified the protest of the Congress.

Resolution VI, on the Official Secrets Bill, was viewed with equal disapproval, as " against the interests of the public, dangerous to individual liberty and retrograde in policy ". Mr. Bishan Narayan Dhar moved the Resolution, saying that no measure of equal importance had ever been so universally condemned. In the Imperial Council Nawab Syed Muhammad and Mr. Gokhale had earned the country's gratitude by denouncing it, "an odious, nay, iniquitous measure," of which "it is impossible to speak with patience or moderation". "Lord Curzon is astonished that this should be described as Russianising the administration. I am astonished that anyone should be so imperfectly informed regarding the Russian Government, as to think that it has got anything in its purely civil laws so arbitrary and so disastrous to the civil liberties of the people as Lord Curzon's Bill, if passed, would be in this country." Running over the changes in the law made by the Bill, the speaker described them as "monstrous, odious and iniquitous in the extreme," and as "calculated to shake our confidence in the justice and fairness of our rulers". "The policy of coercion and distrust is a mistaken, a suicidal policy." Mr. Murlidhar seconded the Resolution, and it was supported by the Hon. Mr. G. Srinivasa Rao and carried. The Bill was, in due course, added to the Coercion Legislation.

Resolution VII, on military expenditure, moved by Mr. N. M. Samarth, seconded by Mr. V. Krishnaswami Iyer, supported by Messrs. Charu Chandra Ghose and Mr. G. A. Natesan, and carried, need not detain us, as it is one of our hardy annuals; but Resolution VIII was a novelty, for it thanked the Government for reducing the Salt Tax and raising the assessable minimum of Income-Tax, thus granting two requests of the Congress: the Resolution was moved by Mr. C. Y. Chintamani, seconded by Miss Balgarnie, and carried.

Mr. J. Choudhuri moved Resolution IX, on the Partition of Bengal, that high-handed measure which nearly led to a revolution, and was annulled by the King-Emperor in 1911. Indians were trying to weld Indian nationalities into a Nation, but Lord Curzon would "divide us and rule". Mr. G. Raghava Rao seconded, and then Mr. V. Krishnaswami Iyer moved an amendment to omit the later part of the Resolution which dealt with a proposal to separate certain districts from Madras. The Amendment was lost and the Resolution carried.

Resolution X condemned the Madras Municipal Bill, said by the Hon. Mr. Krishna Nair, the mover, to be "highly reactionary, retrograde and revolutionary": the Corporation consisted of 24 men elected by the people and 8 nominated; the Bill reduced the popular representatives to 16, and gave 8 to associations wholly or mainly composed of Europeans. A similar Bill had ruined the Calcutta Municipality. Mr. A. C. Parthasarathi Naidu seconded, saying that the Bill reduced Local Self-Government to a sham, and carefully analysing the provisions of the Bill. The Resolution was carried.

Resolution XI, recommending the election of certain gentlemen to Parliament, and Resolution XII thanking the Government for the Co-operative Credit Societies Bill were carried. The President then put from the Chair the Omnibus, Resolution XIII, and Resolution XIV, the usual vote of thanks to Sir William Wedderburn and the British Committee. Mr. Surendranath Bannerji moved the re-appointment of Mr. A. O. Hume and Mr. D. E. Wacha, adding the Hon. Mr. G. K. Gokhale as a second Joint General Secretary. Resolution XV fixed the next sitting of the Congress at Bombay, and with the usual votes of thanks the Nineteenth Session of the National Congress found its ending.

RESOLUTIONS

Sorrow of Congress

I. Resolved—That this Congress desires to put on record its sense of the deep and irreparable loss sustained by India by the deaths of Lord Stanley of Alderley and Mr. W. S. Caine, the memory of whose services the people of India will always cherish with gratitude.

That this Congress also wishes to place on record its deep regret at the death of the Raja of Ramnad, who has always been a distinguished benefactor of the Congress.

Public Service

II. (*a*) That this Congress, concurring with previous Congresses, again records its deep regret that the labours of the Public Service Commission have practically proved void of any good result to the people of this country; that while the recommendations of the Commission did not secure full justice to the claims of the people of the country to larger and more extended employment in the higher grades of the Public Service, the Government have not even carried them out in their integrity, and have not extended the principle of appointing Indians to new appointments since created from time to time, and in Special Departments such as the Salt, Opium, Medical and Police Departments, the Survey Department of the Government of India, the Government Telegraph Department, the Indo-British Telegraph Department, the Mint Department, the Postal Department, and the Foreign Department.

(*b*) That in the opinion of this Congress the recent policy of the heads of departments and of the authorities responsible for Railway administrations proscribing the appointment of Indians in the Public and the Railway Services is a grave violation of the pledges and assurances given by the Government.

(*c*) That in the opinion of this Congress in order to arrest the economic drain that is caused by the present system of appointments by the Government, to secure to the people of the country the invaluable benefit of the experience and knowledge which a training in the Public Service affords, and to introduce economy in the administration, a policy of free employment of the Natives of the soil in all branches of the Service, is imperatively demanded.

Permanent Settlement

III. That this Congress views with alarm the tendency to increase the land revenue assessment every time there is a revision, and declares its firm conviction that the policy of raising the assessment so frequently and so heavily is increasing the poverty of the agricultural population of this country and rendering them still further unfit to withstand the periodical visitations of bad seasons and famines than they are now. This Congress, therefore, prays that the Permanent Settlement be extended to such parts of the country as are now ripe for it, as laid down in the Secretary of State for India's despatches of 1862 and 1867 on the subject; and that Settlements for longer periods be made, and judicial and legislative restrictions on over-assessments be imposed, in those parts of India where Government may still deem it inadvisable to extend the Permanent Settlement.

Indians in the Colonies

IV. That this Congress views with grave concern and regret the hard lot of His Majesty's Indian subjects living in British Colonies in South Africa, Australia and elsewhere, the great hardships and disabilities to which they are subjected by the Colonial Governments, and the consequent degradation of their status and rights as subjects of the King, and protests against the treatment of Indians by the Colonies as backward and uncivilised races; and it prays that, in view of the great part the Indian settlers have played in the development of the Colonies and the economic advantages which have resulted both to India and to the Colonies from their emigration to and stay in the latter, the Government of India will be pleased to ensure to them all the rights and privileges of British citizenship in common with the European subjects of His Majesty, by enforcing, if necessary, such measures as will render it impossible for the Colonies to secure Indian immigrants except on fair, equitable and honourable terms; and that in view to the great importance of the principle of equal treatment to all His Majesty's subjects, His Majesty's Government should devise adequate measures to ensure that position to Indian emigrants in all the British Colonies.

Education

V. That this Congress, while welcoming any wisely considered scheme for the reform of the educational policy of

Government, is of opinion that the Universities Bill, if passed into law, will have, as recommended in the report of the Universities Commission, the effect of restricting the area of education and completely destroying the independence of the Universities upon which largely depend their efficiency and usefulness, and of turning them practically into departments of Government.

That this Congress is of opinion that the provisions of the Bill will not remove the shortcomings of the present system of higher education but that provision for funds and improvement in the standard of teaching by the agency of a superior class of teachers are imperatively needed in the interests of higher education.

That this Congress prays for the following modifications:

(*a*) That each University should be dealt with by a separate Act.

(*b*) That in the case of the older Universities the number of ordinary Fellows should not be less than 200, of whom at least 80 should be elected by registered graduates and 20 by the members of the Faculties, and that, in the case of the Universities of Allahabad and of the Panjab, a similar provision should be made.

(*c*) That the ordinary Fellows should hold office as at present for life, but should be liable to disqualification for absence during a fixed period.

(*d*) That the provision of a statutory proportion for the heads of Colleges on the Syndicate be omitted.

(*e*) That all graduates of ten years' standing in a Faculty be declared eligible to vote.

(*f*) That the section making it obligatory upon Colleges which apply for affiliation or have been affiliated to provide for suitable residential quarters for students and professors and for the permanent maintenance of the Colleges be omitted.

(*g*) That as regards affiliation and disaffiliation the decision should, instead of being the direct act of Government as under the Bill, be as at present the act of the University, subject to the sanction of Government.

(*h*) That as regards the inspection of Colleges it should be conducted by persons specially appointed by the Syndicate, unconnected with the Government Educational Department or any aided or unaided College.

(*i*) That the power of making bye-laws and regulations should as at present be vested in the Senate, subject to the sanction of the Government.

Coercion

Official Secrets Bill

VI. That this Congress views with entire disapproval the Official Secrets Bill now before the Supreme Legislative Council inasmuch as it is uncalled for, against the interests of the public, dangerous to individual liberty and retrograde in policy, and prays that the Government of India may be pleased to confine its scope to the disclosure of Naval and Military secrets

Military

VII. (*a*) That this Congress reiterates its opinion that the scope of the measures, which have been undertaken from time to time for increasing the army in India, for armaments and fortifications with a view to the security of India, not against domestic enemies, or against the incursions of warlike peoples of adjoining countries, but to maintain the supremacy of British Power in the East, and on which millions of Indian money have been spent, reach far beyond the Indian limits in that the policy that has dictated these measures is an Imperial policy; and that, therefore, the Indian Army Charges, which not only include the cost of the native army but also that of the British forces amounting to about one-third of the whole British army which, forms the Imperial Garrison in India, are excessive and unjust, especially having regard to the fact that the Colonies which, are equally dependent upon and indebted to the mother-country for their protection, contribute little or nothing towards the Imperial military expenditure.

(*b*) That inasmuch as large bodies of British troops have with perfect safety and without imperilling the peace of the country, been withdrawn for Service outside the statutory limits of India, this Congress is of opinion, that the Indian tax-payers should be granted substantial relief out the British Exchequer towards the cost of maintaining in India the present strength of the European army.

(*c*) That this Congress protests most emphatically against the manner in which the Indian revenues have been charged with £786,300 per annum for the increased cost of the recruitment of the British army, in spite of the Viceroy of India and his Council having strongly condemned such a charge as being injurious to Indian interests, and as calculated to retard many urgent measures of domestic reform now under contemplation or in course of initiation.

(*d*) That this Congress reiterates its conviction that inasmuch as the army amalgamation of 1859 has all along been the cause of a considerable portion of the unjust aud excessive burden of Indian military expenditure, the time has come when steps should be taken to have that system wholly abolished.

Thanks of Congress

VIII. That this Congress tenders its thanks to the Government of India for the relief granted to the poorer classes of the country by the reduction of the Salt-Tax and by raising the assessable minimum for Income-Tax, and prays that the Government of India be pleased to make a futher reduction in the Salt-Tax.

XII. That this Congress tenders its thanks to the Government of India for the introduction of the Co-operative Credit Societies' Bill into the Viceregal Legislative Council, and trusts that the measure may be so enacted as to achieve the objects the Government has in view.

[And see XIV]

Partitions

IX. That this Congress views with deep concern the present policy of the Government of India in breaking up territorial divisions which have been of long standing and are closely united by ethnological, legislative, social and administrative relations, and deprecates the separation from Bengal of Dacca, Mymensingh, Chittagong Divisions and portions of Chota Nagpur Division, and also the separation of the District of Ganjam and the agency tracts of the Ganjam and Vizagapatam Districts from the Madras Presidency.

Madras Municipality

X. That this Congress is of opinion that the policy of the Madras Municipal Bill, now before the local Legislative Council, is not in consonance with the principles of local Self-Government in India laid down in the time of Lord Ripon, and it desires to point out that the interests of the rate-payers of the City would not be adequately served by a lesser representation than that of twenty-four members. That, if the elective franchise is to be given to associations and institutions, it is of opinion that the institutions and associations should be such as possess a direct interest in the administration of the Municipal affairs of the City, and that the number assigned to them should be very limited. That the Madras Railway and the Port Trust are not bodies to whom such representation should be assigned, but that it should be extended only, if at all, to bodies like the Chamber of Commerce, the Traders Association, and the University, by giving each of them the power of returning one member.

Parliamentary Representation

XI. That this Congress desires to accord its most cordial support to the candidature of Mr. Dadabhai Naoroji for North Lambeth, Mr. W. C. Bannerji for Walthamstow, Sir Henry Cotton for Nottingham, and Sir John Jardine for Roxburghshire, and appeals to the electors of these constituencies that, in the interests of the people of India, they will be pleased to return them to Parliament, so that they may not only loyally serve them, but represent in some manner the people of a country which, though a part of the British Empire, has no direct representative in the British Parliament.

Confirmation of Previous Resolutions

XIII. That this Congress concurs with previous Congresses in strongly advocating: [1902 (*a*)—(*j*)].

(*k*) That the necessity is urgent for the complete separation of Executive and Judicial functions, so that in no case shall the two functions be combined in the same officer;

(*l*) That the simultaneous holding in India and in England of all examinations for all Civil branches of the Public Service in India, at present held only in India, should be conceded;

(*m*) That an enquiry into the economic condition of the Indian ryot, as urged by the members of the Famine Union in England, in their appeal to the Secretary of State for India, should be instituted.

Thanks of Congress and Congress Work

XIV. That this Congress desires to convey to Sir William Wedderburn and the other members of the British Committee its most grateful thanks for their disinterested services in the cause of our political advancement.

And that a sum of Rs. 10,500 be assigned for the expenses of the British Committee, and that the several Congress circles do contribute the amount allotted to each.

That the following gentlemen be appointed Secretaries for the Circles against which their names appear and be responsible for the sums due by the respective Circles, and that the money be paid in advance in two half-yearly instalments:

BENGAL:	BOMBAY:
Babu Surendranath Bannerji.	Hon. Mr. P. M. Mehta.
Babu Baikunthanath Sen.	Mr. D. E. Wacha.
Hon. Mr. Bhupendranath Basu.	Hon. Mr. G. K. Gokhale.

MADRAS

Hon. Mr. G. Srinivasa Rao.
Hon. Mr. Vasudeva Iyengar.
Mr. V. Ryru Nambier.
Mr. G. Raghava Rao, Berhampur.

BERAR AND THE CENTRAL PROVINCES:

Mr. R. N. Mudholkar.

N. W. PROVINCES & OUDH:

Hon. Pandit M. M. Malaviya.
Mr. Ganga Prasad Varma.
Mr. S. Sinha.

CAWNPORE:

Mr. Prithwinath Pandit.

PANJAB

Mr. Harkishan Lal.

Formal

XV. That this Congress re-appoints Mr. A. O. Hume, C. B., to be General Secretary, and Mr. D. E. Wacha to be Joint General Secretary, and appoints the Hon. Mr. G. K. Gokhale as additional Joint General Secretary for the ensuing year.

XVI. That the Twentieth Indian National Congress do assemble, on such day after Christmas Day, 1904, as may be later determined upon, at Bombay.

CHAPTER XX

THE Twentieth National Congress, closing the second decade of this powerful organisation met in Bombay on the 26th, 27th and 28th of December, 1904, in a large Pavilion on the Crescent Site. The Congress met under the gloom created by Lord Curzon's policy, rightly characterised in the Official Report of the Congress as "repressive and re-actionary"; there had grown up a feeling

> of deep resentment. . . . when a series of repressive measures—both legislative and administrative—were forced by him on the country in the teeth of the fiercest opposition from the public. . . . Long before the Congress of last year met, it had come to be very generally recognised that whatever may be said in favour of Lord Curzon's administration, the educated classes of the country, at any rate, had in him no friend, and that their aspirations would receive at his hands not merely cold neglect, but actual repression. . . The situation made the Congress of 1904 one of unusual importance.

The gathering was the largest since 1895, 1010 delegates registering their names. They were divided as follows:

Bombay (548), Sindh (44), Kathiawar (26)	618
C. P., Berar, Secunderabad and Hyderabad	104
Madras	104
Bengal (99) and Assam (3)	102
U. P.	54
Panjab	28
	1,010

The Hon. Sir Pherozeshah M. Mehta, who had received the K.C.I.E., the Chairman of the Reception Committee, after asking a choir of ladies to sing the Congress Anthem, warmly welcomed the delegates, and congratulated them on the presence of Sir William Wedderburn and Mr. Samuel Smith, M.P. The Congress voiced once in each year the public opinion of the country, and the surest testimony to its value was the very policy of reaction and retrogression which it provoked. The possession of India was "a blessing to England if administered in the spirit of righteousness, a curse if in the seductive spirit of worldliness". On the whole, England had chosen wisely and well, but while many grievances—which take more than a page of the Report to enumerate—continue, there would be "two parties about England in India". Political agitation there would be.

> The only question is whether we should suppress and bottle up our feelings, and hopes, and aspirations and our grievances in the innermost recesses of our own hearts, in the secret conclaves of our own brethren, or deal with them in the free light of open day. The former course would be preferred by the prophets of despair. We, gentlemen, prefer the latter, because we have faith in the ultimate wisdom, beneficence and righteousness of the English people.

Mr. Surendranath Bannerji proposed Sir Henry Cotton as President, focussing in a few eloquent sentences his great services to India. Mr. C. Sankaran Nair seconded, Pandit Madan Mohan Malaviya supported, and Sir Henry Cotton took the Chair amid loud cheers. A gift for the Congress of Rs. 4,000, collected by *The Gujarati*, and a handsome silver salver were presented to Sir Henry by its Editor, Mr. I. S. Desai.

After thanking the Congress for the honour done to him, the President said that the Congress was "the voice and brain of the country," that the work of educating the country was carried on by other agencies, and that the function of the Congress was "to give united and authoritative expression to views on which there is already a consensus of opinion in the country ". The public opinion of England needed to be moved.

> Internal agitation in Ireland was the necessary stepping-stone of reform, but by itself it accomplished little; it was only when Irish agitation forced itself upon English Liberal statesmen, and was supplemented by a powerful phalanx of opinion in England, that any concessions were allowed to the sister island. And so it is in the case of India. The remedy for both countries is the same.

After noting the growth of National feeling, Sir Henry Cotton quoted with approval the words of the Hon. Mountstuart Elphinstone, words which some officials in Bombay would certainly consider seditious now, except perhaps if they knew it was a quotation: he spoke in the freer days of 1850:

> I conceive that the administration of all the departments of a great country by a small number of foreign visitors, in a state of isolation produced by a difference in religion, ideas and manners, which cuts them off from all intimate communion with the people, can never be contemplated as a permanent state of things. I conceive, also, that the progress of education among the Natives renders such a scheme impracticable, even if it were otherwise free from objection.

"Every thinking man," added Sir Henry, "must know that these words are true," and the connection between India and England would last. Lord Cromer had said the same, and had declared that the Government must adapt their system to the changes taking place in educated Indians, "if they do not wish to see it shattered by forces which they have themselves called into being, but which they have failed to guide and control". Sir Henry bade his hearers avoid depression, and not to submit with resignation to the policy of the Government, and he held up, as the ideal, India taking rank as a Nation among the Nations of the East. Autonomy is the key-note of England's true relations with her Colonies, and "the key-note also of India's destiny". "Complete autonomous States which are federated together and attached by common motives and self-interest to a central Power," such was "the tendency of Empire". The ideal for India was "a Federation of free and separate States, the United States of India".

The President then dealt with the economic problem, condemned the "drain" and the exploitation of the country by English capital, urged the substitution of Indian for European officials, and the reconstitution of the Indian Civil Service, with other special reforms, protested against the Partition of Bengal, and the treatment of Indians in the Transvaal, and concluded by bidding his hearers labour with hope and courage in the cause they had embraced.

The strong and outspoken discourse aroused the greatest enthusiasm, and was closed amid vociferous applause. The Subjects Committee was approved, and the Congress adjourned.

On the second day, Mr. Surendranath Bannerji brought forward Resolution I, which dealt with Indians in the Public Service, saying that it was extraordinary that, 150 years after the birth of British rule in India, they should be obliged to protest against a policy "inconsistent with the great traditions of the British rule in the East, and with the honour of the British name in this country". The promises made had only been eluded until now, but by Lord Curzon's Resolution of 24th May, 1904, they were openly repudiated, and, by a bitter irony, on the birthday of the Queen, whose Proclamation was set at naught. "Under the new policy, race is the test of qualification. Under the old policy, merit was the test of qualification." The reactionary policy of Lord Curzon tore up the Proclamation of the Queen.

Lord Curzon from his place in the Imperial Council (I am quoting the substance of what he said), declared that by our environments, our heritage and our up-bringing we are unequal to the responsibilities of a high office under the British rule. I venture to say, Sir, that never was a deeper affront offered to the people of India by the representative of the Sovereign. It is bad enough to repudiate the Proclamation, but it is adding insult to injury to cast a slur upon the people of this country. In your name and on your behalf, Gentlemen, I desire to record my most emphatic protest against this assumption of our racial inferiority. Are Asiatics inferior to Europeans? Let Japan answer. Are Indians inferior to Europeans? Let Lord George Hamilton answer, and

Lord George Hamilton is not a friend of the people of this country. Gentlemen, are we the representatives of an inferior race, we, who are the descendants of those who, in the modern world, while all Europe was steeped in superstition and ignorance, held aloft the torch of civilisation? Are we the representatives of an inferior race, from whose shores, forsooth, went forth those missionaries who have converted two-thirds of the human race into moral superiority?

Mr. Bannerji then gave a number of figures, showing the percentage of Indians in the Service, pointed to the fact that they had 14 per cent of employments carrying Rs. 1,000 and upwards, and 17 per cent of employments carrying Rs. 500 and upwards. "Only 14 or 17 per cent of the higher appointments fall to our lot, although the country is ours, the money is ours, and the bulk of the population is ours." Then followed some stinging comparisons between the position of Asiatics in India and in other countries under white rule, and he once more appealed to the pledges given in the Proclamation of the Queen.

Mr. G. Subramania Iyer seconded, and remarked that Indians were worse off than in 1833, and that while Lord Lytton broke the Queen's promises by what he called "subterfuges," Lord Curzon openly said that the principles and policy of British rule in India were not those laid down in the Queen's Proclamation of 1858. We must hold to the liberties and privileges conferred on us by statute also, and "hold them in such a way that not only the English Nation but the whole world will say that India should be free".

In supporting the Resolution, the Hon. Mr. Krishnan Nair gave a historical sketch, showing how much more equal was the treatment of Indians in the past than under Lord Curzon. Mr. G. Abdul Kasim spoke on Muhammadan agreement. Mr. Hussain Badruddin Tyabji brought more statistics proving the injustice under which Indians suffered. The Resolution was then carried.

Resolution II urged the claims of Higher Education and thanked the Government for aiding Primary Education. India needed manual training and the establishment of Polytechnics. Mr. D. G. Padhya moved it, and Mr. R. P. Karandikar seconded, pointing to the splendid example set by Japan. He pressed the need for agricultural training, and quoted Mr. Arthur Balfour's speech on Ireland, pointing out how "one by one each of her nascent industries was either strangled at its birth or handed over gagged and bound to the jealous custody of the rival interest in England, until at last every fountain of wealth was hermetically sealed," so that the whole Nation threw itself on the land. Dr. H. S. Gour followed, condemning the Universities Act, which sealed up the portals of knowledge "with golden locks which would open only to golden keys". Lord Curzon would "make education the privilege of the rich and not the birthright of the poor". We are told that an oriental people should be governed in the oriental way, but if so, oriental Kings gave education free.

Mr. C. Y. Chintamani said that Lord Curzon asked us to consider education apart from political and other questions, but that was impossible, for, as Mr. Morley had said, the questions of education "touch the moral life and death of Nations". Lord Curzon's educational measures were political, and he was swayed in them mainly by political considerations. A section of educated Indians was found inconvenient, and they were to be politely suppressed. The Government sent out circulars introducing the new policy by instalments while the public were discussing the Report and they believed it to be under consideration. The Senates, now the Act was passed, had been Europeanised and officialised, and under the word "efficiency" the Indian and non-official element was suppressed. Mr. G. A. Natesan complained of the "policy of distrust and retrogression," and gave figures to show that in five years 6,223 graduates had been produced, 1,242 a year out of a population of 300 millions! The Resolution was carried.

Resolution III, on the "deplorable poverty of the people" and suggesting remedies, was moved by Mr. R. N. Mudholkar, who compared the state of the people, "on the whole sound," with the necessaries and comforts of life, and exporting a large amount of merchandise, "when there was nothing but anarchy and misrule in this land," with the present poverty, where the highest figure, Lord Curzon's, was Rs 30 per head per year, or one and a half annas (1½d.) a day, out of which Rs. 3½ was paid in taxation. He showed how Indian manufactures had been killed by the East India Company and the Government by prohibitive duties, and the industrial population was forced on to the land, making agriculture the staple industry. He then dealt with land assessment, with the efforts to introduce the mill industries, and the action of Lord Salisbury, who "directed that steps should be taken to protect the British manufacturers against the competition of the Indian manufacturers". The result of the whole policy was the poverty of the Indian masses.

The Hon. Mr. L. A. Govindaraghava Iyer seconded the Resolution, dealing with the necessity for Permanent Settlement and for a judicial check on taxation of improvements made by the ryot. The Resolution was supported by the Hon. Mr. G. K. Parekh, Messrs. R. V. Mahajani, K. Natarajan, Maneckji K. Patel, and carried.

Resolution IV, in view of the alarming indebtedness of the peasantry, repeated the request of the previous Congress for an enquiry into the condition of a few typical villages. It was moved by the Hon. Mr. H. S. Dixit, seconded by the Hon. Mr. V. C. Desikachari, supported by Rai Parvatishankar Choudhuri, Dr. Joseph Benjamin, and carried.

Resolution V brought up once more the condition of Indians in the Colonies, and Messrs. Madanjit and Baroacha told the oft-repeated story of South African sufferings, from their own experiences, and Dr. Munji, from his experience as a Civil Surgeon in the Boer War, added his testimony. The carrying of the Resolution closed the second day's work.

On the third day, the President moved from the Chair Resolution VI, expressing the sorrow of the

Congress for the deaths of Mr. J. N. Tata and of that true friend of India, William Digby. He then called on Sir William Wedderburn to move an important Resolution (No. XV) out of its order, desiring that as a General Election was approaching in England a deputation should be sent from India to bring the claims of India before the electors and the candidates. He urged two special points as of primary importance : the revival of the old custom of an enquiry into the state of India every 20 years, and the placing of the salary of the Secretary of State for India on the British Estimates. Mr. B. G. Tilak seconded, and urged that an agitation must be made in England, for there the judges sit who would decide our case, and as the Government of India was impervious, they must reach the English people, and there should be a permanent political mission in England. Mr. S. Sinha, in supporting, laid stress upon the importance of the English becoming personally acquainted with Indians. The Resolution was carried.

Sir Balchandra Krishna moved the seventh Resolution, asking that the cost of the Secretary of State for India should be placed on the British Estimates. The Colonies had their Secretary and their office free ; India paid nearly 34 lakhs of rupees for hers. The Hon. Mr. G. Srinivasa Rao seconded, Mr. M. K. Padhya supported; he urged that the Secretary of State was responsible to no one—not to the Indian people who paid him, not to the House of Commons because it did not pay him. The Resolution was carried.

Resolution VIII dealt with the artificial surpluses, raised largely by the appreciation of the rupee, and urged reduction of taxation and the devotion of part of the accumulated funds to Education, Medical Relief, and the helping of Local and Municipal Boards. It was moved by Mr. G. K. Gokhale, who remarked on the extraordinary surpluses during the last six years, amounting to 30 crores of rupees, and asked how these arose. He showed that they arose from the value of the rupee being enhanced, so that raising the money wanted for the foreign charges in silver and paying in gold, the Indian Government saved some 5 crores of rupees a year. The high level of taxation was unfair and should be lowered, and the money gained by over-taxation returned to the people on the lines suggested. Dewan Bahadur Ambalal Sakarlal Desai seconded, and pressed the return of the needlessly high surpluses to the people. Mr. G. Subramania Iyer followed and remarked that Sir Antony MacDonnell had said before the Currency Committee that the enhancement of the value of the rupee would be a new burden on the people, but he said that it was safe to add it, because the people of India did not know it would operate in that way, while an addition to direct taxation was dangerous and impolitic. The poor who have suffered most by the forced appreciation should benefit by the surpluses created. The Resolution was carried.

Resolution IX claimed enlarged representation, and was moved by Mr. V. Krishnaswami Iyer, who referred to the enlargement of the Councils in 1892, and the power then given to discuss the Budget; but the Budget having been settled before the discussion, the members had only to state their opinions and read their little essays, the discussion being a farce. Pandit Madan Mohan Malaviya seconded, and said the reforms were good as far as they went, but more power should be given to the Councils and they should be enlarged. Would not the Government show a little more trust in the Indian people? "We have our minds imbued with the ideas of freedom through a body of English literature . . . . In our own country we are anxious to feel that we are really a part and parcel of the great British Empire which we love because of its love of freedom." Mr. Jehangir B. Petit followed, pointing out that educated Indians had shown themselves worthy of fuller representation and power, enumerating the results, beneficial to the country, that they had brought about. They had justified themselves by their achievements. It would be a proud day for England when she gave to India "the inestimable boon of Self-Government, to which all human beings have a birth-right and which is long overdue". The Resolution was carried.

Resolution X was on Tibetan affairs and the Forward Policy, that fruitful source of waste of life and treasure. It was moved by Mr. N. A. Wadia, who remarked that they were struggling "to maintain the small modicum of constitutional privilege conceded by Parliament nearly 50 years ago". He condemned the policy which went beyond the Indian borders: the brave peasants of Tibet fought for the freedom of their soil from the foot of the foreigner, "with a patriotism as pure, with love of independence as tenacious, with contempt for danger and for death as admirable as any recorded in ancient or modern annals". The speaker proceeded with a powerfully reasoned argument against Lord Curzon's mischievous missions, and urged that the employment of Indian troops outside India without the consent of Parliament was illegal.

Lala Murlidhar seconded, Mr. N. B. Ranade supported, and the Resolution was carried.

Police Reform came up once more in Resolution XI, and was moved by Mr. Vijayakumar Bose, seconded by Mr. Sris Chandra Sarbadhikari, supported by Mr. V. G. Joshi, and carried.

Resolution XII on Military Expenditure was very briefly moved and seconded by Messrs. N. M. Samarth, and G. R. Abhyankar, and carried. Then followed the separation of Judicial and Executive functions as Resolution XIII, moved, seconded and supported by Messrs. Harischandra Rai Vishandas, N. K. Ramaswami Iyer, and Kaliprasanna Roy, and carried.

Resolution XIV, on the Partition of Bengal, was moved by the Hon. Mr. Ambikacharan Mozumdar, seconded by Mr. A. Choudhuri, and supported by Mr. Binai Kumar Rai, and the Hon. Baikunthanath Sen, Bengali gentlemen, who all felt too strongly to do more than speak a few sentences. It was carried after a brief expression of sympathy from Mr. R. N. Mudholkar.

Mr. S. Sinha moved Resolution XVI, urging the election to Parliament of Mr. Dadabhai Naoroji, Sir Henry Cotton and Mr. John Jardine in the interests of India. Mr. V. P. Vaidya seconded and it was carried.

Mr. D. E. Wacha moved, and the Hon. Mr. D. N. Bose seconded Resolution XVI, the annual vote of thanks to Sir William Wedderburn and the British Committee. The President then moved Resolution XVIII re-appointing Mr. A. O. Hume, Mr. D. E. Wacha, and the Hon. Mr. G. K. Gokhale as General and Joint General Secretaries. He also moved Resolution XIX, appointing a Committee to report by the 1st of July, 1905, on the question of the constitution of the Congress. Resolution XX fixed Benares for the Congress of 1905. Resolutions XXI and XXII thanked the Reception Committee and the President, and Sir Henry Cotton, answering with a few words of grateful thanks, brought the Twentieth National Congress to an end.

RESOLUTIONS

Employment of Indians in the Public Service

I. (*a*) That in the opinion of this Congress, the principles and policy enunciated by the Government of India in their Resolution, dated 24th May 1904, on the subject of the employment of Indians in the higher grades of the Public Service, are inconsistent with those laid down in the Parliamentary Statute of 1833 and the Proclamation of 1858 by the late Queen-Empress, and this Congress enters its respectful but emphatic protest against an attempt to explain away pledges solemnly given by the Sovereign and Parliament to the people of this country, and to deviate from arrangements deliberately arrived at by the Government after a careful examination of the whole question by a Public Commission.

(*b*) That this Congress is of opinion that the true remedy for many existing financial and administrative evils lies in the wider employment of Indians in the higher branches of the country's service; and while concurring with previous Congresses in urging that immediate effect should be given to the Resolution of the House of Commons of 2nd June, 1893, in favour of holding the competitive examinations for service in India simultaneously in England and in India, this Congress places on record its firm conviction that the only satisfactory solution of this question is to be found in the reorganisation of the Indian Civil Service, which should be reconstituted on a decentralised basis, its judicial functions in the meantime being partly transferred to persons who have been trained in the profession of Law.

(*c*) That this Congress deplores the abolition of the competitive test for the Provincial Service in most Provinces of India. Past experience has amply established the fact that a system of Government nomination degenerates, in the special circumstances of this country, into a system of appointment by official favour, and this, by bringing unfit men into the Service, impairs the efficiency of the administration, and in addition unfairly discredits the fitness of Indians for high office. This Congress, therefore, respectfully urges the Government of India to restore the competitive test for the Provincial Service, wherever it has been abolished.

Education

II. That this Congress, while thanking the Government of India for the increased outlay on Primary Education, promised in their Resolution of March last, and for the institution of ten Technical scholarships for the study of technical arts and industries in foreign countries, repeats its protest of last year against the retrograde policy adopted by Government in regard to Higher Education, as calculated to officialise the governing bodies of the Universities and to restrict the scope of University Education generally; and the Congress places on record its emphatic opinion that in view of the large surpluses which the Government are now realising year after year, it is their clear duty to make a much larger allotment than at present out of public funds for educational expenditure so as

(*a*) to spread primary education more widely among the mass of the people, and to make a beginning in the direction of free and compulsory education;

(*b*) to make due provision for imparting instruction in manual training and in scientific agriculture;

(*c*) to provide for the better manning and equipment of Government Colleges and High Schools so as to make them really model institutions;

(*d*) to establish at least one central fully-equipped Polytechnic Institute in the country, with minor Technical Schools and Colleges in different Provinces.

Economic Situation

III. That this Congress is of opinion that the deplorable poverty of the people of this country is mainly due to the drain of wealth from the country that has gone on for years, to the decay of indigenous arts and industries, to over-assessment of land, and to the excessively costly character of the system of administration. And the Congress recommends the following among other remedial measures :

(*a*) That Government be pleased to afford greater encouragements to education, as indicated in the previous resolution.

(*b*) That the Permanent Settlement be extended to such parts of the country as are now ripe for it, in accordance with the conditions laid down in the Secretary of State for India's Despatches of 1862 and 1867 on the subject; and that where Government may still deem it inadvisable to introduce the Permanent Settlement, judicial restrictions be imposed on over-assessment.

(*c*) That steps be taken to employ a much larger number of Indians in the higher branches of the Public Service.

Indebtedness of the Peasantry

IV. Resolved—That in view of the alarming indebtedness of the peasantry of the country and of the fact that large numbers of them are forced to throw themselves on State help at the first touch of scarcity, this Congress again earnestly endorses the suggestion put forward by the Famine Union in London that a careful inquiry be directed by Government into the condition of a few typical villages in different parts of India.

Indian Emigrants to British Colonies

V. (*a*) That the Congress, while noting with satisfaction the relaxation of restrictions recently ordered by the Government of the Australian Commonwealth in the case of Indian visitors to Australia, places on record its deep regret that Indian Settlers—subjects of His Majesty the King-Emperor—should continue to be subjected to harassing restrictions and denied the ordinary rights of British citizenship in His Majesty's Colonies.

(*b*) In particular, this Congress records its most emphatic protest against the threatened enforcement, in an aggravated form, of the anti-Indian legislation of the late Boer Government of the Transvaal by the British Government. In view of the fact that one of the declared causes of the recent Boer War was the treatment meted out to the Indian subjects of the King-Emperor by the

Government of that Republic, and in view also of the admitted loyalty of Indian Settlers in South Africa and the great help rendered by them during the War, this Congress fervently prays that the British Parliament will insist on a just and equal treatment being secured to Indian settlers in that Crown Colony.

(c) In this connection the Congress tenders its sincere thanks to the Government of India and the Secretary of State for India for their firm stand in the interests of Indian emigrants, and the Congress earnestly trusts that they will not relax their efforts in the matter till a satisfactory solution is reached.

Deaths of Mr. J. N. Tata and Mr. W. Digby

VI. That this Congress places on record its sense of profound sorrow at the death of Mr. J. N. Tata, whose great services to the industrial development of India as also his enlightened philanthropy and patriotism the country will gratefully remember. This Congress also records its deep grief at the death of Mr. William Digby, in whom the people of India have lost an earnest and devoted champion of their cause.

Secretary of State's Salary

VII. That this Congress, while protesting against the injustice of charging the cost of the India Office in London to the revenues of this country, when the Colonies are exempted from any share of the cost of the Colonial Office, places on record its opinion that the whole of tho salary of the Secretary of State for India should be borne on the English Estimates.

Surpluses

VIII. (a) That, in the opinion of this Congress, the large and recurring surpluses of the last six years—amounting in all to about twenty millions sterling—so far from being the result of any increased prosperity of the people, are only an indication of the fact that the level of taxation in the country is maintained much higher than is necessary, inasmuch as these surpluses have been rendered possible mainly, if not exclusively, by the artificial appreciation of the rupee, and the consequent saving of between three and four millions a year on the Home remittances of the Government of India.

(b) That both for the sake of giving relief to the classes which have suffered most from the currency policy of the Government and to remove from the path of Government a direct temptation to increase expenditure, which the existence of large surpluses year after year undoubtedly constitutes, this Congress strongly urges (1) a further reduction in the salt duty; (2) a reduction in the land revenue demand of the State in those Provinces where the agriculturists have had a series of calamitous years; and (3) the abolition of the excise duties on cotton goods.

(c) That till such reduction is effected, the Congress urges that part of the surpluses be devoted to purposes which would directly benefit the people, such as the promotion of scientific, agricultural, and industrial education, and increased facilities of Medical relief, and that the rest be employed in assisting Local and Municipal Boards, whose resources have been seriously crippled by famine and by the annual recurrence of plague, to undertake urgently-needed measures of sanitary reform and the improvement of means of communication in the interior.

Representation

IX. That in the opinion of the Congress, the time has arrived when the people of this country should be allowed a larger voice in the administration and control of the affair of their country by

(a) The bestowal on each Province or Presidency of India of the franchise to return at least two members to the English House of Commons.

(b) An enlargement of both the Supreme and Provincial Legislative Councils—increasing the number of non-official members therein, and giving them the right to divide the Council in all financial matters coming before them—the Head of the Government concerned possessing the power of veto.

(c) The appointment of Indian representatives (who shall be nominated by the elected members of the Legislative Councils) as Members of the India Council in London and of the Executive Councils of the Government of India and the Governments of Bombay and Madras.

Tibetan Affairs and Forward Policy

X. That this Congress expresses its profound regret that in the case of the recent Tibetan Expedition the object of the Act of 1858, in providing that India's revenues shall not be spent outside the Statutory limits of India, except to repel foreign aggression, without the previous sanction of Parliament, was frustrated in practice by the Government continuing to describe the Expedition as a "Political Mission," till it was no longer possible for Parliament to withhold its sanction to the required expenditure, and that Indian revenues were thus unjustifiably deprived of the protection constitutionally secured to them. This Congress further places on record its regret that the House of Commons refused to contribute from the Imperial Exchequer even a portion of the cost of that Expedition, when it was in furtherance of Imperial interests and to carry out an Imperial policy that the Expedition had been undertaken.

The Congress protests strongly against this injustice and all the more because it apprehends that the Tibetan Expedition was but part of a general forward policy, which, with the Missions to Afghanistan and Persia, threatens to involve India in foreign entanglements, which cannot fail to place an intolerable burden on the Indian revenues and prove in the end disastrous to the best interests of the country.

Police Reform

XI. This Congress places on record its deep regret that the Report of the Police Commission has still been withheld by the Government from the public, though it is now two years since the Commission reported, and though portions of it have found their way into the columns of papers beyond the reach of the Official Secrets' Act.

In view of the great urgency of a thorough reform of the Police force of the country, in view further of the large public interests involved in a satisfactory solution of the question and the obvious necessity in consequence of giving the public ample opportunity to express its views before the authorities proceed to formulate a scheme of reform, in view, finally, of the fact that all public criticism expressed after the subject has been considered by both the Government of India and the Secretary of State for India is bound to be virtually ineffective, this Congress earnestly urges the publication of the Commission's Report without any further delay.

Military Expenditure

XII. (*a*) That this Congress regards with grave alarm the heavy and continuous increase that has been taking place year after year in the Military burdens of the country and that in the opinion of this Congress the present Military Expenditure of India is beyond her capacity to bear.

(*b*) That the Congress can only contemplate with dismay all further proposals to throw fresh burdens on the revenues of India in connection with Army expenditure, and it enters its earnest protest against throwing the cost of the proposed Army reorganisation scheme of Lord Kitchener on the Indian Exchequer.

(*c*) That as the strength of the Army maintained in India and the measures that are from time to time adopted to improve its efficiency are determined, not by a consideration of the military needs and requirements of India, but for upholding British Supremacy in the East, as moreover, large bodies of British troops have, in recent years, been temporarily withdrawn, with perfect safety and without imperilling the peace of the country, for service outside the statutory limits of India, this Congress is of opinion that the time has come when the British Parliament should seriously consider the justice and policy of making a substantial contribution towards Army Charges in India.

Separation of Judicial and Executive Functions

XIII. That this Congress, concurring with previous Congresses, appeals to the Government of India and the Secretary of State not to delay any longer the Separation of Executive and Judicial Functions in the administration of Criminal Justice, the desirability of which has been frequently admitted by Government and the practicability of effecting which with a very inappreciable increase of expenditure, if any, has been repeatedly shown.

The Partition of Bengal

XIV. That this Congress records its emphatic protest against the proposals of the Government of India, for the Partition of Bengal in any manner whatsoever. That the proposals are viewed with great alarm by the people, as the division of the Bengali Nation into separate units will seriously interfere with its social, intellectual and material progress, involving the loss of various constitutional, and other rights and privileges which the Province has so long enjoyed and will burden the country with heavy expenditure which the Indian tax-payers cannot at all afford.

The Congress is of opinion that no case has been made out for the Partition of Bengal, but if the present constitution of the Bengal Government is considered inadequate for the efficient administration of the Province, the remedy lies not in any redistribution of its territories, but in organic changes in the form of the Government, such as the conversion of the Lieutenant-Governorship of Bengal into a Governorship with an Executive Council like that of Bombay and Madras.

Delegation to England

XV. That, looking to the near approach of a General Election in England, and to the vital importance, at this crisis, of bringing the claims of India before the Electors, before the Parliamentary Candidates, and before the political leaders, it is expedient that the Congress should depute trustworthy and experienced representatives nominated by the different Provinces to be present in England for this purpose, before and during the election; and that a fund of not less than Rs. 30,000 should be raised to meet the necessary expenses of such Deputation.

Election of Members to the British Parliament

XVI. That this Congress desires to accord its most cordial support to the candidatures of Mr. Dadabhai Naoroji for North Lambeth, Sir Henry Cotton for Nottingham, and Sir John Jardine for Roxburghshire, and appeals to the electors of these constituencies that in the interests of the people of India, they will be pleased to return them to Parliament, so that they may not only loyally serve them, but represent in some manner the people of a country which, though a part of the British Empire, has no direct representative in the British Parliament.

Thanks to the British Committee

XVII. That this Congress desires to convey to Sir William Wedderburn and the other members of the British Committee its most grateful thanks for their disinterested services in the cause of our political advancement.

And that a sum of £700 be assigned for the expenses of the British Committee and that the several Congress circles do contribute the amount allotted to each.

Appointment of General Secretary and Joint General Secretaries

XVIII. That this Congress reappoints Mr. A. O. Hume, C. B., to be General Secretary and Mr. D. E. Wacha and the Hon. Mr. G. K. Gokhale to be Joint General Secretaries of the Congress for the ensuing year.

Constitution of the Congress

XIX. That the question of the Constitution of the Congress be referred for report to a Committee consisting of the following gentlemen:

BOMBAY:

Sir P.M. Mehta
Mr. D. E. Wacha.
Hon. Mr. G. K. Gokhale.
Hon. Mr. Ibrahim Rahimtulla.

PANJAB:

Lala Lajpat Rai.
Mr. Dharmadas.
Lala Harkishan Lal.

MADRAS:

Mr. C. Sankaran Nair.
Mr. Krishnaswami Iyer.
Mr. M. Viraraghava Chari.
Nawab Syed Mahomed.

UNITED PROVINCES:

Babu Gangaprasad Varma.
Hon. Pandit Madan Mohan Malaviya.
Mr. S. Sinha.

BENGAL:

Babu Surendranath Bannerji.
Hon. Mr. Ambikacharan Mazumdar.
Babu Baikunthanath Sen.
Mr. Abdul Kasim.

BERAR AND CENTRAL PROVINCES

Mr. R. M. Mudholkar.
Mr. M. V. Joshi.
Mr. M. K. Padhya.

The Next Session of the Congress

XX. That the Twenty-first Indian National Congress do assemble, on such day after Christmas Day, 1905, as may be later determined upon, at Benares.

XXI. Thanks to the Reception Committee and those who have in various ways assisted it.

By the President.

XXII. Thanks to the President.

President's reply in closing the proceedings.

CHAPTER XXI

IN the sacred City of Kashi, the modern Benares, the Twenty-first National Congress gathered together. Says the Official Report:

> The Congress met at a great crisis in the political fortunes of this country. Never since the dark days of Lord Lytton's Viceroyalty had India been so distracted, discontented, despondent; the victim of so many misfortunes, political and other; the target for so much scorn and calumny emanating from the highest quarters—its most moderate demands ridiculed and scouted, its most reasonable prayers greeted with a stiff negative, its noblest aspirations spurned and denounced as pure mischief or solemn nonsense, its most cherished ideals hurled down from their pedestal and trodden under foot—never had the condition of India been more critical than it was during the second ill-starred administration of Lord Curzon. The Official Secrets Act was passed in the teeth of universal opposition. It was condemned by the whole Press—Indian and Anglo-Indian—protests from all quarters poured in, but Lord Curzon was implacable, and the Gagging Act was passed. Education was crippled and mutilated; it was made expensive and it was officialised; and so that most effective instrument for the enslavement of our National interest, the Indian Universities Act, was passed, and the policy of checking if not altogether undoing the noble work of Bentinck, Macaulay and Lord Halifax, which for more than half a century has been continued with such happy results to the country, came in full swing.

On the 27th, 28th, 29th and 30th of December, 1905, 758 delegates gathered on the noble cliff of Rajghar, dominating Gangamai's rolling flood, and the eye, looking upwards, rested on the great curving bank, the Crescent Moon, crowned with temples and stately dwelling-places. They came thither as follows from:

Bengal	209
U. P.	203
Panjab (104) and N. W. F. P. (1) ...	105
C. P. (44), Berar (16) and Secunderabad (3)	64
Bombay (95) and Sindh (16)	110
Madras (64) and Mysore (1)	65
Burma	2
	758

(The list gives 757, but No. 606 is repeated in error.)

Munshi Madho Lal was the Chairman of the Reception Committee, and made a very brief speech of welcome, asking Pandit Bishambharnath to propose the President-elect. Very warm were the words with which he proposed and Mr. Romesh Chandra Dutt seconded the Hon. Mr. Gopal Krishna Gokhale; they were followed by Sardar Gurucharan Singh, Mr. R. N. Mudholkar and Mr. G. Subramania Iyer, and then the idol of India took the Presidential chair amid resounding cheers, and delivered one of the most notable speeches to which the Congress had listened during the twenty-one years of its existence.

Mr. Gokhale remarked that he was called to take charge of the vessel of the Congress with rocks ahead and angry waves beating around, and invoked the Divine guidance. He then, after a few words of homage to the Prince and Princess of Wales, then visiting India, and of respectful welcome to the new Viceroy and Lady Minto, turned to the administration of Lord Curzon, just closed. Stern and scathing was his verdict:

> Gentlemen, how true it is that to everything there is an end! Thus even the Viceroyalty of Lord Curzon has come to a close! For seven long years all eyes had constantly to turn to one masterful figure in the land—now in admiration, now in astonishment, more often in anger and in pain, till at last it has become difficult to realise that a change has really come. For a parallel to such an administration, we must, I think, go back to the times of Aurangzebe in the history of our own country. There we find the same attempt at a rule excessively centralised and intensely personal, the same strenuous purpose, the same overpowering consciousness of duty, the same marvellous capacity for work, the same sense of loneliness, the same persistence in a policy of distrust and repression, resulting in bitter exasperation all round. I think even the most devoted admirer of Lord Curzon cannot claim that he has strengthened the foundations of British rule in India. . . . . To him India was a country where the Englishman was to monopolise for all time all power, and talk all the while of duty. The Indian's only business was to be governed, and it was a sacrilege on his part to have any other aspiration. In his scheme of things there was no room for the educated classes of the country; and having failed to amuse them for any length of time by an empty show of taking them into his confidence, he proceeded in the end to repress them. Even in his last farewell speech at the Byculla Club in Bombay, India exists only as a scene of the Englishman's labours, with the toiling millions of the country—eighty per cent of the population—in the background. The remaining twenty per cent, for aught they are worth, might as well be gently swept into the sea!

Mr. Gokhale tore into shreds the attempt to separate the educated from the uneducated Indians, and pointed out that the suggestion that the former were opposed to the latter was "unreal and ridiculous," and that the useful measures of which Lord Curzon boasted had been persistently urged by the Congress. Turning to the Partition of Bengal, he denounced it as "a cruel wrong," and indignantly flung back Lord Curzon's false assertion that the agitation was "manufactured," declaring that nothing more intense, widespread and spontaneous had been seen in Indian political agitation. Mentioning the remarkable men who had come forward against the Partition, he exclaimed:

> If the opinions of even such men are to be brushed aside with contempt, if all Indians are to be treated as no better than dumb, driven cattle; if men, whom any other country would delight to honour, are to be thus made to realise the utter humiliation and helplessness of their position in their own, then all I can say is: "Goodbye to all hope of co-operating in any way with the bureaucracy in the interests of the people!" I can conceive of no graver indictment of British rule than that such a state of things should be possible after a hundred years of that rule! .... The tremendous upheaval of popular feeling which has taken place in Bengal in consequence of the Partition, will constitute a landmark in the history of our National progress. For the first time since British rule began, all sections of the Indian community, without distinction of caste or creed, have been moved by a common impulse and without the stimulus of external pressure, to act together in offering resistance to a common wrong. A wave of true National consciousness has swept over the Province and, at its touch, old barriers have, for the time at any rate, been thrown down, personal

jealousies have vanished, other controversies have been hushed! Bengal's heroic stand against the oppression of a harsh and uncontrolled bureaucracy has astonished and gratified all India, and her sufferings have not been endured in vain, when they have helped to draw closer all parts of the country in sympathy and in aspiration. A great rush and uprising of the waters such as has been recently witnessed in Bengal cannot take place without a little inundation over the banks here and there. These little excesses are inevitable when large masses of men move spontaneously—especially when the movement is from darkness into light, from bondage towards freedom —and they must not be allowed to disconcert us too much. The most astounding fact of the situation is that the public life of this country has received an accession of strength of great importance, and for this all India owes a deep debt of gratitude to Bengal.

Speaking of the Swadeshi movement, Mr. Gokhale justified the boycott as a political weapon, to be used only at the last extremity, and with strong popular feeling behind it.

> The devotion to Motherland, which is enshrined in the highest Swadeshi, is an influence so profound and so passionate that its very thought thrills and its actual touch lifts one out of oneself. India needs to-day above everything else that the gospel of this devotion should be preached to high and low, to Prince and to peasant, in town and in hamlet, till the Service of Motherland becomes with us as overmastering a passion as it is in Japan.

Turning then to the Congress movement, Mr. Gokhale traced it to the National consciousness quickened by the beloved Lord Ripon. "Hope at that time was warm and faith was bright" that by urging reforms Indians could win a steady progress towards political emancipation. "Much had happened to chill that faith and dim that hope," yet the people now realised "the idea of a United India working for her salvation". Advance would be gradual, but the resources of the country must be devoted to it, and the people educated. For a hundred years England had ruled India, but four villages out of every five were without a school-house, and seven children out of eight grew up in ignorance. "India should be governed first and foremost in the interests of the Indians themselves. This result will be achieved only in proportion as we obtain more and more voice in the Government of our country."

. . . . That the Charter Act of 1833 and the Queen's Proclamation of 1858 have created in the eyes of reactionary rulers a most inconvenient situation is clear from a blunt declaration which another Viceroy of India, the late Lord Lytton, made in a confidential document and which has since seen the light of day. Speaking of our claims and expectations based on the pledges of the Sovereign and the Parliament of England, he wrote: "We all know that these claims and expectations never can or will be fulfilled. We have had to choose between prohibiting them [the Natives of India] and cheating them, and we have chosen the least straightforward course. . . . . Since I am writing confidentially, I do not hesitate to say that both the Government of England and of India appear to me up to the present moment unable to answer satisfactorily the charge of having taken every means in their power of breaking to the heart the words of promise they had uttered to the ear." We accept Lord Lytton as an unimpeachable authority on the conduct of the Government in evading the fulfilment of the pledges. We deny his claim to lay down that our "claims and expectations never can or will be fulfilled".

Our whole future, it is needless to say, is bound up with this question of the relative position of the two races in this country. The domination of one race over another —especially when there is no great disparity between their intellectual endowments or their general civilisation —inflicts great injury on the subject race in a thousand insidious ways. On the moral side, the present situation is steadily destroying our capacity for initiative and dwarfing us as men of action. On the material side, it has resulted in a fearful impoverishment of the people. For a hundred years and more now India has been for members of the dominant race a country where fortunes were to be made, to be taken out and spent elsewhere. As in Ireland the evil of absentee landlordism has in the past aggravated the racial domination of the English over the Irish, so in India what may be called absentee capitalism has been added to the racial ascendancy of Englishmen. A great and ruinous drain of wealth from the country has gone on for many years, the net excess of exports over imports (including treasure) during the last forty years amounting to no less than a thousand millions sterling. The steady rise in the death-rate of the country—from 24 per thousand, the average for 1882-84, to 30 per thousand, the average for 1892-94, and 34 per thousand, the present average—is a terrible and conclusive proof of this continuous impoverishment of the mass of our people. India's best interests —material and moral—no less than the honour of England, demand that the policy of equality for the two races promised by the Sovereign and by Parliament should be faithfully and courageously carried out.

Mr. Gokhale then turned to the bureaucracy, and bitterly blamed the system, adding that "the bureaucracy is growing frankly selfish and openly hostile to their [the educated classes] national aspirations. It was not so in the past." And he spoke of the different feeling within living memory, when the rulers looked forward to India's Self-Government. It was pretended that the people were indifferent, but "what the educated Indians think to-day, the rest of India thinks to-morrow".

Lastly, Mr. Gokhale advised concentration on selected portions of the Congress programme: (1) a larger and larger share in administration and control, by a steady substitution of Indians for Europeans; (2) improvement in methods of administration; (3) re-adjustment of financial arrangements; and (4) measures to improve the condition of the people. An elaboration of these brought his splendid speech to a close.

The approval of the Subjects' Committee was given, and the Congress adjourned.

On the second day, after noting some telegrams of good wishes, the President moved from the Chair the first Resolution of welcome to T. R. H. the Prince and Princess of Wales, and it was enthusiastically carried.

Resolution II, on the further reform of the Legislative Councils, was moved by the Hon. Mr. J. Choudhuri, who remarked that recent legislation would have been very different had the Supreme Council been more than a debating society. Indians practically said to the officials: "That is our suggestion: reason is on our side: justice is on our side: the votes are on your side: do just as you please." The Hon. Mr. L. A. Govindaraghava Iyer seconded in a weighty speech, pointing out that England's chief aim was not merely to govern India efficiently but "to make her Self-Governing," and for this larger representation was needed. Messrs. R. P. Karandikar, G. S. Khaparde, Ali Muhammad Bhimji, and Surendranath Bannerji supported, and the Resolution was carried.

Resolution III was on Excise Policy and Administration, and was ably moved by Sir Bhalchandra Krishna, seconded by Mr. G. A. Natesan, supported by Mr. B. S. Bhatia and carried.

Resolution IV dealt with representation, but on lines different from those of Resolution II, for it asked that each Province in India should return two members to the House of Commons, that three Indians should be placed on the India Council, two in the Viceroy's Executive Council, and one in the Executive Councils of Bombay and Madras. Mr. G. Srinivasa Rao moved the Resolution in a short speech, Mr. S. R. Das formally seconded it, Mr. Fazal Husain supported it, and it was unanimously carried.

Mr. Ambalal Desai moved Resolution V, suggesting a revival of Parliamentary enquiries into the condition of the country, and the placing of the Secretary of State's salary on the British estimates. He recalled the value of the enquiries on the renewals of the East India Company's Charter, and such enquiries might mitigate present evils. Mr. Tarapada Bannerji seconded, laying stress on the importance of such enquiries. Mr. V. Krishnaswami Aiyar supported, noting that when the Government of India had been transferred to the Crown, serious misgivings had been felt as to Parliamentary control, and they had been justified. Good might come out of such enquiries as were proposed, as the knowledge obtained would touch the heart of the British people. The Resolution was carried.

Resolution VI dealt with the Public Service question, and was moved by Mr. N. M. Samarth, who dealt severely with Lord Curzon's insolent treatment of the Proclamation of 1858, saying that "happily for his Lordship and unhappily for India, we are not living in the days of Burke and Sheridan. Otherwise one could well imagine the fate that would probably have befallen the late Viceroy on his return to England, after trifling with the Queen's Proclamation." Pandit Bishan Narayana Dhar seconded, pointing to the eminent Indians who were "debarred from holding high appointments in the Public Service of their own country". Mr. J. Simeon and the Hon. Mr. K. R. Guruswami Aiyar supported, and the Resolution was carried. The Congress then adjourned.

On the third day, Mr. G. Subramania Iyer moved Resolution VII, dealing with the fashion in which the artificial surpluses were disposed of, and referred to Mr. Gokhale's speech in the previous year as the basis of his own. Mr. R. N. Mudholkar seconded, deploring the unsoundness of Indian finance, and pointing out that expenditure grew from military extravagance, and high berths for Europeans, while education was starved. Mr. Mathura Das supported, and the Resolution was carried.

Mr. H. A. Wadia moved Resolution VIII, on the hopeless subject of military expenditure, and asked that the 10 millions sterling sanctioned for military purposes be spent in education and in reducing the ryots' burdens. On speaking for "the voiceless millions," he said, "it is not so much a right that we desire to assert as a sacred duty which we aspire to perform". Mr. V. Ryru Nambier seconded, urging that a large army was not needed to secure internal peace; what was an army in a population of 300 millions? The loyalty of these was India's defence. After speeches from Messrs. N. B. Ranade and Krishna Baldev Varma, the Resolution was carried.

Resolution IX was on the South African troubles growing worse each year, the conditions of the Indians being far worse than under the Boers, urged Mr. Madanjit. Mr. B. N. Sarma spoke out boldly, warning England that in the Empire there could not be permanently a racial supremacy, one race dominating another. "If we are true to ourselves, then the race which has produced the great philosophers, the greatest statesmen and the greatest warriors shall not crouch for this or that favour at the hands of other people. It is then and then alone that the South African problem, as well as other Indian problems will find their best solution." Well spoken indeed. Then, and only then.

Dr. B. S. Munji remarked that Indians as a Nation were boycotted, both in and out of India, Foreigners in India dominated and ruled, and Indians in foreign countries were ruthlessly boycotted. "Our rulers do not believe that we are men." The Resolution was carried.

Mr. Romesh Chandra Dutt gave a charm even to our old friend the separation of Judicial and Executive functions, embodied in Resolution X, and

34

the Hon. Mr. Setalwad duly seconded it. Dr. Satish Chandra Bannerji supported, urging the need to make British justice sound. Mr. Bishnupada Chatterji added some instances of the miscarriages of justice, and the Resolution passed—as usual.

Police Reforms were entrusted to their old champion, Mr. S. Sinha, and he moved Resolution XI, and said how bitterly the Police Commission had disappointed them, constituting a special Police Service from which Indians should be excluded, Lord Curzon's *corps d'élite*, reserved to Europeans. Messrs. Jogiah, Ishwar Saran, Nargunti Kar, A. C. Parthasarathi Naidu, and Kaliprasanna Kavyabisharad, all spoke to it, and the Resolution was carried.

Resolution XII against the Partition of Bengal was moved by Mr. Surendranath Bannerji, as soon as the shouts of "Bande Mataram" allowed him to speak. With passionate eloquence he voiced the anger of his people, and declared that agitation should never stop until the Partition was cancelled. He proved to be a true prophet, and the cancellation in 1911 proved what agitation could do, even in India, under coercion and an autocracy. He described the grief and excitement in Calcutta: "the shops were closed, the domestic hearth was not lit, food was not cooked". The Government was busy "forging instruments of repression, laying the foundation for the inauguration of a reign of terror". Meetings were prohibited, Sankirtan processions stopped, the singing of "Bande Mataram" punished, boys prosecuted and sent to gaol. They believed God was with them, and

" men fortified by such belief and working under such conviction are irresistible and invincible; there is no danger which they are not ready to brave, no difficulty which they are not prepared to surmount".

Mr. A. Choudhuri seconded in a witty speech, and Messrs. Baikunthanath Sen, C. V. Vaidya (Rao Bahadur), S. Sinha, Hadayat Bakshi, Abdul Kasim, R. N. Mudholkar (Rao Bahadur) and Nussuruddin, voiced, in one indignant protest after another, the anger and determination of India. Not often has the National Congress witnessed such a scene of excitement.

Then came Resolution XIII, protesting against the repressive measures adopted to crush the antagonism that Lord Curzon's tyranny had created. Pandit Madan Mohan Malaviya showed, in moving it, that not one act of violence had been committed by the people, in spite of all that had occurred. No protest was heeded, and as a last measure of despair the boycott of foreign goods was adopted. Then came a series of repressive measures; "persecution is the only word that you can use" for the measures adopted. Earnestly he hoped that the Government would put an end to the boycott by removing its cause.

Lala Lajpat Rai, seconding, congratulated Bengal on its splendid opportunity of heralding a new political era for the country. The English had taught them how to resist when they had a grievance, and the English expected them to show more manliness in their struggles for liberty. They must show that they were "no longer beggars, and that we are subjects of an Empire where people are struggling to achieve that position which is their right". If other Provinces followed the example of Bengal the day was not far distant when they would win.

Messrs. H. A. Wadia, W. D. A. Khare, V. Krishnaswami Aiyar—who recounted the example of Ireland and of China—A. H. Gaznavi—who exposed the violent and hysterical behaviour of Mr. Bamfylde Fuller, his threats, and his rudeness to respectable men, whom he rated and insulted like a bully, "bloodshed might be necessary," he said, and the Gurkhas had been brought to check the state of affairs—Panday Ramsaran Lal and G. S. Khaparde all spoke, the Resolution was passed, and the meeting adjourned.

The Congress met for the fourth time on December 30th, and the President called on Mr. Heramba Chandra Maitra to move Resolution XIV on Education, which protested against the policy of officialising and restricting education, thanked the Government for some special grants made, though insufficient to meet the country's needs, and urged the recommendations made by the Industrial Education Committee, and the establishment of a Polytechnic Institute, with affiliated schools and colleges. The mover made a weighty and impressive speech, remarking that amid the exciting topics of the time the perennial importance of education must not be overlooked. Higher education was openly restricted by the Government, who regarded one college student to every 11,000 of the population as too large a proportion. The

University Commission said that it was better to have a comparatively small number well educated than a large number inadequately educated.

> Is it better that a few men should have a surfeit of luxury and millions should starve, than that all should be moderately fed? Is it better that a few healthy strong giants should stride across the face of the country, and others should be so many skeletons? Is it better that there should be a few saints in the country and the rest should be blackguards, than that all men should be of fairly good character?

The question could not be better put. The view taken by the University Commission is opposed to every modern theory of Society, though it is easy to see why it should be the view of a foreign Government, determined to keep a Nation in bonds. Mr. Maitra said with impassioned eloquence:

> We are denied admission into South African Republics; we are denied admission into Australia. Are we also to be denied admission into the Republic of Letters? Are we not to be admitted freely to the franchises of the citizenship of the great Republic of Letters? . . . . We claim, we demand, that we should be helped to believe that the British Government in India is a wise and humane dispensation and not a scourge for the punishment of the people for their former sins. That is all we demand and ask for in this Resolution. The noblest service which one man can render to another, next to helping in the belief in the glory and goodness of God, is to unfold the doors of the temple of culture to a man, and the cruellest wrong that one can do for another is to withhold from him the boon of education, which is a solace to him in the days of sorrow, which is an augmentation in the days of joy, which is always a friend and companion. We demand that England shall not be deliberately guilty of that cruel wrong.

Mr. D. G. Pandhya seconded and, after many sound arguments against the officialising of education, remarked that "the aim is to manufacture in India, to manufacture from colleges and schools, submissive slaves who will be willing instruments in the hands of despots who live upon the people of this country". Dr. Nilratan Sircar, supporting, advocated industrial education, pleading for an adaptation of technical education as in Japan, America and Germany. Messrs. M. K. Patel, Ramananda Chatterji—who said that India's political salvation depended on mass education—and Nareschandra Sen supported the Resolution, which was carried.

Mr. B. G. Tilak, "who was received with an ovation," says the Report, moved Resolution XV on Famine, Poverty, Economic Enquiry and Land Revenue; he urged the duty of Government to deal with the causes of poverty, to ensure prosperity; Governments would not be needed if there were universal well-being, any more than doctors would be wanted if there were no disease. Pandit Gokarnath seconded, Messrs. N. K. Ramaswami Aiyar, Sanktu Prasad, Rambhuj Dutt, and K. N. Deskmukh supported, and the Resolution was carried.

The Hon. Mr. G. K. Parekh moved and Mr. Ali Muhammad Bhimji seconded, Resolution XVI, to relieve the Muhammadan pilgrims of the Bombay quarantine in view of the 10 days' quarantine at Kamran. The Resolution was supported by Moulvi Abdul Kayum and Mr. G. S. Khare, and passed.

Resolution XVII, the Omnibus, was put from the Chair. Mr. K. Venkata Rao proposed and Mr. J. N. Roy seconded Resolution XVIII, supporting Mr. Dadabhai Naoroji's candidature at South Lambeth; and Mr. D. A. Khare moved and Mr. K. Narayana Rao seconded Resolution XIX, thanking Mr. G. K. Gokhale and Lala Lajpat Rai for their great services in England. Mr. M. V. Joshi then moved Resolution XX, appointing Mr. Gokhale to be the Delegate of the Congress to urge the more pressing proposals of the Congress on the authorities in England. Mr. C. Vijiaraghavachari seconded, and Sister Nivedita supported the Resolution, urging the Congress to remember the birth of Nationality in Europe, an impulse against the Napoleonic movement, a century before; now history was repeating itself, and India must speak for the salvation of Europe, for the English Empire must be Imperialism or Nationality, Slavery of Nations or Freedom for the peoples of the earth.

Resolution XXI appointed a Standing Committee to promote the objects of the Congress throughout the year. Resolution XXII re-appointed the Secretaries; Resolution XXIII thanked Sir William Wedderburn and the British Committee. Then Mr. Yatindranath Choudhuri invited the next Congress to Calcutta, the Congress gladly accepting.

Finally, Pandit Madan Mohan Malaviya, in words of deepest gratitude and admiration, voiced the love and trust of India in the vote of thanks to the President, endorsed by tumultuous applause;

Mr. Surendranath Bannerji seconded, and Mr. Gokhale very briefly replied. Thus had the Twenty-first National Congress its ending.

RESOLUTIONS

Message of Welcome to Their Royal Highnesses the Prince and Princess of Wales

I. Resolved—That this Congress, representing His Majesty's Indian subjects of all races, creeds and communities, most humbly and respectfully offers its loyal and dutiful welcome to Their Royal Highnesses the Prince and Princess of Wales on the occasion of their visit to India.

The Congress is deeply touched by the expressions of Their Highnesses' sentiments of cordial good-will towards the people of India, is confident that the personal knowledge gained during the present tour will stimulate their kindly interest in the welfare of its people, and it expresses the fervent hope that His Royal Highness will be graciously pleased to submit, to His Majesty the King-Emperor, the earnest prayer of this Congress that the principles of the Queen's Proclamation be enforced in the Government of this country.

(*a*) That the President do submit the above resolution to His Royal Highness by wire.

Representation

II. Resolved—That in the opinion of this Congress the time has arrived for a further expansion and reform of the Supreme and Provincial Legislative Councils, so that they may become more representative of the people, and the non-official members thereof may have a real voice in the Government of the country. The Congress recommends an increase in the number of non-official and elected members and the grant to them of the right of dividing the Councils in financial matters coming before them; the head of the Government concerned possessing the power of veto.

IV. Resolved—That in the opinion of this Congress the time has arrived when the people of India should be allowed a larger voice in the administration and control of the affairs of their country by:

(*a*) The bestowal on each of the Provinces of India the franchise to return at least two members to the British House of Commons.

(*b*) The appointment of not less than three Indian gentlemen of proved ability and experience as members of the Secretary of State's Council.

(*c*) The appointment of two Indians as members of the Governor-General's Executive Council and of one Indian as a member of the Executive Councils of Bombay and Madras.

Excise

III. Resolved—That (*a*) this Congress, while thanking the Government of India for the appointment of a Committee to enquire into Excise Administration in the several Provinces of the country, regrets that its composition is exclusively official, and that, therefore, it cannot inspire full public confidence;

(*b*) this Congress, concurring in the opinion of previous Congresses, expresses its deliberate conviction that the recognition of the principle of local option in practical administration and a large reduction in the number of existing liquor-shops are conditions precedent to any satisfactory reform in Excise Administration;

(*c*) this Congress respectfully urges on the Government of India the desirability of speedily carrying out the principal proposals contained in Sir Fredrick Lely's memorandum of last year on Excise Administration;

(*d*) that the Congress begs to protest against the virtual shelving, by the Government of India in its executive capacity, of the Bengal Excise Bill, which has been welcomed as a sound and progressive piece of temperance legislation.

Periodical Enquiries

V. Resolved—That this Congress is of opinion that to enable the Parliament to discharge more satisfactorily its responsibility in regard to the Government of India, periodical Parliamentary enquiries into the condition of India should be revived, and the salary of the Secretary of State for India should be placed on the British estimates.

Public Service

VI. Resolved—(*a*) That, in the opinion of the Congress, the principles and policy enunciated by the Government of India in their Resolution, dated 24th May, 1904, on the subject of the employment of Indians in the higher grades of the Public Service, are inconsistent with those laid down in the Parliamentary Statute of 1833 and the Proclamation of 1858 by the late Queen-Empress, and this Congress enters its respectful but emphatic protest against an attempt to explain away pledges solemnly given by the

Sovereign and Parliament to the people of this country, and to deviate from arrangements deliberately arrived at by the Government after a careful examination of the whole question by a Public Commission.

(*b*) That this Congress is of opinion that the true remedy for many existing financial and administrative evils lies in the wider employment of Indians in the higher branches of the country's service; and while concurring with previous Congresses in urging that immediate effect should be given to the Resolution of the House of Commons of 2nd June, 1893, in favour of holding the competitive examinations for the Civil Services simultaneously in England and in India, this Congress places on record its firm conviction that the only satisfactory solution of this question is to be found in the re-organisation of the Indian Civil Service, which should be reconstituted on a decentralised basis, its judicial functions in the meantime being partly transferred to persons who have been trained in the profession of law.

(*c*) That this Congress, concurring in the opinion of the last Congress, deplores the abolition of the competitive test for the Provincial Service. Past experience has amply established the fact that a system of Government nomination degenerates, in the special circumstances of this country, into a system of appointment by official favour, and thus by bringing unfit men into the Service, impairs the efficiency of the administration and, in addition, unfairly discredits the fitness of Indians for high office. This Congress, therefore, respectfully urges the Government of India to restore the competitive test for the Provincial Service.

Finance

VII. Resolved—That this Congress, while appreciating the action of the Government of India in applying a portion of its surplus revenues last March to some of the purposes recommended by the Congress, is of opinion that the financial relief given by it to the tax-payers of this country during the last three years has been most inadequate, and the Congress regrets that advantage has been taken of recent surpluses to increase largely the military expenditure of the country, raise the salaries of European officials in several departments and create a number of new posts for them. The Congress urges that any surplus that may arise in the future should, in the first place, be utilised for purposes of remission of taxation, and, secondly, be devoted to objects directly benefiting the people, such as imparting scientific, industrial and agricultural education, providing increased facilities of medical relief and assisting Municipal and Local Boards with grants to undertake urgently needed measures of sanitary reform, and the improvement of means of communication in the interior.

Military

VIII. Resolved—(*a*) That this Congress, while recording its emphatic protest against any change which weakens the supremacy of the Civil control over the Military authorities, is of opinion that the necessary Civil control cannot be adequately exercised until and unless the representatives of the tax-payers are placed in a position to influence such control.

(*b*) That this Congress earnestly repeats its protest against the continued increase in the military expenditure, which is unnecessary, unjust and beyond the capacity of the Indian people.

(*c*) That this Congress is distinctly of opinion that as the military expenditure of this country is determined, not by its own military needs and requirements alone but also by the exigencies of British supremacy and British policy in the East, it is only fair that a proportionate share of such expenditure should be met out of the British Exchequer and shared by the Empire at large, instead of the whole of such expenditure falling on a part of the Empire which is the poorest and the least able to bear it.

(*d*) That in view of the changed position of affairs in Asia, due to the recent war between Russia and Japan and the Anglo-Japanese Treaty, this Congress earnestly urges that the large expenditure of 10 millions sterling sanctioned last year for the Re-organisation scheme be not now incurred, and the money be devoted to an extension of education in all its branches and reduction of the ryot's burdens.

Indians in British Colonies

IX. Resolved—That (*a*) this Congress, while expressing its sense of satisfaction at the passing by the Australian House of representatives, of a Bill to amend the Law of Immigration so as to avoid hurting the susceptibilities of the people of India, again places on record its sense of deep regret that British Indians should continue to be subjected to harassing and degrading restrictions and denied the ordinary rights of British citizenship in His Majesty's Colonies. The Congress particularly protests against the enforcement by the British Government of disabilities on the Indian settlers in the Transvaal and Orange River Crown Colonies, which were not enforced even under the old Boer rule, in spite of declarations by His Majesty's Minister that the treatment of the Indian subjects of the King-Emperor by the Boer Government was one of the causes of the late war;

(*b*) in view of the important part the Indian settlers have played in the development of the Colonies, their admitted loyalty and peaceful and industrious habits, their useful and self-sacrificing services during the recent war, and, above all, the great constitutional importance of the principle of equal treatment of all citizens of the Empire anywhere in the King's Dominions, this Congress respectfully, but strongly, urges the Government of India and His Majesty's Government to insist, by prohibiting, if necessary, the emigration of indentured labour and adopting other retaliatory measures, on the recognition of the status of Indian emigrants as British citizens in all the Colonies.

Legal

X. Resolved—(*a*) That in the opinion of this Congress a complete separating of Judicial from Executive functions must now be carried out without further delay; (b) that this Congress, concurring with previous Congresses, urges that the Judicial Service, in all parts of the country, should be recruited from the Legal profession more largely than at present, as the system of appointing Civilians without special legal training to high judicial offices does not lead to satisfactory administration of justice in the Muffasal.

Police

XI. Resolved—That this Congress, while noting with satisfaction some useful reforms recommended by the Police Commission, regrets that adequate measures have not been adopted to materially improve the efficiency and the honesty of the Police Service.

That this Congress records its conviction :

(1) That competitive examinations for the recruitment of the Police Service in the higher grades should be thrown open to all classes of British subjects instead of being confined to candidates of British birth, and that such examinations should be held simultaneously in England and in India.

(2) That educated Indians should be largely employed in the higher grades in order to secure efficiency in work.

(3) That enlistment in the Provincial Service should be by competitive examinations.

(4) And lastly, that District Officers, who are the heads of the Police, should be relieved of judicial work and of all control over the Magistracy of the District.

Coercion

The Partition of Bengal

XII. Resolved—That this Congress records its emphatic protest against the Partition of Bengal in the face of the strongest opposition on the part of the people of the Province.

That having regard to the intense dissatisfaction felt by the entire Bengali community at the dismemberment of their Province and their manifest disinclination to accept the Partition as an accomplished fact, this Congress appeals to the Government of India and to the Secretary of State to reverse or modify the arrangements made in such a manner as to conciliate public opinion, and allay the excitement and unrest manifest among large masses of the people.

That this Congress recommends the adoption of some arrangement which would be consistent with administrative efficiency, and would place the entire Bengali community under one undivided administration either by the appointment of a Governor and Council, or by the adoption of some other administrative arrangement that may be thought desirable.

Repressive Measures

XIII. Resolved—That this Congress records its earnest and emphatic protest against the repressive measures which have been adopted by the authorities in Bengal after the people there had been compelled to resort to the boycott of foreign goods as a last protest, and perhaps the only constitutional and effective means left to them of drawing the attention of the British public to the action of the Government of India in persisting in their determination to partition Bengal, in utter disregard of the universal prayers and protests of the people.

[See XVII, 6.]

Education

XIV. Resolved—(*a*) That this Congress repeats its protest against the present policy of the Government of India in respect of High and Secondary education, as being one of officialising the governing bodies of the Universities and restricting the spread of education.

(*b*) That this Congress, while thanking the Government of India for the special grants made this year to Primary and High Education, again places on record its firm conviction that the material and moral interests of the country demand a much larger expenditure than at present on all branches of education, and a beginning in the direction of Free Primary Education.

(*c*) That in the opinion of this Congress the recommendations of the Committee on Industrial Education should be promptly carried out by the Government for the better provision of Technical Education to the youth of the country. The Congress especially urges the Government to order an Industrial Survey as recommended by the Committee, and as suggested by the Government of India itself in its Home Department Resolution No. 199, dated 18th June, 1888, as a necessary preliminary to the introduction of an organised system of Technical education in the several Provinces.

(*d*) That at least one central fully-equipped Polytechnic Institute should be established in the country with minor technical schools and colleges in the different Provinces.

Poverty

XV. Resolved—That this Congress deplores fresh outbreaks of famine in several parts of the country, and holding that the frequent occurrences of famines are due to the great poverty of the people, which forces large numbers of them to throw themselves on State help at the first touch of scarcity, it again urges the Government of India and the Secretary of State to institute a detailed enquiry into the economic condition of a few typical villages in different parts of India.

(1) This Congress is of opinion that the property of an agricultural country like India cannot be secured without a definite limitation of the State demand on land, such as was proposed by Lord Canning in 1862, or by Lord Ripon in 1882.

(2) It regrets that Lord Curzon, in his Land Resolution of 1902, failed to recognise any such limitation, and declined to accept the suggestions of the Right Hon. Sir Richard Garth and other memorialists.

(3) It holds that a reasonable and definite restriction of the State-demand, and not the restriction on tenants' rights, such as has found favour in recent years, is the true remedy for the growing impoverishment of the agricultural population.

Quarantine at Bombay

XVI. Resolved—That having regard to the fact that there is ten days international quarantine in existence at Kamran, this Congress holds that the quarantine of five days imposed at the port of Bombay upon the Musalman pilgrims before embarking for Jedda is unnecessary and vexatious, and produces a feeling of discontent; this Congress, therefore, prays that the quarantine imposed at Bombay be entirely abolished.

Provincial Grievances

XVII. Resolved—That this Congress, concurring with previous Congresses, strongly urges—

(1) The constitution of the Panjab into a Regulation Province.

(2) The expansion and reform of the Panjab Legislative Council in accordance with the Indian Council Act of 1892.

(3) The establishment of a Chartered High Court of Judicature in the Panjab.

(4) The Enactment of Legislation for Berar by the Supreme Legislative Council and not by Executive order of the Governor-General in Council.

(5) The restoration, to the people of the Central Provinces of the right to elect their representative on the Supreme Legislative Council instead of his being nominated by the Government.

(6) The cancellation of the Government of India Notification of 25th June, 1891, in the Foreign Department, gagging the Press in territories under British administration in Native States as being serious infringement of the liberty of the Press in those tracts.

India and the General Election

XVIII Resolved—That this Congress desires to accord its most cordial support to the candidature of Mr. Dadabhai Naoroji for North Lambeth, and appeals to the electors of that constituency to return him to Parliament

Thanks of Congress

XIX Resolved— That this Congress desires to record its sense of high appreciation of the manner in which the Hon Mr G. K Gokhale, C I. E, and Lala Lajpat Rai discharged the onerous duties imposed on them in England

XXIII Resolved—That this Congress desires to convey to Sir William Wedderburn, Bart, and the other members of the British Committee, its most grateful thanks for their disinterested services in the cause of India's political advancement

Appointment of the Hon. Mr. Gokhale as Delegate to England

XX Resolved— That in view of the importance of urging the more pressing proposals of the Congress on the attention of the authorities in England at the present juncture, the Congress appoints its President, the Hon Mr. Gopal Krishna Gokhale, C I E, as its delegate, and deputes him to proceed to England for this purpose

Congress Work

XXI. Resolved—That a Standing Committee of the Congress be appointed to promote the objects of the Congress and to take such steps during the year as may be necessary to give effect to the Resolutions of the Congress.

That the following gentlemen be appointed members of the Standing Committee for the year 1906

(1) Hon. Sir Pherozeshah Mehta, K.C.I.E. (Bombay).
(2) Hon. Daji Abaji Khare (Bombay).

(3) G. Subramania Iyer Esq. (Madras).
(4) Hon. Nawab Syed Muhammad (Madras).
(5) Surendranath Bannerji, Esq (Calcutta).
(6) A. Choudhuri Esq. (Calcutta).
(7) Maulvi Abdul Kasim (Burdwan).
(8) S. Sinha Esq. (Bankipur).
(9) Hon. Pandit Madan Mohan Malaviya (Allahabad).
(10) Munshi Ganga Prasad Varma (Lucknow).
(11) Lala Lajpat Rai (Lahore).
(12) Lala Harkishan Lal (Lahore).
(13) Rao Bahadur R. N. Mudholkar (Amraoti); with
(14) D. E. Wacha Esq. (Bombay); and
(15) Hon. Mr. G. K. Gokhale, C.I.E. (Poona).
} as Secretaries of the Committee.

Formal

XXII. Resolved—That this Congress re-appoints A. O. Hume Esq., C.B., to be General Secretary, and D. E. Wacha Esq. and the Hon. Mr. G. K. Gokhale, C.I.E., to be Joint General Secretaries for the ensuing year.

XXIV. Resolved—That the Twenty-second Indian National Congress do assemble, on such day after Christmas Day, 1906, as may later be determined on at Calcutta.

CHAPTER XXII

NEVER before nor since 1906, has the Congress seen such a gathering as that which assembled at Calcutta on the 26th, 27th, 28th and 29th of December in that memorable year. A huge Pavilion was erected by the Russa Road, Bhowanipur, seating 16,000 persons, with wide passages that gave standing room to another 4,000; Bengal had been roused from end to end, all India sympathised with her wrongs, and 1,663 delegates came to show their love. They came from:

Bengal	686
U. P.	187
Panjab	139
C. P. (90), Berar (60), Jaipur (1), Indore (1), Secunderabad (6), Bangalore (2) ...	160
Bombay	262
Madras	221
Burma	8
	1,663

Only once has this number been overtopped, in the memorable Congress of 1889, to which Charles Bradlaugh came, and never have the delegates been so evenly distributed as on this occasion.

The welcome given to the President-elect and past Presidents, as they came on to the platform with the Chairman of the Reception Committee, Dr. Rash Behari Ghosh, rang out from 20,000 throats, and when silence was obtained, Mr. Narendranath Sen, the patriot Editor of *The Indian Mirror*, opened the proceedings with a prayer, and two men choirs and a third of 30 young girls, sang National songs. Then Dr. Rash Behari Ghosh welcomed the delegates, and spoke with deep sorrow in that the year had robbed Bengal of two of her best beloved, W. C. Bannerji and Ananda Mohan Bose, leaders sorely needed now, compassed as they were with dangers and darkness. They had been afflicted by floods and famine, but far worse were the political perils around them. Lord Curzon had found India comparatively contented, and had left her fermenting with unrest, and his parting gift was the Partition of "a Province, for which he had always dissembled his love".

The Partition of Bengal was followed by Russian methods of Government, with this difference, that the officials who devised them wero Englishmen, while the Russian official is at least the countryman of those whom he governs or misgoverns. The singing of national songs and even the cry of "Bande Mataram" were forbidden under severe penalties. This ordinance was fittingly succeeded by the prosecution of schoolboys, the quartering of military and punitive police, the prohibition and forcible dispersion of public meetings, and these high-handed proceedings attained their crown and completion in the tragedy at Barisal, when the Provincial Conference was dispersed by the Police, who wantonly broke the peace in order, I imagine, to keep the peace. Now, though we are a thoroughly loyal people and our loyalty is not to be easily shaken because it is founded on a more solid basis than mere sentiment, I have no hesitation in saying that we should be less than men if we could forget the tragedy of that day, the memory of which will always fill us with shame and humiliation. And this leads me to remark that it was not cowardice that prevented our young men from retaliating. It was their respect for law and order—their loyalty to their much reviled leaders that kept them in check. All this has now happily been put an end to. But as soon as the cloud began to lift, those Anglo-Indians who are obliged to live in this land of regrets merely from a high sense of duty were seized with the fear that their monopoly of philanthropic work might be interrupted, and immediately commenced a campaign of slander and misrepresentation which in virulence and mendacity has never been equalled. I. C. S.'s in masks and editors of Anglo-Indian newspapers forthwith began to warn the English people that we were thoroughly disloyal, ferreting out sedition with an ingenuity which would have done no discredit to the professors of Laputa.

He then spoke of Swadeshism, in which "you see the cradle of a New India. To speak of such a movement as disloyal is a lie and calumny. We love England, with all her faults, but we love India more. If this is disloyalty, we are, I am proud to say, disloyal." He closed with some wise words of counsel to the younger men, furious with the wrongs they suffered, of grave warning to England, coupled with a declaration of his belief in her justice.

Raja Peary Mohan Mukerji proposed, the Hon. Nawab Syed Muhammad seconded, Mr. C. Sankaran Nair—remarking that "the people of this country have resolved to take the development of its resources into their own hands"—supported the election of Mr. Dadabhai Naoroji, who took the chair amid a scene of unparalleled enthusiasm. The noble veteran spoke a few words of thanks, and then gave his speech to Mr. Gokhale to read, his 82 years not permitting him to address an audience of 20,000 people.

The President, as is his wont, interspersed his speech with deadly quotations, buttressing every position he took up. He regarded the work of the Congress as twofold: "First and most important is the question of the policy and principles of the system of Government under which India is to be governed in the future." Secondly, to watch the present system of administration, and introduce reform till it was "radically altered and based upon right principles and policy". He addressed himself chiefly to the first. Then he built up his argument. Indians "are British citizens, and are entitled to and claim all British citizens' rights". The first of these is Freedom. Gladstone said: "Freedom is the very breath of our life ..... We stand for liberty, our policy is the policy of freedom." The first grant of Bombay to the East India Company in 1669, declared all living thereon and their descendants to be free as though "living and born in England". The Boers, in 1901, were called fellow-citizens, and had already reached Self-Government; India had not obtained it 200 years after her becoming connected with England. When objection was raised to his name on the register of electors in England, the Revising Barrister had brushed it aside, on the ground that as an Indian he was a British citizen. The Queen's letter to Lord Derby, bidding him draw up the Proclamation of 1858, desired him to point to the privileges "the Indians will receive in being placed on an equality with the subjects of the British Crown". She bound herself to Indians "by the same obligations of duty which bind us to our other subjects," and she telegraphed a message to be read in open Darbar that "the great principles of liberty, equity and justice are secured to them". Edward VII, in 1906, said that he hoped that "throughout my dominions the grant of free institutions will be followed," etc. These rights were due to them, as a reparation for all they had suffered. Moreover the British "would not allow themselves to be subjected for a single day to such an unnatural system of Government as the one which has been imposed upon India for nearly a century and a half".

He then claimed for Indians in India all the control that Englishmen had in England. This was a necessity, in order to remedy the great economic evil which was at the root of Indian poverty. It was "absolutely necessary" for the progress and welfare of the Indian people. "The whole matter can be comprised in one word, Self-Government, or Swaraj, like that of the United Kingdom or the Colonies." When should a beginning be made which should automatically develop into full Self-Government? At once. "Not only has the time fully arrived, but had arrived long past."

Simultaneous examinations should at once be held for the Public Service, so as to change the administration from foreign to Indian, and then transferred entirely to India. Free and compulsory education must be given. Representation, real and living, must be granted. Were Indians to remain "under the barbarous system of despotism, unworthy of British instincts, principles and civilisation"? Just financial relations must "be established at once. They require no delay or preparation. It only needs the determination and will of the British Government to do justice." If the British made up "their mind to do their duty" they could "devise means to accord Self-Government within no distant time". He did not despair, but they must work, and agitate both in England and India.

Agitation is the life and soul of the whole political, social and industrial history of England. It is by agitation the English have accomplished their most glorious achievements, their prosperity, their liberties and, in short, their first place among the Nations of the world. The whole life of England every day, is all agitation. You do not open your paper in the morning but read from beginning to end it is all agitation—Congresses and Conferences, Meetings and Resolutions without end—for a thousand and one movements local and national. From the Prime Minister to the humblest politician, his occupation is agitation for everything he wants to accomplish. The whole Parliament, Press, and Platform is simply all agitation. Agitation is the civilised peaceful weapon of moral force, and infinitely preferable to brute physical force, when possible. . . . . . Agitate; agitate means inform. Inform, inform the Indian people what their rights are and how and why they should obtain them, and inform the British people of the rights of the Indian people, and why they should grant them. If we do not speak they say we are satisfied. If we speak we become agitators! The Indian people are properly asked to act constitutionally, while the Government remains unconstitutional and despotic.

Finally, he appealed for union between Hindus and Muhammadans, for Indian emancipation depended on this. Social Reform and Industrial progress were also needed.

> Self-Government is the only and chief remedy. In Self-Government lie our hope, strength and greatness. . . . . . I do not know what good fortune may be in store for me during the short period that may be left to me, and if I can leave a word of affection and devotion for my country and countrymen I say: Be united, persevere, and achieve Self-Government, so that the millions now perishing by poverty, famine and plague, and the scores of millions that are starving on scanty subsistence may be saved, and India may once more occupy her proud position of yore among the greatest and civilised Nations of the West.

Bande Mataram was sung, by the girls' choir, the audience standing, and the Congress adjourned, after the Subjects Committee had been elected.

The second day saw an equally crowded Pavilion, and after the singing of patriotic songs, Mr. D. E. Wacha read some messages of goodwill from W. T. Stead, Dr. Rutherford, a number of members of Parliament, and, most interesting of all, from Natal and the Transvaal, sending little contributions to the Congress, and from "the Indian inhabitants of German South Africa, sending Rs. 285 to help the cause of their Motherland".

The President then moved Resolution I, of grief over the heavy death-roll of the year, Mr. W. C. Bannerji, Mr. Justice Budruddin Tyabji, and Mr. Ananda Mohan Bose, all ex-Presidents of the Congress, and Mr. Viraraghavachariar, one of the leading workers in Madras.

Resolution II dealt with the wrongs inflicted on Indians in the Colonies, and was moved by Mr. P. R. Sundara Aiyar, lamenting that there were 50,000 Indian slaves in Natal, and many others elsewhere in Africa, and saying that British Indians were discriminated against, Portuguese and French Indian subjects having more rights. Lord Lansdowne had said that "among the many misdeeds of the South African Republic, I do not know that any fills me with more indignation than its treatment of these Indians". That was before the War. The Resolution was seconded by Mr. H. A. Wadia, supported by Mr. Madanjit, Mr. C. Y. Chintamani and Mr. Lalit Mohan Ghosal, and carried.

The Hon. Mr. B. N. Sarma moved Resolution III on the necessity for retrenching Indian expenditure, and showed that between 1893-94 and 1906-07 the gross expenditure had risen from 90 crores of rupees to 134 crores of rupees annually. The net expenditure in 1861-62 was 34 crores, and in 1884-85 it was 41 crores, an increase of 16 per cent, while the growth of population was 14 per cent. But if we take from 1884-85 to 1904-05, we find the increase of expenditure was 70 per cent, and of population, at the highest, of 18 per cent. The currency policy of the Empire made the silver in the rupee worth only 12 annas, so that the ryot, to pay Rs. 3 in taxation, had to sell produce worth Rs. 4. During these twenty years, military expenditure had risen from 17 crores to 32 crores, almost cent. per cent. And of this, nearly 7 crores was spent in England. With this great increase of military expenditure went the worst famines ever known in British India, causing some 11 million deaths. Contrast this with the 2 million pounds spent in education, while England spent 16 millions on education in her own land.

Mr. G. A. Natesan seconded, and pointed out that of the 90 crores of military expenditure 70 crores had been spent on wars outside the Indian frontiers and in parts of India and elsewhere, all against the real interests of India. The Welby Commission had recommended that England should contribute to the cost and that was agreed to, but the pay of British soldiers in India was raised, which took from India thrice the contribution made by England. Sir Henry Brackenbury said, before that Commission :

> If it were desired to maintain British Rule in India only for India's sake, then, I think, it would be fair to make India pay to the utmost farthing that could be shown was due to Britain's rule over India ; but I cannot but feel that Britain's interest in keeping India under British rule is enormous. India affords employment to thousands of Britons. India employs millions of British capital, and Indian commerce is of immense value to Great Britain. Therefore it seems to me that, India being held by Great Britain, not only for India's sake, Great Britain should pay a share of the expenditure for this purpose ; and in estimating what that share should be, I think that England should behave generously England is a rich country, and India is a poor country.

Mr. N. M. Ranade supported, urging that the Government should repeal the Arms Act and give permission for Volunteering, and should give fuller employment to Indians, so reducing expenditure. The Resolution was carried.

Resolution IV, separation of Judicial from Executive Functions, was moved by the Hon. Mr. Krishnan Nair, seconded by the Hon. Mr. Ambikacharan Mozumdar, supported by seven other speakers, despite its familiarity, and carried. Mr. Mozumdar said that he was chosen as seconder, because there was probably no other man in the Congress " who possesses the asinine patience of talking more than twelve times, and each time only to stocks and stones ". Yet people ask why we want Home Rule! The Resolution was carried with one dissentient.

Khan Bahadur Moulvi Muhammad Yusuf moved Resolution V, asking that a Commission should be appointed by the Government, which should see if the decisions of the Privy Council against the validity of the Wakf-i-ala-aulad were consonant with the law, usages, and sentiments of Muhammadans, and if they were not, that steps should be taken to legalise the Musalman view. The Hon. Mr. Baikunthanath Sen seconded, pointing out that the decisions had curtailed the power of Muhammadans to make provision for their children. Mr. A. M. Jinnah, supporting, welcomed the Resolution as showing that the Musalmans could make known their grievances through the Congress. Moulvi Abdul Kasim and Mr. S. B. Patel supported, and the Resolution was carried. The Congress adjourned.

The third day began with National songs, and the arrival of H. H. the Gaekwar of Baroda, accompanied by his Prime Minister, Mr. R. C. Dutt, was warmly welcomed.

Nawab Khuja Athikulla of Dacca moved Resolution VI, against the Partition of Bengal, and declared that Hindus and Muhammadans should enter a united protest against it.

Mr. Surendranath Bannerji seconded, expressing their disappointment with the biographer of Cobden and Bright, but making excuses for him as breathing an undiluted bureaucratic atmosphere. Sir William Wedderburn asked them to wait.

> Wait we must; what else can we do? Waiting upon the will of our rulers has been our lot for the last three centuries. We shall certainly wait; but not in meek submission to the will of our rulers as the decree of an inexorable fate, but with the firm resolve to overcome that fate, and work out our salvation. Our rulers must recognise the new spirit, born, it may be, of the huge blunder of the Partition, vibrating through our hearts, uplifting us to a higher plane of political effort. We are, Sirs, no longer Orientals of the old type, content to grovel under the weight of an overmastering fate, but we are Orientals of the new school, enfranchised by English culture and English influences, revivified by the example of China, Japan, and last, but not the least, of Persia, and as Orientals of the new school we believe that Nations by themselves are made.

The Resolution was supported by Mr. R. N. Mudholkar, who declared that Bengal was divided because it was too strong for the bureaucracy, and that until re-union was conceded "we shall go on agitating, striving, and doing everything that lies within the limits of law till we obtain redress of our grievances". After two more gentlemen had spoken, the Resolution was carried.

The Hon. Mr. Ambikacharan Mozumdar moved Resolution VII, declaring that in view of the little voice the people had in administration, and the lack of consideration shown by Government to their representations, the Boycott was legitimate as a protest against Partition. Mr. Bepin Chandra Pal seconded in a vigorous speech, and said that it was not a mere boycott of goods, but one of honorary offices and associations with the Government in East Bengal. Not one leader of the people would associate with the Lieutenant-Governor in any legislative work. The Hon. Mr. L. A. Govindaraghava Aiyar justified the use of the Boycott in Bengal, but did not think it could be used ordinarily in other Provinces. Mr. A. Choudhuri pointed out that the Resolution was limited to Bengal, that was smarting under a great injury, and had a right to use the Boycott as a political weapon.

The Hon. Pandit Madan Mohan Malaviya, in supporting, said that Bengal was justified in using the Boycott as a weapon, but the Congress could not be committed to the view of Mr. Pal and the extension of the Boycott, as he described it. He hoped the other Provinces would never be driven to the necessity of using it, but that reforms needed would be gained without it. The Hon. Mr. Gokhale said that they were bound only by the Resolutions of the Congress, and the Resolution declared that the boycott movement marking the resentment of the people against the Partition of Bengal was and is legitimate. They were not bound by individual speeches. The Resolution was carried with one dissentient and one neutral.

Mr. Naoroji left the Hall for half an hour, and his place was taken by Mr. R. C. Dutt. Resolutions VIII and IX were postponed, and the Resolutions on Education taken.

Resolution X protested against the educational policy of the Government, restricting the spread of higher education, and asked for free education, to be gradually made compulsory, larger grants, technical education, and the removal of the restrictions on private enterprise in education. It was moved by Dewan Bahadur Ambalal S. Desai, seconded by Mr. Raghubar Dayal, supported by Mr. C. Karunakara Menon, Messrs. M. K. Padhya, S. V. Khare, Harischandra Vissevdas, G. A. Patel, and carried.

Resolution XI declared that the time had come to organise National Education, Literary, Scientific and Technical, for both boys and girls, on National lines and under National control. This Resolution was appropriately moved by Mr. Hirendranath Datta, the Hon. Secretary of the National Council of Education. He said that Self-Government was a three-faced deity, political, industrial and educational. He quoted as describing Indian education what had been said of Irish:

"Departments of Education in Ireland, primary, secondary, university, are directly controlled by the British Government. The language of Ireland, the history of Ireland, the economics of Ireland, the possibilities and rights of Ireland find no place in the curriculum." Exactly the same here. "Education in Ireland encumbers the intellect, chills the fancy, and enervates the body. It destroys the fancy. It does not acquaint the youth with the traditions of his country, nor does it afford him facilities for physical culture."

After describing what they were doing in Bengal, he concluded :

> Trust not your education to aliens. In Native souls and Native hands, the only hopes of succour rest.

Mr. M. P. Venkatappiah seconded, and laid stress on the self-reliance embodied in the resolution, and it struck the note of Nationalism. The Resolution was supported by Messrs. S. K. Nair, C. V. Vaidya, J. N. Roy, Prof. V. G. Bijapurkar, Moulvi Ismail Hasan Sheraji, and Mr. M. K. Patel, and was carried.

Resolution VIII was then moved by Rao Bahadur P. Ananda Charlu; it advocated Swadeshi, and the veteran politician urged its adoption specially by the well-to-do, and suggested an association of rich men who should give bounties to industries, as the Government would not do it. The Hon. Pandit Madan Mohan seconded, pointing out that the raw material left the country and came back as manufactured goods; if they were free, they would adopt protection, as all countries did when industries were nascent. It was a religious as well as a patriotic duty to support indigenous industries. Mr. B. G. Tilak supported, saying that they, the middle classes, were the greatest consumers of foreign goods. Self-help, determination and sacrifice were needed. Lala Lajpat Rai urged that Indians should keep their capital in their own hands and utilise it, and arrange for the distribution of the articles they produced. Messrs. Khaja Muhammad Noor Golam Ahmed Khan and V. R. Joshi supported, and the Resolution was carried.

Then came Resolution IX, demanding Colonial Self-Government, and laying down four steps to it, to be taken immediately (this, in 1906). The speeches were very short, the time being late, so Mr. A. Choudhuri only added a few sentences in moving, and the Hon. Mr. L. A. Govindaraghava briefly pointed to the action, in the Philippine Islands, of the United States. Dr. S. K. Mullick remarked that a paper had said that the English had come here like the Aryans and Mughals, and had come to stay; then let them, like their predecessors, identify themselves with the people. Messrs. Bomanji Patel, V. A. Pandit, S. B. Mitra, A. Ramanna, P. C. Maitra, all supported. Mr. M. A. Jinnah proposed and Mr. M. Abdul Kasim seconded an amendment, cancelling a reservation in the original Resolution, regarding the backward class; it was supported by Mr. Hafiz Abdul Rahim and accepted, and the amended Resolution was carried.

The President moved from the Chair the Resolution re-appointing Messrs. Hume, D. E. Wacha and G. K. Gokhale, which was duly carried (and should be Resolution XI A.) He moved also Resolution XII, thanking Sir William Wedderburn and the British Committee, and the Congress adjourned.

On meeting on the fourth day, the Congress was startled by the news that the Rt. Hon. Mr. Samuel Smith, who had been present on the first day, having come to India to preside at the All-India Temperance Conference, had suddenly passed away.

Mr. Surendranath Bannerji moved a Resolution of sorrow (No. XIII), seconded by Sir Balchandra, and put with a few words from the President, who had known him for 40 years. It was carried by the audience standing.

Mr. C. Vijiaraghavachari moved Resolution XIV, on Permanent Settlement, and protesting against the view that the Land tax was rent. Land in India had never belonged to the King; the Sages had said that the world belonged to those who were born on it; private property was gained by cultivation, and the King, who was ordained for protection, received a share from the cultivators for his services. The idea that land belonged to the King was western and feudal, not Indian. Mr. Gokaran Misra seconded, and Mr. Mehta Bahadurchand supported. Mr. Raoji Govind drew attention to the shortening of the period between Settlements in Hoshangabad, his district. It had been 30 years; it was now 12. When it came under Britain, the Government took Rs. 2,56,600; it rose after 20 years to Rs. 2,70,000. After 30 years it was reduced to Rs. 1,88,000, as the people could not pay, and was again reduced to Rs. 1,68,000. During the last 30 years, it rose, with cesses, to Rs. 4,87,944, and at the current Settlement to Rs. 9,30,257. In 1893-94, under the last, Government took as tax Rs. 4,87,000 out of Rs. 11,33,000, rents paid by tenants, leaving Rs. 6,46,000 to the Malguzars. In 1896, the re-Settlement, the tenant-rents were Rs. 11,42,000, and the Government took Rs. 9,30,000, leaving only

Rs. 2,12,000. Mr. Desmukh added a few words on the land policy of Lord Curzon, "destructive to the people and suicidal to the Government," and the Resolution was carried.

Mr. G. Subramania Iyer moved, Mr. Baikunthanath Sen seconded, and Pandit Ramanath supported, Resolution XV, conveying the thanks of the Congress for his services in England to Mr. Gokhale, who answered in a short speech, when the great ovation which greeted him had subsided, saying what strong hope he felt from the advent of the new Government to power, with a democratic House of Commons.

Then the Hon. Mr. D. A. Khare moved Resolution XVI, containing a Constitution for the Congress, to be tried for a year; it recommended (*a*) the formation of Provincial Congress Committees, which should form District Committees; (*b*) An All-India Congress Standing Committee; (*c*) two alternative schemes for selecting a President; and (*d*) A Subjects Committee for settling the programme of the Congress each year. Four members spoke supporting it and it was carried, the delegates from each Province being asked to send up names for the All-India Committee. Most of this was incorporated in the Constitution framed in 1908.

A vote of thanks to the President was proposed by Mr. Lal Mohan Ghose, and he was garlanded and bestrewn with flowers amid thunders of applause. A Swadeshi umbrella from Poona was unfurled and held over him for a moment, and then he said a few words of thanks. He reminded them that, in its 22nd Session, the Congress had placed before itself a definite goal—Self-Government, Swaraj. Now it was for the younger generation to reach it. The Hon. Mr. Chitnavis invited the Congress to Nagpur, for its 1907 meeting, and the Twenty-second National Congress "dispersed amidst scenes of the wildest enthusiasm and rejoicings".

Alas! Coercion was to do its deadly work during the approaching year. The seeds sown by Lord Curzon were to ripen into their harvest of dragon-teeth. The strongest and furthest-sighted men were to hold to their old ideals of constitutional work and steady progress. Others, maddened by the repressive measures adopted, were to cause a partition worse than that of Lord Curzon, a division of the National Party, one part holding to the group that refused to despair of appealing to the House of Commons, and the other which became frankly antagonistic to all co-operation with the British Government. And beyond these, loomed up the Anarchist Party with the bomb and revolver for its methods, the incarnation of blind hatred, without constructive policy, the mad efforts of lads, dreaming of winning Liberty for their country, and succeeding only in committing a few useless crimes. In the scales of History shall all these be weighed, Government, Moderates, Extremists, Anarchists, and to each shall be assigned their own place.

RESOLUTIONS

Condolence

I. Resolved—That this Congress desires to place on record its sense of the great loss which the Congress and the country at large have sustained by the death of Mr. W. C. Bonnerji,

Mr. Justice Budruddin Tyabji, and Mr. Ananda Mohan Bose, ex-Presidents of the Congress, and Mr. M. Viraraghava Chariar of Madras. Their great public services and the example of duty and of self-sacrificing devotion which they presented in their lives entitle them to the lasting gratitude of the country;

That a copy of the foregoing Resolution be forwarded to the families of the late Messrs. Bannerji, Tyabji, Bose, and M. Viraraghava Chariar, over the signature of the President of the Congress.

Indians in the Colonies

II. Resolved—That this Congress, while noting with satisfaction the action of the Imperial Government in disallowing for the present the proposed Ordinance against British Indians in the Transvaal, desires to give expression to its grave apprehension that unless the Imperial Government continues to extend its firm protection to the British Indian Community, the policy of the Ordinance is almost certain to be enforced as soon as arrangements under the Constitution recently granted are completed;

That this Congress also places on record its sense of deep regret and indignation that the people of this country should be subjected to harassing and degrading restrictions and denied the ordinary rights of British citizenship in His Majesty's Colonies, and the Congress expresses its firm conviction that such a policy is fraught with serious danger to the best interests of the Empire.

Finance

III. Resolved—That this Congress renews its protest against the excessive and alarming growth of military charges in recent years and their undue preponderance in the public expenditure of the country;

That this Congress is of opinion that, as the military expenditure of the country is determined, not solely by its own military needs and requirements, but also by the exigencies of British supremacy and British policy in the East, it is only fair that a reasonable share of such expenditure should be borne by the British Exchequer;

That this Congress strongly urges that by a substantial reduction of military expenditure and by the steady substitution of the Indian for the European agency in the Public Service, funds should be set free to be devoted to the promotion of education in all its branches, to improve sanitation and to the relief of the ryot's burdens, such as a further reduction of the Salt-tax, a reduction of the Land Revenue demand of the State, and measures for dealing with agricultural indebtedness.

Separation of Judicial and Executive Functions

IV. Resolved—That in the opinion of this Congress the separation of the Judicial from the Executive functions, which is admittedly necessary in the interests of good government and sound judicial administration, should no longer be deferred.

Validity of Wakf-i-ala-aulad

V. Resolved—That in view of the general opinion amongst Muhammadans that the recent decisions of the Privy Council against the validity of the "wakf-i-ala-aulad" are against the Muhammadan Law, this Congress is of opinion that a Commission should be appointed by the Government to enquire whether the Privy Council has not erred in its decisions, having regard to the law, usage and sentiments of the Muhammadan people; and, if it be found that the decisions are erroneous, this Congress urges that steps should be taken to give legal effect to the right view.

Partition of Bengal

VI. Resolved—That this Congress again records its emphatic protest against the Partition of Bengal, and regrets that the present Government, while admitting that there were errors in the original plan, and that it went wholly and decisively against the wishes of the majority of the people of Bengal, is disposed to look upon it as a settled fact, in spite of the earnest and persistent protest of the people, and their manifest disinclination to accept it as final;

That this Congress, composed of representatives from all the Provinces of this country, desires earnestly to impress upon the British Parliament and the present Liberal Government that it will be not only just, but expedient, to reverse or modify the Partition in such a manner as to keep the entire Bengali-speaking community under one undivided administration, and thus restore contentment to so important a Province as Bengal.

Boycott Movement

VII. Resolved—That having regard to the fact that the people of this country have little or no voice in its administration, and that their representations to the Government do not receive due consideration, this Congress is of opinion that the Boycott Movement inaugurated in Bengal by way of protest against the Partition of that Province, was, and is, legitimate.

Swadeshi

VIII. Resolved—That this Congress accords its most cordial support to the Swadeshi movement, and calls upon the people of the country to labour for its success, by making earnest and sustained efforts to promote the growth of indigenous industries and to stimulate the production of indigenous articles by giving them preference over imported commodities even at some sacrifice.

Self-Government

IX. Resolved—That this Congress is of opinion that the system of Government obtaining in the Self-Governing British Colonies should be extended to India, and that, as steps leading to it, it urges that the following reforms should be immediately carried out:

(*a*) All examinations held in England only should be simultaneously held in India and in England, and that all higher appointments which are made in India should be by competitive examination only;

(*b*) The adequate representation of Indians in the Council of the Secretary of State and the Executive Councils of the Viceroy, and of the Governors of Madras and Bombay;

(*c*) The expansion of the Supreme and Provincial Legislative Councils, allowing a larger and truly effective representation of the people and a larger control over the financial and executive administration of the country;

(*d*) The powers of Local and Municipal bodies should be extended and official control over them should not be more than what is exercised by the Local Government Board in England over similar bodies.

Education

X. Resolved—That this Congress repeats its protest against the policy of the Government in respect of High and Secondary Education, as being one of officialising the governing bodies of the Universities, and restricting the spread of education. This Congress is of opinion that the Government should take immediate steps for (1) making Primary Education free and gradually compulsory, all over the country, (2) assigning larger sums of money to Secondary Education (special encouragement being given where necessary to educationally backward classes), (3) making the existing Universities more free from official control, and providing them with sufficient means to take up the work of teaching, and (4) making adequate provision for Technical Education in the different Provinces, having regard to local requirements.

National Education

XI. Resolved—That in the opinion of this Congress the time has arrived for the people all over the country earnestly to take up the question of National Education, for both boys and girls, and organise a system of education—Literary, Scientific and Technical—suited to the requirements of the country, on National lines and under National control.

Thanks of Congress

XII. Resolved—That this Congress desires to convey to Sir William Wedderburn, Bart., and the other members of the British Committee, its most grateful thanks, for their disinterested services in the cause of India's political advancement.

XV. Resolved—That this Congress records its sense of high appreciation of the eminent public service rendered by the Hon. Mr. G. K. Gokhale, C.I.E., during his recent visit to England, as the Delegate of the Congress.

Condolence

XIII. Resolved—That this Congress desires to place on record its sense of the deep sorrow and of loss to India of the sudden death of the Rt. Hon. Mr. Samuel Smith, and that a copy of the foregoing resolution be communicated to the members of his family.

Permanent Settlement

XIV. Resolved—That this Congress is of opinion that the prosperity of an agricultural country like India cannot be secured without a definite limitation of the State demand on land, such as was proposed by Lord Canning in 1862, or by Lord Ripon in 1882; and it regrets that Lord Curzon, in his Land Resolution of 1902, failed to recognise the necessity of any such limitation and declined to accept the suggestions of Sir Richard Garth and other memorialists in the matter. The Congress holds that a reasonable and definite limitation of the State demand is the true remedy for the growing impoverishment of the agricultural population.

This Congress respectfully protests against the view that the Land Revenue in India is not a tax, but is in the nature of rent.

Congress Work

XVI. Resolved—That this Congress adopts tentatively for one year the following recommendations of the Standing Committee of the Congress appointed at Benares last year:

1. *Provincial Congress Committees*

(*a*) The Committee recommends that each Province should organise at its capital, a Provincial Congress Committee in such manner as may be determined at a meeting of the Provincial Conference, or at a special meeting, held for the purpose, of representatives of different districts in the Province.

(*b*) The Provincial Congress Committee should act for the Province in all Congress matters and it should be its special care to organise District Associations throughout the Province for sustained and continuous political work in the Province.

2. Central Standing Congress Committee

The Committee recommends that the Congress should appoint every year a Central Standing Committee for all India, to carry out the Resolutions of the Congress, and to deal with urgent questions that may arise and which may require to be disposed of in the name of the Congress, and that this Committee should consist of:

12	members from	Bengal, Behar, Assam and Burma
8	" "	Madras
8	" "	Bombay
6	" "	United Provinces
6	" "	Panjab
4	" "	Central Provinces
2	" "	Berar

the President of the year and the General Secretaries being, ex officio, members in addition.

3. Selection of President

In the matter of the selection of President in future years, the Committee recommends that the following scheme should be adopted:

The Provincial Congress Committee of the Province in which the Congress is to be held should organise a Reception Committee in such manner as it deems proper for making arrangements for the Congress Session, and the choice of the President should, in the first instance, rest with the Reception Committee, if, after consulting Provincial Congress Committees, the Reception Committee is able to make the choice by a majority of at least three-fourths of its members. If, however, no such majority can be obtained to support the nomination of any person, the question should be referred to the Central Standing Committee of the Congress, and the decision of this Committee should be final.

4. Subjects Committee

The Committee recommends that the Subjects Committee, appointed at each Session of the Congress to settle its programme of work, should consist of:

25	representatives of	Bengal, Behar, Assam and Burma
15	" "	Madras
15	" "	Bombay
10	"	United Provinces
10	" "	Panjab
6	" "	Central Provinces
4	" "	Berar

and 10 additional members for the Province in which the Congress is held, elected by the delegates attending the Congress from the respective Provinces in such manner as they may deem proper; and that the President of the year, the Chairman of the Reception Committee of the year, all ex-Presidents and all ex-Chairmen of Reception Committees who may be present at the Congress, the General Secretaries of the Congress, and the local Secretaries of the Congress for the year, should, in addition, be ex-officio members of the Subjects Committee.

Formal

XVII. Resolved—That the next Congress assemble at Nagpur.

CHAPTER XXIII

PART I

We come to the saddest episode in the story of the Congress, the split in the National party. The invitation to Nagpur for the Congress of 1907 had been accepted by the Calcutta Congress, but some local disagreements having supervened, which made the holding of the Congress there difficult, if not impossible, the All-India Congress Committee, elected under the tentative Constitution passed at Calcutta, decided that the Twenty-third National Congress should be held at Surat, and some historic French gardens on the banks of the Tapti, forming French territory, were taken, and a charming city of tents was made with a large Pavilion. The whole country was in a state of turmoil and excitement, and the signs of cleavage of the National party into Right and Left Wings, indicated in the last chapter, had grown marked. Yet all seemed well as the delegates poured in from all sides, some 1,600 in all; but no list of them seems to have survived.

Dr. Rash Behari Ghose had been duly elected President of the Congress under the tentative

Constitution of 1906, and the first sign of discord was the suggestion that Lala Lajpat Rai, just released after his deportation, should be elected as President, as a protest against his unfair treatment by the Government. That staunch patriot, however, refused to be made into a battle-flag, and absolutely declined to be elected President in so irregular a fashion. Then a rumour spread that the four militant Resolutions of the Calcutta Congress, on Self-Government, Boycott, Swadeshi and National Education, were not to be put before the Subjects Committee. Whence the rumour came, none knew, but rumours rise and spread easily in an excited crowd. The Congress met on December 26th, 1907, and the Pandal, holding 7,000 people, was packed. The President-elect received an enthusiastic ovation, a few cries of hostility being drowned in the roar of cheering. The Chairman of the Reception Committee, Mr. Tribhuvan Das Malvi, welcomed the delegates in a short speech, of which the most noteworthy passage referred to the sad condition of the country:

> Since the Congress met last year, we have passed through very troublous times indeed. Eminent Indians have been seriously suspected of and charged with the highest offences against the State, exciting sedition, rioting and the like, in most cases without justification. Somehow the idea became prevalent among the ruling class that the present year, being the 50th year since the Indian Mutiny, Indians were preparing for a similar revolt, and a sort of panic seized them. To check this imaginary revolt all sorts of repressive and re-actionary measures were taken. Old obsolete enactments, of the existence whereof even no one ever dreamed, were brought into requisition for the purpose of punishing people for

undefined offences assumed to have been committed, without giving any notice to the victims of the charges laid at their doors, or giving them an opportunity of meeting those charges. The people in certain localities were assumed to harbour treasonable intentions, and meetings were prohibited in those districts, at first for a time, and we have now a very dangerous statute in the shape of the Seditious Meetings Act, capable of general application throughout the country by a notification in the Government *Gazette*, thrust upon us.

It is all this coercive legislation, with the revival of the old wicked laws which place every man's liberty at the mercy of a frightened official, which renders intelligible the attitude of the Left Wing, that nothing but opposition to a Government which stoops to such measures is consistent with self-respect, or offers any prospect of relief.

Dewan Bahadur Ambalal S. Desai proposed Dr. Rash Behari Ghose as President. Beyond some cries of "No, No," there was little interruption, but a tumult broke out when the old favourite of the Congress, Mr. Surendranath Bannerji, arose to second. The party of shouters seems to have been small, about 30 according to *The Statesman*, but they made so much noise, aided by the shouts of "Order" of the vast majority, that it was impossible to hear Mr. Bannerji, and the Chairman adjourned the meeting till the next day, hoping hot feelings would die down.

The Congress met again on the 27th, and the warm greeting of a huge majority showed the feeling of the delegates. Mr. Surendranath Bannerji finished his speech, Pandit Motilal Nehru supported his proposal, and Dr. Rash Behari Ghose was elected, and took the chair amid vociferous applause. Mr. B. G. Tilak then came to the platform and said he wished to move an amendment, either about an adjournment, or to the Presidential election. An argument ensued. Mr. Tilak attempted to address the delegates, who refused to listen to him, upholding the authority of the President, who had ruled him out of order. The platform was charged by men armed with sticks, a heavy shoe was flung at and struck Sir Pherozeshah Mehta and Mr. Surendranath Bannerji, the President declared the meeting adjourned, and the police cleared the Hall—a sad page in the glorious history of the Congress; but the Congress was saved by the statesmanlike action of Sir Pherozeshah Mehta, Mr. Gokhale, Mr. D. E. Wacha, Dr. Rash Behari Ghose, Pandit Madan Mohan Malaviya, Mr. V. Krishnaswami Iyer, and many others.

They met, and drew up the following notice, calling a National Convention on the next day, December 28th:

The 23rd Indian National Congress having been suspended *sine die* under painful circumstances, the undersigned have resolved with a view to the orderly conduct of future political work in the country to call a Convention of those delegates to the Congress who are agreed:

(1) That the attainment by India of Self-Government similar to that enjoyed by the Self-Governing members of the British Empire, and participation by her in the rights and responsibilities of the Empire on equal terms with those members is the goal of our political aspirations.

(2) That the advance towards this goal is to be by strictly constitutional means, by bringing about a steady

reform of the existing system of administration, and by promoting National Unity, fostering public spirit, and improving the condition of the mass of the people.

(3) And that all meetings held for the promotion of the aims and objects above indicated have to be conducted in an orderly manner, with due submission to the authority of those that are entrusted with the power to control their procedure, and they are requested to attend at 1 p.m. on Saturday the 28th of December, 1907, in the Pandal lent for the purpose by the working Committee of the Reception Committee of the 23rd Indian National Congress.

Signed :

RASH BEHARI GHOSE	NORENDRANATH SEN
PHEROZESHAH M. MEHTA	AMBALAL SAKERAL DESAI
SURENDRANATH BANNERJI	V. KRISHNASWAMI IYER
G. K. GOKHALE	TRIBHOVANDAS N. MALVI
D. E. WACHA	MADAN MOHAN MALAVIYA

And many others.

Over 900 of the delegates subscribed to the above and attended the meeting. If the Congress was not to be slain by violence, some one had to act, and the delegates who originally signed the notice sprang into the breach. The approval of a large majority of the delegates present legitimatised the calling of the Convention, and, if a majority is to rule, the Convention was the child of the 23rd National Congress.

Sir Pherozeshah Mehta proposed Dr. Rash Behari Ghose to the chair. The motion was seconded by Mr. Surendranath Bannerji, and supported by Lala Lajpat Rai and others. It was carried unanimously, and Dr. Rash Behari, taking the chair, called on Mr. Gokhale to move the Resolution appointing a Committee to draw up a Constitution for the Congress.

Mr. Gokhale moved over a hundred names of leading Congressmen present; Dewan Bahadur Govindaraghava Aiyar seconded, Mr. A. Choudhuri supported. It was carried unanimously, Sir Pherozeshah Mehta, Messrs. Gokhale and Wacha were appointed Secretaries, and Dr. Ghose dissolved the Convention, the bridge which carried the Congress from its old system to the new. It has been said that the Surat riot shows the unfitness of Indians for Self-Government; it seems to us that the quickness of recovery, the prompt action, the business-like procedure, were far better proofs of their fitness than the conducting of peaceable meetings. To meet an unexpected emergency, to grapple with it, and to secure the continuity of the Congress showed statesmanship and judgment, and we should like to know what better procedure could have been followed.

The Convention Committee met at Allahabad on the 18th and 19th of April, 1908, and drew up a Constitution for the Indian National Congress. They also drew up a set of Rules for the conduct of meetings. Articles I and II are the vital ones, and run as follows:

Article I.—The objects of the Indian National Congress are the attainment by the people of India of a system of Government similar to that enjoyed by the Self-Governing Members of the British Empire, and a participation by them in the rights and responsibilities of the Empire on equal terms with those members. These objects are to be achieved by constitutional means, by bringing about a steady reform of the existing system of administration, and by promoting national unity, fostering public spirit, and developing and organising the intellectual, moral, economic and industrial resources of the country.

[This is the famous " Creed ".]

Article II.—Every delegate to the Indian National Congress shall express in writing his acceptance of the Objects of the Congress as laid down in Article I of this Constitution, and his willingness to abide by this Constitution, and by the Rules of the Congress hereto appended.

The Madras Congress of 1908 was held under this Constitution, which was formally laid on the table. This Constitution, with the Rules, was submitted to the Congress at Allahabad in 1910, and a Resolution was there passed referring various proposed amendments to a Sub-Committee, which was ordered to report before the end of October, 1911, the report to be laid before the Congress of that year. It was so laid, and was further amended and adopted by the Congress of Calcutta in 1911; it was still further amended, and passed as amended, by the Congress of Bankipur in 1912.

They thus became the Congress Constitution and Rules, being accepted by the body which is the only National Congress in the field, and is accepted as the National Congress in India, and in the whole world outside India.

A few adherents of the Stuarts may deny that the acts which placed the Guelphs on the British Throne were constitutional, but the controversy is academical. The succession of the Guelphs is a *fait accompli*. So with the National Congress. It was, it is, and it will be. Most Indians are grateful to the majority, who foiled the revolution of 1907, and carried on the succession. " Law is silent amid the clash of arms."

They did the best they could under abnormal circumstances, and the Nation, by continuing to send up its delegates year after year, has confirmed their action.

An attempt to find a path of reconciliation was made in 1914, and failed. By whose fault it is once more idle to dispute. The Congress, however, appointed a Committee to consider amendments to the present rule under which the Left Wing refuses to come in. At the time of writing, the Committee has not met, but if it make any amendment, and the Congress approve it and the Left Wing accept it, it can only be acted on in 1916. Practical politicians work from the *status quo,* and the Congress door is open to all who accept its present Constitution. It would seem reasonable for the Left Wing to imitate the Irish party, who, while denouncing the Act of Union on the platform, accepted it as a *fait accompli* in politics, came in under it into the Houses of Parliament, and then proceeded to fight for Home Rule. That is the democratic way of carrying on political battles. Above all, in meetings, where a President has been duly elected, as at Surat, his ruling must be obeyed, otherwise the meeting, as at Surat, becomes a mob. The *sine qua non* of a Democracy is order, under laws made by itself. Dr. Rash Behari Ghose had been elected under the tentative Constitution of 1906, passed by the whole Congress, and no one had any right to challenge it. That was the primary unconstitutional action, out of which the further trouble grew; the Congress, adjourned by him as President, met under him again at Madras, still the 23rd Congress, composed of a crowd of the same delegates and of others added to them by the Nation, the final Court of Appeal, thus preserving the succession.

PART II

The Twenty-third National Congress, adjourned at Surat, met at Madras, on the 28th, 29th and 30th December, 1908. The Pandal had been erected in the Elphinstone Grounds, Mount Road; it met under the Constitution and Rules drawn up by the Committee appointed by the National Convention at Surat, and the signing of Article I was necessary for admission as a delegate. 626 delegates attended, distributed as follows:

Madras	404
Bombay	134
United Bengal	36
U. P.	23
C. P. and Berar	18
Panjab	7
Burma	4
	626

Dewan Bahadur K. Krishnaswami Rao, C.I.E., the Chairman of the Reception Committee, after welcoming the delegates, said a few words on the reforms proposed by Lord Morley, on which the opinion of Congress should be expressed. For the first time they met under a Constitution, drawn up by the Committee appointed at Surat; Mr. Hume,

Sir William Wedderburn and Mr. Dadabhai Naoroji had approved both the Constitution and the Rules, but they were of course subject to modification by the Congress. In concluding, the Chairman expressed the grief of India for the loss of two great men, Rai Bahadur P. Ananda Charlu, C. I. E., and Sir V. Bhashyam Iyengar, C. I. E. He called on Nawab Syed Muhammad to move that the Hon. Rash Behari Ghose take the Chair.

The Nawab Sahab proposed the motion, which was seconded by Rao Bahadur R. N. Mudholkar, supported by Sir Bhalchandra Krishna and carried by tumultuous applause.

The President began by alluding to the Surat trouble, and justifying the course taken to preserve the Congress. Turning to the condition of India, he spoke of the "succession of repressive laws, and deportations under a lawless law" as sapping the most robust optimism; but now the clouds had broken, and representative Government was to be granted, and Indians were to "have an effective voice in directing the policy of the Government". "We shall now have something like a constitutional Government in the place of an autocratic and irresponsible administration." Some unfortunate repressive laws had been passed, with the natural result of secret crime; that which happened in other countries happened in India, and a few began to dally with treason. "Coercion and even the appearance of coercion tend to create only distrust and suspicion." There had been during the year some twenty prosecutions for sedition, and as many convictions, and when feeling runs high every editor or speaker convicted of sedition is regarded as a martyr. Sedition was a vague offence, and might be made to cover any political agitation. In India, where a man tried for sedition had not the defence of a jury, " a prosecution can only be justified when the public peace is imperilled by wild writings or speeches ". He hoped that, ere long, a successor of his in that chair would " be able to congratulate the country on the repeal of Regulation III of 1818, a barbarous relic from the past—an unweeded remnant which ought to have been extirpated long long ago ". [Dr. Ghose refers to the odious *lettre de cachet* system, which still stains our legislation. But we are not likely to get rid of it till we have Home Rule. Autocracy does not readily part with its unconstitutional weapons.]

The President looked forward to the day when a successor should announce the gaining of Self-Government, but he thought it far off :

> A younger generation will take up the work, who will, I trust, have some kindly thoughts for those who too, in their day, strove to do their duty, however imperfectly, through good report and through evil report, with, it may be, a somewhat chastened fervour, but, I may say without boasting, a fervour as genuine as that which stirs and inspires younger hearts.

The delegates were then asked to elect their delegates for the Subjects Committee, and the Congress adjourned.

The second day opened with the reading of a message from Mr. Keir Hardie, brought by Dr. Clark, M.P., who had come as a delegate.

The President then moved Resolution I, tendering loyal homage to the King-Emperor, and respectfully welcoming the message of His Majesty, confirming the Proclamation of 1858. The Resolution was carried amid loud applause.

Resolution II, expressing the deep satisfaction with which Lord Morley's Despatch, outlining the Reform proposals, had been received, and hoping that the Reforms would be worked out in the liberal spirit in which they had been conceived, was moved by Mr. Surendranath Bannerji. He said that in the early days they had only asked for a little expansion of the Legislative Councils, but now things had changed; Asia was throbbing with new life; Japan had become a World-Power; China and Persia were seeking representative institutions. India hoped the Reforms would widen out in the future. In Bengal there was a growing feeling of the uselessness of constitutional agitation, since no efforts had availed to get rid of the Partition, but he still clung to constitutional means. And they should all welcome these Reforms, as a message of conciliation. They would be able to do something under the new conditions. In Bengal nine respectable men had been deported:

> To arrest nine respectable persons, to snatch them away from their families and detain them in prison without a complaint or a charge, and without affording them the opportunity of explanation or defence is a proceeding abhorrent to minds wedded to constitutional methods of procedure and to the canons of law and justice.

Under the proposed Reforms they would at least be able in such cases to challenge the Government in the Council. The Rules to be framed under the scheme were all-important. They might make it successful, or bring about its total failure.

The Hon. Pandit Madan Mohan Malaviya seconded the Resolution, expressing their warm gratitude for the instalment of Reform offered to them, though it did not go as far as they wished. Let nobody imagine the Reforms were final. They must ask for more and more.

Rao Bahadur R. N. Mudholkar supported, and pointed to the definite gains in the proposals made. Dewan Bahadur L. A. Govindaraghava, in view of the opposition to Lord Morley in England, thought they should express their view that the proposals were conceived in a generous spirit; the Reforms were substantial though not large. Lala Harkishan Lal and Mr. Jehangir B. Petit supported, the latter laying stress on the work done in England by Mr. Gokhale. Mr. M. A. Jinnah, the Rev. Dr. R. A. Hume, Pandit Gokarannath Misra and Dr. Clark also supported, the latter expressing the hope—doomed to failure—that they might in the next Congress be as pleased with the Act as they were with the outline of the proposals. "The Russian bureaucrat had got to go; the Turkish bureaucrat has got to go; the Indian bureaucrat has got to go also. . . . If the bureaucrat is bad in Europe, he is bad here also." The Resolution was carried.

The President then put from the Chair Resolution III, expressing detestation of the deeds of violence committed, and it was carried.

Resolution IV brought up once again the ill-treatment of British Indians in South Africa. [It will be noticed that under the rule of another Nation, no grievance is redressed without years of agitation and pleading, if redressed at all. Hence the constant repetition of the same Resolutions.] It was moved by Mr. Mushir Hasan Kidwai, who had been elected as delegate of the Johannesburg British Indian Association and the Hamidia Islamic Society there to the Congress and the All-India Muslim League, to represent their wrongs. He made an admirable and forcible speech.

The passion of earth-hunger has been on Europe for a long time past and there is hardly a corner of the world where the white man has not penetrated and which he would not like to make his own. Will the whole world then become the white man's and all the coloured men have to move away from it? If the Transvaal is to be dubbed a white man's country, why should not then also Egypt, or India, or Algiers? I fail to see, gentlemen, the logic of this arbitrary theory that a white man's country should be a forbidden land for coloured men. Nor would the argument that the Indians should not be allowed to live in a country in which Europeans also live because they lower the standard of living, hold water for a moment. The necessary corollary of that proposition would be, that Asiatics may object to Europeans and Americans living in their midst, as their influence and example would lead them to live in a style unsuited to the circumstances of their country. Would the Europeans leave Asia on the ground that the coloured man's continent ought to remain the coloured man's continent? The more you raise the standard of living, the more you increase pauperism. In India the poor people who could live comfortably on an income of Rs. 2 a month have now to starve on that income, thanks to the raising of the standard of living. I do not know what western moralists would say, but an Eastern would unhesitatingly prefer an all-round low standard of living, if it would render the ordinary comforts of life accessible in a larger degree to the poor masses and make a slender income suffice for a respectable living. My standard of living, for instance, is higher than was that of my grandfather, but when I go to my people and my tenants, and see them struggling hard for their very existence, living in worse houses than they used to and on less sufficient food, I stand self-condemned for the selfish folly of spending more on my own living than I might.

He caustically said :

Just imagine what any section of the Europeans resident in China would do, if they were put to similar worrying insults by the Chinese Government.

Mr. C. Y. Chintamani, in seconding, pointed to the effect on the public mind in India of the continued ill-treatment of Indians in South Africa. The Resolution was supported by Mr. Ibrahim Noordien Muquadam, Dr. U. L. Desai, Mr. G. K. Gadgil, and Dr. Clark, M. P., and carried.

The Hon. Mr. Krishnan Nair moved Resolution V, appealing for the reversal of the Partition of Bengal, and it was seconded by Mr. Ambikacharan Mozumdar, from whom we must cull one paragraph which is always true of Indian as of other despotisms :

As regards new facts, well, they are painfully in evidence in the unrest which is surging from one end of the country to the other, and marking its ravages both in Upper India as well as in the Deccan, and latterly in the ugly developments which have disgraced the Indian public and blotted the Indian administration. Violence and lawlessness we hate ; anarchism we detest. But it seems impossible not to feel the force of the circumstance which has given monstrous birth to the insane bomb-maker. And, gentlemen, what has been the remedy applied to this state of things—Repression, Repression, and nothing but Repression. But, gentlemen, if anarchism has in every age and in every country failed to achieve the salvation of any people, repression has likewise nowhere succeeded in restoring peace and order, and in this country repression has so far only succeeded in converting prison-houses into martyrdoms. How long, oh, how long, will this intolerable state of things continue? If the Partition is a settled fact, the unrest in India is also a settled fact, and it is for Lord Morley and the Government of India to decide which should be unsettled to settle the question.

The Resolution was supported by Messrs. Dharmdas Suri, Harichandra Vishindas, and was carried.

Resolution VI accorded the cordial support of the Congress to the Swadeshi movement, and was moved by Mr. Dipnarrain Singh, who pointed out that the Muhammadan weavers in Bengal had, that year, been able to resist the famine because of the movement. The Resolution was seconded by Mr. K. Perrazu, supported by Messrs. Iswara Saran, G. K. Chitale, R. V. Mahajani and carried.

Mr. V. V. Jogiah moved Resolution VII, a protest against the imposition of new Military charges on India, the latest of £300,000, on the recommendation of the Romer Commission, the Report of which the Government refused to lay on the table of the House. He noted the growth of the expenditure, from nearly 11 crores and odd in 1857 to nearly 32 and odd in 1906-07. Pandit Rambhaja Datta Choudhuri formally seconded, the Resolution was carried, and the Congress rose.

The third day's proceedings began with an invitation to a garden party from the Raja of Kollengode, and a telegram from South Africa, nearly 2,000 Indians having suffered imprisonment in the Transvaal. Then came our old Separation of Judicial and Executive Functions, as Resolution VIII, moved by Dr. Satish Chandra Bannerji, seconded by Mr. R. Sadagopachariar, supported by Messrs. Bishunpada Chatterji and Govindarao Apaji Patil, and carried.

Pandit Rambhuj Dutt Choudhuri moved Resolution IX, asking that the army might be thrown open to Indians in its higher grades. It was seconded by Mr. Narayana Menon, supported by Mr. Govinda Shai Sharma and carried.

Next came Resolution X, demanding the repeal of the Bengal Regulation III of 1818, and other similar Regulations in other Provinces, and asking that the recently deported persons might be given an opportunity of meeting the charges made against them, or else be set at liberty. Mr. Syed Hasan Imam moved the Resolution, the necessity for which was, and still is, a disgrace to British rule in India. The speaker, after showing that there were no circumstances which justified the seizure of peaceable citizens and dragging them away from their homes without charge or trial, spoke of the nine recent arrests and of the previous arrest of Lala Lajpat Rai. "Unexplained deportations shook the faith of the most loyal in the justice of a law that hides its proceedings from public gaze." Babu Bhupendranath Basu seconded, as a close personal friend of some of those deported; they were his fellow-workers for many years. "Are we to be imprisoned, are we to be deported, are we to be arrested, without being given even an opportunity of explaining our conduct?" There had been lately the Midnapore trial, where elderly men, some of the highest men in Indian Society, had been thrown into prison, and when they were brought to trial it was found that "the whole prosecution under which the men were subjected to indescribable ignominy was based upon the information of a drunken debauchee picked up in the streets of Midnapore," information that had to be abandoned.

Mr. P. L. Raj Pal supported in a few words, and then Dr. Tej Bahadur Sapru pointed out that in no other country in the British Empire did such a law exist as that which they desired to be repealed. The spirit of it was

> against the very first principles of English jurisprudence, and it is opposed to all the traditions of the English Constitution. I would go further, and say that it constitutes a very great menace to our liberty. It stands hanging over our heads like the sword of Damocles.

The Resolution was put and carried.

Resolution XI expressed the hope that Acts VII and XIV of 1908 would not long remain on the Statute Book, and was moved by Mr. P. R. Sundara Aiyar. Act VII allowed the summary attachment of newspaper presses, and Act XIV made it punishable for any person to subscribe to an association that was condemned; the word "knowingly" was suggested as an amendment before "subscribe," but it was rejected. If such legislation were necessary, it should only be passed for a short period, and brought up for renewal if the necessity continued, as in Ireland. Mr. S. Sinha seconded, Mr. M. Ramchand supported, and the Resolution was passed.

The President put from the Chair Resolution XII, on legislation in the Central Provinces and Behar. Carried.

Mr. C. Karunakara Menon moved Resolution XIII, asking for an enquiry into the causes of the high prices of food-stuffs. It was seconded by Mr. A. C. Parthasarathi Naidu and carried.

Resolution XIV, on Education, was moved by Mr. A. Choudhuri, seconded by Rao Bahadur K. G. Desai, supported by Messrs. Parameshwar Lal and Utamlal Trivedi, and Dr. Nilratan Sircar, and carried.

The President put from the Chair Resolution XV, on Permanent Settlement, and XVI, on the loss sustained by the deaths of Messrs. Kalicharan Bannerji, Alfred Webb, Bansilal Singh, Pandit Bishambarnath, and Rao Bahadur P. Ananda Charlu. Both carried.

The Hon. Mr. Gokhale then moved Resolution XVII, comprising messages of congratulation to Mr. A. O. Hume on the Reforms; and to Sir William Wedderburn on his recovery from serious illness, and thanking him for all his work; thanking also the British Committee. He made a long and eloquent speech, dwelling on the new responsibilities imposed on them by the Reforms, and on the need to co-operate with Government under the new conditions. The Resolution was carried without any further speaking, and Dr. Clark responded.

Resolution XVIII appointed the members of the All-India Congress Committee; Resolution XIX thanked the Reception Committee; and XX appointed Messrs. D. E. Wacha and the Hon. Mr. D. A. Khare, General Secretaries. Resolution XXI accepted Lahore for the meeting of the Congress in 1909. Then the Hon. Mr. V. Krishnaswami Aiyar moved a vote of thanks to the President and Dr. Ghose responded; he sounded a note of warning, for since his presidential speech news had come from England of the gathering of ominous clouds in the political sky.

Our enemies—did I say our enemies? I ought to have said the enemies of the English people, the enemies of English rule in India, are trying to thwart Lord Morley's Reform scheme. It is therefore our duty to make organised efforts here, as well as in England, to counteract the mischievous action of mischievous bureaucrats, who, even in their retirement, in the very home of free institutions, have not lost their re-actionary instincts. The leopard may change his spots, but there is no hope, take my word for it, for the sun-dried bureaucrat. The fetters are not taken off his mind even in the free atmosphere of England. Once a bureaucrat, always a bureaucrat.

The warning proved to be but too true; the Reforms were spoiled.

The Twenty-third National Congress dissolved.

RESOLUTIONS

To the King-Emperor

I. Resolved—That the Indian National Congress tenders its loyal homage to His Gracious Majesty the King-Emperor and respectfully welcomes the message sent by His Majesty to the Princes and Peoples of India on the Fiftieth Anniversary of the memorable Proclamation issued in 1858 by his Illustrious Mother, Victoria the Good.

That this Congress begs to record its satisfaction that the interpretation placed by it upon the Pledge contained in that "Great Charter" of 1858 has been upheld by His Majesty.

That this Congress gratefully welcomes the pronouncement made by His Majesty that the time has come when the principle of representative institutions, which from the first began to be gradually introduced in India, may be prudently extended, and that the politic satisfaction of the claim to equality of citizenship and greater share in legislation and government made by important classes in India, representing ideas that have been fostered and encouraged by British Rule, will strengthen, not impair, existing authority and power.

That the Congress looks forward with confidence to a steady fulfilment by those in authority under the Crown in letter and in spirit of the pledges and assurances contained in the Great Charter of 1858 and in His Majesty's Message of 1908.

Minto-Morley Reforms

II. Resolved—That this Congress desires to give expression to the deep and general satisfaction with which the Reform proposals formulated in Lord Morley's despatch have been received throughout the country; it places on record its sense of high statesmanship which has dictated the action of the Government in the matter, and it tenders to Lord Morley and Lord Minto its most sincere and grateful thanks for their proposals.

That this Congress is of opinion that the proposed expansion of the Legislative Councils and the enlargement of their powers and functions, in the appointment of Indian members of the Executive Councils with the creation of such Councils where they do not exist, and the further development of Local Self-Government, constitute a large and liberal instalment of the reforms needed to give the people of this country a substantial share in the management of their affairs and to bring the administration into closer touch with their wants and feelings.

That this Congress expresses its confident hope that the details of the proposed scheme will be worked out in the same liberal spirit in which its main provisions, as outlined in the Secretary of State's despatch, have been conceived.

Outrages

III. Resolved—That this Congress places on record its emphatic and unqualified condemnation of the detestable outrages and deeds of violence which have been committed recently in some parts of the country, and which are abhorrent to the loyal, humane and peace-loving nature of His Majesty's Indian subjects of every denomination.

Indians in British Colonies

IV. Resolved—That this Congress views with the greatest indignation the harsh and humiliating and cruel treatment to which British Indians, even of the highest respectability and position have been subjected by the British Colonies in South Africa, and expresses its alarm at the likelihood of such treatment resulting in far-reaching consequences of a mischievous character calculated to cause great injury to the best interests of the British Empire, and trusts that the Imperial Parliament, when granting the new Constitution to South Africa, will secure the interests of the Indian inhabitants of South Africa.

That this Congress begs earnestly to press upon the British Parliament and the Government of India, the desirability of dealing with the Self-Governing Colonies in the same manner in which the latter ruthlessly deal with Indian interests, so long as they adhere to the selfish and one-sided policy which they proclaim and practise, and persist in their present course of denying to His Majesty's Indian subjects their just rights as citizens of the Empire.

That this Congress, while aware of the declaration of responsible statesmen in favour of allowing the Self-Governing Colonies in the British Empire to monopolise vast tracts of undeveloped territories for exclusive white settlements, deems it right to point out that the policy of shutting the door and denying the rights of full British citizenship to all subjects of the British Crown, while preaching and enforcing the opposite policy in Asia and other parts of the world, is fraught with grave mischief to the Empire and is as unwise as it is unrighteous.

Partition of Bengal

V. Resolved—That this Congress earnestly appeals to the Government of India and the Secretary of State for India to reverse the Partition of Bengal, or to modify it in such a manner as to keep the entire Bengali-speaking community under one and the same administration.

That this Congress is of opinion that the rectification of this admitted error will restore contentment to the Province of Bengal, give satisfaction to the other Provinces, and instead of impairing, will enhance the prestige of His Majesty's Government throughout the country.

Swadeshi

VI. Resolved—That this Congress accords its most cordial support to the Swadeshi Movement, and calls upon the people of the country to labour for its success by making earnest and sustained efforts to promote the growth of industries capable of development in the country, and respond to the efforts of Indian producers by giving preference, wherever practicable, to Indian products over imported commodities, even at a sacrifice.

VII. Resolved—That this Congress enters its emphatic protest against the fresh burden of £300,000 which the British War Office has imposed on the Indian Exchequer for military charges on the recommendation of the Romer Committee, the proceedings of which the Under-Secretary of State for India has refused to lay on the table of the House of Commons, in contravention of previous practice in such matters.

That this Congress views with the greatest regret the repeated imposition of military charges by the British War Office on the Indian tax-payer from the date of the Army Amalgamation Scheme of 1859, in regard to which imposition the Government of India has repeatedly remonstrated.

That this Congress respectfully urges upon the attention of His Majesty's Government the necessity of revising the Army Amalgamation Scheme of 1859 in the light of the experience of the last fifty years, and the desirability of laying down a fair and reasonable principle which shall free the Indian Exchequer from unjust exactions of this character.

IX. Resolved—That this Congress prays that the high recognition of the valour and fidelity of the Indian troops by His Majesty the King-Emperor in his Message to the Princes and Peoples of India should include the throwing open to Indians of higher careers in the Army, from which, as this Congress has repeatedly pointed out, they have been hitherto excluded.

Legal

VIII. Resolved—That this Congress records its satisfaction that the proposal for the separation of Executive and Judicial functions has received the sanction of the Government in some definite shape for the Province of Bengal; but is at the same time of opinion that the scheme should also be extended throughout the country, and that it will not succeed in its object unless and until the entire Judicial Service be placed directly and absolutely under the High Court or Chief Court, as the case may be, even in matters of promotion and transfer.

Coercion

Lettres de cachet

X. Resolved—That having regard to the recent deportations, and the grave risk of injustice involved in Government action based upon ex parte and untested information, and having regard to the penal laws of the country, this Congress strongly urges upon the Government the repeal of the Bengal Regulation III of 1818 and similar Regulations in other Provinces of India; and it respectfully prays that the persons recently deported in Bengal be given an opportunity of exculpating themselves, or for meeting any charges that may be against them, or be set at liberty.

Acts of 1908

XI. Resolved—That this Congress deplores the circumstances which have led to the passing of Act VII of 1908 and Act XIV of 1908, but having regard to their drastic character and to the fact that a sudden emergency alone can afford any justification for such exceptional legislation, this Congress expresses its earnest hope that these enactments will only have a temporary existence in the Indian Statute Book.

Provincial Grievances

XII. Resolved—That this Congress urges upon the Government the necessity of:

(*a*) placing in regard to legislative and administrative matters the Province of Berar on the same footing as the Provinces included in British India; and

(*b*) establishing a Legislative Council for the combined territory of the Central Provinces and Berar.

High Prices of Food-stuffs

XIII. Resolved—That this Congress is of opinion that having regard to the high prices of food-stuffs for the past several years, and the hardships to which the middle and poorer classes are put thereby, an enquiry should be instituted by Government into the causes of such high prices, with a view to ascertain how far and by what remedies such causes could be removed.

Education

XIV. Resolved—That this Congress is of opinion that the Government should take immediate steps:

(*a*) to make Primary Education free at once and gradually compulsory throughout the country,

(*b*) to assign larger sums of money to Secondary and Higher Education (special encouragement being given where necessary to educate all backward classes),

(*c*) to make adequate provision for imparting Industrial and Technical Education in the different Provinces, having regard to local requirements, and

(*d*) to give effective voice to the leaders of Indian public opinion in shaping the policy and system of Education in this country.

In the opinion of this Congress the time has arrived for people all over the country to take up earnestly the question of supplementing existing institutions and the efforts of the Government by organising for themselves an independent system of Literary, Scientific, Technical, and Industrial Education, suited to the conditions of the different Provinces in the country.

Permanent Settlement

XV. Resolved—That this Congress is of opinion that the prosperity of an agricultural country like India cannot be secured without a definite limitation of the State demand on land, and it regrets that Lord Curzon in his Land Resolution of 1902 failed to recognise the necessity of any such limitation, and declined to accept the suggestions of Sir Richard Garth and other memorialists on the matter.

This Congress holds that in Provinces where the Permanent Settlement does not now exist, a reasonable and definite limitation of the State demand and the introduction of Permanent or a Settlement for a period of not less than sixty years, are the only true remedies for the growing impoverishment of the agricultural population.

This Congress emphatically protests against the view that the Land Revenue in India is not a tax but is in the nature of rent.

Grief of Congress

XVI. Resolved—That this Congress records its sense of the great loss which the country has sustained in the death of:

Mr. Kalicharan Bannerji,
Pandit Bishambarnath,
Mr. Alfred Webb,
Mr. Bunsilal Singh, and
Rai Bahadur P. Ananda Charlu.

Congratulations and Thanks

XVII. Resolved—(*a*) That the following message be addressed by the Congress to Mr. A. O. Hume.

This Congress sends you its cordial greetings and congratulations. The reforms announced by Lord Morley are a partial fruition of the efforts made by the Congress during the last twenty-three years, and we are gratified to think that to you, as its father and founder, they must be a source of great and sincere satisfaction.

(*b*) This Congress offers its sincere congratulations to Sir William Wedderburn, Bart., on his recent recovery from a serious illness and takes this opportunity to give expression to its deep gratitude for the unflagging zeal and devotion, and the love, patience and singleness of purpose with which he has laboured for the Indian cause during the last twenty years, and which has been largely instrumental in securing for Congress' views and representations the favourable consideration which they have received in England.

(*c*) This Congress desires to convey to members of the British Committee its grateful thanks for their disinterested and strenuous services in the cause of India's political advancement.

XIX. Resolved—That this Congress accords its most hearty thanks for the hospitality with which the Reception Committee has received the delegates and the perfection of the arrangements made for their comfort during their stay in Madras. The Congress also thanks the Captain, Lieutenants and Members of the Congress Corps for the trouble they have taken in looking after the comforts of the delegates, and in being very diligent in preserving order throughout the session.

Formal

XVIII. Resolved—That the following gentlemen are appointed members of the All-India Congress Committee. (*List omitted*).

XX. Resolved—That Mr. D. E. Wacha and the Hon. Mr. Daji Abaji Khare be appointed General Secretaries for the ensuing year.

XXI. Resolved—That the next Congress assemble at Lahore.

CHAPTER XXIV

THE Twenty-fourth National Congress met in Lahore, in the Bradlaugh Hall, on the 27th December, 1909. There was a great chill over the country, in consequence of the way in which the Minto-Morley Reforms had been wrecked by the rules made for their carrying out; the Panjab was restless and sullen; the number of delegates dropped to 243, and only 76 came from the Panjab itself; the Official Report describes the Hall as "fairly well filled". The delegates were distributed as follows:

Madras	20
Bombay (27), Sindh (30)	57
Bengal	20
C. P. and Berar	6
U. P.	64
Panjab	76
	243

Lala Harkishan Lal, the Chairman of the Reception Committee welcomed the President-elect and the delegates. His speech was in the minor key, for the Congress had been attacked on all sides; some said it was disloyal at heart, others that it excited the young and so caused tendencies which would lead to violence; others said its day was over. The Muslim League and the Hindu Conference had both assailed it. Hence the smallness of their gathering. He condemned the Council Regulations as unjust and impolitic, and disapproved of the Land Legislation embodied in the Acts of 1900, 1905 and 1907. He called on Mr. Surendranath Bannerji to propose that Pandit Madan Mohan Malaviya should take the Chair.

Surendranath Babu welcomed him as President, as one of the earliest and most devoted of Congressmen; he remembered him in 1886, when he made his first speech, which marked him out as a future leader, and that promise had been fulfilled. They owed him special thanks, in that though suffering from the effects of malarial fever, he had stepped forward to fill the vacancy suddenly occurring in the Presidentship of the Congress, an act of devoted self-sacrifice. Mr. G. K. Parekh seconded, Dewan Bahadur L. A. Govindaraghava Aiyar and Raizada Bhagat Ram supported, and Pandit Madan Mohan Malaviya took the Chair amid loud applause.

The President alluded to the sudden resignation of Sir Pherozeshah Mehta, the duly elected President, only six days before the Congress, and the great disappointment caused. He had had no time for preparation, but would try to do his best. They had to mourn the loss of Mr. Lalmohan Ghose and Mr. Romesh Chandra Dutt, and also of that true friend of India, the Marquis of Ripon. The President then turned to the total change of feeling among educated

Indians: at the last Congress they had hailed the Reforms with joy; the Regulations, issued five weeks before the present Congress, had caused widespread disappointment and dissatisfaction. He then sketched the history of the claim for representative Government from 1876, when Messrs. Surendranath Bannerji and Ananda Mohan Bose had established the Indian Association of Calcutta, which had representative Government among its objects. The most striking feature of the Reforms was the admission of Indians to the Executive Councils of the Viceroy and of the Governors of Madras and Bombay. The United Provinces, with a population of 48 millions, far larger than either Madras (38 millions) or Bombay (19 millions), was not given an Executive Council. The Regulations had introduced religion into politics, and had differentiated electorates by religious beliefs. Muhammadan minorities were given separate electorates and were allowed also to vote in the general electorates, while Hindu minorities in the Panjab and Assam enjoyed no such electorates. Further a Muhammadan who paid an income-tax on Rs. 3,000 a year, money or land revenue, had a vote. But the non-Muhammadan paying on three lakhs of rupees had no vote. Muhammadan graduates of five years standing had a vote; non-Muhammadan graduates of thirty years had none. Again, only members of Municipal and District Boards were eligible to the Provincial Councils. The President pointed out the many other defects, such as the nominations which made the "non-official majority" a farce, except in

Bengal, thanks to Sir Edward Baker. He then spoke on a number of other questions, expressed the deep sorrow of the Congress for the murders of Sir William Curzon-Wylie, Dr. Lalkaha and Mr. Jackson, and for the attempt on the life of the Viceroy, condemned the deportations, the Partition of Bengal, and the Panjab Land Alienation Act. He concluded a fine speech —when did Pandit Madan Mohan speak otherwise than finely ?—by defending the Congress, and deprecating sectarianism, and then moved from the Chair the first three Resolutions, grieving for the loss of Messrs. Lalmohan Ghose and Romesh Chandra Dutt, and for that of the Marquis of Ripon, and thanking the Government for appointing the Hon. Sir S. P. Sinha a member of the Viceroy's Executive Council, and the Right Hon. Mr. Amir Ali a member of the Privy Council.

The delegates from each Province were then requested to elect the Subjects' Committee, and the Congress adjourned.

On the second day the first place was given to the Regulations under the India Council Act of 1909, and Mr. Surendranath Bannerji moved Resolution IV, embodying the Congress view. It ran :

That this Congress while gratefully appreciating the earnest and arduous endeavours of Lord Morley and Lord Minto in extending to the people of this country a fairly liberal measure of constitutional reforms, as now embodied in the India Councils' Act of 1909, deems it its duty to place on record its strong sense of disapproval of the creation of separate electorates on the basis of religion and regrets that the Regulations framed under the Act have not been framed in the same liberal spirit in which

Lord Morley's despatch of last year was conceived. In particular the Regulations have caused widespread dissatisfaction throughout the country by reason of :

(*a*) the excessive and unfairly preponderant share of representation given to the followers of one particular religion ;

(*b*) the unjust, invidious, and humiliating distinctions made between Muslim and non-Muslim subjects of His Majesty in the matter of the electorates, the franchise, and the qualifications of candidates ;

(*c*) the wide, arbitrary and unreasonable disqualification and restrictions for candidates seeking election to the Councils ;

(*d*) the general distrust of the educated classes that runs through the whole course of the Regulations ; and

(*e*) the unsatisfactory composition of the non-official majorities in the Provincial Councils, rendering them ineffective and unreal for all practical purposes.

And this Congress earnestly requests the Government so to revise the Regulations, as soon as the present elections are over, as to remove these objectionable features, and bring them into harmony with the spirit of the Royal Message and the Secretary of State's despatch of last year.

Mr. Surendranath Bannerji pointed out :

It is no exaggeration to say that the Rules and Regulations have practically wrecked the Reform scheme as originally conceived with a beneficence of purpose and a statesmanlike grasp that did honour to all that are associated with it . . . Who wrecked the scheme ? Who converted that promising experiment into a dismal failure ? The responsibility rests upon the shoulders of the bureaucracy . . . . Is the bureaucracy having its revenge upon us for the part we have played in securing these concessions ?

One point he strongly urged was the disqualification of many of the most distinguished men by the qualifications demanded for eligibility. Further, the non-official majority was a delusion, for nominees of the Government usually voted with the Government. Still, let them not abandon hope.

> Let us see to it that, in the depths of our desperation, we do not forget the immemorial traditions of our race, or renounce the unalterable faith which is ours in the ultimate triumph of constitutional and righteous means for the attainment of National regeneration.

Dewan Bahadur L. A. Govindaraghava Iyer seconded the Resolution, dealing especially with his own Province, and showed that to say there was a non-official majority in Madras was "a travesty of truth". Mr. Harichandrai Vishandas said that the pæans of praise sung in chorus in the last Congress were a little too previous, and the benedictions of their leaders were premature. Mr. Syed Hasan was against all communal representation. The Hon. Munshi Ganga Prasad Varma analysed the effect of the Regulations in the U. P. Mr. J. B. Petit showed that religious and race hatreds would be aroused by the Regulations; if one minority were represented, others should be. The Resolution was further supported by Messrs. Rajpal Kane, Pandit Gokarannath Misra, Messrs. Rambhuj Dutt Choudhuri, Harnam Das, and A. Choudhuri, and unanimously carried.

Resolution V, urging the formation of Executive Councils in the United Provinces, the Panjab, Eastern Bengal, Assam, and Burma, was moved by Dr. Tej Bahadur Sapru, who rapidly outlined the history of Agra in respect to this question, and showed the absurdity of a Province containing 48 millions of people being governed by one man, a Lieutenant-Governor, without an Executive Council. Dewan Lachmi Narain seconded the Resolution, and it was supported by Lala Hakamchand and Moulvi Abdul Qasim, and carried.

Resolution VI criticised the Panjab Regulations under the Act, and Mr. Sundar Singh Bhatia, moving it, said that the educated community of the Panjab was in a state of profound disappointment, bordering on despair. For the first time a barrier was raised between Muhammadans and non-Muhammadans, the Hindus were relegated to a subordinate position, and, in spite of all their efforts, were thrown back. Under Muhammadan rule, the highest offices were open to Hindus; now they were sent to a back seat. Lala Dharmdas Suri seconded, and the Resolution was carried.

Mr. C. Y. Chintamani moved Resolution VII, complaining of the treatment of the Central Provinces and Berar, which had not even a Legislative Council, Berar being peculiarly unfortunate in that in disabilities it was British territory, but from privileges it was excluded as belonging to the Nizam. Mr. N. A. Dravid seconded, saying that Berar was held from the Nizam on a perpetual lease, which was a doom of perpetual disfranchisement. Being under British administration, they have no rights under the Nizam, and not being British subjects they could not be represented in British India. The Resolution was carried and the Congress adjourned.

On the third day, Mr. Bhupendranath Basu moved Resolution VIII, asking for a modification of the

Partition of Bengal, and appointing Mr. Surendranath Bannerji and himself as a deputation to England, to lay the question before the authorities and the public. He said the Bengalis would not rest until they were re-united, for the boys of eastern and western Bengal were now separated, brought up under different ideals of manhood. East Bengal was police-ridden, tyrannised over, boys were arrested, and thousands of lads were being driven into the camp of the extremists, filled with bitter hostility. The speaker concluded with a passage of splendid and moving eloquence, declaring that Bengal would never admit its cause was lost:

> I stand before you, I, a Bengali from Bengal, one of a very small number of men who have been able to come to your Province to attend this Congress. I stand before you, I stand at the bar of my own country, I stand before the best and the highest men in all India, I stand like a neophyte at the altar which you have raised for the worship of our Mother, to plead for a cause which to others may seem to be lost, to re-vitalise what to others may seem a vanished hope. Gentlemen, so long as the Bengali race will last, so long as the blood which flows through our veins courses through generations yet unborn, so long as the picture of a United India remains on our vision, so long as the mighty rivers of my native Province flow on in their majesty and glory to the sea, so long as the fields and meadows of East Bengal wave in all their verdant glory, our cause will not be lost. So long as the inspiriting strains of Bande Mataram put new heart into generations of Bengalis yet to come, our cause will not be lost. For the moment we may have suffered defeat. For the moment the question seems to be settled, but, God willing, we shall yet turn the defeat into victory.

And they did.

Mr. K. Ekambara Iyer seconded, Mr. Parameshwar Lal supported the Resolution and it was carried.

Resolution IX was moved by the Hon. Mr. G. K. Gokhale, and embodied the cry for help from the Indians in South Africa. He sketched the history of the Indians in the Transvaal under the Boers, the Crown, and the Colonial Government. He then described the endless negotiations and the breaches of faith, and the long patient struggle of the Indians led by Mr. Gandhi; now the Congress said to the Government of India that "they have made endless representations, but so far they have produced no effect. The time has come for retaliation." The Indians in South Africa were engaged in the passive resistance struggle:

What is the passive resistance struggle? It is essentially defensive in its nature, and it fights with moral and spiritual weapons. A passive resister resists tyranny by undergoing suffering in his own person. He pits soul force against brute force; he pits the divine in man against the brute in man; he pits suffering against oppression, pits conscience against might; he pits faith against injustice; right against wrong.

Mr. Dipnarrain Singh seconded, and Mr. G. A. Natesan supported. Mr. Natesan has made this question his own, and he spoke eloquently out of a full heart and a mind stored with facts. Mr. Malik Girdharilal, Mr. Iswara Saran, Pandit Dey Rattan, and Messrs. C. R. Naidu and Lutchman Panday followed. Then Mr. H. S. L. Polak, the delegate from the Transvaal, spoke, urging India to sympathise with and to support the men who were suffering for India's honour. Mr. Surendranath Bannerji called for monetary help, and a collection was made amid great enthusiasm; Rs. 15,000 were soon collected, and in half an hour another Rs. 3,000 were added. The Resolution was formally carried.

Mr. A. Choudhuri moved Resolution X, calling for the repeal of the Regulations giving the power to deport and to keep in prison persons without trial. Mr. H. S. Dixit seconded, and Mr. A. S. Krishna Rao supported the Resolution, and it was carried.

Resolution XI, on opening the higher grades in the Army to Indians, was moved by Mr. Senathi Raja, seconded by Sardar Gurmukh Singh, and carried.

Lala Sangam Lal moved Resolution XII, which asked for a Commission to enquire into the results of the laws restricting alienation of land, as grave dissatisfaction was being caused by their operation in the Panjab. He traced the history of the Panjab in relation to the large class of yeomen proprietors there, and showed how the causes which were working elsewhere in India to impoverish the agriculturists were also operating in the Panjab, and the land legislation was based on a mistaken idea. Lala Bhana Ram seconded, and Mr. Mathra Das, Lala Ram, Sardar Mehr Singh Chawla, and Mr. B. V. Vidwans all supported, and the Resolution was carried.

Mr. N. M. Samarth moved Resolution XIII on the Public Service, noting that Lord Morley had repudiated Lord Curzon's translation of the Proclamation of 1858, for, in the Royal Message of 1908, he said that the Proclamation aimed at "obliterating all distinctions of race". Rai Bahadur Khandu Bai Desai seconded, Dr. Ranjit Singh spoke for the Medical Service, and the Resolution was carried.

Resolution XIV was moved by Mr. Peter Paul Pillai, and dealt with the high prices of food-stuffs, and asked for a Commission of Enquiry. Professor V. G. Kale seconded, and it was supported by Mr. Wacha and Pandit Govind Sahai Sharma, and carried.

The President moved from the Chair Resolution XV on the Swadeshi Movement; XVI on Education; XVII on the Separation of Judicial and Executive Functions; all of which were carried.

Resolution XVIII asked for an enquiry into the dissatisfaction existing in the N. W. P. Frontier Province, and it was moved by Mr. Purushottam Lal. Mr. Sunder Singh Bhatia, in seconding, pointed out that there was no security for life or property for Hindus in that Province, and that there was a special form of trial, called Jirga, in which a number of Sardars, without any knowledge of criminal law, tried and sentenced men to long terms of imprisonment. The Resolution was carried.

The President put from the Chair Resolution XIX, thanking Mr. Hume, Sir William Wedderburn and Sir Henry Cotton; Resolution XX, appointing the All-India Committee as elected; Resolution XXII, re-electing Messrs. D. E. Wacha and D. A. Khare as General Secretaries; Resolution XXIII, thanking the few volunteers who had done the work usually done by students ten times their number, coming forward when a circular from the educational authorities forced the students to withdraw.

Dr. Tej Bahadur Sapru then invited the Congress to meet in Allahabad in the following year, and the invitation was accepted.

With the vote of thanks and the President's final speech, the Twenty-fourth Congress ended.

RESOLUTIONS

The Grief of Congress

I. Resolved—That this Congress desires to place on record its sense of the great and irreparable loss which the country and the community has sustained by the deaths of Mr. Lalmohan Ghose and Mr. Romesh Chandra Dutt, both past Presidents of the Congress. Their services to the country will always remain enshrined in the grateful recollection of their countrymen.

II. Resolved—That the Congress records its sense of the great loss that this country has sustained by the death of the Marquis of Ripon, who by his beneficent, progressive, and statesmanlike policy, as Viceroy of India, earned the lasting esteem, affection and gratitude of all classes of His Majesty's subjects.

Thanks of Congress

III. Resolved—That this Congress thanks the Government of His Imperial Majesty for appointing the Hon. Mr. S. P. Sinha as a member of His Excellency the Governor-General's Executive Council and the Rt. Hon. Mr. Amir Ali as a member of the Privy Council.

[See XIII].

XXI. Resolved—That this Congress desires to convey to Sir William Wedderburn, Mr. A. O. Hume, Sir Henry Cotton, and other members of the British Committee, its grateful thanks for their disinterested and strenuous services in the cause of India's political advancement.

XXIII. Resolved—That the thanks of this Congress be given to the volunteers, who supplied the place of the students, withdrawn by the Educational Authorities.

Representation

[For Resolution IV, on Council Reforms, see pp. 494, 495].

Executive Councils

V. Resolved—That this Congress while regretting that Cl. 3 of the India Councils Bill, under which power was to be given to the Governor-General in Council to create Executive Councils to assist the heads of the Government in the United Provinces, the Panjab, Eastern Bengal, Assam and Burma, was not passed as originally framed, earnestly urges that action may be taken at an early date under the Act to create Executive Councils in the above-named Provinces.

Panjab

VI. Resolved—That this Congress records its opinion that the Regulations framed for the Panjab, under the Reform scheme, fail to give satisfaction for the following reasons, *viz.*—

(*a*) In that the numerical strength of the Council provided for in the Regulations is not sufficient to allow an adequate representation to all classes and interests of the population, nor is it commensurate with the progress made by this Province, in matters social, educational, industrial and commercial.

(*b*) In that the elected element prescribed by the Regulations for the Local Council is unduly small and altogether insufficient to meet the needs and requirements of this Province, and compares very unfavourably with that accorded to other Provinces, not more advanced.

(*c*) In that the principle of protection of minorities, which has been applied in the case of non-Muhammadans in Provinces where they are in a minority, has not been applied in the case of non-Muhammadans who are in a minority in the Panjab, both in the Provincial and Imperial Councils.

(*d*) In that the Regulations, as framed, tend practically to keep out non-Muhammadans from the Imperial Council.

Berar and C. P.

VII. Resolved—That this Congress desires to give expression to the dissatisfaction produced among the people of the Central Provinces and Berar by the decision of the Government not to establish a Provincial Legislative Council for those territories, and by the exclusion of Berar from participation in the election of two members of the Imperial Legislative Council by the landholders and members of District and Municipal Boards of the Central Provinces, and this Congress appeals to the Government to remove the aforesaid complaints at an early date.

Local Self-Government

XVIII. Resolved—That this Congress expresses its satisfaction that the Secretary of State has recognised that the Local Self-Government Scheme of 1882, has not had a fair trial, and has pressed on the Government of India the necessity of an effectual advance in the direction of making local, urban and rural bodies really self-governing, and it expresses the earnest hope that the

Government will be pleased to take early steps to make all Local Bodies, from village panchayats upwards, elective, with elected non-official chairmen, and support them with adequate financial aid.

The Partition of Bengal

VIII. Resolved—That this Congress earnestly appeals to the Government of India and the Secretary of State for India, not to treat the question of the Partition of Bengal as incapable of reconsideration, but to take the earliest opportunity so to modify the said Partition as to keep the entire Bengali-speaking community under one and the same administration.

That this Congress humbly submits that the rectification of this admitted error will be an act of far-sighted statesmanship. It will restore contentment to the Province of Bengal, give satisfaction to other Provinces, and enhance the prestige of His Majesty's Government throughout the country.

That this Congress appoints Messrs. Surendranath Bannerji and Bhupendranath Bose to proceed to England as a deputation, to lay the question of the Partition before the authorities and public there.

South Africa

IX. Resolved—That this Congress expresses its great admiration of the intense patriotism, courage and self-sacrifice of the Indians in the Transvaal, Muhammadan and Hindu, Zoroastrian and Christian—who, heroically suffering persecution in the interests of their country, are carrying on their peaceful and selfless struggle for elementary civil rights against heavy and overwhelming odds.

That this Congress offers its warmest encouragement to Mr. M. K. Gandhi and his brave and faithful associates, and calls upon all Indians of whatever race or creed to help them unstintedly with funds; and in this connection the Congress begs to convey to Mr. R. J. Tata its high appreciation of the patriotic instincts which have inspired his munificent donation of Rs. 25,000 to his suffering countrymen in South Africa in their hour of need and trial.

That this Congress begs earnestly to press upon the Government of India the necessity of prohibiting the recruitment of indentured Indian labour for any portion of the South African Union, and of dealing with the authorities there in the same manner in which the latter deal with Indian interests, so long as they adhere to the selfish and one-sided policy which they proclaim and practise, and persist in their present course of denying to His Majesty's Indian subjects their just rights as citizens of the Empire.

That this Congress protests against the declaration of responsible statesmen in favour of allowing the Self-Governing Colonies in the British Empire to monopolise vast undeveloped territories for exclusive white settlement, and deems it its duty to point out that the policy of shutting the door in these territories and denying the rights of full British citizenship to all Asiatic subjects of the British Crown, while preaching and enforcing the opposite policy of the open door in Asia, is fraught with grave mischief to the Empire and is as unwise as it is unrighteous.

Coercion

Lettres de cachet

X. Resolved—That, having regard to the grave risk of injustice in Government action based upon ex-parte and untested information, and to the sufficiency for reasonably preventive and punitive purposes of other provisions on the Statute Book of the country, this Congress urges upon the Government the repeal of the old Regulations relating to deportation, and prays that the persons who were last year deported from Bengal be set at liberty without further detention, or be given an opportunity to meet the charges, if any, that may be against them, and for which they have been condemned unheard.

Military

XI. Resolved—That this Congress protests against the continued exclusion of the children of the soil from higher military careers, and in urging that such careers be thrown open to them, suggests the establishment of Military Colleges, at which Indians may receive the training necessary to qualify them for His Majesty's commission in the Army.

[See XIX (*b*)].

Land Laws

XII. Resolved—That having regard to the grave dissatisfaction caused by the operation of the Land Alienation and allied Acts among large sections of the community in the Panjab and elsewhere, this Congress is of opinion that the time has arrived for instituting a thorough and detailed enquiry into the policy and working of the laws restricting alienation of land in Provinces where such laws are in operation; and urges Government to appoint a mixed Commission of officials and representative non-official Indians to institute an enquiry, in order to ascertain whether the legislation has really benefited the interests of agriculture and of the class intended to be benefited by it, and whether it has given rise in actual operation to anomalies, hardships and disabilities, calculated to injure the growth and prospects of the agricultural industry, and cause discontent among any particular class or section of the community.

Public Service

XIII. Resolved—(*a*) That this Congress gratefully recognises the efforts that have been made during the last three years by the Secretary of State for India and the Viceroy to give gracious effect to the policy, laid down in the great Charter of 1858, and reiterated in His Majesty's message of last year, of obliterating distinctions of race in conferring higher offices on the people of India in the Public Service of the country.

That this Congress, however, is strongly of opinion that in order to carry out this policy effectively, the Resolution of the House of Commons of 2nd June, 1893, should be given effect to, and all examinations held in England only should be simultaneously held in India and in England, and all first appointments for the higher branches of the Public Service, which are made in India, should be by competitive examination only.

(*b*) That this Congress thanks the Secretary of State (1) For his despatch regarding the employment in the superior posts of the Civil Medical Service of qualified medical men, not belonging to the Indian Medical Service, and earnestly requests the Government of India to take early action in the direction pointed out by the Secretary of State. (2) That in the interests of the public, the medical service and the profession, as well as for the sake of economy in expenditure, this Congress, concurring with previous Congresses, urges the constitution of a distinct Indian Civil Medical Service, wholly independent of the Indian Military Medical Service.

High Prices of Food-stuffs

XIV. Resolved—That this Congress is of opinion that, having regard to the high prices of food-stuffs current during the past several years, and the hardships to which the middle and poorer classes in particular are put thereby, an enquiry by a properly constituted Commission should be instituted by the Government into the causes of such high prices, with a view to ascertain how far and by what remedies that evil could be removed or its effects minimised.

Swadeshi

XV. Resolved—That this Congress accords its most cordial support to the Swadeshi Movement, and calls upon the people of the country to labour for its success by making earnest and sustained efforts to promote the growth of industries, capable of development in the country, and to respond to the efforts of Indian producers by giving preference whenever practicable to Indian products over imported commodities, even at a sacrifice.

Education

XVI. Resolved—That this Congress is of opinion that the Government should take immediate steps :

(*a*) to make Primary Education free at once and gradually compulsory throughout the country ;

(*b*) to assign larger sums of money to Secondary and Higher Education (special encouragement being given where necessary to educate all backward classes) ;

(*c*) to make adequate provision for imparting Industrial and Technical Education in the different Provinces, having regard to local requirements ; and

(*d*) to give effective voice to the leaders of Indian public opinion in shaping the policy and system of Education in this country.

That in the opinion of this Congress the time has arrived for people all over the country to take up earnestly the question of supplementing existing institutions and the efforts of Government, by organising for themselves an independent system of Literary, Scientific, Technical, and Industrial Education, suited to the conditions of the different Provinces in the country.

Separation of Judicial and Executive Functions

XVII. Resolved—(*a*) That this Congress places on record its sense of regret that notwithstanding the hopes held out by Government that the Executive and Judicial functions were soon to be separated, no effective steps have been taken in that direction, and this Congress, concurring with previous Congresses, urges a complete separation of the two functions without delay.

(*b*) That this Congress, concurring with previous Congresses, urges that the Judicial Service in all parts of the country should be recruited mainly from the legal profession.

Permanent Settlement

XIX. Resolved—That this Congress, concurring with previous Congresses, urges :

(*a*) A reasonable and definite limitation to the State demand on land, and the introduction of a Permanent Settlement, or a Settlement for a period of not less than sixty years in those Provinces where short periodical Settlement revisions prevail, as, in the opinion of this Congress, that is the only means of ameliorating the present unsatisfactory economic condition of the agricultural population ; and (*b*) A reduction of the annually growing military expenditure which now absorbs nearly one-third of the Empire's revenue, leaving an inadequate portion only of the balance available for the many objects of popular utility, specially Education and Sanitation, which are yet greatly starved.

N. W. F. Province

XX. Resolved—That in view of the prevalence of serious dissatisfaction among the people of the N. W. Frontier Province with the character of the administration under which they live, this Congress earnestly urges the Government of India to order a public enquiry into their complaints, and take steps to remedy the disadvantages under which they labour as compared with the population of the Panjab.

Formal

XXII. Resolved—That Mr. D. E. Wacha and Mr. Daji Abaji Khare be appointed General Secretaries for the ensuing year.

XXIV. Resolved—That the next meeting of the Indian National Congress be held at Allahabad after Christmas, 1910.

CHAPTER XXV

The Twenty-fifth National Congress met at Allahabad on the 26th, 27th, 28th, and 29th December, 1910. The Congress Pavilion was pitched on a plot of ground opposite the Fort, and it was quaintly designed with twenty-five sides and twenty-five doors, with a picture of a President over each door. 636 delegates attended, and some 4,000 visitors gathered to take part in the proceedings. The delegates were distributed as follows:

Madras	121
Bombay (80), Sindh (58)	138
Bengal	85
U. P.	202
Panjab	27
C. P.	16
Berar	8
Behar	39
	636

It will be noticed that the Central Provinces and Berar are here definitely separated, and we miss Burma from the roll.

Sir William Wedderburn had been elected as President, and he came over from England in the hope of surmounting the difficulties that were dividing the National Party, on one side from the Surat trouble, on the other from the wedge driven in between the Hindus and the Muhammadans by introducing the religious question into electioneering. The Hon. Pandit Sunderlal, as Chairman of the Reception Committee, welcomed the President and the delegates, and was able to say that both the Civil and Military authorities had helped the Committee in making the necessary arrangements. After reference to several losses of the old pillars of the Congress, he welcomed Sir William Wedderburn, whose ceaseless labours for India's welfare had made him beloved by every Indian. Then followed a touching reference to the passing away of H. I. M. Edward VII and loyal homage to his successor, with a word of gladness for the promised visit of the new King-Emperor and his Consort. The changes in the Viceroyalty and the Secretaryship of State were noted, and the attention of the new Viceroy, Lord Hardinge, was called in a few brief sentences to the claims of Education, the Separation of Judicial and Executive functions, and the need for the establishment of an Executive Council in the U. P. Sir William Wedderburn was going to hold a Conference of Hindus and Muhammadans; it was noteworthy that in District and Municipal Boards in the U. P where there were no separate electorates, out of 663 members of District Boards, the common electorate had returned 445 Hindus and 189 Muhammadans, and in 965 Municipalities 562 were Hindus and 310 Muhammadans, showing that in a Province where only one-seventh of the population were Muslims, Hindus had voted for them in large numbers. Sir John Hewett had said that it would be a great pity to disturb their amicable relations by introducing religious differences into elections.

Mr. Surendranath Bannerji moved that Sir William Wedderburn take the Chair in a speech of warm and grateful praise for his long and devoted services to India. The motion was seconded by Mr. D. E. Wacha, supported by the Hon. Rao Bahadur R. N. Mudholkar, the Hon. Mr. N. Subba Rao, the Hon. Lala Harkishan Lal, Mr. Yusuf Hasan, and the Hon. Pandit Madan Mohan Malaviya, and he was installed amid enthusiastic cheers.

The President began by asserting his faith in the future destiny of India. "India deserves to be happy." They had reason for hope in the reforms lately introduced, and these should result in a spirit of conciliation and co-operation. The chief differences were: (1) between European officials and educated Indians; (2) between Hindus and Muhammadans; and (3) between Moderates and Extremists. He then dealt with these seriatim, making far too little of the "indiscriminate house-searchings, prosecutions and other processes in pursuit of offences"; then urging harmony under (2) and (3).

The President next classified Congress work as: (1) constructive work in India, educating and organising public opinion; (2) representations to Government; and (3) propaganda in England. The latter he urged very strongly. The newborn spirit of self-reliance was good, but it should not degenerate into dislike of people from other lands. The "United States of India," under the ægis of the British Empire, need not be very long in coming, if the leaders of India worked hand in hand with the British people.

Mr. D. E. Wacha read telegrams from Mr. Dadabhai Naoroji, Dr. Rash Behari Ghose and others, and Mr. D. A. Khare asked the delegates to elect their representatives on the Subjects Committee. The Congress rose for the day.

The second day opened with the President putting the first three resolutions from the Chair. Resolution I was an expression of profound grief for the death of King Edward VII, which was passed standing and in silence. Resolution II offered the homage of the Congress to King George V, and welcomed the proposed visit of the King and Queen, and passed by acclamation. Resolution III welcomed the new Viceroy, Lord Hardinge, and appointed a Committee to draw up an Address to him from the Congress, and named the deputation to wait upon him to present it. Sir William Wedderburn noted that it was for the first time that the Congress was to "be received in friendly personal recognition by a Viceroy"—the first, we may add, of many acts whereby Lord Hardinge showed his sympathy with Indian feeling. The Resolution was unanimously carried.

Resolution IV, on the appointment of the Law Member to the Viceroy's Executive Council being limited to members of the English Bar, and urging that Advocates and Vakils should also be eligible, was moved by the Hon. Mr. S. Sinha, who pointed out that it was unwise to restrict the field of choice, and noted that Dr. Rash Behari Ghose was a Vakil, and was certainly not below a Barrister in qualifications. Rao Bahadur B. N. Sarma seconded, remarking on the eminent Vakils who had adorned the profession in Madras. The Resolution was carried.

Mr. G. A. Natesan was once more called to move the Resolution on Indians in the Colonies (No. V), and said that the sufferings of Indians in South Africa were indeed well known to them all. He urged the duty of the British Government to protect its subjects, and praised the heroism of the passive resisters. Mr. Manilal Doctor seconded, and spoke of the oppression suffered by Indians in Mauritius. The Resolution was supported by Mr. Raghunandan Prasad and Mr. Debi Prasad, and carried.

Resolution VI, supporting the Swadeshi Movement, was moved by Mr. C. Y. Chintamani, who urged the duty of educated people to help indigenous industries by using their products. The imports of foreign goods increased, and even shawls were being brought in from abroad; purchase of Home goods should be made easy by setting up Swadeshi stores, for, as Mr. Ranade had said, India had "come to be regarded as a plantation of England, growing raw produce to be shipped by British agents in British ships, to be worked into fabrics by British skill and capital, and to be re-exported to India by British merchants to their corresponding British firms in India through their British agents ".

Mr. Jitendralal Bannerji seconded, and urged that at every sacrifice Home goods should be used. The Resolution was supported by Messrs. Dwarkanath, D. V. Krishna Rao, Sachindra Prasad Basu, and Lokamal Chellaram, and carried.

Mr. Jogendranath Mukerji moved Resolution VII, urging the Separation of Judicial and Executive functions, and adding the proposal that the Judicial Service should be recruited mainly from the legal profession. He recalled the recommendation of separation by the Police Commission of 1863, the Memorial of Lord Hobhouse and others in 1889; Lord Curzon included it in his twelve reforms, but did nothing, and Lord Morley in 1908 gave it his sanction. Still no effective steps had been taken. The Hon. Mr. Braj Kishore seconded, giving a story from his own district: a Mahant rang bells in his temple, and this annoyed the Magistrate; so he bade his orderly lodge a complaint, and the case came up before him, whereupon he convicted and fined the Mahant, and gave part of the fines to the orderly.

Mr. C. P. Ramaswami Aiyar said that speech on the subject ought to be needless under British rule, as the British had always been peculiarly jealous of any executive interference with the administration of their laws. But for the theory that the Collector was to be responsible for law and order and also ought to dispense justice, no pleading for such reform would have been necessary under the British Crown. On the second part, he need only say that in filling up the office of Judge it seemed to be thought that no training was necessary. No one was allowed to masquerade as a doctor without training, nor was an engineer entrusted with a locomotive without training, but "to administer justice, the one *sine qua non* is that nothing need be known of the principles of law". The Resolution was carried.

The second day's work came to an end with Resolution VIII, demanding Executive Councils for the U. P. and the Panjab. It was moved by Pandit Gokharannath Misra, who briefly sketched the history of the creation of these Councils; in Lord Morley's Indian Councils Bill, a clause was provided to give them to the major Provinces, but Lord Curzon and Lord Macdonnell succeeded in mutilating the Bill, though passed in the Commons, when the Bill was before the Lords. Strong protests were made, but, as usual, no attention was paid to them. Mr. P. L. Rajpal seconded in a vigorous speech, the Resolution was carried, and the Congress adjourned.

On the re-assembling of the Congress on the third day, Dr. Gour moved Resolution IX on Local Self-Government. When Lord Ripon in 1882 planned the Local Self-Government scheme, all thought the people were to be entrusted with effective power in administering local affairs, but when he left, there was reaction; official Chairmen, Collectors and Tahsildars were appointed to District and Taluq Boards, and took over all power. Things went from bad to worse till the Decentralisation Commission was appointed. The

Congress asked that all Local Bodies, from Village Panchayats upwards, should be made elective, and all chairmen and secretaries should be elected.

The Hon. Mr. G. Raghava Rao seconded, and laid special stress on the election of non-official chairmen. Mr. M. Ramchandra Rao dealt specially with the financial aspect, and after a Hindi speech from Munshi Sankata Prasad, the Resolution was carried.

Mr. Ambikacharan Mozumdar moved Resolution X, protesting against the Partition of Bengal. It was no "dead issue," as it had been called, and smart expressions did not stamp out vital grievances. There was no "settled fact" in politics, and it was useless to charge them with sedition. "When there is a rupture between a settled Government and its people, the presumption is generally against the former." A great man had said that "a Nation is not governed when it has perpetually to be conquered," and the Bengalis were not well governed, if they had to be continually repressed. God grant that Lord Hardinge might open a new era. [The prayer was granted.] Dewan Bahadur C. Karunakara Menon seconded, and Mr. Nibaran Chandra Das Gupta supported. He said that the wail of Bengal was no longer heard because the people were muzzled by repressive measures; remove the muzzle, and the cry would again be heard. The Resolution was carried.

Resolution XI embodied the old grievances of Indians in the Medical Service; it was moved by

Sir Bhalchandra Krishna, seconded by Dr. Ranjit Singh, supported by Dr. H. D. Pant, and carried.

Mr. J. Choudhuri moved Resolution XII, praying that the Seditious Meetings Act should not be re-enacted on its expiry, and that the Press Act should be at once removed. "Public meetings and public speeches are becoming a thing of the past. Thus, it is a measure of first-rate coercion for suppressing the expression of public opinion."

> It is a shame and a scandal that the British Government should not only curtail the liberty of the press, but frame a law which will interfere with the setting up of new printing presses, and thus indirectly check the spread of knowledge in this benighted country. . . The law of sedition in this country is elastic enough. If the law would go any greater length, then all our liberties—individual, personal and communal—will be at an end.

Mr. A. S. Krishna Rao seconded, and pointed out the unfairness of presuming guilt against a publisher by demanding security before he had committed any fault. Mr. Dwarkanath, supporting, said that these measures had paralysed the public life of India. People were afraid of joining any public movement. The C. I. D. "is a real terror to the people," for "our public men are always at the mercy of the members of the C. I. D." Mr. Yusuf Hasan also supported, and the Resolution was carried.

The Resolution (XIII) on Elementary Education was moved by Mr. V. V. Jogiah Pantulu, seconded by Mr. Ganpati Krishna Chitale, supported by Pandit Hirdaynath Kunzru, and carried.

Resolution XIV, asking for a Commission of Enquiry into Expenditure, was moved by Mr. N. M. Samarth, seconded by Mr. N. A. Dravid, and carried.

Resolution XV. dealt with the Council Regulations, and the mover, Dr. Satish Chandra Bannerji, spoke of the bitter disappointment caused by the Regulations which had wrecked the Reform scheme. Dr. Tej Bahadur Sapru seconded, asking that the Regulations might at least deal equally with all communities. Rai Bahadur M. Adinarayana Iyah and the Hon. Mr. Harchandrai Vishandas supported, and Nawab Sadiq Ali Khan made a strong appeal to his fellow-Muslims to be united and patriotic, "and, for the sake of certain paltry gains in the Services or in the Councils, do not sacrifice the larger hopes of an ampler day". Shaik Faiz and Mr. Yusuf Hasan supported, but on the latter saying that it was not honest of the Muslim League to demand an unfair amount of representation, he was checked by the President, and Mr. Surendranath Bannerji, supported by loud cheers, dissociated the Congress and himself from the remarks made. The Resolution was carried.

A gentleman wishing to move an amendment was ruled out of order, not having sent it in.

Resolution XVI, deprecating the extension of communal representation to Local Bodies was moved by the Hon. Mr. M. A. Jinnah, who merely said it embodied his views. The Hon. Mr. Muzharal Haq seconded, urging Hindus and Muslims to join hands. Mr. Syed Hasan Imam supported and it was carried.

Mr. G. K. Devadhar moved Resolution XVII, urging the formation of Conciliation Boards wherever disturbances over religious celebrations were feared. Mr. Ramkumar Goenka seconded, and the Resolution was carried.

Three Resolutions were then put from the Chair and carried : XVIII, on reforms in the C. P. and Berar ; XIX, on reforms in the Panjab ; XX, on the desirability of reducing cable rates between England and India. The Congress adjourned.

On the fourth day, Resolution XXI, on Higher and Secondary, Industrial and Technical Education, was moved by Mr. A. B. Patro, seconded by Mr. Pulin Chandra Das, supported by Messrs. Devi Prasad Sukla, V. R. Dixit, and Ramakant Malaviya, and carried. Then the President put from the Chair Resolution XXII, Simultaneous Examinations ; XXIII, the Omnibus ; XXIV, asking Lord Hardinge to show clemency to purely political prisoners ; XXV, referring some amendments in the Congress Constitution to a Sub-Committee, to report to the next Congress ; and XXVI, the All-India Congress Committee.

Mr. Surendranath Bannerji then moved the thanks of the Congress to Sir William Wedderburn, Mr. A. O. Hume, Sir Henry Cotton and the members of the British Committee (Resolution XXVII), and asked for Rs. 39,000, and got Rs. 40,000 there and then, also carrying the Resolution. The President put from the Chair a message of sympathy to the Indians in the Transvaal, one of affection to Mr. Hume and the G. O. M. Resolution XXVIII, re-election of

General Secretaries and Resolution XXIX, fixing the next meeting of the Congress in Calcutta, on the invitation of Mr. Bhupendranath Basu were carried.

The Hon. Mr. G. K. Gokhale moved Resolution XXX, conveying the thanks of the Congress to the President in a very eloquent and beautiful speech; Pandit Motilal Nehru seconded, and it was carried by acclamation. The Hon. Pandit Sunderlal, C. I. E., garlanded the President, who received a tremendous ovation in his closing speech.

The Twenty-fifth National Congress then dissolved.

RESOLUTIONS

"The King is Dead"

I. Resolved—That this Congress desires to give expression to its profound grief at the sudden and untimely demise of His Most Gracious Majesty King Edward VII, whose beneficent reign will ever be memorable in the annals of India for the steps taken to obliterate race distinctions in making appointments to high office, and for the measures of constitutional reform adopted with a view to associate the people of this country with the administration of their affairs.

"Long Live the King"

II. Resolved—That this Congress offers its humble homage and duty to the King-Emperor George V on his accession and begs to tender to His Majesty an assurance of its profound loyalty and attachment to his august throne and person. The Congress expresses its deep and heartfelt joy at the announcement of the proposed visit of their Most Gracious Majesties, King George and Queen Mary, to India, in 1911.

Delegation to Lord Hardinge

III. Resolved—That (*a*) this Congress in offering its warm and respectful welcome to His Excellency Lord Hardinge, Viceroy and Governor-General of India, begs to convey to His Excellency an earnest assurance of its desire to co-operate loyally with the Government in promoting the welfare of the people of the country;

(b) this Congress resolves that a sub-Committee consisting of the following gentlemen be appointed to prepare an address to be presented to His Excellency in the name of the Congress by a deputation headed by the President:

The President.
The Ex-Presidents present.
The General Secretaries.
Hon. Mr. Bhupendranath Basu (United Bengal).
Mr. Ambikacharan Mozumdar (United Bengal).
Hon. Mr. N. Subba Rao (Madras).
Hon. Mr. T. V. Seshagiri Iyer (Madras).
Hon. Mr. M. H. Jinnah (Bombay).
Mr. N. M. Samarth (Bombay).
Pandit Bishan Narayan Dhar (United Provinces).
Nawab Sadiq Ali Khan (United Provinces).
Mr. Syed Hasan Imam (Behar).
Dr H. S. Gour (Central Provinces).
Hon. Rao Bahadur R. N. Mudholkar (Berar).
Hon. Mr. Harkishan Lal (Panjab).
Pandit Rambhuj Dutt Choudhuri (Panjab).

Legal

IV. Resolved—That in view of the fact that Section III of the Indian Councils Act of 1861 is understood in practice to limit appointment to the Office of Law Member of the Viceroy's Executive Council to members of the English Bar, thereby greatly restricting the field from which a selection may be made, this Congress urges that the said section be so amended as to allow of Advocates, Vakils, and Attorneys-at-Law of Indian High Courts being appointed to that office.

VII. Resolved—That (a) this Congress places on record its sense of regret that notwithstanding the hopes held out by the Government that the Executive and Judicial functions were soon to be separated, no effective steps have been taken in that direction, and, concurring with previous Congresses, urges a complete separation of the two functions without delay;

(b) this Congress, concurring with previous Congresses, urges that the Judicial Service in all parts of the country should be recruited mainly from the legal profession.

Indians in the Colonies

V. Resolved—That (a) this Congress expresses its great admiration of the intense patriotism, courage, and self-sacrifice of the Indians in the Transvaal—Muhammadan and Hindu, Zoroastrian and Christian, who, heroically suffering persecution in the interests of their countrymen, are carrying on their peaceful and selfless strugggle for elementary civil rights against heavy and overwhelming odds, and urges the Imperial Government to adopt a firm and decisive attitude on the question, so as to remove a great source of discontent amongst the people of India;

(*b*) this Congress begs earnestly to press upon the Government of India the necessity of prohibiting the recruitment of indentured Indian labour for any portion of the South Africa Union, and of dealing with the authorities there in the same manner as the latter deal with Indian interests, so long as they adhere to the selfish and one-sided policy, which they proclaim and practise, and persist in their present course of denying to His Majesty's Indian subjects their just rights as citizens of the Empire;

(*c*) this Congress protests against the declarations of responsible statesmen in favour of allowing the Self-Governing Colonies in the British Empire to monopolise vast undeveloped territories for exclusive white settlement, and deems it its duty to point out that the policy of shutting the door in these territories against, and denying the rights of full British citizenship to, all Asiatic subjects of the British Crown, while preaching and enforcing the opposite policy of the open door in Asia, is fraught with grave mischief to the Empire and is as unwise as it is unrighteous.

Swadeshi

VI. Resolved—That this Congress accords its most cordial support to the Swadeshi Movement, and calls upon the people of the country to labour for its success by making earnest and sustained efforts to promote the growth of industries capable of development in this country, and to respond to the efforts of Indian producers by giving preference, wherever practicable, to Indian products over imported commodities, even at a sacrifice.

Executive Councils

VIII. Resolved—That this Congress earnestly recommends that speedy action be taken under the Indian Councils Act to establish Executive Councils in the United Provinces of Agra and Oudh and in the Panjab.

Local Self-Government

IX. Resolved—That this Congress expresses its satisfaction that the Secretary of State has recognised that the Local Self-Government scheme of 1882 has not had a fair trial, and has pressed on the Government of India the necessity of an effectual advance in the direction of making Local, Urban, and Rural bodies really Self-Governing, and it expresses the earnest hope that the Government will be pleased to take early steps to make all Local Bodies from Village Panchayats upwards, elective, with elected non-official Chairmen, and to support them with adequate financial aid.

The Partition of Bengal

X. Resolved—That (*a*) this Congress earnestly appeals to the Government of India and the Secretary of State for India not to treat the question of the Partition of Bengal as incapable of reconsideration, but to take the earliest opportunity so to modify the said Partition, as to keep the entire Bengali-speaking community under one and the same administration ;

(*b*) this Congress humbly submits that the rectification of this admitted error will be an act of far-sighted statesmanship. It will restore contentment to the Province of Bengal, give satisfaction to other Provinces, and enhance the prestige of His Majesty's Government throughout the country.

Public Service

Medical

XI. Resolved—That (*a*) this Congress thanks the Secretary of State for his Despatch regarding the employment in the superior posts of the Civil Medical Service, and earnestly requests the Government of India to take early action in the direction pointed out by the Secretary of State for India ;

(*b*) in the interests of the public, the medical service, and the profession, as well as for the sake of economy in expenditure, this Congress, concurring with previous Congresses, urges the constitution of a distinct Indian Civil Medical Service wholly independent of the Indian (Military) Medical Service.

Simultaneous Examinations

XXII. Resolved—That this Congress is of opinion that the Examination held in England for the Indian Civil Service should be simultaneously held in England and in India, and that all higher appointments which are made in India should be made by Competitive Examinations only.

Confirmation of Previous Resolutions

(1) *Police*

XXIII. Resolved—That (*a*) Competitive Examinations for the recruitment of the Police Service in the higher grades should be thrown open to all classes of British subjects, instead of being confined to candidates of British birth, and such examinations should be held simultaneously in England and in India.

(*b*) educated Indians should be largely employed in the higher grades in order to secure efficiency in work ;

(*c*) enlistment in the Provincial Service should be by Competitive Examination ; and lastly, (*d*) the District Officers who are the heads of the Police should be relieved of Judicial work and all control over the Magistrates of the Districts.

(2) *Permanent Settlement*

That a reasonable and definite limitation to the State demand on land and the introduction of a Permanent Settlement or a Settlement for a period of not less than sixty years in those Provinces where short periodical Settlements or Revisions prevail, are, in the opinion of the Congress, the only means of ameliorating the present unsatisfactory conditions of the agricultural population.

(3) *Military Expenditure*

That in the opinion of this Congress, a reduction is urgently needed of the annually growing Military Expenditure which now absorbs nearly one-third of the Empire's revenue, leaving only an inadequate portion of the balance available for many objects of public utility, especially Education and Sanitation, which are yet greatly starved.

Coercion

Press

XII. Resolved—That having regard to the state of the country since the passing of the Seditious Meetings Act and the Indian Press Act, this Congress earnestly prays that the former be not re-enacted at the expiry of its term, and that the latter be removed from the Statute Book without delay.

Education

Elementary Education

XIII. Resolved—That in the opinion of this Congress the time has arrived when a substantial beginning should be made in the matter of Elementary Education—free and compulsory—throughout the country.

XXI Resolved—That this Congress is of opinion that the Government should take early steps:

Secondary and Higher

(*a*) to assign larger sums of money to Secondary and Higher Education (especial encouragement being given where necessary to educate all backward classes);

Industrial and Technical

(*b*) to make adequate provision for imparting Industrial and Technical Education in the different Provinces, having regard to local requirements; and

National Control

(*c*) to give effective voice to the leaders of Indian public opinion in shaping the policy and system of Education in this country.

Popular Duty

That in the opinion of this Congress the time has arrived for people, all over the country, to take up earnestly the question of supplementing existing institutions and the efforts of the Government, by organising for themselves an independent system of Literary, Scientific, Technical and Industrial Education, suited to the conditions of the different Provinces in the country.

Finance

XIV. Resolved—That having regard to the enormous growth that has taken place in the public expenditure of the country, this Congress urges that a mixed Commission of enquiry composed of officials and non-officials, be appointed to enquire into the causes which have led to this increase and to suggest remedies.

[And see XXIII (3)].

Representation

XV. Resolved—That while recognising the necessity of providing for a fair and adequate Representation in the Legislative Councils for the Muhammadan and other communities where they are in a minority, this Congress disapproves the Regulations promulgated last year to carry out this object by means of separate electorates, and in particular urges upon the Government the justice and expediency of modifying the Regulations framed under the Indian Councils Act of 1909, before another election comes on, so as to remove anomalous distinctions between different sections of His Majesty's subjects in the matter of the franchise and the qualifications of candidates and the arbitrary disqualifications and restrictions for candidates seeking election to the Councils. The Congress also urges a modification of the Regulations, where necessary, relating to the composition of non-official majorities in the Provincial Councils, so as to render them effective for practical purposes.

Separate Electorates

XVI. Resolved—That this Congress strongly deprecates the expansion or application of the principle of Separate Communal Electorates to Municipalities, District Boards, or other Local Bodies.

Provincial Reform (C. P. and Berar)

XVIII. Resolved—That this Congress is of opinion that the time has come for the establishment of a Provincial Legislative

Council for the Central Provinces and Berar, and for according to Berar, which is now held by the Government on a permanent tenure, the status and privileges which are accorded to Provinces included in British India.

Provincial Reform (Panjab)

XIX. Resolved—That this Congress records its opinion that the Regulations framed for the Panjab under the Reform Scheme fail to give satisfaction for the following reasons, namely:

(*a*) that the numerical strength of the Council provided for in the Regulations is not sufficient to allow an adequate representation to all classes and interests of the population, nor is it commensurate with the progress made by that Province in matters Social, Educational, Industrial and Economical;

(*b*) that the elected element prescribed by the Regulations for the Local Legislative Council is unduly small, and altogether insufficient to meet the needs and requirements of that Province, and compares unfavourably with those accorded to other Provinces;

(*c*) that the proportion of nominated members of the Panjab Legislative Council is inequitable and out of proportion to the ratio of the different sections of the population; and

(*d*) that the Regulations, as framed, tend practically to keep out non-Muhammadans from the Imperial Legislative Council.

Conciliation Boards

XVII. Resolved—That in view of the disturbances that have occurred from time to time in this country on occasions of religious celebrations, this Congress urges the Government to form Conciliation Boards at places where disturbances are apprehended, and to take timely and adequate measures for the prevention of such disturbances.

Reduction of Cable Rates

XX. Resolved—That in the opinion of this Congress it is extremely desirable on more than one ground that the rate of cable messages between England and India should be still further reduced, so as to offer greater facilities to the trade and to the press, and, at the same time, stimulate traffic in those messages.

Political Prisoners

XXIV. Resolved—That having regard to the great improvement which has taken place in the general situation of the country, as recognised by the late Viceroy and other high authorities, this Congress respectfully appeals to His Excellency Lord Hardinge to signalise the commencement of a new administration by an act of clemency to those who are undergoing imprisonment for purely political offences. In the opinion of this Congress, such an act of clemency will have the undoubted effect of facilitating the return of the country to normal conditions, and will lead to a further improvement in the relations between the Government and the people.

Congress Constitution

XXV. Resolved—That the Amendments suggested by the United Bengal Provincial Congress Committee and such other amendments as may be suggested by other Committees be referred to a Sub-Committee, consisting of the members of the All-India Congress Committee and two members elected by each of the Provincial Congress Committees, who are members of a Congress organisation, for consideration and report before the end of October, 1911, the Sub-Committee to meet at Allahabad and their report to be laid before the next Congress for consideration.

Formal

XXVI. Resolved—The following gentlemen are nominated to form the ALL-INDIA CONGRESS COMMITTEE for 1911 (list omitted).

XXVIII. Resolved—That Mr. D. E. Wacha and Mr. Daji Abaji Khare be appointed General Secretaries for the ensuing year.

XXIX. Resolved—That the next Congress be held at Calcutta.

Thanks of Congress

XXVII. Resolved—That this Congress desires to convey to Sir William Wedderburn, Mr. A. O. Hume, Sir Henry Cotton, and other members of the British Committee, its grateful thanks for their disinterested and strenuous services, and it takes this opportunity to make an earnest appeal to the Indian public to place adequate funds at the disposal of the Committee to enable it to carry on its work with vigour.

XXX. Resolved—That our most cordial thanks be accorded to our President Sir William Wedderburn, for the great trouble he has taken in coming out to India to preside over this assembly, and for his devoted labours in guiding aright the deliberations of this Congress.

[See IX, XI.]

CHAPTER XXVI

The Twenty-sixth National Congress met in Calcutta, on the 26th, 27th and 28th of December, 1911, met in the full joy of the reunited Bengalis, whose long suffering had been crowned with triumph, and who had heard the Partition of Bengal annulled by the King-Emperor's own lips in the great Coronation Durbar at Delhi. 446 delegates had gathered in Calcutta on that joyous occasion, and they were grouped as follows :

Bombay	26
Panjab	3
U. P.	94
Madras	136
Behar	23
C. P.	7
Berar	9
Bengal	148
	446

The Hon. Mr. Bhupendranath Basu, the Chairman of the Reception Committee, welcomed the President-elect and the delegates, and then, recalling the vow of October 16th, 1905, that, come what might, the people of Bengal should not be divided, he spoke of the Royal announcement, redressing a grave wrong.

They would welcome the King-Emperor on his coming among them, "not only as our King and Emperor, but as our deliverer". They welcomed also the Queen-Empress, and also the Secretary of State for India, Lord Crewe, and he paid a graceful tribute to Lord Hardinge, "that statesman, lonely and serene, ... who saw the wrong and did the right". He spoke with deep regret of the removal of the seat of Government from Bengal after its connection of 150 years with British Power. He then turned to the necessity that the Congress should continue its work, despite the Legislative Council reforms, since the Congress had to build the Nation, and to be a centre, round which all could gather. He touched briefly on the various differences between Indians, but they had a common consciousness as Indians, the sense of oneness of which the Congress was a symbol. Their sense of Nationality would not weaken their tie with England, but rather strengthen it.

Mr. Surendranath Bannerji, in a very brief speech, moved that Pandit Bishan Narayan Dhar should take the Chair. The motion was seconded by Rao Bahadur R. N. Mudholkar, supported by Mr. G. K. Gokhale, the Hon. Nawab Syed Muhammad, and Pandit Rambhuj Dutt Choudhuri, and warmly carried.

The President said that they had hoped to have had Mr. Ramsay Macdonald as their President, but his wife's untimely death had called him away, and he himself had been asked unexpectedly to take his place. He then referred to the death of the Nizam of Hyderabad, mourned through the whole country;

that of Sir Charles Dilke, who had always shown himself a friend of India; and the loss, especially to Bengal, of Norendranath Sen and Mr. Shishir Kumar Ghosh. Then followed some grateful words to Lord Hardinge, and deep loyalty to the King-Emperor, who had annulled the Partition of Bengal. He spoke approvingly of the transfer of the capital to Delhi, as likely to vivify the Panjab, glanced at the creation of the new Province of Behar, and hoped the creation there of an Executive Council presaged the granting of one to the U. P. Turning to the Government here, he spoke gratefully of the benefits of British rule, the peace and order, the gift of education: "faulty as it is in many respects, and greatly as it needs to be reformed and renovated from top to bottom, it is still the greatest gift of Providence to my race". "The root-cause," he said,

> of most of our misfortunes, which, if not corrected, forebodes serious disasters in the future, is the growth of an unsympathetic and illiberal spirit in the bureaucracy towards the new-born hopes and ideals of the Indian people. While a new India has gradually been rising up, that spirit too has been growing, and so the critical situation has arisen: on the one hand, the educated classes, filled with new knowledge and conscious of new political rights, but hampered by the bars and fetters of a system perhaps good enough for other days but now obsolete; on the other, the bureaucracy with its vested interests, its domineering habits, its old traditions of obsolete and unquestioned authority, suspicious of knowledge and averse to innovation like every close corporation, cut off from the people by its racial exclusiveness, and wedded to a paternal system of Government under which it has so long enjoyed power and pelf but which is discordant with the more liberal ideals of the present day.

He strengthened this contention by giving a long list of the cases in which the bureaucracy had worked against Indian interests. After condemning the coercive policy, the President turned to the Regulations which had wrecked the Reforms, and subjected them to a searching analysis, and he complained that all attempts to unite Hindus and Muhammadans were opposed by the Anglo-Indian press.

> When under the advice of Sir William Wedderburn and H. H. the Aga Khan, the representatives of the two communities were about to meet at Allahabad a year ago, with the object of reconciling their differences, an Anglo-Indian paper, which is believed to be an organ of the Civil Service, remarked: "Why do these men want to unite the two communities, if it is not to unite them against the Government?" This one remark throws a ghastly light upon the political situation in India.

The President declared against the introduction of communal representation into Local Bodies, and commented sarcastically on the Burn circular in favour of it; the circular advocated separate electorates for Muhammadans while also allowing them to vote in mixed electorates, as this would be helpful in maintaining friendly relations between the two communities. "I will only say that this solicitude for promoting our unity is rather a heavy draft upon our credulity." The employment of Indians in the Public Service, "which has been before the Government for nearly a century," the proposal to found Hindu and Muslim Universities which he warmly praised, the Elementary Education Bill of Mr. Gokhale, the status of Indians in the Colonies—all came under review. The President, in conclusion, spoke ringing words on the "ideal of Self-Government within the Empire".

> Our agitation, in order to be effective must be National not sectarian, persistent not spasmodic, directed by intelligence and wisdom and not impulsive and reckless. Enthusiasm is good, and idealism is good, and even crying for the moon is sometimes good; and I for one sympathise with those who are called visionaries and dreamers, for I know that in every active and reforming body there is always an extreme wing that is not without its uses in great human movements. I know that moderation sometimes means indifference, and caution timidity, and I hold that India needs bold and enthusiastic characters—not men of pale hopes and middling expectations, but courageous natures, fanatics in the cause of their country.

The President ended amid loud applause, and the Congress adjourned to the following day.

On the assembly of the Congress on the second day, some letters and telegrams having been read, the President moved from the Chair the first Resolution of loyal homage to the King-Emperor and Queen-Empress on their visit, and it was carried with hearty cheers and telegraphed to His Majesty.

Resolution II thanked His Majesty and also the Government of India and the Secretary of State for annulling the Partition of Bengal. It was moved by Mr. Surendranath Bannerji in a grateful speech, in which he dwelt on the wisdom of the action taken, and rejoiced that all India, which had helped the Bengalis in their struggle, now shared in the joy of their triumph ; he concluded with a hope that India would form "part and parcel of the Self-Governing States of a great, free and federated Empire, rejoicing in our indissoluble connection with England, and in the enjoyment of the inestimable blessing of new-born freedom".

The Hon. Rao Bahadur R. N. Mudholkar seconded the Resolution, praising the courage of the Secretary of State and the Viceroy in facing the opposition in England, and gratefully recognising the noble courage of the King, who had risked personal opprobrium by announcing the reversal.

The Resolution was supported by Mr. C. P. Ramaswami Aiyar, who pointed to the importance of the issue raised in the question—whether the people should be consulted, or the Government should act in an arbitrary and secret fashion. A question supposed to be settled had been re-opened by constitutional agitation, and they now knew that when a wrong had been done, right agitation would redress it. The Resolution was further supported by Mr. Muralidhar Rai and Mr. D. E. Wacha, who voiced the sympathy of Bombay, and by Mr. Ambikacharan Mozumdar, who in the course of an admirable speech, said:

Gentlemen, on this day of universal rejoicing when every heart in India in general and in Bengal in particular is beating in unison with reverence and devotion to the British Throne and overflowing with revived confidence and gratitude towards British statesmanship, I will not—I dare not—recount the painful records and recall the bitter memories of the past 5 years. Let the dead past bury its dead. Let suspicion and distrust, malice and rancour, rage and repression—those evil spirits that revel in darkness—vanish from the land, and let cavil and calumny be hushed into silence. Groping our way through the darkness of defeat and despair, we have by the grace of God at last emerged into the breaking sunshine of success. Gentlemen, some of us never faltered—no, not even in the darkest days of our trials and tribulations—in our hope, in our conviction and in our faith in the ultimate triumph and vindication of British justice. In that hope we have lived, in that conviction we have worked and in that faith we have patiently suffered and waited. We had read English history in vain, if we had failed to grasp the one great lesson it teaches, that though British statesmanship has blundered in many places it has ultimately failed nowhere. British conscience, however much darkened at times by other considerations, has invariably vindicated itself by rebelling at the end against proved tyranny, injustice and oppression to suffering humanity. The nation of Howard and Wilberforce, of Edmund Burke and Ewart Gladstone, of Henry Fawcett and John Bright, of Bentinck, Canning and Ripon, cannot perpetrate a wrong, and if it ever does, it will that day cease to be the greatest nation that it is on the surface of the earth.

Messrs. Muhammad Ali Choudhuri and Rambhuj Dutt Choudhuri further supported, and the Resolution was passed. The agitation, carried on from 1905 to 1911 has taught two great lessons: first, that where India demands justice insistently and refuses to be silenced, she must succeed, however apparently hopeless the task; secondly, that when Britain reverses a policy of wrong and nobly does the right, she strengthens, she does not weaken, the ties between India and herself. India is too mighty to be refused when she speaks out, and when her children, as in Bengal, are ready to suffer ; England is too just to refuse, when she sees earnestness and the will which demands redress. The final outcome is thus a mutual advantage, drawing the two Nations together, not rending them apart.

Resolution III, thanks for the formation of the Province of Behar and the expression of the wish that the Bengali-speaking districts should all be under one administration, was moved very briefly by Dr. Tej Bahadur Sapru, seconded by Mr. Parameshvarlal, supported by Messrs. Ananda Charan Rai, Anath Bandhu Guha, and A. Choudhuri, and carried.

Resolution IV asked for the removal from the Statute Book of the Seditious Meetings Act, Press Act, and the deportation without trial Regulations. It was moved by the Hon. Rai Bahadur Baikunthanath Sen in a powerful speech, urging the necessity of getting rid of repressive measures. Mr. Daji Abaji Khare seconded, and put the case in a nutshell :

> Now let us consider what was the effect of these Acts. That effect was very well portrayed in one of the speeches delivered in the Supreme Legislative Council. These Acts, it must be conceded, practically killed political life in India. There were many meetings held, but for what ? They gave instructions for collecting subscriptions, for memorials, for congratulations and for similar things, but there were no meetings to protest against wrongful or illegal acts, there was no agitation against measures which were not liked by the people. There were no speeches against any of these things either delivered from the platforms or any letters published in the public print, because almost everyone was afraid that if he came within these laws or transgressed the laws there was a chance of his being held up not under the ordinary law

but under these darkening laws which no doubt were laws but were the most illegal of laws. You may pass anything and call it a law, but all the same they are illegal laws which ought never to have been on the Statute Book. They should not blot the Statute Book which is framed under the ægis of the greatest politicians of England.

I therefore say that these statutes were not required, they are not certainly required now and the sooner they are abolished the better for everyone concerned. Of course we say that you passed them because you thought that the times were such that the Government required such measures, but now with the modification of the Partition these times have gone by, and we say that whatever occasion there was, whatever case there may have been in favour of these Acts, that is all finished and therefore you must take away these statutes.

As regards the deportation regulations, no doubt they are the old standing regulations of 1813, no doubt it has been said that almost every Government has in its armoury of weapons some regulations of this kind for removing dangerous people at a moment's notice. I can quite conceive that in exceptional times when there is danger of a revolution in the country, such regulations may properly be used, but I do not concede that there was such a danger; and although a weapon may be good, I do not concede that the arms which wielded these weapons were arms that ought to have been trusted with these weapons. A knife may be very good, but if you entrust it into improper hands it is bad. It would be better to take away the knife from such hands, or to see that the person who holds it is more reasonable. So far as these regulations are concerned, in every case in which there has been deportation the Government were forced to admit that they took steps and deported these people entirely on no ground whatever. A common policeman makes a report, that report is forwarded by his superior to a superior officer, and it passes from one to the other until ultimately it is sent up to the Government, and it is taken to be gospel by the Government. In this way the liberty of the most respectable man and the most law-abiding citizen will be threatened without his knowledge, and without the man having any notice of what is going on. Regulations like that, which are worked by such machinery, require to be removed forthwith. Therefore we pray that these regulations be abolished and that the future history of India should not be allowed to be darkened with such shameful measures.

Rao Bahadur G. Srinivasa Rao supported, and the Resolution was carried.

Resolution V amended the Congress Constitution; Mr. Bhupendranath Basu brought up the Report of the Sub-Committee appointed by the previous Congress, and the Subjects Committee having approved it, it was submitted to the Congress and passed.

The Hon. Mr. M. S. Das moved Resolution VI, supporting the Swadeshi Movement; it was seconded by Mr. S. K. Nair, supported by Messrs. Sasanka Jihan Rai and Dwarkanath, and carried.

Resolution VII urged the necessity of immediate measures being taken to promote Sanitation; it was moved by Dr. Sarat K. Mullick, seconded by Dr. J. N. Ghose, supported by Kaviraj Jatindranath Sen, and carried.

Resolution VIII, practically identical with Resolution IX of the previous Congress, was moved by Mr. A. P. Patro, seconded by Mr. N. A. Dravid, and carried.

Mr. D. E. Wacha moved Resolution IX, bringing up once more the vital question of the enormous growth in public expenditure, and dealt with it in his own exhaustive fashion. The kernel of his speech was in the pregnant sentence:

> The expenditure has grown during the last 10 years by $1\frac{1}{2}$ per cent more than the revenue. This is a frightful state of things. If you are a business man, and your income is only growing at the rate of one per cent and you are spending three, the inevitable result will be that your house will be in bankruptcy. This is exactly the state of things in which the Government finds itself.

Mr. Pramathanath seconded, and the Resolution was carried.

Resolution X, praying for the abolition of the countervailing excise duties on Indian cotton, handicapping the growth and expansion of the Indian cotton industry, was proposed by Mr. D. A. Khare, seconded by Lala Gobardhan Das, and carried. The sitting closed with the passing of Resolution XI, on the familiar question of Land Settlements, moved by the Hon. Mr. M. S. Das, seconded by Mr. V. Venkateswarlu, and supported by Mr. Pantulu.

The third day opened with sad and startling news —the sudden and unexpected death of the Hon. Mr. V. Krishnaswami Aiyar, which deprived the National party of one of its pillars. A message of condolence was at once wired to his family.

Resolution XII, supporting the Hon. Mr. Gokhale's Elementary Education Bill, then before the Supreme Legislative Council, was appropriately moved by the Hon. Dewan Bahadur L. A. Govindaraghava Aiyar, one of the best friends of education in Madras. He said that the opposition of the Local Government rendered the support of the Congress all the more necessary, and this was the chief reason for putting forward this special resolution, in addition to a more general one. He reviewed the arguments put forward against the Bill, and shattered them one by one. Strangest spectacle of all was the objection that compulsion would bring odium on the Government, the Government which had passed the Seditious Meetings Act and the Press Act! Mr. R. P. Karandikar seconded the Resolution, and pointed out that the boys asked for education; they were helpless and should be helped. The Resolution was supported by Dr. Gour, Dr. Satish Chandra Bannerji—who regarded education as the question of questions, for the National Ideal could not be reached without it—Rao Bahadur V. R. Pandit, Mr. Jitendralal Bannerji—who said that Mr. Gokhale had exhausted the subject, and they could only repeat his arguments and figures—and the discussion was closed by the Hon. Mr. Gokhale, who noted the approval with which the Bill had been met on all sides. Without compulsion universal education was impossible. To be successful it must be introduced gradually in areas where primary education was valued. The Central Government would not introduce it, so they must move the local bodies. If the Bill were defeated, they must agitate with all their might and main, and they would presently win, and lay the foundation of a noble Democracy. The Resolution was carried.

Resolution XIII urged a modification of the Regulations under the Indian Councils Act of 1909.

Mr. A. Choudhuri moved it, giving practical illustrations of the working of the "non-official majority"; Mr. V. Naidu seconded it, Pandit Rambhuj Dutt Choudhuri supported it, and it was carried.

Resolution XIV, against separate electorates for Local Bodies, brought up again the arguments of the previous year. It was moved by Pandit Gokarannath Misra, seconded by Munshi Narayan Prasad, and carried.

Resolution XV, the Separation of Judicial and Executive functions, was put from the Chair and carried.

The Subjects' Committee brought up another Resolution (XVI) on the Congress Constitution, as there existed much difference of opinion as to the amendments thereon, and it was decided that the All-India Congress Committee should consider and report to the next Congress what further modifications should be made in the Constitution and Rules, Article I being kept intact. Carried.

Mr. Hasan Imam invited the next Congress to Bankipur and the invitation was accepted. The proposal (Resolution XXXIII) was interjected at this point, as Mr. Imam was ill and was obliged to leave.

Resolution XVII dealt with the old question of Police Reform: it was no fault of the Congress if Resolutions were instances of perpetual motion, for the Government was an instance of perpetual immobility. The Hon. Mr. Karandikar moved, Mr. Birendranath Sasmal seconded, Messrs. V. N.

Jakatdan, Samasamudran Pillai and Bishnupada Chatterji supported, and it was carried.

The President moved Resolution XVIII on Education and it was carried.

In Resolution XIX the Congress recorded again its "emphatic opinion" in favour of Simultaneous Examinations, and Mr. V. V. Jogiah recalled the Act of 1833, and the enforcement in 1853, and the Queen's Proclamation, *und so weiter*. Mr. Kane seconded, and the Resolution was carried once more.

The Hon. Mr. S. Sinha proposed, Dr. Tej Bahadur Sapru seconded, Resolution XX, asking for an Executive Council and a Governor for the U. P. Carried.

Resolution XXI, Release of Political Prisoners; Resolution XXII, Executive Council for the Panjab; Resolution XXIII, Council and status of British Province for C. P. and Berar, were all put from the Chair.

Messrs. P. C. Bannerji and G. Sarma moved and seconded Resolution XXIV, the hoary request of opening the higher grades of the Army to Indians. Carried. Is it any wonder that we want Home Rule, when India has been vainly asking for thirty years for the removal of preposterous injustices?

Resolution XXV was brand-new, and asked that all Indian High Courts should have direct relations with the Government of India such as had the High Court of Fort William (Calcutta); it was moved by Mr. Pravas Chandra Mitra. Control exercised by

Local Governments over High Courts, he said, was not desirable, and he gave details to show that the prestige and independence of the High Courts would be increased by the proposed change. Mr. Atul Chandra Rai seconded, and the Resolution was carried.

Having thus refreshed itself with novelty, the Congress returned to its old friends, and the President put from the Chair Resolution XXVI, Indians in the Medical Service; Resolution XXVII, Law Membership; and Resolution XXVIII, Reduction of Cable Rates.

Indians in the Colonies made up Resolution XXIX, moved by Mr. J. Choudhuri—great Charter of 1858 again—seconded by Mr. C. Y. Chintamani, supported by Dr. Manilal and Mr. Sorabji Sapurji, one of the passive resisters, who had been to gaol eight times, and was going back immediately in case he were wanted again. Mr. H. S. L. Polak, the gallant Jewish gentleman who, as a member of an oppressed race, felt for the woes of other oppressed races, made a fine speech full of facts. 3,500 sentences of hard labour had been endured by the passive resisters, who were treated so badly, Mr. Gandhi among them, that they were unrecognisable when they came out. Boys and men were deported penniless. Businesses were ordered to be removed and so ruined. Men were forced to re-indenture, because they had not means to pay the tax for excuse. And so on. The Resolution was carried.

Then came three more Resolutions from the Chair: Resolution XXX, re-appointing the General Secretaries; Resolution XXXI, the thanks of Congress to Sir William Wedderburn, Mr. A. O. Hume, Sir Henry Cotton, and the British Committee; Resolution XXXII, appointing the All-India Congress Committee, as elected by the Provincial Congress Committees.

Mr. A. Choudhuri then moved a vote to the President, carried with hearty cheers. He spoke a few grateful words in reply, and the Twenty-sixth National Congress dissolved.

RESOLUTIONS

Welcome to Their Majesties

I. Resolved—That this Congress in humble duty respectfully tenders its most loyal homage to the Throne and Person of their Imperial Majesties, the King-Emperor and the Queen-Empress, and feels confident that their visit to India will be productive of lasting benefit to the people of this country.

Thanks of Congress

The Re-Uniting of Bengal

II. Resolved—That this Congress respectfully begs leave to tender to His Imperial Majesty the King-Emperor a humble expression of its profound gratitude for his gracious announcement modifying the Partition of Bengal. The Congress also places on record its sense of gratitude to the Government of India for recommending the modification and to the Secretary of State for sanctioning it. In the opinion of this Congress, this administrative measure will have a far-reaching effect in helping forward the policy of conciliation with which the honoured names of Lord Hardinge and Lord Crewe will ever be associated in the public mind.

The Creation of the Province of Behar

III. Resolved—That this Congress desires to place on record its sense of profound gratitude to His Majesty the King-Emperor for the creation of a separate Province of Behar and Orissa under a

Lieutenant-Governor in Council, and prays, that in re-adjusting the provincial boundaries, the Government will be pleased to place all the Bengali-speaking districts under one and the same administration.

Sanitation

VII. Resolved—That this Congress, while thanking the Government for having initiated a system of Scientific Enquiry into the circumstances affecting the origin and progress of plague, malaria and other diseases, urges the necessity of immediately taking in hand such practical measures as the opening of congested areas, the reclamation of silted rivers, the clearing of jungles, the draining of water-logged areas, and better provision for the supply of pure drinking water throughout the country.

XXXI. Resolved—That this Congress desires to convey to Sir William Wedderburn, Mr. A. O Hume, Sir Henry Cotton and other members of the British Committee its grateful thanks for their disinterested and strenuous services, and it takes this opportunity to make an earnest appeal to the Indian public to place adequate funds at the disposal of the Committee to enable it to carry on its work with vigour.

[And see VIII and XXVI.]

Coercion

IV. Resolved—That this Congress respectfully repeats its protest against the Seditious Meetings Act and the Press Act, and prays that, in view of the loyal enthusiasm evoked by the Royal visit, and the official pronouncements about an improvement in the general situation, these measures, as well as the Regulations authorising deportations without trial, may now be removed from the Indian Statute Book.

Release of Political Prisoners

XXI. Resolved—That, in view of the gratifying improvement in the general situation of the country, this Congress respectfully submits that the advent to India of Their Imperial Majesties may be signalised by the release of those who are undergoing imprisonment for purely political offences; such an act will be appreciated throughout India, and will deepen the feelings of profound gratitude and loyalty which the Royal visit has evoked.

Congress Constitution

V. Resolved—That the Constitution and Rules of the Indian National Congress as amended by the Sub-Committee appointed at the last Session of the Congress be adopted.

XVI. Resolved—That the All-India Congress Committee be asked to consider and report to the next Congress what further modifications may be made in the Constitution and Rules with a view to promote the objects of the Congress as laid down in Article I of the Constitution, keeping that article intact.

Swadeshi

VI. Resolved—That this Congress accords its most cordial support to the Swadeshi Movement and calls upon the people of India to labour for its success by making earnest and sustained efforts to promote the growth of indigenous industries by giving preference, whenever practicable, to Indian products over imported commodities, even at a sacrifice.

Local Self-Government

VIII. Resolved—That this Congress expresses its satisfaction that the Secretary of State has recognised that the Local Self-Government scheme of Lord Ripon has not had a fair trial, and the Congress expresses the earnest hope that the Government may be pleased to take early steps to extend the application of the principle of election in the constitution of all Local Bodies, and to confer upon them the right of electing non-official chairmen, and further that they may be provided with adequate financial aid by the State.

Finance

IX. Resolved—That having regard to the enormous growth that has taken place in the public expenditure of the country, this Congress urges that early steps be taken towards effective retrenchment in all the spending departments for the Imperial and the Provincial Governments and specially the Military Department.

Excise Duties and Cotton

X. Resolved—That this Congress is of opinion that the countervailing Excise Duties on Indian Cottons are handicapping the growth and expansion of the Indian manufacturing industry, and earnestly prays to the Government of India that they may be abolished at an early date.

Permanent Settlements

XI. Resolved—That a reasonable and definite limitation to the demand of the State on Land and the Introduction of a Permanent Settlement directly between the Government and holders of land in ryotwari areas, or a settlement for a period of not less than 60 years in those Provinces where short periodical settlements or revisions prevail, will, in the opinion of this Congress, substantially help in ameliorating the present unsatisfactory condition of the agricultural population.

Education

Mr. Gokhale's Bill

XII. Resolved—That this Congress accords its whole-hearted support to the principles of the Hon. Mr. Gokhale's Elementary Education Bill and expresses its earnest hope that the Government will be pleased to afford the necessary facilities for the further stages of this Bill in Council.

Higher and Technical Education

XVIII. Resolved—That in the opinion of this Congress the time has arrived for people all over the country to take up earnestly the question of supplementing existing institutions and the efforts of the Government by organising for themselves an independent system of Literary, Scientific, Technical and Industrial Education, suited to the conditions of the different Provinces of India.

This Congress further is of opinion that the Government should take early steps :

(*a*) to assign larger sums of money to Secondary and Higher Education (special encouragement being given where necessary to educate all backward classes) ;

(*b*) to make adequate provisions for imparting Industrial and Technical Education in the different Provinces, having regard to local requirements ; and

(*c*) to give effective voice to the leaders of Indian public opinion in shaping the policy and system of Education in this country.

Representation

XIII. Resolved—While recognising the necessity of providing for a fair and adequate representation in the Legislative Council for the Muhammadan and other communities where they are in a minority, this Congress disapproves of the Regulations promulgated in 1909 to carry out this object by means of separate electorates, and in particular urges upon the Government the justice and expediency of modifying the Regulations framed under the Indian Council's Act of 1909 before another election comes on, so as to remove anomalous distinctions between different sections of His Majesty's subjects in the matter of the franchise, and the qualifications of candidates and the arbitrary disqualifications and restrictions for candidates seeking election to the Councils. This Congress also urges a modification of the Resolutions, where necessary, relating to the composition of non-official majorities in the Provincial Councils so as to render them effective for practical purposes.

Separate Electorates

XIV. Resolved—That this Congress strongly deprecates the extension of the principle of Separate Communal Electorates to Municipalities, District Boards or other Local Bodies.

Council and Governor

XX. Resolved—That this Congress strongly urges upon the Government the justice of creating an Executive Council in the United Provinces at as early a date as may be practicable, and it further expresses an earnest hope that those Provinces will soon be placed under a Governor, as Madras, Bombay and Bengal.

Council for the Panjab

XXII. Resolved—That this Congress expresses its earnest hope that the Government will be pleased to appoint an Executive Council for the Panjab.

Councils for C. P. and Berar

XXIII. Resolved—That this Congress is of opinion that the time has come for the establishment of a Provincial Legislative Council for the Central Provinces and Berar, and for according to Berar, which is now held by the British Government on a permanent tenure, the status and privileges which are accorded to Provinces included in British India.

Legal

Separation of Judicial and Executive Functions

XV. Resolved—(*a*) That this Congress places on record its sense of regret that notwithstanding the hopes held out by the Government some time ago that the Executive and Judicial functions were soon to be separated, no effective steps have yet been taken in that direction, and, concurring with previous Congresses, it urges that any scheme of Separation to be really effective must place all the judiciary completely under the control of the highest civil courts in every Province in respect of pay, promotion and transfer.

(*b*) This Congress, concurring with previous Congresses, urges that the Judicial Service in all parts of the country should be recruited mainly from the legal profession.

High Courts

XXV. Resolved—That this Congress is strongly of opinion that all the High Courts in India should have the same direct relations with the Government of India alone as the High Court of Fort William in Bengal at present time.

Law Membership

XXVII. Resolved—That in view of the fact that Section III of the Indian Councils Act of 1861 is understood in practice to limit appointment to the office of Law member of the Viceroy's Executive Council to members of the English Bar only, thereby greatly restricting the field from which a selection may be made, this Congress urges that the said section be so amended as to allow Advocates, Vakils and Attorneys-at-Law of Indian High Courts being appointed to that office.

Public Service

Police

XVII. Resolved—That this Congress desires to place on record its deliberate opinion that the reforms in the Police system which have been effected under the recommendations of Sir Andrew Fraser's Commission have not produced the results which had been anticipated, as is evident from the judicial findings of the highest courts in some recent cases, and they have not improved the quality or the efficiency of the police force, including the village police. This Congress is of opinion that the pay and prospects of the Indian officers are not sufficient to attract the best men to the Service, and it strongly protests against the practical exclusion of Indians of a better class from the higher offices of trust and responsibility, and records its conviction that no real improvement in the methods of Police investigation can be effected unless confessions are made inadmissible, except when made at trial.

Simultaneous Examinations

XIX. Resolved—That this Congress records its emphatic opinion that the present differentiation of the Civil Service into (1) the Imperial Service recruited in England, mainly from Europeans; and (2) the Provincial Services recruited in India, mainly from Indians, is opposed to the declarations made in the statutes of 1833 and 1870 and the Queen's Proclamation of 1858, and that such differentiation should be abolished as early as possible and that Indians should be afforded equal opportunities with Europeans, for appointment to posts now reserved for the Imperial Service, by the holding of Simultaneous Examinations in England and India under conditions calculated to secure the best men for the posts.

Military

XXIV. Resolved—That this Congress is strongly of opinion that the injustice of keeping the higher ranks of the Army closed against the people of this country should remain no longer unredressed, and this Congress expresses its earnest hope that the general expectation in the country that, before His Imperial Majesty the King-Emperor leaves the shores of India, a more liberal policy under which commissions in the army will be granted to selected Indians will be announced, will not be disappointed.

Medical

XXVI. Resolved—(*a*) That this Congress while thanking the Secretary of State for his despatch regarding the employment of Indians in the superior posts of the Civil Medical Service, regrets that no action has as yet been taken in the matter.

(*b*) In the interests of the public, and the medical service and the profession, as well as for the sake of economy in expenditure, this Congress, concurring with previous Congresses, urges the constitution of a distinct Indian Medical Service wholly independent of the Indian (Military) Medical Service.

Reduction of Cable Rates

XXVIII. Resolved—That in the opinion of this Congress, and in the interests of the newspaper press and of trade and commerce, it is extremely desirable that the rate of Cable Messages between England and India should be further reduced, so as to bring it into line with the rate which, under recent arrangement, has been announced to come into force between England and Canada and Australia from the ensuing year.

Indians in the Colonies

XXIX. Resolved--(*a*) That this Congress, anticipating the forthcoming legislation of the Provincial Settlement recently arrived at, cordially congratulates Mr. Gandhi and the Transvaal Indian Community upon the repeal of the anti-Asiatic Legislation of the Province regarding registration and immigration, and expresses its high admiration of the intense patriotism, courage and self-sacrifice with which they—Muhammadan and Hindu, Zoroastrian and Christian —have suffered persecution in the interests of their countrymen, during their peaceful and selfless struggle for elementary civil rights against overwhelming odds.

(*b*) Whilst appreciating the endeavours that have been made from time to time to secure the redress of the grievances of the Indians of South Africa and other British Colonies, this Congress urges that, in view of the avowed inability of His Majesty's Government to adopt a firm and decisive attitude in this matter, the Government of India should take such retaliatory measures as may be calculated to protect Indian self-respect and the interests of

Indian residents in those parts of the Empire, and thus remove a great source of discontent among the people of this country.

(*c*) This Congress further protests against the declaration of responsible statesmen in favour of allowing the Self-Governing Colonies in the British Empire to monopolise vast undeveloped territories for exclusive white settlements, and deems it its duty to point out that the policy of shutting the door in these territories against, and denying the rights of full British citizenship to, all Asiatic subjects of the British Crown, while preaching and enforcing the opposite policy of the open door in Asia is fraught with grave mischief to the Empire and is as unwise as it is unrighteous.

(*d*) Whilst thanking the Government of India for the prohibition to the recruitment of indentured Indian labour for South Africa, this Congress is strongly of opinion that in the highest National interests, the system of indentured labour is undesirable and should be abolished, and respectfully urges the Government to prohibit the further recruitment of Indian labour under contract of indenture, whether for service at home or abroad.

Formal

XXX. Resolved—That Messrs. D. E. Wacha and D. A. Khare be appointed General Secretaries for the ensuing year.

XXXII. Resolved—That the following gentlemen do form the ALL-INDIA CONGRESS COMMITTEE for the next year (list omitted).

XXXIII. Resolved—That the next Congress be held at Bankipur.

CHAPTER XXVII

Most unfortunately, something went wrong with the reporters at this meeting and there is no Official Record of the Twenty-seventh Congress at Bankipur, in December, 1912. The President was Mr. R. N. Mudholkar, and the Constitution and Rules of the National Congress were there again passed as amended. It would be well, if possible, to make even a skeleton Report, with the Resolutions at least. Some papers, making this possible, must be in the hands of Messrs. D. E. Wacha and D. A. Khare.

CHAPTER XXVIII

THE Twenty-eighth National Congress met in Karachi, Sindh, on the 26th, 27th and 28th December, 1913. The Pavilion was dignified and well decorated, and each of the sixteen gates was ornamented with a motto descriptive of the objects of the Congress—an original idea. The delegates were 550 in number, distributed as follows:

Bombay and Sindh	264
U. P.	13
Panjab	10
Behar	4
Madras	33
Bengal	22
Canada	3
Sindh (Reception Committee)	201
	550

Some notable figures were absent from the Congress. The heart-affection which killed him in 1915 kept Mr. Gokhale away, and Sir Pherozeshah Mehta, Mr. Surendranath Bannerji and Pandit Madan Mohan Malaviya were all absent.

The Hon. Mr. Harchandrai Vishindas, the Chairman of the Reception Committee, welcomed the

President-elect and the delegates, and gave a short sketch of Sindh and its special difficulties, such as its decennial revision Settlements and its irrigation problem. He then turned to the various questions which lay before the Congress for discussion, and finally called on the delegates formally to elect the Hon. Nawab Syed Muhammad Bahadur as President. The proposal was moved by Rao Bahadur R. N. Mudholkar, seconded by Rai Baikunthanath Sen, supported by Mr. Gopaldas Jhamatmal and Pandit Rambhuj Dutt Choudhuri, and carried with acclamation.

After speaking of the necessity of the continued work of the Congress, he alluded to the King-Emperor's message on leaving India, and urged that the unity hoped for by His Majesty should be sought, and that Muhammadans, Christians, Parsis and Hindus, should advance together, rather than in separate groups. He noted the *rapprochement* of Hindus and Musalmans, as shown by the hope expressed by the All-India Muslim League that the leaders on both sides should meet periodically "to find a *modus operandi* for joint and concerted action in questions of public good". He next spoke of the troubles of the Indians in South Africa, then reaching their climax, and he advised retaliatory measures against South African whites, such as shutting out Natal coal, and closing the door of the Civil Service against them. He then turned to the India Council and the need for its radical reform; it must be only an advisory, not an administrative body. He repeated the condemnation of the

Regulations which had spoiled the reforms, showed how dilatory was the action of Government with regard to Local Self-Government, emphasised the enormous importance of Primary and Technical Education, and the need of Permanent Settlement to relieve the grave economic situation. The President alluded also to the Public Service Commission then in India, and urged the granting to Indians of Commissions in the Army, quoting some recent remarks on the subject by Lord Minto in London, the previous year, relating his efforts to bring it about. He then said a few words, fraught with deep emotion, on "the subversion of the Ottoman power in Europe and the strangling of Persia," and expressed the grief with which all the Muslims had felt the blow to their Turkish brethren. He concluded with an earnest plea that Hindus and Musalmans should clasp hands, and work for the Motherland. "The tide of National Unity .... by God's grace, will surely sweep away in its majestic onward course the unnatural and artificial barriers of race, colour and religion."

The President resumed his seat amid loud applause.

The second day's work began with the moving from the Chair of Resolution I, regretting the deaths of Mr. J. Ghosal and Mr. Justice P. R. Sundara Aiyar. It was passed standing.

Resolution II, dealing with the Indians in South Africa, was moved by Dewan Bahadur L. A. Govindaraghava Aiyar, and seconded by Lala Lajpat Rai in Hindustani. It was supported by six more speakers, who urged the arguments so familiar to us all, and was carried.

The second day began with the moving of Resolution III, the Separation of Judicial and Executive Functions, by Mr. C. P. Ramaswami Aiyar, who quoted Sir Harvey Adamson's condemnation of a judge having the police organisation at his back; Mr. R. C. Dutt and Sir Pherozeshah Mehta had showed that the reform would not entail extra expenditure. A re-distribution of functions among munsiffs, magistrates and judges could be made without greater cost. Mr. K. C. Ganguli seconded, complaining that the Congress had passed an annual resolution since 1886, but the bureaucracy opposed it. Messrs. Lalchand Navalrai and Abdul Rahman supported, and the Resolution was carried.

Resolution IV welcomed the adoption by the Muslim League of the ideal of Self-Government for India, and the declaration of the necessity of harmonious co-operation, to be found by the leaders deciding on joint concerted action. It was proposed by Mr. Bhupendranath Basu, saying that Hindus and Muhammadans must concentrate their attention on the one united ideal, for the India of to-day was not the India of the Hindu or the Muslim, nor of the Anglo-Indian, much less of the European, but the India in which all had a share. "If there have been misunderstandings in the past, let us forget them." If they were united, "the India of the future will be a stronger, nobler, greater, higher, aye, and a brighter India than was realised by Ashoka in the plenitude of his power, a better India than was revealed to Akbar in the wildest of his visions".

Rao Bahadur R. N. Mudholkar seconded, and said that the Congress and the League now stood on a common platform, and could work together. Mr. Jehangir B. Petit said that many had thought that Hindus and Muslims would never unite, but that if they did they would be a powerful instrument for good and a force to be reckoned with. Mr. D. A. Khare said that Self-Government would be won by the brotherhood of Hindu and Muslim. Mr. Mathradas Ramchand further supported, and Mr. C. Gopala Menon welcomed the pronouncement of the Muslim League as marking an important epoch in the history of the Congress. Mr. D. E. Wacha said that the Congress had entered on a new Nativity and with the new Star they would achieve new success. The Resolution was carried with great applause.

Resolution V was on the Reform of the India Council. It was moved by Mr. M. A. Jinnah, who pointed out that the Council was composed of old officials who had served in India, and non-official India had no voice. The Secretary of State was responsible to nobody, and was a greater Mughal than any Mughal who had ever ruled in India. Mr. N. M. Samarth seconded, and said that the Secretary of State for India should be accountable to Parliament as was the Secretary for the Colonies, and one-third of the Council should be elected by Indians. The Hon. Mr. Krishna Rao supported, and gave a short review of the changes that had taken place in the constitution of the Council. The Resolution was further supported by Messrs. Gopaldas Jhamatmal and Surendranath Mallik, and carried.

The Congress then adjourned.

On meeting for the third session, the Congress took up a new question, the "continuous journey clause" of the Canadian Privy Council Order, No. 920. The ingenuity of this clause was that it forbade Indians to enter Canada unless they had made a continuous journey from India, and they could not make a continuous journey because there was no direct boat-service and the Steamship Companies refused through booking. Hence it forbade the entry of any Indian into Canada, and prevented any Indian already there from bringing over his wife and family. [It was this Order which caused the chartering of the *Komagatu* and the subsequent troubles.] The Resolution (VI) was moved by Sardar Nand Singh Sikra, who, himself a Sikh, spoke for his brethren in Canada, but pointed out that all India suffered in the suffering of Sikhs in Canada and Indians in South Africa, and "we join hands as one United Nation, and with one heart and one voice we condemn the Colonial atrocities". The Chief Justice of British Columbia had condemned as illegal the Federal Orders in Council, but that did not seem to help them much. General Swayne had explained the real reason of the exclusion. He said:

One of those things that make the presence of East Indians here, or in any other white Colony, politically inexpedient, is the familiarity they acquire with the whites, the instance of which is given by the speedy elimination of caste in this Province, as shown by the way all castes help each other. These men go back to India, and preach ideas of emancipation, which, if brought about, would upset the machinery of law and order. While this emancipation may be a good thing at some future date, the present time is premature for the emancipation of caste.

Is then the whole Empire in a conspiracy against Indian freedom, and is caste to be a weapon in the hands of the bureaucracy to prevent her emancipation?

The Sardar Sahab was one of the three delegates elected by the Canadian Sikhs on February 22nd, 1913, to go to the Congress and represent their grievances.

Mr. Krishna Kumar Mitra seconded, remarking that it would be better for Canadians to say openly that they would not admit Indians rather than pass so cowardly a law. Mr. Ayub Khan and Pandit Rambhuj Dutt Choudhuri supported, and the Resolution was carried.

Resolution VII was on the Public Service Commission, and was very full, laying down the grievances under which Indians suffered and suggesting changes. It was moved by Rai Baikunthanath Sen Bahadur, who remarked on the charges levelled by witnesses before the Royal Commission against Indians; it was said they had defects in moral character, and were lacking in physical endurance, administrative efficiency and power of initiative. He brought in rebuttal the districts in East Bengal where there were anarchical disturbances, and while those managed by British Civilians were much disturbed, those in charge of Bengali Civilians were kept quiet. He asked for the cases where Indians had failed. Witnesses from English commercial houses naturally preferred their own kith and kin and depreciated Indians.

The Hon. Dr. Nilratan Sarkar seconded, and took the sound ground that Indians had a birthright to serve their own country, and that non-Indians should be admitted only when necessary and for a short time. But in the Public Services, "the upper branch is synonymous with European, and the lower with Indian. This is as indefensible in principle as it is mischievous in practice." "We are to remain content as a Nation of assistants." He illustrated Indian efficiency with various examples, and remarked that Dr. Pal Roy had no equal in India, "but he is to remain all his life in the Provincial inferior Service". Messrs. V. V. Jogiah Pantulu and Mathradas Ramchand supported the Resolution and it was carried.

Mr. Bhupendranath Basu moved Resolution VIII, asking for the repeal of the Press Act. He pointed out that in 1837, Sir Charles Metcalfe had liberated the Indian Press; Lord Lytton replaced fetters in 1878 with his Vernacular Press Act, but Mr. Gladstone repealed it. When Sir Herbert Risley spoke in 1910 in favour of introducing the present Press Act, he had destroyed several papers, such as the *Gugantar*, and had said that in the 47 cases instituted by Government under the old law of sedition, a conviction had been secured in every one. What more did they want? The Law Member, who certainly believed what he said, had laid stress on the right of appeal to the High Court, but in a late case the High Court had said that a forfeiture was invalid and illegal, but the High Court had no power to interfere. So there was "a special law of a very drastic nature without any safeguards," and it was "a wet cloth on all expressions of public opinion". "Situated as the Government of India is, foreign in its composition and aloof in its character, that law is a source of great peril." Mr. Dalvi, seconding, quoted Sir L. Jenkins, the Chief Justice, in the *Comrade* case, who said that it is difficult to see to what lengths the operation of these sections may not be plausibly extended by an ingenious mind.

Mr. J. Choudhuri, supporting, gave his own case as editor of a legal journal, the *Calcutta Weekly Notes*. His printer and publisher died, and he had to find a new one, and was running backwards and forwards between his office and the Presidency Magistrate's Court before his declaration was accepted. The C.I.D. could find nothing against the printer, except that his knowledge of English was not as perfect as it might be! Sir Herbert Risley had said that the Press Act would not affect existing papers, and that the administration of the law would not be in the hands of the Police. Both assurances were false. When a declaration is made the magistrate hands over the papers to the C.I.D., and the *Habul Matin*, an existing paper, was called on to furnish security.

Mr. Kishindas Jhamrai supported the Resolution, and it was carried.

Resolution IX, on Permanent Settlement, was moved by the Hon. Mr. A. S. Krishna Rao, seconded by Rao Bahadur Hiranand Khemsing, supported by Mr. Mathradas Ramchand, and carried.

Then followed a series of Resolutions, put from the Chair: X, Army Commission; XI, Education (including a protest against the veto by the Government of India of three lecturers, Messrs. Rasul, Subravardi and Jayaswal, on the ground of their connection with politics); XII, High Courts; XIII, Swadeshi; XIV, Indentured Labour; XV, Local Self-Government; XVI, Council Regulation; XVII, Executive Councils for U. P. and Panjab; XVIII, authorising the All-India Congress Committee to arrange a deputation to England, to represent Indian views on: (1) Indians in S. Africa and the Colonies; (2) Press Act; (3) Reform of the India Council; (4) Separation of Judicial and Executive Functions; (5) Important Questions on which Congress has expressed opinion; XIX, Thanks to Sir William Wedderburn and members of the British Committee. These Resolutions, put *seriatim*, were really our old friend the Omnibus.

Resolution XX, was an expression of deep regret at the retirement of Messrs. Wacha and Khare, from the office of Secretaries, and thanks for their work. Rai Baikunthanath Sen Bahadur voiced the gratitude of the Congress to the eminent veteran, who had acted for 18 years, with great self-denial and ability.

Mr. Khare had worked well for 6 years. Mr. C. P. Ramaswami Aiyar seconded, saying that the greatness of the Congress was largely due to its Secretaries. The Resolution was carried with cheers, and then the Hon. Mr. Harchandrai Vishindas proposed and Mr. D. G. Dalvi seconded the election of the Hon. Nawab Syed Muhammad Bahadur and Mr. N. Subba Rao Pantulu as General Secretaries for the ensuing year. Carried.

Mr. N. Subba Rao invited the Congress to Madras, and Resolution XXII decided the acceptance.

The vote of thanks to the Chair was moved by Mr. Ghulamali G. Chayla, seconded by Mr. Bhupendranath Basu, supported by Mr. Lakamal Chellaram and Mir Ayab Khan, and carried by acclamation. The President's brief reply closed the proceedings, and the Twenty-eighth National Congress dissolved.

RESOLUTIONS

Grief of Congress

I. Resolved—That this Congress desires to place on record its sense of the great loss sustained by the country by the death of Mr. J. Ghosal, who was a staunch worker in the Congress cause, and Mr. Justice P. R. Sundara Aiyer.

Indians in South Africa and Canada

South Africa

II. Resolved—(*a*) That this Congress enters its emphatic protest against the provisions of the Immigration Act in that they violate the promises made by the Ministers of the South African Union, and respectfully urges the Crown to veto the Act and requests the Imperial and Indian Governments to adopt such measures as would ensure to the Indians in South Africa just and honourable treatment.

(*b*) That this Congress expresses its abhorrence of the cruel treatment to which Indians were subjected in Natal in the recent strikes, and entirely disapproves of the personnel of the Committee appointed by the South African Union to enquire into the matter, as two of its members are already known to be biassed against Indians and as it does not include persons who command the confidence of Indians in South Africa and here.

(*c*) That this Congress tenders its most respectful thanks to His Excellency the Viceroy for his statesmanlike pronouncement of the policy of the Government of India on the South African question.

(*d*) That this Congress requests the Imperial and Indian Governments to take the steps needed to redress the grievances relating to the questions of the £3 tax, indentured labour, domicile, the Educational test, validity of Indian Marriages and other questions bearing on the status of Indians in South Africa.

(*e*) That this Congress expresses its warm and grateful appreciation of the heroic struggle carried on by Mr. Gandhi and his co-workers, and calls upon the people of this country of all classes and creeds to continue to supply them with funds.

Canada

VI. Resolved—That this Congress strongly protests against prohibition of immigration, resulting from the operation of the Canadian Privy Council Order No. 920, generally known as the "Continuous Journey Clause," as the order in question has practically the effect of preventing any Indian, not already settled there, from going to Canada, inasmuch as there is no direct steamship service between the two Countries, and the Steamship Companies refuse through booking, and further subjects the present Indian Settlers in Canada to great hardship by precluding them from bringing over their wives and children. This Congress, therefore, urges upon the Imperial Government the necessity of securing the repeal of the said Continuous Journey Regulation.

Legal

Separation of Judicial and Executive Functions

III. Resolved—That this Congress, concurring with previous Congresses, urges the early Separation of Judicial from Executive Functions in the best interests of the Empire and prays that any scheme of Separation that may be undertaken to be really effective must place all judiciary solely under the control of the highest Court in every Province.

High Courts

XII. Resolved—That this Congress is strongly of opinion that all the High Courts of India, inclusive of non-chartered High Courts, should have the same direct relation with the Government of India alone, as the High Court of Fort William in Bengal has at the present time. The Congress is, further, of opinion that the Chief Judge of unchartered High Courts should be appointed from the members of the bar.

[See VII *c*, 3.]

Union for Self-Government of Congress and Muslim League

IV. Resolved—That this Congress places on record its warm appreciation of the adoption by the All-India Muslim League of the ideal of Self-Government for India within the British Empire, and expresses its complete accord with the belief that the League has so emphatically declared at its last sessions that the political future of the country depends on the harmonious working and co-operation of the various Communities in the country which has been the cherished ideal of the Congress. This Congress most heartily welcomes the hope expressed by the League that the leaders of the different communities will make every endeavour to find a *modus operandi* for joint and concerted action on all questions of national good and earnestly appeals to all the sections of the people to help the object we all have at heart.

India Council Reform

V. Resolved—That this Congress is of opinion that the Council of the Secretary of State for India, as at present constituted, should be abolished, and makes the following suggestions for its reconstruction:

(*a*) That the salary of the Secretary of State for India should be placed on the English Estimates.

(*b*) That, with a view to the efficiency and independence of the Council, it is expedient that it should be partly nominated and partly elected.

(*c*) That the total number of members of the Council should not be less than nine.

(*d*) That the elected portion of the Council should consist of not less than one-third of the total number of members, who should be non-official Indians chosen by a constituency consisting of the elected members of the Imperial and Provincial Legislative Councils.

(*e*) That not less than one-half of the nominated portion of the Council should consist of public men of merit and ability unconnected with the Indian administration.

(*f*) That the remaining portion of the nominated Council should consist of officials who have served in India for not less than

10 years and have not been away from India for more than two years.

(*g*) That the character of the Council should be advisory and not administrative.

(*h*) That the term of office of each member should be five years.

Public Service

VII. Resolved—(*a*) That this Congress places on record its indignant protest against, and emphatically repudiates, as utterly unfounded, the charges of general incompetence, lack of initiative, lack of character, etc., which some of the witnesses, among whom this Congress notices with regret some of the highest administrative officers, have freely levelled at Indians as a people.

(*b*) That this Congress begs to express its earnest hope that the Royal Commissioners will, alike on grounds of justice, national progress, economy, efficiency and even expediency, see fit to make recommendations which will have the certain effect of largely increasing the present very inadequate proportion of Indians in the high appointments in the Public Services of their own country; thus redeeming the solemn pledge contained in the Charter Act of 1833 and the Royal Proclamation of 1858.

(*c*) In particular, this Congress places on record its deep conviction:

(1) that justice can never be done to the claim of the people of this country unless the examinations for the recruitment of the superior offices of the various Services be held in India as well as in England;

(2) that the age limit in the case of candidates for the Indian Civil Service should not be lowered, as such a step will operate to the disadvantage of Indian candidates as well as prove detrimental to efficiency;

(3) that the Judicial and Executive Services and Functions should be completely separated and the Judicial Service recruited from the legal profession and placed in subordination to the High Court instead of to the Executive Government;

(4) that such restrictions as exist at present against the appointment of persons other than members of the Indian Civil Service to certain high offices be removed;

(5) that any rule or order which, in terms or in effect, operates as a bar against the appointment of an Indian as such to any office under the Crown for which he may otherwise be eligible, should be rescinded as opposed to the Act and the Proclamation hereinbefore mentioned;

(6) that the division of Services into Imperial and Provincial be abolished and the conditions of Services be equalised as between Indians and Europeans, and that in case the division be maintained, the recruitment of the Executive branch of the Provincial Civil Service be made by means of an open competitive examination instead of by nomination ;

(7) that in case the said division be maintained, the Indian Educational and other Services be recruited in India as well as England, and Indians of the requisite attainments be appointed thereto both directly and by promotion from the respective Provincial Services ;

(8) that civil medical posts should not be filled by the appointment of members of the Military I.M.S. or I.S.M.D., and a distinct and separate Indian Civil Medical Service should be constituted therefor and recruited by means of a competitive examination held in India as well as England; educational and scientific appointments, however, being filled by advertisement in India and abroad;

(9) that the present scale of salaries is sufficiently high and should not be raised, and further, that exchange compensation allowance should be abolished, as it has been a costly anomaly since exchange was fixed by statute ; and

(10) that the people of those dominions of the Crown, where they are not accorded the rights of British citizens, should be declared ineligible for appointments in India.

Coercion

Press

VIII. Resolved—That this Congress reiterates its protest against the continuation of the Indian Press Act on the Statute Book, and urges that the same be repealed, specially, in view of the recent decision of the High Court of Calcutta, which declares that the safeguards provided by the Act are illusory and incapable of being enforced.

Permanent Settlement

IX. Resolved—That this Congress is strongly of opinion that a reasonable and definite limitation to the demand of the State on land and the introduction of a Permanent Settlement directly between Government and land-holders in ryotwari-areas, or a settlement for a period of not less than 60 years in those Provinces where shorter periodical settlements on revision prevail will substantially help in ameliorating the present unsatisfactory condition of the Agricultural population.

Military

X. Resolved—That this Congress again respectfully points out to the Government of India the injustice of keeping the higher ranks in the Army closed against the people of this country, and urges that the same should remain no longer unredressed.

[And see VII *c*, 8.]

Education

XI. Resolved—(*a*) That this Congress, while thanking the Government of India for its donation of larger grants towards the extention of Primary Education in India, is strongly of opinion that a beginning should now be made for introducing Free and Compulsory Education in some selected areas.

(*b*) That the Congress, while approving of the proposals by Government for introducing teaching and residential Universities, is strongly of opinion that that system should supplement, and not replace, the existing system of University Education, as otherwise the progress of Higher Education among the poorer classes will be seriously retarded.

(*c*) That this Congress reiterates its prayer to Government to make adequate provision for imparting Industrial and Technical Education in the different Provinces, having regard to local requirements.

(*d*) That this Congress records its strong protest against the action of the Government of India vetoing the selection by the Calcutta University of Messrs. Rasul, Suhravardi and Jayaswal, as lecturers, on the ground of their connection with politics; as the bar of politics is so general as to lend itself to arbitrary exclusion of the best scholarship from the lecturer's chair, so detrimental to the interests of Education in the country.

Swadeshi

XIII. Resolved—That this Congress accords its most cordial support to the Swadeshi Movement, and calls upon the people of India to labour for its success, by making earnest and sustained efforts to promote the growth of indigenous industries, by giving preference, wherever practicable, to Indian products over imported commodities, even at a sacrifice.

Indentured Labour

XIV. Resolved—That owing to the scarcity of labour in India, and the grave results from the system of Indentured Labour, which reduces the labourers, during the period of their indenture, practically to the position of slaves, this Congress strongly urges the total prohibition of recruitment of labour under indenture, either for work in India or elsewhere.

Representation

XV. Resolved—That this Congress expresses its regret that the recommendations of the Decentralisation Commission, with regard to the further development of Local Self-Government, have not yet been given effect to, and urges that the Government of India may be pleased to take steps, without delay, to increase the powers and resources of Local Bodies.

XVI. Resolved—That this Congress records its sense of keen disappointment that at the last revision of the Legislative Council Regulations, the anomalies and inequalities, rectification of which the four previous Congresses strongly urged upon the Government, were not removed. And in order to allay the widespread dissatisfaction caused by the defects complained of, and in view of the experience of the last four years, this Congress earnestly prays that—(1) there should be a non-official majority in the Imperial Legislative Council; (2) there should be a majority of elected members in all Provincial Councils; (3) the system of voting by delegates be done away with, where it still exists; (4) the franchise be broadened by simplifying the qualifications of electors, basing it on education, property or income; (5) the Government should not have the power arbitrarily to declare any person ineligible for election on the ground of his antecedents or reputation; (6) no person should be held ineligible for election on the ground of dismissal from Government Service, or of conviction in a criminal court, or from whom security for keeping the peace has been taken, unless his conduct has involved moral turpitude; (7) no property or residential qualification should be required of a candidate, nor service as member of a Local Body; (8) a person ignorant of English should be held ineligible for membership; (9) it should be expressly laid down that officials should not be allowed to influence elections in any way; (10) Finance Committees of Provincial Councils should be more closely associated with Government in the preparation of the Annual Financial Statements; (11) there should be a Finance Committee of the Imperial Legislative Council as in the case of Provincial Legislative Councils; (12) the right of putting supplementary questions should be extended to all members and not be restricted to the member putting the original question; (13) the strength of the Panjab Council be raised from 26 to 50, and more adequate representation be allowed to the Panjab in the Imperial Council.

And further, this Congress, while recognising the necessity of providing for a fair and adequate representation in the Legislative Councils for the Muhammadans or the other communities where they are in a minority, disapproves of the present regulations to carry out this object by means of separate electorates.

XVII. Resolved—That the Congress again urges that an Executive Council, with an Indian member, be established in the United Provinces at an early date, and is of opinion, that a similar Council should be established in the Panjab too.

Deputation to England

XVIII. Resolved—That the All-India Congress Committee be authorised to arrange for a Deputation consisting, as far as possible, of representatives from different Provinces, to England, to represent Indian views on the following subjects:

(1) Indians in South Africa and other Colonies;
(2) Press Act;
(3) Reform of the India Council;
(4) Separation of Judicial and Executive Functions;
(5) And important questions on which Congress has expressed opinion.

Thanks of Congress

XIX. Resolved—That this Congress records its sense of high appreciation of the services of Sir William Wedderburn and other members of the British Committee, and resolves that the organisation of the British Committee and *India* should be maintained.

[See II *c*, XI *a*, XX.]

Retirement of General Secretaries

XX. Resolved—That this Congress expresses its sense of deep regret at the retirement of Mr. D. E. Wacha and Mr. D. A. Khare, from the office of its General Secretaries, and begs to place on record its sense of warm appreciation of the very signal and distinguished Services rendered by the former for 18 years, and the latter for 6 years, to the cause of the Congress.

Formal

XXI. Resolved—That the Hon. Nawab Syed Muhammad Bahadur and Mr. N. Subba Rao Pantulu be appointed General Secretaries for the next year.

XXII. Resolved—That the Congress of the year 1914 be held in the Province of Madras.

CHAPTER XXIX

The Twenty-ninth National Congress met in Madras on the 28th, 29th, and 30th December, 1914. The Pavilion was erected in the grounds of Doveton House, Nungambaukam, and, draped in white, with flower-wreathed pillars and decorated with many flags, the portraits of their Imperial Majesties and the Royal Arms, the whole appearance was light and graceful. The delegates rose to the number of 866, the largest number that had assembled since 1907. They were grouped as follows :

Madras	748
Bombay and Sindh	54
Bengal	38
U. P.	12
Berar	5
C. P.	2
Behar	5
Panjab	0
Burma	2
	866

The Reception Committee was a very large one, 355 in number, and the arrangements made by them were very satisfactory.

The platform was very crowded with all the notabilities of Madras when the President-elect came in, in procession, escorted to the Pavilion door by a guard of Congress Volunteers on cycles. He was accompanied by many of the Congress leaders and the six Secretaries of the Reception Committee, and was received by Sir S. Subramania Iyer, the Chairman of the Reception Committee. He said a few words of welcome, and then gave his speech to be read by Mr. K. N. Iyah Iyer. Instead of reviewing the questions which the Congress was to discuss, the Chairman took up certain points of wide importance. He urged the desirability of winning the co-operation of the landed aristocracy, who ought not to hold themselves aloof from the National work, sharing as they did the advantages resulting from it. Next, attention should be given to the improvement of the village life, the organic unit of administration; there should be a network of village Panchayats, as under the Chola dynasty, yet nothing had been done in this Presidency, despite the report of the Decentralisation Committee, now five years old. Loan Societies must also be started, to relieve the ryot from his indebtedness, while there should be storage facilities for grain, and sufficient fixity of tenure. Turning to the Congress the Chairman protested against the idea that it should come to an end, for it was the centre of Indian Nationality, but its work should continue during the year, and funds should be raised for the purpose. Finally, he urged that India should rise to the full height of her spiritual stature, should abstain from the greed of exploiting the best spots of earth for herself, and conquer by love, not hate. They must unite and unify, despite the prejudice so widely shown against the coloured race. The Sovereign had shown deep sympathy with India, and an abiding care for her welfare, and India must prove worthy of his love, sympathy and care.

The formal election of Mr. Bhupendranath Basu as President was moved by Mr. Surendranath Bannerji, who described him and himself as lifelong friends, comrades, co-workers, and companions in arms. He told of the services rendered by the President-elect in the troublous times of the Partition, and warmly welcomed him to the Chair. The Hon. Nawab Syed Muhammad seconded, speaking of the useful work Mr. Basu had done in England. The motion was supported by Rao Bahadur R. N. Mudholkar and Mr. Samarth, and carried by acclamation.

The President spoke of the difficulties under which the Congress met, a devastating War, in which Britain and India were fighting side by side in the cause of honour, liberty and justice. One of the chief functions of the Congress was to act as His Majesty's Opposition, and that could not be effectively discharged at the moment. Britain did not come as an invader to India, but gained power by treaties with Princes and People, the Princes becoming Allies, and the People equal subjects, of the Crown, under solemn Charters and Statutes. This was apt to be forgotten. He then alluded to the Deputation to England and the India Council Bill, rejected by the House of Lords, though it fell short of Indian expectations. India wants to abolish the Council, but it would be wise to press for the Reforms advocated in the Congress. Also he desired to see constituted a Parliamentary Committee, which might be kept furnished with information on Indian affairs.

The Government of the country was still vested in a foreign Civil Service, there being only 70 Indians out of a cadre of 1,400 men. This Service remained while all the higher officers came and went, and it was responsible to no one. They form the Executive Council of the Viceroy, save for one Indian member; the India Council, save for two. They are thus their own Court of Appeal. Six Governments out of nine are furnished by them with rulers. All the great Departments of State are under their control. They would be more than human if they did not desire to remain as they are:

> Against this state of things we have a people rapidly awakening to self-consciousness; thousands of our boys are receiving education on western lines in Indian Universities based on western models; hundreds of them are daily flocking to the Universities of Europe, America and Japan, and on their return home spreading the knowledge that they have acquired. You may chain Prometheus, but the fire is lighted and cannot be extinguished. India wants a higher life, a wider sphere of activity and usefulness. India wants that her Government should be consistent with her growing self-respect and intellectuality. India wants that the presumption which has all along existed, and which the Board of Directors in 1833 made a vain attempt to dispel, namely, that the Indians can only rise to a certain limit, should be removed from the precincts of her Court, as it has been from the Statute Book, and

the door to her Services should not be closed by artificial barriers against her own sons. India wants that her children should have the same rights of equal citizenship as other members of the Empire. India wants the removal of vexatious hindrances on the liberty of speech and freedom of the Press, fruitless and dangerous alike to the Government and the people. And, above all, India wants that her Government should be an autonomous Government under the British Empire. Then only the great benefits, which have emanated from British rule and which carry with them the memory of doles, will be sweetened with the sweat of her brow.

The President declared :

The Indian bureaucracy do not offer us any constructive programme for the future of India, no land of promise to her children. They are content to work for the day and take no thought for the morrow. An autocratic Viceroy or Secretary of State may put extra steam into the machinery of the Indian Government, or try to shut the safety-valve, but the great fly-wheel is not easily disturbed. And the bureaucracy have given us honest and conscientious workmen, not troubled, it may be, with the visions of the future, but they have reason to be well pleased with their work: they have given us internal peace and guarded us from external aggression; the blessings of an ordered administration are apparent on every side. Why should India resent? Her Government has always been that of one man's sway whether she was an Empire or broken into small States of varying dimensions. Why should she object to the Government of an outside bureaucracy? My answer is: the days of the lotus-eater are gone, the world is swinging onward on the uplifting ropes of time, and in Europe, the war of nations, now in progress, will knock off the last weights of mediæval domination of one man over many, of one race over another; it is not possible to roll back the tide of wider life which is flowing like the warm Gulf Stream through the gateways of the West into the still waters of the East. You may abolish the study of English history and draw a sponge over all its enthralling story of freedom; you may bar Milton and Burke, Mill and Spenser; you may bend the Indian Universities to your will if you like, fetter their feet with obstructive statutes, but you cannot bar the imponderable influences of an expanding world. If English rule in India meant the canonisation of a bureaucracy, if it meant perpetual domination and perpetual tutelage, an increasing dead-weight on the soul of India, it would be a curse to civilisation and a blot on humanity. But I am doing injustice to a large body of Civil Servants who have loyally accepted the recent reforms and who seek to remain true to the traditions of Munro and Elphinstone.

Separation from England was not desirable, and none save a few youths desired it. Neither subordination nor separation was wanted, but "a joint partnership on equal terms". The Constitution for India should be modelled on that of the United States of America or the Commonwealth of Australia, modified to suit India, and with a representative of the Crown at its head. Some special changes were needed:

The right to carry arms, the right to bear commissions in the Army, and lead our men in the cause of the Empire, the right to form volunteer corps in the defence of hearth and home, how long will these be denied to the Indian people? How long will India toddle on her feet, tied to the apron strings of England? Time it is that she stood on her legs for herself as well as for England. What could be more humiliating to India and to England alike, if England were obliged in the hour of some great danger, as Imperial Rome was in her day, to leave India unarmed and untrained to the use of arms, and, as her civil population is, a prey to internal anarchy and external aggression? What commentary would it be on 150 years of British rule in India, that England found the people strong though disunited and left them helpless and emasculated? And, on the other hand, what could be more glorious both for India and England than that India, strong in her men, strong in her faith, should stand side by side with England, share her troubles and her dangers and be joint defenders of their common heritage.

How different would England's position have been to-day, had she trusted India. She would have had a wall of men against which Germany would have hurled itself in vain. England is now pouring out wealth and men in defence of her plighted word to Belgium. And what of India? India's claim "is not a prayer, but a call in the name of the people of India, enforced by the moral sense of mankind, which, if religions are not mere myths and their teachings empty shibboleths, will survive the clash of arms and the fate of Nations". The President concluded:

Brother delegates, it is no use looking backward; no use in vain regrets. Let us be ready for the future, and I visualise it. I see my country occupying an honoured and proud place in the comity of nations. I see her sons sitting in the Councils of our great Empire, conscious of their strength, and bearing its burden on their shoulders as valued and trusted comrades and friends, and I see India rejuvenated and re-incarnate in the glories of the future broadened by the halo of the past. What does it matter if a solitary raven croak from the sand banks of the Jumna and the Ganges? I hear it not, my ears are filled with the music of the mighty rivers, flowing into the sea scattering the message of the future. Brother delegates, let us live as the ancients lived, in the purity of heart, so that the message may be fulfilled; let us forget the narrow barriers of man's creation; let us be humble and forget the pride of self; let us step across the barriers of prejudice; let us always be with our hand on the plough, preparing the soil for the harvest of the future; let our heart-strings be attuned to God and Country and then no power on earth can resist the realisation of that message, the fulfilment of the Destiny that is ours. And assembled in this tabernacle of the people, let us pray to Him, who knoweth all hearts, to grant us grace and strength that we may deserve and bear this future and this destiny.

The Congress then adjourned, after cheering to the echo a speech filled with the new life throbbing through India.

On the second day, the first duty was to move from the Chair three Resolutions of sorrow: I, Condolence with the Viceroy for the terrible bereavements he had suffered; II, the great loss to the country in the death of Gangaprasad Varma, the staunch worker and stainless gentleman; III, the deaths of Mr. Amberal Sakerlal Desai and Mr. Bishnupada Chatterji, both good Congressmen. The Resolutions were passed in silence, the audience standing.

Resolution IV, expressing the loyalty of the Congress to the Throne was arranged to fit in with the visit to the Congress of H. E. the Governor of Madras, who was greeted by the rising of the Congress and hearty applause. It was the first visit ever paid by the Representative of the Crown to the Congress.

The Resolution was moved by Mr. Surendranath Bannerji, who eloquently voiced the loyalty of India, it being a fit time to declare it when the Empire was engaged in War, and the Congress spoke in the name of the Nation. Dewan Bahadur L. A. Govindaraghava Aiyar seconded, and spoke of the ingrained loyalty of the Hindu heart to which loyalty was part

44

of religion. Mr. Mehta, C.I.E., the Hon. Mr. S. B. Upasani, Pandit Gokarannath Misra, Mr. Harikishan Sinha, Mr. N. A. Dravid, Mr. Gopaldas Chamatmal, and Mr. M. D. Devadoss further voiced the same idea, each in his own way; the Resolution was then carried, and H. E. the Governor left, after a few words of thanks from the President, amid the loud cheers of the audience.

Mr. A. P. Patro, who had begun to move Resolution V, on the despatch of the Indian Expeditionary Force, a minute before the arrival of H. E. the Governor, then resumed his speech, expressing the pride felt by Indians in the recognition of their share in the Empire in that they were called to its defence. Mr. Jogendranath Bose seconded, Mr. G. K. Gadgil, Pandit Iqbal Narain Musaldan, and Mr. D. V. Prakasa Rao supported, and the Resolution was carried.

Rao Bahadur R. N. Mudholkar moved Resolution VI, urging the Government to open the higher ranks of the army to Indians, to establish Military Schools and Colleges and to allow Indians to volunteer. This had been urged by the Congress from its beginning; H. R. H. the Duke of Connaught had urged the first two points; Lord Kitchener was said to have been in favour of admitting Indians as far as majors, and it was thought that the King would have announced this in 1911. Now, the pressing need had arisen. For over 80 years the Statute of 1833 had remained unfulfilled, and the pledge of the Proclamation of the Queen in 1858 was still unredeemed. There was no legal bar to Indians volunteering. Some of his friends were Volunteers. But their names were taken off the list in 1898, without reason given.

Mr. J. Choudhuri seconded, and urged that India was surrounded by powerful eastern Nations, and should be organised for self-defence. Messrs. Senathi Raja, K. Venkata Reddi, R. V. Gupta, A. C. Parthasarathi Naidu, all supported, and the Resolution was carried.

Resolution VII, asking for the modification of the Arms Act, was moved by Mr. A. P. Sen, who gave instances of the hardships suffered. In a raid upon a house in Oudh, two members of the household, out of seven, were killed. There were 10 armed robbers, 7 unarmed persons. In another case a "Baron of Oudh" had his licence to bear arms cancelled, because he refused to give evidence in a police prosecution. Mr. C. P. Ramaswami Aiyar seconded, quoting Milton who said that no Nation was a free Nation unless its citizens were trained to the use of arms. Lord Roberts said that a man was not fully a citizen, if he was unable "to defend himself, his home and his liberties". That was the right they asked. The Rules framed under the Act made galling distinctions of race and creed, and they deprecated such distinctions. It was the duty of England to grant their demand. The periodical renewals, "which operate as galling reminders of the servitude of the people, should be removed for ever. In fine, we ask that we should be treated as self-respecting citizens of the Empire, and be given opportunities of developing to the best advantage the manhood in us."

Mr. Krishnadas Rai laid stress on the ravages of wild animals, the destruction of valuable crops, and the consequent running of large tracts of land to waste. Dacoits were becoming numerous because they knew whole villages were unarmed and they could plunder at pleasure. Bomb-throwers and dacoits had their way; the police could not defend the people, and the people were not allowed to defend themselves. While the English papers talked of Indian loyalty, the magistrates here were busy in confiscating, on technical grounds, the few licensed guns possessed. Mr. S. Somasundaram Pillai supported and the Resolution was carried.

Resolution VIII defined what was meant by "Reciprocity" between India and the Colonies, and was moved by Mrs. Annie Besant. She said Confucius advised people to recompense evil with justice, and justice lay behind reciprocity. There had been talk of a reward due to India's loyalty, but "India does not chaffer with the blood of her sons and the proud tears of her daughters in exchange for so much liberty, so much right. India claims the right, as a Nation, to justice among the Peoples of the Empire. India asked for this before the War. India asks for it during the War. India will ask for it after the War, but not as a reward but as a right does she ask for it. On that there must be no mistake." She then asked them not to try to limit the right of the Colonies to be masters in their own houses, for India would have that same right soon. Whatever rule a Colony made as to the entry of Indians, that rule should India make as to the entry into India of people of that Colony. Again, India might exclude imports where her people were excluded. Imports from Australia to Madras were as much in a year as Rs. 13,40,000. After saying that the indenture system must be stopped, she concluded: "India is growing in the sense of her own dignity. She is not content to be any longer a child in the nursery of the Empire. . . . She is showing the responsibility of the man in Europe. Give her the freedom of the man in India." The Hon. Mr. P. Kesava Pillai seconded in a few sentences, pointing out that as long as Indians were treated as inferiors in their own country, the Colonists would not treat them as equals. Mr. Hridayanath Kunzru dealt with the Canadian difficulties. If the Indian Government would notify that aliens in India will be treated as Indians are treated abroad, that would exercise a wholesome influence on them.

The Resolution was put and carried, and the Congress adjourned.

On the third day, Resolution IX, on the Protection of Indian Industries, was moved by the Hon. Mr. K. R. V. Krishna Rao. He urged that the State ought to help Home Industries, but that nothing could be done unless the Governments were allowed to regulate their own tariffs. Prof. V. G. Kale seconded, and urged that poverty could only be removed by industrial advancement, and that needed the direct assistance of the State. Mr. J. C. Chakravarti supported, and said the War had shown our utter helplessness in the industrial world. Mr. G. K. Devadar urged industrial autonomy, so as not to be so dependent on other countries. Mr. S. K. Nair further supported, and the Resolution was carried.

Mr. Surendranath Bannerji moved Resolution X, claiming Self-Government for India, in a long and eloquent speech. India took her stand on the Proclamation of 1858, and called on the Government to give effect to the Despatch of 25th August, 1911, until "India would consist of a number of administrations, autonomous in all provincial affairs, with the Government of India above them, and possessing powers to interfere in case of mis-Government". Mr. Bannerji quoted a letter from the Chairman of an English organisation for the introduction of a federal system of Government, in which he asked "India to organise her strength for this movement, and educate her public both in India, and all parts of the world". The speaker urged his audience to "formulate your scheme, press it upon the attention of the British public, and I am confident that your appeal will not fall upon needless ears".

Mr. Sadhu Ganapathi formally seconded, Mrs. Annie Besant supported, urging the younger, "who will be part of the Self-Governing Nation," to practise the science and art of Government in the Local Bodies, however crippled they might be by officials. The drudgery of learning local administration prepared a man for wider power. Provincial autonomy was a step to complete Self-Government. She then vindicated India's worthiness of freedom, and asked Congress to formulate a definite scheme of Self-Government, to present to England after the War.

Mr. Suweshchandra Bose supported, and urged that India could be a pillar of strength to England, and after the War she should press her claim to Self-Government.

Resolution XI, on India Council Reform, was moved by Mr. A. S. Krishna Rao, seconded by Mr. K. M. Choudhuri, supported by Mr. P. C. Mitra, and carried.

Mr. G. A. Natesan moved Resolution XII rejoicing over the partial settlement of the South African troubles, but he pointed out that the question was not really solved. Mr. S. Prasad Basu seconded, Messrs. Lakshminarasimha and Ramakantam Malaviya supported, and the Resolution was carried.

Resolution XIII, asking for the total Prohibition of Indentured Labour, was moved by Mr. F. G. Natesan, in an impassioned speech, seconded by Mr. Totaram Senadhya from the Fiji Islands and carried.

The President then put from the Chair Resolution XIV, Separation of Judicial and Executive Functions; XV, Swadeshi; XVI, Press Act; XVII, Permanent Settlement; XVIII, Separate Electorates; XIX, sending a message of greeting to Indian troops; XX, asking for an extension of Lord Hardinge's term of Office; XXI, Reference to a Committee of two amendments to Article XX of the Constitution; XXII, Thanks to Sir William Wedderburn and the British Committee; XXIII, re-election of

Nawab Sahab Syed Muhammad and Mr. N. Subba Rao as General Secretaries.

Resolution XXIV thanked the Deputation which went to London for its good work. The Deputation consisted of Messrs. Bhupendranath Basu, M. A. Jinnah, N. M. Samarth, S. Sinha, Mazaral Haq, the Hon. Mr. B. N. Sarma and Lala Lajpat Rai. The Hon. Mr. K. Chidambaranadha Mudaliar seconded the Resolution, and it was carried.

Resolution XXV approved the All-India Committee for the ensuing year. Resolution XXVI accepted the invitation to Bombay for the next Congress, offered by Sir Vitaldas Damodar Thackersay.

Mr. S. Srinivasa Iyengar then moved a vote of thanks to the President, and it was carried with great enthusiasm. The President made an earnest and graceful speech in answer, and the Twenty-ninth National Congress dissolved.

RESOLUTIONS

Grief of the Congress

I. Resolved—This Congress desires to express its heart-felt and respectful sympathy with H. E. Lord Hardinge in the bereavements he has sustained by the death of his wife and of his eldest son. All India mourns with His Excellency in his great sorrow.

II. Resolved—That this Congress desires to place on record its sense of the profound sorrow and irreparable loss the country has sustained by the untimely death of Babu Ganga Prasad Varma who was a devoted worker in the cause of the Congress from its earliest days, and whose memory will be cherished with grateful affection by his friends and colleagues and by his countrymen at large for his many distinguished services.

III. Resolved—That this Congress desires to express its deep sorrow for the death of Mr. Amberal Sakerlal Desai, and of Babu

Bishnu Pada Chatterji of Bengal, who were devoted and distinguished workers in the Congress cause, and who rendered it valuable service.

Loyalty to the Throne

IV. Resolved—(*a*) That this Congress desires to convey to His Majesty the King-Emperor and the people of England its profound devotion to the Throne, its unswerving allegiance to the British connection, and its firm resolve to stand by the Empire, at all hazards and at all costs.

(*b*) That this Congress places on record the deep sense of gratitude and the enthusiasm which the Royal Message, addressed to the Princes and Peoples of India at the beginning of the War, has evoked throughout the length and breadth of the country, and which strikingly illustrates His Majesty's solicitude and sympathy for them, and strengthens the bond which unites the Princes and Peoples of India to His Royal House and the person of His Gracious Majesty.

Military

The Indian Expeditionary Force

V. Resolved—That this Congress notes with gratitude and satisfaction the despatch of the Indian Expeditionary Force to the theatre of war, and begs to offer to H. E. the Viceroy its most heart-felt thanks for affording to the people of India an opportunity of showing that, as equal subjects of His Majesty, they are prepared to fight shoulder to shoulder with the people of other parts of the Empire in defence of right and justice, and the cause of the Empire.

Military Training and Volunteers

VI. Resolved—That this Congress urges on the Government the necessity, wisdom, and justice, of throwing open the higher offices in the Army to Indians, and of establishing in the country Military Schools and Colleges where they may be trained for a military career as officers in the Indian Army. In recognition of the equal rights of citizenship of the people of India with the rest of the Empire, and in view of their proved loyalty so unmistakably and spontaneously manifested, and the strongly expressed desire of all classes and grades, to bear arms in the service of the Crown and of the Empire, this Congress urges upon the Government the necessity of re-organising the present system of volunteering, so as to enable the people of this country, without distinction of race or class, to enlist themselves as citizen-soldiers of the Empire.

Arms Act

VII. Resolved—That in view of the hardship entailed by the Arms Act (XI of 1878) as at present administered, and the unmerited slur which it casts upon the people of this country, this Congress is of opinion that the said Act and the rules made thereunder should be so modified that all restrictions as to the possession and bearing of arms shall apply equally to all persons residing in or visiting India; that all licences issued under the rules shall be granted once for all, shall operate within the provincial jurisdiction within which they are issued, shall be revocable only on proof of misuse, and shall not require yearly or half-yearly renewals.

Indian Troops

XIX. Resolved—That this Congress rejoices to place on record its deep sense of gratification and pride at the heroic conduct of the Indian Troops whose deeds of valour and conspicuous humanity and chivalry in the Great War, are winning the respect of civilised mankind for the mother country and resolves to send a message of hearty and affectionate greetings to them and their comrades in arms, with fervent prayers for their well-being and success.

The President be requested to cable the above Resolution to the Indian Troops, through the proper channels.

Reciprocity

VIII. Resolved—That this Congress begs to convey to H. E. the Viceroy the profound gratitude of the people of India for the sympathetic manner in which he has handled the questions connected with the emigration of Indians abroad, and while welcoming H. E.'s suggestion of Reciprocity as the underlying basis of negotiations with the Colonies, this Congress desires to record its conviction that any policy of Reciprocity to be effective and acceptable to the people of India, must proceed on the basis that the Government of India should possess and exercise the same power of dealing with the Colonies as they possess and exercise with regard to India.

Industries

IX. Resolved—That in view of the present exceptional circumstances and in order to promote the material prosperity of the country, this Congress urges that immediate measures be taken by Government to organise and develop Indian Industries.

Self-Government

X. Resolved—That in view of the profound and avowed loyalty that the people of India have manifested in the present crisis this Congress appeals to the Government to deepen and perpetuate it, and make it an enduring and valuable asset of the Empire, by removing all invidious distinctions here, and abroad, between His Majesty's Indian, and other subjects, by redeeming the pledges of Provincial autonomy contained in the Despatch of the 25th, August 1911, and by taking such measures as may be necessary for the recognition of India as a component part of a federated Empire, in the full and the free enjoyment of the rights belonging to that status.

India Council Reform

XI. Resolved—That this Congress records its opinion that the Council of the Secretary of State for India should be abolished and pending its abolition makes the following suggestions for the amendment of its constitution.

(*a*) That the salary of the Secretary of State for India should be placed on the English estimates.

(*b*) That, with a view to the efficiency and independence of the Council, it is expedient that it should be partly nominated and partly elected.

(*c*) That the total number of members of the Council should be not more than nine.

(*d*) That the elected portion of the Council should consist of not less than one-third of the total number of members, who should be non-official Indians, chosen by a constituency consisting of the elected members of the Imperial and Provincial Legislative Councils.

(*e*) That the election of Indians to the Council should be direct, and not of a panel of elected members as proposed in Lord Crewe's Bill.

(*f*) That not less than one-half of the nominated members of the Council should consist of public men unconnected with the Indian Administration.

(*g*) That the remaining portion of the nominated members of the Council should consist of officials who have served in India for not less that ten years and have not been away from India for more than two years.

(*h*) That no distinction whatever with regard to salary or allowance should be made between the Indian members and their colleagues in the Council.

(*i*) That the character of the Council should be purely advisory as heretofore and that no change in the methods and procedure should be made which may convert or tend to convert it in any manner whatsoever into an administrative body.

This Congress regrets the summary rejection of the Council of India Bill of 1914.

South Africa

XII. Resolved—(*a*) That this Congress begs to offer to H. E. the Viceroy, its respectful thanks for the noble and courageous stand made by him in the cause of our people in S. Africa; and, while expressing its grateful appreciation of the efforts of the Government of India, in obtaining relief in respect of some of the most pressing grievances of our Indian fellow subjects and of the firm advocacy in the cause of India of Sir Benjamin Robertson, this Congress begs to place on record that no settlement can be wholly satisfactory or be deemed final, which does not secure equality of treatment between His Majesty's Indian and other subjects in S. Africa, and respectfully urges on the Government of India that steps may be taken as early as circumstances will permit to bring about such equality of treatment.

(*b*) That this Congress places on record its warm appreciation of, and admiration for, the heroic endeavours of Mr. Gandhi and his followers, and their unparalleled sacrifice in their struggle for the maintenance of the self-respect of India and the redress of Indian grievances.

(*c*) That this Congress further expresses its gratitude to Messrs. Pollak and Kallenbach for their voluntary sacrifice and suffering in the cause of India, and to the Rev. Mr. Andrews for his help under circumstances of great difficulty.

(*d*) And, lastly, that this Congress records its appreciation of the invaluable services of the Hon. Mr. Gokhale throughout the struggle in bringing about the present settlement.

Indentured Labour

XIII. Resolved—That owing to the scarcity of labour in India and the grave consequences resulting from the system of Indentured Labour which reduces the labourers, during the period of their indenture, practically to the position of slaves, this Congress strongly urges the total prohibition of recruitment of labour under indenture, either for work in India or elsewhere.

Legal

XIV Resolved—That this Congress, concurring with previous Congresses, urges the early separation of Judicial and Executive Functions in the best interests of the Empire and prays that any scheme of Separation that may be undertaken, to be really effective, must place all the Judiciary solely under the control of the highest Court in the Province.

Swadeshi

XV. Resolved—That this Congress accords its most cordial support to the Swadeshi Movement and calls upon the people of India to labour for its success by making earnest and sustained efforts to promote the growth of indigenous industries, by giving preference, wherever practicable, to Indian products over imported commodities, even at a sacrifice.

Coercion

XVI. Resolved—That this Congress reiterates its protest against the continuation of the Indian Press Act on the Statute Book and urges that the same be repealed, specially in view of the decision of the Calcutta High Court which declares that the safeguards provided by the Act are illusory and incapable of being enforced.

Permanent Settlement

XVII. Resolved—That this Congress is strongly of opinion that a reasonable and definite limitation to the demand of the State on land and the introduction of a Permanent Settlement directly between the Government and land-holders in ryotwari areas, or a settlement for a period of not less than 60 years in those Provinces where shorter periodical settlements on revision prevail, will substantially help in ameliorating the present unsatisfactory condition of the agricultural population.

Representation

Separate Electorates

XVIII. Resolved—That this Congess while deprecating the creation of Separate Electorates in the Imperial and Provincial Legislative Councils urges on the Government that the said system should not in any case be extended to the local bodies, as it will prove injurious to the development of national unity and the fostering of the national ideal.

Extension of Lord Hardinge's Term of Office

XX. Resolved—That this Congress begs to place on record its high appreciation of the services rendered to India by H. E. the Viceroy and expresses the hope that his tenure of the office may be extended for such time as, after the cessation of the War, may be necessary for a proper settlement of the great and far-reaching issues affecting the future position of India as a component and equal part of the Empire.

Congress Constitution

XXI. Resolved—That the following two amendments suggested for the consideration of the Subjects Committee of this Congress, be referred by the General Secretaries of the Congress to a Committee consisting of three members, to be nominated by each Provincial Congress Committee; with the General Secretaries as ex-officio members, the said Committee to meet at such time and place as may be fixed by them, in consultation with the Secretaries of the Provincial Congress Committees, and to report to the All-India Congress Committee in regard to the said amendments for such action, if any, as the All-India Congress Committee may deem fit to suggest to the next Congress.

The said two amendments are:

At the end of Article XX of the Constitution of the Indian National Congress Organisation now in force, add the following words:

"If such a meeting be not called, it shall be called, for the election of delegates, within one month of the Congress, in any town or district on the requisition of not less than 20 householders over 21 years of age to the Provincial or District Congress-Committee, in which the town of the requisition is situate"

2. In Article XX of the Constitution of the Indian National Congress Organisation now in force make the following alterations:

(I) at the end of clause (4) delete the word "and";
(II) at the end of clause (5) for the stop, substitute a comma;
(III) and add the words:

"And public meetings convened under the auspices of any association which has, as one of its objects, the attainment of Self-Government by India on Colonial lines within the British Empire by constitutional means"

Thanks of Congress

XXII. Resolved—That this Congress records its sense of high appreciation of the services of Sir William Wedderburn and other members of the British Committee, and resolves that the organisation of the British Committee and *India* should be maintained.

XXIV. Resolved—That this Congress acknowledges with deep gratitude the services rendered at great personal sacrifice by the Deputation which went to England last summer on behalf of the Congress to place before the Secretary of State for India the views of the Congress on the India Council Bill of 1914 and other important questions.

[See IV (*b*), V, XII, XIX and XX.]

Formal

XXIII. Resolved—That the Hon. Nawab Syed Muhammad Bahadur and Mr. N. Subba Rao Pantulu be appointed General Secretaries for the next year.

XXV. Resolved—That the following gentlemen form the All-India Congress Committee for 1915 (list omitted).

XXVI. Resolved—That the next Congress meet in Bombay.

APPENDIX

THE TWENTY-SEVENTH CONGRESS

CHAPTER XXVII[1]

The acceptance of Bankipur as the seat of the Twenty-seventh Congress had been made on the invitation of Mr. Hasan Imam, but his raising to the Bench deprived India of his political services, while opening to him a valuable line of activity. The Chairmanship of the Reception Committee was assigned to Mr. Mazarhal Haque, known all over India for his courageous advocacy of Indian claims in the Supreme Legislative Council. The pavilion was much admired, and had 28 gates, each named after a famous person or place in the history of Magadha, and there the Congress met on December 26th, 1912. The pavilion seated 5,000 persons of whom 207 were delegates:

Madras	19
Bombay	10
Berar	13
C. P.	1
Panjab	4
U. P.	67
Bengal	35
Behar	58
	207

[1] We had relied on a statement of an old Congressman, to the effect that the Report of the Twenty-seventh Congress had not been published. Mr. Ashesh Kumar Bannerji kindly sets us right, and sends a copy of the Report. As the book is "locked up" we print the summary as an Appendix.

The President's procession having entered, and the members being seated on the dais, the Hon. Mr. Haque delivered the Welcome Address. He made a feeling allusion to the outrage at Delhi, and to the passing away of two great Congressmen, Allan Octavian Hume, and Krishnaswami Iyer. Then came a swift sketch of Behar history, and a reference to the happy absence of any Hindu-Muhammadan question in Behar. After a survey of the unfortunate position taken up by English statesmen towards Turkey, and the wise sympathy shown by the Viceroy and the Presidency Governors, and Sir Charles Bayley and Sir James Meston, he voiced the gratitude of the Muhammadans to Mr. Surendranath Bannerji for the sympathy shown in *The Bengalee.* He concluded by calling on Mr. Surendranath Bannerji to move the formal election of the Hon. Rao Bahadur R. N. Mudholkar.

The veteran Bengali patriot was followed by the Hon. Mr. G. K. Gokhale, the Hon. Pandit Madan Mohan Malaviya, the Hon. Mr. N. Subba Rao, Lala Harkishan Lal, Mr. Ambikacharan Mozumdar, and the Hon. Maharaja-Kumar of Tikari, and the proposal was unanimously carried.

The President, after a few words of gratitude, spoke of the Delhi outrage with sympathy for the victim and detestation of the crime. He then passed on to the ideal of the Congress, a united and Self-Governing India, an India in which jarring creeds should be harmonised, all faiths should be unified, and in which life should be spiritualised. Then he laid India's love and gratitude on the tomb of Mr. Hume, and offered her sympathy to Turkey. Turning to National politics, he laid stress on the entrance of Indians into the Executive Councils, and hailed the Viceregal Despatch of August 25th, 1911, which promised larger measures of Self-Government to the Provinces, " until at last India would consist of a number of administrations autonomous in all provincial affairs, with the Government of India above them all, and possessing power to interfere in case of misgovernment, ordinarily restricting their function to matters of Imperial concern ". He then pointed out the changes necessary in the Council Regulations, and protested against the system of separate electorates, while approving the representation of minorities. He next raised the question of the representation of India in the House of Commons. Pondicherry sent a representative to the French Chamber, and Goa to the Portuguese, but the infinitely larger interests of British India were ignored. This section of the subject was completed by the urging of decentralisation, and of the creation of divisional and district Advisory Boards.

After a glance at the miserable condition of Indian immigrants into the Colonies, the President turned to the position of Indians here, and accurately pointed out that the scant consideration shown to them abroad was the reflection of their political status at home. He ran over the familiar grievances in the Civil Service, Simultaneous Examinations, Education, Public Works, etc., commissions in the army—all questions occupying the minds of the people. The Congress itself should be improved by the discussion in detail of three or four subjects only, by men who had studied them. The Congress must put forth more sustained energy, and we must remember that social advance and moral and spiritual regeneration must accompany political growth. Only thus can our Motherland become free and great.

A change in the ordinary sequence of Congress work was made by the introduction at this point of a Resolution—moved by the Hon. Mr. Surendranath Bannerji, seconded by Mr. D. E. Wacha, and supported by Lala Lajpat Rai, the Hon. Pandit Madan Mohan Malaviya, the Hon. Mr. N. Subba Rao, the Hon. Mr. Krishna Sahai and Mr. Syed Muhammad Ismail, who all voiced the sorrow and indignation of the Congress for the Delhi outrage—expressing the sympathy and affection felt for the Viceroy. A telegram was ordered to be sent, and the Subjects' Committee being approved, the Congress adjourned.

The second day's proceedings began by the recital of a poem on unity between Hindus and Muslims. Then came Resolution II, expressing the grief of the Congress for the death of Mr. Allan Octavian Hume, feelingly moved by the Hon. Mr. Bhupendranath Basu, who recounted his great services to India, seconded by the Hon. Pandit Motilal, and carried in silence, standing. The Viceroy's reply to the Congress telegram, bringing "his warmest thanks to the Indian National Congress for their kind message of sympathy and for their expression of regard," was then read.

The Hon. Mr. G. K. Gokhale moved Resolution III, while congratulating the Indians in South Africa for some alleviation of their sufferings, protested against the reservation of huge tracts of land for white settlement, and demanded the abolition of indentured labour. Mr. Gokhale explained the private nature of his visit to South Africa, and explained that the restriction of immigration was not a restriction on the Indians but on the Executive, imposing on the latter the admission of an irreducible minimum. He then went over the remaining grievances, and urged the Indians at home to support solidly their South African brethren. The Resolution was seconded by the Hon. Pandit Madan Mohan Malaviya, and supported by the Hon. Mr. Mazaral Haque, Lala Lajpat Rai, the Hon. Mr. Harchandrai Bishandas, Messrs. Pramathanath Bannerji, Madanjit, C. Y. Chintamani and Kedarnath, and carried.

The fourth Resolution expressed the satisfaction of the Congress at the appointment of the Public Service Commission—a Resolution passed rather too soon—and outlined certain necessary reforms. It was moved by the Hon. Mr. Subba Rao, tracing the simultaneous examination question from 1850 onwards, when the reform was recommended by a Committee appointed by the Secretary of State. The Hon. Rai Bahadur Baikunthanath Sen seconded, expressing a pious hope that the new Commission might do better than its predecessor. Dr. D. Saryadhikari, Pandit Gokarannath Misra, Mr. D. G. Dalvi, Dr. Nilratan Sarkar, Dr. R. Ranjit Singh, Pandit Hridaynath Kanzru, and the Hon. Mr. Dwarkarnath, all supported, and the Resolution was carried.

The fifth Resolution on Swadeshi was moved by Mr. Ambikacharan Mozumdar, who said that though Swadeshi had begun in revenge and retaliation, it had now struck its root into the firm ground of love and patriotism. If Indians loved their country, they should stick to the Swadeshi vow. "Every pie that you spend on a foreign article is a robbery of the limited resources of the country." The Resolution was seconded by Mr. V. V. Jogiah, and carried unanimously.

The Congress adjourned.

On the third day, Resolution VI, on Local Self-Government, was moved by Mr. S. V. Narasimha Rao. He pointed out that Lord Ripon's Resolution of 1882 was intended to use Local Self-Government "as a means of political and popular education". After 25 years, Lord Morley found that the scheme had never been given a fair trial, and urged the Government of India in 1908 to shape their policy on the principle laid down by Lord Ripon. The most important recommendation is the establishment of Village Panchayats, Lord Morley pointing out that "the village in India has been the fundamental and indestructible unit of the social system, surviving the downfall of dynasty after dynasty".

Mr. N. A. Dravid seconded, and Mr. Arikshan Sinha supported, giving various local details to show the need for reform. The Resolution was carried.

Resolution VII endorses the Despatch of the Government of India to the Secretary of State of August 25th, 1911, and challenges the interpretation put on it. The Hon. Mr. Surendranath Bannerji, in moving it, said that Provincial Autonomy was a stage on the road to Self-Government. Some said Self-Government was a dream, but the dreams of one age were the realities of the next. Mr. D. A. Khare, in seconding, said the Despatch must be read in the obvious meaning of the words, and not in the words of Lord Crewe. Mr. Shashanka Jivan Roy supported, and the Resolution was carried.

Resolution VIII expressed the regret of the Congress that the Council Regulations had not been improved, and asked for 13 definite amendments to them. It was moved by the Hon. Mr. S. Sinha. The Resolution was seconded by Mr. Dwarkanath, and supported by the Hon. A. S. Krishna Rao, Mr. Surendranath Mallick, Pandits Rambhuj Dutt Choudhuri and Gokarannath Misra, Dr. Tej Bahadur Sapru, who moved, and Mr. C. Y. Chintamani, who seconded, an amendment excluding those who voted in separate electorates from voting in general electorates. The Hon. Mr. Mazaral Haque appealed to them to withdraw the amendment for the sake of peace, and they did so. The Resolution was carried with one dissentient.

Resolution IX, asking for Executive Councils for the U. P. and the Panjab, was moved by the Hon. Pandit Motilal Nehru, seconded by Munshi Chail Bihari Lal, and Resolution X, thanking the Government for establishing Legislative Councils for the C. P. and Assam, moved by Rao Bahadur R. A. Mundle, and seconded by Mr. G. N. Kane, were carried.

Resolution XI, against the introduction of separate electorates for Local Bodies, and Resolution XII, asking that the Law Membership should not be restricted to Barristers, were put from the chair and carried.

Mr. Sachindra Prasad Bose next moved Resolution XIII on Education. He said that the whole subject had been so thoroughly discussed the previous year that there was nothing to add. The Government knew that if the masses were educated things could not go on as they were. The Congress needed the strength which came from the people behind it. Mr. C. P. Ramaswami Aiyar seconded, and urged that they should agitate as one man until Mr. Gokhale's Bill was passed into law. In education India was far below Russia. India needed residential and teaching Universities, diffusing the light of knowledge through the land. The Resolution was supported by the Hon. Mr. Ramanbhai Mahipatram, Mr. R. C. Ghose, and Mr. A. B. Patro, and carried.

Mr. G. K. Devadhar moved XIV, an important Resolution on Sanitation, pointing out the duties of Government and of the educated class. It was literally a question of life and death, yet both Government and the educated showed much indifference. Dr. Ranjit Singh seconded, urging the spread of simple hygienic knowledge. The Resolution was carried.

Resolutions XV and XVI, on Public Expenditure and Land Settlement, were put from the Chair and passed. Then the Hon. Mr. C. V. S. Narasimha Raj moved Resolution XVII, the familiar grievance of the exclusion of Indians from the higher ranks of the army. It was seconded by Mr. Prakasa Rao, and carried. The President moved from the Chair Resolution XVIII, asking that High Courts might be directly related to the Government of India.

Resolution XIX, conveying the thanks of the Congress to Mr. Gokhale for his services in South India, was moved by Dr. Tej Bahadur Sapru, seconded by Mr. Krishna Sahay, and carried by acclamation, the whole audience rising to its feet and cheering.

Resolution XX, accepting the Constitution and Rules of the Congress, as amended by the All-India Congress Committee, was put from the Chair and carried. The only important change was giving to Congress Committees and their affiliated associations the right to call public meetings for the election of delegates.

Resolution XXI resolving that the British Committee and *India* should be maintained, was carried. Resolution XXIII passed the All-India Congress Committee as elected by the Provincial Committees. Resolution XXII, reappointing Messrs. Wacha and Khare as General Secretaries was passed with acclamation. The invitation to Karachi was accepted unanimously, and, with the vote of thanks to the President and his reply, the Twenty-seventh National Congress came to its ending.

RESOLUTIONS

Sorrow of Congress

I. Resolved—That this Congress desires to place on record its sense of horror and detestation at the dastardly attempt made on the life of His Excellency the Viceroy, who has by his wise and conciliatory policy and earnest solicitude to promote the well-being of the millions of His Majesty's subjects entrusted to his care, won the esteem, the confidence, the affection and the gratitude of the people of India. The Congress offers its respectful sympathy to Their Excellencies Lord and Lady Hardinge and fervently prays that His Excellency may have a speedy recovery and restoration to health.

II. Resolved—(*a*) That this Congress places on record its sense of profound sorrow for the death of Mr. Allan Octavian Hume, C.B., the father and founder of the Indian National Congress, for whose lifelong services, rendered at rare self-sacrifice, India feels deep and lasting gratitude, and in whose death the cause of Indian progress and reform has sustained an irreparable loss.

(*b*) The President be requested to cable this resolution to Sir William Wedderburn, Baronet, Chairman of the British Committee of the Indian National Congress, with the request that he may convey to Mrs. Ross Scott, Mr. Hume's daughter, the sympathy of the Congress in her great bereavement.

Indians in the Colonies

III. Resolved (*a*) That this Congress, anticipating the forthcoming legislation of the provisional settlement recently arrived at, cordially congratulates Mr. Gandhi and the Transvaal Community upon the repeal of the anti-Asiatic legislation of the Province regarding registration and immigration, and expresses its high admiration of the intense patriotism, courage and self-sacrifice with which they—Muhammadan and Hindu, Zoroastrian and Christian—have suffered persecution in the interest of their countrymen during their peaceful and selfless struggle for elementary Civil rights against overwhelming odds.

(*b*) Whilst appreciating the endeavours that have been made from time to time to secure the redress of the grievances of the Indians of South Africa and other British Colonies, this Congress urges that in view of the avowed inability of His Majesty's Government to adopt a firm and decisive attitude in this matter, the Government of India should take such retaliatory measures as may be calculated to protect India's self-respect and the interest of Indian residents in those parts of the Empire, and thus remove a great source of discontent among the people of this country.

(*c*) This Congress further protests against the declarations of responsible statesmen in favour of allowing the Self-Governing

Colonies, in the British Empire, to monopolise vast undeveloped territories for exclusive white settlements, and deems it its duty to point out that the policy of shutting the door in those territories against, and denying the right of full British citizenship to, all the Asiatic subjects of the British Crown, while preaching and enforcing the opposite policy of the open door in Asia, is fraught with grave mischief to the Empire and is as unwise as unrighteous.

(*d*) Whilst thanking the Government of India for the prohibition of the recruitment of indentured Indian labour for South Africa, this Congress is strongly of opinion that in the highest National interest, the system of indentured labour is undesirable and should be abolished, and respectfully urges the Government to prohibit the further recruitment of Indian labour under contract of indenture whether for service at home or abroad.

(*e*) That the President do dispatch the following message to Mr. Gandhi: "The Congress reaffirms last year's resolution, expresses its warmest appreciation of your efforts, and assures you and your fellow workers of the country's whole-hearted support."

Public Service

IV. Resolved—(*a*) That this Congress records it sense of satisfaction at the appointment of the Royal Commission on Indian Public Service, and while expressing its regret at the inadequacy of the non-official Indian element thereon, trusts the deliberation of the Commission will result in the just recognition of Indian claims to appointments in the various departments of the Public Service.

(*b*) This Congress urges the introduction of the reforms outlined below:

(1) The holding of the open Competitive Examination for the Indian Civil Service and Public Services now recruited in England simultaneously in India and in England.

(2) The recruitment of the Public Services as a rule by means of Competitive Examinations and not by a system of nomination.

(3) The abolition of the division of Services into Imperial and Provincial as now constituted, and the equalisation of the conditions of service as between Europeans and Indians.

(4) The abrogation of all rules, orders, notifications and circulars which expressly or in effect debar Indians as such from any appointment in any department.

(5) The removal of restrictions against the appointment of persons other than members of Indian Civil Service in certain high and miscellaneous offices.

(6) The complete Separation of the Executive and Judicial functions and services. The creati n of a distinct Judicial Service to be recruited from among members of the legal profession, and a proportionate curtailment of the cadre of the Indian Civil Service.

(7) The constitution of a distinct Indian Civil Medical Service for Civil Medical Service for Civil Medical appointments and the restriction of members of the Indian Medical Service to military posts only, the designation of the Indian Medical Service to be changed to Indian Military Medical Service.

(8) The closing of all Indian Services to the natives of those British Colonies where Indians are not elegible for service.

Swadeshi

V. Resolved—That this Congress accords its most cordial support to the Swadeshi Movement and calls upon the people of India to labour for its success by making earnest and sustained efforts to promote the growth of indigenous, industries by giving preference, wherever practicable, to Indian products over imported commodities, even at a sacrifice.

Local Self-Government

VI. Resolved--That this Congress expresses its regret that the recommendations of the Decentralisation Commission with regard to the further development of Local Self-Government, have not yet been given effect to, and urges that the Government of India may be pleased to take steps without delay to increase the powers and resources of Local Bodies.

Provincial Autonomy

VII. Resolved—That this Congress records its satisfaction at the recognition by the Government of India in their Despatch to the Secretary of State for India, dated the 25th August, 1911, of the necessity of introducing autonomous form of administration in the different Provinces of this country, and begs to record its respectful protest against the interpretation sought to be put upon the Despatch, which is contrary to its letter and spirit.

Representation

VIII. Resolved—(*a*) That this Congress records its sense of keen disappointment that at the last revision of the Legislative Council Regulations, the anomalies and inequalities, the rectification of which the previous Congress strongly urged upon the Government, have not been removed. And in order to allay the widespread dissatisfaction caused by the defects complained of, and in view of the experience of the last three years, this Congress earnestly prays that—

(1) There should be a non-official majority in the Imperial Legislative Council;

(2) There should be a majority of elected members in all Provincial Councils;

(3) The system of voting by delegates be done away with where it still exist;

(4) The franchise be broadened by simplifying the qualification of electors basing it on education, property or income;

(5) The Government should not have the power arbitrarily to declare any person ineligible for election on the ground of his antecedents or reputation;

(6) No person should be held ineligible for election on the ground of dismissal from Government Service, or of conviction in a criminal court, or from whom security for keeping the peace has been taken, unless his conduct has involved moral turpitude:

(7) No property or residential qualification should be required of a candidate, nor service as member of a Local Body;

(8) A person ignorant of English should be held ineligible for membership;

(9) It should expressly be laid down that officials should not be allowed to influence elections in any way;

(10) Finance Committees of Provincial Councils should be more closely associated with Government in the preparation of the annual financial statements;

(11) There should be a Finance Committee of the Imperial Legislative Council as in the case of Provincial Legislative Councils;

(12) The right of putting supplementary questions should be extended to all members, and not to be restricted to the member putting the original question;

(13) The strength of the Panjab Council be raised from 26 to 50 and more adequate representation be allowed to Panjab in the Imperial Council.

Separate Electorates

XI. Resolved—That this Congress strongly deprecates the extension of the principle of Separate Communal Electorates to Municipalities, District Boards or other Local Bodies.

Executive Councils for the United Provinces and the Panjab

IX. Resolved—That this Congress again urges that an Executive Council with an Indian member be established in the United

Provinces at an early date, and is of opinion that a similar Council should be established in Panjab too.

Thanks of Congress

X. Resolved—That this Congress thanks the Government for the establishment of Legislative Councils in the Central Provinces and Assam and is of opinion that the former administration should be raised to the status of a Lieutenant-Governor's charge.

XIX. Resolved—That this Congress puts on record its high appreciation of the valuable work done by the Hon. Mr. Gokhale, C.I E., in his visit to South Africa undertaken at the invitation of our countrymen in that Colony.

XXI. Resolved—That this Congress records its sense of high appreciation of the services of Sir William Wedderburn and the other members of the British Committee, and resolves that the organisation of the British Committee and *India* should be maintained.

Law Membership

XII. Resolved.—That in view of the fact that Section III of the Indian Councils Act of 1861 is understood in practice to limit appointment to the office of Law Member of the Viceroy's Executive Council to members of the English Bar only; thereby greatly restricting the field from which a selection can be made, this Congress urges that the said Section be so amended as to allow of Advocates, Vakils and Attorneys-at-Law of Indian High Courts being appointed to that office.

Education

XIII. Resolved—(*a*) That while expressing its satisfaction and thankfulness that Government have announced a more active educational policy, this Congress regrets the defeat of the Hon. Mr. Gokhale's Elementary Education Bill, and affirms its conviction that the introduction of a measure of Free and Compulsory Education is essential to secure a rapid extension of Elementary Education.

(*b*) This Congress cordially approves of the movement for the establishment of teaching and residential Universities in India.

Sanitation

XIV. Resolved—(*a*) That this Congress, while thanking the Government for having initiated a system of scientific enquiry into the origin and progress of plague, malaria and other diseases, urges the necessity of immediately taking in hand such practical measures as the necessity of congested areas, the reclamation of silted rivers, the clearing of jungles, the draining of waterlogged areas, and better provision for the supply of pure drinking water throughout the country.

(*b*) And this Congress exhorts Local Bodies and Public Associations to systematically educate public opinion in matters relating to sanitation and hygiene, and facilitate the working of those measures that are inaugurated with a view to check the spread of disease and the increase of mortality and to secure better health and sanitation of urban and rural areas.

Financial

XV. Resolved—That, having regard to the enormous growth that has taken place in the public expenditure of the country, the Congress urges that early steps be taken towards effective retrenchment, in all the spending department, of the Imperial and the Provincial Governments and specially the Military Department.

Land Settlement

XVI. Resolved—That a reasonable and definite limitation to the demand of the State on land and the introduction of a Permanent Settlement directly between the Government and holders of land in ryotwari areas, or a Settlement for a period of not less than 60 years in those Provinces where short periodical settlements or revisions prevail, wlll in the opinion of this Congress substantially help in ameliorating the present unsatisfactory condition of the agricultural population.

Military

XVII. Resolved—That this Congress is strongly of opinion that the injustice of keeping the higher ranks in the army closed against the people of India and the exclusion of certain races and castes from the lower ranks as well should be abolished.

High Courts

XVIII. Resolved—That This Congress is strongly of opinion that the High Courts in India should have the same direct relation with the Government of India alone as the High Court at Fort William in Bengal has at the present time.

Constitution of Congress

XX. Resolved—That the Constitution and Rules of the Indian National Congress organisation, as amended by the All-India Congress Committee, be adopted.

Formal

XXII. Resolved—That the following gentlemen form the All-India Congress Committee for 1918 (list omitted).

XXIII. Resolved—That Messrs. D. E. Wacha and D. A. Khare be re-appointed Secretaries for the ensuing year.

XXIV. Resolved—That the next Congress be held in Karachi.

STATEMENT GIVING THE MAIN DATES CONNECTED WITH THE INDIAN NATIONAL CONGRESS FROM ITS INCEPTION IN 1885 TO 1914

No.	Date	Place	Total No. of Delegates (Registered)	No. of Spectators	Chairman of the Reception Committee	General and Joint General Secretaries	Name of the President	No. of Resolutions passed	Subject of Resolutions in each Congress
1	28-12-85	Bombay	72				W. C. Bonnerji	9	3, 11, 18, 25, 35, 38
2	28-12-86	Calcutta	434		Dr. Rajendralala Mitra	A. O. Hume (by implication)	Dadabhai Naoroji	15	21, 25, 35, 38
3	28-12-87	Madras	607	3,000	Rajah Sir T. Madhava Rao	do.	Budruddin Tyabji	11	9, 21, 25, 38, 43
4	26-12-88	Allahabad	1,248	5,000	Pandit Ayodhyanath	do.	Mr. Yule	17	1, 9, 11, 21, 25, 31, 34, 35, 38, 43
5	26-12-89	Bombay	1,889	4,000	Pherozeshah M. Mehta	A. O. Hume (by appointment)	Sir William Wedderburn	15	1, 16, 20, 25, 35, 38, 43
6	26-12-90	Calcutta	677	7,000	Manamohan Ghose	do.	Sir Pherozeshah Mehta	15	1, 11, 16, 20, 38, 43
7	28-12-91	Nagpur	812	3,200	C. Narayanasami Naidu	1. A. O. Hume (gl.) 2. Ayodhyanath (jt.gl.)	P. Ananda Charlu	18	9, 15, 21, 25, 31, 38, 43
8	28-12-92	Allahabad	625	2,800	Pandit Bishambernath	do. do.	W. C. Bonnerji	22	8, 9, 14, 15, 20, 21, 25, 34, 35, 38
9	27-12-93	Lahore	867	3,200	Sardar Dayal Singh	do. 2. Ananda Charlu (jt. gl.)	Dadabhai Naoroji	23	8, 9, 12 14, 15, 20, 21, 23, 24, 34, 38
10	26-12-94	Madras	1,163	4,000	P. Rangiah Naidu	A. O. Hume	Mr. Alfred Webb	27	8, 9, 10, 14, 15, 18, 20, 21, 23, 33, 35, 38, 43
11	27-12-95	Poona	1,584		S. M. Bhide	do.	Surendranath Bannerji	26	9, 14, 15 16, 20, 21, 23, 33, 35, 36, 38, 43
12	28-12-96	Calcutta	784		Sir Romeshchandra Mitra	1. A. O. Hume (gl.) 2. D. E. Wacha (jt. gl.)	Muhammad Rahimtullah Sayani	24	9, 10, 13, 14, 20, 21, 24, 35, 38, 43
13	27-12-07	Amraoti	692		Khaparde	do.	Sir C. Sankaran Nair	21	6, 13, 14, 20, 21, 25, 33, 35, 38, 40
14	29-12-98	Madras	614		N. Subba Rao	do.	Ananda Mohan Bose	27	6, 9, 10, 14, 20, 21, 25, 30, 33, 35, 41
15	27-12-99	Lucknow	740	3,500	Bansi Lal Singh	do.	Romeshchandra Dutt	21	1 9, 13, 14, 20, 21, 25, 30, 33, 35, 38
16	27-12-1900	Lahore	567		Kali Prasanna Roy	do.	N. G. Chandravarkar	25	1, 9, 10, 13, 19, 20, 21, 25, 26, 35, 38

List of important Resolutions passed during 29 years on the following subjects

1. Abkari 2. Agriculture 3. Annexation of U. Burma 4. Boycott 5. Cable charges and Telegrams 6. Coercive Measures 7. Conciliation Boards 8. Economic Condition 9. Education 10. Emigration, Indians in Colonies 11. Enquiries 12. Executive and Bench 13. Famine 14. Finance 15. Forest 16. Grievances and Supply 17. High prices of Food-stuffs 18. India Council 19. Industries 20. Land Tenure, Permanent Settlement 21. Law 22. Loyalty 23. Medical 24. Migration 25. Military 26. Mining Industry 27. Official Secrets Bill 28. Outrages 29. Partition of Bengal 30. Plague 31. Police 32. Political Prisoners 33. Press 34. Prostitution 35. Public Service Simultaneous Examination 36. Railway 37. Reciprocity 38. Representation Legislative Councils 39. Sanitation 40. Sedition 41. Self-Government 42. Swadeshi 43. Taxation, Salt-Income 44. Tibetan Affairs 45. Union for Self-Government between the Congress and the Muslim League

N.B.—Formal Resolutions on congratulations, condolences, Congress Constitution and most appointments, etc., have been omitted.

Nos. in the penultimate col. refer to Resolutions numerically detailed in the last col.

No.	Date	Place	Total No. of Delegates (Registered)	No. of Spectators	Chairman of the Reception Committee	General and Joint General Secretaries	Names of the President	No. of Resolutions passed	Subject of Resolutions in each Congress	List of important Resolutions passed during 29 years on the following subject
17.	28-12-01	Calcutta	896		Maharajah Bahadur Jagndindranath Rai Bahadur	1. A. O. Hume (gl) 2. D. E. Wacha (subsequently became the President)	D. E. Wacha	33	2, 8, 9, 10, 14, 19, 21, 24, 25, 26, 35	
18	23-12-02	Ahmedabad	471		Ambalal Desai	do.	Surendranath Bannerji	23	8, 9, 10, 14, 21, 23, 25, 31, 43	
19	28-12-03	Madras	538	5,500	Nawab Syed Muhammad Sahab Bahadur	do.	Lal Mohan Ghose	16	9, 10, 20, 25, 27, 29, 35, 38, 41	
20	26-12-04	Bombay	1,010		Sir P. H. Mehta	1. A. O. Hume (gl.) 2. D. E. Wacha 3. G. K. Gokhale (jt. gl.)	Sir Henry Cotton	22	8, 9, 10, 14, 21, 25, 29, 31, 35, 38, 44	
21	27-12-05	Kashi or Benares	758		Madho Lal	do.	G. K. Gokhale	25	6, 8, 9, 10, 14, 21, 25, 31, 35, 38, 39, 43	
22	26-12-06	Calcutta	1,663	20,000	Dr. Rash Behari Ghose	do.	Dadabhai Naoroji	17	4, 9, 10, 14, 20, 21, 29, 41, 42	
23	26-12-07	Surat	1,600	5,400	Tribhuvan Das Malvi		Dr. Rash Behari Ghose			
	28-12-07						do.			
	28-12-08	Madras	626		Dewan Bahadur K. Krishnaswami Row		do.	21	6, 9, 10, 20, 21, 28, 29, 38, 42	
24	27-12-09	Lahore	243		Harikishan Lal	1. D. E. Wacha 2. D. A. Khare	Madan Mohan Malaviya	24	6, 9, 10, 17, 20, 21, 25, 29, 35, 38, 42	
25	26-12-10	Allahabad	636	4,000	Pt. Sundar	do.	Sir William Wedderburn	30	5, 6, 7, 9, 10, 14, 21, 32, 38	
26	26-12-11	Calcutta	446		Bhupendranath Basu	do.	Bishen Narayan Dhar	33	5, 6, 9, 10, 14, 20, 21, 23, 25, 29, 31, 35, 38, 39, 41, 42, 43	
27	26-12-12	Bankipur		4,500	Mazarbul Huque	do.	R. N. Mudholkar	24	9, 10, 12, 14, 20, 21, 25, 30, 35, 38, 41, 42	
28	26-12-13	Karachi	550		Harischandra Vishandas	do.	Nawab Syed Muhammad Bahadur	22	9, 10, 18, 20, 21, 25, 33, 35, 38, 42, 45	
29	28-12-14	Madras	866		Sir S. Subramania Iyer	1. Syed Muhammad 2. N. Subba Rao	Bhupendranath Basu	26	6, 10, 18, 19, 20, 21, 22, 25, 37, 41, 42	

INDEX

NOTE

1. For the purpose of this Index all the Resolutions are numbered *seriatim* and are referred to by their numbers. The numbers in brackets following the names of Movers, etc., of Resolutions indicate the Congress.

2. Where any person has taken part in the Congress activities in any particular capacity, such capacity is indicated. In other cases, the names only are given.

3. When a subject has been discussed by the Congress as the object of a Resolution the names of the mover, seconder, supporter and other speakers have been indicated. Subjects not discussed as the objects of Resolutions, but only referred to in any other connection, are mentioned without further particulars.

4. The following abbreviations have been used to economise space.

   1. A.I. = Agent for the sale of the newspaper *India*
   2. B.C. = British Committee
   3. C.A.B. = Committee on Address to Mr. Bradlaugh
   4. C.C. = Congress Committee
   5. C.C.C. = Committee for considering the continuance or otherwise of the Congress
   6. C.I. = Committee on Industries
   7. C.L.T. = Committee to represent grievances in Land Tenure to the Viceroy

8. C.P.P. = Committee for presentation of a petition to Parliament
9. C.R.E. = Congress Representative in England
10. D.H. = Delegate before Lord Hardinge
11. D.V. = Deputation to the Viceroy
12. E.C. = Education Committee
13. F.C. = One of the Fathers of the Congress
14. I.C.C. = Indian Congress Committee
15. M. = Mover of a Resolution
16. M.A. = Mover of an Amendment
17. P.L.C. = Panjab Land Alienation Committee
18. Pr. = Proposer of a Resolution
19. P.S.C. = Public Service Committee
20. R. = Resolution number
21. R.C. = Rules Committee
22. S.C. = Subjects Committee
23. S.C.C. = Standing Counsel of the Congress
24. S.C.M. = Secretary for the Circle formed for collection of money for the Congress
25. Sc. = Seconder of a Resolution
26. Sc.A. = Seconder of an amendment
27. Sp. = Speaker in Connection with a Resolution
28. Spp. = Supporter of a Resolution
29. Spp.A. = Supporter of an Amendment
30. Su.C.C. = Surat Congress Committee

INDEX TO HISTORICAL INTRODUCTION

1. SUBJECTS

2. NAMES

INDEX TO RESOLUTIONS

GENERAL INDEX

INDEX OF NAMES

ADDENDUM TO THE INDEX

INDEX TO THE 27TH CONGRESS RESOLUTIONS

GENERAL INDEX

INDEX OF NAMES

BIBLIOGRAPHY TO INTRODUCTION

TITLE	AUTHOR	PUBLISHERS	DATE
Prosperous British India	William Digby	T Fisher Unwin, London	1901
Poverty and Un-British Rule in India	Dadabhai Naoroji	Swan Sonnenschein, London	1901
Economic History of British India	Romesh Chandra Dutt	Kegan Paul, Trench, Trubner & Co., London	1902
Government of India	Sir Courtenay Ilbert	Clarendon Press, Oxford	1915
Law of Municipal Corporations in British India	P Duraiswami Iyengar	Guardian Press, Madras	1913
Imperial Gazetteer of India, Vols II and IV		Clarendon Press, Oxford	1907 & 1908
New India	H J S Cotton	Kegan Paul Trench & Co.	1885
Indian National Congress		G A. Natesan & Co., Madras	
Speeches of G K. Gokhale		do	
The Struggle between the Mahrattas and the Mogals	Mukund Wamanrao Burway	Printed at The Tatva-Vivechaka Press, Bombay	1914
A Brief History of the Indian People	W W. Hunter	Morrison & Gibb, Edinburgh	1881
The Indian Empire, Its People, History, and Products	Sir William Wilson Hunter	W. H. Allen & Co., Ltd., London	1893

Title	Author	Publishers	Date
Travels and Travellers in India, A.D. 1400—1700	Edward Farlay Oaten	Kegan Paul, Trench, Trubner & Co., London	1909
Progress of the Madras Presidency during the last forty years of British Administration	Dewan Bahadur S. Srinivasa Raghavaiyangar	Printed by the Supt., Govt. Press, Madras	1893
India. Forty years of progress and reform: being a sketch of the life and times of Behramji M. Malabari	R. P. Karakaria	Henry Frowde. Oxford University Press, Warehouse, London, E. C.	1896
India and Her People	Swami Abhedanand	The Vedanta Society, New York	1906
Rise of the Maratha Power	M. G. Ranade	Punalekar & Co., Bombay	1900
'The Arya Samaj": An account of its aims, doctrine and activities with a biographical Sketch of the Founder	Lajpat Rai	Longmans, Green & Co.	1915
A History of Civilisation of Ancient India in 2 Vols. [Based on Samskrit Literature.] (B.C. 2000 to 320.) (B.C. 320 to A.D. 1000.)	Romesh Chandra Dutt	Kegan Paul, Trench, Trubner & Co., Ltd.	1893
An Essay on the Civilisation of India, China and Japan	G. Lowes Dickinson	J. M. Dent & Sons, Ltd.	1914

Title	Author	Publishers	Date
Voyages de Bernier	François Bernier	Paul Marret Amsterdam	1699
Tavernier's Travels in India (originally published in French in 1676)	Jean Baptiste Tavernier	Bangabasi Office, Calcutta	1905
Early History of India (including Alexander's campaigns)	Vincent A. Smith	Clarendon Press, Oxford	1908
History of Indian Shipping and Maritime Activity from the earliest times	Radhakumud Mookerji	Longmans, Green & Co., London	1912
Critical and Historical Essays in 2 Vols.	Lord Macaulay	Longmans, Green, Longmans Roberts & Green, London	1864
Manual of the Administration of the Madras Presidency in 3 Vols.		Printed at the Govt. Press, Madras	1885 & 1893
The Imperial Gazetteer of India: Vol. II Historical, Vol. IV Administration	Published under the Authority of His Majesty's Secretary of State for India in Council	Clarendon Press, Oxford	1907 & 1908
Children of the Motherland	Annie Besant and others	The Board of Trustees, Central Hindu College, Benares	1906
Indian Unrest	Sir Valentine Chirol	Macmillan & Co., London	1910

ERRATA

Page	Line		For	Read
XLVI	11	from top	Suraj	Suja
LI	5	from bottom	Imperial Council	The Viceroy's Council
167	5	from top	IV	III
,,	6	,,	V	IV
278	5	from bottom	IX	X
,,	2	,,	X	XI
320	2	,,	XIII	XXIII
360	11	,,	VI	VII
362	11	from top	Amhalal	Ambalal
386	5	,,	XV	XVI
406	8	,,	XVI	XVII
501	11	,,	XVIII	XX
,,	22	,,	XIX read, Permanent Settlement, XXI	
,,	23	From "Resolution XX" to end of line 24—to be deleted.		
603	8	from bottom	XXIII	XXII
,,	6	,,	XXII	XXIII

Printed by Annie Besant at The Vasanṭā Press, Adyar, Madras.